Course	Introduction to Theatre
Course Number	**DRAM 1101**
	University of Connecticut
	Drama Department

http://create.mheducation.com

ISBN-10: 1308190638   ISBN-13: 9781308190631

Contents

Credits

About *Theatre: Brief Version*

Cohen's insider's guide to the world of theatre puts students in the front row

INVITING STUDENTS INSIDE THE PROCESS

Coverage of design, acting, and directing, and photo essays, provide a behind-the-scenes look at professional theatre artists performing their craft.

ILLUSTRATING LIVE THEATRE

More than 250 theatre photographs from five continents, most of them showing recent stage productions, bring to life many exciting theatre companies and productions.

What's New

New sections on eight major theatre professionals:

- A photo essay on scene designer Scott Pask (*Hair, The Coast of Utopia, The Book of Mormon*), in "Designers and Technicians."
- Full sections on leading contemporary directors Silviu Purcarete (Romanian), Julie Taymor (American), and Katie Mitchell (English), in "Global Theatre Today."

Full sections on leading contemporary playwrights Theresa Rebeck and Sarah Ruhl, in "The Playwright," Wendy Wasserstein, in "The Modern Theatre," and Yasmina Reza, in "Global Theatre Today."

Entirely new sections on:

- Theatre beyond Theatre—site-specific and "immersion" theatrical formats, in "Global Theatre Today."
- Directorial Adaptation—how today's directors increasingly adapt the texts of classic and even modern plays, in "The Director."
- Performance Studies—the growing study of performance in everyday life, in "The Critic."
- Puppet Performance—the increasing use of "actors" made of metal, wood, and fabrics, in "Global Theatre Today."
- Updated scholarship in all areas and extensive revisions, in "Global Theatre Today."

BRINGING PRACTITIONERS AND STAGING TO LIFE

Spotlight and Stagecraft sidebars offer insights about acting, staging, and theatre history.

ONLINE LEARNING CENTER (www.mhhe.com/cohenbrief10e)

Support for Instructors

- The **Instructor's Manual** includes learning objectives, an overview and outline, a list of significant names and terms, and suggested written works and videos that can serve as lecture launchers for each chapter.

- The **Test Bank,** organized by chapter, contains multiple-choice, true-false, and essay questions for in-class quizzes and testing. The Test Bank is also available in **EZ Test,** McGraw-Hill's flexible and easy-to-use electronic program that allows instructors to create tests keyed to the book's content.

- New **Lecture PowerPoints** highlight key points of each chapter.

Support for Students

- *Enjoy the Play!* is a brief guide that leads students through the complete theater-going experience. It offers tips on everything from buying tickets to what to look for when watching a play. It also provides guidelines for writing a theatre report.

- **Quizzes** include multiple-choice, true-false, and essay questions to help students test their comprehension of the material, and **Internet Exercises** encourage students to explore theatre on the Web.

- **Flashcards** help students review and learn important theatrical terms.

Letter from the Author

What's it like to be on the inside of a theatrical performance? Have you ever wondered? Well, to those of us who work in theatre, it's called "magic time."

I described such a phenomenon in the preface I wrote for the very first edition of this book, more than thirty years ago.

> At this moment, I am sitting in a darkened theatre during a technical rehearsal for a play I am directing. The action onstage has been put on hold for a few minutes while a pair of spotlights are being refocused, and I am trying to use the time to write this preface—but my eye is continually being pulled away from my pages by the dance of light now playing upon the stage. I am dazzled by its violet and amber hues, its sharp shafts of incandescence, and I gaze with admiration at the technicians who, above my head, are adjusting their instruments with precision. Looking around me, I see the sound designer carefully setting controls on her console, the scenery and costume designers seeing how their work appears in the lights and whispering to each other over their headsets, the stage managers recording lighting and sound cues in their promptbooks, and the actors standing patiently on the stage and going over their lines in their heads while they await the stage manager's cue for the rehearsal to resume.
>
> Though all is relatively still and nothing but whispers can be heard, I am utterly hypnotized by these goings-on. The stage seems to be pulsing with torrents of passion and exhilaration just waiting to be unleashed. I am utterly alive with excitement—and can only look back to these cold words I have written with dismay. How can I even think to express my love of theatre in these pages? How can I hope to share with you readers the awe and the thrill that course through my body when I engage in theatre's many mysteries?
>
> For the theatre is not merely a body of plays, a collection of skills, or a collaborative art form. It is a life. It is people. It is people making art out of themselves. It has been the living reenactment of the human adventure for more than three thousand years, and never so alive as it is today. Live theatre transcends by light-years anything that could be said or written about it, and I only hope I can do it justice.

Well, I continue to feel every bit of this exhilaration today. By this time, I have staged more than a hundred productions as a director. But I have also worked as a producer, actor, stage manager, and lighting designer in both professional theatres and universities, and I have published more than four hundred play reviews, articles, plays, and translations, as well as more than a dozen books on acting, directing, and dramatic literature—and just about everything in between. In the theatre, I am a throwback, a jack-of-all-trades in a field that is becoming increasingly specialized.

But my deepest connection to theatre is simply as a playgoer. Having been bitten by the drama bug when seeing my first professional play—the Broadway musical *Where's Charley?* starring Ray Bolger in 1948—I have seen well over a thousand theatre productions, in almost every state in the nation and in thirty-some countries around the world. And in each of this book's editions, I have sought to express the exhilaration I have experienced when seeing theatre as much as when working to create it.

I am always asked how this book has changed over its more than three decades. This edition includes more than one hundred new or significantly revised pages, and eighty new photos that I have personally taken or selected from stage productions mounted during the three years since the previous (ninth) edition went to press. New theatre artists, new technologies, new plays and productions, and new movements and trends constitute the bulk of the revisions, but the most important overall change in the current era has been the extraordinary increase in theatre as a truly global art. For this edition, for example, I traveled to England, France, Germany, Romania, Poland, and Italy to see and report on new theatre companies and productions—and in the same period I saw at least an equal number of stunning theatrical events that were touring here to the United States, and to other countries I was visiting as well. The "theatre world" is now a world of theatre, multicultural and accessible, coming to life right before our eyes.

Lights up! Curtain up! Enjoy the show wherever you are!

—**Robert Cohen**

Introduction

I T IS EVENING IN MANHATTAN. On Broadway and the streets that cross it—from 42nd to 54th— marquees light up, "Performance Tonight" signs materialize in front of double doors, and beneath a few box-office windows placards announce "This Performance Completely Sold Out." At Grand Central and Penn stations, trains disgorge suburbanites from Greenwich, Larchmont, and Trenton; students from New Haven and Philadelphia; day-trippers from Boston and Washington. Up from the Times Square subways troop denizens of the island city and the neighboring boroughs. At the Duffy Square "TKTS" booth, hundreds line up to buy the discount tickets that go on sale a few hours before curtain time for those shows with seats yet to be filled. Now, converging on these few midtown blocks of America's largest city, come limousines, restaurant buses, private cars, and taxis, whose drivers search for a curbside slot to deposit their riders among the milling throng of pedestrians. Financiers and dowagers, bearded intellectuals, backpack-toting teenagers, sleek executives, hip Harlemites, arm-in-arm widows, out-of-town tourists and conventioneers, between-engagement actors, celebrities, honeymooners, and the precocious

young—all commingle in this bizarre aggregation that is the New York Broadway audience. Even during (and perhaps *especially* during) troubled times in this vibrant city, it is as bright, bold, and varied a crowd as is likely to assemble at any single place in America.

It is eight o'clock. In close to forty theatres within two dozen blocks of each other, houselights dim, curtains rise, and spotlights pick out performers whose lives center on this moment. Here a hot new musical, here a star-studded revival of an American classic, here a contemporary English comedy from London's West End, here a new play fresh from its electrifying Seattle or Chicago premiere, here a one-woman show, here an offbeat off-Broadway musical moving to larger quarters, here a new avant-garde dance-drama, here a touring production from eastern Europe, and here the new play everyone expects will capture this year's coveted Pulitzer Prize. The hours pass.

It's 10:30. Pandemonium. All the double doors open simultaneously, as if on cue, and once again the thousands pour out into the night. At nearby restaurants, waiters stand by to receive the after-theatre onslaught. In Sardi's private upstairs room, an opening-night cast party gets under way; downstairs, the patrons rehash

Plays were often the sources of films in the early days of cinema, but now major films are increasingly turned into plays—and very successful ones (*The Lion King, The Producers, Newsies*), too. This scene is from the 2012 London premiere of the musical, *Top Hat,* a stage adaptation of the 1935 Fred Astaire–Ginger Rogers RKO movie that brilliantly recreates the original music and lyrics of Irving Berlin. Tom Chambers plays Jerry Travers (center) in the production, which was directed by Matthew White, with scenery by Hildegard Bechtler and costumes by Jon Morrell.

the evening's entertainment and sneak covert glances at the celebrities around them and the actors heading for the upstairs sanctuary to await the reviews that will determine whether they will be employed next week or back on the street looking for new jobs.

Now let's turn back the clock. It is dawn in Athens, the thirteenth day of the month of Elaphebolion in the year 458 B.C. From thousands of low mud-brick homes in the city, from the central agora, from temples and agricultural outposts, streams of Athenians and visitors converge on the south slope of the Acropolis, Athens's great hill and home of its grandest temples. Bundled against the morning dampness, carrying breakfast figs and flagons of wine, they pay their tokens at the entrance to the great Theatre of Dionysus and take their places in the seating spaces allotted them. Each tribe occupies a separate area. They have gathered for the Great Dionysia festival, which celebrates the greening of the land, the rebirth of vegetation, and the long sunny days that stretch ahead. It is a time for revelry, for rejoicing at fertility and all its fruits. And it is above all a time for the ultimate form of Dionysian worship: the theatre.

The open stone seats carved into the hillside fill up quickly. The crowd of seventeen thousand here today comprises not only the majority of Athenian citizens but also thousands of tradesmen, foreign visitors, slaves, and resident aliens. Even paupers are in attendance, thanks to the two obols apiece provided by a state fund to buy tickets for the poor; they take their place with the latecomers on the extremities of the *theatron,* as this first of theatres is called. Now, as the eastern sky grows pale, a masked and costumed actor appears atop a squat building set in full view of every spectator. A hush falls over the crowd, and the actor, his voice magnified by the wooden mask he wears, booms out this text:

I ask the gods some respite from the weariness
of this watchtime measured by years I lie awake . . .

And the entranced spectators settle in, secure in the knowledge that today they are in good hands. Today they will hear and see a new version of a familiar story—the story of Agamemnon's homecoming and his murder, the revenge of that murder by his son, Orestes, and the final disposition of justice in the case of Orestes' act—as told in the three tragedies that constitute *The Oresteia*. This magnificent trilogy is by Aeschylus, Athens's leading dramatist for more than forty years. The spectators watch closely, admiring but critical. Tomorrow they or their representatives will decide by vote whether the festival's prize should go to this work, or whether the young Sophocles, whose plays were presented in this space yesterday, had better sensed the true pulse of the time. Even forty years later, the comic playwright Aristophanes will be arguing the merits and demerits of this day's work.

It is noon in London, and Queen Elizabeth I sits on the throne. Flags fly boldly atop three of the taller buildings in Bankside, across the Thames, announcing performance day at The Globe, The Rose, and The Swan. Boatmen have already begun ferrying theater-goers

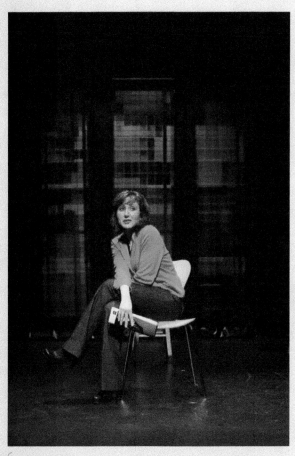

Theatre is not always—or even often—grandiose. New York actress Andrea Caban wrote, produced, and performed the only role in this acclaimed solo performance of *Questions My Mother Can't Answer*, which was seen on an American tour in 2012, following its much-lauded Manhattan debut. The production may have cost less than a thousandth of the production of *Top Hat*, but its theatrical thrills were every bit as high.

across the river, where The Globe will present a new tragedy by Shakespeare (something called *Hamlet*, supposedly after an old play by Thomas Kyd), and The Rose promises a revival of Christopher Marlowe's popular *Dr. Faustus*.

Now, at The Globe, two thousand spectators have arrived for the premiere. A trumpet sounds, then sounds again, then builds into a full fanfare. Members of the audience, standing on the ground before the stage or seated in bleachers overlooking it, exchange a few final winks with their friends old and new—covert invitations to postperformance intimacies perhaps—and turn their attention to the platform stage. Through a giant door a guard bursts forth, lantern in hand. "Who's there?" he cries. In two thousand

imaginations, the bright afternoon has turned to midnight, London's Bankside has given way to the battlements of Denmark's Elsinore, and a terrified shiver from the onstage actor has set up an answering chill among the audience. A great new tragedy has begun its course.

It is midnight in a basement in the East Village, or in a campus rehearsal room, or in a coffee shop in Pittsburgh, Seattle, Sioux Falls, or Berlin. Across one end of the room, a curtain has been drawn across a pole suspended by wires. It has been a long evening, but one play remains to be seen. The author is unknown, but rumor has it that this new work is brutal, shocking, poetic, strange. The members of the audience, by turns skeptics and enthusiasts, look for the tenth time at their programs. The lights dim. Performers, backed by crudely painted packing crates, begin to act.

What is the common denominator in all of these scenes? They are all theatre. There is no culture that has not had a theatre in some form, for theatre is the art of people acting out—and giving witness to—their most pressing, most illuminating, and most inspiring concerns. Theatre is at once a showcase and a forum, a medium through which a society displays its ideas, fashions, moralities, and entertainments, and debates its conflicts, dilemmas, yearnings, and struggles. Theatre has provided a stage for political revolution, for social propaganda, for civil debate, for artistic expression, for religious conversion, for mass education, and even for its own self-criticism. It has been a performance ground for priests, witch doctors, intellectuals, poets, painters, technologists, philosophers, reformers, evangelists, jugglers, peasants, children, and kings. It has taken place in caves, fields, and forests; in circus tents, inns, and castles; on street corners and in public buildings grand and squalid all over the world. And it goes on incessantly in the minds of its authors, its actors, its producers, its designers, and its audiences.

Theatre is, above all, a *living* art form. It does not simply consist of "plays" but also of "playing," and a play is not simply a series of "acts" but a collectivity of "acting." Just as *play* and *act* are both noun and verb, so theatre is both a thing and a happening, a result and a process: fluid in time, rich in feeling and human experience.

And above all, theatre is *live:* an art that continually forms before our eyes and is continually *present* to an

Lee Breuer is one of America's most celebrated avant-garde stage directors, so it was a surprise when France's Comédie Française, the oldest classical repertory theatre in Europe (founded in 1680), invited him in to stage their first-ever non-European play: Tennessee Williams's great—and very *non*-avant-garde—American classic, *Streetcar Named Desire*. Breuer's 2012 production went yet further abroad, transporting the play's setting to classical Japan, with exquisitely painted *dogugaeshi* screens, lavishly embroidered kimonos, and masked *kuroko* stagehands.

audience even as it is *presented* by its actors. In fact, this very quality of "presentness" (or, in the actor's terminology, "stage presence") defines every great theatrical performance.

Unlike the more static arts, theatre presents us with a number of classic paradoxes:

It is spontaneous, yet it is rehearsed.
It is participatory, yet it is presented.
It is real, yet it is simulated.
It is understandable, yet it is obscure.
It is unique to the moment, yet it is repeatable.
The actors are themselves, yet they are characters.
The audience believes, yet it does not believe.
The audience is involved, yet it remains apart.

The theatre's actors "live in the moment" during performance yet carefully study, plan, and rehearse the details of their roles beforehand. And the audience responds to this performance by rooting for dramatic "characters" to achieve their goals, then applauding the "actors" who play those roles during the curtain call. Yet these paradoxes do not represent a flaw or weakness in the logic of theatrical construction; rather, they show the theatre's essential strength, which lies in its kinship and concern with the ambiguity and irony of human life. For it is *we*—the people of the real world—who are at the same time spontaneous yet premeditating, candid yet contriving, unique yet self-repeating, comprehensible yet fundamentally unknown and unknowable. The theatre shows us, and *is* us, in all of our living complexity.

Theorists of dramatic literature and of dramatic practice often ignore the theatre's paradoxes in their attempts to "explain" a play or the art of the stage. In this they do a disservice to art as well as to scholarship, for to "explain" the theatre without reference to its ambiguities is to remove its vital dynamic tension—in other words, to kill it. And although much valuable information can certainly be discovered at an autopsy table, it is information pertinent only to the appearance and behavior of a corpse.

In this book we shall not be concerned with corpses. Our task will be the harder one—to discover the theatre in being, *alive* and with all its paradoxes and ambiguities

Theatre is, above all else, a living art, and its greatest performers live their roles physically, emotionally, and often passionately while playing them. In this internationally celebrated Australian production of Anton Chekhov's *Uncle Vanya*, which was brought to New York by the Lincoln Center Festival in 2012, Richard Roxburgh and Cate Blanchett throw both their bodies and feelings into the desperately confused characters of Uncle Vanya and his ex-brother-in-law's wife Yelana, whom the hapless Vanya loves. Guided by acclaimed Hungarian director Tamas Ascher, the production creates a stunning mélange of tragic despair and rip-roaring humor. Chekhov, as Ms. Blanchett says in a TV interview, "creates epic moments in peoples' very small domestic lives," and these veteran actors fill such epochal instants with their own flesh and blood eight times a week.

intact. From time to time it will be necessary for us to make some separations—between product and process, for example—but we must bear in mind at all times that these separations are conveniences, not representations or facts. In the end we shall be looking at the theatre as part of the human environment and at the ways in which we fit into that environment—as participants and observers, artists and art critics, role models and role players, actors and persons. As such, this book about the theatre is also about ourselves.

Chapter 1

What Is Theatre?

WHAT IS THEATRE? The word comes from the Greek *theatron,* or "seeing place." A theatre is a place where something is seen.

Today we use the word *theatre* in many ways. We use it to describe the building where plays are put on: the architecture, the structure, the space for dramatic performance—the place where "something is seen." We also use it to indicate where films are shown, as in "movie theatre." And we use it metaphorically to refer to a place where wars and surgeries occur: the "theatre of operations" and the "operating theatre." These are all examples of the "hardware" definition of *theatre.*

The "software" definition—the *activity* involved in theatre—is far more important. For *theatre* also refers to the players (and owners, managers, and technicians) who perform in such a space and to the plays that such a company produces. When we speak of "the Guthrie Theatre," we are referring not merely to a building in Minneapolis, but also to the stage artists and administrators who work in that building and to the body of plays produced there. We also are referring to a body of ideas—a vision—that animates the Guthrie Theatre artists and the plays they produce. *Theatre,* in this sense, is a combination of people and ideas—and the works of art that result from this collaboration. ▶

We also use the word *theatre* to summon the professional *occupation*—and often the passion—of thousands of men and women all over the world. It is a vocation and sometimes a lifetime devotion. *A Life in the Theatre* is the title of one theatre artist's autobiography (Tyrone Guthrie, in fact, for whom the Guthrie Theatre in Minneapolis is named), as well as the title of a play about actors by the contemporary American dramatist David Mamet. But *A Life in the Theatre* could also be the title for the unrecorded biographies of the theatre artists who have dedicated their professional lives to perfecting the special arts of acting, directing, designing, managing, and writing for "the theatre" in all the senses described above.

Theatre as a building, a company, an occupation—let's look at all three of these usages more closely.

THE THEATRE BUILDING

A theatre is not always an enclosed structure. The most ancient Greek *theatron* was probably no more than a circle of bare earth, where performers chanted and danced before a hillside of seated spectators. The requirements for building such a theatre were minimal: finding a space to act and a space to watch and hear.

As theatre grew in popularity and importance, however, its simplicity required further elaboration. Attention had to be given to seating larger and larger numbers of people, so the hillside soon became an ascending bank of seats, each level providing a good view of the acting area. And as the *theatron* grew, attention had to be paid to *acoustics* (from the Greek *acoustos*, "heard"), so the sounds coming from the stage would

National theatre buildings in many European countries, generally supported by their governments, are often palatial. The National Theatre in Cluj, Romania, is regarded as the most beautiful building in this Transylvanian capital, which indicates the prominence of live theatre in that country.

be protected from the wind and directed (or reflected) toward the *audience* (from the Latin *audientia*, "those who hear").

Often these spaces—for performing and for seeing and hearing—can be casually defined: the audience is up there, the actors are down there. Occasionally, the spaces are merged together, with the actors mingling—and sometimes interacting—with the watchers and listeners. When the practice of selling tickets and paying actors began (more than twenty-five hundred years ago), these spaces became more rigidly separated.

Theatre buildings may be elaborate structures. Greek theatres of the fourth century B.C.—the period immediately following the golden age of Greek playwrights—were gigantic stone edifices, some capable of holding up to seventeen thousand spectators. Magnificent three-story Roman theatres, complete with gilded columns, canvas awnings, and intricate marble carvings, were often erected for dramatic festivals in the later years of the Republic—only to be dismantled when the festivities ended. Grand free-standing Elizabethan theatres dominate the London skyline in illustrated sixteenth-century pictorial maps of the town. Opulent proscenium theatres were built throughout Europe and in the major cities of the United States in the eighteenth and nineteenth centuries. Many remain in full operation today, competing with splendid new stagehouses of every description and serving as cultural centers for metropolitan areas around the world. Theatres (the buildings) are fundamental to urban architecture, just as theatre (the art) is to contemporary life.

THE COMPANY, OR TROUPE, OF PLAYERS

Theatre is a collaborative art, usually involving dozens, even hundreds, of people working closely together on a single performance. Historically, therefore, theatre practitioners of various specialties have teamed up in long-standing companies, or troupes. Since the fourth century B.C., such troupes of players (actors or, more literally, "playmakers") have toured the countrysides and settled in cities to present a repertory of plays as a means of earning a livelihood. Generally such players have included actor-playwrights and actor-technicians, making the company a self-contained production unit capable of writing, preparing, and presenting whole theatrical works that tend to define the company itself. Some of these troupes—and the works they produced—have become legendary: for example, the Lord Chamberlain's Men of London, which

This watercolor depicts the opulent interior of Booth's Theatre in New York at its 1869 opening. This grand "temple of theatre" was built by America's finest actor of the time, Edwin Booth (the brother of Lincoln's assassin). Booth staged and performed in a classical repertory of Shakespearean plays at his theatre for four years. The side boxes, similar to those that still exist in older Broadway theatres, had poor sight lines: spectators electing to sit there were interested more in being seen than in seeing the play. The luxurious seating in the orchestra made this a particularly comfortable and elegant place to see classic theatre. Charles Witham, Booth's original stage designer, painted this watercolor; part of Witham's scenery (a street scene) is visible onstage.

counted William Shakespeare as a member; and the Illustrious Theatre of Paris, founded and headed by the great actor-writer Molière. The influence of these theatre companies has proven more long-lasting than the theatre buildings that, in some cases, physically survived them. They represent the genius and creativity of theatre in a way that stone and steel alone cannot.

Shakespeare's Globe has been meticulously reconstructed near its sixteenth-century location on the south bank of London's Thames River. The reconstruction was spearheaded by the late Sam Wanamaker, an American actor who labored many years to acquire the funding and necessary permits (the theatre has the first thatch roof laid in London since the Great Fire of 1666). This is scholarship's best guess as to the specific dimensions and features of The Globe in Shakespeare's time. Since its 1997 opening this Globe has produced a summer repertoire of the plays of Shakespeare's age, seen on a stage much like the stages they were written for.

THE OCCUPATION OF THEATRE

Theatre is also the *occupation* of its practitioners. It is a vocation for professionals and an avocation for amateurs, yet in either case, theatre is *work*. Specifically, it is that body of artistic work in which actors impersonate characters in a live performance of a play. Each aspect of theatre as occupation—work, art, impersonation, and performance—deserves individual attention.

Work

The "work" of theatre is indeed hard work. Rehearsals alone normally take a minimum of four to six weeks, which are preceded by at least an equal amount of time—and often months or years—of writing, researching, planning, casting, designing, and creating a production ensemble. The labors of theatre artists in the final weeks before an opening are legendary: the seven-day work-week becomes commonplace, expenditures of money and

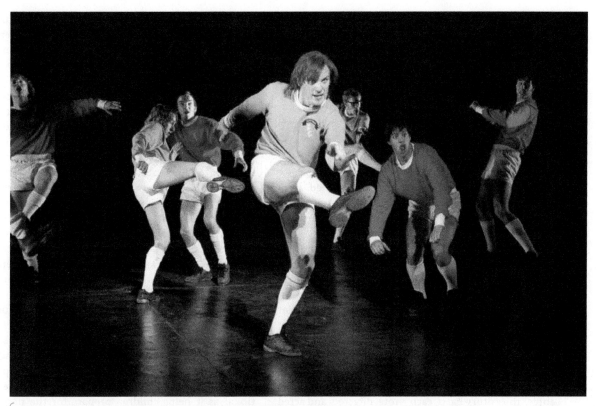

Games and serious theatre have always been related, and some plays combine these different "playing" motifs. Richard Greenberg's *Take Me Out* takes place in a baseball locker room in America, David Storey's *The Changing Room* in a rugby locker room in England. Pictured here, Andrew Lloyd Webber's musical *The Beautiful Game* takes place in Northern Ireland, on a soccer field, where it portrays contemporary violence and religious intolerance rampant between English and Irish teenagers in recent decades.

spirit are intense, and even the unions relax their regulations to allow for an almost unbridled invasion of the hours the ordinary world spends sleeping, eating, and unwinding. The theatre enterprise may involve hundreds of people in scores of different efforts—many more backstage than onstage—and the mobilization and coordination of these efforts are in themselves giant tasks. So when we think of the "work" embodied in the theatrical arts, we must think of work in the sense of physical toil as well as in the loftier sense of *oeuvre*, by which the French designate the sum of an artist's creative endeavor.

The work of the theatre is generally divisible into a number of crafts:

Producing, which includes securing all necessary personnel, space, and financing; supervising all production and promotional efforts; fielding all legal matters; and distributing all proceeds derived from receipts

Directing, which includes controlling and developing the artistic product and providing it with a unified vision, coordinating all of its components, and supervising its rehearsals

Acting, in which actors perform the roles of characters in a play

Designing, in which designers map out the visual and aural elements of a production, including the scenery, properties, costumes and wigs, makeup, lighting, sound, programs, advertising, and general ambience of the premises

Building, in which carpenters, costumers, wigmakers, electricians, makeup artists, recording and sound engineers, painters, and a host of other specially designated craftspeople translate the design into reality by constructing and finishing, in detail, the "hardware" of a show

Crewing, in which technicians execute in proper sequence and with carefully rehearsed timing the light and sound cues and the shifting of scenery, as well as oversee the placement and return of properties and the assignment, laundering, repair, and changes of costumes

Stage managing, which includes the responsibility for "running" a play production in all its complexity in performance after performance

House managing, which includes the responsibility for admitting, seating, and providing for the general comfort of the audience

And, above all, there is *playwriting*—and for musical theatre, *composing*—which are in a class by themselves. These crafts of theatre are normally executed away from the theatre building and its associated shops. Indeed, they may take place continents and centuries away from the productions they inspire.

Of course, the work of the theatre need not be divided exactly as the preceding list indicates. In any production, some people perform more than one kind of work; for example, many of the builders also crew. And it is not uncommon for playwrights to direct what they write, for directors to act in their own productions, and for designers to build at least some of what they design. On some celebrated occasions multitalented theatre artists have taken on multiple roles at the same time: Aeschylus, in ancient Greece, and Molière, in seventeenth-century Paris, each wrote, directed, and acted in their own plays, and probably designed them as well; William Shakespeare was a playwright, actor, and co-owner of the Lord Chamberlain's Men in Elizabethan times; Bertolt Brecht revolutionized both playwriting and acting when writing and directing his plays in Berlin after World War II; and Mel Brooks, in our own century, wrote the text and lyrics, composed the music, and produced his 2001 Broadway show, *The Producers.*

Theatre is also work in the sense that it is not "play." This distinction is more subtle than we might at once imagine. First, of course, recall that we ordinarily use the word *play* in describing the main product of theatre work: while children "play games," adults may "play roles" or "put on a play." This is not merely a peculiarity of the English language, for we find the French *jeu,* the German *Spiel,* the Hungarian *játék,* the Chinese *xi,* and the Latin *ludi* all share the double meaning of the English *play,* referring both to children's games and to dramatic plays and playing. This association points to a relationship that is fundamental to our understanding of theatre: theatre *is* a kind of playing, and it is useful for us to see how and why this is so.

Theatre and games have a shared history. Both were developed to a high level of sophistication in Greek festivals: the Dionysian theatre festivals and the Olympian game—or sport—festivals were the two great cultural events of ancient Greece, each embodying the legendary Greek competition for excellence. The Romans merged sports and theatre in public circuses, where the two were performed side by side, often in competition with each other. And more than a millennium later, the Londoners of Shakespeare's time built "playhouses" that could accommodate dramatic productions on one day and bear-baiting spectacles (somewhat akin to bullfights) on the next. The association—and popularity—of dramatic and sports entertainment continues today, where dramatizations (sitcoms, detective and courtroom dramas, even TV commercials) and games (spectator sports, quiz shows, reality shows) dominate television fare around the world. Meanwhile, professional athletes and stage entertainers are among the foremost (and most highly paid) celebrities of the modern age. Many a retired sports hero has even found a second career in the other type of play: acting.

This link between games and theatre is formed early in life, for "child's play" usually manifests both gamelike and dramalike aspects. Much child's play includes dressing up and acting out, where children create improvisations they may call "playing cops and robbers." Like drama, this kind of play is also educational as it helps children prepare for the necessary role-playing of adult life. Structured games are similarly instructional: hide-and-seek, for example, a playful and engrossing game, also offers an opportunity to act out one of childhood's greatest fears—the terror of separation from the parent, or "separation anxiety," as psychologists term it. Hide-and-seek affords the child a way of dealing with separation anxiety by confronting it "in play" until it loses much of its frightening power. Such "child's play" is grounded in serious concerns, and through the act of playing the child gradually develops means of coping with life's challenges and uncertainties. The theatre's plays and playing often serve the same role for adults.

Drama and games are likewise linked in that they are among the very few occupations that also attract large numbers of wholly *amateur* "players," individuals who seek no compensation beyond sheer personal satisfaction. This is because both drama and games offer wonderful opportunities for intense physical involvement, friendly competition, personal self-expression, and emotional engagement, all within limits set by precise and sensible rules. And both sport and drama generate an audience for their activities because the energies and passions expressed by each—common enough on children's playgrounds but rarely seen in daily adult life—can prove immensely engaging to nonparticipating spectators.

Nevertheless, the theatre must be distinguished from child's play, and from sports as well, because theatre is by its nature a calculated act from beginning to end. Unlike adult games, which are open-ended, every theatre performance has a preordained conclusion. The Yankees may not win the World Series next year, but Hamlet definitely will die in the fifth act. The work of the theatre, indeed, consists in keeping Hamlet *alive* up to that point—brilliantly alive—to make of that foreordained end a profoundly moving, ennobling, and even surprising climax.

We might say, finally, that *theatre is the art of making play into work*—specifically, into *a work of art*. It is exhilarating work, to be sure, and it usually inspires and invigorates the energies and imaginations of all who participate; it transcends more prosaic forms of labor just as song transcends grunts and groans. But it is, ultimately, work. That is its challenge.

Art

The word *art* brings to mind a host of intangibles: creativity, imagination, elegance, power, aesthetic harmony, and fineness of form. We expect a work of art to capture something of the human spirit and to touch upon familiar, but intellectually elusive, meanings in life. Certainly great theatre never fails to bring together many of these intangibles. In great theatre we glimpse not only the physical and emotional exuberance of play, but also the deep yearnings that propel humanity's search for purpose, meaning, and a life well lived.

Art, of course, is a supreme pursuit of humanity, uniquely integrating our emotions with our intellects and our aesthetics with our revelations. Art is empowering both to those who make it and to those who appreciate it. Art sharpens thought and focuses feeling; it brings up reality against imagination and presses creativity to the ever-expanding limits of human potential. Although life may be fragmented, inconclusive, and frustrating, a beautiful painting, choral hymn, jazz rendition, or dance recital can provide us with near-instant integration, synthesis, and satisfaction. We might find similar values in religion as well, but art is accessible without subscribing to any particular set of beliefs; it is, for everyone, an open-ended response to life's unending puzzles. It is surely for this reason that all great religions—both Eastern and Western—have employed art and artworks (including dramatic art) in their liturgies and services from the earliest of times.

Impersonation

The theatrical art involves actors impersonating characters. This feature is unique to the theatre and separates it from art forms such as poetry, painting, sculpture, music, performance art, cabaret acts, and like activities. Further, impersonation is the single most important aspect of the theatre; it is its very foundation.

Try to imagine what extreme conceptual difficulties the ancient creators of the theatre encountered in laying down ground rules for dramatic impersonation. How was the audience to distinguish the character being portrayed from the actor playing the character? Even today, TV fans write letters to characters in their shows, asking how they could possibly have fallen in love with some other character, and film buffs swap theories on what befalls Leonardo DiCaprio's character at the end of *Inception*. Given this confusion between the real actor and the fictional character he or she plays—even now, in what we like to think of as a sophisticated age—it is easy to see why the ancients had to resolve the problem of actor-character separation before the theatre could become a firmly established institution.

The solution the ancient world found was the mask. Western theatre had its true beginning that day in ancient Greece when an actor first stepped out of the chorus, placed an unpainted mask over his face, and thereby signaled that the lines he was about to speak were "in character." The mask provides both a physical and a symbolic separation between the impersonator (the actor) and the impersonated (the character), thus aiding onlookers in temporarily suspending their awareness of the "real" world and accepting in its place the world of the stage. In a play, it must be the *characters* who have apparent life; the actors themselves are expected to disappear into the shadows, along with their personal preoccupations, anxieties, and career ambitions. This convention of the stage gives rise to what Denis Diderot, an eighteenth-century French dramatist (and author of the world's first encyclopedia), called the "paradox of the actor": when the actor has perfected his or her art, it is the *simulated* character, the mask, that seems to live before our eyes, while the real person has no apparent life at all. The strength of such an illusion still echoes in our use of the word *person*, which derives from the Latin word (*persona*) for mask.

But of course we know the actor does not die behind the mask, and herein lies an even greater paradox: we believe in the *character*, but at the end of the play we applaud the *actor*. Not only that—as we watch good theatre we are always, in the back of our

Masks were fundamental to ancient theatre and often appear in contemporary productions, particularly in revivals of such classic works. Christina Uribe's masks, sculpted in the ancient Greek tradition, were employed in this Greek/French production of Sophocles' *Antigone* directed by Philippe Brunet for his Demodocos company, which since 1995 has been devoted to the pursuit of what Brunet calls "Dionysian mystery theatre." The production, with costumes by Florence Kukucka, was featured at the "off" schedule of France's 2008 Avignon Theatre Festival; shown here are two chorus members.

minds, applauding the actor. Our appreciation of theatre rests largely on our dual awareness of actor and character and on our understanding they live inside the same skin.

Masks were used throughout the ancient Greek theatre period, and as we shall see in the pages that follow, they were also staples of many other theatres of the past, including the masquerade dramas of Nigeria, the *nō* and *kyōgen* drama of Japan, and the *commedia dell'arte* of Italy. They are still seen onstage today, not only in stagings of these historic forms but in expressionist and avant-garde productions. But beyond the mask's physical presence, the *idea* of masking—of hiding the performer while displaying the character—remains at the heart of impersonation. As such, the mask endures—often as the back-to-back masks of comedy and tragedy that adorn a theatre company letterhead—as the most fundamental symbol of theatre itself.

Performance

Theatre is performance, but what, exactly, does *performance* mean? Performance is an action or series of actions taken for the ultimate benefit (attention, entertainment, enlightenment, or involvement) of someone else. We call that "someone else" the audience.

Presentational styles make little pretense of mimicking ordinary life. Here, director Susan Stroman creates a wonderful farcical moment in *The Producers* as "theatre queen" director Roger De Bris (played in drag by Gary Beach) desperately tries to keep his wig on. Facial expressions around the room focus the action and intensify the hilarity. Matthew Broderick and Nathan Lane (*at left*) are the producers of the musical's title. De Bris's hangers-on (with the gaping Roger Bart as his "common-law assistant," Carmen Ghia) are perfectly arranged on the stairs by director Stroman to capture every possible droll expression. Scenic design is by Robin Wagner, costumes by William Ivey Long, and lighting by Peter Kaczorowski.

A strictly private conversation between two people is simply "communication." If, however, they engage in a conversation to impress or involve a third person who they know is in a position to overhear it, the communication becomes a "performance" and the third person becomes its "audience."

Obviously, performance is a part of everyday life; indeed, it has been analyzed as such in a number of psychological and sociological works. When two teenage boys wrestle on the schoolground, they may well be performing their physical prowess for the benefit of their peers. The student who asks a question in the lecture hall is frequently "performing" for the other students—and the professor performs for the same audience in providing a response. Trial lawyers examining witnesses invariably perform—often drawing on a considerable repertoire of grunts, snorts, shrugs, raised eyebrows, and disbelieving sighs—for the benefit of that ultimate courtroom audience, the jury. Politicians kiss babies for

the benefit of parents (and others) in search of a kindly candidate. Even stony silence can be a performance—if, for example, it is the treatment a woman metes out to an overly eager admirer. We are all performers, and the theatre only makes an art out of something we all do everyday. The theatre expands our everyday performances into a formal mode of artistic expression.

The theatre makes use of two general modes of performance: presentational (or direct) and representational (or indirect). *Presentational* performance is the basic stand-up comedy or nightclub mode. Presentational performers directly and continuously acknowledge the presence of audience members by singing to them; dancing for them; joking with them; and responding openly to their applause, laughter, requests, and heckling. Dramatic forms of all ages have employed these techniques and a variety of other presentational methods, including asides to the audience, soliloquies, direct address, and curtain calls.

This production of Bertolt Brecht's sharply satirical *Threepenny Opera*, directed by Robert Wilson at the Berliner Ensemble theatre (which Brecht founded in 1949), follows Brecht's representational concepts, with its bold colors, super-white faced actors facing front, and deliberately artificial lighting. The production played in New York City in 2011.

Representational performance, however, is the more fundamental mode of drama that certainly makes drama "dramatic" as opposed to simply "theatrical." In representational performance, the audience watches behavior that seems to be staged as if no audience were present. As a result, the audience is encouraged to concentrate on the *events* that are being staged, not on the nature of their presentation. This allows members of the audience to "believe in" the play and forget the characters are really actors and the apparently spontaneous events are really a series of scripted scenes. This belief—or, to borrow Samuel Taylor Coleridge's famous double negative, this "willing suspension of disbelief"—attracts audience participation through empathy: our feeling of kinship with certain (or all) of the characters, which encourages us to identify with their aspirations, sympathize with their plights, exult in their victories, and care deeply about what happens to them. When empathy is present, the audience experiences what is often called the "magic" of theatre. Well-written and well-staged dramas make people *feel*, not just think; they draw in the spectators' emotions, leaving them

feeling transported and even somewhat changed. This is as much magic as our current world provides.

Occasionally, presentational and representational styles are taken to extremes. In the late nineteenth century, the representational movement known as *realism* sought to have actors behave onstage exactly as real people do in life, in settings made as lifelike as possible (on one occasion, a famous New York restaurant was completely disassembled and reconstructed on a stage, complete with its original moldings, wallpaper, furniture, silverware, and table linens). At times the representational ideal so dominated in certain theatres that actors spoke with their backs to audiences, directors encouraged lifelike pauses and inaudible mumblings, playwrights transcribed dialogue from fragments of randomly overheard conversations, and house managers timed intermissions to the presumed time elapsing in the play's story.

Rebelling against this extreme representationalism, the twentieth-century German playwright-director Bertolt Brecht created its opposite: a presentational style that, seeking to appeal directly to the audience on a variety of social and political issues, featured openly visible lighting instruments; signs, songs, slide projections, and speeches addressed directly to the audience; and a "distanced" style of acting intended to reduce emotional empathy or theatrical "magic." Those extremes, however, exist more in theory than in practice. During naturalistic performances, we are always aware that we are watching actors perform for us, and the plays of Brecht and his followers, despite his theories, generate empathy when well performed. For the fact is that theatrical performance is always both presentational and representational, though often in different degrees.

Two other aspects of performance distinguish theatre from certain other forms of performance: theatre is *live* performance, and in most cases it is a *scripted* and *rehearsed* event.

Live Performance   In contrast to video and cinema (although sometimes employing elements of both), the theatre is a living, real-time event in which performers and audience mutually interact, each fully aware of the other's immediate presence. This distinction turns out to be extremely important. Distinguished film stars, particularly those with theatre backgrounds (as most have), routinely return to the live dramatic stage despite the substantially greater financial rewards of film work, and they invariably prefer stage acting because of the immediate audience response theatre provides, with its corresponding sensations of excitement and "presence." Beyond question, fundamental forces are at work in live theatre.

The first of these forces is the rapport existing between actor and audience. Both are breathing the same air; both are involved, at the same time and in the same space, with the stage life depicted by the play. Sometimes their mutual fascination is almost palpable: every actor's performance is affected by the way the audience yields or withholds its responses—its laughter, sighs, applause, gasps, and silences. Live theatrical performance is always—even in naturalistic theatre—a two-way communication between stage and house.

And second, live theatre creates a relationship among the audience members. Having arrived at the theatre as individuals or in groups of two or three, audience members quickly find themselves fused to a common experience with total strangers: laughing at the same jokes, empathizing with the same characters, experiencing the same revelations. This broad communal response is never developed by television drama, which is played chiefly to solitary or clustered viewers who (because of frequent commercials) are

Some actors prefer to act only on stage, and others only on camera, but most actors seek to do both. The lure of the stage is hard for actors to resist, despite its significantly lower pay. Katie Holmes and John Lithgow, embracing joyously in this 2008 Broadway revival of Arthur Miller's World War II drama *All My Sons,* have extensive film and TV credentials—Holmes with more than 150 TV episodes and films, and Lithgow with more than 250, but they came with unequal stage experience. This was Lithgow's twenty-first Broadway role, and Holmes's first. Nevertheless, "Holmes makes a fine Broadway debut," said the *New York Daily News* reviewer (as did your author), even playing opposite Lithgow and many distinguished veterans of the stage.

only intermittently engaged; nor is it likely to happen in movie houses, where audience members essentially assume a one-on-one relationship with the screen and rarely (except in private or group-oriented screenings) break out in a powerful collective response, much less applause. In contrast, live theatrical presentations generate audience activity that is broadly social: audience members arrive at the theatre at about the same time, they mingle and chat during intermissions, and they all depart together, often in spirited conversation about the play. Moreover, they communicate *during* the play: laughter and applause build upon themselves and gain strength from the recognition that others are laughing and applauding. The final ovation—unique to live performance—inevitably involves the audience applauding *itself,* as well as the performers, for understanding and appreciating the theatrical excellence they have all seen together. And plays with political themes can even generate collective political response. In a celebrated example, the Depression-era *Waiting for Lefty* was staged as if the audience were a group of union members; by the play's end the audience was yelling "Strike! Strike!" in response to the play's issues. Obviously, only a live performance could evoke such a response.

Finally, live performance inevitably has the quality of *immediacy.* The action of the play is taking place *right now,* as it is being watched, and anything can happen. Although in most professional productions the changes that occur in performance from one night to the next are so subtle only an expert would notice, the fact is that each night's presentation is unique and everyone present—in the audience, in the cast, and behind the scenes—knows it. This awareness lends an excitement that cannot be experienced while watching films or video, which are wholly "in the can" before they are viewed. One reason for the excitement of live theatre, of course, is that mistakes can happen in its performance; this possibility occasions a certain abiding tension, perhaps even an edge of stage fright, which some people say creates the ultimate thrill of the theatre. But just as disaster can come without warning, so too can splendor. On any given night, each actor is trying to better her or his previous performance, and no one knows when this collective effort will coalesce into something sublime. In this way, the immediacy of live performance creates a "presentness," or "presence," that embodies the fundamental uncertainty of life itself. One prime function of theatre is to address the uncertainties of human existence, and the very format of live performance presents moment-to-moment uncertainty right before our eyes. Ultimately, this "immediate theatre" helps us define the questions and confusions of our lives and lets us grapple, in the present, with their implications.

Scripted and Rehearsed Performance Theatre performances are largely prepared according to written and well-rehearsed texts, or play scripts. In this way they are often distinguished from other forms of performance, such as improvisation and performance installations. Although improvisation and ad-libbing may play a role in the preparation process, and even in certain actual performances, most play productions are based on a script that was established before—and modified during—the play's rehearsal period, and most of the action is permanently set during these rehearsals as well. Mainstream professional play productions, therefore, appear nearly the same night after night: for the most part, the Broadway production of *Wicked* that you see on Thursday will be almost identical to the show your friend saw on Wednesday or your mother saw last fall. And if you were to read the published text, you would see on the page the same words you heard spoken or sung on the stage.

But the text of a play is not, by any means, the play itself. The play fully exists only in its performance—in its "playing." The script is merely the record the play leaves behind after the audience has gone home. The script, therefore, is to the play it represents only what a shadow painting is to the face it silhouettes: it outlines the principal features but conveys only the outer margins of the complexity, color, smell, and spirit of the living person.

And published scripts are an imperfect record at that. Often they carry over material left out of the actual production, or they include new material the author thought of after the production was over. The published texts of Shakespeare's plays include differing versions of many of his plays, including two versions of *King Lear* written several years apart. When American dramatist Tennessee Williams published his *Cat on a Hot Tin Roof* after the play's premiere, he included both the third act he originally wrote and the third act written at director Elia Kazan's request, which was actually used, and he invited readers to select their preferred version. Moreover, even a fixed script is often as notable for what it lacks as for what it contains. Plays published before the twentieth century rarely have more than rudimentary stage directions, and even now a published play tells us almost nothing about the play's nonverbal components. How can a printed text capture the bead of sweat that forms on Hamlet's brow as he stabs Polonius, or Romeo's nervous laugh as he tries to part dueling adversaries, or the throbbing anxiety in Beatrice's breast when she first admits to Benedick that she loves him? The published text gives us the printed, but not the spoken, word: it largely fails us in providing the sounds and inflections of those words, the tones and facial expressions of the actors, the color and sweep of costumes, the play of light and shadow, the movement of forms in space—and the audience response to all this—that come together in a living production.

What, then, is the chief value of play scripts? They generate theatrical productions and provide an

○Spotlight

Film Stars on Stage Acting

The vast majority of film stars got their start acting onstage in high school, college, or small theatres near their hometowns. Many of them—including the most successful—return to live stage performing. Film and TV stars Al Pacino, Scarlett Johansson, Daniel Radcliffe, Samuel L. Jackson, Andrew Garfield, Frances McDormand, Vanessa Redgrave, Kiefer Sutherland, Edie Falco, Ellen Barkin, Catherine Zeta-Jones, Jude Law, Denzel Washington, Laura Linney, and Christopher Walken all found themselves acting on Broadway in recent seasons. Why would these actors, plus the likes of David Hyde Pierce, Katie Holmes, Jane Fonda, Matthew Broderick, Jeremy Irons, Anne Hathaway, Frank Langella, James Gandolfini, Geoffrey Rush, John Lithgow, Christian Slater, Anthony Hopkins, Ethan Hawke, Meryl Streep, and Kevin Spacey, leave Hollywood for such vastly lower-paying stage work? Here are some of their replies:

I love acting for the camera. But in film your performance doesn't really belong to you. It belongs to the director and the editor and the producers. Onstage [in Arthur Miller's A View from the Bridge*], the audience saw everything I had, not some reshaped version of it. The same arc was there every night, of course, and yet it was a living, breathing thing.*

—SCARLETT JOHANNSON

Theater is about authenticity. It's in front of you; you feel it. It's so hard to feel stuff anymore from film. . . . It can get very remote.

—MERYL STREEP

If my movie career was totally terminated, I would be saddened and disappointed . . . but if that were to happen with the live theater, it would be devastating. [Theatre] is like a fountain that I have to return to.

—PATRICK STEWART

One of the glorious things about the theatre is that it cannot be preserved. You can't look at it again; it's live. . . . Cinema's dead. You can laugh, you can cry, you can shout at the screen and the movie will carry on. But an audience in the theatre, whether it knows it or not, is affecting the performance. . . . That's the stream of life at its best, isn't it?

—IAN MCKELLEN

In film, the challenge is to be able to shape a performance when the process is so piecemeal. And the absolute joy of being onstage is you get to surf that wave. It's a much more muscular experience.

—CATE BLANCHETT

There is only so long you can go from film to film. Theatre is a more raw experience. For an actor a live audience is creative inspiration.

—JUDE LAW

My primary focus is theatre. It's the most satisfying place to be as an actor.

—KEVIN SPACEY

Acting on stage was the best life experience I've had.

—BEN AFFLECK

I love the stage, and I love being on stage, and the rush and the fear and all of that.

—DANIEL RADCLIFFE

Nothing was going to stand in my way of doing that play.

—ASHLEY JUDD, EXPLAINING WHY SHE TURNED DOWN THE TITLE ROLE IN HOLLYWOOD'S *CATWOMAN* TO BE ONSTAGE IN A NEW YORK REVIVAL OF *CAT ON A HOT TIN ROOF*

---

invaluable, albeit imperfect, record of performances past. Two-and-a-half millennia of play productions have left us a repository of thousands upon thousands of scripts, some awful, many ordinary, a few magnificent. This rich store puts us in touch with theatre history in the making and allows us a glimpse back at the nature of the originals in production. It also suggests ways in which the plays of yesterday can serve as blueprints for vital theatre today.

This, then, is the theatre: buildings, companies, and plays; work, art, impersonation, and performance; living performers and written, rehearsed scripts. It is a production; an assemblage of actions, sights, sounds, ideas, feelings, words, light, and, above all, people. It consists of playing and, of course, plays.

What is a play? That question deserves a separate chapter.

Chapter **2**

What Is a Play?

A PLAY IS, ESSENTIALLY, WHAT HAPPENS in theatre. A play is not a thing but an event. Other theatrical events may be created onstage—performance art, rock concerts, stand-up comedy, poetry readings, storytelling, and cabaret performances—and we will discuss some of these alternate theatrical presentations elsewhere. From the distant past to the present day, however, the theatre's basic unit has always been the play.

The play supplies the theatre's *drama,* a word whose origin is from the Greek *dran,* "something done." The word *theatron,* we remember, means "seeing place," and the two companion terms *theatron* and *dran* help us understand the essence of theatre: something is both done and communally witnessed. A play, then, is *action,* not just words in a book.

Action, however, is not merely movement. It is argument, struggle, persuasion, terror, seduction, sound, music, dance, speech, and passion. It comprises all forms of living human energy, including language, spatial dynamics, light, color, sonic shocks, aesthetic harmonies, and "remarkable things happening" from moment to moment. ▶

Yet a play does not merely produce (or reproduce) live action; drama frames and focuses such action around a particular conflict that lends it meaning and significance. As Shakespeare's Macbeth says, life may be "a tale told by an idiot, full of sound and fury, signifying nothing," but drama, which is also full of sound and fury, signifies all sorts of things—if not exactly answers, then at least perspectives, vocabularies, illuminating arguments, and revelations. Conflict, generally between characters but also within them, shapes the action into purposeful, meaningful human struggles, the composite of which contains dramatic stories against which we can judge our own endeavors. A play presents cautionary tales or characters that can serve as role models; it offers themes, ideas, and revelations we can accept, scorn, or store for future contemplation. Fundamentally, a play is a piece of life that has been animated, shaped, and framed to become a work of art. It provides a structured synthesis—sometimes a critique and sometimes a celebration—of life's glories and confusions.

Yet a play is also a piece of literature. In the West there has been a reading audience for plays at least since the time of the ancient Greeks, and play collections, such as Shakespeare's works, have been published since the Renaissance. Today, plays are often printed in literary anthologies, intermixed with poems, short stories, and even novels. But drama should not be thought of as merely a "branch" of literature; it is foremost a live performance, of which some repeatable aspects (chiefly, the words) may be captured in a written and published text. Continuing with the arboreal metaphor, drama would have to be considered the "trunk" of the literary tree, not merely a branch. Certainly no other literary form—novel, epic poem, lyric poem, short story—has the same sustained level of literary excellence over twenty-five centuries as does the written dramatic work of Aeschylus, Sophocles, Euripides, Aristophanes, Marlowe, Shakespeare, Jonson, Chikamatsu, Racine, Corneille, Lope de Vega, Calderón, Molière, Congreve, Goethe, Schiller, Ibsen, Wilde, Chekhov, Shaw, O'Neill, Pirandello, Giraudoux, Sartre, Brecht, Beckett, Williams, Wilson, and so on.

Finally, as we learned in the chapter titled "What Is Theatre?", a play is "playing," and those who create plays are "players." The theatrical play contains root notions of "child's play" in its acting out and adventurism, of dressing up in its costumes and props, and of the thrill of sportive competition in its energy and abandon. Like all play, drama is an exhibition, and in a real sense its players are willingly exhibitionistic. These are not simply literary characteristics.

CLASSIFYING PLAYS

Plays may be volatile, but they are also contained. They are framed, with a beginning and end, and no matter how original, they can be classified in a variety of ways, most fundamentally by *duration* and by *genre*. Although those categories were emphasized more in the past than they are today, they still play a part in our understanding of drama.

Duration

How long is a play? American playwright Arthur Miller admitted that when he first thought of writing for the theatre, "How long should it be?" was his most pressing question. The answer is far from obvious. And the fact that Arthur Miller had to puzzle over a play's duration makes it clear it has implications beyond being merely a technical consideration.

Historically, in Western drama, a "full-length" play has usually lasted between two and three hours. This is not an entirely arbitrary period of time; it represents roughly the hours between lunch and dinner (for a matinee) or between dinner and bedtime. The Jacobean playwright John Webster wrote that the actor "entertains us in the best leisure of our life, that is between meals, the most unfit time either for study or bodily exercise." Webster was thinking of the afternoon performances in the outdoor theatres of his day (c. 1615). A few years earlier, speaking of candlelit evening performances at court, Shakespeare's Theseus, in *A Midsummer Night's Dream*, asks for a play "to wear away this long age of three hours between our after-supper and bed-time." Elsewhere, however, Shakespeare refers to "the two-hours traffic of our stage" (in and about *Romeo and Juliet*), and in fact the average running time for the plays appearing on Broadway in 2012 was two hours and one minute—and for musicals two hours 26 minutes. Shakespeare's sense of an audience's patience was much like our own.

But plays can be much shorter or longer. One-act plays of an hour or less, or even popular "ten-minute plays," are occasionally combined to make a full theatre program. Short plays, which have existed since ancient times, can be presented in lunchtime theatres, dramatic festivals, school assemblies, social gatherings, street entertainments, cabaret performances, or other nontraditional settings. The shortest play on record is probably Samuel Beckett's *Breath*, which can be performed in one minute. There are exceptionally

Aristotle's exemplary model of catharsis in ancient Greek tragedy is the act of Oedipus blinding himself at the climax of Sophocles' *Oedipus Tyrannos*, during which, offstage, the Theban ruler stabs through his eyeballs with his dead wife's brooches. In this 2009 French production, Bruno Ouzeau, as Oedipus, returns to the stage appropriately bloodied after this brutal act. But since this is a dramatic tragedy and not a horror film, the blood is portrayed in a stylized rather than a realistic manner, as would have been the case with the original actor of Sophocles' play, who while offstage would have replaced his standard "tragic mask" with a special mask painted with bloody eye sockets.

long plays as well, particularly in Asia, where traditional Chinese theatre can last all day and Indian dance-dramas last all night. In recent decades, eight- or nine-hour productions have proven popular in the West, such as Tom Stoppard's *Coast of Utopia* in London and New York, Peter Brook's *Mahabharata* in Paris, Peter Stein's production of Aeschylus's *Oresteia* in Berlin, and Tony Kushner's *Angels in America* in New York. (At the extreme end of this spectrum, Robert Wilson's *Ka Mountain* was once performed over 168 continuous hours.) In short, Miller's question does not have a precise answer.

Genre

Genre provides a more subjective basis of classification than duration, and the term brings with it certain critical perspectives. *Genre* is directly derived from the Old French word meaning "kind" (it is also the root word for *gender*). So to classify a play by genre is to say what kind of play it is.

Why do we care? Why don't we simply don't call a play a play? Mainly because knowing what kind of play it is lets people know whether they want to see it or read it. Just as there are different kinds of movies—comedies, westerns, action films, horror films, documentaries—there are different genres of plays.

Historically, the first defined dramatic genres were *tragedy* and *comedy*. We are probably most familiar with comedy because of its popularity in films: we can easily recall moments and scenarios from movies that make us laugh just by thinking about them or describing them to friends. Tragedy, though, is not nearly as common in films, nor even in contemporary theatre. But many of the great masterpieces of theatre are so labeled—from ancient Greek times through the eras of Shakespeare and Racine—and tragedy deserves serious discussion.

A *tragedy* is a profoundly serious play. A tragedy always ends in the death of one or more of its main characters and focuses on a universal theme about human life and society. Tragedy was first described by the Greek philosopher Aristotle (384–322 B.C.) in his monumental work *Poetics,* where he uses Sophocles' *Oedipus Tyrannos (Oedipus the King)* as his main example. In Aristotle's construction, the central character of a tragedy, the *protagonist,* is a person of high rank or stature. During the play, the protagonist undergoes a decline of fortune, which leads to his or her suffering and usually to death. Integral to tragedy, according to Aristotle, is the protagonist's *self-recognition (anagnorisis* in Greek) of a fundamental flaw (*hamartia*). Self-recognition makes the protagonist reverse course (*peripeteia*) and thus leads to the protagonist's demise. This dire outcome elicits pity and terror from the audience and then a purging of those emotions (*catharsis*) aroused by the play's events.

In Aristotle's prime example, Oedipus, king of Thebes, realizing that his city is suffering from the plague because the killer of the late King Laius is still on the loose, vows to find and destroy him. Soon, however, Oedipus discovers that he himself, being impulsive by nature (his fundamental flaw), had killed Laius some years ago, thinking him a stranger he ran into at a crossroads. He then finds out (his self-recognition) that Laius was also his father, whom he had never met, and that by marrying Laius's widow Jocasta, he had married his own mother. Jocasta kills herself at this discovery. Wracked with shame, Oedipus plucks out his eyes with brooches pulled from her gown, thus precipitating the emotional release—the catharsis—of the audience.

Struggle, self-recognition, and catharsis are central to tragic drama, elevating the genre above mere sadness or sentimentality. Tragedy is neither pathetic nor maudlin; it involves a bold, aggressive, heroic attack

Shakespeare took Sophocles' blinding motif one step further in his tragedy *King Lear,* some two thousand years later. Lear's friend, the Duke of Gloucester, is brutally blinded onstage by Lear's daughter and her husband. Here, Japanese actor Kazunori Akitaya plays the blinded Gloucester in a stylized production by the Globe Theatre of Tokyo.

against huge, perhaps insurmountable, odds. Tragic protagonists (Medea, Hamlet, Macbeth, King Lear) are always flawed in some way; indeed, Aristotelian tragic theory insists they *must* be so, or at least acting in ignorance. But they are heroes, not victims. Their instigation of the play's action and their discoveries during its course bring the audience to deep emotional and intellectual involvement at the play's climax—and then great relief at its conclusion.

The notion of *protagonist* (Greek: "carrier of the action") is complemented by the notion of *antagonist* ("opposer of the action"), which gives tragedy its

Arthur Miller's *Death of a Salesman* is often considered the American theatre's finest tragedy, since its protagonist, the likeable but morally flawed Willy Loman, experiences a decline of fortune that eventually leads to his suicide. Here, in a dream sequence from the much-heralded 1999 Goodman Theatre production, Brian Dennehy as Willy (*center*) leans on the shoulders of his two sons (played by Kevin Anderson and Ted Koch), not as they are now but as he remembers them from better days.

fundamental conflict and character struggle. Tragic protagonists go forth against superhuman antagonists—gods, ghosts, fate—and their struggle, though doomed, takes on larger-than-life proportions. Through the heat of such conflict, they assume superhuman force and offer the audience a link outwardly to divine mysteries—or inwardly to the unconscious mind. The goal of tragedy is therefore to ennoble, not sadden, us. The tragic heroes we admire will fall, but not before they heroically challenge the universe. They carry us to the brink of disaster, but it is *their* disaster, not ours—at least, not yet. Experiencing a tragedy allows us to contemplate and rehearse in our own minds the great conflicts that may await us.

Can a modern play be termed a tragedy? Playwright Arthur Miller's *Death of a Salesman* (1947)—whose protagonist, an ordinary American salesman, commits suicide after realizing he has failed to fulfill his familial obligations—has often been considered an attempt at

tragedy. Miller named his protagonist "Willy Loman" (i.e., *low man*) to challenge the classical idea that a protagonist must be of high rank. The antagonists Willy faces in the play are not gods but faceless bureaucrats, insensitive children, and an impersonal capitalistic economic system. Is the play a tragedy? Ultimately, *you,* the audience, must decide. The classification of plays into genres is not a science but a matter of opinion. Even Shakespeare made fun of scholars who treated genres as absolute categories to be applied to each and every work.

The fact is that genres are mainly important to play producers and publishers who want to let the public know what sort of drama they are being asked to attend or read. The editors of the first edition (the First Folio) of Shakespeare's complete dramatic works divided them into tragedies, comedies, and histories. The last category refers to plays about England's kings that were more or less based on historical accounts. But some of

Stagecraft

Genre-ly Speaking

Shakespeare has brightly parodied the division of plays into genres, a practice that in his time was already becoming almost an affectation. In *Hamlet,* Polonius describes an acting company as "The best actors in the world, either for tragedy, comedy, history, pastoral, pastoral-comical, historical-pastoral, tragical-historical, tragical-comical-historical-pastoral; scene individable, or poem unlimited."

those "histories" could be construed as tragedies—and vice versa—and some of the comedies include scenes as tragic as anything in Shakespeare's (or the world's) dramatic repertoire.

Kevin Spacey plays the "hunch-backed" King Richard III in Shakespeare's history play of that name. At London's Old Vic Theatre, 2011; directed by Sam Mendes, with costumes by Catherine Zuber.

Comedy is a very popular genre and has been a staple of the theatre since ancient times. Playwrights of all eras have written comedies—sometimes with serious themes, sometimes with particularly dark humor (whereupon they may be classed as *dark comedy*). At yet other times playwrights have no purpose other than to create continuous hilarity through common devices like full-stage chases, mistaken identities, lovers hiding in closets or under tables, sexual puns, switched potions, clever disguises (often transsexual), misheard instructions, and sheer physical buffoonery; such works are usually labeled *farce.* Comedies have been immensely popular in all ages, but because they are topical, about ordinary life rather than larger-than-life heroes, they usually lose their popularity sooner. And because they rarely probe as deeply into human destiny as do tragedies, they offer less fertile ground for academic scholarship and hence are less frequently published in anthologies, examined in scholarly literature, or placed into college course syllabi. Nevertheless, some comedies (particularly those of Shakespeare and Molière) are considered true masterpieces of human observation, and comedy's place in the theatre world is every bit as secure as tragedy's—and as popular as it was in the days of Aristophanes—the great comic playwright of ancient Greece.

Other genres are defined from time to time, and playwrights often have fun creating genres of their own, but none have any truly definitive value. The *history play,* mentioned briefly above, did not die with Shakespeare. It has come into the modern era as the occasional play about a historical figure; examples include George Bernard Shaw's *Saint Joan,* Bertolt Brecht's *Galileo,* and Alan Bennett's *The Madness of George III.* More common today is the *documentary drama,* which is a play that makes use of actual documents—court records, for example, or transcribed interviews, or, to take a recent example, oral histories of witnesses to the attacks of September 11th, performed on stage for the event's 10-year anniversary. *Tragicomedy,* as the name implies, attempts to blend the two original genres. Maintaining a serious theme but varying the approach from serious to humorous, while leaving the hero alive at the end, tragicomedy relaxes tragedy's larger-than-life scale and is sometimes known as "tragedy that ends happily." *Melodrama,* whose heyday was the nineteenth century, is outwardly serious, embellished with spectacular stagings and flamboyant dialogue (e.g., "Curse their old families—a bilious, conceited, thin lot of dried up aristocracy. I hate 'em. It makes my blood so hot I feel my heart hiss!"), along with highly suspenseful, contrived plotting. Presenting a simple and finite confrontation between good and evil, rather than a complex exposition of universal human aspirations and sufferings, melodramas cannot sustain unpleasant endings or generate catharsis. When performed today, they are almost always staged as parodies of their originals and are played for laughs. The *musical,* of course, is a major genre—the most commercially successful genre in the American theatre today—and is the subject of a later chapter in this book.

(*Left*) *Satire* is a dramatic style as old as Aristophanes, who brazenly ridiculed Socrates, Euripides, and contemporary Athenian politicians in his Greek comedies. Comedian Will Ferrell wielded a satirical pen in writing and starring in *You're Welcome America: A Final Night with George W. Bush,* which opened on Broadway in 2009 weeks before the end of the president's final term. Ferrell achieved success by depicting what he considered the president's limitations with light-hearted comic banter rather than direct attacks.

While he also writes serious drama (*Copenhagen, Democracy*), British playwright Michael Frayn is generally considered the greatest farceur in English language theatre today. Frayn's 1982 backstage farce *Noises Off* (the title refers to a common stage direction in nineteenth-century theatre) is already considered a classic; former *New York Times* drama critic Frank Rich said it "is, was, and probably always will be the funniest play written in my lifetime." This 2012 production was directed by Lindsay Posner at London's Old Vic Theatre; the actors—who are playing the roles of actors—are, from left to right, Celia Imrie, Karl Johnson, Jonathon Coy, Janie Dee, and Amy Nuttall.

Potentially there are as many theatrical genres as the imaginative playwright (or the diligent critic) wishes to define. "An Anti-Play," "A Conversation in One Act," "A Grim Comedy," and "A Tragic Farce" are a few of the "genres" modern authors—generally with tongue in cheek—have invented and claimed for one or another of their dramatic works. Certainly, no system of classification should obscure the fact that every play is unique; the grouping of any two or more plays into a common genre is only a convenience for purposes of comparison and analysis. But applying genres can help us comprehend the broad spectrum of purposes to which plays may be put, and help us to perceive important similarities and differences between individual works. For the theatre artist, awareness of the possibilities inherent in each genre—together with knowledge of the achievements made in each—stimulates the imagination and aids in setting work standards and ambitions.

DRAMATURGY: THE CONSTRUCTION OF DRAMA AND DRAMATIC PERFORMANCE

A play is action, but it is *patterned* action. Unlike the action of, say, a street riot, dramatic action has clearly identifiable components and a specified beginning and ending. Even when improvised or radically experimental, a play's dramatic action tends to be crafted in well-understood compositional patterns. We call these patterns a play's *dramaturgy*.

Action provides a play's thrills and excitement; dramaturgy provides momentum and meaning, allowing the action to become increasingly compelling and significant as the play heads toward its eventual climax and resolution. Dramaturgical devices lead an audience to see the play's action as *consequential* rather than as a random series of events. The most successful dramaturgy, even when buried deep within a play's dialogue and appearance, can create a profound engagement with the audience's thoughts, fantasies, and feelings.

Students of drama often visualize two intersecting axes along which they can analyze a play's dramaturgy: a "vertical" axis composed of the play's various components—the elements that make up its essential fabric—and a "horizontal" axis that records the temporal structure of the performance (the order and timing of what happens). Both perspectives are immensely useful to scholars, appreciators, and creators of drama.

Drama's Components: The Vertical Axis

The division of plays into components is an ancient analytical practice begun by Aristotle. He identified six components of a tragedy (by which he meant a generally serious drama): plot, characters, theme, diction, music, and spectacle—in that order of importance. With some modification and elaboration, Aristotle's list still provides a helpful breakdown of the major elements of most dramas, although the importance of each component is a matter of continuing controversy.

Plot Although we may think of *plot* as synonymous with *story*, the meanings of the two words are actually quite different. The *story* is simply the narrative of what happens in the play, as might be described by someone who has seen it. *Plot* refers to the mechanics of storytelling: the sequencing of the characters' comings and goings; the timetable of the play's events; and the specific ordering of the revelations, reversals, quarrels, discoveries, and actions that take place onstage. (The word comes from the written "platte," or "plotte," that was hung on the backstage wall of sixteenth-century English theatres to remind the actors of the play's order of events, entrances, and exits.) Plot is therefore the *structure of actions*: both outer actions (such as Romeo stabbing Tybalt) and inner ones (such as Romeo falling in love with Juliet).

Perhaps Aristotle listed plot foremost among drama's six elements because it essentially makes drama dramatic. Creating a compelling plot is often the most demanding test of a playwright's skill, for plot normally keeps the audience involved (and *increasingly* so) during the play's two-plus-hour duration.

The primary demands of plot are logic and suspense. To satisfy the demand for logic, the actions portrayed must be plausible, and events must follow one upon another in an organic, rather than arbitrary, fashion. To create and sustain suspense, however, these actions must set up expectations for further actions, leading the audience inescapably toward an ending that may be sensed but is never wholly predictable. Perhaps the most palpable examples of plot elements can be found in "well-made plays," a genre of farce and melodrama in the late nineteenth century that relied heavily on intricately and precisely crafted dramas. Many plays today retain elements of these forms—or, in some cases, the forms themselves.

Characters Characters are the human figures who undertake the actions of the plot. Their potency in the theatre is measured by our interest in them *as people*.

The most brilliant plotting cannot redeem a play if the audience remains indifferent to its characters; therefore, the fundamental demand of a play's characters is that they make the audience *care*. Characters cannot be mere stick figures, no matter how elaborately detailed. The great dramatic characters of the past—Hamlet, Juliet, Uncle Vanya, and Blanche DuBois, to name a few—evoke personalities as vivid and memorable as those of good friends (and hated enemies). They are whole beings, indelibly human, alive with the attributes, feelings, and expectations of real people. We can identify with them. We can sympathize with them.

Character depth is what gives a play its psychological complexity, sensuality, and warmth. Without character depth we cannot experience love, hate, fear, joy, hope, despair—or indeed any of the emotions we expect to derive from theatre. And a theatre devoid of the emotions that stem from the humanness of its characters would soon be a theatre without an audience.

Theme A play's theme is its abstracted intellectual content. The theme may be described as the play's overall statement: its topic, central idea, or message. Some plays have obvious themes, such as Euripides' *The Trojan Women* (the horrors of war) or Molière's *The Bourgeois Gentleman* (the foolishness of social pretense). Other plays have less clearly defined themes, and the most provocative of these plays have given rise to much scholarly controversy. *Hamlet, Oedipus Tyrannos,* and *Waiting for Godot* all suggest many themes, and each play has spawned fierce debates about which is central.

Nothing demands that a play have a single theme, however, or that a theme be reducible to any straightforward intellectual generalization. Indeed, plays that are too obviously theme-intensive are often considered too propagandistic or academic for theatrical success: "If you want to send a message," one Broadway saying goes, "use Western Union." (Today we would say, "Text me.") Moreover, although the themes of plays address the central questions of society and humanity, a play's theatrical impact normally hinges—at least in the Aristotelian model—on the audience's engagement with its plot and characterization.

Nevertheless, a play must have *something* to say, and that something must seem pertinent to the audience. Otherwise why would we leave the outside world, filled as it is with actions and "scenes," to come to the theatre? Further, the play's theme or themes must be sufficiently focused and limited to give the audience at least some insight. Plays that try to say nothing—or, conversely, everything—rarely have even a modest impact

no matter how entertaining or well plotted they may be. Thus playwrights working in every genre—tragedy, comedy, melodrama, musical comedy, or farce—have from the beginning of theatrical history learned to narrow and focus their field of intellectual investigation.

Diction Aristotle's fourth component, diction, does not refer to the pronunciation of spoken dialogue, as its contemporary definition might suggest. More crucially, it refers to the literary character of a play's text, including its tone, imagery, cadence, and articulation, and to the playwright's use of literary forms and figures of speech such as verse, rhyme, metaphor, apostrophe, jest, and epigram.

The value of poetry has been well established from the theatre's beginning; indeed, until fairly recent times, most serious plays were written largely in verse. Today, although the use of verse is relatively rare, all plays continue to demonstrate carefully crafted language. Many, such as those by Tom Stoppard and Richard Greenberg, feature brilliant repartee, stunning epigrams, witty arguments, and dazzling tirades. Other, quite different, sorts of plays may feature rough-textured slang, local dialects, and crude vulgarities, or a poetry of silences and nearly inarticulate mutterings—dictions that can be no less effective than flamboyantly crafted verbal pyrotechnics.

The diction of a play is by no means the creation of the playwright alone. It is very much the product of the actor as well, and for that reason throughout the history of Western theatre, an effective stage voice has been considered the prime asset of the actor. Even today, the study of voice is a primary course at most schools and conservatories of acting. The chief aim of such study is to create an acting voice capable of dealing in spectacular fashion with the broad palette of dramatic diction demanded by the works of the world's most noted playwrights. (See the chapter titled "The Actor" for more on vocal technique.)

Music When discussing music, Aristotle's fifth component, we should remember that plays in Aristotle's time were sung or chanted, not simply spoken. That mode of presentation has all but disappeared, yet music, more broadly understood, remains directly or indirectly present in all plays performed today.

Such music can take many forms. Songs are common in the plays of Shakespeare, as well as in the works of many modern writers. Many naturalistic dramatists work familiar songs into their scripts, sometimes by having the characters sing, at other times by having them play recordings onstage. Anton Chekhov and

Spectacle can be simple but still profound. The image of the aged Nagg and Nell in their ashcans, trying to kiss, in Samuel Beckett's grimly absurdist *Endgame* is unforgettable. Shown here are Liz Smith and Geoffrey Hutchings in their 2004 performance at London's Albert Theatre.

Tennessee Williams both make extensive use of offstage music, as with the military marching band heard in *The Three Sisters*, or the dance-hall music in *Streetcar Named Desire*, respectively. More subtly, the music of a play may include a live or electronically prerecorded sound score, created and implemented by a sound designer who can provide anything from incidental music between scenes to a full soundscape that intensifies the play's emotional range, punctuates its action, intensifies its rising suspense and climaxes, and moves its audience to an ever-deepening engagement. Not all of this is necessarily tuneful: vocal tones, footsteps, sighs, shouts, railroad whistles, gunshots, animal cries, the hubbub of crowds, the shrill ring of a telephone, and amplified effects (heartbeats, heavy breathing, otherworldly harmonies) may combine into a sonic orchestration of such dramatic force that it can thrill even persons wholly unacquainted with the language of the dialogue.

Spectacle   Aristotle's sixth component, spectacle, encompasses the visual aspects of production: scenery, costumes, lighting, makeup, properties, and the overall *look* of the theatre and stage. It would be wrong to infer that *spectacle* is synonymous with *spectacular*, for some productions are quite restrained in their visual artistry. Rather, *spectacle* here refers to its etymological root, meaning "something seen." Although this point may seem obvious, it is crucial. Theatre is as much a visual experience as it is an aural, emotional, and intellectual experience: the ancient Greeks clearly had this in mind when they chose the name *theatron* ("seeing place") to designate the site of their performances.

Much as the cinema has been called the art of moving pictures, the theatre might be called the art of fluid sculpture. This sculpture is fashioned from both human bodies in motion and still or moving scenery and props—natural and manufactured items of dramatic and decorative importance, illuminated by natural or artificially modulated light. Such sculpture moves in time as well as in space. And although it primarily supports the plot, characters, and theme of a play, spectacle has an artistic appeal and an artistic heritage all its own. Certainly some ardent patrons of the theatre pay more attention to settings and costumes than to any other aspect of a play, and dramatic visual effects—such as the chandelier that crashes to the ground at the end of the first act of *Phantom of the Opera*—have occasionally become the most noted highlight of a production.

Memorable visual elements can be both grand and prosaic, imposing and subtle. Nineteenth-century romanticism, which survives today primarily in the form of grand opera, tends to favor elaborate palaces, impressive crowd scenes, parades of circus animals, and lavish, overscale costumes. In contrast, twentieth- and twenty-first-century dramas are more likely to be dressed in domestic environments and archetypal images: Jimmy and Cliff reading newspapers while Alison irons a shirt in John Osborne's *Look Back in Anger;* Laura playing with her glass animals in Tennessee Williams's *The Glass Menagerie;* Mother Courage pulling her wagon in Brecht's *Mother Courage;* and Nagg and Nell peeking out of ashcans in Samuel Beckett's *Endgame.* In the long run, the conceptual richness and precision of a play's visual presentation are far more telling than grandeur for its own sake.

Conventions   To those six Aristotelian components we shall add a seventh, discrete, category that Aristotle apparently never saw reason to consider: theatrical conventions. The agreement between audience and actor—by which the audience willingly suspends its disbelief and accepts the play as a new and temporary "reality"—entails our unthinkingly accepting a set of conventions such as "when the stage lights fade out, the play (or act) is over." Other common conventions of the Western stage over the centuries have included the following:

- When an actor turns directly away from the other actors and speaks to the audience, the other characters are presumed not to hear him or her. This is the convention of the *aside* (a line addressed directly to the audience, unheard by the other characters).

- When actors all leave the stage and then they or others reenter (particularly when the lights change), time has elapsed. And if one actor then says to another, "Welcome to Padua," we are now in Padua even if in the previous scene we were in Verona.

- When actors "freeze," we are seeing some sort of "dream state" (of one of the characters, presumably), and the words we hear are to be considered a character's thoughts, not audible speech.

We can recognize conventions most clearly in theatres unlike our own (that is probably why Aristotle, knowing no theatre but his own, never thought of defining them). In the *wayang kulit* shadow puppet theatre of Bali, for example, the play is over when the "tree of life" puppet, previously seen only in motion, comes to a standstill at the center of the stage. In the ancient *noh* drama of Japan, the audience realizes that words sung by chorus members are to be considered speeches spoken by the actors who are dancing, and the audience interprets gestures with a fan to indicate wind, rain, or the rising moon. In the Chinese *xiqu,* or traditional opera, a character entering the bare stage while holding a boat paddle is understood to be rowing across a river, and one entering with a whip is understood to be riding a horse.

According to one Chinese theatre convention, a man paddling with an oar signifies "boatman," "boat," and "water" alike. Here, famed Shanghai actor Liu Yilong portrays the boatman ferrying his passengers in *The Meeting by the Lake,* a classic work of the Chinese *xiqu* (traditional opera) form.

Theatrical conventions permit shorthand communication with the audience without the encumbrance of extensive physical elaboration or acting-out. If a locale can effectively be changed by the convention of a simple light shift instead of by moving a ton of scenery, the theatre saves money and the audience saves time. Thus stage violence is usually executed conventionally (that is, with little physical mayhem) rather than with lifelike (or cinematic) verisimilitude. The near-impossibility of realistically portraying severed torsos, rupturing intestines, or bleeding limbs onstage ordinarily outweighs any dramatic advantage in actually doing so; most theatrical conventions of violence can be accepted fully if performed with emotional and psychological, if not physical, authenticity.

Each theatrical era sets up its own system of conventions, which the audience will accept without the slightest reflection. In modern times, playwrights and directors have deliciously exploited the theatrical conventions of the past or invented new ones. Peter Shaffer's *Black Comedy*, which is set in a room during a complete blackout, employs a convention that Shaffer attributes to the Chinese: when the lights are on, they are "off," and when they are off, they are "on." Eugene O'Neill's *Strange Interlude* and Steven Berkoff's *Kvetch* give us to understand that when the actors "freeze" and speak, we in the audience—but not the other characters in the play—hear their unspoken thoughts. Jean Anouilh's *Antigone* uses a variation on the Greek device of the chorus: a single man speaks with the author's voice as the characters onstage freeze in silence. Arthur Miller's *After the Fall* places an imaginary psychiatrist in the midst of the audience, and the play's protagonist repeatedly interrupts the action of the drama to address his analyst in highly theatrical therapy sessions. Indeed, there is no formal requirement for the establishment of theatrical conventions except that audiences must "agree" to suspend disbelief and accept them. And they do.

The seven vertical components of every play—Aristotle's six plus the conventions that frame them—are the raw material of drama. All are important. Indeed, the theatre could not afford to dispense with any of them. Some plays are intensive in one or more components; most great productions show artistry in all. Balancing these components in theatrical presentations is one of the primary challenges facing the director, who on one or another occasion may be called upon mainly to clarify and elaborate a theme, find the visual mode of presentation that best supports the action, develop and flesh out the characterizations to give strength and meaning to the plot, heighten a musical tone to enhance sensual effect, or develop the precise convention—the relationship between play and audience—that will maximize the play's artistic impact. For as important as each of these components is to the theatrical experience, it is their combination and interaction, not their individual power, that are crucial to a production's success.

Drama's Timeline: The Horizontal Axis

The action of a dramatic performance plays out over time. The horizontal axis of dramaturgy focuses on *temporal structure*. Here, this term refers to much more than the events contained within the play's script. It pertains to three major groupings of a performance: *preplay*, *play*, and *postplay*. The play itself,

quite properly, receives the most attention from drama scholars and theorists, but the surrounding preplay and postplay have been part of the overall theatrical experience from the theatre's earliest days and also merit attention.

Preplay   Preplay begins with the attraction of an audience. Theatre has had this responsibility in every era, for there can be no "seeing place" (*theatron*) without those who see.

The procession is one of the oldest known ways of publicizing the theatre. The circus parade, which still takes place in some of the smaller towns of Europe and the United States, is a remnant of a once-universal form of advertisement for the performing arts that probably began well in advance of recorded history. The Greeks of ancient Athens opened their great dramatic festivals with a *proagon* (literally, "pre-action") in which both playwrights and actors were introduced at a huge public meeting and given a chance to speak about the plays they were to present on subsequent days. The Elizabethans flew flags atop their playhouses on performance days, enticing hundreds away from their commercial and religious activities. The lighted marquees of Broadway theatres around Times Square and of London theatres in the West End are modern-day equivalents of those flags, signaling their entertainments to passersby. Today, posters, illustrated programs, multicolor subscription brochures, full-page newspaper advertisements, staged media events, elaborate press releases, and, in New York, flashy television commercials summon patrons out of the comfort of their homes and into the theatre. Far from being an inconsequential aspect of theatre, publicity today occupies a place of fundamental importance in the thinking of theatrical producers, and it commands a major share of the budget for commercial theatrical ventures.

Once gathered at the theatre's door, the audience remains a collection of individuals preoccupied with their daily concerns. Now the theatre must shift their focus to the lives of dramatic characters and transform the spectators into a community devoted to the concerns of the play. Ushers may lead them into the audience area, showing them to their seats and providing them with written programs that will prepare them for the fiction they are about to see. Preshow music or sound effects may be used to set a mood or tone, while stage lights may "warm" a curtain or illuminate the revealed stage and scenery with a romantic or eerie glow, creating the anticipation of dramatic actions about to take place. There may be some visible

Posters—on theatre walls, in subway stations and shop windows, and on special billboards—around theatre towns are universal for advertising current theatre productions. Here, in Tokyo's downtown Ginza district, theatergoers study posters advertising the new production at the Kabuki-za theatre, the world's outstanding showcase for Japanese kabuki drama.

stage activity, such as a ticking clock or flickering carnival lights, or perhaps a few actors engaged in quiet pre-show activity as incoming audience members observe the scene. In most cases there will be much to look at, but unlike moviegoers, the audience for a live theatre production will be aware of *itself* because the seating area is fully illuminated and audience members are free to greet and chat with each other. As a live art, theatre's liveliness in part results from the fact that audience members are always part of the action and share their responses—laughter, sighing, and applause—with the actors as well as with one another.

Finally, a swift conclusion to the transition begins, usually with an announcement for audience members to turn off their cell phones so the outside world will remain sealed out for the show's duration. Then the houselights dim, and (if all goes well) the audience is transported into the world of the play. In the familiar theatrical saying, "It's magic time."

Play In contrast to staged events such as performance art and stand-up comedy, a play normally contains a structured sequence of identifiable elements. Here again, Aristotle affords some help, telling us that drama has a beginning, a middle, and an end. In his *Poetics*, Aristotle even proffers some details about these elements, all in the context of his first dramatic component: plot. We can elaborate on Aristotle's beginning, middle, and end somewhat, for four fairly consistent features are routinely recognized in the orderly plot sequencing of a conventionally Aristotelian dramatic experience: exposition, conflict, climax, and denouement.

The exposition No important play has ever begun with a character dashing onstage and shouting, "The house is on fire!" At best such a beginning could only confuse members of the audience, and at worst it could cause them to flee in panic. At that point they would have no way of knowing what house is on fire, or why they should care about it. Most plays, whatever their style or genre, begin with dialogue or action calculated to ease us, not shock us, into the concerns of the characters with whom we are to spend the next two hours or so.

Exposition is a word not much in favor now, coming as it does from an age when play structure was considered more cut and dried than it is today. But it remains a useful term, referring to the background information the audience must have in order to understand what's going on in the action of a play.

In the rather mechanical plotting of "well-made plays," the exposition is handled with little fanfare. A few characters—often servants (minor figures in the action to follow)—discuss something that is about to happen and enlighten one another (and, of course, the audience) about certain details around which the plot will turn. Consider these lines from the opening scene of Henrik Ibsen's 1884 classic, *The Wild Duck*:

PETTERSEN, *in livery, and* JENSEN, *the hired waiter, in black, are putting the study in order. From the dining room, the hum of conversation and laughter is heard.*

PETTERSEN: Listen to them, Jensen; the old man's got to his feet—he's giving a toast to Mrs. Sorby.

JENSEN: (*pushing forward an armchair*) Do you think it's true, then, what they've been saying, that there's something going on between them?

PETTERSEN: God knows.

JENSEN: He used to be quite the lady's man, I understand.

PETTERSEN: I suppose.

JENSEN: And he's giving this party in honor of his son, they say.

PETTERSEN: That's right. His son came home yesterday.

JENSEN: I never even knew old Werle had a son.

PETTERSEN: Oh, he has a son all right. But he's completely tied up at the Hoidal works. In all the years I've been here he's never come into town.

A WAITER: (*in the doorway of the other room*) Pettersen, there's an old fellow here …

PETTERSEN: (*mutters*) Damn. Who'd show up at this time of night?

After a few more lines, Pettersen, Jensen, and the waiter make their exits and are seen no more. Their function is purely expository—to pave the way for the principal characters. Their conversation is a contrivance intended simply to give us a framework for the action and impart information to the audience.

In contrast, the exposition of nonrealistic plays can be handled more directly. It was the Greek custom to begin a play with a prologue preceding the entrance of the chorus and the major play episodes; the prologue was sometimes a scene and sometimes a simple speech to the audience. Shakespeare also used prologues in some of his plays. In one particularly interesting example, Shakespeare's *Romeo and Juliet*, the play begins with an actor identified as "Chorus" who comes onstage and addresses the audience directly, telling us where the play is presumed to take place (the city of Verona), explaining what the theatre's stage doors are to represent (the "two households" of the leading characters), and previewing the characters and plot:

CHORUS: Two households, both alike in dignity,
In fair Verona, where we lay our scene,
From ancient grudge break to new mutiny,
Where civil blood makes civil hands unclean.
From forth the fatal loins of these two foes
A pair of star-crossed lovers take their life;
Whose misadventured piteous overthrows
Do with their death bury their parents' strife.
The fearful passage of their death-marked love,
And the continuance of their parents' rage,
Which, but their children's end, nought could remove,
Is now the two hours' traffic of our stage;
The which if you with patient ears attend,
What here shall miss, our toil shall strive to mend.

By saying "our toil," the Chorus presents himself not as a character but as a member of the acting company, reminding the audience that putting on a "play" requires "work" from the actors as well as "patient ears" from the audience. In today's theatre, of course, some of the exposition the Chorus shares with us (normally the setting, at least) will instead be in a printed program distributed as we enter.

The conflict   Now is the time for the character to enter shouting, "The house is on fire!" It is a truism that drama requires conflict; in fact, the word *drama*, when used in daily life, implies a situation fraught with conflict. No one writes plays about characters who live every day in unimpaired serenity; no one would ever choose to watch such a play. Conflict and confrontation are the mechanisms by which a situation becomes dramatic.

Why is this so? Why is conflict so theatrically interesting? The reasons have to do with plot, theme, and character. Plot can hold suspense only when it involves alternatives and choices: Macbeth has strong reasons to murder King Duncan and strong reasons not to. If he had only the former or only the latter, he would project no real conflict and we would not consider him such an interesting character. We are fascinated by such a character's actions largely in light of the actions he rejects

Drama requires conflict, and Shakespeare's tragedy *Othello* is filled with it: between father and daughter, soldiers and officers, and, fatally, husbands and wives. In the Royal Shakespeare Company's 2009 production directed by Kathryn Hunter, Patrice Naiambana as Othello furiously hurls Natalia Tena as Desdemona to the ground in a jealous rage as the conflict between them escalates.

and the stresses he has to endure in making his decisions. In other words, plot entails not only the actions of a play but also the inactions—the things that are narrowly rejected and do *not* happen. A character's decision must proceed from powerfully conflicting alternatives if we are to watch this behavior with empathy instead of mere curiosity. In watching a character act, the audience must also watch the character *think,* and a playwright gets the character to think by putting him or her into conflict.

Conflict may be set up between characters as well as within them; it may be reducible to one central situation, or it may evolve out of many. Whatever the case, conflict throws characters into relief and permits the audience to see deeply into their humanity and

personality. To see a character at war with herself or in confrontation with another allows insight into how that character *works,* and this is the key to our caring about them.

The theme of a play is often a simple abstraction of its central conflict. In Sophocles' *Antigone,* for example, the theme is the conflict between divine law and civil law; in *Death of a Salesman,* it is the conflict between Willy's reality and his dreams. Conflicts are plentiful in farces and comedies as well; the conflicts inherent in a "love triangle," for example, have provided comic material for dramatists for the past two millennia. Many of the more abstract philosophical conflicts—independence versus duty, individuality versus conformity, idealism versus pragmatism, integrity versus efficiency, pleasure versus propriety, progress versus tradition, to name a few—suggest inexhaustible thematic conflicts that appear in various guises in both ancient and contemporary plays.

The playwright introduces conflict early in a play, often by means of an "inciting incident" in which one character poses a conflict or confrontation either to another character or to himself. For example:

FIRST WITCH: All hail, Macbeth, hail to thee, Thane of Glamis!

SECOND WITCH: All hail, Macbeth, hail to thee, Thane of Cawdor!

THIRD WITCH: All hail, Macbeth, that shalt be King hereafter!

BANQUO: Good sir, why do you start, and seem to fear

Things that do sound so fair?

In this, the inciting incident of Shakespeare's *Macbeth* (which follows two brief expository scenes), a witch confronts Macbeth with the prediction that he will be king, thereby posing an alternative that Macbeth has apparently already considered, judging from the startled response that elicits Banquo's comment.

Once established, conflict is intensified to crisis, usually by a series of incidents, investigations, revelations, and confrontations. Sometimes even nonevents serve to intensify a conflict, as in the modern classic *Waiting for Godot* in which two characters simply wait, through two hour-long acts, for the arrival of a third, who never comes. Indeed, with this play, Samuel Beckett practically rewrote the book on playwriting technique by showing how time alone, when properly managed, can do the job of heightening and developing conflict in a dramatic situation.

The climax Conflict cannot be intensified indefinitely. In a play, as in life, when conflict becomes insupportable, something has to give. Thus every play, be it comic, tragic, farcical, or melodramatic, culminates in some sort of dramatic explosion.

As we have seen, Aristotle described that dramatic explosion, in tragedy, as a *catharsis,* a cleansing or purification. The catharsis releases the audience's pity and thereby permits the fullest experience of tragic pleasure, washing away the terror that has been mounting steadily during the play's tragic course. The ultimate example of catharsis, for classical Greek tragedy, accompanies Oedipus's gouging out his own eyes as he recognizes his true self.

For most dramatic forms, however, the climax need not be so explicitly gruesome. It is simply the conflict of a play taken to its most extreme—the moment of maximum tension. At the climax, a continuation of the conflict becomes unbearable, impossible: some sort of change is mandated. Climaxes in modern plays do not, as a rule, involve death or disfiguration (although there are exceptions: Peter Shaffer's celebrated *Equus* reaches its climax with the blinding of six horses, and Edward Albee's *The Zoo Story* climaxes with one character's impaling himself on a knife held by another). Instead, climaxes inevitably contain elements of recognition and reversal, and usually the major conflicts of a play are resolved by one or more of these elements. William Gibson's *The Miracle Worker,* for example, climaxes when the young Helen Keller, a blind, deaf, mute, and until the end uncontrollable child, finally says a word ("wawa"—which we understand to mean "water") for the first time, and the audience experiences a catharsis of long-delayed joy.

The denouement The climax is followed and the play is concluded by a denouement, or resolution (the word in French means "un-knotting"), in which a final action or speech, or even a single word or gesture, indicates that the passions aroused by the play's action are now stilled and the conflicts are over. The tenor of the denouement tends to change with the times. In the American theatre of the 1950s and 1960s, for example, a sentimental and message-laden denouement was the rule: in Robert Anderson's *Tea and Sympathy,* a teacher's wife prepares to prove to a sensitive boy that he is not a homosexual; in Dore Schary's *Sunrise at Campobello,* a future American president makes his way on crippled legs to a convention platform. In the current theatre—in this existential age that looks with suspicion on tidy virtues and happy endings—more ironic and ambiguous denouements prevail. The denouements of contemporary theatre, as a result, find it harder to let the audience "off the hook," favoring instead a lingering sense of unease. For many plays, a lack of neat dramatic conclusions parallels a lack of real-life solutions since the issues raised by the best of contemporary drama are themselves not amenable to complete resolution; at the end of Tony Kushner's epic *Angels in America,* for instance, we attain a satisfying degree of emotional release from witnessing the characters' astonishing journeys, but we are reminded starkly that the real tragedy of AIDS continues to play out in the world offstage.

But while a denouement may be indeterminate, it must still provide at least some lucidity concerning the problems raised by the play, some vision or metaphor of a deeper and more permanent understanding. Perhaps the final lines of *Waiting for Godot,* although premiering in 1953, best represent the denouement of the current age:

ESTRAGON: Well, shall we go?

VLADIMIR: Yes, let's go. *They do not move.*

Postplay   The last staged element of a theatrical presentation is the *curtain call,* during which the actors bow and the audience applauds. This convention—customary in the theatre at least since the time of the Romans—plays an important but often overlooked role in the overall scope of theatrical presentation.

The curtain call is *not* simply a time for the actors to receive congratulations from the audience, although many actors today seem to think it is. Indeed, the actor's deeply bowed head was originally an offer for his patron—the nobleman who had paid for the performance—to lop off that head with his sword if the actor had not provided satisfaction! The curtain call remains a time in which the actors show their respect for the audience that patronizes them. And aesthetically, it is a time in which the audience allows itself to see the other side of the "paradox of the actor." The curtain call liberates the audience from the world of the play. Indeed, when there is no curtain call, audiences are often disgruntled, for this convention fulfills the last provision of the mutual agreement that characterizes the theatre itself: the agreement by which the audience consents to view the actors as being the characters they have agreed to impersonate. It is at the curtain call that actors and audience can acknowledge their mutual belonging in human society, can look each other in the eye and say, in effect, "We all know what it is to experience these things we've just seen performed. We must all try to understand life a little better. We are with you." In the best theatre, this communication is a powerful experience—and it becomes even more powerful when the entire audience leaps to its collective feet in a standing ovation. Such a response becomes a sort of audience participation for theatergoers, who physically express their enthusiasm not only to the performers but also to fellow audience members standing and cheering around them.

What follows the curtain call? The audience disperses, of course, but the individual audience members do not die. Through them the production enjoys an extended afterlife—both in talk and in print—in late-night postmortems at the theatre bar, probing conversations on the morning after, and in the coming days' published and online reviews, actor appearances on television talk shows, letters to the editors of local newspapers, and scholarly articles and books seen weeks, months, or years later. Indeed, in a theatre devoted to community interaction, such as Los Angeles's Cornerstone (see the chapter titled "Global Theatre Today"), the end of the play is the beginning of a hoped-for new life of political change. The theatre is a place of intellectual and emotional public stimulation; it should be expected that the stimulation a provocative production provides would generate both animated discussion and illuminating commentary.

Both the post-show chat and the formally published analysis are examples of what we may call *dramatic criticism,* which is the audience's contribution to the theatre. Criticism is as ancient as Aristotle and as contemporary as the essays and lectures that are presented daily in newspapers, journals, books, and academies all over the world. But criticism is not solely an expert enterprise; criticism—which combines analysis and evaluation—is everybody's job. We look further at this key aspect of the theatre's art in the chapter titled "The Critic."

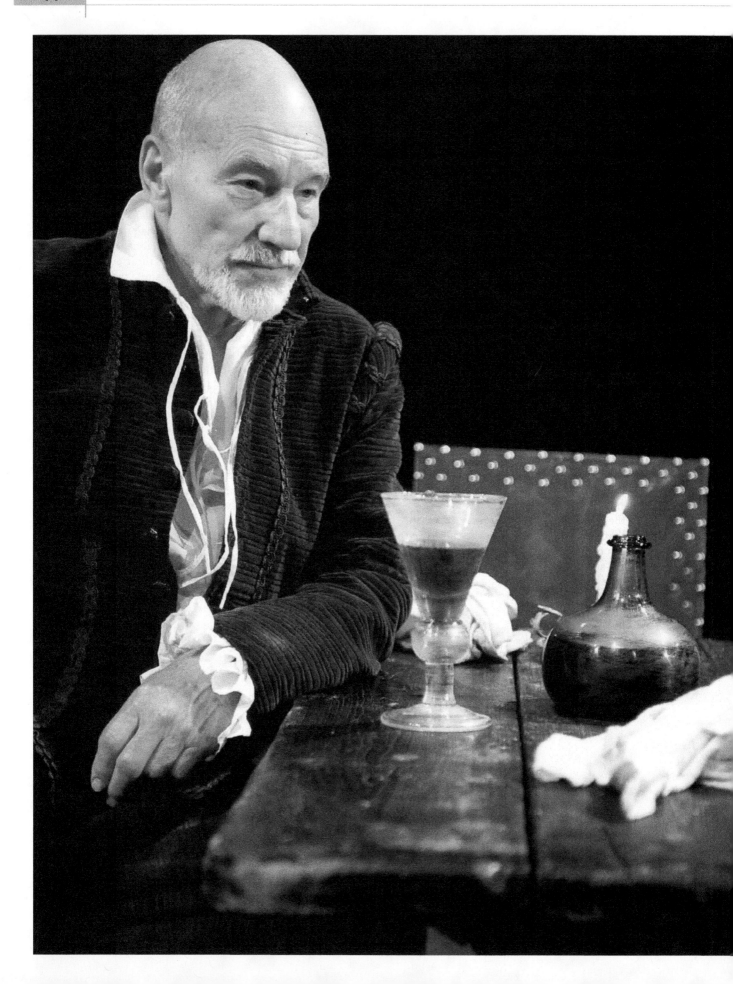

Chapter 3

The Actor

SHE STANDS ALONE IN THE darkness, waiting in the wings, listening with one ear to the insistent rhythms of the dialogue played out upon the stage immediately beyond. Her heart races, and she bounces lightly on the balls of her feet, fighting the welling tension, exhilarated by the sense of something about to engulf her.

The stage ahead of her is ablaze with light; dazzling colors pour on from all possible directions. The energy onstage is almost tangible: it is there in the eyes of the actors, the pace of the dialogue, the smell of the makeup, the sparkle of perspiration glittering in the lights, the bursts of audience laughter and applause, the sudden silence punctuated by a wild cry or a thundering retort.

She glances backward impatiently. Other actors wait in the backstage gloom. Some perform knee bends and roll their necks against the tension. Some gaze thoughtfully at the action of the play. Some stare at the walls. In one corner a stage manager, his head encased in electronic equipment, his body hunched over a dimly lighted copy of the script, whispers commands into an intercom. The backstage shadows pulse with anticipation.

Suddenly the onstage pace quickens; the lines, all at once, take on a greater urgency and familiarity. It is the cue . . . if only there were time to go to the bathroom . . . it is the cue . . . she takes a deep ▶

The Antoinette Perry Awards, more commonly known as the Tonys, are the theatrical equivalent of the film world's Oscars in the United States. Determined by a vote of 700 judges from the press and the theatre community, the Tony's are considered the highest honor for stage performers on Broadway, and emotions run high during the nationally televised award announcements, particularly for the acting prizes. Here Nikki James receives the 2011 Tony for Best Featured Actress in a Musical for her portrayal of Nabalungi in *The Book of Mormon*.

breath, a deeper breath, a gasp . . . *it is the cue.* She bounds from the dimness into the dazzle: she is onstage, she is an actor!

Acting is perhaps the world's most bewildering profession. At the top, it can be extraordinarily rewarding. The thrill of delivering a great performance, the roar of validation from an enraptured audience, the glory of getting inside the skin of the likes of Hamlet, Harpagon, and Hecuba—these are excitements and satisfactions few careers can duplicate. Nor are the rewards purely artistic and intellectual; audience appreciation and the producer's eye for profit can catapult some actors to the highest income levels in the world, with salaries in the millions of dollars for actors achieving "star" status in films. And the fame that can follow is legendary: the private lives of the most universally admired actors become public property, their innermost thoughts the daily fare of television talk shows and fan magazines.

And yet, for all the splendor and glamor, the actor's life is more often than not an anxious one, beset by demands for sacrifice from every direction: psychological, financial, and even moral. Stage fright—the actor's nemesis—is an ever-present nightmare that often increases with experience and renown. Fear of failure, fear of competition, fear of forgetting lines, fear of losing emotional control, fear of losing one's looks, fear of losing one's audience—this list of concerns is endemic to acting as to no other profession.

Nor are the economic rewards in general particularly enticing. The six- and seven-figure salaries of the stars bear little relation to the scale pay for which most actors work; actors often realize less income than the janitors who clean the theatres they perform in. And although the stars billed "above the title" may be treated like celebrities or royalty, the majority of actors are freely bullied by directors, bossed about by stage managers, capriciously hired and fired by producers, dangled and deceived by agents, squeezed and corseted by costumers, pinched by wig dressers, poked and powdered by makeup artists, and disparaged by press agents. Certainly no other profession entails more numbing uncertainties and sacrifices, nor measures its rewards in such extreme and contradictory dimensions.

WHAT IS ACTING?

Since the first published discussions of acting, more than two thousand years ago, theatre theorists and practitioners have recognized two different and seemingly contradictory notions of what acting really is. The first notion is that an actor creates a performance *externally,* first by imagining how his or her character should walk, talk, and behave, and then by imitating these imagined behaviors when performing the character. The second notion is that acting is created *internally,* by concentrating not on imitating behavior but actually *experiencing* it, and thereby "living the part" while performing it.

These different modes require quite different approaches. The external method is often called "technical" because actors employing it have spent years mastering their performing techniques, which include vocal skills (articulation, resonance, and projection), an appreciation for spoken rhetoric

Belfast-born Kenneth Branagh is best known in the United States for his Shakespearean films (*Hamlet, Henry V, Much Ado About Nothing, Love's Labor's Lost, Othello*). He is deeply admired on the British stage for his dramatic passion, clearly apparent here in his 2008 performance in the title role of Chekhov's *Ivanov*, directed by Michael Grandage for London's Wyndham's Theatre.

(phrasing, persuasive argumentation, building crescendos, and fiery perorations) plus verse speaking, an ability to speak a variety of regional dialects and foreign accents flawlessly, and physical dexterity that allows for complete control over their every movement. Such an actor will also seek to master a wide variety of performance modes, such as singing, dancing, mime, fencing, and the like, and will study human behaviors from a broad range of historical periods, countries, and social classes, so as to apply them when creating characters in a variety of dramatic styles.

The internal method, by contrast, asks the actor to enter into the mind and emotional state of the character being played. Such an actor will be expected to

think the character's thoughts, *feel* the character's feelings, *try* to win the character's goals, and, when called for, *cry* the character's (real) tears. He or she thus tries to "be" the character on stage, not to just present the audience with a made-up imitation of an imagined individual. "Act from the outside" is the implicit slogan of the externally shaped actor; "act from the inside" is the slogan of the internally propelled one.

Which is the "best" method? Twenty-five hundred years of debate has not completely resolved this, but most actors and directors and their teachers today insist that *both* of these notions—when integrated—are vital to great acting. Great acting, therefore, comes from both the inside and the outside, and the apparent contradiction between these two approaches is not a debate but a paradox. And the paradox has been known since the beginning of theatre.

The Paradox of Acting—from Socrates to Stanislavsky

It is often thought that ancient drama was performed in an entirely technical manner—mainly because Greek and Roman actors wore elaborate masks, elevated shoes, and flowing gowns. But one ancient Roman actor named Aesopus became so overwrought when performing the revenge of Orestes that he ran his sword through a stagehand who unhappily strayed into his line of sight. Another, named Polus, brought the ashes of his own dead son onstage with him so that, in playing the character of Electra, he could cry real tears lamenting the death of his fictional brother. They were obviously acting "from the inside," at least at those times. Indeed, this was well understood in ancient times. The Roman poet Horace (65–8 B.C.) wrote, "In order to move the audience, you must first be moved yourself," and this adage was repeated by commentators on acting right up through the Renaissance. So it is clear that ancient actors, at least at key moments in their performances, felt the emotions of their characters, and certainly, in the case of Polus, developed techniques to do so.

The paradox of acting was itself described in this famous ancient dialogue in which the philosopher Socrates inquired of the rhapsodist (poetic reciter) Ion as to what role real emotion played in his recitations:

SOCRATES: Tell me, Ion, when you produce the greatest effect upon the audience... are you in your right mind? Or are you not carried out of yourself [and]... seem to be among the persons or the places of which you are speaking?

No American actress in the past thirty-five years—indeed, probably no actress anywhere—has come close to equaling the achievement, both artistic and commercial, of Meryl Streep. Quickly moving from her Yale Drama School acting M.F.A. degree into five Broadway shows between 1975 and 1977, Streep crossed into films and by 2012 had received more Academy Award nominations (seventeen) than any other performer. But Streep remains closely connected to the stage through the New York Shakespeare Festival, where, in 2001, she played Madame Arkadina in Chekhov's *The Seagull*. She is shown here in 2006 in one of the most demanding roles in modern theatre: the seventeenth-century war-profiteer Anna Fielding (Mother Courage) in Brecht's *Mother Courage and Her Children*. Audiences lined up from the early morning hours, rain or shine, to see Streep's three-and-a-half-hour outdoor performance in Central Park's Delacorte Theatre. She received nearly unanimous praise for fully capturing Anna's hardbitten cynicism, raucous exuberance, and capitalist fervor—as well as for belting out Brecht's audacious songs with tremendous élan. The script was adapted by Tony Kushner, and the direction of this New York Shakespeare Festival production was by George C. Wolfe.

ION: Socrates, I must frankly confess that at the tale of pity my eyes are filled with tears, and when I speak of horrors, my hair stands on end and my heart throbs.

So Ion was not only feeling the emotions of his roles, he was imagining himself in the presence of the fictional characters he was speaking of. But he was also aware, during the very moments his eyes were filled with tears, of the effects his performance was having on the audience:

SOCRATES: . . . and are you aware that you produce similar effects on most of the spectators?

ION: Only too well; for I look down upon them from the stage, and behold the various emotions of pity, wonder, sternness, stamped upon their countenances when I am speaking.

Thus Ion considered his acting both from the inside (his whole body experienced the story he was describing) and from the outside (he was, at the same time, checking out the audience's reaction). This inside *and* outside nature of acting is thus a paradox; when reciting, Ion is simultaneously both inside and outside the fiction of his performance.

"There is no definitive *Hamlet*," says Jude Law, "because you don't play Hamlet, Hamlet plays you. You come out in him." Law played the title role of the play in London and on New York's Broadway in 2009, explaining to an interviewer that he let his emotions in each scene drive the next one, "almost as if he were improvising." Here he gives Hamlet's "To be or not to be" soliloquy in a winter snowfall; the production was directed by Michael Grandage.

Much of the study of acting since Ion and Horace, therefore, has not been whether the actor should get inside the role (or, we might say, cry real tears), but how to do it. The Roman orator Quintilian (A.D. 35–100) envisioned his wife's and children's imaginary deaths with such "extreme vividness" as to become "so moved" during his oration that he would be brought to tears, turn pale, and exhibit "all the symptoms of genuine grief." Quintilian's treatise on performance—and its privileging of these inside techniques—was widely cited up through the Renaissance; an eighteenth-century French critic even proposed that only actors who were truly in love should play lovers onstage.

Yet true to acting's paradox, Quintilian also acknowledged that he created his performances with a "regularity and discipline promised by calculation," and he cautioned fellow performers that "it is never correct to employ the left hand alone in gesture" and that "the hand [must not] be raised above the level of the eyes." And this notion of regularity and discipline

became championed in the eighteenth century by the French essayist Denis Diderot, whose 1773 "Paradox of Acting" proclaimed the radical thesis that "a great actor . . . must [only be] an unmoved and disinterested onlooker." Diderot argued fiercely that it is better for an actor to imitate anger than to actually be angry, and that actors should therefore play from the head, not from the heart. "Actors impress the public not when they are furious, but when they play fury well," he declared, explaining that "actors who play from the heart . . . are alternately strong and feeble, fiery and cold. . . . Tomorrow they will miss the point they have excelled in today. . . . But the actor who plays from thought . . . will be always at his best; for he has considered, combined, learned and arranged the whole thing in his head." Diderot beautifully represents the rationalist view of the European Enlightenment, which sought to demystify both medieval superstition and Renaissance idealism, and his viewpoints circulated widely in Europe and America through the nineteenth

Stagecraft

Basic Acting Exercises

Acting is easier to understand by doing it than by reading about it. Even if you have never acted before, the following four acting exercises can help you understand what acting is, from the inside and the outside.

REACH

Stand on your right foot; reach as high as you can with your left hand. Imagine there is something you greatly desire above your head: a beautiful jewel, a wad of thousand-dollar bills, or "the key to your true love's heart." Now reach again, and *really try to get it!*

This is the simplest acting exercise there is, and it illustrates the difference between presentational (outside) and representational (internal) acting methods. When you're only asked to reach as high as you can, you will respond by acting from the outside since you will reach only because you were told to. This is not even acting—it's simply calisthenics. But when you *really try* to get something—even though it is imaginary—you will be acting from the inside because you are trying to achieve the goals of some imaginary character. And the goals will come from your imagination: What kind of a jewel was it? How many thousand-dollar bills?

Reach for an imagined lover! Imagine Rapunzel in her tower prison—or Leonardo diCaprio in chains—or the boy or girl you were hopelessly in love with in junior high school. By trying to reach and rescue this idol, you will put yourself into the role of a character and, in Stanislavsky's phrase, you will be able to "live the life of your character" for a few seconds—or, in a play, for two hours and a half. If you can commit fully to this, you will probably have stretched your arms out farther, breathed harder, found your pulse beating faster, and felt, when you were done, exhausted—and/or exhilarated.

SHADOWBOX

Make two fists; then, bouncing from foot to foot, with one fist held up to protect your chin, jab at an imaginary opponent with the other fist, extending your arm fully each time. As you do this, shout "BAM!" with every jab.

Continue to bounce from foot to foot, dodging your imaginary opponent's imaginary blows ("Rope-a-dope," Muhammad Ali called this). When you see an (imaginary) opening, hit your opponent with your other fist—a potentially knockout punch known as a cross (a "right cross" if done with your right fist).

With every cross, shout "POW!" Use "BAM!" and "POW!" to cheer yourself on, to frighten an (imaginary) opponent into submission, and to encourage any witnesses to cheer for you (which will frighten your opponent even more).

DANCE

Balancing on the balls of your feet, step forward on one foot while extending the same-side arm, wrist forward, in the same direction, letting your fingers follow after the wrist has reached its maximum extension. The movement is identical to throwing a Frisbee. At the moment when the fingers follow (or the imaginary Frisbee is released), cry "Dance!" Repeat with the other leg and arm, and keep repeating, in alternation, crying "Dance!" with each move.

Continue, switching to the word "Ballet!" As you step on your right foot, go up on the toes of your left foot, and vice versa. Say "Ballet!" in a way that encourages others to appreciate the beauty of ballet (whether or not you find it beautiful). Continue, switching to the word "L'amour!" (French for "love," pronounced "la-MOOR!") and imagining that you are casting beautiful flower petals—as love tokens—at the feet of beautiful people. Say "L'amour!" in a way that encourages others to think you a wonderful and imaginative lover (whether or not you think you are). *Exult* in your magnificent ballet moves and your beautiful tossing of flower petals.

Did those last two exercises make you feel a bit foolish? Good—for that means you are learning what it means to perform behaviors beyond what you do in your everyday life. Actors do things all the time that would appear ridiculous if they did them in daily life—such as behave like an ass in *A Midsummer Night's Dream* or cry like a witch in *Macbeth*—yet these actors must believe in what they're doing, and believe they *want* to do those things. The "shadow-box" and "dance" exercises involve doing something you're asked (by a stage direction or director) to do, but finding a reason to make it seem like something you *want* to do, no matter how foolish you might have thought it when you were first asked to do it.

century and remain influential in some measure in classical theatre training in the modern era, particularly in France and England.

In the American theatre, however, the inside method has increasingly held sway since the visits to the United States of Russian actor-director Konstantin Stanislavsky (1863–1938) and his Moscow Art Theatre in 1924 and 1925. Astounding American audiences with an intensely realistic and convincing acting style in New York and thirteen other cities, Stanislavsky's system of acting—described as the actor "living the life of his or her character on stage"—turned many American actors into Stanislavsky disciples. When taken up by various American acting teachers, particularly Lee Strasberg in New York, Stanislavsky's system became "the Method"—with a capital M. As taught by Strasberg at the Group Theatre in the 1930s and at the Actors Studio from 1951 until his death in 1982, variations of the Method became core beliefs of actors such as Paul Newman, Ann Bancroft, Al Pacino, James Dean, Dustin Hoffman, and Marilyn Monroe, and the Method became world renowned through the success of these actors on the stage and, more notably worldwide, in American films.

CONTENTLESS SCENE: WHAT DID YOU DO LAST NIGHT?

Here is a short dialogue exchange written for two actors. It has no fixed content: it takes on meaning only when it becomes part of a context, which, in this exercise, can be any of the seven situations listed below. To perform this exercise, one person memorizes the lines of role A and the other of role B. Then the players choose any of the seven situations and "perform" the scene accordingly. This exercise is best experienced in a classroom where half of the participants learn one role and half the other and each participant tries the scene several times, changing both situations and partners on each occasion.

The Dialogue

A: Hi!

B: Hello.

A: How's everything?

B: Fine. I guess.

A: Do you know what time it is?

B: No. Not exactly.

A: Don't you have a watch?

B: Not on me.

A: Well?

B: Well what?

A: What did you do last night?

B: What do you mean?

A: What did you do last night?

B: Nothing.

A: Nothing?

B: I said, nothing!

A: I'm sorry I asked.

B: That's all right.

The Seven Situations

1. A is a parent; B is a teenager. The scene takes place at the breakfast table. B is eating a bowl of cereal, and A is entering the room.
2. A and B are a young married couple. Last night, after an argument, B left the apartment. It is now the following morning. A is washing dishes. B returns.
3. A and B (same sex) are roommates. Both have been involved with the same boy (or girl) during the past few weeks, both are still interested in pursuing the relationship, and both are somewhat suspicious of the other's secrecy. They meet while returning to their room after a night's absence.
4. A and B are classmates who have been romantically interested in each other for some time. They meet in a cafeteria by accident, and A sits down next to B.
5. A and B (same sex) are auditioning for an important role. It is rumored that the director plays favorites in casting. A and B meet at the bulletin board to await the announcement of callbacks.
6. A and B are siblings. B has recently been released from a psychiatric unit after a suicide attempt. After B has stayed out all night, A finds B in the waiting room of a bus depot.
7. A and B are friends. B has recently been released from a psychiatric unit after maniacally attacking a friend with a butcher knife. A, aware of this, comes upon B in an isolated spot.

When variations on contentless scenes are performed, with the actors switching partners each time, several things become evident.

In this exercise, the content is created entirely by the situation and what the actors bring to it from their own imaginations. It is happening in real time, therefore, and being experienced at the same time it is being performed. The words are instruments of the action, not the dictator of plot, character, or behavior. Thus the acting becomes a way of creating a spontaneously changing relationship, and the plot develops entirely out of what happens between you and your acting partner.

These exercises should teach you a little bit about acting, and they should be fun: they should allow you to move outside your own environment and into the lives of others who are both you and not you at the same time. This is the paradox of acting.

Acting Today

In the current era, most of the fire has gone out of the inside/outside debate, and the distinction between European and American actors has largely diminished. Today's French and British actors study Stanislavsky's inner methods as well as external classical techniques, while American actors are trained in voice, speech, movement, and period styles along with their focus on "being real," "living the part," "being in the moment," "owning the role," and "personalizing their roles"—all colloquial references to inner, or Method, approaches.

So we will follow this history with expanded discussions of inner and outer techniques and how they have come together in the current era.

ACTING FROM THE INSIDE: THE STANISLAVSKY LEGACY

Stanislavsky's major pronouncements on living the life of the character were first conveyed to a public audience not in Russian but in English, as translated by Elizabeth Hapgood and published as *An Actor Prepares* in New York in 1936. This slender text presented a valuable though incomplete version of Stanislavsky's basic system of realistic acting, and it had a profound and immediate impact, becoming the core textbook of the American acting style for decades to come. Since 2008, however, it has been superseded by a more accurate and more complete translation by Jean Benedetti entitled *An Actor's Work,* which also includes Stanislavsky's following text, called *Building a Character* in its initial (1949) English appearance. All quotations of Stanislavsky in the following pages are from the Benedetti translation.

In the beginning of *An Actor's Work,* Stanislavsky writes, "Our prime task is . . . to create the inner life of the character." We can do this, he says, by "bringing our own individual feelings to it, endowing it with all the features of our own personality."

By "inner life" Stanislavsky meant the ambiguity of emotion, the mystery of love and death, and the confusion of experience. To create this life onstage, Stanislavsky sought to identify the separate steps of the actor's preparation. Primary to his vision was that the actor must base the performance in pursuing his or her character's *task* (in Russian, *zadacha,* which can also be translated as "problem" or, as by Hapgood, "objective"). The character's task is different from the actor's task. The actor's task may be to get a standing ovation from the audience, or a good review in the local press; but the character's task for, let's say, Juliet is to win Romeo's love or, at other times, to win her father's respect, the friar's blessing, or the nurse's assistance. By concentrating on *winning these tasks* (instead of on "being a great actress") during her performance, Stanislavsky discovered, the actress can lose her stage fright, throw herself into her character, and convincingly represent Juliet as a real and whole person rather than simply presenting her as a fictional—though admirable—Renaissance teenager. Identifying the character's tasks and asking the actor to actually try to *achieve* them while acting is Stanislavsky's key to this process.

Stanislavsky was not the first person to propose this strategy, but he was the first to systematically investigate how to carry it out. He spoke of a character's *motivations* for acting, and he advanced the notion that every move onstage must be seen to correspond to what the *character* (and not just the playwright or director or even the actor) is striving to achieve: "Everything that happens onstage must occur for *some reason or other.* When you sit there, you must also sit for a reason, not merely to show yourself off to the audience."

Stanislavsky had many dictates within this basic belief. He asked actors to enter a circle of "solitude" to avoid shamelessly playing to the audience, and urged them to maintain a deep concentration on the other actors onstage: Your "tasks are . . . directed toward the other actors, not to the audience," he proposed. He established the concept that the play's text was accompanied by a profound "subtext" of meanings hidden beneath the lines, which was revealed *unconsciously* by actors when they were concentrating on their tasks and the characters around them. He despised empty theatricality, whereby the actor relies on showing off theatrical gimmicks and brazenly seeks to generate audience approval.

Stanislavsky was deeply, almost obsessively, concerned with the actor's emotion. In the writings of nineteenth-century French psychologist Théodule Armand Ribot, he had read that "all memories of past experiences are recorded by the nervous system and . . . may be evoked by an appropriate stimulus." So in his earlier years he experimented with recalling his own past emotional states and developed an acting technique now called *emotion memory* (or "emotional recall" or "affective memory") whereby mentally substituting remembered situations from his own life into the action of the play could allow him to reach the emotional levels the play required. By this method, Stanislavsky sought to make his own acting natural, truthful, and emotionally vivid for the performer and audience alike.

No country—not even Russia—has been as influenced by Stanislavsky's teaching as the United States. Even before his 1924 tour, two of Stanislavsky's disciples, Richard Boleslavski and Maria Ouspenskaya, had moved to New York and founded the American Laboratory Theatre, bringing Stanislavsky's system to the attention of hundreds of young New York actors. One of these was Strasberg, an Austrian immigrant who, along with other Stanislavsky devotees—Harold Clurman, Clifford Odets, Elia Kazan, Morris Carnovsky, Stella Adler, and Sanford Meisner—formed the Group Theatre in 1931 to revolutionize not only American theatre but American acting.

The Group did not outlive the decade, but by the 1950s, all the first believers had developed major theatre careers (Odets as a playwright, Kazan and Clurman as directors, the others as actors and acting teachers). The Actors Studio, created by Kazan and others in 1947 and headed by Strasberg from 1951, became the temple of American theatre—with the Method as its Bible and emotion memory as its First Commandment. The Actors Studio dominated the New York acting scene and quickly spread to Hollywood to become the gold standard of American acting both on the stage and in film.

Actress Ann Hathaway (*left*) had the task of playing the young woman Viola in Shakespeare's *Twelfth Night*—who spends all but the first and last moments of the play pretending to be a young man named Cesario, even after falling in love with the handsome Count Orsino (Raúl Esparza, *right*). How did Hathaway prepare for the Cesario scenes? From the outside, at least in part—by putting a rolled-up pair of socks down her trousers and getting used to thinking of it as part of her anatomy. "I'd be lying if I said that I haven't walked around my apartment with a sock shoved down the front!" she explained. "All of a sudden, you just understand. You stand differently and it's just like, yeah!" The highly successful 2009 New York production was directed by Daniel Sullivan.

Perhaps because Strasberg's Method privileged actors over the script—making their own feelings as much the "subject" of the play as their characters' actions—American actors and not a few celebrities flocked to his school. Other American acting teachers who had been with the Group, notably Adler, Meisner, and Carnovsky, while notably deviating from Strasberg's commitment to emotion memory, perpetuated Stanislavsky's ideal in their classes as well.

ACTING FROM THE OUTSIDE

Although Stanislavsky was committed to his primary principles of developing the inner life of the character, he never excluded the need to also create characters through external or technical means. He began

his theatrical career, in fact, as a highly technical performer. Born to an aristocratic family, he had performed in plays, operettas, and operas from the age of six, often in large, fully equipped theatres that his family had built in their Moscow home and their country estate. As a singer, he had studied with a Bolshoi Opera star; indeed, he was so promising that the renowned composer Pyotr Tchaikovsky proposed writing an opera for him. Like Quintilian, he prized true emotion but also recognized the necessity for rational control in performance, and the second half of his *An Actor's Work* mainly concerns external acting techniques.

"Feeling . . . does not replace an immense amount of work on the part of our intellects," Stanislavsky wrote in this section (which was unknown in the West until 1949), after which he went on to examine elocution, resonance, and rhetorical phrasing, even describing them with operatic terms. "Begin the speech quietly," he advises at one point. "Speak slightly louder after the first line, the next line louder still, until you reach *forte*. If you increase power step by step, you will ultimately reach *forte-fortissimo*." Elsewhere he explains that "upward inflections can be of definite shapes and heights: in intervals of a third, a fifth, or an octave." It is hard to imagine acting instructions more "technical" than these.

Indeed, by the middle of his career, Stanislavsky had even discarded emotion memory from his system, replacing it by a focus on *physical action* as the key to truthful acting. He began to reproach his actors for excessive wallowing in their own emotion: "What's false here? You're playing feelings, your own suffering, that's what's false. I need to see the event and how you react to that event, how you fight people—how you react, not suffer. . . . To take that line . . . is to be passive and sentimental. See everything in terms of action!" Even Stanislavsky understood that technical mastery is at least one critical part of career success in acting, for it is obvious that actors must be heard and understood in the back row, and must fulfill the basic expectations that the text promises and the production's director seeks to create—that, for example, Prometheus be seen as fiery, Juliet as romantic, and Monsieur Jourdain as comical. Beyond that, a professional actor should be able, at times, to amuse, electrify, delight, seduce, and thrill a paying audience—not just be heard and seen by them. And that requires the level of trained and perfected skills called "virtuosity."

THE ACTOR AS VIRTUOSO

The characters of drama are rarely mundane. They are exemplary, and so must be the actors who portray them. To deliver the genius of Hamlet, for example, an actor must *embody* that brilliance of mind. Similar resources are required to create the fury of Lear, the fervor of Saint Joan, the bravura of Mercutio, the heroic charisma of Hecuba. The despair of Willy Loman in *Death of a Salesman* must be conveyed in his body, worn out by carrying display cases every day for forty years; by his voice, made desperate from trying daily to cover up his obvious, increasing failures; and by his gestures, riddled with the uncertainties of a man who can no longer distinguish between real-time events and his memories of the past. Outsized characters, whether in classical dramas or modern realism, demand outsized abilities and the capacity to project them throughout a crowded

auditorium. Such characters draw the audience into the play's world: they not only "entertain" the audience but become archetypes of the play's themes and ideas. We are not only depressed by Willy's pain, we are fascinated by it, and we learn from it as we become determined not to suffer his fate ourselves—if we can help it!

Acting virtuosity involves many areas, as discussed above, but there are two that dominate: a magnificently expressive voice and a splendidly supple body. These are the tools every actor strives to attain, and when brilliantly honed they are valuable beyond measure.

Throughout history, the actor's voice has received the greatest attention. Greek tragic actors were awarded prizes for their vocal abilities alone, and many modern actors, such as Liev Schreiber, Patrick Stewart, James Earl Jones, Rachel Weisz, Helen Mirren, and Meryl Streep are celebrated for their stunning voices, which may be, by turns, resonant, mellow, sharp, musical, stinging, poetic, seductive, compelling, lulling, and dominating. A voice that can articulate complex ideas rapidly and explain subtleties clearly and convincingly, rivet attention while conveying nuances, thunder with rage and flow with compassion can hold audiences spellbound.

The actor's use of her or his body—the capacity for movement—is the other fundamental element of virtuoso technique. Most of the best actors are strong and flexible; all are capable of great physical self-mastery and are artists of body language. The effects that can be achieved through precise and subtle stage movement are as numerous as those that can be achieved through voice: the gifted and well-trained actor's arched eyebrow, toss of the head, flick of the wrist, whirl of the hem, or shuffle of the feet can command electric attention. But bold movements, too, produce indelible stage moments: Helene Weigel's powerful chest-pounding when, as Mother Courage, she loses her son; Laurence Olivier's breathtaking fall from the tower as Coriolanus; Paul Scofield's audacious upheaval of the laden dinner table, crashing pewter plates and beer mugs to the floor in Peter Brook's production of *King Lear*—these are sublime theatricalizations that are remembered long after the deaths of those who performed them.

Theatrical virtuosity has made somewhat of a comeback in the American theatre since the mid-twentieth century, when Stanislavsky's *An Actor Prepares* went on sale, the Actors Studio had its heyday, and Hollywood's *East of Eden* (James Dean) and *On the Waterfront* (Marlon Brando)—along with European cinéma vérité (cinema of truth)—held sway in the film world. Why? In part because audiences continued to demand, on the live stage at least, clarity of speech, elegance of movement,

English-born but American-schooled actor Mark Rylance is one of the most versatile and accomplished actors in both of these countries today. After ten years (1995–2005) as the artistic director and principal actor of the Globe Theater in London, Rylance concentrated on his acting and quickly became recognized as one of the most accomplished and versatile actors on the American and English stages. His brilliant, quirky Broadway performances as the unapologetic, alcoholic ex-Hippie, "Rooster" (*top photo*), in Jez Butterworth's 2011 *Jerusalem* ("a seismic performance" raved the *New York Times*), the would-be lover Robert in 2008 Marc Camoletti's *Boeing Boeing*), and the effusively uncouth "playwright" Valere in David Hirson's 2010 *La Bête* (*bottom photo*), won him a pair of Best Actor Tony Awards and near-universal praise for both his farcical genius and unsettling tragic dimensions.

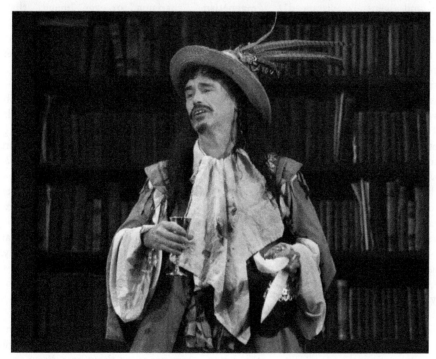

and iconic rather than ordinary characters. Also, in part, because drama itself was changing. The theatre of alienation propounded by Bertolt Brecht, which prioritized the dialectic of social and political ideologies over the search for inner truth of individual characters; along with the nonlinear structures, multidisciplinary styles, and metatheatrical techniques of our postmodern age, have occasioned a comeback for singing, dancing, circus

Actors Kristin Scott Thomas and Peter Sarsgaard create emotionally intense interactions between the famous but distant actress, Arkadina, and her equally aloof paramour, the manipulative and rakish novelist Trigorin, in Anton Chekhov's *The Seagull,* a performance *New York Times* senior critic Ben Brantley called "the finest and most fully involving production of Chekhov that I have ever known." The 2008 Broadway production was directed by Ian Rickson.

techniques, direct address, and a generally "distanced" style of acting in many modern dramatic stagings. Multiskilled, multitalented, and multifaceted performers—men and women who can play multiple roles of both sexes and all ages, in plays with no costume or makeup changes deemed necessary—are in demand as never before. The actor is now as often seen as a versatile "performer" as he or she is viewed as a fixed "character"—and thus must be rich in talent and performing skills, capable not merely of depicting everyday life but of fashioning an artful and exciting theatrical expression of it.

It seems clear, then, that great acting today demands *both* a convincing inner life for the character *and* virtuoso skills that can deliver that character with some or all of these theatrical ideals: clarity, excitement, vivacity, charm, sex appeal, a sense of danger, and a sense of exhilaration—along with a profound engagement with the dramatic text, its issues and ideas, and its production. Virtuosity for its own sake, possibly appealing in the cabaret or lecture hall, can only create performances of depth, complexity, and theatrical power when coupled with the convincing impersonation of a character's inner life.

MAGIC

Are conviction and virtuosity all there is to great acting? Probably not.

Almost all theatergoers, directors, and critics find a final acting ingredient, often called "presence," "magnetism," "charisma," or even "magic," that has been felt by audiences throughout the centuries. It is a quality that, though impossible to precisely define, is universally felt—a quality we cannot explain except to say we know when we are under its spell.

What is it? We must always remember that the earliest actor was not a technician of the theatre but a priest—and that he (and in those days it was almost certainly a "he") embodied not ordinary men but gods. We may witness this apparent transcendence directly today in certain tribal dramas in which a shaman or witch doctor is accepted by cocelebrants as the possessor of divine attributes or as one possessed by them. The greatest actors convey a hint of the divine. Elevated upon a stage and bathed in light, charged with creating an intensity of feeling, a vivid characterization, and a well-articulated eloquence of verbal and physical mastery, the actor at his or her finest becomes what we metaphorically consider an extraterrestrial being, a "star," or, in the French expression, a *monstre sacré* ("sacred monster").

This quality of "presence"—the ability not merely to "be present" but to project an aura of magic, of the divine—does not come about as a direct result of studying realistic impersonation or technical virtuosity. It is more surely a factor of the actor's inner confidence, which, though usually bred from the actor's mastery of his or her craft, cannot be taught as part of craft training. It is perhaps frustrating to find that this final measure of acting depends so heavily on an elusive, largely inexplicable goal, but it is also true that every art incorporates elements that must remain as mysteries. The best acting, like any art, ultimately transcends the reach of pure descriptive analysis; it cannot be acquired mechanically. The best acting strikes chords in the deepest, most inaccessible reaches of our brains, where it rings with a resonance we do not fully understand and evokes an ancient reality we no longer remember. We should extol, not lament, this fact.

BECOMING AN ACTOR

How does one become an actor? Many thousands ask this question every year; many thousands, indeed, act in one or more theatrical productions every year. The training of actors is a major activity in hundreds of colleges, universities, conservatories, and private and commercial schools across the United States today; and theories of actor-training constitute a major branch of artistic pedagogy.

Essentially, actor-training entails two distinct phases: development of the actor's approach to a role (largely creating the character's inner life) and developing the actor's vocal and physical instrument (largely concerning virtuosity). There is no general agreement—indeed, there is substantial debate—on the order in which these phases should occur, but there is now widespread understanding that both are necessary and that the two are interrelated.

The Approach

By the twenty-first century, an integrated, or fusion, technique has become nearly universal in actor-training in the West. The first element of this approach to acting is Stanislavsky's primary principle: the actor creates her or his performance through the pursuit of the character's zadacha, or task to be accomplished. Whether *zadacha* is translated as "objective," "intention," "problem," "victory," "want," or (this author's choice) "goal," the basic point—that the actor fully embodies (enters into) a role by pursuing the character's goal (to marry, to revenge), rather than by pursuing the actor's own goal (to get a standing ovation, to get a better part in the next production)—is widely accepted. This goal focuses the actor's energy, displaces her stage fright, aligns her with the character, and allows her to use all her technical skills to win the struggle that propels her words and actions.

Most contemporary teachers, including this author, also insist that these goals be achievable only through

other characters in the play, so that acting is, in almost all cases, *interacting* with other people. Juliet does not simply want "to marry" but "to marry Romeo"; Hamlet wants not just "to revenge" but to "revenge his father's death by killing Claudius." The acting thus becomes *enlivened;* it occurs in real time onstage, with moment-to-moment *live* interplay between all the actors involved.

The second element of the actor's approach is the identification of the *tactics* necessary to achieve goals and avoid defeat. Romeo woos Juliet by composing love poems to her and reciting them fetchingly; he silences Mercutio's jibes by wittily humoring him. Hamlet secures Horatio's aid by speaking warmly to him, he turns his mother's mind against her husband by chastising her, he disorients Polonius through clever wordplay and feigned insanity, and he steers his girlfriend Ophelia out of harm's way (he believes) by frightening her. By means of these tactics Romeo and Hamlet try to make their goals come to fruition, and the voices and bodies of the actors who play them with committed vigor should pulse with anticipation, excitement, and alarm. Actors who play tactics boldly and with enthusiasm, and who allow themselves to believe that they will *win* their goals (even if the play dictates that they will not), convey the theatre's greatest intangible: *hope.* Hope achieved—as when the young deaf and blind Helen Keller finally utters the word "wawa" as her teacher splashes water on her hands in the final moments of William Gibson's *The Miracle Worker*—can be overwhelmingly thrilling. Hope dashed—as when Jim O'Connor tells Laura that he won't be able to invite her on a date in Tennessee Williams's *The Glass Menagerie*—can be unbearably poignant. It is in the alternation of these sorts of climaxes that great theatrical impact is achieved.

The third and most complicated element of the actor's approach requires research into the *style* of the play and the *mode* of performance that will govern the production, in which each role is but a single integer. Some plays, and some productions, invite—indeed, require—direct confrontation with the live audience. Others assume an environment in which the entire cast of characters expects and rewards elegantly refined speech, while still others assume an environment in which such speech is ridiculed as pretentious. Some plays contain several "worlds" of characters—Shakespeare's *A Midsummer Night's Dream,* for example, features aristocrats, "mechanicals" (common laborers), and fairies—and the actor's approach must lead to a deep and clear understanding of the nature of each of the play's separate or inclusive worlds.

The Actor's Instrument

The actor's instrument is the actor's *self*—her mind, mettle, and metabolism are the materials of her performance. The actor's voice is the perfectly tuned violin to be played; her body is the sculpting clay to be molded. An actor is a portrait artist working from inside the subject's self, creating characters with her or his own organs, hormones, and neurons. It is obvious that a great artist requires first-rate equipment. For the actor this means a responsive self: disciplined yet uninhibited and capable of rising to the enormous challenges of great roles.

The training of the actor's instrument is then both physiological and psychological; for that reason it must be accomplished under the personal supervision of qualified instructors. In the past, acting instructors were invariably master actors who took on younger apprentices; even today, students of classical French and Japanese acting styles learn their art by relentless imitation of the actors they hope to succeed. In America and many parts of Europe, however, acting instruction has expanded to include a great many educational specialists who may or may not have had extensive professional acting experience themselves; indeed, some of the most celebrated and effective acting teachers today are play directors, theatrical innovators, and academics.

No one, however, has yet discovered the art of training an actor's instrument simply by reading books or thinking about problems of craft!

Voice and Speech   Voice and speech, quite naturally, are the first elements of the actor's physiological instrument to be considered: "Voice, voice, and more voice" was the answer Tommaso Salvini, the famed nineteenth-century Italian tragedian, gave to the question "What are the three most important attributes of acting?" We already have discussed the importance of vocal skills in the acting profession. Voice- and speech-training programs are aimed at acquainting the actor with a variety of means to achieve and enhance these skills.

The basic elements of voice (breathing, phonation, resonance) and of speech (articulation, pronunciation, phrasing)—as well as their final combination (projection)—are all separate aspects of an integrated voice-training program. Such a program ordinarily takes three years or longer, and many actors continue working on voice and speech all their lives.

As devoted as teachers and scientists have been to the problems of perfecting voice and speech, however, a certain mystery still surrounds much of their work. Even the fundamental question of how the voice actually works is a subject of fierce dispute among specialists in anatomy and physiology. Moreover, the processes involved in breathing and speaking have acquired a certain mystique. For example, the dual meaning of *inspiration* as both "inhalation" and "spirit stimulus" has given rise to a number of exotic theoretical dicta that border on religiosity.

Movement   Movement is the second element of the actor's physiological instrument. Movement training typically involves exercises and instruction designed to create physical relaxation, muscular control, economy of action, and expressive rhythms and movement patterns. Dance, mime, fencing, and acrobatics are traditional training courses for actors; in addition, circus techniques and masked pantomime have become common courses.

Most actors work out regularly. Longtime British stage and film star Laurence Olivier, for example, contended into his senior years that only sheer physical strength could provide the actor with the stamina needed to "hold stage" without strain or fatigue. In America, leading actress Jane Fonda became such a fitness buff as to create a series of training videos to share her discoveries.

Control of the body permits an actor to stand, sit, and move on the stage with alertness, energy, and seeming ease. Standing tall, walking boldly, turning on a dime at precisely the right moment, extending the limbs joyously, sobbing violently, springing about uproariously, and occupying a major share of stage space (metaphorically becoming "larger than life") are among the capacities of the actor who has mastered body control through training and confidence.

Economy of movement, often taught through mime, permits the conveyance of subtle detail by seemingly inconspicuous movement. The waggle of a finger, the flare of a nostril, the quiver of a lip can communicate volumes in a performance of controlled movement. The beginning actor is often recognized by uncontrolled behaviors—fidgeting, shuffling, aimless pacing, and nervous hand gestures—that draw unwanted audience attention. The professional understands the importance of physical self-control and the explosive potential of a simple movement that follows a carefully prepared stillness. Surprise, one of the actor's greatest weapons, can be achieved only through the actor's mastery of the body. Collective movement, involving continuous physical contact between two or more people, is often taught through dance, contact improvisation, and even theatre games, all ways to release actors from their individual isolation and make them part of a creative and physically interactive ensemble. And

Photo Essay: Actor Sir Patrick Stewart

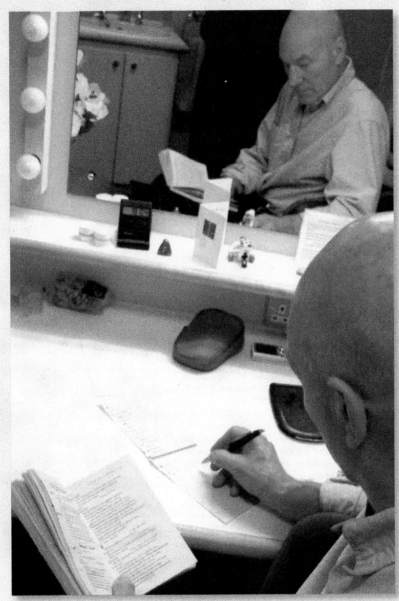

1. In his dressing room, Stewart is making out a chart (in green) specifying where he is to make his entrances in the many different scenes of *Antony and Cleopatra*. During each performance he must leave the stage many times, going to his dressing room to change costume before reentering somewhere else each time. He feels safer with this "cheat sheet" on his dressing-room table to remind him of the location of each new entrance.

Patrick Stewart is known worldwide because of his 176 episodes as Captain Jean-Luc Picard on television's *Star Trek* and his continuing role of Professor Charles Xavier in the *X-Men* films, but he began his continuously ascending acting career with sixteen years of playing largely classical performances with England's Royal Shakespeare Company (RSC), and has, during the course of a fifty-year career, performed in more than 100 stage productions on Broadway, London's West End, and regional American theatres including Minneapolis's Guthrie, Washington's Shakespeare Theatre Company, the New York Shakespeare Festival, and Los Angeles' Ahmanson and Huntington Theatres. And his post–*Star Trek* stage career is certainly his greatest, including stunning performances in the major classical roles of Othello, Macbeth, Prospero, Claudius, Malvolio, and Mark Antony (in *Antony and Cleopatra*) together with equally celebrated New York and London performances as Vladimir in Samuel Beckett's *Waiting for Godot* (London West End, 2009), Robert in David Mamet's *A Life in the Theatre* (Broadway, 2012), and William Shakespeare himself in Edward Bond's *Bingo* (London's Old Vic, 2010). In 2010, he was knighted Sir Patrick Stewart by the Queen of England.

With numerous film and television credits along with his stage work, Stewart is convinced that each medium can be a lead-in to all the others. "Sitting in all those thrones of England on the stage at Stratford-upon-Avon was nothing less than a preparation for sitting in the captain's chair of the *Enterprise*," he said in an interview in early 2007. "This is an exaggeration, of course, but there are parallels," he insists, referring to his two long-standing artistic "homes"—England's RSC and America's *Star Trek*.

"*Star Trek* isn't written in naturalistic dialogue," Stewart continues. "It has a certain heightened quality, a tonality which is not like *CSI* or any of those contemporary shows. It has a five-act structure, which very much follows classical principles. And the bridge set is like an Elizabethan stage: it had a huge opening; the 'view screen' where the audience is; entrances, down left and right and up

2.

3.

4.

2. From his dressing room, Stewart checks with the wig room—92 steps up—to see if his wig is ready. London's Novello Theatre, where the performance takes place, has dozens of individual dressing rooms scattered throughout the building's five backstage floors. The telephone is essential for communications with stage management before and during the show.

3. Onstage, the actors prepare with a physical and vocal warmup, led by voice coach Lyn Darnley (*standing*). Lying on the floor with the rest of the cast, Stewart is sounding his vowels as Darnley directs.

4. In the makeup and wig room, Fiona Matthews applies Antony's graying hairpiece with tiny dabs of spirit gum adhesive. Becoming bald at age nineteen, Stewart, at first embarrassed, soon discovered it could be a theatrical asset. "Most of my hair went within a year," he told the *London Independent*, "and I was very depressed. But it was possibly one of the best things that could have happened. And of course it means I've got a head that's the perfect block for wearing hairpieces. I'm a wigmaker's dream." For Antony, Stewart felt the wig a necessity, in particular to justify the line "the curled Antony."

left and right; and a raised area at the back with its own entrances. It is a very theatrical set, basically a stage format that hasn't changed much since the sixteenth century. And it is costume drama: no jeans or T-shirts, and, as with Elizabethan costumes, we have no pockets! No place to put our hands! And finally, the nature of the relationships of the principal cast very much conforms to what you might find in a Shakespearean history play. So there are many parallels!"

Stewart is also deeply involved in theatre education, currently serving as chancellor at the University of Huddersfield and as the Cameron Mackintosh Visiting Professor of Theatre at Oxford. And he is widely known to U.S. theatre students through his many visits to American campuses, first through the RSC's "theatre-go-round," which visited the University of California at Irvine in 1968, and for a dozen years thereafter as the joint founding director of the ACTER group of British performers (now called Actors from the London Stage) who have toured American colleges annually since 1976.

One of the remarkable aspects of Patrick Stewart's career is his easy crossover between English drama (by Shakespeare, Harold Pinter, and Tom Stoppard, among others) and American drama (by Arthur Miller, Edward Albee, and David Mamet). Born in the north of England, he had to lose his Yorkshire accent before acting even in classic English plays, so finding the proper dialect was always part of his actor's preparation. Even today, forty-plus

5. Wig on, Stewart applies the "pathetic little makeup that I use" to play Mark Antony. He uses no base makeup, only a few very simple lines accented with an eyebrow pencil. Forty-five minutes before curtain, Stewart makes his final preparation, with light exercise and meditation, all intended to lead him to the ideal state of readiness for his first entrance.

6. Stewart as Mark Antony and Harriet Walker as Cleopatra in the 2006–2007 production of Shakespeare's *Antony and Cleopatra*, produced by the Royal Shakespeare Company and directed by Gregory Doran at London's Novello Theatre. The costumes were designed by Kandis Cook.

years into his professional acting career, Stewart joins the cast in preperformance warmups that tone not only his voice but the particular diction of the play he is in.

For his first American plays, Stewart admits, "the biggest handicap was the accent. I was very aware of this in an early movie where I played an American and they wrote in a line about me saying, 'Oh, he was born in England.' Whenever you hear a line like that, you know it's about the accent!" Stewart attributes his now-polished American accent to vocal coach (and New York University faculty member) Deborah Hecht, "who completely transformed my experience and confidence in speaking American. That was for [Arthur Miller's] *Ride down Mount Morgan* on Broadway. We were aiming at sort of a cultivated, cultured, New York Jewish accent, and she brought me to a point where I felt so good with it that I felt physically like a different person. The accent changed the way I moved, the way I behaved; certainly the rhythms of speech changed. And she was very, very precise with me, very exact. I worked with her again on [Edward Albee's] *Who's Afraid of Virginia Woolf?* and I went to her again for a film role. Once I had 'slipped sideways' into feeling like an American, everything became much easier. Indeed, a year ago, when we started to rehearse *Antony and Cleopatra* (in England), I was perpetually teased by stage management for my American vowels!"

Stewart obviously loves acting. "It's the liberty of total freedom, where I can be not myself—yet also purely myself. It is a kind of possession, where something takes over and I become everything I would like to be, and find a liberty to 'play' while knowing at the same time that there will be no consequences. Nobody's going to say, 'Oh, stop being a child! Stop being so selfish, so self-obsessed! Pull yourself together!'"

"I thank God that I am an actor," Stewart concludes. "And that I spend my days in the company of people who behave with such dignity, honesty, and openness. That's what's truly meant by 'theatrical'—not something merely flashy, but doing what actors must do to help people understand what is really going on."

7. The actor plays a playwright: Patrick Stewart here performs the role of the aging William Shakespeare contemplating his future at a local pub after his retirement to Stratford-upon-Avon, in Edward Bond's *Bingo*, directed by Angus Jackson for London's Old Vic Theatre in 2012.

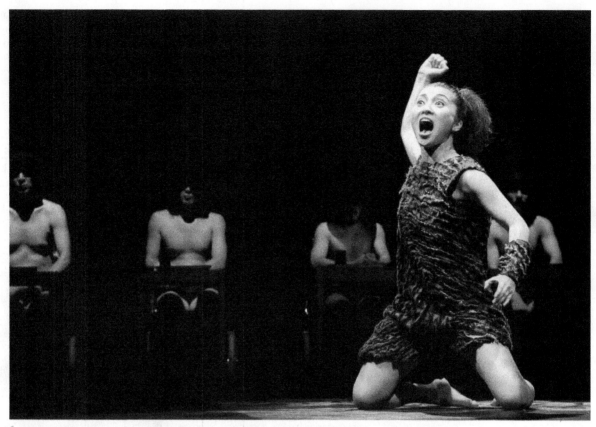

Tadashi Suzuki, the founder/director of the Suzuki Company of Toga (Japan), is widely admired around the world for his intense, nō- and kabuki-inspired productions of ancient Greek tragedies, which showcase the supreme vocal and physical control techniques he has developed among his actors. Suzuki's most noted trademark is seen in his actors' feet, which are most often stamping rather than walking, shuffling, or tiptoeing. This production of his *Electra* (adapted from the opera libretto by Hugo von Hofmannsthal) placed the barefoot and bare-chested male chorus in wheelchairs, however; it was seen on tour in Poland in 2009.

specialty movements, as with period dance and various forms of combat (hand-to-hand, fencing with a variety of weapons, gun battles) are also standard parts of actor training for today's theatre—and film.

All of these are components of an actor's physiological training, and the basic instructional technique for all of them is nearly identical to athletic training: demonstration, memorization, repetition, and constant drilling. This is where the actor learns that to be part of a "play" requires a tremendous amount of what can only be called "work."

The Psychological Instrument   The psychological gift of *imagination,* and the willingness and ability to use it in the service of art, is an even more important component of the actor's instrument. At the first level, an actress must use her imagination to make the

artifice of the theatre real enough to herself to convey a sense of reality to the audience: painted canvas flats—even in a Brechtian "distanced" production—must be imagined as brick walls, an offstage jangle must be imagined as a ringing onstage telephone, and a young actress must be imagined as a mother or grandmother.

At the second, far more important, level, the actor must imagine himself in an interpersonal situation created by the play: in love with Juliet, in awe of Zeus, in despair of his life. This imagination must be broad and all-encompassing: the successful actor is able to imagine himself performing and even relishing the often unspeakable acts of his characters, who may be murderers, despots, or monsters; insane or incestuous lovers; racial bigots, atheists, devils, perverts, or prudes. To the actor, nothing must be unimaginable; the actor's

Annette Bening plays the title role—a woman who murders her children—in Euripides' *Medea* in this 2009 production of the Greek tragedy staged by the distinguished Croatian director Lenka Udovicki for UCLA-Live in Los Angeles. Backed by a chorus largely composed of UCLA and California Institute of the Arts students and alumni, Bening draws upon extensive stage training and experience to blend her decidedly contemporary fire and intelligence with the play's ancient Greek text—and its horrific context. "Annette has something inside of her that is very noble and yet warm," says Udovicki about her chosen actor for the title role. "She has the inner and outer beauty. Things are not black and white, or shallow. There is a depth. She really defends her characters." Costumes were designed by Bjanka Adzic Ursulov; the setting, with its sand floor, was by Richard Hoover.

imagination must be a playground for expressive fantasy and darkly compelling motivations.

At the third, deepest, level, the actor's imagination must go beyond the mere accommodation of an accepted role pattern to become a creative force that makes characterization a high art, for each actor creates his or her role uniquely—each Romeo and Juliet is like none other before them, and each role can be uniquely fashioned with the aid of the actor's imaginative power. The final goal of creating a character is to make it fresh by filling it with the pulse of real blood and the animation of real, on-the-spot thinking and doing. The actor's imagination, liberated from stage fright and mechanical worries, is the crucial ingredient in allowing the actor to transcend the everyday and soar toward the genuinely unique and original.

The liberation of imagination is a continuing process in actor training. Exercises and theatre games designed for that purpose are part of most beginning classes in acting, and many directors use the same exercises and games at the beginning of play rehearsal periods. Because the human imagination tends to rigidify in the course of maturation—the child's imagination is usually much richer than that of the adult—veteran professional actors often profit from periodic mind-expanding or imagination-freeing exercises and games.

Discipline   The fourth and final aspect of an actor's instrument, and to a certain extent the one that rules them all, is simply discipline. As the late actress Maureen Stapleton once put it, "Actors are the only people, good or bad, hot or cold, who show up on time." This remains true today.

Artistic discipline keeps an actor within the established bounds and at the same time ensures artistic agility. The actor is not an independent artist, like a playwright or a composer or a sculptor. The actor works in an ensemble and is but one employee (paid or unpaid) in a large enterprise that can succeed only as a collaboration of many persons. Although actors are sometimes considered by the public to be egotistical or "divas" (temperamental), the truth is almost always the opposite: professional actors are among the most disciplined of artists, and the more professional they are, the more disciplined they are.

The actor, after all, leads a vigorous and demanding life. Makeup calls at 5:30 A.M. for film actors and both nightly and back-to-back weekend performances for stage actors make for exceedingly challenging schedules. Further, the physical and emotional demands of the acting process—the need for extreme concentration in rehearsal and performance, for physical health and psychological composure, the need to be both the instrument and the initiator of her or his performance, and the extraordinary demands of interacting with fellow performers at a profound level of mutual emotional and intellectual involvement—do not permit casual or capricious behavior among the members of a professional cast or company. So despite what you might read in the celebrity-gossip magazines, the discipline of professional actors is always at a very high level, and making calls (for rehearsals, costume fittings, photographs, makeup, auditions, and performances) at required times, learning lines, and memorizing stage movements well before stipulated deadlines are absolute requirements for anyone hoping to have a career in this field.

THE ACTOR'S ROUTINE

In essence, the actor's professional routine consists of three stages: audition, rehearsal, and performance. In the first, the actor gets a role; in the second, the actor learns the role; and in the third, the actor produces the role, either night after night in a theatre or in one or many "takes" in a film or video. Each of these stages imposes special demands on the actor's instrument and on his or her approach.

Audition

Auditioning is the primary process by which acting roles are awarded to all but the most established professionals. In an audition the actor has an opportunity to demonstrate to the director (and/or producer or casting director) how well he or she can fulfill an available role. To show this, the actor is usually asked to present either a memorized monologue or a reading from the play being produced. Every actor who is seriously planning for a career in the theatre will prepare several monologues to have ready when audition opportunities arise. For the most part these

will be one- or two-minute speeches from plays, although sometimes short narrative cuttings from novels, short stories, and poems are used. Each monologue must be carefully edited for timing and content (altering the text to make a continuous speech out of two or three shorter speeches is generally permissible), after which the piece is memorized and practiced. Any "staging" of the monologue should be flexible enough to adjust to the size of the audition space (which might be a stage but could just as well be an agent's office) and should not rely on costuming or the use of large props or furniture. Auditions sometimes specify two contrasting monologues (perhaps one in verse and one in prose, or one classical and one modern). These audition pieces are as essential as calling cards for actors seeking a place at regional repertory theatres or Shakespeare festivals, and should be carefully developed and rehearsed to be performed with assurance and poise.

Readings from a script present different opportunities since the actor will be reading aloud from the actual play that is going into production. Most often, the actor will be able to study the script in advance; in "cold reading" situations, however, the actor may be given the script just prior to the audition. Actors must train how to give excellent readings in both of these circumstances if they are to make progress toward a professional career.

The qualities a director looks for at an audition vary from one situation to another, but generally they include the actor's ease at handling the role; naturalness of delivery; physical, vocal, and emotional suitability for the part; and spontaneity, power, and charm. Most directors also look for an actor who is well-trained and disciplined and capable of mastering the technical demands of the part, who will complement the company ensemble, and who can convey that intangible presence that makes for "theatre magic." In short, the audition can show the director that the actor not only knows her or his craft but also will lend the production a special excitement.

Rehearsal

Plays are ordinarily rehearsed in a matter of weeks: a normal period of rehearsal ranges from ten weeks for complex or experimental productions to just one week for many summer stock operations. Much longer rehearsal periods, however, are not unheard of; indeed, the productions of Stanislavsky and Brecht were frequently rehearsed for a year or more. Three to five weeks, however, is the customary rehearsal period for American professional productions—but these are forty-hour weeks, and they usually are followed by several days (or weeks) of previews or out-of-town tryouts, with additional rehearsals between performances.

During the rehearsal period the actor learns the role and investigates, among other things, the character's biography; the subtext (the unspoken communications) of the play; the character's thoughts, fears, and fantasies; the character's goals; and the world envisioned by the play and the playwright. The director will lead discussions, offer opinions, and issue directives with respect to some or all of these matters; the director may also provide reading materials, pictures, and music to aid in the actor's research.

The actor must memorize lines, stage movements ("blocking"), and directed stage actions ("business"—scripted or seemingly unconscious physical behaviors) during the rehearsal period. He or she must also be prepared to rememorize these if they are changed, as they frequently are: in the rehearsal of new plays it is not unusual for entire acts to be rewritten between rehearsals and for large segments to be changed, added, or written out overnight.

Memorization usually presents no great problem for young actors, to whom it tends to come naturally (children in plays frequently memorize not only their own lines but everyone else's, without even meaning to); however, it seems to become more difficult as one gets older. But at whatever age, memorization of lines remains one of the actor's easier problems to solve, contrary to what many audience members think. Adequate memorization merely provides the basis from which the actor learns a part; the actor's goal is not simply to get the lines down but to do it *fast* so most of the rehearsal time can be devoted to other things.

The rehearsal period is a time for experimentation and discovery. It is a time for the actor to get close to the character's beliefs and intentions, to steep in the internal aspects of characterization that lead to fully engaged physical, intellectual, and emotional performance. It is a time to search the play's text and the director's mind for clues as to how the character behaves and what results the character aims for in the play's situation. And it is a time to experiment, both alone and in rehearsal with other actors, with the possibilities of subtle interactions that these investigations develop.

Externally, rehearsal is a time for the actor to experiment with timing and delivery of both lines and business—to integrate the staged movements (given by the director) with the text (given by the playwright) and to meld these into a fluid series of actions that build and illuminate by the admixture of the actor's own personally initiated behavior. It is a time to suggest movement and business possibilities to the director (assuming the director is the sort who accepts suggestions, as most do nowadays) and to work out details of complicated sequences with the other actors.

It is also a time to "get secure" in both lines and business by constant repetition—in fact, the French word for rehearsal is *répétition*. And it affords an opportunity to explore all the possibilities of the role—to look for ways to improve the actor's original plan for its realization and to test various possibilities with the director.

Thus the rehearsal of a play is an extremely creative time for an actor; it is by no means a routine or boring work assignment—and for this reason some actors enjoy the rehearsal process even more than the performance phase of production. At its best, a rehearsal is both spontaneous and disciplined, a combination of repetition and change, of trying and "setting," of making patterns and breaking them and then making them anew. It is an exciting time, no less so because it invariably includes many moments of distress, frustration, and despair; it is a time, above all, when the actor learns a great deal about acting and, ideally, about human interaction on many levels.

Performance

Performing, finally, is what the theatre is about, and it is before an audience in a live performance that the actor's mettle is put to the ultimate test. Sometimes the results are quite startling. The actor who has been brilliant in rehearsal can crumble before an audience and completely lose the "edge" of his or her performance in the face of stage fright and apprehension. Or—and this is more likely—an actor who seemed fairly unexciting in rehearsal can suddenly take fire in performance and dazzle the audience with unexpected energy, subtlety, and depth: one celebrated example of this phenomenon was achieved by Lee J. Cobb in the original production of Arthur Miller's *Death of a Salesman* in which Cobb had the title role. Roles rehearsed in all solemnity can suddenly turn comical in performance; conversely, roles developed for comic potential in rehearsal may be received soberly by an audience and lose their comedic aspect entirely.

Sudden and dramatic change, however, is not the norm as the performance phase replaces rehearsal. Most actors cross over from final dress rehearsal to opening night with only the slightest shift; indeed, this is generally thought to be the goal of a disciplined and professional rehearsal schedule. "Holding back until opening night," an acting practice occasionally employed over the past century, is universally disavowed today, and opening-night recklessness is viewed as a sure sign of the amateur, who relies primarily on guts and adrenaline to get through the evening. Deliberate revision of a role in performance, in response to the first waves of laughter or applause, is similarly frowned upon in all but the most inartistic of theatres today.

Nevertheless, a fundamental shift does occur in the actor's awareness between rehearsal and performance, and this cannot and should not be denied; indeed, it is essential to the creation of theatre art. The shift is set up by elemental feedback: the actor is inevitably aware, with at least a portion of her mind, of the audience's reactions to her own performance and that of the other players; in any acting performance, there is always a subtle adjustment to the audience that sees it. The outward, and usually unconscious, manifestations of this adjustment are usually all but imperceptible: the split-second hold for a laugh to die down, the slight special projection of a certain line to ensure it reaches the back row, the quick turn of a head to make a characterization or plot transition extra clear.

In addition, the best actors consistently radiate presence—that quality, so difficult to define, that makes both the character and the "self" of the actor especially vibrant and "in the present" for the audience. It is the quality of an actor who can take the stage and acknowledge, in some inexplicable yet indelible manner, that he or she is there *to be seen and heard.* Performance is not a one-way statement given from the stage to the house; it is a two-way, interparticipatory communication between the actors and the audience members in which the former employ text and movement and the latter employ applause, laughter, silence, and attention.

Even when the audience is silent and invisible—and, owing to the brightness of stage lights, the audience is frequently invisible to the actor—the performer feels its presence. There is nothing extrasensory about this: the absence of sound is itself a signal, for when several hundred people sit without shuffling, coughing, or muttering, their silence betokens a level of attention for which the actor customarily strives. Laughter, gasps, sighs, and applause similarly feed back into the actor's consciousness—and unconsciousness—and spur (or sometimes, alas, distract) his efforts. The veteran actor can determine quickly how to ride the crest of audience laughter and how to hold the next line just long enough that it will pierce the lingering chuckles but not be overridden by them; he also knows how to vary his pace or redouble his energy when he senses restlessness or boredom on the other side of the curtain line. The art of "reading an audience" is more instinctual than learned. It is not dissimilar to the technique achieved by the effective classroom lecturer or TV talk-show host or even by the accomplished conversationalist. The timing it requires is of such complexity that no actor could master it rationally; he or she can develop it only through experience—both on the stage and off.

Professional stage actors face a special problem unknown to their film counterparts and seldom experienced by amateurs in the theatre: the problem of maintaining a high level of spontaneity through many, many performances. Some professional play productions perform continuously for years, and actors may find themselves in the position—fortunately for their finances, awkwardly for their art—of performing the same part eight times a week, fifty-two weeks a year, with no end in sight. Of course the routine can vary with vacations and cast substitutions; and in fact very few actors ever play a role continuously for more than a year or two, but the problem becomes intense even after only a few weeks. How, as they say in the trade, does the actor "keep it fresh"?

Each actor has her or his own way of addressing this problem. Some rely on their total immersion in the role and contend that by "living the life of the character" they can keep themselves equally alert from first performance to last. Others turn to technical experiments—reworking their delivery and trying constantly to find better ways of saying their lines, expressing their characters, and achieving their objectives. Still others concentrate on the relationships within the play and try with every performance to "find something new" in each relationship as it unfolds onstage. Some actors, it must be admitted, resort to childish measures, rewriting dialogue as they go or trying to break the concentration of the other actors. This sort of behavior is abhorrent, but it is indicative of the seriousness of the actor's problems of combating boredom in a long-running production and the lengths to which some actors will go to solve them.

The actor's performance does not end with the play, for it certainly extends into the postplay moments of the curtain call—in which the actor-audience communion is direct and unmistakable—and it can even be said to extend to the dressing-room postmortem in which the actor reflects on what was done today and how it might be done better tomorrow. Sometimes the postmortem of a play is handled quite specifically by the director, who may give notes to the cast. More typically, in professional situations, the actor simply relies on self-criticism, often measured against comments from friends and fellow cast members, from the stage manager, and from reviews in the press. There is no performer who leaves the stage in the spirit of a factory worker leaving the plant. If there has been a shift up from the rehearsal phase to the performance phase, there is now a shift down (or a letdown) that follows the curtain call—a reentry into a world in which actions and reactions are likely to be a little calmer. There would be no stage fright if there were nothing to be frightened *about,* and the conquering of one's own anxiety—sometimes translating as conquering of the audience—fills the actor at the final curtain with a sense of awe, elation . . . and emptiness. It is perhaps this feeling that draws the actor ever more deeply into the profession, for it is a feeling known to the rankest amateur in a high school pageant as well as to the most experienced professional in a Broadway or West End run. It is the theatre's "high," and because it is a high that accompanies an inexpressible void, it leads to addiction.

THE ACTOR IN LIFE

Acting is an art. It can also be a disease. Professional actors are privileged people. They get to live the lives of some of the world's greatest and best-known characters: Romeo, Juliet, Phèdre, Cyrano, Saint Joan, and Willy Loman. They get to fight for honor, hunger for salvation, battle for justice, die for love, kill for passion. They get to die many times before their deaths, duel fabulous enemies, love magnificent lovers, and live through an infinite variety of human experiences that, though imaginary, are publicly engaged. They get to reenter the innocence of childhood without suffering its consequences and to participate in every sort of adult villainy without reckoning its responsibility. They get to fantasize freely and be seen doing so—and they get paid for it.

Millions of people want to be actors. It looks easy, and, at least for some people, it *is* easy. It looks exciting, and there can be no question that it is exciting, very exciting; in fact, amateurs act in theatres all over the world without any hope of getting paid merely to experience that excitement. Acting addicts, as a consequence, are common. People who will not wait ten minutes at a supermarket checkout stand will wait ten years to get a role in a Hollywood film or a Broadway play. The acting unions are the only unions in the world that have ever negotiated a *lower* wage for some of their members in order to allow them to perform at substandard salaries. To the true acting addict there is nothing else; acting becomes the sole preoccupation.

The addicted actor—the actor obsessed with acting for its own sake—is probably not a very good actor, however, for fine acting demands an open mind, a mind capable of taking in stimuli from all sorts of directions and not merely from the theatrical environment. An actor who knows nothing but acting has no range. First and foremost, actors must represent human beings, and to do that they must know something about humankind. Thus the proper study of acting is life, abetted but not supplanted by the craft of the trade. Common sense, acute powers of observation and perception, tolerance and understanding for all human beings, and a

Keira Knightley plays Célimène as a Hollywood starlet in this updated 2009 London production of Molière's *The Misanthrope*. The production was adapted by Martin Crimp and directed by Thea Sharrock, who had decided to "get a real film star playing the part of a film star." Happily, Knightley—whose father is a stage actor and whose mother is a playwright—proved a very accomplished stage actress as well.

sound general knowledge of one's own society and culture are prime requisites for the actor—as well as training, business acumen, and a realistic vision of one's own potential.

A lifetime professional career in acting is the goal of many but the accomplishment of very few. Statistically, one's chances of developing a long-standing acting career are quite small. Only those individuals possessed of great talent, skill, persistence, and personal fortitude stand any chance of succeeding—and even then it is only a chance. But the excitement of acting is not the exclusive preserve of those who attain lifetime professional careers; on the contrary, it may be argued that the happiest and most artistically fulfilled actors are those for whom performance is only an avocation. The excitement of acting, finally, is dependent not on monetary reward, a billing above the title, or the size of one's roles, but on the actor's deepest engagement with dramatic action and theatrical expression—which comprise the very heart of the theatre experience.

Chapter 4

The Playwright

AT HOME, AS I GAZE at my computer screen, I am the total master of my stage. Actions cascade through my head; whole characters pop into my imagination; great speeches, scenes, and visions flow directly from my brain to my fingers to the words leaping onto my screen. They are *my* ideas, *my* people, *my* language, and *my* play that will soon be resounding through theatre walls around the world; it will be *me* up there receiving the critics' raves, press interviews, and speaking invitations as a result of my play's success; it will be *me* mounting the stage to accept my 'best play' award, perhaps even sitting one day in Stockholm, next to my fellow Nobel Prize winners—this year's Einstein and Marie Curie who, like me, have also rocked the modern world.

"But that's only at home. In the theatre, I am the loneliest of figures. I huddle inconspicuously in the back row, taking notes in the dark. I am unnoticed by the actors and, indeed, rarely allowed to speak directly to them. The designers look at me with condescension and suspicion. At the end of the rehearsal, when I politely offer to share my notes with the director, she glares at me. And when she finally listens, it's with a noncommittal face and a dismissive agreement that, yes, she'll 'think about all of this tomorrow.' ▶

"I am totally convinced that the theatre is nothing more than an instrument for massacring my manuscript!"

This monologue is imaginary—and perhaps a bit extreme. Playwrights, by their creative natures, generally have vivid imaginations, which can and often do lead to both mania and paranoia. But this inner monologue expresses the great fear of every playwright, reflecting the paradox of theatrical creation: the playwright is both the most central and the most peripheral figure in the theatrical event.

The playwright is central in the most obvious ways. She or he provides the point of origin for nearly every play production: the script, which is the rallying point around which the director or producer gathers the troops. Yet that point of origin is also a point of departure. The days when a Shakespeare or a Molière would read his text to actors, and then coach them in its proper execution, are long gone. What we have today is a more specialized theatrical hierarchy in which the director is interposed as the playwright's representative to the actors and designers. More and more, the playwright's function is to write the play and then disappear, for once the script has been printed, duplicated, and distributed, the playwright's physical participation is relegated mainly to serving as the director's sounding board and script reviser. Indeed, the playwright's mere physical presence in the rehearsal hall can become an embarrassment, more tolerated than welcomed—and sometimes not even tolerated.

Fundamentally, today's playwright is considered an independent artist whose work, like that of the novelist or poet, is executed primarily if not exclusively in isolation. There are exceptions, of course. Some playwrights work from actors' improvisations, and others participate quite fully in rehearsals, even to the point of serving as the initial director of their plays (as Edward Albee, Sam Shepard, and Neil LaBute often do) or, more extraordinarily, by acting in them (as Athol Fugard and August Wilson have done).

But the exceptions, in this case, do not disprove the rule; since the age of romanticism, the image of the playwright has turned increasingly from that of theatre coworker and mentor to that of isolated observer and social critic. In the long run, this change should occasion no lamentation, for if theatre production now demands collaboration and compromise, the art of the theatre still requires individuality, clarity of vision, sharpness of approach, and devotion to personal truth, if it is to challenge the artists who are called upon to fulfill it and the audiences who will pay money to experience it.

Therefore, the *independence* of the playwright is generally her or his most important characteristic. Playwrights must seek from life, from their own lives—and not from the theatrical establishment—the material that will translate into exciting and meaningful and entertaining theatre, and their views must be intensely personal, grounded in their own perceptions and philosophy, in order to ring true. We look to the theatre for a measure of leadership, for personal enlightenment derived from another's experience, for fresh perspectives, new vision. Simple mastery of certain conventional techniques will not suffice to enable a playwright to expand our lives.

WE ARE ALL PLAYWRIGHTS

Playwriting is not just something we learn. It's something we already do. All of us. Every day—or night.

Every night, dreams come to us in our sleep. Or, rather, they *seem* to come to us: in fact, we create them, for each of us has our own "playwright-in-residence" somewhere in the back of our minds, churning out a nightly mixture of vivid, believable, and sometimes terrifying fantasies that create half-real, half-imagined characters, idealized settings, surprising plot complications, nostalgic visions, and often nightmarish climaxes and reversals. The situations and characters of our dreams are our own creations, drawn from our careful observations, colored by our unconscious phobias and fancies, and stylized into associations of words, scenes, and "stagings" that ring with the deep resonance of our innermost plans, fears, and secrets.

Of course there's more to playwriting than dreaming up characters and a story. As dreamers, we are only beginning playwrights. What happens next is the subject of this chapter.

LITERARY AND NONLITERARY ASPECTS OF PLAYWRITING

Because drama is a foundational form of literature (and is taught in departments of literature) and because many dramatic authors begin (or double) as poets or novelists, it may seem as if playwriting is primarily a literary activity. It is not. Understanding the word's origin helps here: *playwright* is not *playwrite*. Writing for the theatre entails considerations not common to other literary forms. Although by coincidence the words *write* and *wright* sound identical, a "playwright" is a person who *makes* plays, just as a

Sometimes the edgiest plays of today arise from the most traditional dramatic forms of the past, as with Sarah Ruhl's *Passion Play*, which received its New York premiere (by the Epic Theatre Ensemble) in a Brooklyn church in 2010. The play depicts a group of actors presenting the medieval Passion Play (the trial and crucifixion of Christ) in three different historical eras—its own (sixteenth-century England), in Oberammergau (Germany) during the time of Hitler's rise, and in late twentieth-century America. Ruhl's play has a relatively long history of its own: she began writing it when still in graduate school, eight years before this production. Mark Wing-Davey directed.

wheelwright is a person who makes wheels. This distinction is particularly important because some plays, or portions of plays, are never written at all. Improvisational plays, rituals, scenes of comic business, and documentary dramas may be created largely or entirely in performance or are learned simply through oral improvisation and repetition. Some are created with a tape recorder and the collaboration of multiple imaginations and may or may not be committed to writing after the performance is concluded. And others, though dramatic in structure, are entirely nonverbal—that is, they include no dialogue, no words, and very little that is written other than an outline of physical actions.

So while drama is one of the literary arts, it is much more than an arrangement of words. It is rather a structured assemblage of vocal and physical interactions, a compilation of the many elements of the theatrical medium: movement, speech, scenery, costume, staging, music, spectacle, and silence. It is a literature whose impact depends on a collective endeavor and whose appreciation must be, in large part, spontaneous and immediate.

A play attains its finished form only in performance upon the stage: the written script is not the final play but the *blueprint* for the play, the written foundation for the production that is the play's complete realization. Some of a play's most effective writing may look very clumsy as it appears in print. Take, for example, the following lines from Shakespeare:

Oh! Oh! Oh!   —*Othello*

Howl, howl, howl, howl!   —*King Lear*

No, no, the drink, the drink. O my dear Hamlet,
The drink, the drink! I am poisoned.   —*Hamlet*

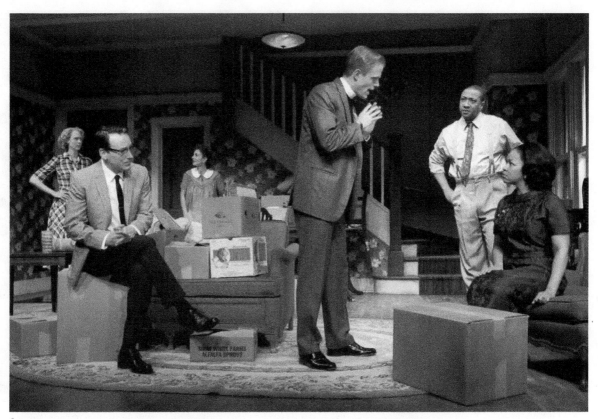

Bruce Norris was awarded the 2012 Tony Award and the 2011 Pulitzer Prize for his *Clybourne Park,* which picks up the story of Lorraine Hansberry's classic 1950's *A Raisin in the Sun* exactly where it left off (see the chapter entitled "Global Theatre Today")—on a day in 1959 in which an African American family is about to move into a home in an all-white Chicago suburban community. Norris's sadly funny sequel begins with the white family moving out of that same suburban home that day, and discussing the situation with their deeply upset neighbors and their black housekeeper and her husband. The Playwrights Horizons premiere production, directed by Pam McKinnon, transferred to Los Angeles's Mark Taper Forum in 2011, where this photo was taken, and reopened on Broadway with the same cast in 2012.

These apparently unsophisticated lines of dialogue in fact provide great dramatic climaxes in an impassioned performance; they are *pretexts for great acting,* the creation of which is far more crucial than literary eloquence to the art of playwriting.

Of course some formal literary values are as important to the theatre as they are to other branches of literature: allusional complexity, descriptive precision, poetic imagery, metaphoric implication, and a careful crafting of verbal rhythms, cadences, and textures all contribute powerfully to dramatic effect. But they are effective only insofar as they are fully integrated within the whole of the theatrical medium—as they stimulate action and behavior through stage space and stage time in a way that commands audience attention and involvement. Mere literary brilliance is insufficient as theatre, as a

great many successful novelists and poets have learned to their chagrin when they attempted to write plays.

PLAYWRITING AS EVENT WRITING

The core of every play is action. Unlike other literary forms, the inner structure of a play is never a series of abstract observations or a collage of descriptions and moralizings; it is an ordering of observable, dramatizable *events.* These events are the basic building blocks of the play, regardless of its style or genre or theme.

Fundamentally, the playwright works with two tools, both representing the externals of human behavior: dialogue and physical action. The inner story and

Pulitzer Prize–winning playwright Suzan-Lori Parks is one of America's most provocative young dramatists, as seen in her *Fucking A,* which, from its title onward, provides in-your-face drama. Paralleling Nathaniel Hawthorne's *The Scarlet Letter* but set in an impoverished, dictator-ruled country, the play treats a young man who has been incarcerated since childhood (played by Mos Def) and his mother (S. Epatha Merkerson), who, having provided abortions to earn money for her son's release, has been branded with a "Fucking A" on her skin. The 2003 New York Public Theatre production was directed by Michael Greif.

Prometheus is chained to his rock. Some are subdued, as when the military regiment in Chekhov's *The Three Sisters* leaves town at the play's end. Some are quite ordinary, as in the domestic sequences depicted in most modern realist plays. But they are always aimed at creating a memorable impression. To begin playwriting, one must first conceptualize events and envision them enacted in such a way as to hold the attention of an audience.

The events of a play can be connected to each other in a strict chronological, cause-effect continuity. This has been a goal of the realistic theatre, in which dramatic events are arranged to convey a lifelike progression of experiences in time. Such plays are said to be *continuous* in structure and *linear* in chronology, and they can be analyzed like sociological events: the audience simply watches them unfold as it might watch a family quarrel in progress in an apartment across the way.

Continuity, however, is by no means a requirement for play construction. Many plays are discontinuous or nonlinear. The surviving plays of ancient Greece are highly discontinuous: choral odes alternate with character-driven episodes in the tragedies, and choral interjections and a direct speech to the audience (*parabasis*) interrupt the action of Old Comedies. Shakespeare's plays are structured in a highly complex arrangement of time shifts, place shifts, style shifts, songs, and subplots ingeniously integrated around a basic theme or investigation of character. And many contemporary plays break with chronological linearity altogether, flashing instantly backward and forward through time to incorporate character memories, character fantasies, direct expressions of the playwright's social manifesto, historical exposition, comic relief, or any other ingredient the playwright can successfully coordinate.

Linear, point-to-point storytelling has not disappeared from the theatre—indeed, it remains the basic architecture of most popular and serious plays. But modern (and postmodern) audiences have proven increasingly receptive to less-conventional structures: the exuberance of the music hall, for instance, inspires the structuring of Joan Littlewood's *Oh, What a Lovely War!;* the minstrel show serves as the basis of David Thompson's book for *The Scottsboro Boys;* and the didacticism of the lecture hall underlies most of the plays by Bertolt Brecht. Nonlinear, discontinuous, and even stream-of-consciousness structures can provide powerful and sustained dramatic impact, provided they still fundamentally portray a dramatization of events that the audience can put together in some sort of meaningful and satisfying fashion.

theme of a play—the psychology of the characters, the viewpoint of the author, the impact of the social environment—must be inferred by the audience from outward appearances, from the play's events as the audience sees them. Whatever the playwright's intended message and whatever the playwright's perspective on the function and process of playwriting itself, the play cannot be put together until the playwright has conceived of an event—and then a series of related events—designed to be enacted on a stage. It is this series of related events that constitutes the play's scenario or, more formally, its *plot.*

The events of drama are, by their nature, compelling. Some are bold and unusual, such as the scene in which

No drama could have a more serious topic than *The Scottsboro Boys*, which (see the chapter titled "Global Theatre Today") treats the true story of nine black teenage boys jailed for a crime they never committed (in fact no crime was committed at all) during the period of racial segregation in the American South. But David Thompson's script for the production, as directed and choreographed by Susan Stroman, transforms the story into a black minstrel show being performed for white audiences, making the irony of the horrific real-life events an agonizing clash of social evil and musical entertainment at the same time. Colman Domingo and Forrest McClendon play the "minstrel" performers, with the jailed prisoners behind them.

THE QUALITIES OF A FINE PLAY

As with any art form, the qualities that make up a good play can be discussed individually. But only in their combination, only in their interaction—only in ways that cannot be dissected or measured—do these qualities have meaning.

Credibility and Intrigue

To say that a play must be credible is not at all to say that it has to be lifelike, for fantasy, ritual, and absurdity have all proven to be enduringly popular theatrical modes. *Credibility* is the audience-imposed demand that requires a play's actions to appear to flow logically from its characters, its situation, and the theatrical context

the playwright provides. In a credible play, what happens in act 2 appears to be a reasonable outgrowth of what happened in act 1.

Credibility requires that the characters in a play appear to act out of their own individual interests, instincts, and intentions rather than serving as mere pawns for the development of theatrical plot or effect, or as empty disseminators of propaganda. Credibility requires that characters maintain consistency within themselves: their thoughts, feelings, hopes, fears, and plans must appear to flow from human needs rather than purely theatrical ones. Credibility also requires that human characters appear to act and think like human beings (even in humanly impossible situations) and not purely as thematic automatons. Credibility, in essence, is a contract between author and audience,

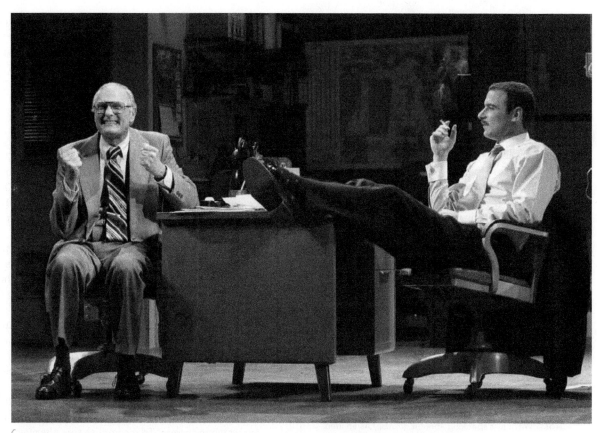

David Mamet won the Pulitzer Prize for his fiery *Glengarry Glen Ross,* portraying the cut-throat competition among employees in a Chicago real estate office. Alan Alda (left) and Liev Schreiber are having it out in this 2005 Broadway revival of the play, directed by Joe Mantello.

whereby the audience agrees to view the characters as "people" as long as the author agrees not to shatter that belief in order to accomplish other purposes.

Thus James Barrie's famous play *Peter Pan,* though undeniably fantastical, creates a cast of characters wholly appropriate to their highly imaginary situation and internally consistent in their actions within the context of their developing experience. All of their aspirations (including those of the dog!) are human ones, and their urgencies are so believable that when Tinkerbell steps out of the play's context to ask the audience to demonstrate its belief in fairies, we are willing to applaud our approval. At that moment, the world of the play becomes more credible, more "real," than that of the audience.

Intrigue is the quality of a play that makes us curious (sometimes fervently so) to see "what happens next." Sheer plot intrigue—which is sometimes called "suspense" because it leaves us suspended (that is,

"hanging")—is one of the most powerful dramatic approaches. Whole plays can be based on little more than artfully contrived plotting designed to keep the audience in a continual state of anticipation and wonder. Plot, however, is only one of the elements of a play that can support intrigue. Most plays that aspire to deeper insights than whodunits or farces develop intrigue in character as well and even in theme. Most of the great plays demand that we ask not so much "What will happen?" as "What does this mean?" Most great plays, in other words, make us care about the characters and invite us to probe the mysteries of the human condition.

Look, for example, at this dialogue from David Mamet's *Glengarry Glen Ross,* in which a disgruntled real-estate salesman proposes to a colleague that they rob their front office, stealing some real-estate "leads" (names of potential customers) they can then sell to a competitor.

MOSS: I want to tell you something.

AARONOW: What?

MOSS: I want to tell you what somebody should do.

AARONOW: What?

MOSS: Someone should stand up and strike back.

AARONOW: What do you mean?

MOSS: *Somebody* . . .

AARONOW: Yes . . . ?

MOSS: Should do something to *them*.

AARONOW: What?

MOSS: Something. To pay them back. (*Pause*) Someone, someone should hurt them. Murray and Mitch.

AARONOW: Somebody should hurt them.

MOSS: Yes.

AARONOW: (*Pause*) How?

MOSS: How? Do something to hurt them. Where they live.

AARONOW: What? (*Pause*)

MOSS: Someone should rob the office.

AARONOW: Huh.

MOSS: That's what I'm *saying*. We were, if we were that kind of guys, to knock it off, and *trash* the joint, it looks like a robbery, and *take* the fuckin' leads out of the files . . . [. . .] (*Pause*)

AARONOW: Are you actually *talking* about this or are we just . . .

MOSS: No, we're just . . .

AARONOW: We're just *"talking"* about it.

MOSS: We're just *speaking* about it. (*Pause*) As an *idea*.

AARONOW: As an idea.

MOSS: Yes.

AARONOW: We're not actually *talking* about it.

MOSS: No.

AARONOW: Talking about it as a . . .

MOSS: No.

AARONOW: As a *robbery*.

MOSS: As a "robbery"?! No.

AARONOW: *Well*. Well . . .

The basic action of this scene could be expressed in just two or three lines of dialogue; but since a conspiracy is being proposed, each character must proceed with extreme caution—as his colleague could turn him in at any time. Since each of the thirty-two short lines, and each of the five indicated pauses, takes the conspiracy one tiny—but precise—step forward, the credibility is exacting while the intrigue builds to an increasingly higher level of tension.

Intrigue draws us into the world of a play; credibility keeps us there. In the best plays the two are sustained in a fine tension of opposites: intrigue demanding surprise, credibility demanding consistency. Combined,

they generate a kind of "believable wonder," which is the fundamental state of drama. Credibility alone will not suffice to make a play interesting, and no level of intrigue can make a noncredible play palatable. The integration of the two must be created by the playwright in order to establish that shared ground that transcends our expectations but not our credulity.

Speakability, Stageability, and Flow

The dialogue of drama is written upon the page, but it must be spoken by actors and staged by directors. Thus the goal of the dramatist is to fabricate actable, stageable dialogue that flows in a progression leading to theatrical impact.

One of the most common faults of beginning playwrights is that their lines lack *speakability*. This is not to say that dramatic dialogue must resemble ordinary speech. No one imagines people in life speaking like characters out of the works of Aeschylus, Shakespeare, or Shaw, or even modern writers like Tom Stoppard or Edward Albee. Brilliantly styled language is a feature of most of the great plays in theatre history, and lifelikeness, by itself, is not a dramatic virtue—nor is its absence a dramatic fault.

Rather, speakability means that a line of dialogue should be so written that it achieves its maximum impact when spoken. To accomplish this, the playwright must be closely attuned to the *audial shape* of dialogue: the rhythm of sound that creates emphasis, meaning, focus, and power. Verbal lullabies and climaxes, fast punch lines, sonorous lamentations, sparkling epigrams, devastating expletives, significant pauses, and electrifying whispers—these are some of the devices of dialogue that impart audial shape to great plays written by master dramatists. Look, for example, at Andrew Undershaft's chiding of his pretentious son, Stephen, in George Bernard Shaw's *Major Barbara*, where Stephen has just said that he knows "the difference between right and wrong."

UNDERSHAFT: You don't say so! What! no capacity for business, no knowledge of law, no sympathy with art, no pretension to philosophy; only a simple knowledge of the secret that has puzzled all the philosophers, baffled all the lawyers, muddled all the men of business, and ruined most of the artists: the secret of right and wrong. Why, man, you're a genius, a master of masters, a god! At twenty-four, too!

No one would call this "everyday speech" as in the David Mamet dialogue quoted earlier. But it is immensely speakable and its cascading sarcasm develops a fiercely intimidating momentum, leaving Stephen

☾Spotlight

Two English Playwrights

The two leading English playwrights of the past fifty years exhibit radically different styles. The plays of Harold Pinter, which are filled with abrupt, almost inexplicable transitions, intense pauses and glances, and elliptical dialogue, create an almost palpable sense of foreboding and spookiness that plunges the audience deeper and deeper into inexplicable moods and reveries. The plays of Tom Stoppard, in contrast, race glibly through brilliant rhetorical flights of language that always manage to stay one step ahead of the audience's capability to follow, keeping the audience breathless while forcing them to remain intellectually alert.

BATES: (*moves to* ELLEN) Will we meet tonight?

ELLEN: I don't know. (*Pause*)

BATES: Come with me tonight.

ELLEN: Where?

BATES: Anywhere. For a walk. (*Pause*)

ELLEN: I don't want to walk.

BATES: Why not? (*Pause*)

ELLEN: I want to go somewhere else. (*Pause*)

BATES: Where?

ELLEN: I don't know. (*Pause*)

BATES: What's wrong with a walk?

ELLEN: I don't want to walk. (*Pause*)

BATES: What do you want to do?

ELLEN: I don't know. (*Pause*)

BATES: Do you want to go somewhere else?

ELLEN: Yes.

BATES: Where?

ELLEN: I don't know. (*Pause*)

—FROM PINTER'S *SILENCE* (1969)

COCKLEBURY-SMYTHE: May I be the first to welcome you to Room 3B. You will find the working conditions primitive, the hours antisocial, the amenities nonexistent and the catering beneath contempt. On top of that the people are for the most part very boring, with interests either so generalized as to mimic wholesale ignorance or so particular as to be lunatic obsessions. Their level of conversation would pass without comment in the lavatory of a mixed comprehensive and the lavatories, by the way, are few and far between.

—FROM STOPPARD'S *DIRTY LINEN* (1976)

speechless and, with a great actor delivering it, the audience breathless.

Speakability also requires that the spoken line appear to realistically emanate from the character who utters it and that it contain—in its syntax, vocabulary, and mode of expression—the marks of that character's milieu and his or her personality. The spoken line is not merely an expression of the author's perspective; it is the basis from which the actor develops characterization and the acting ensemble creates a play's style. Thus the mastery of dramatic dialogue writing demands more than mere semantic skills—it requires a constant awareness of the purposes and tactics underlying human communication, as well as of the multiple psychological and aesthetic properties of language.

Stageability, of course, requires that dialogue be written so it can be spoken effectively upon a stage, but it requires something more: dialogue must be conceived as an integral element of a particular staged situation in which setting, physical acting, and spoken dialogue are inextricably combined. A stageable script is one in which staging and stage business—as well as design and the acting demands—are neither adornments for

the dialogue nor sugar-coating for the writer's opinions but are intrinsic to the very nature of the play.

Both speakability and stageability are contingent upon human limitations—those of the actors and directors as well as those of the audience. Speakability must take into account that the actor must breathe from time to time, for example, and that the audience can take in only so many metaphors in a single spoken sentence. Stageability must reckon with the forces of gravity and inertia, which both the poet and the novelist may conveniently ignore. The playwright need not simply succumb to the common denominator—all the great playwrights strive to extend the capacities of actors and audience alike—but still must not forget that the theatre is fundamentally a human event that cannot transcend human capabilities.

A speakable and stageable script flows rather than stumbles; this is true for nonlinear plays as well as for more straightforwardly structured ones. *Flow* requires a continual stream of information, and a play that flows is one that is continually saying something, doing something, and meaning something to the audience. To serve this end, the playwright should address such technical problems as scene-shifting, entrances and exits, and act breaks (intermissions) as early as possible in the scriptwriting process. Furthermore, in drafting scenes, the writer should be aware that needless waits, arid expositions (no matter how "necessary" to the plot), and incomprehensible plot developments can sink the sturdiest script in a sea of audience apathy.

Richness

Depth, subtlety, fineness, quality, wholeness, and *inevitability*—these words are often used in reference to plays we like. They are fundamentally subjective terms, easier to apply than to define or defend, for the fact is that when a play pleases us—when it "works"—the feelings of pleasure and stimulation it affords are beyond the verbal level. Certainly *richness* is one of the qualities common to plays that leave us with this sense of satisfaction—richness of *detail* and richness of *dimension.*

A play that is rich with detail is not necessarily one that is rife with detail; it is simply one whose every detail fortifies our insight into the world of the play. For going to a play is in part a matter of paying a visit to the playwright's world, and the more vividly created that world, the greater the play's final impact. In Margaret Edson's *Wit,* for example, Vivian, a terminally ill English professor, addresses the audience from her hospital bed. Her tone is professorial, and her vocabulary is filled with medical terminology, little of which the average audience member will understand, but in the context of an intellectual woman

Language is everything for Edward Albee, whose awards include three Pulitzer Prizes and three Tonys (one for Lifetime Achievement). Albee's language ranges from the brilliant wit of a Tom Stoppard to the hidden menace of a Harold Pinter. There are only two characters in his 1959 one-act *The Zoo Story,* his first produced work, but they became so vivid in theatergoers' memories that Albee brought them back in a new play, initially called *Peter and Jerry* and now *At Home in the Zoo,* which acted as a prequel to the original. Shown here in its 2004 world premiere production, this most recent of his plays, directed at the Hartford Stage by Pam MacKinnon, featured Frank Wood (seated) as Peter and Frederick Weller as Jerry, as they meet and talk in Central Park—with (eventually) tragic results.

struggling against a fatal disease, Edson's dialogue creates an immensely compelling and affectingly detailed portrait:

VIVIAN: I don't mean to complain, but I am becoming very sick. Very, very sick. Ultimately sick, as it were.

In everything I have done, I have been steadfast, resolute—some would say in the extreme. Now, as you can see, I am distinguishing myself in illness.

I have survived eight treatments of Hexamethophosphacil and Vinplatin at the *full* dose, ladies and gentlemen. I have broken the record. I have become something of a celebrity. Kelekian and Jason [*her doctors*] are simply delighted. I think they foresee celebrity status for themselves upon the appearance of the journal article they will no doubt write about me.

But I flatter myself. The article will not be about *me*, it will be about my ovaries. It will be about my peritoneal cavity, which, despite their best intentions, is now crawling with cancer. What we have come to think of as *me* is, in fact, just the specimen jar, just the dust jacket, just the white piece of paper that bears the little black marks.

Vivian's free use of seven-syllable words, her refining of words on the spot (from "very sick" to "very, very sick" to "ultimately sick"; from "steadfast" to "resolute"), her public style of presentation ("ladies and gentlemen"), her parallel phrases ("I have . . . I have . . . I have . . . ," "just the . . . just the . . . just the . . . "), her alliteration of consonants ("just . . . jar . . . just . . . jacket, just"), and her use of antithesis ("white piece of paper . . . little

Margaret Edson's *Wit*—about an English professor dying of cancer—began as a script "tossed over the transom" at South Coast Repertory in California by the yet-unknown playwright; it was soon premiered by that company and not long after was awarded the 1999 Pulitzer Prize. This 2012 Broadway revival featured Cynthia Nixon as Dr. Vivian Bearing; Michael Countryman plays one of her doctors. It was directed by Lynn Meadow for the Manhattan Theatre Club.

black marks") tell us volumes about her character and how she is "distinguishing" herself in illness. Richness of linguistic detail lends a play authority, an aura of sureness. It surrounds the play's characters as a city surrounds homes and gives them a cultural context in which to exist. It also lends specificity: specific people are engaged in specific tasks in a specific place. Going to (or even reading) a play rich with texture is like taking a trip to another world—and it is an adventure no travel agent could possibly book.

Richness is not an easy quality to develop in writing. It demands of its author a gift for close observation, an uninhibited imagination, a consummate vocabulary, and an astute sense of what to leave out as well as what to include. A person who can recollect personal experiences in great detail, who can conjure up convincing situations, peoples, locales, and conversations, and who is closely attuned to nuance can work these talents into the writing of plays.

Depth of Characterization

Depth of characterization presents perhaps the greatest single stumbling block for novice playwrights, who tend either to write all characters "in the same voice" (normally the author's own) or to divide them into two camps: good characters and bad. Capturing the depth, complexities, and uniqueness of real human beings, even seemingly ordinary human beings, is a difficult task.

Depth of characterization requires that every character possess an independence of intention, expression, and motivation. Moreover, these characteristics must appear sensible in the light of our general knowledge of psychology and human behavior. In plays as in life, all characters must act from motives that appear reasonable to *them* (if not to those watching them or to those affected by them). The writer should bear in mind that every character is, *to himself or herself,* an important and worthwhile person, regardless of what other people think. Thus even the great villains of drama—Shakespeare's Richard III, Claudius, and Iago, for example—must be seen to believe in themselves and in the fundamental "rightness" of their causes. Even if we never completely understand their deepest motivations (as we can't fully understand the motives of real villains such as Hitler, Caligula, or John Wilkes Booth), we should be able to sense at the bottom of any character's behavior a validity of purpose, however twisted or perverse we may find it.

The realistic theatre—Chekhov, Williams, Miller, and the like—has provided many works in which the psychological dimensions of the characters dominate all other aspects of the theatrical experience. Look, for example, at this speech of Big Mama in Tennessee Williams's *Cat on a Hot Tin Roof:*

BIG MAMA: [*outraged that her son-in-law, Gooper, is offering her a written trusteeship plan which would give him and his wife control over the estate of Big Daddy, Mama's ailing husband*] Now you listen to me, all of you, you listen here! They's not goin' to be any more catty talk in my house! And Gooper, you put that away before I grab it out of your hand and tear it right up! I don't know what the hell's in it, and I don't want to know what the hell's in it. I'm talkin' in Big Daddy's language now; I'm his *wife,* not his *widow,* I'm still his *wife!* And I'm talkin' to you in his language an'—

Williams has brilliantly crafted Big Mama's rage with aggressive verbs ("grab," "tear"), local vernacular ("they's"), clause repetitions ("I'm his wife . . . I'm still his wife"), loaded adjectives ("catty"), profanities rare for a southern woman ("hell"), dialectical contractions ("goin'", "talkin'"), and individual word emphases as marked by italics. But he has also undermined her rage by having her admit to assuming her husband's vocabulary—so that while she states that she's not Big Daddy's widow, her language indicates she knows, even if only unconsciously, that it will soon be otherwise.

Modern dramatists have even made psychotherapy part of their dramatic scheme in many cases. Psychiatrist characters appear (or are addressed) in plays such as Williams's *Suddenly, Last Summer,* Miller's *After the Fall,* Peter Shaffer's *Equus,* and the 1941 American musical *Lady in the Dark,* each of which portrays a principal character undergoing psychotherapy and discussing what he or she learns. Certainly the psychological sophistication of modern theatre audiences has afforded playwrights expanded opportunities to explore and dramatize characters' psyches, and has helped to make the "case study" drama a major genre of the current theatre.

Gravity and Pertinence

Gravity and *pertinence* are terms used to describe the importance of a play's theme and its overall relevance to the concerns of the intended audience. To say a play has gravity is to say simply that its central theme is one of serious and lasting significance in humanity's spiritual, moral, or intellectual life. The greatest dramas—comedies as well as tragedies—are always concerned with what is called the human predicament: those universal problems—aging, discord, regret, insecurity, rejection, loss—for which we continually seek greater lucidity. Gravity does not mean somberness, however; it requires only a confrontation with the most elemental tasks of living. When an audience truly understands and identifies with a play's experiences, even the darkest tragedy radiates power and illumination.

Look, for example, at Bynum's speech in August Wilson's *Joe Turner's Come and Gone.* Bynum is what Wilson calls a rootworker (conjuror). A younger man, Jeremy, has just praised a woman as knowing "how to treat a fellow," and Bynum chastises him for his shallowness:

> You just can't look at it like that. You got to look at the whole thing. Now, you take a fellow go out there, grab hold to a woman and think he got something 'cause she sweet and soft to the touch. It's in the world like everything else. Touching's nice. It feels good. But you can lay your hand upside a horse or a cat, and that feels good too. What's the difference? When you grab hold to a woman, you got something there. You got a whole world there. You got a way of life kicking up under your hand. That woman can take and make you feel like something. I ain't just talking about in the way of jumping off into bed together and rolling around with each other. Anybody can do that. When you grab hold to that woman and look at the whole thing and see what you got... why she can take and make something of you. Your mother was a woman. That's enough right there to show you what a woman is. Enough to show you what she can do. She made something out of you.

Using only simple words (see, for a direct contrast, Vivian's speech in *Wit*), Wilson's Bynum probes at the heart of a profound subject: the most meaningful relationship between a man and a woman. When these lines are well acted, their impact stays with us long after we leave the theatre.

Pertinence refers to the play's touching on current audience concerns, both of-the-moment and timeless. Plays about current political situations or personalities are clearly pertinent; they may, however, quickly become outdated. Plays whose concerns are both ephemeral and universal, however, such as Miller's *The Crucible*—which, in treating the Salem witch trials of 1692, pertains as well to the McCarthy trials of the 1950s and to corrupt investigations in all eras—will have a more enduring relevance. The greatest plays are not merely pertinent to a given moment but also serve as archetypes for all time.

Roger Robinson plays the spellbinding healer Bynum Walker, a freed slave with mysterious insights, and Marsha Stephanie Blake is Mattie, a lost young woman seeking love but not knowing where to find it, in this 2009 Broadway revival of August Wilson's *Joe Turner's Come and Gone,* directed by Bartlett Sher. Costumes are by Catherine Zuber.

Compression, Economy, and Intensity

Compression, economy, and intensity are also aspects of the finest plays. *Compression* refers to the playwright's skill in condensing a story (which may span many days, even years, of chronological time) into a theatrical time frame. *Economy* relates to an author's skill in eliminating or consolidating characters, events, locales, and words in the service of compression. Unlike other literary or visual art forms that can be examined in private and at the leisure of the observer, a play must be structured to unfold in a public setting and at a predetermined pace.

Many beginning playwrights attempt to convert a story to a play in the most obvious way: by writing a separate scene for every event described in the story (and sometimes including a different setting and supporting cast for each scene). Economy and compression, however, require that most stories be restructured in order to be dramatically viable. If the play is to be basically realistic, the playwright has traditionally reworked the story to have all the events occur in one location, or perhaps in two locations with an act break between to allow for scenery changes. Events that are integral to the story but cannot be shown within the devised settings can simply be reported (as in Shaw's *Misalliance,* for example, in which an airplane crash occurs offstage as the onstage characters gawk and exclaim). More common today is the use of theatrical techniques that permit an integration of settings so events occurring in various places can be presented on the same set without intermission, or an integration of characters by which an actor, by a sudden change in voice or posture or mannerism, switches from playing one character to another.

The effects of economy and compression are both financial and aesthetic. Obviously, when scenery changes and the number of actors are held to a minimum, the costs of production are minimized as well. But beyond that, compression and economy in playwriting serve to stimulate intrigue and focus audience expectation: a tightly written play gives us the feeling that we are on the trail of something important and that our quarry is right around the next bend. Thus, economy and compression actually lead to *intensity,* which is one of the theatre's most powerful attributes.

Dramatic intensity can take many forms. It can be harsh, abrasive, explosive, eminently physical, or overtly calm. It can be ruminative, tender, or comic. But whenever intensity occurs and in whatever mood or context, it conveys to the audience an ineradicable feeling that this moment in theatre is unique and its revelations are profound. Intensity does not come about by happy accident, obviously, but neither can it be simply injected at the whim of the playwright. It must evolve out of a careful development of issues, through the increasing urgency of character goals and intentions and the focused actions and interactions of the plot that draw characters and their conflicts ever closer to some sort of climactic confrontation. A play must spiral inward toward its core—that is, its compression must increase and its mood must intensify as it circles toward its climax and denouement. Too many tangential diversions can deflect a play from this course, rendering it formless and devoid of apparent purpose.

Celebration

Finally, a great play celebrates life; it does not merely depict or analyze or criticize it. The first plays were presented at festivals that—though perhaps haunted by angry or capricious gods—were essentially joyful celebrations. Even the darkest of the ancient Greek tragedies sought to transcend the more negative aspects of existence and to exalt the human spirit, for the whole of Greek theatre was informed by the positive (and therapeutic) elements of the Dionysian festival: spring, fertility, and the gaiety and solidarity of public communion.

The theatre can never successfully venture too far from this source. A purely didactic theatre has never satisfied either critics or the public, and a merely grim depiction of ordinary life has little to offer this art form. Although the word *theatrical* usually suggests something like "glittery" or "showy," it better accords with the theatre's most fundamental aspirations: to extend our known experience, to illuminate life, and to raise existence to the level of art—the art of theatre.

This celebration can easily be perverted. Dramas intended to be merely "uplifting"—with a reliance on happy endings and strictly noble sentiments—or written in self-consciously "elevated" tones do not celebrate life; they merely whitewash it. The truest and most exciting theatre has always been created out of a passionate, personal vision of reality and deep devotion to expressing life's struggles and splendors, for the theatre is fundamentally an affirmation. Writing, producing, and attending plays are also acts of affirmation: attesting to the desire to share and communicate, and celebrating human existence, participation, and communion. Purely bitter plays, no matter how justly based or how well grounded in history or experience, remain incomplete and unsatisfying as theatre, which simply is not an effective medium for nihilistic conveyance. Even the bleakest of modern plays radiates a persistent hopefulness—even joyousness—as archetypally represented by Samuel Beckett's two old men who sing, joke, and entertain each other, and us as well, in the forlorn shadow of a mostly leafless tree while waiting for a probably nonexistent Godot.

THE PLAYWRIGHT'S PROCESS

How does one go about writing a play? It is important to know the elements of a play (as discussed in the chapter titled "What Is a Play?") and the characteristics of the best plays—credibility, intrigue, speakability, stageability, flow, richness, depth of characterization, gravity, pertinence, compression, economy, intensity, and celebration—as discussed in the preceding sections. But that is not enough; one must still confront the practical task of writing.

The blank sheet of paper is the writer's nemesis. It is the accuser, the goad and critic that coldly commands action even as it threatens humiliation. There is no consensus among writers as to where to start. Some prefer to begin with a story line or a plot outline. Some begin with a real event and write the play to explain why that event occurred. Some begin with a real character or set of characters and develop a plot around them. Some begin with a setting and try to animate it with characters and actions. Some begin with a theatrical effect or an idea for a new form of theatrical expression. Some write entirely from personal experience. Some adapt a story or a legend, others a biography of a famous person, others a play by an earlier playwright; others simply expand upon a remembered dream.

A documentary might begin with a transcript of a trial or a committee hearing. Other documentary forms might begin with a tape recorder and a situation contrived by the playwright. Some plays are created out of actors' improvisations or acting-class exercises. Some are compilations of material written over the course of many years or collected from many sources.

The fact is, writers tend to begin with whatever works for *them* and accords with their immediate aims. On the one hand, because playwrights usually work alone, at least in the initial stages, they can do as they please whenever they want: there is no norm. On the other hand, certain steps can be followed as introductory exercises in playwriting, and these may in fact lead to the creation of an entire play.

Dialogue

Transcription of dialogue from previous observation and experience—in other words, the writing down of *remembered dialogue* from overheard conversations or from conversations in which the author has participated—is step one of a fundamental playwriting exercise; probably most finished plays contain such scenes. Because we remember conversations only selectively and subjectively, a certain amount of fictionalizing and shading inevitably creeps into these transcriptions; and often without even meaning to do so, authors also transform people in their memory into characters in their scenes.

Writing scenes of *imagined dialogue* is the logical step two, for all the author need do now is to extend the situation beyond its remembered reality into the area of "what might have happened." The dialogue then constructed will be essentially original yet in keeping with the personalized "characters" developed in the earlier transcription. The characters now react and respond as dramatic figures, interacting with each other freshly and under the control of the author. Many fine plays have resulted from the author's working out, in plot and dialogue, hypothetical relations between real people who never confronted each other in life; indeed, many plays are inspired by the author's notion of what *should* have happened among people who never met. In this way, the theatre has often been used as a form of psychotherapy, with the patient-playwright simply acting out—in imagination or with words on paper—certain obligatory scenes in life that never occurred.

Conflict

Writing scenes of *forced conflict* makes the dialogue *dramatic* and becomes a third step in the exercise and the first step toward the creation of a play. Events such as discovery, victory, rejection, revelation, separation, or death become climactic scenes in a play and define its structure. If a writer can create a convincing scene of high conflict that gets inside *each* of the characters involved and not merely one of them, then there is a good chance of making that scene the core of an exciting play—especially if it incorporates some subtlety and is not dependent entirely on shouting and denunciation. What is more, such a scene will be highly actable in its own right and thus can serve as a valuable tool for demonstrating the writer's potential.

Exercises that result in scripted scenes—even if only a page or two in length—have the advantage of allowing the writer to test her or his work as it progresses, for a short scene is easily producible: all it requires is a group of actors and a modest investment of time, and the playwright can quickly assess its impact. Moreover, the performance of such a scene can sometimes generate enthusiasm for the theatrical collaboration needed for a fuller theatrical experience.

But the beginning playwright should bear in mind that intrigue, thematic development, compression, and even credibility depend on a carefully built structure and that it is an axiom of theatre that most playwriting is in fact *rewriting*—rewriting aimed principally at organizing and reorganizing the play's staged actions and events.

A strong dramatic structure compels interest and attention. It creates intrigue by establishing certain expectations—both in the characters and in the audience—and then by creating new and bigger expectations out of the fulfillment of the first ones. A good dramatic structure keeps us always wanting more until the final curtain, and at the end it leaves us with a sense of the inevitability of the play's conclusion, a sense that what happened onstage was precisely as it had to be. A great structure makes us comfortable and receptive; we feel in good hands, expertly led wherever the play may take us. And we are willing, therefore, to abandon ourselves to a celebration of vital and ineffable matters.

THE PLAYWRIGHT'S REWARDS

There will always be a need for playwrights, for the theatre never mutes its clamor for new and better dramatic works. Hundreds of producers today are so anxious to discover new authors and new scripts that they will read (or instruct an associate to read) everything that comes their way; so a truly fine play need not go unnoticed for long. Moreover, playwrights are the only artists in the theatre who can bring their work to the first stage of completion without any outside professional help at all; they do not need to be auditioned, interviewed, hired, cast, or contracted to an agent in order to come up with the world's greatest dramatic manuscript.

The rewards that await successful playwrights can be very fulfilling. Playwrights receive compensation according to their commercial success; they may acquire influence and prestige on the basis of their personal vision, for while the public may adore an actor or admire a director or designer, it *listens* to the playwright who truly has something to say. The impact of playwrights such as Arthur Miller, Lillian Hellman, Tennessee Williams, Lorraine Hansberry, Tony Kushner, August Wilson, David Mamet, and Lynn Nottage on American social thought and cultural mores, for example, is easily measurable. At its best, playwriting is more than a profession and more than just another component of the theatrical machine. It is a creative political act that enlarges human experience and enriches our awe, understanding, and appreciation of life.

Some plays, particularly in the contemporary postmodern era, dispense altogether with conventional structure in favor of a collage of events, images, and poetic perceptions. Sarah Kane's last play, *4:48 Psychosis,* treats disorientation, death, and despair in an entirely nonlinear way—with no attempt to convey a coherent plotline or even an identification of who the characters are or who speaks which lines. Even the first half of the title is meaningless: Kane says 4:48 is simply the time she usually wakes up in the morning. Nonetheless, and although the playwright died before it was performed, the play is now produced all over the world, usually drawing high praise for its poetic beauty and intensely portrayed psychological complexities. Illustrated is a moment of extreme anguish from Poland's TR Warsawa company's production, performed at the Edinburgh International Theatre Festival in 2007. Magdalena Cielecka is the suffering central (but unnamed) character.

Structure

Developing a complete play demands more than stringing together a number of scenes, of course, and at some point in the scene-writing process the playwright inevitably confronts the need for structure. Many playwrights develop outlines for their plays after writing a scene or two; some have an outline ready before any scenes are written or even thought of. Other playwrights never write down anything except dialogue and stage directions yet find an overall structure asserting itself almost unconsciously as their writing progresses.

A SAMPLING OF CURRENT AMERICAN PLAYWRIGHTS

Literally hundreds of American playwrights are producing works on professional American stages today, and several have international reputations. In this section, we focus on six contemporary writers, all under 60 at the time of publication, who have made major impacts on the national theatre scene and from whom we may eagerly expect to see new and important works in the decades ahead. One is Neil LaBute, who is featured in this chapter's photo essay. The others are Tony Kushner, David Henry Hwang, Lynn Nottage, Theresa Rebeck, and Sarah Ruhl.

Tony Kushner

Surely no play has burst upon the contemporary American theatre scene with such thrilling panache as the seven-hour, two-part *Angels in America* by Tony Kushner (born 1956). Initially commissioned by the Eureka Theatre in San Francisco, *Angels* was subsequently developed at the Mark Taper Forum in Los Angeles and (part one only) at the National Theatre in London. The two parts had separate openings on Broadway in 1993 (under the direction of George C. Wolfe) and received rapturous critical acclaim. Part one, *Millennium Approaches,* took the Tony Award and Pulitzer Prize in 1993, and part two, *Perestroika,* took the Tony in 1994—an unprecedented achievement. By 1995 the play had fully entered the international repertoire and was featured in major productions in theatre capitals and drama festivals throughout the world.

Angels fully merits this extraordinary attention: it is a masterpiece of modern drama; many critics consider it the finest American play of the present generation. Dealing unstintingly with the AIDS crisis, Kushner has laid bare still-unsettled issues in American culture that touch upon race, religion, gender, politics, economics, and sexual orientation. Pairing a heterosexual couple (Joe and Harper Pitt, Mormons from Utah) with a homosexual couple (Louis Ironson, a New York Jew, and Prior Walter, afflicted with both AIDS and a lineage that goes back to the *Mayflower*), Kushner interweaves their stories and shakes up their lives within a vast medical-political "America," which is run in Kushner's imagination by Roy Cohn—the (real) self-hating, self-baiting, sometime gay Jewish lawyer in raging self-denial right up to his awful AIDS-ravished demise. A black nurse (male) and a white angel (female) also

Tony Kushner's brilliant, two-part *Angels in America* is thought by many critics to be the finest American play in years or even decades. A complex work of comedy, sagacity, and fantasy, it casts a wicked eye on American politics, religion, economics, medicine, and racial and sexual bigotry—but it is also a moving story of human affection and alienation. In this 1993 Broadway production, an angel visits the AIDS-afflicted Prior Walter.

play sustained roles in this adventure, which is additionally peopled with another twenty-five characters, real and imagined and all played by the eight actors in the cast: a rabbi, an Eskimo, a travel agent, a real-estate saleswoman, the ghost of Ethel Rosenberg, various doctors, nurses, angels, and a man we are told is "the world's oldest Bolshevik." What is astonishing about Kushner's work is its explosive humor; this is one of the funniest American plays of the twentieth century. But it's also one of the saddest. Though not meant for all audiences (rejected by many theatre producers in conservative cities, the play includes frontal nudity, grisly depictions of AIDS suffering, savage religious satire, the blatant miming of homosexual acts, and a good deal of in-your-face hurling of loathing invectives), *Angels* has a transporting and transforming effect on spectators who are attuned to its rhythms and subject. Most claim to come out of the seven-hour performance ennobled. Many more experienced the same feelings when a cable-television version of the play, directed by Mike Nichols, premiered on HBO in 2003.

Born in New York City and raised in Louisiana, Kushner was known, pre-*Angels*, mainly for his clever adaptation of Pierre Corneille's French classic *The Illusion*, and for his sadly wistful *A Bright Room Called Day*, about a family trying to respond to the Nazi takeover of their homeland. After *Angels*, Kushner's interests again went overseas, with *Slavs! Thinking about the Longstanding Problems of Virtue and Happiness* (1995), a satirical comedy about Russian communism, and *Homebody/Kabul* (2001), a three-act, sixteen-actor, three-and-a-half hour intellectual extravaganza written in English, French, Pashto, Dari, Arabic, Esperanto, and international computerese. Set in London, Kabul, and the Afghan desert, *Homebody/Kabul* spans a global, mythic history that covers the history of central Asia, from Cain's burial to the present day. Astonishingly prescient ("You love the Taliban so much? . . . don't worry, they're coming to New York!" cries a Pashtun woman in lines written months before the devastating 9/11 attack), *Kabul* also exemplifies its author's genius for combining the foreign with the familiar, the ancient with the contemporary, and dope-laden ecstasy with passionate intellectuality. Has there ever before been a play in which the word *dichlorodiphenyltrichloroethane* came trippingly off a character's tongue? Or the verbal compound *synchitic expegeses*?

Kushner scored three more times following *Kabul*, and the variety of his topics, settings, and styles continues to be extraordinary. His 2003–2004 *Caroline, or Change* is a full-on Broadway musical: it concerns a black maid in a 1960s Jewish Louisiana family much like Kushner's own. *Caroline* digs deeply but without polemic into America's complex race relations, finding, amid the misery, nuances of grace, humor, and hope. On Broadway it received six Tony nominations and afterward enjoyed a good run at London's National Theatre. His subsequent adaptation of Bertolt Brecht's classic of epic theatre, *Mother Courage*, premiered at Shakespeare in the Park with Meryl Streep in the title role and became the must-see event of the 2006 summer season in New York. And his *Intelligent Homosexual's Guide to Capitalism and Socialism with a Key to the Scriptures* opened in Minneapolis at the Guthrie Theater in 2009 and had a successful run at New York's Public Theatre in 2011. Despite its exotic title and multiracial, ambisexual cast of characters, it is a straightforward dysfunctional family drama so realistic in its writing that it often seems an homage to Anton Chekhov and George Bernard Shaw—who are referenced in the text, which also has covert allusions to the playwright's American realistic forebears: Williams, Miller, O'Neil, and Albee.

A giant among American playwrights since *Angels in America*, Kushner seems dedicated to build upon that stature for decades to come.

David Henry Hwang

Growing up in San Gabriel, California, David Henry Hwang (born 1957) began writing—"on a lark," he says—while an undergraduate at Stanford University. His first play, *FOB* (for "Fresh Off the Boat"), is a biting, honest, angry reaction to hidden (and not-so-hidden) American racism; it was first produced at Stanford and subsequently at the Eugene O'Neill Theatre Center in Connecticut and at the New York Public Theatre, for which it received the Obie Award.

Hwang's subsequent *M. Butterfly* (1988), his most celebrated work, explores the bizarre (and apparently true) relationship between a French diplomat and his Chinese mistress: bizarre because the mistress is revealed during the play to be—unbeknownst to the diplomat—a male in disguise. Hwang's main subject is "Orientalism," the ingrained sense of deprecation with which Western culture views the East. In *Butterfly*, Hwang, himself of Chinese heritage, brilliantly interweaves gritty Western romanticism (including portions of the Puccini opera that gives the play its name) with Asian theatre and *xiqu* (Chinese opera) technique, lending it current-political and timeless-mythic proportions. *Butterfly* won Hwang the Tony Award in 1988 and international fame. His subsequent *Golden Child* (1998), a play about a traditional Chinese family assimilating to Westernizing influences after World War I, was also a Broadway critical success, earning its author another Tony nomination for best play.

Hwang's prominence continues in the twenty-first century. His fascinating, semiautobiographical *Yellow Face*, premiering at the Mark Taper Forum in Los Angeles in 2007, treats his own efforts, since *M. Butterfly*, to increase the profile of Asian theatre artists in the American theatre (and the many paradoxes inherent in seeking to define what is truly "Asian" in America's increasingly multiethnic culture). And his *Chinglish*, which opened on Broadway in 2011, is a surprisingly comic examination of the difficulties inherent in translation, both linguistic and cultural. Hwang is even more widely known for his recent work as a librettist—as the author of "books" (spoken texts) for operas and musicals. Opera fans know his librettos for Unsuk Chin's *Alice in Wonderland*, Howard Shore's *The Fly*, and Philip Glass's *The Sound of a Voice*, which

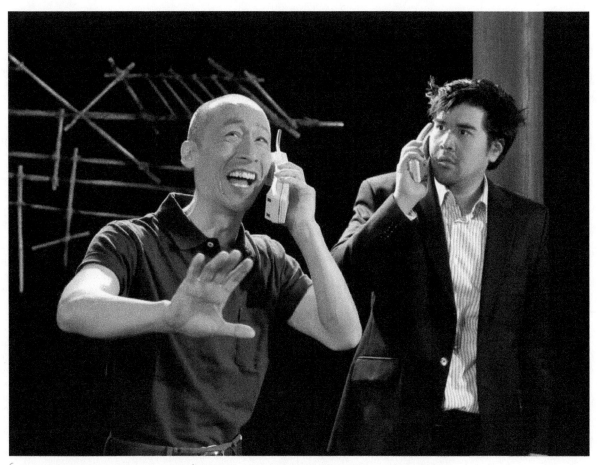

David Henry Hwang's *Yellow Face* is a semiautobiographical work in which the author is represented by a character known only as DHH, Hwang's own initials, while Hwang's father is likewise known only by his initials, HYH. Francis Jue (*left*), and Pun Bandhu play the two roles in this 2009 production of the play at TheatreWorks in Palo Alto, California, directed by the company's artistic director, Robert Kelly.

have premiered in Munich, Paris, and Cambridge (Massachusetts), respectively, since 2007. Broadway-goers know his libretti for the Disney productions of *Aida* and *Tarzan*, and his own adaptation of Rodgers and Hammerstein's *Flower Drum Song*, which played on Broadway after a Los Angeles premiere. Like Kushner and Mamet, Hwang moves gracefully and effectively from spoken to musical drama and is eager to create theatre within a great variety of styles.

Lynn Nottage

When she received the 2009 Pulitzer Prize for Drama with *Ruined*, Lynn Nottage reached an important milestone not only in her career but also in her life. Born in Brooklyn in 1964, Nottage began writing plays and

stories when she was eight years old. She first studied playwriting as an English concentrator (major) with Pulitzer-winner Paula Vogel at Brown University, then went to Yale, receiving her M.F.A. in playwriting in 1989. But rather than heading straight into theatre, Nottage spent her next four years at Amnesty International, soon becoming the national press officer of this preeminent worldwide organization dedicated to human rights. Thus *Ruined*, the capstone of her dramatic work so far, sprang not only from her playwriting experience but also from her deep commitment to social justice.

Ruined was conceived, Nottage says, as a contemporary adaptation of Brecht's *Mother Courage* but written from a woman's point of view and omitting Brecht's notion of emotional estrangement. Set in the

Photo Essay: Playwright Neil LaBute

With his twenty-one plays on and off Broadway since 1989, Neil LaBute is one of America's most prolific and admired playwrights. In 2006, in his Los Angeles-area home, Neil LaBute chatted with the author about his life as a working writer of films and plays. Excerpts from the conversation follow (RC indicates Robert Cohen; NL, Neil LaBute).

RC: Where do you do your writing?

NL: Anywhere the feeling seizes me. I do a lot of writing on airplanes. I usually fly at night, and most of the time I stay up and write. But I find that I can write in most places: I'll perch on any windowsill or sit down in the grass or wherever. I don't feel I have to write from eight in the morning 'til noon, or anything like that; I write only when I feel compelled to. Usually I circle around my computer like a shark, closing in until I say, "I have to do this" and then sit down and begin.

RC: What are your usual starting points? Do you get captured by a story or . . . ?

NL: Sometimes it's a story, but it could be as simple as a line of dialogue you have in your head. It may come to you in bed, like "Let's hurt somebody!" I thought of that line and said, "That's a provocative notion. What does

that *mean*? What are we going to *do* with that?" And so one script [*In the Company of Men*, LaBute's first film] sprang from that. By the time I made the film, I ended up putting it at the end of the first scene rather than the beginning, but that line was the catalyst for the whole script. Maybe then comes a character. Or an idea. In one case it was: "I want to say something about art." So who's going to do this? "It's going to be an artist and a girl." So who does she need to work with? And then characters come to me: *The Shape of Things* grew out of that kind of dialogue with myself. Sometimes it's simply a title. I admired the title of the Amy Mann song "This Is How It Goes." But what does that title *mean*? I ask myself these kinds of questions, and very often something grows out of it: in that case it was something about (*pause*) the flexibility of truth.

Places I tend not to look for material are those right in front of me. I don't look at "me" to give me inspiration. I don't say, "Oh, this is a great story from my youth" or about my parents, or how they got together, and I don't look in the newspaper for stories—which are usually more amazing than the ones I come up with,

actually. What's in the newspaper is breathtaking stuff, it's real. For me it always seems to come just from my imagination, but I never know where it's going to take me next.

RC: One thing I always see in your writing is peer pressure: how groups of people transform us and affect what we do. Does this come from personal experience or . . . ?

NL: Well, I suppose it does, I mean, it can't help but start there, but I've still never written from personal experience. My interest is in the two selves that we have, the public and private self, the worlds that people juggle a lot of time just from being out there in the world: being one kind of person while trying to be another person. Or being "this" person and knowing this group over here won't like me if they know "this" about me, so trying to keep "this" person from them. The fact that this often leads to us becoming a smoldering wreck because of trying to maintain this deception is fascinating stuff.

RC: Betrayal and deception also seem common themes.

NL: Yes, a lot of what I write is about people being betrayed, or people who have a confession—one-person

Neil LaBute has had well over a dozen of his plays produced in London and New York, but *reasons to be pretty*, which opened at the off-Broadway Lucille Lortel Theater in 2008, was, after some revisions and recasting, his first to make it to Broadway, where it was highly praised and nominated for a 2009 Tony Award. The play treats contemporary romantic relationships and the seemingly simple words that can propel—or destroy—them, such as this moment from the Lortel premiere when Steph (Alison Pill) is upset that Greg (Thomas Sadoski) has called her face "ordinary."

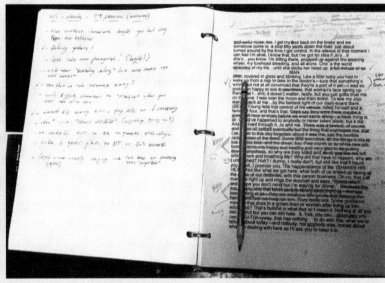

2.

1. Neil LaBute is working on the *Wrecks* script in his Los Angeles–area office, with his extensive DVD collection shelved above him. The painting on the wall is a color rendition of W. Eugene Smith's well-known photograph "Walk to Paradise Garden," which LaBute bought at a flea market. "I thought it was the perfect thing for my office," the playwright says, "because the characters are turned away from us, and I always felt that was how I write, that you can never know a person completely, and they always have their back turned to you in a way."

1.

2. Writing is rewriting. LaBute's *Wrecks* script looks at first like something of a wreck itself, but it shows the extraordinary amount of revision most writers do to perfect their scripts. *Wrecks,* at the time this photo was taken, had already had its world premiere in Ireland and a run in New York, both directed by the author. Even so, LaBute continues to work on it—deleting, adding, and revising individual lines and making notes on each page of the manuscript.

3. A one-time professor of drama, LaBute often returns to the classroom. Here he is working with a student from the University of California–Irvine on a writing/acting exercise of his own invention.

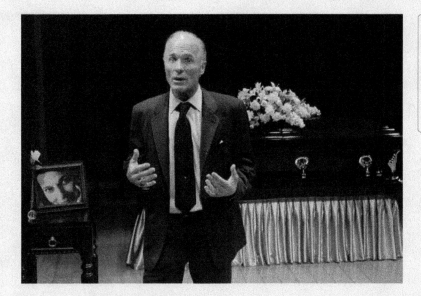

4. LaBute's play *Wrecks* is about a man who, grieving at his wife's funeral, gradually lets us into his secrets. The play's tragic dimension (its title—like LaBute's *Medea Redux*—echoes Greek tragedy, in this case *Oedipus Rex*) is not obscured by its contemporary dialogue. Ed Harris here plays the solo role, under LaBute's direction, at the Public Theatre in New York in 2006.

monologues which are a kind of confession: "I can't tell anybody else what I've done, so I'm telling you…" In fact, that's what's going on in [my 2006 play] *Wrecks*, which is a kind of moral exploration that [actor Ed] Harris nightly makes to an audience. He talks glowingly about love and I believe that he believes in it, but the big question for me is can you love somebody that you have deceived from the day you met them? And I don't know the answer to that. That's the beauty of being a writer: I don't have to know things. Fuck, I don't know! (*Laughter*) But I *do* love the investigation.

I don't write from a place of knowledge. I'm not saying, "I'm going to raise this question just so I can shove an answer down your throat." It's not like I already have this figured out; it's going to take a lot of writing for me to finally say, "This is what I think." Most times I think to myself, if an audience wonders why I've written something, "Why are you asking me? I only thought of the question. I wouldn't have written it if I had an answer!" For me, it's all about "what if?" And "why?" And sometimes by the end I'm even farther away from the answer than when I began.

RC: One thing I love about your work is the sense of deferral. We're pulled into the play and then certain

surprises come to us and we've discovered the play isn't what we thought it was. How much of that do you discover as you're writing the play—and how much of the ending have you prepared?

NL: Well, hopefully there's a place where [the ending] reveals itself to me. Sometimes I'm clear in knowing where I want to go, but I still don't know how the journey's going to happen. Like I knew where I was heading with *Wrecks* because of the kind of story that it was—I had the Greek model so the process was different—but exactly when that moment was going to drop, and where he's going to allow us to go, and how that reversal will work I didn't know until I'd written it. To answer the question: sometimes an ending is present as I begin writing, sometimes not. It's always an adventure.

You know, I'm not always working toward clarity. Sometimes I'm working toward the grayest area possible, because that's what I find attractive. Why do we always have to know everything? That's what is fascinating to me about people, and art. I love that a play could be shit to one person and art to somebody else and that they can both be right. It's when somebody tries to tell me their opinion is more valid than mine is

when I get upset. I like to believe that just about everything can be more than one thing; I'm a big believer in "subjectivity."

RC: Like you said earlier, the flexibility of truth.

NL: Mm-hmm.

RC: Last question: Any thoughts to say to an emerging, young playwright, somebody who wants to try to write a play?

NL: There was a great quote and I often, as a teacher, would give it to students. It was [Russian dramatist Anton] Chekhov writing to [Maksim] Gorky around the turn of the [twentieth] century and all he said was, "Write, write, write." There's just no way around it, other than sitting down and writing. I know a lot of people talk about being writers, but I know far fewer who actually give me a manuscript to read. And to me, that's the only mark of being a writer. Not that they worked at the Geffen [Theatre] or the Public [Theatre] or in London or if they've been published—it's just that they have *written* something, you know? That's the springboard for everything else, that you actually have something on paper. So, don't fear it, but wrestle your thoughts to the ground, do your best. That's the only thing that I've ever really done, is to sit down and write.

Democratic Republic of Congo at the height of that central African nation's seemingly eternal series of brutal conflicts—ongoing, in some form, since 1998 and globally known for its extreme sexual violence against women—the play's action takes place in a small-town bar and brothel run by "Mama Nadi," the "Mother Courage" of the play, who doggedly seeks to create a survivable wartime environment for herself and those around her. Mama Nadi profits by prostituting women who have come to her establishment for shelter, but she also creates for them, as best she can, a haven of respect and security. "My girls [would] rather be here, any day, than back out there in their villages where they are taken without regard. They're safer with me," Mama Nadi insists to her would-be critics. And the stories we hear from these women are indeed horrifying, particularly from the beautiful but now semicrippled young Sophie, who, having been raped by soldiers' bayonets in her native village, has been deemed "ruined" for life. Sophie's is only one of the many stories that Nottage—and the director Kate Whoriskey—heard when they went to Africa and interviewed raped and mutilated Congolese refugees while researching this play. "Their husbands had rejected them," Nottage explained. "Their communities had rejected them. Friends didn't want to take them in because they had leakage and smelled of urine. They needed money for medical expenses and operations, and the only thing they could do was turn to prostitution." Yet the grimness of the play's situations are transcended in Nottage's beautifully executed script (and in Whoriskey's finely tuned direction of its world premiere), for *Ruined* is also suffused with the warmth, beauty, music, and even humor of contemporary African life. "I also wanted to show the beauty, how gorgeous [Africa] is," Nottage has said. "I believe in engaging people emotionally because I think they react more out of emotion . . . [than by being] preached to." Nottage succeeded: *Ruined* elicits tears and joy as well as ideas and social engagement as it captivates its audience. When the play opened—first at Chicago's Goodman Theatre in 2008 and then at New York's Manhattan Theatre Club in 2009—it received rave press reviews and its powerful impact led to the formation of social-action groups in both cities and soon around the country, each group seeking new ways of remedying the human tragedies that have become endemic in parts of central Africa. Obviously, Nottage's four years with Amnesty International was no mere intermission in her playwriting career but rather its booster rocket.

Ruined is Lynn Nottage's masterwork to date; in addition to the Pulitzer Prize, it received the Lucille Lortel Award, the Outer Critics Circle Award, and the increasingly important Independent Theatre Bloggers Award. Pictured are Condola Rashad (*left*) as the "ruined" bar singer Sophie, and Cherise Booth (*standing*) and Quincy Tyler Bernstine as, respectively, Josephine and Salima, two of the bar's "girls" who have been forced into prostitution to survive.

Nottage's earlier works show the trajectory of her progress. *Crumbs from the Table of Joy*, premiering at off-Broadway's Second Stage in 1995, is a family drama set in her own hometown of Brooklyn in 1950. There, a divorced African American father of two teenage girls has fallen under the influence of the era's most extreme radio evangelist, Father Divine—an ultra-puritan who claimed he was God himself—and has fled from the sexual overtures of his deceased wife's sister and into the arms of a white German immigrant lady whom he met in a subway car. The play, which is mainly a coming-of-age narrative of the older sister, Ernestine, is perhaps more accomplished in its well-drawn white and black characters than in its overall dramatic impact. It had strong runs at major theatres around the country (South Coast Repertory, Steppenwolf Theatre Company, Baltimore's Centerstage), and it put Nottage squarely on America's cultural map.

Intimate Apparel, which premiered at Baltimore's Centerstage in 2003, is another period play; set in 1905, it centers on Esther, a thirty-five-year-old unmarried black seamstress who lives and works in New York. Esther's specialty is designing and sewing women's intimate apparel, including wedding garments, which by the time the play opens have graced most of her friends at the boardinghouse where she lives. The time has come, Esther now feels, to find a husband of her own. And so she does, or thinks she does, through a chance correspondence with a man from Barbados who is now in Panama working on the construction of the Panama Canal. The core story is from the playwright's own family history: Nottage's great-grandmother was a seamstress who arrived in New York in 1902 and eventually corresponded with—and married—just such a Barbadian. Nottage departs from her family history early on, however, bringing in a panoply of diverse characters, black and white, including Esther's landlady, two of her customers (a prostitute and a society lady), and an Orthodox Jew who supplies her fabrics. "I am drawn to the interplay of voices on a stage," Nottage said in an interview in the program for *Intimate Apparel*'s premiere, and the interplay here is not only between individuals but among races, creeds, countries, and social mores. With seventeen productions mounted in 2006, *Apparel* became the most-produced play in America's theatres that year, and its New York premiere received a best-play award from the New York Drama Critics Circle and the Outer Critics Circle and led to a 2007 MacArthur "genius" fellowship in recognition of her "original voice in American theatre." With a Pulitzer Prize now heading her résumé, Nottage is clearly a playwright who will be a force in the American theatre for decades to come.

Theresa Rebeck

Many of America's best mid-century playwrights—Clifford Odets, Tennessee Williams, and Arthur Miller—were drawn to Hollywood after their biggest Broadway hits, either by transposing their plays into films (Williams's *Streetcar Named Desire* and *Cat on a Hot Tin Roof*) or writing original films of their own (Miller's *The Misfits*). For Theresa Rebeck, however,

Theresa Rebeck's 2011 *Seminar* was her first Broadway show, a brilliantly caustic comedy featuring Alan Rickman as Leonard, a novelist-turned-writing teacher, and Hamish Linklater as Martin, his most rebellious student.

stage, film, and television have been joint ventures since her career began, after receiving graduate degrees (an M.F.A. in playwriting and a Ph.D. in dramatic literature) from Brandeis University in the late 1980s. At the time of writing, Rebeck has written eighteen full-length plays, twenty-two one-acts, and more than fifty films and television episodes (the latter for shows including *L.A. Law*, *Law & Order*, *NYPD Blue*, *First Wave*, *Third Watch*, *Brooklyn Bridge*, and *Dream On*) and was in the process of opening three new plays (*Poor Behavior* at the Mark Taper Forum in Los Angeles, *Dead Accounts* at Cincinnati's Playhouse in the Park, and *Seminar* on Broadway) along with several episodes on TV's *Smash*, for which she is also the series' executive producer. She has been nominated for a Pulitzer Prize and has won many national and regional awards. This is a writer who is at the very top of her many games.

Rebeck's initial dramas sported a sharp-witted and essentially comical feminist edge. Her first play to gain public attention, *Spike Heels* in 1992, centers on "Georgie," a classy modern secretary who oscillates between her shy neighbor and her sexually over-aggressive boss; the *New York Times* critic noted that "the drop-dead shoes of the title are at once an emblem of Georgie's erotic appeal to men and symbolic shackles that keep her in subjugation and pain." These themes carry over in Rebeck's *Bad Dates,* which was her first work to gain broad national attention, becoming "wildly popular" according to *American Theater,* which ranked it the fifth most popular play in America in the season following its off-Broadway 2003 premiere at Playwrights Horizons. *Bad Dates* presents a fashion-conscious Manhattan woman, Haley, who chats with us while dressing—and redressing, as she manages twenty-some onstage costume changes and forty shoe changes—for a series of "bad dates" she has with various men. And Rebeck's *The Scene* (2006), which presents Clea, a sexpot from Ohio recently transplanted to New York and its high-powered and male-dominated theatre/TV talk show scene, also intertwines social satire, professional jealousy, sexual electricity, and near-farcical comedy in roughly equal measures. By now, anyone familiar with TV's *Sex and the City* knows the territory of these three plays, but Rebeck all but invented it.

Rebeck seems to be drifting away from her feminist-centered themes these days. Her most recent success is *Seminar,* which, premiering on Broadway at the end of 2011, features the central character of Leonard (played, in its premiere, by Alan Rickman), an acerbic novelist who, after being accused of plagiarism and no longer in favor, is reduced to giving private writing seminars for a stiff $5,000 fee. Four young New Yorkers in their mid-twenties—two men and two women—have signed up for his latest class, which is held in the lofty Park Avenue apartment of one of the women. With a cruel but comically wry wit, Leonard trashes all of their work, often viciously. As always in Rebeck's work, sexual complications abound, but in *Seminar* they are not central to the play's theme or major action, and the final scene is a reconciliation between Leonard and his most promising but antagonistic (male) student. And, earlier that season, Rebeck's *O Beautiful,* commissioned by the University of Delaware's theatre department, was produced on that campus; this work centers on current American politics, specifically focusing on abortion, school bullying, America's founding fathers, and the otherworldly

intervention of Jesus Christ. With Rebeck's increasingly wide coverage of major issues in contemporary life, coupled with her superb dramaturgical craftsmanship—developed in part from years of writing for films and television—her work can be expected to excite audiences for decades to come.

Sarah Ruhl

With her Pulitzer-nominated *The Clean House* in 2004, her MacArthur "genius" award in 2006, and her widely produced *Dead Man's Cell Phone* in 2008, the highly unconventional Sarah Ruhl has made quite an inroad into the American theatre. And with her 2009 Broadway hit, *In the Next Room or the vibrator play,* which earned her nominations for both a Tony Award and a second Pulitzer, Ruhl has clearly entered the top tier of current American dramatists.

Ruhl was born in Illinois in the mid-1970s. Educated at Brown, she received her B.A. and then an M.F.A in playwriting, the latter while studying (as had Lynn Nottage) under Pulitzer Prize–winning dramatist Paula Vogel. National attention came with her play *The Clean House,* which premiered at Yale Repertory Theatre in 2004 and, after being performed at other regional theatres, received widespread exposure with the play's Lincoln Center debut in New York, directed by Bill Rauch (who had also staged the Yale premiere). *Clean House* is, by turns, charming, delightful, and bewildering. Set in a coolly luxurious American living room, it centers at first around two sisters, Lane and Virginia, a doctor and a germophobe, and Lane's Brazilian housekeeper Matilde—who hates housecleaning. Soon Ruhl brings in Lane's surgeon husband and one of his cancer patients, an Argentinean who is now his mistress, and the plot not only thickens, it begins exploding. The women fight, make up, and fight again. Charles flees to Alaska to find a tree that he believes may cure cancer. Since the plot is multilayered and absurd, the actors double in various parts (at least in the New York production), and a healthy portion of the play's language is Spanish and Portuguese—with no subtitles—the play may be seen as more tantalizing than gripping, but it is certainly provocative and entertaining throughout, acutely touching serious contemporary issues in America's social environments.

Dead Man's Cell Phone moves Ruhl into a purely metaphysical world. It begins when Jean, its central character, finds herself irritated by a ringing cell phone in the luncheonette where she is dining. Since its apparent owner is not picking it up, she wanders over to his table to complain, only to realize that he's not being rude;

Sarah Ruhl's *In the Next Room or the vibrator play* received great acclaim in its Broadway appearance in 2009–2010. Its key action shows a late-nineteenth-century doctor treating female patients' "hysteria" with the newly invented electric vibrator, which not only "cures" but delights his patients. Known for her witty dialogue and off-beat, semicomical characters (see later in this chapter), Ruhl's play—and its surprising central "prop"— wonderfully penetrate the miscommunications between men and women on matters of sexual intimacy, then and now. Les Waters directed this Lincoln Center production; Maria Dizzia is the patient and Michael Cerveris the doctor. The period costumes—petticoats and all—were designed by David Zinn.

he's just dead. Not knowing quite what to do, she picks up his ringing phone and answers it: one of the most astonishing opening sequences in the history of theatre! Refusing to tell the caller that the intended receiver has died, she becomes his receptionist/secretary, telling callers what she thinks they want to hear. One thing leads to another and soon Jean is dining with the dead man's family, coupling with his brother in the back room of a stationery store, heading off to "the airport in South Africa" to surgically remove her kidney in its waiting room, and even meeting up with the dead man himself in a laundromat located in heaven—cyberspace and paradise having joined hands. Like *The Clean House, Cell Phone*'s plot is abstract and convoluted, but the validity of the play's social issues (e.g., Does modern technology bring us together or keep us apart?), the elegant novelty of Ruhl's spoken dialogue ("Life is essentially a very large Brillo pad"), and the surprises of its ever-twisting

action create a comic and an altogether engaging potpourri of rare entertainment.

In the Next Room or the vibrator play—which became Ruhl's first Broadway venture—displays a more coherent and intriguing plot (at least through the first act), and is her greatest public success to date. Its first act is pure dynamite. In a suburban New York home in the late 1880s, a "Dr. Giving" has discovered he can "cure" women from "hysteria" and other emotional "diseases" by applying the newly invented electric vibrator to their lower regions. And when the vibrator doesn't do the trick, the added manual insertion of his nurse's finger in those quarters will trigger the appropriate reactions. But as neither the nineteenth-century medical establishment nor its polite society has yet associated the resulting orgasmic spasms with the ecstasies of sexual pleasure, the play's first act, which takes place for the most part under discreet sheets in the "operating room" (the "next room" of the title), becomes a comedy of manners—or mis-manners—since all pretenses of propriety have gone delightfully awry amidst the women's unfamiliar shrieks and tears of joy. Even those being "cured" have no idea what is going on beneath their corsets, drawers, chemises, and petticoats. But they know they like it, and they insist on more of these "treatments."

But other events are taking place in the Givings' adjacent parlor, where the doctor's wife, unable to breast-feed her new baby, has engaged a wet nurse to perform these tasks. And the humor darkens when, trying to be polite, the wife cannot stop calling attention to the nurse's dead baby, and then apologizing clumsily for her inopportune remarks. The dissonance between the women increases as the disparity rises between the poor, black nurse and the rich, white wife; by intermission, at which time tears, emotions, and milk are flowing abundantly in one room and electrically generated orgasms are activated in the other, we get the full impact of the main (but often overlooked) title of this play and find ourselves struggling with a genuinely unique—and highly dramatic—visual dialectic: a female, nurse-prioritized "living" room on the left, where hormones and feelings rule, and a male, doctor-dominated "science" room on the right, where the latest technology—Thomas Edison's electricity—is blithely imposed to "cure" the most ancient of human-to-human interactions. One of the most brilliant first-act closings in theatre history.

Not all of the play's admirers (including your author) are comfortable with the play's act 2, however, which begins with the entrance of a new character: a handsome young painter who, coming in for treatment of his own, elicits the doctor's wife's adoration in the parlor; it seems to be the start of a wholly new play rather than the climactic events of one already well under way. But conventional Aristotelian structure (exposition, conflict, climax, denouement) is remote from Ruhl's stated objectives, at least so far, and she is not concerned with the tight plotting of many of her predecessors. "I try to interpret how people subjectively experience life," she told John Lahr in an interview. Ruhl is creating a new dramaturgy, and perhaps a new theatre. And the theatre world is enchanted. Sarah Ruhl is "the darling of the American theatre scene," said director Mark Wing-Davey back in 2008, and this remains true today.

Chapter **5**

Designers

and

Technicians

WHEN AN ACTOR FIRST STEPPED onto the stage as Jocasta in Sophocles' Greek tragedy *Oedipus Tyrannos,* he (and it was a he—all Greek actors of that time were men) wore clothing similar but not identical to what he would wear in the marketplace. It was similar in the sense that it was robe-like, but different because the shape and perhaps color of the garments indicated that he was to be seen as a "she." And not only a she, but a *royal* she. This is the basic purpose of design: to transform something so it may be seen, by a willing viewer, as something else—in this case a fifth-century B.C. male commoner as the tenth-century B.C. Queen of Thebes.

There would have been other differences too. The robe's sleeves would have been narrower than the sleeves of an everyday gown, so the actor's movements could be clearly seen from the back of the amphitheatre. And the actor also would have worn a mask, enlarging his face, amplifying his voice, and providing a fixed expression that even from a long distance could be quickly seen as both powerful and tragic. ▶

Thus when the costumed and masked "Jocasta" strode through the giant *skene* (stagehouse) door onto the sun-drenched stage, the audience saw not an actor walking onto a platform but a tragic queen leaving the royal palace to greet her equally gowned and masked husband, King Oedipus, grieving with his citizens on the palace steps.

Nothing in the text of *Oedipus* refers to the clothing, mask, or door just described. Yet these elements, creating the *look* of the play, are absolutely crucial to the drama in its performance. They constitute its *design:* its costumes (gowns), scenery (door, wall), makeup (mask), lighting (sun), and sound (voice as amplified through the mask). And that design has aesthetic, as well as dramatic, characteristics: color, scale, line, balance, harmony, punctuation, surprise. All these design elements came into play with the first drama, and all have even greater importance today.

The playwright creates the play's words, and the actors execute its actions and impersonate its characters, but the theatre designers determine what both the stage and the characters look like. Indeed, design comprises most of what we see when we go to the theatre—and much of what we hear. Designers, and the technicians who implement their ideas, create what the actors wear, what they sit on, and what they stand before. They determine how the actors are illuminated and how they—and the play around them—sound. Sometimes they even create—as with incense—what we smell. The playwright may create the words of a play and the actors may speak them, but the designers and technicians create the play's scenery, costumes, properties, lighting, sound score, sound amplification, and special aromas and effects.

THE DESIGN PROCESS

The initial framework for design is the play itself. The action Sophocles outlined in *Oedipus* implies a door, and most designers provide one. The action requires a chorus and characters that enter and leave the staging area, so suitable points of entry/exit are created as well. Sometimes—even in ancient times—characters fly in or out of sight, so machines are designed and built to execute these superhuman actions.

Today, of course, scenery, lighting, and costumes can create realistic-looking environments, such as living rooms and Roman piazzas, barrooms and butcher shops—and imagined locales such as Satan's Hell or the Never Never Land of *Peter Pan*. They also can create uniquely conceived visualizations that layer interpretations and social, political, or aesthetic references to the scripts they accompany. Sound designs can create scores that enhance (or contrast with) the play's actions by means of musical or other sonic themes, thereby underlining romance, tension, or grief. Or sound designs can punctuate and disrupt the play's actions with the cacophonous noise of traffic, jungle cries, or warfare.

The first stage in creating a play's design is a conceptual one, during which design *ideas* emerge from the designers' reading of the script, researching its historic, intellectual, and stylistic context, and imagining its potential impact on the expected audience. These ideas are shared with the play's director (who may have initiated this process with ideas of his or her own), with the playwright (if a living playwright is part of the conceptual process), and with the production designers in other areas. Although the director normally oversees these conversations, artistic collaboration is absolutely fundamental to this conceptual period of a play production's creation.

For the visual designer, conceptual ideas may be almost instantly translated into mental images, both general and specific. Such images may be expressed first in words—such as "gloomy clouds," "El Greco blues," "delicate archways," "broken bottles," "black, black, black"—but they will soon lead to stabs at representation: quick sketches, photos torn from magazines, color samples and swatches. The sound designer may likewise contemplate resonances of "medieval chanting," "random gunfire," "baroque harpsichords," or "winds in the reeds," and then compose or hunt down sounds that could give others on the design/directing team a sense of where they are heading at this stage.

Gradually, a comprehensive design emerges from the repeated sharing and building upon these contributions, normally guided—with a hand that may be sometimes quite gentle and sometimes quite firm—by the director and, of course, the budget. For the visual designer, a physical presentation of proposed designs normally involves colors (primary, earthy, gloomy, pastel), textures (rough, shiny, delicate, steely), shapes (angular, spiraling, blockish, globular), balance (symmetrical, natural, fractal), scale (towering, compressed, vast), style (realistic, romantic, period, abstract, expressionist), and levels of detail (gross, fine, delicate), as rendered in drawings, digitized representations, three-dimensional models, fabric samples, and other media. For the sound designer, designs may move in the direction of music underscoring (retreating brass bands, lush violins, ominous chords), ambient noises (distant sirens, gunfire, ocean breakers), and enhanced, reverberated, or digitally manipulated live sounds (voices, footsteps, door slams), gathered into digitized recording media.

Thomas Umfrid's realistic scenery for a production of Noel Coward's *Hay Fever*, a comedy set in a well-to-do theatrical family's English country home in the mid-1920s, is beautifully realized for this production at the 2003 Utah Shakespeare Festival. Umfrid's set forcefully projects the action of the play through a skillful arrangement of staircase, doors, and landing. The showy flapper-age costumes were designed by Kevin Alberts, and the posh lighting was designed by Lonnie Alcaraz.

All these representations are shared among the artistic and technical staff, analyzed for cost and required labor in construction, and evaluated for their individual merit as well as their joint impact. How will the final, synthesized design *look*? How will it propel the *action* of the play? What will it communicate to the expected *audience*? How will it tie the actors to the audience, the drama to the theatre in which it is staged, and the play's events to the real life that goes on outside the theatre's door?

Those are the questions the designer considers from the initial moment of conception to the opening performance.

WHAT DESIGN DOES

Theatrical design in the twenty-first century presents a wide-open field for artistic creativity. While a play normally has thousands of lines for the actors to speak, and hundreds of implicit or explicit stage directions

The traditional elements—fire and water—can be major scenic pieces, as exemplified in this astonishing 2005 Icelandic production of George Büchner's 1839 *Woyzeck,* staged by Reykyavik's Vesturport Theatre with a water-filled, stage-wide fish tank in which Woyzeck drowns his girlfriend, Marie, and eventually himself. The play is a German pre-expressionist classic about the impoverishment of working-class life in the nineteenth century. Woyzeck, modeled on a real person, is an uneducated army private, tormented by officers and doctors, taunted by his girlfriend, and cuckolded by his company's drum major. His watery murder and subsequent suicide constitute the play's grim climax. Ingvar E. Sigurdsson is Woyzeck; Nina Dogg Filippusdottir, beneath him, is Marie. Gisli Orn Gardarsson directed.

for the director to stage, it rarely provides more than brief descriptions for its setting or costumes. At the beginning of *Waiting for Godot,* for example, playwright Samuel Beckett simply writes, "A country road. A tree. Evening." He then launches directly into the opening dialogue, leaving us to wonder: What sort of road should this be? What sort of tree? Where is it in relation to the road? And how dark an "evening" is it? Later in the play Beckett provides another stage description: "The light suddenly fails. In a moment it is night. The moon rises at back, mounts in the sky, stands still, shedding a pale light on the scene." But how is all this accomplished? How much darker does the stage get? What does the "moon" look like: full? crescent? How quickly does it rise? How suddenly does it stop? And

what is it made of: projected light? a wooden cutout on a wire? And if a wire, is it meant to be seen or should it be invisible to the audience? Or is the moon simply a lantern carried by an actor—as in the "Pyramus and Thisbe" play embedded in Shakespeare's *A Midsummer Night's Dream*?

And what do *Godot*'s actors *wear*? We read in the dialogue of bowlers, boots, and coats, but what do these garments look like? What colors should they be? How worn? Are they clean or dirty? well-fitted or too large? or too small?

More questions: How *old* should the characters appear to be? Should any have long hair? facial hair? fat bellies? missing teeth? And what sounds might surround them: birds? wind? passing cars or airplanes?

Most Americans can imagine what a shabby motel room on California's Mojave Desert might look like, but Bunny Christie's scenic and costume design for this 2006 London production, with lighting by Mark Henderson, beautifully sets up the bleak but sensual atmosphere (notice the red dress and the blue and yellow light pouring through the closed blinds) for the action of Sam Shepard's explosive drama of lust and longing, *Fool for Love,* which is set in such a locale. Though deceptively "realistic" in apparent detail, the room looks like no actual motel room in the world. Juliette Lewis is the intensely passionate May, and Martin Henderson is her on-and-off boyfriend Eddie. Lindsay Posner directed at the Apollo Theatre.

sounds of war? nothing? Should the characters' voices sound natural? be amplified? Should they reverberate?

And what *else* might be there besides the road, tree, and moon?

Those sorts of initial questions are posed and addressed by the production's designers and the technicians who execute their designs. But they also lead to questions of a different order. What are the dominant *feelings* the audience might be expected to experience when they first see the stage? What feelings should be evoked afterward? Should audience members find the environment mundane? shocking? hopeful? depressing? Is the environment human or otherworldly? ancient or futuristic? archetypal or unpredictable? What *world* should the audience enter when the curtain or lights come up and the play begins?

There are certainly as many designs for *Waiting for Godot* as there are designers to tackle this particular script, and the same is true of any play. No matter how detailed the playwright's directions may be, the design team and their collaborators ordinarily shape the production's visual and audio elements as they see fit.

SCENERY

Scenery is usually what we first see—either when the curtain rises in a traditional proscenium production or as we enter the theatre if there is no curtain—and the scene designer is usually listed first among designers in a theatre poster or program. Scenery, however, is a relatively new design area. Costume, makeup, and masks are far more ancient. Scenery was not needed at all in

Contemporary eastern European design is almost always radically abstracted from realism. In his design for *Waiting for Godot*, Romanian Silviu Purcarete (who also directed) set aside Beckett's stage directions entirely and created a setting of iron scaffolding and plastic sheeting. The play's iconic tree was raised above the actors' heads; only its roots were shown. A prompter sat on the stage, following the script and playing a gong. At the end of each act a three-piece combo appeared at the rear of the stage—at the end of act 1 wearing full-body bunny costumes, at the end of act 2 bare-headed and hacking furiously at their instruments rather than playing them. The staging certainly emphasized the play's "absurdity" but was oddly affecting as well.

the Egyptian *Abydos Passion Play* or the Greek dithyramb, and it probably played little part in early Greek or Roman drama, save to afford entry, exit, and sometimes expanded acting space (such as platforms that rolled onto the stage) or to provide a decorative backdrop (by painted panels or rotating prisms) later in the period. In much Asian theatre, scenery remains rare or even nonexistent; this is the case in most Chinese xiqu and—apart from the elaborate stage-house itself—in Japanese nō drama as well. Nor was scenery of paramount importance in the outdoor medieval or public Elizabethan theatres, apart from a few painted set pieces made to resemble walls, trees, caves, thrones, tombs, porches, and the occasional "Hellmouth." Prior to the seventeenth century, most of drama's scenic aspects were part of, or dictated by, the architecture of the theatre structure itself.

The development of European indoor stages, artificially illuminated, fostered the first great phase of scene design: a period of painted, flat scenery. Working indoors, protected from rain and wind, the scenic designers of Renaissance court masques and public spectacles were for the first time able to erect and position painted canvases and temporary wooden structures without fear of having the colors run and the supports blow away. And with the advent of controllable indoor lighting in the nineteenth century (first by gas, then by electricity), designers could illuminate settings and acting areas as they wished, leaving other parts of the theatre building, such as the audience area, in the dark for

the first time. By that time designers could create both realistic illusion and extravagant visual spectacle—and have the audience focus on their work without worrying about the weather outside the theatre doors.

The result was that a new class of theatre artists came to public consciousness. Early designers such as Sebastiano Serlio (1475–1554), Aristotile da Sangallo (1481–1551), and Giacomo Torelli (1608–1678) in Italy, Inigo Jones (1573–1652) in England, and the Frenchman Jean Bérain (1637–1711) became as prominent as the playwrights whose plays they designed. Indoor stage scenery, painted in exquisite perspective, took on even greater sophistication under the artists of the Royal and Romantic eras in the eighteenth and nineteenth centuries. The proscenium format, which was created primarily to show off elegant settings, has largely dominated theatre architecture ever since.

The painted flat scenery that the proscenium gave rise to has been only one of many competing scenic formats in the modern era, usually divided into two general categories. *Realistic* scenery attempts to depict, often in great detail, a specific time and place in the real world where the play's events are presumed to take place. *Metaphoric* scenery favors, instead, visual images that seek to evoke (or to suggest, abstract, or make a visual statement about) the production's intended theme, mood, or social/political implications. Metaphoric scenery tends to remind us—at least when we first see it—that we are in a theatre, not in a bedroom or butcher shop, and

The arch frames the action.

Backstage activity is concealed.

Proscenium

Unencumbered acting space

Varied viewing perspective

Thrust

Actors (and audiences) can enter from all 4 corners.

The action is truly surrounded.

Arena

A simple space able to adapt to a variety of staging styles

"Experimental" atmosphere

Black Box

Illustrated here are the four basic staging formats: proscenium, thrust, arena, and black box. Deciding where to locate the stage in relation to the audience is the first consideration in theatre design. Drawing by John Von Szeliski.

seeks to draw us more deeply into the play's larger issues and concerns. And although stage design today most often combines realism with metaphor—these terms are best described as end points on a continuum rather than purely exclusive categories—these complementary design goals have each contributed mightily to the important position of scenery in the theatrical experience today.

Realistic settings carry on the tradition of illusionism established in eighteenth-century painted scenery. At that time, an ingeniously arranged assembly of "wings" (vertical, flat scenery pieces standing left and right of the stage), "borders" (horizontal, flat scenery pieces hung above the stage), and "drops" (short for *backdrops:* large, flat scenery pieces at the rear of the stage), painted in perspective, created the lifelike illusion of offices, dining rooms, servants' quarters, and factory yards of many a dramatist's imagination. By the nineteenth century, this "wing-and-drop set," as it was known, yielded to the "box set": a three-dimensional construction of interconnected hard-covered "flats" (representing the walls and occasionally the ceilings of a real room), which was then filled with real furniture and real properties taken from ordinary real-world environments. The box set is very much alive today and is indeed a major scenic format

for contemporary domestic drama (particularly comedy) on New York's Broadway, in London's West End, and at many community and college theatres across America. Though no longer voguish (it rarely wins design awards), the box set fulfills the staging requirements of a great many domestic comedies, thrillers, and serious, linearly structured dramas, particularly those requiring interior settings. Moreover, by adding three-dimensional features, they allow for acting and playwriting opportunities unachievable in wing-and-drop scenery, providing solid, three-dimensional staircases to descend, doors to slam, windows to climb through, bookcases to stash revolvers in, and grandfather clocks to hide characters in. Public fascination with realistic scenery reached its high-water mark in the ultrarealistic "theatre of the fourth wall removed" of the late nineteenth century, during which the box set was used to such advantage that it helped foster a uniquely architectural theory of theatre—that it should represent life exactly as it is normally lived, but with one wall removed so the audience could look in upon it.

Metaphoric scenic design, in contrast, tends to be more conceptual than literal, more kinetic than stable, more theatrical than photographic. The use of scenic metaphor is hardly new. In the 4,500-year-old *Abydos Passion Play*, two maces represent Set's testicles, and a

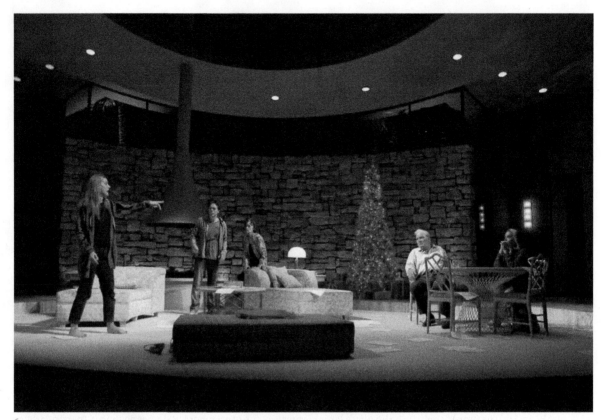

More thematic than literal, this setting by John Lee Beatty for the Broadway production of Jon Robin Baitz's 2011 *Other Desert Cities* abstracts the main elements—furniture, fireplace, overhead lamps, and curved stone wall—of a contemporary living room for a wealthy retiree (Lyman Wyeth, played by Stacy Keach, seated second from right) in Palm Springs, California. Costumes were designed by David Zinn and the lighting by Kenneth Posner; the other actors, left to right, are Rachel Griffiths, Thomas Sadoski, Judith Light, and Stockard Channing.

red stone indicates the Eye of Horus. In his prologue to *Henry V*, Shakespeare apologizes for the "unworthy scaffold" of his stage and begs his audience to use their "imaginary forces" to complete his scenic illusion—which during that play probably included a door opening under the stage balcony where the audience could imagine the English army storming "unto the breach" of a castle wall in France. These are scenic "abstractions" in the most elemental sense: they present reality by a sign rather than by *trompe l'oeil* ("eye-deceiving") realism.

The modern sense of metaphoric scenery began with the theoretical (and occasionally practical) works of designers Adolphe Appia (1862–1928) and Edward Gordon Craig (1872–1966), both of whom urged the fluid use of space, form, and light as the fundamental principle of dramatic design. Today, aided by technological advances in motorized, computer-controlled lighting and scene-shifting, the movement toward a more conceptual, abstract, and kinetic scenography has inspired impressive stylizations around the world. Shafts and walls of light, transparent "scrims," sculptural configurations, wall-size photo and video projections, mirrored and burlapped surfaces, "floating" walls and rising staircases, and "found" or "surreal" environments have all become major scenic media over the past fifty years. Sometimes these scenic designs go far beyond the stage itself. For her design for the 2010 Broadway emo-rock musical *Bloody Bloody Andrew Jackson*, for example, designer Donyale Werle surrounded the audience on all sides and over their heads with blood-red lights and drapes, 500 cat food cans, junk shop rubble, and what Werle called lots of "animals, beer and porn," including a huge (and fake) dead horse, hung upside down over the awed spectators in the center rows. The impact was to implicate the entire audience as complicit in the reckless and often corrupt

Theatre design is not limited to stage scenery, costumes, and lighting. Scenic designer Donya Werle made over the Bernard Jacobs Theatre from floor to ceiling (including an upside-down stuffed horse) for the 2010 Broadway rock musical *Bloody, Bloody Andrew Jackson.*

behavior of our country's seventh president. Such metaphoric settings rarely establish clear, specific locales, but they are powerfully effective in establishing moods, styles, and in cases like *Andrew Jackson,* violent emotional reactions.

Postmodern design elements made their appearance in the theatre of the 1980s and 1990s. Because the postmodern emphasizes disharmonies and associations, it travels a somewhat different path from the departures of modernist innovators such as Craig and Appia. Much as postmodernism, as a dramatic movement, suggested the "death of isms"—that is, a lack of any single, overarching idea or set of rules—postmodern design is identifiable by its conscious disruption of unifying stylistic themes, replacing them with what at first may seem random assemblages of different and unrelated styles. We can think of postmodern design as "quoting" historical periods or intellectual sources to disrupt the linear flow of consistent imagery or effect. Postmodern design also tends to reconfigure, or blatantly refer to, the theatre facility itself with (for example) painted scenery deliberately made to look scenic, particularly in contrast to seemingly arbitrary found objects strewn about the set, and with theatrical devices meant to comment on—and to mock—their own "theatricality."

Successful postmodern design is not merely an intellectual exercise, however. Its ability to combine disparate historical elements and highlight theatrical artifice can, at its best, surprise and provoke the audience while resonating with the deeper themes of the play. Bob Crowley's setting for Tom Stoppard's *The Invention of Love* (see the photo in the chapter titled "Global Theatre Today"), portraying the English poet and classical scholar A. E. Housman, is a postmodern deconstruction of Roman architectural and sculptural forms, reflected in the River Styx in Stoppard's version of the classical Hades (the mythological Greek world of the dead). And Richard Hudson's 1997 *The Lion King* (see the same chapter) filled Broadway's New Amsterdam Theatre—stage and house alike—with multiple and ingenious recapitulations of African, Asian, and American avant-garde design in a joyous celebration of the theatre's truly global virtuosity.

The best scenic design today is so much more than mere "backing" for the action of a play. It is instead the visual and spatial architecture of the play's performance, an architecture that when fully realized is *intrinsic to the play's action:* it is the place *where* the play exists; it also determines exactly *how* the play exists and, along with other factors, helps reveal the play's deepest meanings.

Stagecraft

Quince's "Significant" Moon

Shakespeare understood and at times apologized for the pictorial limitations of the scenery of his time ("Piece out our imperfections with your thoughts," he advised the audience in the prologue to *Henry V*). But he also appreciated its capacity to signify—rather than merely depict realistically—the world of his plays. In Shakespeare's *A Midsummer Night's Dream*, the character Peter Quince is seen directing a production of "Pyramus and Thisbe" with a group of amateur actors and pondering the "hard things" this play requires, mainly the effect of moonshine in a bedroom chamber. One actor, finding that the moon will be shining on the night of performance, suggests they simply open the window and let the real moon shine in. Quince, however, prefers that an actor hold up a lantern to "disfigure, or to present" the moon. The created "scenic" moon is preferred to the real one because it *signifies* moonshine; it is intentional and consequently meaningful rather than accidental and therefore meaningless. To indicate a "wall" in the same play—the other "hard thing"—Quince refrains from bringing in a real wall and instead has another actor put on "some plaster or some loam" so as "to signify wall."

Life may be a tale, as Shakespeare's Macbeth says, "full of sound and fury, signifying nothing," but the theatre tells tales that signify a great many things. Thus scenery's function is not merely to depict but to signify—to "make a sign," to be "significant."

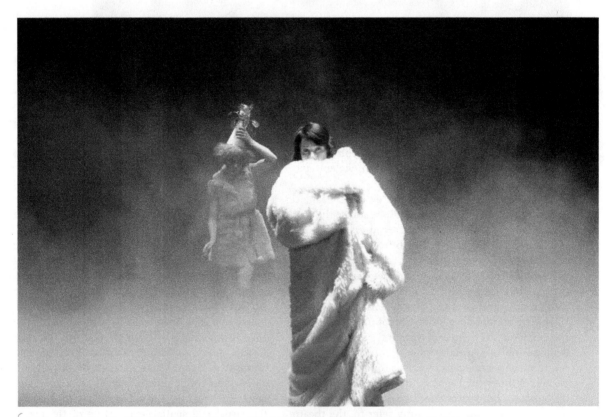

The "scenery" designed by Katrin Brack for Chekhov's *Ivanov*, as produced by Berlin's Volksbühne in a 2008 Los Angeles tour, consisted almost entirely of stage fog. Within a towering rectangular surround of white fabric, Brack created a "wall of mist" that billowed up from the floor, dividing the stage in half so characters could make their entrances and exits by simply walking forward or back through the fog. Because the play, Chekhov's first, is largely about a Russian community beset by depression, despair, and anxiety, Brack's setting—with great support from Henning Streck's lighting—completely captured the confusion of the characters and the malaise of their pre-Revolutionary society. Bulgarian-born Dimiter Gottscheff was the director.

Scenic Materials

Scene designers begin their work with the words of the text and the images in their minds, but at a certain point they begin to concentrate on the materials

Ming Cho Lee's great realistic setting for Patrick Meyer's adventure drama *K-2* portrays a ledge in the Himalaya mountains. It even feels cold.

with which a design will be physically realized. The traditional materials they have been using over the past four centuries—wood, canvas, and paint—were in the twentieth century extended to include nearly every form of matter known to (or created by, or found by) humankind: metals, plastics, masonry, and fabrics; earth, stone, fire, and water; fog, smoke, rain, light projections, and live animals.

Platforms, flats, and draperies are traditional building blocks of stage scenery and remain important. The *platform* is perhaps most fundamental: all theatre requires is "two boards and a passion," goes an old adage (variously attributed to Molière, Lope de Vega, and Ben Jonson, among several others), and the boards represent the platform stage that elevates the actor above the standing audience. Multiple platforms can create different height levels that provide actors with elevated spaces where they can be seen over the heads of other actors and stage furniture. A stage setting with several well-designed platform levels, normally with the highest at the rear of the (proscenium) stage, permits the audience to see dozens of actors simultaneously. *Flats*—sturdy wooden frames covered in various hard surfaces (such as plywood) and then painted or otherwise treated (pierced with doors and windows, adorned with paintings or moldings)—can realistically represent walls, ceilings, or pretty much any flat surface a designer might wish. *Drapery* is the great neutral stuff of stage scenery: black hanging drapes are conventional to mask (hide) backstage areas and overhead lighting instruments, and a stage curtain (typically but not necessarily dark red) may separate the stage from the audience to indicate, with its rise and fall, the play's (or act's) beginning and end.

In addition to these three primary components of stage settings, unique special objects, or *set pieces*, frequently become focal points for an overall setting design or even for the action of a play. The tree in *Waiting for Godot*, for example, is the primary scenic feature of that play's setting, symbolizing both life and death. The moment when Vladimir and Estragon "do the tree"—a kind of exercise in which each man stands on one leg with the tree between them—is a profound moment of theatre in which set piece and actors coalesce in a single image echoing the triple crucifixion on Calvary, where, as Vladimir recollects earlier in the play, two thieves died alongside Christ. Similarly, the massive supply wagon hauled by Mother Courage, in Bertolt Brecht's epic play of that name, gives rise to a powerful visual impression of struggle and travail that may last long after the characters' words are

The horticultural set, dominated by a giant beehive at its center, was designed by Tim Hatley and proved the virtual star of Charlotte Jones's *Humble Boy,* which played at the New York City Center in 2003.

forgotten. And what would *Prometheus Bound* be without its striking cliff (however it may be designed), onto which Prometheus is bound by iron chains? No matter how stylized this element may have been in its original realization, it must have radiated to the Athenian audience a visual poetry every bit as eloquent as the verbal poetry with which the play's author supported it. Such unique set pieces tax the imagination of author, director, designer, and scene technician alike, and the masterpieces of scenic invention can long outlive their makers in the memory of the audience.

A host of modern materials and technological inventions add to the primary components from which scenery is created. *Light* as scenery (as opposed to stage lighting, discussed later) can create walls, images, even (with laser holography) three-dimensional visualizations. Banks of sharply focused light sent through dense atmospheres (enhanced by electronically generated haze that simulates smoke, dust, or fog) can create trenches of light that have the appearance of massive

solidity yet can be made to disappear at the flick of a switch. Image *projections* (see later in this chapter) can provide visuals either realistic or abstract, fixed or fluid, precise or indefinite. *Scrim,* a loosely woven, gauzy fabric long a staple of theatre "magic," is opaque when lit from the audience's side but almost transparent when lit from behind, and is thus employed to make actors and even whole sets seem to instantly appear or disappear, simply with the flick of a switch on the light board.

Stage machinery—power-driven turntables, elevators, hoists, fully tilting stage floors (or "decks"), effortlessly gliding rooms (on "wagons"), and the like—can create a virtual dance of scenic elements to support and accompany the dramatic action. The ancient Greeks well understood the importance of such mechanical devices and used flying machines and rolling carts to deliver gods and corpses to the onstage action. More tricks and sleight-of-hand techniques were invented in the medieval theatre (where they were called "trucs" and

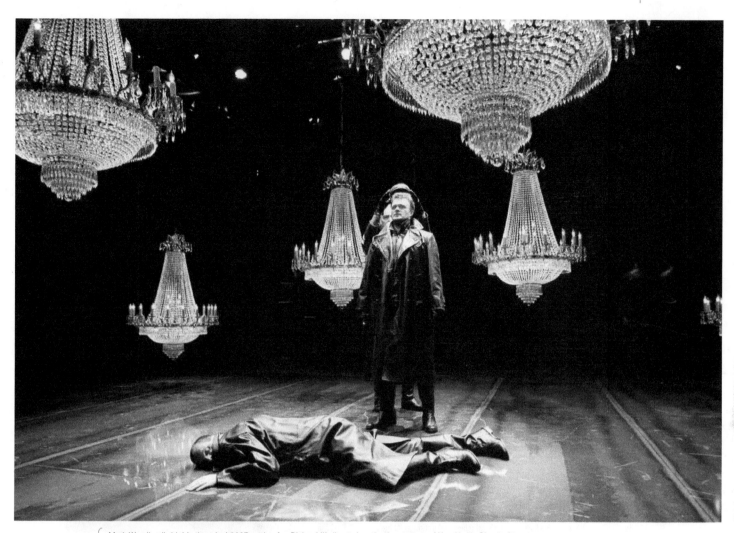

Mark Wendland's highly theatrical 2007 setting for *Richard III*, directed on the thrust stage of New York's Classic Stage Company by Brian Kulik and Michael Cumpsty—who also played Richard (seen here being crowned)—was largely made up of hanging chandeliers, which rose and fell to change the varying locales of the play. "Day, yield me not thy light; nor, night, thy rest!" cries Richard, which may have sparked interest in Wendland's design motif.

"feynts"), imparting a certain sparkle of mystery that Shakespeare picked up—*Macbeth* includes three mysterious "Apparitions," a reappearing "Ghost," and the stage direction "Witches vanish." Today, the choreography of these appearances and disappearances, and even the gliding of the scenery during scene changes, may be as much a part of the performance as the scenery itself.

Sound is also considered by the scenic designer, who must plan for the actors' footfalls as well as for the visual elements around them. The floor of a Japanese nō stage, for example, is meant to be stamped on, and it must be designed and constructed to produce a precisely "tuned" vibration. The European scenographer Joseph Svoboda designed a stage floor for *Faust* that could be either resonant or silent, depending on the arrangement of mechanisms concealed underneath. When Faust walked upstage, his steps reverberated; when he turned and walked downstage, his steps were suddenly silent—and we knew that the devil Mephistopheles had taken his body.

Properties (*props*) and *furniture* are often handled by separate artists, usually called prop masters, working under the guidance of the scene designer. They are crucial not only in establishing realism but also in enhancing mood and style. Although furniture often functions in the theatre as it does in real life—to be sat on, lain on, kicked over in a fit of anger—it also has a crucial stylistic importance. Often stage furniture is designed and built in imaginative ways to convey a special impact. Properties such as ashtrays, telephones,

(*Above*) Neil LaBute's *The Mercy Seat,* about a couple who were presumed killed in the September 11, 2001, World Trade Center attack but who were actually having a secret affair in an apartment across town, lends itself to both realistic and highly stylized stagings. Robert Jones's entirely realistic setting beautifully sets off Sinead Cusack's effusive exhilaration as Abby (with John Hannah as Ben) in London's Almeida Theatre production of 2003.

(*Right*) Alex Hard's setting for the Zurich Schauspielhaus production of *The Mercy Seat* in the same year (2003) focuses on the situation rather than on the characters, making the play—as directed by Christina Paulhofer—less personal but more intensely political.

letters, and tableware are usually functional in realistic plays, but they can have aesthetic importance and symbolic significance, such as the poisoned "union" (pearl) that Claudius throws into Hamlet's drink, or the map of England that King Lear divides to give his daughters. How these props are designed helps shape the contours of the plot and the audience's perception of the characters. Some props are even raised to titular importance, such as the glass figurines in Tennessee Williams's *Glass Menagerie* and the adding machines in Elmer Rice's *Adding Machine.* No prop is too small, or too insignificant, to escape the scene designer's and/ or prop master's attention.

The Scene Designer at Work

The scene designer's work inevitably begins with several re-readings of the play, normally followed by research on the play and its original period (and the periods in which it may be set), a consideration of the type of theatre in which the play is to be produced, and extensive discussions with the director and other members of the design and production team. Scenic design usually is a collaborative process engaging the director, other designers, the principal technical staff, and whoever establishes and manages the budget.

The discussion phase normally proceeds almost simultaneously with the designer's preparation of a series of visualizations, which may begin with collected illustrations (for example, clippings from magazines, notations from historical sources, color ideas, spatial concepts) and move on to sketches of individual settings, *storyboards* that illustrate how the sets will be rearranged or used in each scene, digital or handcrafted color renderings of the set elements, and often three-dimensional models, which will help the director and design team fully understand how the set will work and be put together. Eventually, these lead to a set of *working drawings* and other materials that will guide the eventual scenic construction.

Throughout the process, of course, the designer must gain the approval of the director and producers and reckon with necessary budgetary constraints and the skills of the construction staff that will execute and install the finished design. Part architect, part engineer, part accountant, and part interpretive genius, the scene designer today is one of the theatre's premier artists.

Bob Crowley, one of the leading scenic designers working today, is pleased to share examples of his design process with readers of this book. Pictured here is his model of the basic classroom setting for Alan Bennett's 2004 *The History Boys*. Although the shape of the classroom is unlike any in the real world, it projects the play's action perfectly. The overhead fluorescent tubes dominating the set are not required for actual lighting but convey the institutional rigidity of modern education, against which both teachers and students struggle to engage—and assert—their basic humanity.

(*Above*) Shown here is Crowley's classroom setting as realized for the Royal National Theatre premiere of *The History Boys*, which went on to receive the English Olivier and Broadway Tony best-play awards.

(*Right*) This is Crowley's model showing his design for the Banks family household—emphasizing the kitchen—in the popular 2004 London and 2006 Broadway musical *Mary Poppins*, for which Crowley received the Tony Award for best design of a musical. The meticulous setting, in which individual rooms can be closed off or revealed by the addition of an exterior facade, provides a focus for the individual areas while still maintaining the overall architecture of the play's center: an integrated English family home.

Photo Essay: Scene Designer Scott Pask

Scott Pask is one of the leading scenic designers in America today. With an undergraduate degree in architecture (University of Arizona) and M.F.A in scene design from the Yale School of Drama, he has built an outstanding design record on and off Broadway, in London, and in regional American theatre, earning six Tony Awards (for *The Pillowman*, each of the three plays that make up *The Coast of Utopia*, and the 2011 hit musical *The Book of Mormon*) in the six years prior to our 2012 interview. Other Pask productions include recent Broadway revivals of *Hair*, *Les Liaisons Dangereuses*, *Nine*, *La Cage Aux Folles*, *Speed the Plow*, *Pal Joey*, and *Promises, Promises*, and the Broadway premieres of important new plays including *A Behanding in Spokane*, *Impressionism*, *The Vertical Hour*, *The Lieutenant of Inishmore*, and *Take Me Out*.

This is how Scott answered some of my questions:

RC: Why did you head into design?

SP: I first trained as an architect, but while pursuing that education, I started thinking about narrative structure and remembering how much I was intrigued with theatre. So I decided to take an elective course at the music theater department at the university, and I loved it. Then I trained in Italy for a semester, studying the architecture and how the Baroque and Renaissance architects explored fluidity and space, and how they manipulated the space to make it more dramatic. That was a huge revelation. So when I finished my degree in architecture I knew what I wanted to do—come to New York and work in theatre design.

I began working with people who were creating performance art projects downtown and in experimental dance companies. Then I interned on a film and afterward did quite a bit of art direction. But as the films were getting bigger and the schedules were getting longer (and I was getting a little older, having been in New York for five years), I realized I had to move with that trajectory in mind if I was going to study theater—and that's when I decided to go to Yale. A kind of "now or never" moment.

1.

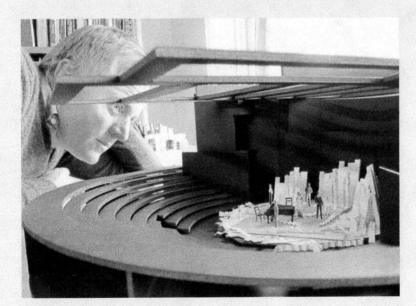

2.

1. Scott Pask at his design table in his studio overlooking New York's Union Square.

2. Pask studies his model for the upcoming (2012) production of Stephen Sondheim's *Merrily We Roll Along* which he is designing for the Cincinnati Playhouse in the Park.

1c... "Two by Two"   THE BOOK OF MORMON

3.

3a... Ugandan Village   THE BOOK OF MORMON

4.

3. Pask's model for the first scene of *The Book of Mormon,* showing the false proscenium, which is seen throughout the play and shown here in the opening Salt Lake City scene.

4. When the action moves to Uganda, Africa, the set model changes radically.

RC: And what is your basic process?

SP: Whether a musical or a dance or film or opera, I have to start with the script. I tend first to do small thumbnails—little sketches to put some thoughts and ideas on the page. And then I research

and start looking at images, whether it's the period of the play or a place for the action. And then I'll storyboard, first very roughly, and then I'll go into a rough model to get spatial relationships and try to articulate some of my ideas in three dimensions. Then I start modeling, talking back and forth with the director and choreographer, showing them the development, hearing their responses, and honing our work to where we want it to head as the model becomes more developed and more detailed.

RC: How did you develop *The Book of Mormon?*

SP: I imagined it as a pageant, which is why the portal for the show is so important ... we are always experiencing the material of the show through that viewfinder. I had been a part of a religious pageant or two while in elementary school, so putting it within the context of that frame seemed important from the beginning.

From there the design moved in stages. The first pageant in the opening moments of the show dissipates, and we're suddenly in a dark blue void singing 'Hello!' and then at a training room with a vista of Utah behind it, all very bright and colorful and shiny. We used metallic automotive paint with an inherent glitter to make it sparkle, to make it all luminous. I collaborated with Brian [MacDevitt, the lighting designer] to give everything a halo—every piece of architecture, each planet, each tree—which would have light emanating from every possible angle. And then we go from these cool colors—the blues, the ice blues, the royal blues of Utah—to a very expressionistic and textured world of Africa (the opposite of the very presentational views of Utah), with warm and darker colors within burnt, distressed portals of tattered and torched fabric wings and borders.

RC: And how about *Hair,* which you first did in Central Park and then moved to Broadway?

SP: We really did four productions of it. First, it was a summer concert in Central Park's Delacorte Theatre, for which we had simply painted the floor black and put in a bandstand since

6. Pask's design for the 2010 Broadway revival of *Hair*, designed as if to suggest that the "Tribe" had created it themselves.

5. Pask's Ugandan village in *The Book of Mormon*, as actually realized on the stage. The splendid costumes were designed by multi-Tony-winning Ann Roth.

8. Pask's setting for the Cincinnati Playhouse in the Park 2009 production of Chekhov's *The Three Sisters*, adapted by Sarah Ruhl, was a masterpiece of utterly decayed splendor. Moving the time period to the early years after the Russian revolution, Pask created a Soviet takeover of the sisters' home, with broken furniture, industrial wiring, fluorescent lighting, crumbling yellowed walls, and misery in every corner. John Doyle directed; Hannah Cabell, in the faded yellow sweater, plays Irina—the only member of the family character who, until the final moments, still has hope.

7. Pask goes to his well-stocked "tool chest" of supplies for model building and materials.

9. Pask's setting and costume design for Martin McDonough's grim 2010 *Behanding in Spokane*, about a man (played here by Christopher Walken) who is still searching for his left hand that was amputated 47 years ago, captures the pathos of the main character's life and environment, exemplified by the brightness of the light behind him—which might be seen as the promise of his long-lost youth. Zoe Kazan plays a con artist who pretends to know where his hand is.

that was about all we had time and money for. But that taught us a lesson about scale; *Hair* has an energy that wants to come into the audience, and when we came back to the Delacorte for a full production the following year, we wanted to embrace the expanse of it, while making the production feel intimate. So I created a semicircular wall nearly midway on the expansive stage that reflected the architecture of the theater. It became something the "Tribe" [the group of 1960s hippies that comprise the cast] climbed over to invade the space, make it theirs, and thus begin their evening. I wanted to have nature as close as possible, so we did tons of planting right behind that constructed wall, to match the existing architecture of the theater. People walked in and said, "They're using the Delacorte without a set?" Many had no idea that our wall was built and distressed to match the existing wooden texture, color, and age [of the theatre], and that there were trees brought in and grass—and that's what it should be: an authenticity of space and a complicity of gesture, an architectural intervention by which the Tribe came in, invaded the space, and put on their show. Because it

had been such a success in the Park, moving into a Broadway theatre that fall created a real challenge. The one thing I had on my side was that energy can be more easily contained onstage indoors, where the play's optimism and hope and excitement can come right at you. Indoors, people are looking up at the stage rather than down onto an amphitheater, and so the wall motif—the architectural intervention—is very important. Indeed, it's the statement of the show. So the tribe came in and threw their rugs down and painted something on the wall and called it their space, claimed it as their own. And by the end, when sunlight and the mural's color has completely faded, and there's snow and they all put coats on, the optimistic commentary has gone away and is replaced by a plea for "let the sun shine in—Please!" I feel that true art can come from a place of upset, from people trying to find their way in the world, and from the "what's-next" of things, so the wall became a character of its own.

RC: So your design is more about narrative and ideas than about decor?

SP: For me *decorative* is a bad word. I'll even look at something of my own work mid-process and think—is that

just decorative?—What is it trying to say? What is it doing?

You can create the realistic elements that are there, but how do you make it theatrical? How do you address the space where we watch the action? In whatever era the play takes place, we all know we're watching it *today*; that's the main thing. That's something I obsess about. Keeping the theatre that I help to create as contemporary and progressive as I can.

RC: Do you have any advice to young potential designers?

SP: I began as an artist and I think art classes are always going to be useful—any class that has you manipulating materials and paint. I also think it's important to develop your visual acuity, to go see exhibitions, to pick up on what art things are happening, to visit cities, travel, find spaces that are inspiring. Go to churches. Go to Washington D.C., and see the Capitol and the museums. There are amazing things at our fingertips useful toward understanding visual perception and space.

But basically, I think design is intuitive. It's about your gut. Intuit as much as you can. Be sensitive to the things around you—and to yourself, and especially to how it relates to the piece you are working on. Listen to what your mind or instincts are telling you.

LIGHTING

The very word *theatre*, meaning "seeing place," implies the crucial function of light. Light is the basic precondition for theatrical appearance. Without light, nothing can be seen.

But stage lighting is not simply used for illumination. The manipulation of light for dramatic effect can be traced back to the earliest surviving plays. *Agamemnon*, by Aeschylus, was staged so the watchman's spotting of the signal fire heralding Agamemnon's return to Argos coincided with the actual sunrise over the Athenian skene (stagehouse). It is also probable that the burning of Troy at the conclusion of Euripides' *Trojan Women* was staged to coincide with the sunset that reddened the Attic sky. Modern plays commonly use light in metaphoric and symbolic ways, such as the blinking neon light that intermittently reddens Blanche's quarters in Williams's *A Streetcar Named Desire*, and the searching *follow-spot* (a swivel-mounted lighting instrument that can be pointed in any direction by an operator) that Samuel Beckett calls for to train upon the hapless, trapped characters in his play, *Play*.

Although it is customary to think of theatre lighting as dating from the invention of electricity, nothing could be more misleading. Lighting has always been a major theatrical consideration. In addition to coordinating the timing of their plays to the sunrise and sunset, the ancient Greeks paid a great deal of attention to the proper orientation of their theatres to take best advantage of the sun's rays. The medieval outdoor theatre, though as dependent on sunlight as the Greek theatre was, made use of several devices to redirect sunlight, including halos made of reflective metal to brighten the faces of Jesus and his disciples. In one production a highly polished metal bowl was held over Jesus' head to concentrate the sun's rays, and surviving

Individual pools of light illuminate the parasols and costumes—and the isolation—of ladies waiting for the soldiers' return at the beginning of *Much Ado about Nothing*. This Indiana Repertory Theatre production was directed by Libby Appel, with lighting design by Robert Peterson.

instructions indicate that when cloudy skies obscured the sun, medieval stagehands would substitute blazing torches for the bowl.

It was in indoor stagings, however, that lighting technology attained its first significant sophistication. In a 1439 production of the *Annunciation* in Florence, one thousand oil lamps were used for illumination, and a host of candles were lighted by a "ray of fire" that shot through the cathedral. One can imagine the spectacle. Leonardo da Vinci designed a 1490 production of *Paradise* with twinkling stars and backlit zodiac signs on colored glass. By the sixteenth century the great festival lighting of indoor theatres, located in manor houses and public halls, served as a symbol of the intellectual and artistic achievements of the Renaissance itself, a mark of the luxury, technical wizardry, and exuberant humanism of the era. People went to theatres in those times simply to revel in light and escape the outside gloom—in much the same way today's moviegoers, from early in the twentieth century, might go to the cinema to escape the heat of summer days.

By the Renaissance, the sheer opulence of illumination was astonishing—even though the entire effect was created simply from tallow, wax, and fireworks. Raphael "painted" the name of his patron, Pope Leo X, with thirteen lighted chandeliers in a dramatic production; Sebastiano Serlio inserted sparkling panes of colored glass (the predecessors of today's *gels*) which, illuminated from behind, created glistening and seductive scenic effects. The "Sun King" of France, Louis XIV, ordered a 1664 presentation at Versailles that featured twenty thousand colored lanterns, hundreds of transparent veils, bowls of colored water, and a massive display of fireworks—all displaying his (presumed) incendiary brilliance.

The inventions of gaslight in the nineteenth century and electric lighting thereafter—first in carbon arcs and "limelight" lighting, later in incandescence, and most recently with light-emitting diodes (LEDs)—have brought stage lighting into its contemporary phase, permitting it to favor the shaping of dramatic action more than simply being ostentatious and "showy." Ease and flexibility of control are the cardinal virtues of both gas and electric lighting. By adjusting a valve, a single operator at a "gas table" could raise or dim the intensity of any individual light or preselected "gang" of lights just as easily as we can raise or lower the fire on a gas range with the turn of a knob today. And with electricity—introduced in American theatres in 1879 and in European theatres the following

year—the great fire hazard of a live flame (a danger that had plagued the theatre for centuries and claimed three buildings a year on average, including Shakespeare's Globe) was at last over. The round-the-clock staffs of fire crews in every major nineteenth-century theatre were dismissed, and the deterioration of scenery and costumes from the heat, smoke, and carbon pollution produced by a live flame similarly came to a halt.

Electrical lighting also had the great advantage of being fully self-starting—it did not need to be relit or kept alive by pilot lights—and it could easily be switched off, dimmed up and down, and rehanged or reconnected simply by fastening and unfastening flexible wires. Within a few years of its introduction, electricity became the primary medium of stage lighting in the Western world, and great dynamo generators—for electricity was used in the theatre long before it was commercially available from municipal power supplies—were installed as essential equipment in the basements of theatres from Vienna to San Francisco.

Electricity provides an enormously flexible form of lighting. The incandescent filament is a reasonably small, reasonably cool point of light that can be focused, reflected, aimed, shaped, and colored by a great variety of devices invented and adapted for those purposes, and electric light can be trained in innumerable ways upon actors, scenery, audiences, or a combination of these to create realistic or atmospheric effects through dimensionality, focus, animation, distortion, diffusion, and overwhelming radiance. Today, thanks to the added sophistication of computer technology and microelectronics, it is not uncommon to see theatres with nearly a thousand lighting instruments all under the complete control of a single technician seated in a comfortable booth above the audience.

Contemporary Lighting Design

Today, the lighting for most productions is conceived and directly supervised by a professional lighting designer, a species of theatre artist who has appeared as a principal member of the production team only since the mid-twentieth century. By skillfully working with lighting instruments, hanging positions, angles, colors, shadows, and moment-to-moment adjustments of intensity and directionality, the lighting designer can illuminate a dramatic production in a variety of subtle and complex ways. The manner in which the lighting designer uses the medium to blend the more rigid design elements (architecture and scenery) with the evolving patterns of the movements of the actors, the colors and fullness of their costumes, and the meanings of the play is normally a crucial factor in a production's artistic and theatrical success.

Visibility and *focus* are the primary considerations of lighting design: visibility ensures that the audience sees what it's meant to see, and focus ensures that it sees this without undue distraction. Visibility, then, is the passive accomplishment of lighting design, and focus is its active accomplishment. The spotlight, a development of the twentieth century, has fostered something akin to a revolution in staging. Contemporary productions now routinely feature a darkened auditorium (a rarity prior to the 1880s) and a deliberate effort to illuminate certain characters (or props or set pieces) more than others—in other words, to direct the audience's attention toward those visual elements that are dramatically the most significant.

Verisimilitude and *atmosphere* also are common goals of the lighting designer, and both can be achieved largely through the color and direction of lighting. Verisimilitude (lifelikeness) is crucial in realistic dramas, where the style generally demands that the lighting appear as if emanating from familiar sources: as from the sun, from "practical" (real) lamps on the stage, or from moonlight, firelight, streetlights, neon signs, or perhaps the headlights of moving automobiles. Atmospheric lighting, by contrast, need not suggest any particular source and can be used simply to evoke a mood appropriate to a scene or to a moment's action: gloomy, for example, or sparkling, oppressive, nightmarish, austere, verdant, smoky, funereal, or regal.

Sharp, bold lighting designs are frequently employed to create highly theatrical effects—from the glittery entertainments of the Broadway musical tradition to harsher experimental stagings like those often associated with the plays and theories of Bertolt Brecht. Brecht's concept of a "didactic" theatre favors bright, cold (uncolored), and deliberately "unmagical" lighting. Brecht suggested, in fact, that the lighting instruments be made part of the setting, placed in full view of the audience; this "theatricalist" use of the lighting instruments themselves is now widespread even in nondidactic plays. Moodier plays may employ dense or unnatural colors, "gobo" templates that break light beams into shadowy fragments (such as leaf patterns), or atmospheric "fog" effects that make light appear misty, gloomy, or mysterious. The Broadway-type musical, in contrast, often makes splashy use of banks of colored footlights and border lights, high-intensity follow-spots that track actors around the stage, "chaser" lights that flash on and off in sequence, and a seemingly fuse-busting incandescence that makes a finale seem to burn up the stage. In fact, this traditional exploitation of light has done as much to give Broadway the name "Great White Way" as have the famous billboards and marquees that line the street.

Stylized lighting effects are often used to express radical changes of mood or event; indeed, the use of lighting alone to signal a complete change of scene is an increasingly common theatrical expedient. Merely by switching from full front to full overhead lighting, for example, a designer can throw a character into silhouette and make her or his figure appear suddenly ominous, grotesque, or isolated. The illumination of an actor with odd lighting colors, such as green, or from odd lighting positions, such as from below, can create mysterious, unsettling effects. The use of follow-spots can metaphorically put a character "on the spot" and convey a specific sense of unspeakable terror. Highly expressive lighting and projections, when applied to a production utilizing only a cyclorama (a scenic backdrop at the rear of the stage, often representing the sky), a set piece, sculpture, or stage mechanism and neutrally clad actors, can create an infinite variety of convincing theatrical environments for all but the most resolutely realistic of plays. It is here, in the area of stylization and expressive theatricality, that the modern lighting designer has made the most significant mark.

The Lighting Designer at Work

The lighting designer ordinarily conceives a design by synthesizing many discrete elements: the action and ideas of the play, discussions with the director and other members of the design team about the approach or concept of the production, the characteristics of the theatre building (its lighting positions, control facilities, and wiring system), the scenery and costume designs, the movements and behavior of the actors, and the available lighting instruments. Occasionally the availability of an experienced lighting crew must also be a consideration. Because not all of these variables can be known from the outset (the stage movement, for example, may change from one day to the next right up to the final dress rehearsal), the lighting designer must be skilled at making adjustments and must have the opportunity to exercise a certain amount of control, or at least to voice concerns with regard to areas affecting lighting problems.

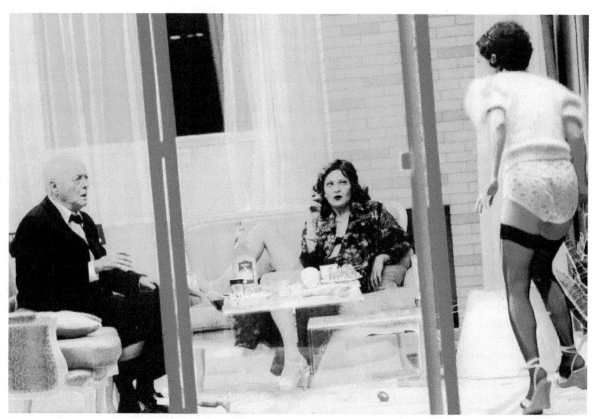

Lighting Designer Rainer Casper's radically contrasting lighting colors—even in the same scene—create wholly different indoor and outdoor environments in Bert Neumann's set for *The Insulted and Injured*.

The lighting by Peter Mumford makes Tim Hatley's setting for Noel Coward's *Private Lives* an enchanting hotel facade, whose Mediterranean-facing balconies offer the promise of an elegant—but perhaps empty—life. Alan Rickman and Lindsay Duncan star in this production on Broadway in 2002.

Shown here is Tom Ruzika's light plot for the 2003 Broadway production of *Six Dance Lessons in Six Weeks* (substantially reduced in size to fit this page). You are looking down from the theatre's ceiling; the stage is at the top of the drawing, and the audience area (the "house") is at the bottom. The gray rectangles on each side indicate the vertical sides of the proscenium; the "CL" symbol is the center line of the stage and house, and each bomb-shaped symbol is an individual and specific lighting instrument. "Practicals" are lighting or other working electrical instruments that are part of the scenery but are also connected ("wired") into the lighting control system (the "board"). The light plot tells the electrical staff where instruments are to be hung, where (roughly) they are to be aimed, and how they are wired to the board.

Ordinarily, the two major preparations required of the lighting designer are the light plot and the cue sheet. A *light plot* is a plan or series of plans showing the placement of each lighting instrument; its type, wattage, and size; its wiring and connection to an appropriate dimmer; its color; and sometimes its physical movement, since lighting instruments are increasingly being electronically programmed to pan, tilt, or change color by remote control. A *cue sheet* is a list of the occasions, referred to by number and keyed to the script of the play (and then to the stage manager's *prompt book*, and eventually his or her *calling book*), to

indicate the precise moments the lights are to move and/or change color or intensity. Both light plot and cue sheet are developed in consultation with the director and other members of the design team, who may take major or minor roles in the consultation, depending on their interests and expertise. Inasmuch as some productions use hundreds of lighting instruments and require thousands of individual cues, the complexity of these two documents can be extraordinary; weeks and months may go into their preparation. In today's theatre the cues resulting from this lengthy process are almost always then programmed into a computer program capable of executing them with the necessary speed and precision.

The lighting designer works with a number of different types of lighting instruments and must know the properties of each well enough to anticipate fully how it will perform when hung and focused on the stage. If you glance up at the grid above the stage or at the pipes above and to the sides of the audience, you will see the huge range of instruments from which the designer makes a selection.

Fixed-focus spotlights are the main instruments for lighting stage action; they come in two main forms. The *ellipsoidal reflector spotlight* (*ERS*—but sometimes called "lekos" by old-timers after the company that popularized them) has a sharply defined conical shape and is the instrument of choice for intense, hard-edged, and closely focused lighting. The circular ERS beam is easy to shape: four shutters can frame it from different sides, an "iris" can tighten its radius, and "gobos"— metal templates—placed into the instrument can project silhouettes of almost any variety. The *fresnel* (pronounced 'fren-ELL') *spotlight,* named for its French-designed lens (originally used in lighthouses), has by contrast a generally less defined and less shapeable beam. It is most often used for general (wash) lighting, backlights, and downlights.

Other common lighting instruments are even less focused. *Parabolic aluminized reflectors,* or *PARs* ("cans"), can be used for color washes and general lighting. *Striplights,* banks of PARs or floodlights, are used to light drops, cycloramas, and other broad areas. Specialty instruments include follow-spots—whose high-intensity and manual operation allow for "following" an actor (for example, during a solo dance number)—and *automated lights,* which can be computer-programmed to instantly change direction, color, and beam size at the mere touch of a button. Though more common in the musical theatre, follow-spots and automated lights are beginning to make an impact in "straight" (nonmusical) theatre as well.

The most exciting new development in lighting technology is the LED, which creates an electroluminescence that can now deliver sufficient lighting intensity and color control to rival many incandescent sources. While costing more at the outset, LEDs prove considerably less expensive in the long run since they are vastly more energy-efficient and environmentally friendly than incandescent bulbs. LEDs are now widely found in PAR cans, strip lights, moving color washes, and the "LED walls" used in large image and video projections (see the Projections section later in this chapter). In the coming years, LEDs may develop sufficient intensity to provide the light source for spotlights and fresnels as well.

Few theatres have the time or space flexibility to permit much on-site experimentation in lighting design; thus the development of the light plot and cue sheet takes place primarily in the imagination and, where possible, in workshop or free experimentation apart from the working facility. This limitation places a premium on the designer's ability to predict instrument performance from various distances and angles and with various color elements installed. It also demands sharp awareness of how various lights will reflect off different surfaces.

Once the light plot is complete, the lighting instruments are mounted (hung) in appropriate positions, attached to the theatre's circuits (wiring system), "patched" to proper control channels (dimmers), focused (aimed) in the desired directions, and colored by the attachment of frames containing "gels" (plastic color media).

Once the instruments are in place and functioning, the lighting designer begins setting the intensities of each instrument for each cue. This painstaking process involves the programming of thousands of precise numerical directions into the computer software from which an operator will execute the cues during performances. And finally, the lighting designer presides over the working and timing of the cues, making certain that in actual operation the lights shift as subtly or as boldly, as grandly or as imperceptibly, as desired to support and complement the play's action and achieve the design aesthetic.

Great lighting design springs out of thousands of details, most of them pulled together in a single final week or two. Gradations of light, difficult to measure in isolation, can have vastly differing impacts in the moment-to-moment focus and feel of a play. Because light is a medium rather than an object, audience members are rarely if ever directly aware of it; they are aware only of its illuminated target. Therefore, the lighting designer's work is poorly understood by the theatergoing public at large. But everyone who works professionally in the theatre—from the set and costume designers to the director to the actor—knows what a crucial role lighting plays in the success of the theatre venture. As the Old Actor says as he departs the stage in off-Broadway's longest-running hit, *The Fantasticks:* "Remember me—in light!" The light that illuminates the theatre also glorifies it; it is a symbol of revelation—of knowledge and humanity—upon which the theatrical impulse finally rests.

📷 Photo Essay: Lighting Designer Don Holder

1.

With two Tony Awards (for the Broadway production of the 1997 *Lion King* and the 2008 Lincoln Center revival of *South Pacific*) on his shelf, and eleven Tony and Drama Desk nominations for his forty Broadway and eighty-six off-Broadway shows to date—which since the last edition include *Spider-Man, Turn off the Dark, Arcadia, The Motherfucker and the Hat, Annie, Leap of Faith,* and *Golden Boy,* not to mention his innumerable regional theatre productions—Don Holder is clearly at the very top of the American lighting design field. In addition, he has had the opportunity to ride and master the entire new wave of technological sophistication that has propelled a truly revolutionary new era of stage design.

Like many designers, Holder became fascinated by lighting at a very young age. A self-admitted "music and drama addict" from the days his parents drove him from their Long Island home into Manhattan to see symphonies, ballets, and Broadway musicals, Holder began to light shows while still in junior high. "I did band concerts, high school plays,

everything I could. I was also the guy at scouting camp who was always lighting the campfires and putting smudge pots on the trails," he remembers. Adoring the outdoors, Holder majored in forestry at the University of Maine's Orono campus, but he also played in jazz bands and the Bangor Symphony during the school year and worked summers as a technician and actor at Maine's Theatre at Monmouth. Inspired by a designer there, he applied for graduate training at Yale Drama School, enrolling first as a stage technician and eventually as a lighting designer under the mentorship of fabled Broadway designer Jennifer Tipton. After Yale, Holder headed directly into a New York career, working first in small off-Broadway and off-off-Broadway companies and then making his Broadway debut with Richard Greenberg's *Eastern Standard* in 1989.

Holder describes his design aesthetic as supportive: "My basic goal is to bring out the play's text, the composer's music, and the director's vision. I strongly feel our job as designers is to adapt our own style and design aesthetic to the specific production; to help tell the story, of course, but also to augment the story's context and style." The path to excellence, however, is in the details. "I suppose I am characterized as meticulous," Holder freely admits. "My work tends to be quite detailed—specific rather than

2.

1. In a workroom above the Mark Taper Forum stage in Los Angeles, where he is designing a production of the musical *Pippin,* Lighting Designer Donald Holder makes final marks on his light plot. Soon he will turn it over to the theatre's electricians to hang and focus the hundreds of lighting instruments that will be used in the show.

2. In the light booth, Holder looks up at stage left (the right side of the stage, as seen from the audience) to see how the lighting will work with the scene as described in his script.

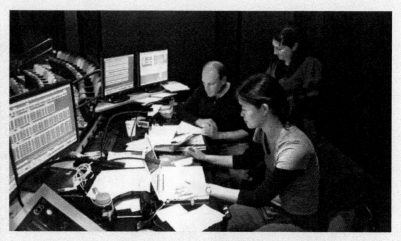

4. As technical rehearsals begin, Holder and his two assistants, in the light booth at the rear of the auditorium, enter the light cues into computers that will be used to operate the lighting during the show.

3. In the front rows of the audience, Holder discusses the scene with *Pippin* director Jeff Calhoun.

5. What time of day is it? And what mood? These are the issues the lighting designer addresses. Holder created the dawn on a tropical island in the South Pacific for the 2007 Broadway revival of the musical by that name, seeking to establish the beauty and tranquility of the scene before the battles of World War II arrived in this part of the world.

7. For Arthur Miller's *A View from the Bridge*, staged at Minneapolis's Guthrie Theatre in 2008, Holder had the delicate task of making Miller's realistic characters seem to "pop out of the scenery" without the audience being aware of how the lighting has so focused their attention on the actors. The background (which in an actual living room would be just as bright) all but disappears. John Arnone designed the scenery and Robert Perdziola the costumes for this production.

6. Holder's lighting for the famous balcony scene in *Romeo and Juliet*, as staged in the New York Public Theatre's outdoor stage in Central Park, isolates the two lovers (played by Oscar Isaac and Lauren Ambrose) against the park's Belvedere Castle and magnificent trees, which are more subtly illuminated. The light also casts subtly romantic reflections in the water-filled seventy-foot round "lake" beneath Romeo's feet, a feature of Mark Wendland's scenic design.

general, layered rather than spare. I'm certainly obsessive about craft—I start with a strong take on each scene and then detail each moment. This means that my lighting tends to be very densely cued and shaped." Holder cites as an example his 2009 production of the musical *Pippin* at the Mark Taper Forum in Los Angeles on which he was working at the time of this interview: "It's just two hours long but it has six hundred light cues. But every detail retains the sense of the big picture."

With a strong background in music, Holder finds himself often engaged in shows "that require a romantic, lyrical, and above all *musical* treatment— but this is not limited to the music in musicals (like *Pippin*) alone. Indeed, he accounts his love of music as a reason why he has often been tapped to design the premieres of August Wilson's "straight" plays. "I think that August's work is so

poetic and operatic, his storytelling is so rich, his sense of history, religion, and magic have such a depth, and there are so many undercurrents running through the body of his work that there's always much more underneath these plays than what you see on the page. I think my style of lighting is well suited to Wilson's work, since so many of his characters seem like they're stepping out of straight dramatic acting and singing arias. His work has a musicality, an operatic quality, a mythic proportion that I simply love. So there's a certain amount of freedom and liberty I can take by stepping out of reality, heightening things, making things larger than life, and responding to the play emotionally rather than intellectually. And so my work becomes very personal."

Holder's career has taken flight during an extraordinary evolution of lighting technology, which has fit exceptionally well with his careful craftsmanship. "When I broke into the theatre, the theatres I worked at were still employing manual dimming systems, so my work was wholly dependent on the skill of the person running it. Indeed, I was at the mercy of the light board operator. And as my work requires every light to be

specifically cued and crafted, I would become despondent when mistakes were made. So I greeted the age of computerized control with open arms. For me it changed everything: my lighting could become more fluid and more creative, and I didn't have to lower my expectations because of technical issues. And then came automated lighting [AL]— motorized moving lights that I first used when I designed *The Lion King*. That show was huge—with scenery constantly flying in and out, an animal parade through the audience to begin the show, and a band that played in the theatre's boxes above the audience. [Director] Julie [Taymor] had conceived the show within a constantly changing skyscape, a "lightscape" actually, that included a whole spectrum of colors—not just three or four—that were to continuously cross-fade with each other. I needed to have six colors on every single surface of the setting! And since I simply didn't have enough space in the theatre to hang all the lights I wanted, or to provide the level of detail and specificity the show required, or even to light the environment—the "dance space on steroids" as we called it—I simply had to use AL. It was incredible—as, for example, in the opening

8. Holder creates light and dark at the same time in this sunset scene from the 2011 Broadway production of Tom Stoppard's *Arcadia*, directed by David Leveaux. The play takes place in two time frames: the present, and 1809, which is pictured here. Since there was no electricity at that time, Holder has created a moonlight ambience to capture the period as well as the atmosphere.

sequence, when several luminous clouds were to rise in sequence while at the same time the sky was changing from twilight to dawn to noon and everything was in a constant state of motion. With AL, one instrument can replace fifty, and so that's how I did it. And when the director wanted to change something, I could do it right from my seat—without ever taking out a ladder or refocusing a light or changing a gel [color agent]. This became a revelation to me!"

Holder thinks of his lighting as both impressionistic and specific. Impressionistic "because the artists I'm most inspired by are the impressionists; they speak to me in a profound way." And specific because "my mantra is craft, sweating the details, really controlling the composition, which must be impeccably crafted." When these two elements are brought together by Holder, the art of stage lighting rises to luminous achievements.

COSTUMES

Costumes have always been a major element in the theatrical experience. They are vehicles for the "dressing-up" that actors and audiences alike have always considered a requirement for the fullest degree of theatrical satisfaction. Costumes serve both ceremonial and illustrative functions.

The Functions of Costume

The first theatrical costumes were essentially ceremonial. The *himation* (a gownlike costume) of an original performer in *Prometheus Bound* was derived from the garment worn by the priest-chanter of the dithyramb; the comic and satyr costumes, with their use of phalluses and goatskins, were likewise derived from more primitive god-centered rites. The priests who first enacted the *Quem Queritis* trope (liturgical text) in medieval Europe simply wore their sacred albs, hooded to indicate an outdoor scene but otherwise unaltered. The actors of the classic Japanese nō drama also wore—and wear today—costumes that relate more to spiritual sources than to secular life. These ancient uses of costuming served primarily to separate the actor from the audience, to "elevate" the actor to a quasi-divine status. They became indeed larger than life in the fourth century B.C. Greek theatre, where principal actors wore thick-soled *kothurnoi* so as to stand much taller than ordinary humans—a literal "dressing-up" that gave their characters a superhuman magnitude.

By the time of the Renaissance, the ceremonial costuming of the ancient theatre had given way, at least in the West, to costumes designed to distinguish individual characters and historical periods. The Italian commedia dell'arte boasted dazzling, highly distinctive costumes so each of its traditional characters—such as Arlecchino with his multi-colored patches, Pantalone with his red tights, red cap and slippers, and Il Dottore with his black cap and ankle-length black coat—could be instantly identified by what they wore. Elizabethan actors were often favored by their patrons with the gift of their cast-off but still elegantly detailed garments. Such costumes valued distinction over historical accuracy: while a 1595 drawing of an Elizabethan production of Shakespeare's *Titus Andronicus* shows the ancient Roman general wearing a toga appropriate to his historical era, it also portrays other male characters wearing standard Elizabethan attire.

Modern costuming, however, is based on an overall design plan. This became important during the

Plays often indicate design colors for symbolic importance. In *A Streetcar Named Desire,* playwright Tennessee Williams emphasizes the raw sexuality of cardplaying New Orleans workingmen by specifying that they wear "bright primary colors," while the delicate lady who visits them has the name of Blanche—French for "white"—and dreams of her deceased gay husband, named Grey. In this 2002 London production, designer Bunny Christie underlines Williams's color symbolism by clothing Glenn Close, as Blanche, in a white dress, white hat, and sheer white gloves and accessorizing her with a sheer white handkerchief and white rosebuds in her hair.

eighteenth and nineteenth centuries, as realism began to arrive in Western theatre. Realism led to an interest in *historical accuracy* in design, which required consistency, and by the early 1800s, painstaking efforts would be made to ensure that the design of *every* costume in a play (along with every prop and set piece) was accurate to its era. Thus a production of *Julius Caesar* would recreate the exact clothing worn in first century B.C. Rome, a *Hamlet* production would mirror the dress and architecture of medieval Denmark, and a costumer for *Romeo and Juliet* would seek to make garments just like those worn in Renaissance Verona.

The passion for historical accuracy no longer dominates the world of costume design, but it left an

Robert Wilson's *Les Fables de La Fontaine* is a hugely imaginative stage re-creation of the stories of France's greatest fabulist. Here Bakary Sangaré plays the Lion and Céline Samie is Circé in "The Lion in Love." The 2005–2006 Comédie-Française production, directed and designed by Wilson, was immensely popular with both adults and children at this historic theatre.

important residue: the *conceptual and holistic approach to a show's overall design*. This approach is no longer historical but *stylistic*. It communicates attitudes, themes, feelings, and ideas rather than historical pictures. And, when historicity is involved, it may be of a period unrelated to the one set by the author: *King Lear,* for example, has been played as variously taking place in medieval Japan, the Iran-Iraq War, and today's Africa. Costume design, in the twenty-first century, is generally an imaginative art that conveys not just a set historical period or a group of stereotyped characters but a view of the world of the play—as it intersects with a view of the world of today.

Modern costume design serves four separate functions. First, it retains at least a hint of the ceremonial magic once conjured by ancient priests and shamans. Even today, costume demonstrates a primordial theatricality. As Theoni Aldredge said of the clothes she designed for *A Chorus Line,* they "had to look real and

yet theatrical enough for an audience to say, 'Okay, I'm in the theatre now.'"

Second, the costumes of a play show us what sort of world we are asked to enter, not only its historical place and period but its social and cultural values as well. The word *costume* has the same root as *custom* and *customary;* as such it indicates the "customary" wearing apparel (or the "habitual habit") of persons living in a particular world. For example, the Mexican American characters in Luis Valdez's *Zoot Suit,* set in the 1940s, are seen as virtual extensions of the overly long pegged trousers and looping watch chains referenced by the play's title. Tennessee Williams, in *A Streetcar Named Desire,* specifically directs the poker players to wear shirts of "bright primary colors," to contrast their primary sexuality with Blanche DuBois's dead (and gay) husband, whom the dramatist had named "Allan Grey." The ensemble of costumes in a dramatic production reveals the social and cultural environment of its collective characters.

Third, the costumes can express the specific individuality of each character's role. They may reveal at a glance, for example, the character's profession, wealth, age, class status, tastes, and self-image. More subtly, costume can suggest the character's vices, virtues, and hidden hopes—or fears. By the judicious use of color, shape, fabric, and even the movement and sound the fabric makes, costume designers can imbue each character with distinct qualities that contrast that character to the others in the play. When Hamlet insists on wearing his "inky cloak" and "suits of solemn black" in his uncle's presence, for example, he silently signifies his refusal to accept his uncle's authority, and his adversarial position vis-à-vis the Danish court. The garments therefore become both a mark of Hamlet's character and a significant action in the play. When Monsieur Jourdain, in Molière's *The Bourgeois Gentleman,* dons his fancy suit with the upside-down flowers and, later, his Turkish gown and grotesque turban, he is proclaiming (albeit foolishly) to his peers that he is a person of elegance and refinement. And Estragon's unlaced boots in *Waiting for Godot* represent—pathetically, to be sure—his great wish to be unfettered, not "tied to Godot" but simply free, fed, and happy.

Finally, and perhaps most practically, the costume serves as wearable clothing for the actor! For a costume, of course, is indeed clothing; it must be functional as well as meaningful and aesthetic. The actor does not model costumes; he or she walks, sits, duels, dances, and tumbles downstairs in them. Indeed, unless the character is a prisoner or a pauper, we are supposed to

(*Left*) "Blood will have blood," says Macbeth after the killing of Duncan. Stage blood is the costume designer's and makeup artist's nightmare, for the costumes (or at least some costumes) have to be worn afresh at the next performance. But blood is fundamental to the theatre, certainly in most tragedies (which stem from rituals involving blood sacrifices), and solutions must always be found. Here Liev Schreiber as Macbeth and Jennifer Ehle as Lady Macbeth try to cover their murderous tracks in Moisés Kaufman's production for Shakespeare in the Park at New York's Delacorte Theatre in 2006.

(*Below*) Blood need not be portrayed realistically. In this *Macbeth* production directed by Mihai Maniutiu at the Romanian National Theatre Festival, the designer Valentin Codoiu created blood-papers that were spewed across the stage floor.

believe that the character actually chose the costume and really *wants* to wear it! Thus the costume designer cannot be content merely to draw pictures on paper but must also design workable, danceable, *actable* clothing, for which cutting, stitching, fitting, and quick changing are considerations as important as color coordination and historical context. For this reason, costume designers generally collaborate very closely with the actors they dress.

The Costume Designer at Work

The costume designer begins, as all designers do, with ideas about the play's action, themes, historical setting, theatrical style, and the impact the play might have on the expected audience. Collaboration with the director, who ordinarily takes a leading role from the start, and with the other designers is important even at this early stage, as ideas begin to be translated into possible fabrics, colors, shapes, and time periods.

Fabrics exist in many textures and weaves and can be cut, shaped, stitched, colored, and draped in innumerable ways. But fabrics can also be augmented (or even replaced) by leather, armor, jewelry, feathers, fur, hair (real or simulated), metallic ornamentation—in fact, any material known to exist. The designer selects or at least oversees the acquiring of all materials. Often costumes are acquired whole. For contemporary plays with modern settings, some or all costumes may be selected from the actors' own wardrobes, purchased from thrift shops, or bought at clothing stores. Costumes have even been solicited as gifts. In a celebrated instance, Louis Jouvet appealed to the citizens of Paris after World War II to donate their fancy prewar clothing to provide costumes for the premiere of Jean Giraudoux's *The Madwoman of Chaillot*. The spectacular garments that poured into the Athénée theatre for that brilliant 1945 Parisian production signaled to the world that France had survived the scourge of Nazi occupation with its devotion to the theatre intact.

It is, however, the production designed and built entirely from scratch that fully tests the measure of the costume designer's imagination and ability. In such productions, the designer can create a unique design, matching his or her conception of the text with hat-to-shoe originality. The comprehensive design for such a production moves from the conceptual period to a developmental one. The designer usually compiles a portfolio of images from his or her research, creates a series of quick sketches (sometimes called

Stagecraft

Importance of Small Details

"The task of subtly distorting uniformity, without destroying the desired illusion, is a difficult one. Anton Chekhov's play *The Three Sisters* presents a case in point. The characters of the male players are clearly defined in Chekhov's writing, but because the men are all wearing military uniforms they are theoretically similar in appearance. One of the few ways in which the designer can help to differentiate between characters is by the alteration of proportion; changes such as these, which do not show enough from the "front" to make the uniforms seem strange to the audience, can be extremely effective, as well as helpful to the actor. In a London production of *The Three Sisters*, Sir Michael Redgrave [as Baron Tusenbach] wore a coat with a collar that was too low; Sir John Gielgud [as Vershinin] one that was too high. No one in the audience was unaware of the characters' individuality, the talents of these actors being what they are, but the small details added to the scope of their performances."

—MOTLEY (THREE ENGLISH DESIGNERS WORKING AS A FIRM)

"roughs"), and assembles various "palettes" of possible color samples, all in the service of giving the director and the entire design team a quick idea of the design's direction without, however, including any specific designs. Once this basic direction is approved by the director, and is seen to be consonant with the work of the entire design team (and the show's budget), the designer proceeds to create actual designs. Generally they take the form of "renderings" (drawings, first in black and white and then in color) supplemented with notes about each costume's accessories, hairstyles, and construction details. Enlarged drawings provide information about items too small to show in a single head-to-toe illustration.

The acquisition of fabrics—the basic medium of the costumer's art—is the crucial next stage. Texture, weight, color, suppleness, and response to draping, dyeing, folding, crushing, twirling, and twisting are all considerations. Velvet, silks, and woolens are the costumer's luxury fabrics; cottons, felt, burlap, and painted canvas are less expensive and often very effective for theatrical use. Contemporary designers, particularly in nonrealistic productions, may also turn to unique and surprising materials: Dean Mogle, for example, adapted hundreds of greyed-down beer bottle caps into his costumes for a Utah Shakespeare Festival production of *Macbeth*. Dyeing, "aging" (making a new fabric appear old and used), and detailing are often achieved with commercial dyes, appliqués, and embroidery, and sometimes with paint, glues, and other special treatments (for example, the costume designers Motley—three women working under a single professional name—simulated leather by rubbing thick felt with moist yellow soap and spraying it down with brown paints). Before large quantities of fabric are ordered, samples or swatches can be pinned to the renderings to forestall the purchase of material at odds with the desired "look."

Costume accessories greatly affect the impact of the basic design. Occasionally they may stand out in such a way as to "make" the costume—or to obliterate it. Hairstyles (including beards and mustaches) and headdresses, because they frame the actor's face, convey a visual message every time the actor speaks a line; they are obviously of paramount importance. Jewelry, sashes, purses, muffs, and other adornments, and official badges of various sorts, have considerable storytelling impact: they "read" to the play's audience a character's rank or role in society. The lowly shoe, if unwisely chosen, can destroy the artistry of a production by being unsuitable for the character or style of the play or by being so badly fitted or so unwieldy that the actor exhibits poor posture or stumbles noisily about the stage.

Whether arrived at through design and fabrication or through careful selection from an army surplus store, good costume design creates a sense of character, period, style, and theatricality out of wearable garments. In harmony with scenery, makeup, lighting, and the play's interpretation, costuming's impact may subtly underline the play's meaning and the characters' personalities, or can scream for attention—and sometimes even become the "star of the show." Not a few musicals have succeeded primarily because the audience "came out whistling the costumes," as a Shubert Alley phrase reminds us. But even in productions of purely naturalistic drama, well-designed and well-chosen costumes can exert a magical theatrical force, and lend a special magnitude to the actor's and the playwright's art.

MAKEUP

Makeup, which is essentially the design of the actor's face, occupies a curiously paradoxical position in the theatre. In much modern production, certainly in the realistic theatre, makeup seems sorely neglected. It tends to be the last design field to be considered. In amateur theatre, makeup is likely to be applied for the first time at the final dress rehearsal—and sometimes not until just before the opening performance. Indeed, makeup is the only major design element whose planning and execution are often left entirely to the actor's discretion.

Makeup, however, is one of the archetypal arts of the theatre, quite probably the first of the theatre's design arts, and it was absolutely fundamental to the origins of drama. The earliest chanters of the dithyramb, like the spiritual leaders of primitive tribes today, invariably made themselves up—probably by smearing their faces with blood or the dregs of wine—in preparation for the performance of their holy rites. Their resulting makeup subsequently inspired the Greek tragic and comic masks that are today the universal symbols of theatre itself. The ancient art of face painting remains crucial to Chinese xiqu, as well as to other traditional Asian, African, and Native American theatre forms.

The reason for makeup's paradoxical role resides in the changing emphasis of theatre aims. Makeup, like costuming, serves both ceremonial and illustrative functions. The illustrative function of makeup is unquestionably the more obvious one today—so much so that we often forget its ceremonial role entirely. Illustrative makeup is the means by which the actor changes her or his appearance to resemble that of the character—or at least the appearance of the character as the author, director, and actor imagines it. Makeup of this sort is particularly useful in helping to make a young actor look older or an old one look younger and in making an actor of any age resemble a known historical figure or a fictitious character whose appearance is already set in the public imagination. Makeup gives Cyrano his great nose and Bardolph his red one; it reddens *Macbeth*'s "bleeding captain" and blackens Laurence Olivier's Othello; it turns the college sophomore into the aged Prospero, the Broadway dancer into one of T. S. Eliot's cats, and Miss Cathy Rigby into Master Peter Pan. Artificial scars, deformities, bruises, beards, wigs, sunburn, frostbite, and scores of other facial embellishments, textures, and shadings can contribute significantly to realistic stagecraft when needed or desired.

A subtler use of makeup, but still within the realistic mode, is aimed at the evocation of psychological traits through physiognomic clues: the modern

Photo Essay: Costume Designer Catherine Zuber

With thirty-seven Broadway shows and fifty-one off-Broadway ones glimmering on her résumé, along with several dozen regional productions around the country and abroad, Catherine Zuber is, as this edition goes to press, probably the most active costume designer in America. Her productions have netted her seven Tony Awards (*The Royal Family, South Pacific, Awake and Sing, The Light in the Piazza*, and all three parts of *The Coast of Utopia*) plus five additional Tony nominations (*Born Yesterday, How to Succeed in Business . . . , Seascape, Dinner at Eight, Twelfth Night*) and a host of other awards and tributes.

Your author met with Zuber in the tiny basement costume shop of the Shoenfeld Theatre on 45th Street, where she was making final adjustments to Jeremy Irons's costume for *Impressionism*.

1. Catherine Zuber shows your author some of the research pictures she has collected for her current design of *Impressionism* in the "costume space" allocated to her in the basement of the Broadway theatre where the play is in technical rehearsals. On the table below the pictures, you can see her black-and-white rendering of the costumes being readied for dress rehearsal.

2. Zuber and First Costume Design Assistant Nikki Moody discuss which of the newly purchased costume items could best be added to the design at this point. "We have been working together for over a year," says Zuber of Moody. "She's terrific; just out of grad school in Boston and a lot of fun."

3. Going over their collection of fabric swatches for the show, Zuber and Assistant Designer Patrick Bevilacqua are delighted to come up with a swatch they both like. "Patrick and I have a great relationship," Zuber explains. "It's a collaboration: I show him a sketch and he interprets it. And when really great assistant designers like Patrick take it a step further, it becomes a *great* collaboration!"

1.

2.

3.

4. In the basement of the theatre, Zuber and Bevilacqua test whether a new skirt goes with the already selected jacket.

5. One of the roles of the costume designer is to rivet audience attention on the play's key characters and moments. Here, as Kelli O'Hara sings the final bars of "I'm Gonna Wash That Man Right Outa' My Hair" in the Broadway revival of *South Pacific*, the actress's bright turquoise swimsuit lights up the stage—and the actress—as it pops out from the six mixed red and orange swimsuits behind her.

This wasn't her only obligation on this day, however. She had just come from a final dress rehearsal of *The Winter's Tale* at the Brooklyn Academy of Music and was about to head to Lincoln Center, where she was designing a gala performance celebrating the Metropolitan Opera's 125th anniversary.

Zuber explained that she had come to her profession from an undergraduate background in art, with a major in photography. But after college graduation and a subsequent move to New Haven, Connecticut, she happened to meet up with several Yale theatre students who, admiring the vintage clothes she liked to wear, encouraged her to design costumes for their extracurricular productions staged at Yale's undergraduate colleges. "I just loved doing this," Zuber exulted, and after a year of designing such shows she assembled a portfolio of her designs and applied to the Yale School of Drama for graduate professional training in the field. Jane Greenwood, a veteran designer who then headed the Yale costume program, was enthusiastic and Zuber was admitted. "I also had a photo portfolio," she adds. "Being a costume designer is not about costumes alone! Learning photography proved extremely helpful because it taught me how to compose an entire image—a picture of the set with characters wearing my costumes in it. Composing such images taught me how to design a show so that my costumed people would appear to *belong* in that world, to hold their own within it rather than disappearing into the scenery. Costumes then become an ensemble of characters within a rectangular image, not just clothes on a rack."

Zuber now moves easily between classic verse dramas (*Twelfth Night, The Winter's Tale*), revivals of modern comedies (*Born Yesterday, The Royal Family*), musicals (*How to Succeed . . . , South Pacific*), historical dramas (*A Man for All Seasons, Coast of Utopia)*, and new plays set in our own times (*Impressionism, Frozen, Doubt*). "I enjoy going from one style to the other," she says, though with contemporary plays "it's sometimes harder to convince the actors to wear certain things, as they all have their own ideas of how they should dress. And that's natural because in a modern realistic play the actors need to stay connected to who they are. But in a period show, actors are more trusting of the designer: there's enough distance from where they are in their everyday life, and who they are playing as a character." Zuber particularly loves designing fantasy plays, "where I have a project that must come mainly from my imagination, and where I can therefore go more 'over the top.' That's absolutely thrilling!"

6.

6. Sometimes costume uniformity is required, as in the case of "uniforms." In *South Pacific*, Zuber has given each sailor a measure of individuality by the way he wears his uniform: with his blue shirt buttoned or unbuttoned and with or without a name or initials printed on it; with his metal dog tags worn or abandoned; with his white hat brim turned up or rolled up or rolled down, or with his hat taken off entirely; and, in the case of one particularly muscular actor (Andrew Samonsky), with a plain white undershirt that stands out in the otherwise "uniform" naval brigade. Lifted by the men and holding a grass skirt is Loretta Ables Sayre as "Bloody Mary," a Polynesian native seller of exotic local products, who wears layered garments and exotic jewelry—all sharply contrasting with the bold masculinity of the sailors.

7. & 8. Every costume designer faces a challenge in Shakespeare's *The Winter's Tale*, since the play takes place in two very different locales: the deeply somber and gloom-ridden court of Sicilia, and the joyous, rustic sheep-shearing festival in far-away Bohemia. (*Above*) In Sicilia, young princess Perdita (Morven Cristie) sees what she thinks is a statue of her long-dead mother, Hermione (Rebecca Hall); Zuber has dressed each in silky white flowing dresses against the black background of the joyless kingdom. (*Below*) In Bohemia, Zuber has costumed the Bohemian country revelry in rough-textured, earth-colored, and multilayered fabrics that play brilliantly against the scenic background of dark blue sky and red, white, and blue balloons. Ethan Hawke (*center*) plays the shifty but entertaining tradesman Autolycus—a "snapper up of unconsidered trifles," Shakespeare tells us—in an unmatched ensemble of shirt, vest, and trousers; a black hat with a bright yellow flower; tall leather boots, one strapped up to his knee; doubly dark sunglasses; and with hair that straggles down to his shirt pockets. His friends strum their guitars in even more casual garb, and the women, under their loosely tied country aprons, wear rugged red, green, and orange skirts that reach the floor.

7.

8.

But no designer works wholly on her own, and Zuber is quick to point out that costume design is a "real collaboration" with those technicians who actually pattern, cut, drape, and sew the costumes that she draws. "Costume designers are very dependent on the people who make the clothes. We show them the sketch and they interpret and build it—and the really great ones take it a step further."

Technology has come to the aid of costume designers as it has all the design arts, and Zuber now finds her process greatly enhanced by Photoshop in particular. "I sketch freehand, then scan it into the computer, and then add color—and if the director doesn't like the color I can change it right away. After that, I can manipulate it any way I want. I can put all the costumes together on one page, and if I see that one character stands out inappropriately, or doesn't stand out enough, I can change this very quickly. When I was designing the last act of *Cherry Orchard* [at the Brooklyn Academy of Music in 2008], I could show the director all the characters onstage together just as they would be in the play. And on a separate page I can trace each individual character's journey so the director can see the character's trajectory through the play, so the director can say 'this character should be messier here,' or something like that. Photoshop is a fantastic tool to show what the designs will look like onstage in all these formats."

Zuber adores her profession: "I love being a costume designer! You're learning something new with each show, meeting new people, and the greatest thing is that it leaves beautiful, indelible memories. Of course, it's a lot of hard work, and while some people coming to New York may have stars in their eyes, they should know it's not very glamorous. Sometimes we have to laugh at how ridiculous our work conditions can be—just look at this room [referring to the cluttered basement workplace] for instance! But if you really have a love for it, and a passion, there's absolutely nothing like it!"

9. Zuber's exuberant 1940s lounging wear for Harry Brock (played by Jim Belushi) and Billie Dawn (Nina Arianda) in Garson Kanin's 1946 *Born Yesterday*, revived on Broadway in 2011, earned her an eleventh Tony nomination.

10. It's not all glamour, of course. Here Zuber's comically exaggerated period "uniforms" for Daniel Radcliffe and company in the "football dance" in Broadway's 2011 *How to Succeed in Business without Really Trying* helped her win her twelfth Tony nomination.

Duelist and would-be lover Cyrano de Bergerac has a large nose—indeed, that's the axis on which the entire plot of Edmond Rostand's romantic-era play of the same name turns. But most actors don't have giant noses, so makeup artists need to be experts in prosthesis—the artificial extension or replacement of human body parts. Here normal-nosed Stephen Rea sports a skillfully created prosthetic proboscis, overseen by Costume Designer John Bright, in a 2004 production of the play at England's National Theatre.

Brian d'Arcy James required ninety minutes to put on his makeup to play the title role in *Shrek* when he starred in the 2008 family-friendly Broadway musical.

no question that we form impressions of a character's inner state on the basis of observable physical characteristics—as Caesar notices and interprets Cassius's "lean and hungry look," so do we. And the skilled makeup artist can go far in enhancing the psychological texture of a play by the imaginative use of facial shapings and shadings.

Still another use of makeup, also within the realistic and practical spectrum, seeks merely to simplify and embolden the actor's features in order to make them distinct and expressive to every member of the audience. This is known as creating a face that "reads" to the house—that is, one that conveys its fullest expression over a great distance. To achieve this effect, the makeup artist exaggerates highlights and shadows and sharply defines specific features such as wrinkles, eyelashes, eyebrows, and jawlines. Such simplified, emboldened, and subtly exaggerated makeup, combined with stage lighting, creates an impression of realism far greater than any that could be achieved by makeup or lighting alone.

makeup artist may try to suggest character by exaggerating or distorting the actor's natural eye placement, the size and shape of her mouth, the angularity of her nose, or the tilt of her eyebrows. There can be

Makeup reflects ancient roots. These young African women have applied bold geometric face paint in a centuries-old design for their performance of a traditional dance-drama of the Ivory Coast based on an ancient hunting ritual. The design, originally intended not merely to entertain an audience but to suggest a magical transformation into the spirit realm, continues to carry at least the resonance of that meaning today.

An entirely different category of makeup can be described as beyond realism altogether, however. This includes makeup that is stylized, ceremonial, or represents the actor as a superhuman presence. The face painting of the traditional Chinese xiqu actor, for example, like the mask of the Japanese nō performer or the African shaman, can endow the person applying it with at least the illusion (and perhaps the inner feeling) of spiritual transcendence. Like the war paint applied in tribal rituals, stylized and ceremonial makeup allows the performer, at least in his or her (and hopefully the audience's) imagination, to become larger than life, to assume divine powers, and to ascend to (and lead the audience to) a higher world. This apparent enhancement of the actor may even be thought of as the "up" in "makeup."

Some obvious examples of such traditional makeup and "making up" are still evident, particularly in European and Asian theatre. The makeup of the circus and the classic mime, two formats that developed in Europe out of the masked commedia dell'arte of centuries past, both use bold colors: white, black, and sometimes red for the mime and an even wider spectrum for the circus clown. Avant-garde and expressionist playwrights also frequently utilize similar sorts of abstracted makeup, as does French dramatist Jean Genet in *The Blacks* (which features black actors in clownish whiteface) and German playwright Peter Handke (whose *Kaspar* features similarly stylized facial painting). And Asian theatre has always relied on the often dazzling facial coloring (and mane-like wigs and beards) of certain characters in Japanese kabuki, Indian kathakali, and Chinese xiqu—not to mention the violently expressive makeup often seen in contemporary avant-garde productions in Tokyo. The American theatre has certainly caught on to these extreme,

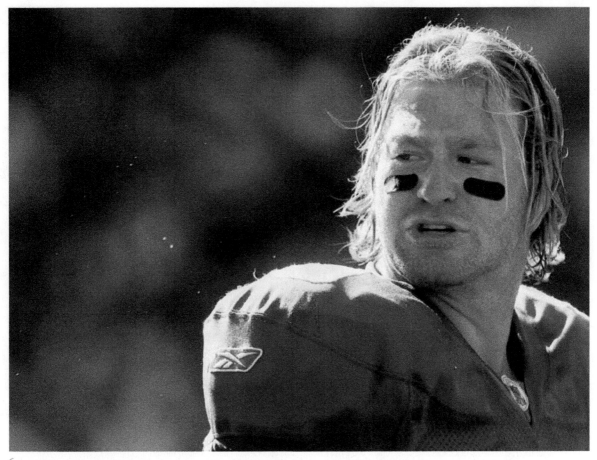

Like many football players, New York Giants tight end Jeremy Shockey applies black grease stripes under his eyes. The technique is often said to protect the player from the glare of the sun, but its real purpose—as with war paint—is to make the player look more menacing, thereby demoralizing the opposition.

and show-stopping, makeup possibilities as well. Actor Patrick Page's make-up, designed by Judy Chin, with which he changes from the character of "Norman" to that of the Green Goblin in *Spider-Man: Turn Off the Dark* (see the chapter titled "Global Theatre Today"), initially took him three and a half hours to apply, although by the time the show opened he could get it down to the necessary three minutes. Page's make-up (by Angelina Avallone) for his title role performance in *The Grinch that Stole Christmas* was similarly elaborate, as was Brian d'Arcy James's (by Naomi Donne) for the title role in *Shrek: the Musical*. As more stage plays are adapted from full-length cartoon films like these, we will certainly be seeing more radical makeups on the live stage.

In some productions, however, particularly in smaller theatres, actors go onstage with no makeup at all. Some directors, particularly in realistically acted plays, approve of this, believing it adds to the naturalness of the characters. Other directors, particularly in musicals or broad comedies, dislike it because they feel the actors' faces will "wash out in the lights." There is no fixed consensus on this debate, but avoiding makeup altogether does bypass the initial reasons for makeup's creation: to announce the actor as a performer and to establish a milieu for acting that is neither realistic nor practical but rather supernatural, mysterious, and calculatedly theatrical. The theatre artists involved, therefore—actors, directors and designers—have serious choices to make in this decision. For in the final analysis, makeup always combines the realistic and symbolic functions of theatre. Even the most stylized makeup is based on the human form, and even the most realistic makeup conveys some theatricality.

Stagecraft

The Makeup Kit

While makeup in high-budget productions may be created and applied by professional makeup artists, most actors in most productions—even on Broadway—design and apply their own, and hence travel to the theatre with a well-stocked makeup kit that consists of a foundation, color shadings, and various special applications.

The foundation is a basic color applied thinly and evenly to the face and neck and sometimes to other parts of the body as well. Creme makeup, formerly (and still commonly) known as greasepaint, is a traditional foundation material; a highly opaque and relatively inexpensive skin paint, it comes in a variety of colors. Cake makeup, or "pancake" as it is also known, is another type of foundation; it is less messy than creme but also less flexible. Cake makeup comes in small plastic cases and is applied with a damp sponge. Most foundation colors are richer and deeper than a Caucasian actor's normal skin color to counteract the white and blue tones of stage lights.

Color shading defines the facial structure and exaggerates its dimensions to give the face a sculptured appearance from a distance; ordinarily, the least imposing characteristics of the face are put in shadow and the prominent features are highlighted. Shading colors—universally called "liners"—come in both creme and cake form and are usually chosen to harmonize with the foundation color, as well as with the color of the actor's costume and the color of the lighting. Shadows are made with darker colors and highlights with lighter ones; both are applied with small brushes and blended into the foundation. Rouge, a special color application used to redden lips and cheeks, is usually applied along with the shading colors. When greasepaints are used, the makeup must be dusted with makeup powder to "set" it and prevent running. A makeup pencil is regularly used to darken eyebrows and also to accentuate eyes and facial wrinkles.

Special applications may include false eyelashes or heavy mascara; facial hair (beards and mustaches, ordinarily made from crepe wool); nose putty and various other prosthetic materials; and various treatments for aging, wrinkling, scarring, and otherwise disfiguring the skin. A well-equipped actor has a makeup kit stocked with glue (spirit gum and liquid latex), solvents, synthetic hair, wax (to mask eyebrows), and hair whiteners—in addition to the standard foundation and shading colors—to create a wide variety of makeup effects.

The theatre, after all, is never so immersed in the ordinary that it could—or should—be wholly mistaken as such. So when an American actor sitting at a makeup table opens little bottles and tubes, moistens Chinese brushes, and sharpens eyebrow pencils, more is going on than simple, practical face-making. Primal forces are at work, linking the actor not merely to the imagined physiognomy of his or her character or to the demands of facial projection in a large arena but also, and more fundamentally, to the primitive celebrants who in ages past painted their faces to assure the world that they were leaving their temporal bodies and boldly venturing into the exalted domain of the gods.

SOUND DESIGN

Music and sound effects have been in use in the theatre since ancient times. Aristotle considered music one of the six essential components of tragedy, and offstage thunder, trumpet "flourishes" and "tuckets," and "the noise of a sea-fight" are all called for in Shakespeare's original stage directions. Before the electronic age, theatres were routinely equipped with such devices as rain drums (axis-mounted barrels that, partly filled with pebbles or dried seeds, made rain sounds when revolved), thundersheets (hanging sheets of tin that rumbled ominously when rattled), and thunder runs (sloping wooden troughs down which cannonballs rolled and eventually crashed). Since 1900, most theatres have also used an electric telephone ringer (a battery-powered bell mounted on a piece of wood) and a door slammer (a miniature doorframe and door, complete with latch) to simulate the sounds of domestic life. All of these "sound effects" were ordinarily created by an assistant stage manager, among his or her many other duties. But the rapid development of audio recording and playback technologies starting in the 1970s and 1980s has led to a virtual revolution in the area of sound design and the emergence of an officially designated sound designer in theatres around the world. Like musical underscoring in cinema and sound balancing and enhancement in rock concerts, theatre sound is now almost entirely an electronic art.

Augmented sound is now routinely used in theatrical performances. Musical theatre and larger theatres increasingly employ electronic sound enhancement to reinforce the actors' voices and create a "louder than life" sonic ambiance for almost all musicals and for many straight plays. In such cases the actors usually wear miniature wireless microphones—often

Photo Essay: Sound Designer Scott Lehrer

When Scott Lehrer received the Tony Award in Sound Design for *South Pacific* in 2008, it was an honor not only for him but for sound design itself, as his award was the first Tony ever awarded in this blossoming field. Yes, Lehrer acknowledges, the Tony was "something of a culmination after working in the mines for many years," but he is also insistent that there have been many other sound design pioneers who should be recognized. "I was just lucky enough to be doing a show the year they initiated these," he modestly declares. But it certainly wasn't just luck: in the next four years he received four more Tony nominations, for his work in *Joe Turner's Come and Gone*, *Finian's Rainbow*, *A View from the Bridge*, and the 2012 Broadway production of *Death of a Salesman*.

Lehrer practiced and studied music when he went to college at Sarah Lawrence in the mid-1970s, first expanding his early love of rock, folk, and jazz and then "getting weird sounds out of synthesizers." Soon he was deep into electronic music, picking up bits of "found sound" and creating sound collages for classmate directors and choreographers to go with their performances. "I became fascinated by the entire world of sound," he explains. "It was all quite new and wonderful." Not limiting himself to drama or dance productions, he created sound for giant public events like New York's SummerStage in Central Park with 100,000 attendees, along with museum exhibitions, live industrial shows, and corporate media. But theatre beckoned strongly when he took a job as sound engineer for the Colonnades Theatre Lab, an avant-garde off-off-Broadway theatre on New York's Lower East Side. "We all worked together there," he remembers, "blending multichannel 'surround sound' into the rehearsals so that the actors would get used to hearing sounds while rehearsing, and would respond to those sounds like they responded to the other actors. Sound simply became part of their world." Lehrer didn't realize how unusual this was at the time, but in the days when offstage sound was mainly created by stage managers operating

1. Sound Designer Scott Lehrer, in the professional sound studio he has built into his apartment in lower Manhattan, builds up possible cues for a new production.

wooden, handheld "door-slamming" devices or executing "needle drops" on long-playing records played over a loudspeaker, he and his colleagues were innovating truly revolutionary techniques.

By 1980, Lehrer had moved up the ladder to off-Broadway, where he worked at many of the finest companies: Circle Repertory, Manhattan Theatre Club, the American Place, and, mainly, Playwrights Horizons, where he describes himself as "almost in residence" for many years. "We were still in the Stone Age as far as equipment was concerned," Lehrer recalls. "We had to be really creative, figure out how to do things with very little money, invent new ways of working."

No theatre technology has advanced as rapidly in the past decades as sound, Lehrer says: "Young people coming into this field today have little idea how new it all is. In just the time I've been doing all this, we've gone from records to tape decks to samplers to digital sound and music sequencers. The speed with which we can create sound design, and the level of control we have over it, have increased almost beyond belief." To create the sound of road construction that director Susan Stroman had thought of adding into her production of

Happiness, at New York's Lincoln Center, for example, Lehrer sent his assistant out to record the jackhammers then hammering away on the street outside. "I handed him my recorder at 10:00, at 10:15 I plugged the recorder into my Pro Tools [digital audio system], by 10:30 I had cleaned it up, and by 10:45 I had it in my QLab [sound software] ready to go into the show. Just a few years ago this would have taken three days!"

By the end of the 1980s, Lehrer was on Broadway, first with Wendy Wasserstein's *The Heidi Chronicles*, which received the Pulitzer Prize and the Tony Award for best play of the year, and soon thereafter designing sound for Tony Kushner's landmark *Angels in America*. By the time of writing he has designed twenty-six shows on Broadway and fifty-one off.

What, aside from a mastery of technology, does it take to be a sound designer? Lehrer does not pretend to have a single aesthetic style; rather he considers himself something of a chameleon and frames his designs in close concert with the context of the play and

2.

3.

the perspective of the director. Working with the playwright/director Richard Nelson, for example, who asks for the sound "to be a part of the storytelling, to be another character in the play," he investigates the sonic ambience of the text. For Nelson's *Franney's Way*, set in an apartment above a jazz club, Lehrer describes his challenge as creating the unseen people downstairs. "What would they be listening to? Jazz, of course, but what kind of jazz? What tempo? Cool or hot, ballad or up-tempo? Saxophone, yes, but Dexter Gordon or John Coltrane? I tried to find the musical style that would convey the ambient emotional feel Nelson wanted." For Terrence McNally's *A Perfect Ganesh*, two older American women are traveling through India. "What sort of music do they hear?" Lehrer asked himself. "There are many regions in India and many local musical forms, and it would be disrespectful to the culture not to represent this. So I have to be an amateur musicologist; I have to listen to everything from the locale, the era, and the culture that the play is seeking to represent."

Lehrer considers sound design a perfect marriage of art and technology. "You have to have something to say. Sound design is not just technical, but you absolutely have to have the skills to do it. While you can't let the technique get in the way, you also have to make it work for you. Sound design takes place in real time. When you're in technical rehearsals, if you don't know the technology you can't keep up with the speed of the rehearsal, and if that happens you simply can't realize your art. You have to control the technology; you can't let the technology control you."

2. Lehrer checks out his extensive CD library for music that might come into play in this new work.

3. At his piano, Lehrer composes a new melody that might be inserted into his design.

4. In the Mitzi Newhouse Theatre in Lincoln Center, technical rehearsals are about to get started for the world premiere of *Happiness*, with Lehrer as sound designer. A "sound table" has been placed in the theatre's auditorium where Lehrer and Drew Levy, his assistant, have set up their computers and audio equipment to create the sound cues that will be executed—and adjusted—for this afternoon's rehearsal.

5. Now, in the theatre's light booth from which the sound will be operated during actual performances, Lehrer confirms that the sound operating system—with the GO button the technician will use to execute the individual cues—is properly set up.

concealed, though in the twenty-first century increasingly visible. The use of live or recorded offstage sounds may establish locale (such as foghorns), time of day (midnight chimes), time of year (birdsong), weather (thunder and rain), and onstage or offstage events (a ringing telephone, an arriving taxi, an angel crashing through the ceiling). Stage sounds can be realistic (an ambulance siren), stylized (an amplified, accelerating heartbeat), stereophonically localized (an airplane heard as crossing overhead from left to right), or pervasive and "in-your-head" (a buzzing mosquito, electronic static, a thousand ringing cell phones).

Music, as well as sound, is often used to evoke a mood, support an emotion, intensify an action, or provide a transition into or between scenes. Music accompanying a play can be composed for the production and played "live" during the performance, or it can be derived from (legally acquired and paid for) copyrighted recordings, which are then played back through a theatre's sound system (or, sometimes, through onstage "prop" boom boxes). Naturally, many combinations are possible. The sound designer designs and oversees the implementation of all of these elements, and, particularly if she or he is also the play's musical composer, this work may be of immense importance in the overall production.

Sound design has rapidly escalated in importance over the past two decades as playwrights and directors have sought to incorporate the new sound technologies that have swiftly expanded the theatrical potential, first with audiotape recording and now with highly complex digital recording, editing, processing, and playback technologies that grow more sophisticated every year. Contemporary sound design is not without its detractors, however. The electronic amplification of speaking and singing voices in musicals and nonmusicals alike is often derided by critics who prefer—or believe they prefer—a more natural unamplified sound. The sound-mixing board, now commonplace in the back orchestra rows of most Broadway and larger regional theatres, is a visual reminder of the contemporary technology that some feel diminishes the "liveness" of "live theatre." Extended musical underscoring in some plays raises objections that it turns drama into cinema and suffuses the articulation of ideas in the syrup of generalized emotion. Nonetheless, sound design—as well as original music composition that makes use of it—has become absolutely fundamental to the production of today's theatre around the globe and is quite definitely here to stay.

The Midas XL8 audio mixer is one of the newest and most elaborate sound consoles on the market, providing user friendly desk operation for the most complex sound-scored productions and concerts, including the 2009 Nobel Prize Ceremony in Oslo and Depeche Mode's "Tour of the Universe," which played worldwide to audiences of up to eighty-five thousand in 2009–2010.

PUPPETS AND PROJECTIONS

In the spring of 2011, the Broadway (Lincoln Center) production of *War Horse* won separate Tony Awards for best play, direction, scenery, costume, and sound design—but took no awards for what everyone left the theatre talking about: its magnificent projections and puppets. These are currently the two fastest growing design areas in theatre, and each has seized an important space in today's theatrical design; clearly, further recognition will soon be coming. We will look at them separately.

Puppets

Puppet theatre began in China two thousand years ago, and has long been used in the Japanese Bunraku and Javanese shadow puppetry, and for supernatural characters in Shakespeare (almost certainly for some of the apparitions the Witches raise up from their cauldron in *Macbeth,* for example), but increasingly they are used to represent human dramatic characters in contemporary plays, such as *Avenue Q,* or as full-sized living animals, as in Julie Taymor's *The Lion King* (see the chapter titled "Global Theatre Today") and *War Horse.* In the latter production, two full-sized "puppet horses," designed, fabricated, and directed by Basil Jones and Adrian Kohler of the Handspring Puppet Company and

The projections that Elaine McCarthy designed for *33 Variations* showed various locales where the play takes place, and, as shown here, a handwritten classical piano score by Ludwig von Beethoven that the terminally ill Dr. Brandt, played by Jane Fonda (right), is researching in the hopes of discovering the composer's motive for creating it. Susan Kellerman plays Brandt's doctor in this 2009 Broadway production, written and directed by Moisés Kaufman.

controlled by expertly trained operators from within the skeletal animal, are seen to prance, gallop, whinny, and rise up on their back feet throughout the production. The effect is certainly spectacular, but what is particularly surprising is that after a few minutes of admiring the technology, the audience settles back and begins to forget the "horses" are puppets and to imagine them instead as real animals. They then empathize with their feelings, and with the feelings of the characters who love them. And when the horses "die" at the end of the play, grown adults in the audience are seen to wipe tears from their eyes. Puppets may not be living things, but when artfully created and manipulated they can evoke great laughter (in *Avenue Q*), awe (in *Lion King*), and genuine emotion (in *War Horse*).

Moreover, unlike those of the past, the puppets in all three productions are controlled by their operators *in full sight of the audience*—by the actors who say their lines in *Avenue Q*, and by puppeteers working within their puppets, their human heads and arms clearly visible as they perform. An open display of theatrical mechanics, we discover again and again, can heighten rather than distract from the intellectual and emotional thrust of the play being performed. Once again, we see the Brechtian idea of making the mechanics of the theatre *part of the show* instead of hidden behind the curtains or proscenium—and this is no longer considered an avant-garde technique, but rather a part of the theatre's mainstream, for at the time of writing, all three of these productions are playing to full houses in New York City.

Projections

Projections were not possible until the development of the steady beam of focused, incandescent, electric light. But by the 1920s, German designer Erwin Piscator was experimenting with projected images as part of his scenic design, while his colleague Bertolt Brecht

Tim Bird's projection design for the 2008 Broadway revival of Stephen Sondheim's *Sunday in the Park with George*, seen behind the actors, was widely considered a major factor in the production's success, spurring a greatly expanded interest in projections as vital contributors to the art of theatrical design.

projected titles on screens to indicate the location (e.g., "*A highway cutting through barren fields*" in his *Mother Courage*) or show supplementary material (e.g., historical maps and documents in his *Galileo*). In America, Tennessee Williams called for "a screen on which were projected magic-lantern slides bearing images or titles" to be used in the production of his new play, *The Glass Menagerie,* in 1944, so as "to give accent to certain values for each scene." (The play's first director, Eddie Dowling, decided not to use this device, but many subsequent directors of the play have done so.)

Today, led by the trend away from strict realism as well as new technological developments (digital imaging, video recording, computer-designed animation), both image and video projections have frequently become integral to theatrical design, and the projection designer (sometimes called the image designer or video designer) has become a new member of theatrical design teams around the world. Wendall K. Harrington has been a particularly important leader in this field, having been credited as projection designer (or video designer or multi-image designer) thirty-five times on

Broadway since his work on *They're Playing Our Song* in 1979, and having created the country's first projection design program at the Yale Drama School in 2010.

Signaling this growth, Tim Bird earned the first-ever Drama Desk Award for outstanding projections and video design for his work on the 2008 Broadway revival of *Sunday in the Park with George,* the celebrated musical about French artist Georges Seurat and his influence on modern art. The first act of this work—which received the Pulitzer Prize—was staged in its 1984 premiere in front of a large painted canvas of Seurat's famous pointillist painting named in the play's title, with the costumed actors taking the positions of the artist's human figures. David Farley's twenty-first-century set design, however, was paired with Bird's animated video of that painting, which was projected on an LED wall at the rear of the stage, allowing the audience to see the painting created from completely blank canvas to finished masterpiece during the act. It was a stunner—by showing Seurat's images as constructed from thousands of discrete "points" of color, it visually, and brilliantly, demonstrated the musical's "pointillist" theme; *Sunday's*

War Horse astonished audiences in London and then in New York by the giant projections of World War I battlefields designed by 59 Productions, and by the amazing, full-sized, puppet horses created by Basil Jones and Adrian Kohler. The New York production won 2011 Tony Awards for Best Play, Best Direction, and Best Scenic, Lighting and Sound Design—but audiences left the theatre thinking mainly about the magnificent horses and the stunning projected images.

composer-creator Stephen Sondheim was heard to say, "if we had the technology when we first staged the show, this is the way we would have wanted to do it."

Not all introductions to new theatre technologies are received as warmly, however, as can be expected for an art form with a five-thousand-year-old history. Finn Ross's projection design for the 2008 Broadway revival of Arthur Miller's *All My Sons*, starring John Lithgow, included newsreels of the period, large videos of wartime soldiers, factory workers, and military planes, plus occasional indications of time and scene changes, and was both praised ("surprisingly effective," "insinuating projections") and damned ("[they do] more to harm the play than bolster it," "don't draw us closer to these people—they push us away"). Similarly, the LED screen behind the 2009 Broadway revival of *Guys and Dolls* was hailed as "majestic and handsomely humanized," and Destin O'Neill's projections on it as "expertly made," but the same critic felt the ultimate impact of

the projections was to overwhelm the characters, who were "upstaged by the fancy video. . . . The wall does all the talking."

Nonetheless, projections are certainly here to stay. David Korins and Zachary Borovay won a 2011 Drama Desk Award for their projections of photos and video clips of football games for the Broadway play, *Lombardi,* about the storied Green Bay Packers coach. And while much of the acclaim for *War Horse* was for the puppets, critics also praised what was behind them: horrific World War I images drawn by the show's scenery and costume designer Rae Smith and projected onto what looked like a giant, war-torn movie screen, created by 59 Productions, at the rear of the Lincoln Center stage.

As projection design becomes more and more common, will it lick its potential problems, such as upstaging the live actors performing in its midst? Probably, as long as it prioritizes art over technology. "What I know about the technology you can fit in a thimble," says

Re-Animator: The musical is a semi-operatic farce staged by Stuart Gordon (who also directed the film of that name) that capitalizes on bizarre magical effects created by Effects Designer John Naulin and Costume Designer Joe Kucharski. The play premiered at the Steve Allen Theatre in Hollywood, California, in 2011; the now-headless Professor Hill is played by Jesse Merlin, who is staring at the body of his Dean's daughter (Rachel Avery), while the Dean, played by George Wendt, looks on from behind.

Theatrical smoke is commonly used with stage lighting to provide atmospheric and supernatural effects, and also to create a level of stylization that permits a suspension of realism—as in a battle scene that would be dangerous to stage with greater physical authenticity. Here, smoke and lighting combine to create the chaos and violence of battle in the Utah Shakespeare Festival production of War of the Roses, a compilation by Howard Jensen of Shakespeare's three plays of Henry VI. Lighting is by Donna Ruzika.

veteran designer Harrington. "The thinking is much more important."

SPECIAL EFFECTS

Theatre "magic" often entails special effects not easily described as simply lighting or sound—fire, explosions, fog, smoke, wind, rain, snow, lightning, spurts of blood, and mysterious arrivals and disappearances, such as what stage directions in Shakespeare's *Tempest* describe as the goddess Juno descending from Mount Olympus and certain nymphs who "heavily vanish" after "a strange hollow and confused noise." And all of these effects must be accomplished without burning down the theatre. (Except, of course, sometimes they do: the firing of an offstage cannon burned down Shakespeare's Globe in 1613.) Commercial devices can help theatre technicians achieve these effects, but each bit of magic requires its own on-the-spot ingenuity to be both credible and effective. And one-of-a-kind tricks, such as having Hans's armor suddenly fall off his body in Jean Giraudoux's *Ondine* and "Professor Hill" bravely holding his decapitated but still-speaking head against his stomach in a stage production of *Re-Animator*, must be individually designed and perfected. Effects designers are not universally employed

in the theatre, but since the growth of spectacular musicals and dazzling entertainments such as Cirque du Soleil (see the chapter titled "Global Theatre Today"), they are clearly in a growth industry.

DIGITAL TECHNOLOGIES IN THEATRE DESIGN

Designers—like other visual artists—have always used the technologies available to them. For centuries, designers have worked with such basic drawing implements as charcoal, colored paints, rulers, squares, and drafting tables. Complicated "drawing machines" came into play during the Renaissance: Leonardo da Vinci invented a

Falling snow is one of the special effects in—and also underlines the major theme and title of—*Snow in June.* The play, which depicts the ghost of a young Chinese girl returning to earth, was inspired by a thirteenth-century Chinese legend. Written by Charles Mee and adapted and directed by Chen Shi-Zheng for the American Repertory Theatre in 2003, *Snow in June* blends ancient Chinese theatre techniques with contemporary technology. The play's accompanying music, composed by Paul Dresher, mixes bluegrass, Tex-Mex, Chinese, and Cajun elements. Scenic design is by Yi Li Ming, costumes are by Anita Yavich, and lighting is by Rick Fisher.

"perspectograph" to help artists transform their perceived earthly realities into two-dimensional sketches and engravings in the early 1500s, and Canaletto's detailed paintings of eighteenth-century Venice were executed with the aid of a room-size "camera obscura." The digital programs of today are only the most recent in a long list of technological tools used by visual artists, but they have become widespread in the theatre.

What does digital design offer that pencil and paper don't? Computers don't think and can't create; they can't (yet) analyze a text, imagine an environment, suggest a costume, conceive a style, or make an audience laugh. But what digital technology *can* do is aid and accelerate the process of artists who do these things. The capacity for digitally combining and configuring (and then reconfiguring) ideas, angles, shapes, colors, spaces, perspectives, and measurements, which designers uncover through research or create through imagination, makes

possible the consolidation of a giant spectrum of experimental and aesthetic possibilities with the speed of light and the assurance of a mathematician. Perhaps no other era of theatre history has seen a technological innovation so successfully balance reality's hard facts with the artist's free-floating imagination.

Digital design has become invaluable to contemporary designers on a variety of levels. First, computer-aided-design (CAD) programs can assist with or even replace much of the drudgery of sheer drawing mechanics. With a click of the mouse, straight lines, angles, circles, shapes, colors, and typefaces can be selected from a menu of choices and placed where desired. Moreover, all of these can be shifted in an instant: colors can be changed, lines lengthened, walls thickened, floors raised, furniture moved, sight lines adjusted, dimensions measured, and texts edited and resized. Individual design elements can be instantly replicated: an elaborately drawn banister post can become a dozen posts with two clicks of a mouse. Indeed, whole drawings can be rescaled, zoomed in or out; individual elements can be rotated or relocated freely about the page. And the resulting working drawings can be shared instantly with design team members working anywhere around the world (as designers often do). Global collaboration has become not merely possible in the digital age, it has become routine.

And there's more. Digital storage allows designers to draw upon vast visual databases: virtual art catalogues of, for example, eighteenth-century chandeliers, Victorian drapery, Roman togas—all digitized for computer retrieval and available (subject to copyright considerations) for incorporation into stage designs. And digitized cutting and pasting allows the designer to *combine* virtual forms. For example, a costume designer can "virtually sew" the sleeves of one digitized garment onto another or even "virtually dress" one digitized actor with a digital costume, giving a view of a fully costumed character without buying a single inch of fabric. Dedicated database programs also permit lighting and sound technicians to save innumerable hours in storing, sorting, and printing the dozens of dimmer schedules, cue sheets, and loudspeaker assignments needed in multiproduction repertory assignments.

Furthermore, in many theatres digitized scenographic modeling has supplemented traditional drawings by creating, on a computer screen, three-dimensional models of the stage set that can demonstrate perspectives from any vantage: the left, right, or center of the house; or from a bird's-eye position that may clarify lighting and offstage storage positions. Designers, directors, and actors can now "walk through" the set while it exists solely as a virtual reality, and they can "light the scenery" in a variety of ways before anything is built—or even before a theatre is rented. The opportunity to digitally "storyboard" scenery, costumes, and lighting, together with text and music and sound, is an extraordinary advance in the art of production planning wherever time and money are involved, as they almost always are.

Finally, of course, digital technology is not merely a preparatory tool for the designer; it is now the very medium by which sound, lighting, and projections are routinely transmitted to the audience. The music and sound that emanate from house speakers have been fully digitized, the still or moving images projected onto screens or LED walls are now pixelated, and the intensity of the lighting instruments—and increasingly their colors and movements as well—are executed today with the aid of highly specialized computer software. And the cues for these operations are, in many theatres, now called from digital promptbooks. Theatre

has definitely entered the digital age, and while the progress will be far faster in some theatres than others, there will be no going back.

THE TECHNICAL PRODUCTION TEAM

Far outnumbering all the other members of the theatre staff—the actors, designers, writers, and directors put together— are the artisans or "technologists" who get the production organized, built, installed, lit, and ready to open, and who then make it run.

Because of their numbers, theatrical technicians are ordinarily organized in a hierarchical structure, headed by stage, house, and production managers, technical directors, and shop supervisors all of whom are charged with guiding and overseeing the work of a virtual army of craftspersons. A typical breakdown of these functions—which you might find detailed in the theatre program of any major theatre—could be something like this:

The *production stage manager* (*PSM*)—previously known simply as the *stage manager*—has existed at least since the eighteenth century. The PSM coordinates the scheduling, staffing, and budgeting of every element of the production, from the acting rehearsals to the building, installation ("load-in"), and operation ("running") of all the design and technical elements. Expert in legal codes, safety procedures, and accounting policies, and sensitive to the varying artistic needs of actors, directors, designers, and technicians, the PSM wrestles with the complex problems of integrating the play's disparate elements—determining, for example, whether the lights should be hung and focused before or after the scenery is installed (there can be reasons for going either way on this) and anticipating how long it will take to train the stage crew or to set the light cues.

The production stage manager coordinates the director's work with that of the actors and the technical and design departments. At the beginning of rehearsals, the PSM is involved primarily in organizational matters: scheduling calls and appointments, recording the blocking of actors, anticipating technical problems of quick costume changes, set shifts, and the like, and organizing the basic "calling" of the show—that is, the system by which lighting, sound, actor-entrance, and scene-shift cues are initiated.

During performance, the PSM is in full charge of the show. He or she observes it (either directly from a booth above the audience, or from the side of the stage, or through one or more video monitors) and physically calls each lighting, sound, and scene-moving

Photo Essay: Broadway Stage Manager Michael McGoff

Michael McGoff has stage-managed five Broadway and nineteen off-Broadway shows since his arrival in New York in 2000. His impressive credits include Shakespeare's *The Winters' Tale* and *Romeo and Juliet* at Shakespeare in the Park, the American premiere of Caryl Churchill's *Drunk Enough to Say I Love You* at New York's Public Theatre in 2008, and the Broadway productions of Richard Brinsley Sheridan's *The Rivals*, Edward Albee's *Seascape*, David Eldridge's *Festen*, Shakespeare's *Cymbeline*, and Simon Gray's *Butley*, starring Nathan Lane, at the Booth, where this author interviewed him two hours before curtain time on a weekday evening in early 2007.

1.

1. Michael McGoff on the *Butley* set at the Booth Theatre in New York's Broadway Theatre District.

2. "The audience is different every night, and so is the play," says McGoff, who must be fully alert to every nuance in the rise and fall of audience laughter and applause, and to the actors' variations in their movements and line deliveries, as he calls cues from his stage manager's console behind the scenes. These cues—for specific (and numbered) shifts in lighting and in sound, for actors' entrances, for the rise and fall of the curtain—all must be timed in precise synchronization with intricate onstage action. The five video monitors on the console capture this action from every possible vantage. Toggle switches above McGoff's hand operate the offstage cue-lights that signal actor entrances. The headset keeps McGoff in continuous contact with the light and sound operators located in distant parts of the theatre and with the stage crew elsewhere behind the scenes. Every two or three days, McGoff turns his console over to an assistant so he can watch the performance from the back of the house and identify moments in the show that may need tweaking to regain their fullest potential.

2.

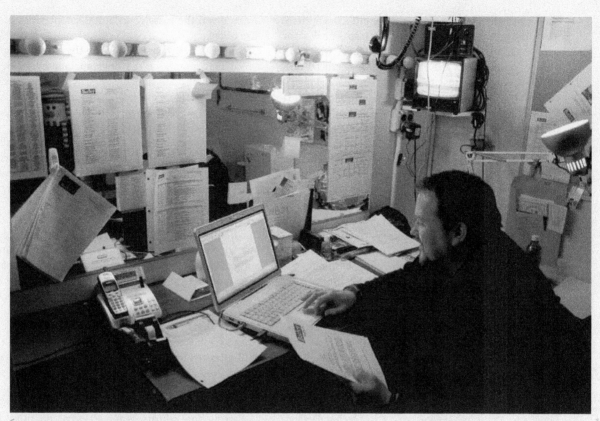

3. "I use my office as a place to focus and communicate with the on-site needs of the show, and also to get in touch with the many off-site service providers, management, producers, public relations and press officers, agents, and so forth," explains McGoff. "The office is placed strategically, allowing me to catch staff going up and coming down the stairs. And when we have guests I can head them off if they are arriving at an inconvenient time. It also puts me where the actors need me, yet it is close to the stage so my crew can call me when they have to."

McGoff's work begins ninety minutes before every performance.

"I use this time to check in with my crew and to see if anything needs to be taken care of before we turn the house over to the house manager. At that point, while my assistant handles the prop preset, I deal with any of the actors' concerns and give them my notes. Some days there aren't very many; on others I can be continuously running up and down the backstage stairs to keep everyone in the loop. All actors take their notes differently; you learn when to invoke the director, when to appeal to logic, when to cut through with the harsh but important truth, and when to just watch it again and wait until tomorrow."

It's time for the visitor to leave: the actors are arriving, and McGoff is beginning his opening setup.

cue—normally through an electronic intercom system. The production stage manager may also signal actor entrances, usually by means of "cue-lights," which are tiny backstage lights the PSM triggers—a crucial task when an entrance must be timed to an onstage physical action that the actor cannot see from backstage. It is the PSM's job and, more important, his or her art to precisely time these cues to create the theatrical impact intended by the director, while also making adjustments for unexpected interruptions such as sustained audience laughter or applause, electrical outages, or actor or technician accidents onstage.

The PSM also maintains the production after its opening performance, conducting understudy and replacement rehearsals when needed, arranging for the cleaning, repair, or replacement of costumes, props, and stage machinery, and in other ways assuming the functions of the director, who, in most professional productions, is no longer present on a regular basis. Indeed, many professional stage directors (including your author) and film directors (including Stephen Spielberg) began their theatrical careers by stage managing their high school or college productions.

Working for the PSM is one or more *assistant stage managers* (ASMs). In rehearsals, ASMs typically set out props, follow the script, prompt actors who are "off book" (no longer rehearsing with script in hand) when they forget their lines, take line notes when actors memorize lines incorrectly, and substitute for actors who may be temporarily away from the rehearsal hall, as for conflicting publicity or costume-fitting appointments. During the performance, with the PSM calling the show from a fixed offstage position, the ASMs—on two-way headset connections—implement the PSM's calls to the actors and crew chiefs, often transmitting them as visual "go" signs for scene shifts, actor entrances, and effect cues. ASMs also serve as the backstage eyes and ears of the PSM, who is always watching the stage.

Technical director (TD) is a term that dates from early in the last century, when a person holding that title was responsible for the scenery, lighting, sound, stage machinery, and just about everything "technical" that was designed to operate onstage. Although the title is still used, the TD is usually now only in charge of the building and operation of scenery and stage machinery. The position requires great knowledge and skill in engineering, drafting, construction, budgeting, and team management (of shops and crews). But it is a high art as well, for every construction and operation the TD oversees is a one-of-a-kind project and must be completed in most cases on an exactly fixed schedule—no small

order, given the massive technical complexities of theatre today.

The TD's first task is to receive the scenic designs—which may simply be drawings augmented by overall dimensions, perhaps supplemented by three-dimensional models—and figure out how their various elements will be constructed. Dozens of factors must be considered and, much of the time, traded off. The cost of materials and labor must be carefully reconciled with the available budget; scenery meant to look light and airy must be engineered with critical concerns for stability and safety; scenery meant to look heavy and gargantuan often must be built to roll or fly offstage at lightning speed—or in a choreography of alternate accelerations and decelerations. During this phase the TD drafts the working drawings for the scenery's construction and exact placement and consults, often daily, with the designer and director as to whether the working drawings will lead to the intended look of the set, and yield scenery that works in the manner each of them has imagined.

Once the scenery is built, the TD oversees its load-in and establishes the manner in which scenery is to be shifted, either by manual pushing and pulling or by computerized mechanical devices. At the end of the play's run, the TD organizes the "strike"—the speedy removal of scenery into storage or the local dumpster.

During final rehearsals and actual productions, *technical crews*, working under the PSM and trained by the TD, hoist, lower, and push scenery pieces exactly on cue to precisely predetermined locations. They shift props and furniture to the right places at the right times. They pull the curtain (if there is one) up and down when cued by the PSM or ASM. In general, they make the carefully preplanned scene changes, prop appearances, and actor entrances appear to flow effortlessly. The technical crews' skills ensure that the audience concentrates on the play's action rather than on the theatre's mechanics. One particularly special "tech" assignment is flying actors through the air, which is usually done by only a few professional companies with patented equipment and expertly trained personnel; the crash-landing of a *Spider-Man* actor during previews in 2010 was a reminder of the potential danger in this field—fortunately, the actor survived his 30 foot fall and returned to the show five months later.

Working in the scene shop—normally under the TD, a *shop foreman*, or a *scenery supervisor*—are production *carpenters* (and master carpenters) and *scenic artists* (painters). They are joined by welders when steel—commonly used today for weight-bearing constructions—is to be joined.

A wider array of specialists is required in the costume shop, (though many costume designers and technologists assume more than one of these roles):

- *Costume director* (or *costume shop manager*), who coordinates the entire operation, supervising personnel, work spaces, and schedules.
- *Dyers,* who dye fabrics to the color specified by the design and may also be skilled at fabric painting, aging, distressing, and other fabric modifications.
- *Drapers,* who drape fabrics on an actor or on a dummy, testing and choosing the way the fabric falls—either with the grain or on the bias—to create the desired look of the eventual garment both at rest and on a moving (and possibly dancing, tumbling, or fencing) actor.
- *Cutters,* who cut the fabric according to the selected grain direction, either from a flat paper pattern or with no pattern at all, often first creating a cheap muslin prototype. (Most often today, draping and cutting are performed by the same person: a draper/cutter.)
- *First hands,* who, working directly for the cutter, correct the pattern after the muslin prototype has been fitted to the actor and then "hand off" the work to stitchers.
- *Stitchers,* who sew the garment.
- *Craft specialists,* who make costumes or costume elements involving more than fabric—armor, belts, masks, and so forth. Specific specialists, such as milliners to make hats and cobblers to make shoes, may be added. Other specialists may be involved in distressing costume elements (making them look older and well used) or adding decorations, such as badges, military ribbons, and gold braid.
- *Hairstylists and wigmakers,* who coif the actors as the designers specify.
- *Wardrobe supervisors,* who ensure that costumes are cleaned and maintained during the run of a show and delivered to the appropriate backstage areas during dress rehearsals and performances. Wardrobe (or storage) supervisors and technicians also oversee the costume storage area and help determine which existing costumes can be taken from storage and rebuilt to serve a new design.
- *Dressers,* who work backstage during dress rehearsals and performances, helping the actors when necessary with quick changes between scenes.

In the area of lighting, *electricians* and *master electricians* hang, focus, and "gel" (put color media in) lighting instruments prior to and during technical rehearsals, and they maintain the lighting technology during the run of a show. *Lighting-board* and *follow-spot operators* execute the lighting cues called by the PSM. For the sound department, one or more *sound engineers* work with the sound designer in recording the sound cues and placing the speakers, and a *soundboard operator* executes the cues during technical and dress rehearsals and performances. And in the makeup room, *makeup artists* may provide assistance to actors requiring it, or they may indeed apply full makeup to the actors as specified by the designers.

Each of these backstage technicians plays an absolutely crucial role in theatrical presentation. The stage fright of the actor playing Hamlet is not necessarily greater than the nervousness of the stagehand who pulls the curtain, for backstage work, though technical, is never merely mechanical. Every stage production poses a host of problems and situations that are new to the people who deal with them and, sometimes, new to the theatre itself. Technological innovation takes place when sound knowledge of craft combines with creative imagination in the face of unanticipated problems. The technical artists of the theatre have always manifested impressive ingenuity at meeting unprecedented challenges in creative ways. Each of the theatre's shops—scene shop, costume shop, prop shop, and makeup room—is therefore a creative artistic studio and a teaching laboratory for all its members, as well as a theatrical support unit.

Indeed, in contemporary theatre, particularly after the "distancing" stage innovations of Bertolt Brecht, the theatre's technology—such as lighting instruments and sound-enhancing devices—has increasingly been taken out of hiding and placed right on the stage itself. And when follow-spot operators and stage managers are placed in direct public view, sound operators and their consoles are plopped in the midst of the audience, and puppeteers are seen visibly manipulating their animals on the stage, the theatre's technicians themselves are increasingly drawn into direct public awareness—and in some cases are invited to take onstage curtain calls with the rest of the cast. Popular fascination with technology, together with diminishing interest in mere realism, has led to a scenography that deliberately incorporates technology as a visible aesthetic component of the theatre itself. Given this trend and the theatre's increasing use of the most recent technical innovations—superhydraulics, lasers and holograms, air casters, wall-size video, moving lights, and projections, to name but a few—the theatre technologist is becoming widely recognized (as cinematographers are in cinema) as not merely implementers but full-fledged stage artists and creators.

Chapter 6

The Director

THE ROOM IS ALREADY FILLED with people when she enters, a bit fussily, with a bundle of books and papers under her arm. Expectation, tension, and even a hint of panic can be sensed behind the muffled greetings, loose laughter, and choked conversation that greet her arrival.

She sits, and an assistant arranges chairs. Gradually, starting at the other end of what has suddenly become "her" table, the others seat themselves. An edgy silence descends. Where are they going? What experiences lie ahead? What risks, what challenges are to be demanded? What feelings, in the coming weeks and months, are going to be stirred to poignant reality?

Only she knows—and if she doesn't, no one does. It is in this silence, tender with hope and fear, that the director breaks ground for the production. It is here that plan begins to become work and idea begins to become art. It is the peak moment of directing and of the director.

That is an idealized scenario, to be sure. There are many directors who deliberately avoid invoking an impression of "mystique" and whose primary efforts are directed toward dispelling awe, dread, or any form of personal tension among their associates. Nonetheless, the picture holds a measure of truth for every theatrical production, for the art of directing is an exercise in leadership, imagination, and control; in the director's hands, finally, rest the aspirations, neuroses, skills, and ideas of the entire theatrical company. ▶

Director Gábor Tompa's 2011 staging of Georg Büchner's nineteenth-century comic political satire, *Leonce and Lena*, set the play in a ruined eighteenth-century chateau and stylized the actors' movements in a brilliant pastiche of aristocratic buffoonery that implied the innate idiocy of royal rule. The production opened at the Hungarian Theatre in Cluj, Romania, and went on to tour in Hungary, France, Germany, Croatia, and Bogota, Colombia. The stunning designs (scenery and costumes) were created by Carmencita Brojboiu.

Directing is an art whose product is the most ambiguous, perhaps the most mysterious, in the theatre. The direction of a play is not visible like scenery or costumes; and unlike the actor's voice or the sound designer's score, it cannot be directly heard or sensed. Yet direction underlies everything we see and hear in the theatre. Utterly absorbed by the final theatrical experience, direction animates and defines that experience. A whole class of theatrical artists in our time has reached international eminence in this particular art. But what, exactly, is involved?

At the *technical* level, the director is the person who organizes the production. He or she schedules the work process and supervises the acting, designing, staging, and technical operation of the play. This is usually the easiest part of the director's job.

At the more fundamental, *artistic,* level, the director inspires a creation of theatre with each production. He or she *conceptualizes* the play, gives it vision and purpose—both social and aesthetic—and inspires the company of artists to join together in collaboration. This is the hard part, the part by which directors earn their reputations.

It is in the conjunction of the technical and the artistic that each director defines the directorial function anew. And it is with one foot in each that the director creates—through an adroit synthesis of text, materials, and available talent—a unique and vivid theatrical experience.

A HISTORICAL OVERVIEW

Play productions have been directed ever since theatre began, but the emergence of a "director"—a person who guides the actors and designers in orchestrating the play's dramatic actions (and who takes credit for doing so)—has been relatively recent. Although playwrights

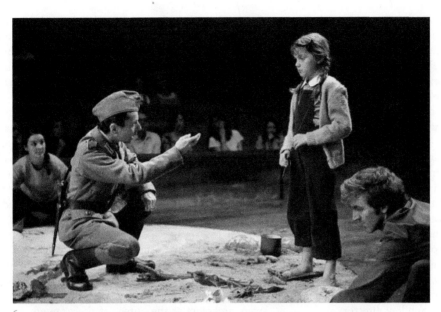

In Ariane Mnouchkine's *Les Éphémères* (*Ephemeral Things*), actors often double as scenery shifters. From a squatting or kneeling position, they silently wheel large "chariots" (wheeled platforms, usually circular) on and off the staging area—an alley between two banks of audience seats. Atop the chariots, the company's 27 actors (including children) perform 75 roles in the 29 loosely interrelated scenes of the two-part production that proved the sensation of New York's 2009 Lincoln Center Theatre Festival. Shown here, a Jewish girl, wearing a cross and disguised as a Christian during the Nazi occupation of northern France during World War II, is being questioned by a German officer. Or is she being interrogated? We cannot be certain, but we see every possibility and contingency going through the characters' minds. In addition to moving the chariots, the scenery shifters provide a nonspeaking chorus of witnesses to the seemingly ordinary but often tragic events the play depicts. Mnouchkine provided the production's concept and direction, but the play was "dreamed upon, invoked, evoked, improvised and devised" by the entire 50-member company of the Théâtre du Soleil (Theatre of the Sun). Everest Canto de Montserrat designed the scenery.

since the time of Aeschylus have been known to direct their own plays, the idea of an independent "director" did not even exist until the nineteenth century and did not become universal until just before the twentieth. Yet today the role of the director has become so significant that many critics and theatergoers speak of the current stage as a "director's theatre." And many directors, particularly in Europe and in film, have become world celebrities—more famous than the actors they direct.

The director's evolution, however, is not simply the rise of one member of the theatrical production ensemble. The emergence of the director has coincided with an expansion of the theatre's perspective from a national to a global art form, and from limited stylistic repertoire to nearly unlimited palette of creative possibilities. Today's playwright, actor, and designer may draw from a vast world of resources, spanning three millennia, six continents, and an ever-increasing host of new technologies. And the role of director has risen accordingly, becoming a vital force in creating unique, tightly focused, and well-shaped productions.

Teacher-Directors

In the earliest days of the theatre and for some time thereafter, directing was considered a matter of instruction. The Greeks called the director the *didaskalos*, which means "teacher," and in medieval times the director's designation, in all the various European languages, was "master." The underlying assumption of this early directing, then, was that the (almost certainly male) teacher had already "mastered" his subject, and was simply required to "teach" the current conventions of acting and design to his less experienced colleagues. The earliest directors, therefore, were basically asked to pass along the techniques of "correct" performance technique within a given style of performance. Often the playwrights themselves served as directors, for—so the reasoning went—who would be better qualified to "teach" a play than the person who wrote it? In Molière's play *The Rehearsal at Versailles*, the seventeenth-century playwright-director delightfully depicts himself staging one of his own plays; this is surely an effective model of the author-teacher-director for the seventeenth century and indeed for much of the theatre's history.

The teacher-director reached a pinnacle of influence, albeit anonymously, during the late Enlightenment and Victorian eras—the eighteenth and nineteenth centuries—partly in response to the remarkable fascination of those times with science, scientific method, and humanistic research. The same dedication to rationalism that fostered a profusion of libraries, museums, and historic preservation also emphasized accuracy, consistency, and precision in the arts. The temper of the times led to major directorial changes in the theatre, for on the one hand audiences were demanding revivals of classic plays—whose authors were no longer around to direct them—and on the other hand they were demanding that these revivals be historically edifying, with a museum-like authenticity. All of this required research, organization, and comprehensive coordination; in other words, it demanded an independent director.

With only a few exceptions, directors before the twentieth century received as little public recognition for their efforts as do present-day museum directors for creating historical dioramas. Sometimes the directing was attributed to a famous acting star, such as the Englishman Charles Kean or the American Edwin Booth, when in fact the work was done by a lesser functionary. In Booth's case, for example, D. W. Waller was the true director; however, his name was all but buried in the program and never appeared in the reviews or publicity. Nevertheless, these teacher-directors who labored largely in the shadows began the art of directing as we know it today. They organized their productions around specific ideas—and dedicated themselves to creating unified and coherent theatrical works by "directing" an ensemble of actors, designers, and technicians toward established ends.

Directors of Realism

The second stage in the development of modern-day directing began toward the end of the nineteenth century and brought to the fore a group of directors who restudied the conventions of theatrical presentation in the age of realism, and strove to make their play productions more lifelike than those of past eras. George II, Duke of Saxe-Meiningen (1826–1914), was among the first of this breed and became known as the first "modern" director. The duke, who headed a provincial troupe of actors in his rural duchy, presented a series of premieres and classical revivals in the late 1870s and 1880s, dazzling the German public with their carefully harmonized acting, staging, and scenery. While historically

"correct" in their designs, the duke's productions created, instead of a star actor surrounded by supporting actors and supernumeraries, a true acting ensemble, all of whom had been all precisely staged and vigorously rehearsed so that each one, even the "spear carriers" (those in nonspeaking parts), appeared to be behaving naturally and individually. The totality of the Meiningen theatre aesthetic, which embraced acting, interpretation, and design, became acclaimed throughout Europe as the troupe toured the continent; by the 1890s, the position of a director that would organize and rehearse an entire company toward a complexly and comprehensively fashioned theatrical presentation was firmly established.

In 1887 André Antoine began a movement of even greater realism in Paris with his Théâtre Libre, and in 1898 Russian actor-director Konstantin Stanislavsky initiated his Moscow Art Theatre, which eventually became the international model of realistic ensemble acting. Both of these directors, who like Meiningen were amateurs at the outset of their careers, went on to develop innovative techniques in acting and actor-coaching based on the duke's staging concepts. Both also theorized and worked pragmatically on the organization of theatre companies, the development of a dramatic repertory, the reeducation of theater-going audiences, and the re-creation of an overall aesthetic of the theatre. Although both Antoine and Stanislavsky were known primarily as naturalists—somewhat to their disadvantage, perhaps, for they had many other interests as well—they were above all idealists who sought to make the theatre a powerful social and artistic instrument for the expression of truth. Their ideals and their commitment practically forced them to expand the directorial function into an all-encompassing and inspirational art.

The importance of these directors—and of certain other pioneers of the same spirit, including Harley Granville-Barker in England, David Belasco in America, and Otto Brahm in Germany—was not merely that they fostered the developing realist and naturalist drama, but also that they opened up the theatre to almost infinite possibilities of psychological interpretation. Once the psychology of the human individual became crucial to the analysis and acting of plays, directors became more than teachers: they became part analyst, part therapist, and even part mystic; their *creative* function in play production increased substantially. The rise of realism in the theatre of the late nineteenth and early twentieth centuries, and the accompanying rise of directors capable of incorporating realistic nuances into highly theatrical productions, brought about an irreversible theatrical renovation that in turn further established the importance of the director.

Directors of Antirealism

Right on the heels of the realist phase of direction came a third phase—one that brought directors to their present positions of power and recognition. This phase arrived with the directors who joined forces with nonrealist playwrights to create the modern antirealistic theatre. These theatre artists demanded that directing aim primarily at the creation of originality, theatricality, and style, and be unrestrained by rigid formulas with respect to verisimilitude or realistic behavior.

Their goal was to create sheer theatrical brilliance, beauty, and excitement, and to lead their collaborators in explorations of pure theatre and pure theatrical imagination.

Paul Fort, one of the first of these third-phase directors, launched his Théâtre d'Art in Paris in 1890 as a direct assault upon the realist principles espoused by Antoine. Similarly, Vsevolod Meyerhold, a one-time disciple of Stanislavsky, began his theatre of "biomechanical constructivism" (an acting method characterized by bold gestures and rapid, near-acrobatic

Because of rigorous censorship under Nazi and Communist regimes, innovative playwriting was practically forbidden throughout most of Eastern Europe from the mid-1930s until the end of the Soviet era in 1989. So during that period it became the job of directors and designers, when staging the few "approved" classics from past centuries, to introduce the penetrating political analogies and revolutionary aesthetics that would convey deep meaning to an audience while still escaping the censors' wary eyes. Although the iron curtain has since fallen, Eastern European directing and design retain their radical slant, as represented by these two twenty-first century productions of Shakespeare's *King Lear* by directors from this part of the world.

(*Above*) Director Lazlo Bocsardi, working with Designer Bartha Jósef on a 2008 *King Lear* production for the Tamasi Aron Theatre of Romania, augmented Lear's dismay at seeing "poor naked wretches" with "looped and windowed raggedness" by placing near-naked young men in individual glass cages elevated on waist-high stilts and framed within bright brass struts, as if the poor wretches of Lear's kingdom had become mannequins in department store showcases. (*Below*) This 2011 production directed by Georgian-born Paata Tsikurishvili for his Synetic Theatre in Washington, D.C., dispensed entirely with the text and told the story of the play in a brutal 95-minute pantomime focusing on the abuse of power. Scene designer Phil Charlwood, costume designer Georgi Alexi-Meskhishvili, and lighting designer Andrew F. Griffin all won Helen Hayes Award nominations for their work on this production.

Katie Mitchell is arguably the most controversial director in London today (see the chapter titled "Global Theatre Today"). Her astonishing stagings infuriate purists because of their modern settings, radically adapted texts and, in this 2007 cut-down production of Euripides' *Women of Troy* at England's Royal National Theatre, frontal nudity, pyromania, ballroom dancing, and women climbing tall ladders in long dresses and high heels. Here Sinead Matthews as a fire-happy Cassandra stares into the future—which is us.

movement) in Moscow to combat the master's realism. The movement toward stylized directing occasioned by these innovators and others like them introduced a lyricism and symbolism, an expressive and abstract use of design, an explosive theatricality, and certain intentionally contrived methods of acting that continue to have a profound effect on today's theatre and its drama.

Perhaps the most influential proponent of this third-phase position of the director, however, was not himself a director at all but an eminent designer and theorist: Edward Gordon Craig. In a seminal essay titled "The Art of the Theatre" (1905), Craig compared the director of a play to the captain of a ship: an absolutely indispensable leader whose rule, maintained by strict discipline, extends over every last facet of the enterprise. "Until discipline is understood in a theatre to be willing and reliant obedience to the manager [director] or captain," wrote Craig, "no supreme achievement can be accomplished." Craig's essay was aimed at a full-scale "Renaissance of

the Art of the Theatre," in which a "systematic progression" of reform would overtake all the theatre arts— "acting, scenery, costuming, lighting, carpentering, singing, dancing, etc."—under the complete control and organizing genius of this newcomer to the ranks of theatrical artistry, the independent director.

The Contemporary Director

Craig's renaissance has arrived: this indeed is the "age of the director," an age in which the directorial function is fully established as the art of synthesizing script, design, and performance into a unique and splendid theatrical event that creates its own harmony and its own ineffable yet memorable distinction. If, as performance theorist J. L. Styan says, "the theatre persists in communicating by simultaneity of sensory impressions," it is above all the director who is charged with inspiring these impressions and ensuring their simultaneity.

Photo Essay: Director Susan Stroman

No director-choreographer has captured turn-of-this-century Broadway audiences and critics of musical theatre better than Susan Stroman, who won Tony Awards for both her direction and choreography of *The Producers* in 2001, and Tony nominations in both of those categories for *Scottsboro Boys* in 2011—along with three Tonys and five nominations for her earlier work in *Crazy for You, Showboat, Contact, Steel Pier, The Music Man, Oklahoma,* and *Young Frankenstein*. Quite an achievement for a University of Delaware theatre major who hit the ground running—or at least dancing—following her 1976 graduation.

The author met up with Stroman in Las Vegas, where she was restaging her Broadway production of *The Producers*—which won more Tony Awards (twelve) than any show in history—for the Paris Hotel and Casino. The show had begun its preview performances the evening before, and Stroman was working with a few actors prior to the full rehearsal, which was to begin in the following hour.

RC: When did you start thinking of being a choreographer?

SS: Always. I'm not one of the people who dance-dance-dancès and then decides to try choreography. Ever since I was a little girl, whether it was classical or rock and roll or an old standard, I visualized music. My father was a wonderful piano player. He would play the piano and I would dance around the living room, but in my head I would be imagining loads of people dancing with lights, sets, and costumes. When I came to New York, I knew I couldn't just "take over"—I would have to come as a song-and-dance gal because I could sing and dance—but I did so always with the idea of going to the other side of the table. So I started to choreograph and direct industrial shows and club acts in small venues— just dabbling in it to see if I could compete. But at a certain point I had to stop being known as a performer, because in New York you have to be

1. Directing and choreographing a musical involves close personal interaction, plus great attention to the details of both script and musical score. Here Stroman (*center*) gathers members of her cast around the orchestral score, which she has laid upon the stage in the convenient spotlight so all can see it (and her) clearly. From left to right behind her are Associate Choreographer Bill Burns and performers Matthew J. Vargo, Shari Jordan, Katrina Loncaric, and Patrick Boyd.

either one thing or another. You have to focus on what you want to be. So I stopped performing and decided to go for it. I was in a Broadway show called *Musical Chairs* and with me was another aspiring fellow, Scott Ellis, who also wanted to be on the other side of the table. We both knew [the musical Broadway team of composer John] Kander and [lyricist Fred] Ebb, and we decided to go to them and ask if they would allow us to mount an off-Broadway production of their *Flora the Red Menace*. This is a good lesson because in any business you need to ask yourself, "what's the worst that can happen?" They can say "no" or they can say "yes," but you won't get anywhere unless you ask the question. So Scott and I went to Kander and Ebb and they said "yes!" We mounted a production of *Flora*, which developed a cult following and launched our

careers. I think we made about three hundred dollars that entire summer. Of course we starved to death, but we had made the leap to the other side. And we have never gone back. It was a wonderful combination of believing in the show, adoring Kander and Ebb, and asking "the question" that led us to get that one really good break. Coincidentally, Kander and Ebb wrote a song in that show called "All I Need Is One Good Break."

That was when things really opened up for me. Hal Prince asked me to choreograph *Don Giovanni* at the New York City Opera, and then we collaborated on the Broadway show *Showboat*. Liza [Minnelli] also saw *Flora*. She asked me to choreograph her show *Stepping Out* at Radio City Music Hall. The key is really to be ready for that break when it happens.

RC: How did you then make your transition to directing?

SS: The transition to directing was very natural. Being a theatre choreographer is very different from being a ballet or modern dance choreographer (although I have done these too—for the New York City Ballet and the Martha Graham company). For choreographing theatre you have to acknowledge the lyric. Everything must center on the plot; your role is to push the plot forward through the choreography. Plus you have to create time period, geographical area, and rich characters. Because of all this, the choreographer is right there with the director from beginning to end. It's not like one job starts where the other one finishes; you're trying to make a total vision together. So it was a very natural transition for me.

The first Broadway show that I directed was *The Music Man*, and that was perfect for me because I love that show. Love it, love it! I grew up in a house filled with music. My father was my real Music Man: he was a salesman and he played the piano. There's a wonderful line in the show where the little boy accuses Harold Hill of lying about being the leader of a band. Harold Hill says, "I always think there's a band, kid." For musical comedy people that line resonates because we grow up thinking that there's always a band—we're always hoping our band is coming around the corner. So for *The Music Man* to be the first Broadway show I directed was very meaningful. The movement in *Music Man* is a very important aspect. When you first meet the characters in Iowa they're very stiff, they don't move at all, but by the end, the entire town is dancing the "Shipoopee." And it's all because Harold Hill has introduced the town to rhythm and music.

RC: How did you come up with the terrific ending?

SS: Closing the book after one of my readings of the script during rehearsals I thought, Well what is this town doing now? What *could* they be doing? Well, perhaps they all took trombone lessons? So for the curtain call I decided the entire

company should play the trombone. What did I have to lose? I'll hire a trombone teacher, they'll either learn it or they won't, and if they don't they'll just come out and bow. After the second week of rehearsal they sounded like a moose herd, and I thought this is never going to happen. And then *I* became the music man! All of a sudden, they had become my kids, and they were playing seventy-six trombones and it sounded beautiful. I was so pleased and proud! And that's how it ended up as the curtain call.

RC: What do you like about directing?

SS: It gives me great pleasure to be in the back of the house and see something I've created affect an audience. Whether it makes them laugh from something they saw in *The Producers* or makes them cry from a moment in *Contact* or—in *Crazy for You*—the audience puts their arms around one another (*laughs*). Even last night at the first preview of our Vegas production of *The Producers*, I saw a lady doubled over with laughter and tumbling into the aisle at the sight of the walker dance with the little old ladies. It gave me such joy to see her laugh.

RC: How do you conceive of some of the darker themes you explore, as in *Contact*?

SS: Oh, I have a million stories in my head. Being allowed to do something like *Contact* was amazing. Lincoln Center is the only place you can do something like that: take an idea and build it into a show. My production of *Steel Pier* only lasted about six months on Broadway, but [Lincoln Center's artistic director] André Bishop saw it and called me. He loved the choreography and said, "If you have an idea I will help you develop it." And to hear those words from a producer is like hearing a beautiful melody! It's unheard of. Usually, they just want you to do a revival, or something safe. And I said, "Well, as a matter of fact I *do* have an idea." A few weeks before I had been to a dance club in NYC's meatpacking district, a swing club where everybody wore black. Out of this sea of black stepped a girl in a yellow dress.

2. Directing often takes the form of one-on-one coaching. Here Stroman works with Burns on the "Ball and Chain" prison number in the final act.

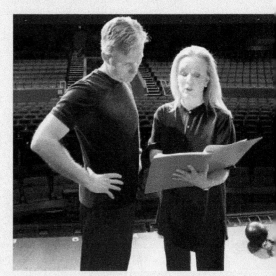

3. Studying the script, Stroman and Vargo go over dialogue.

4. Stroman works individually with the actors as they rehearse, fine-tuning choreographic gestures, expressions, and focus points (where actors are to look).

I got obsessed watching her, and I thought to myself, "She's going to change some man's life tonight." I thought she was quite bold—a New Yorker wearing yellow—so when André asked if I had an idea, I said, "I absolutely have an idea," and so I started to develop a story about the girl in the yellow dress. I called my friend John Weidman, who wrote *Assassins* and *Pacific Overtures*. We went into the rehearsal rooms of Lincoln Center with eighteen dancers, and we created a story about someone who, if he doesn't make contact that night, will die. It was remarkable to have the opportunity to develop this work from the visuals and concepts in my mind. Before it opened, I thought, "Well, there'll be a handful of people that will get this," but it took the city by storm. The girl in the yellow dress was on every bus

in Manhattan! It clearly has a very universal theme.

RC: Do you have any advice for a young person aspiring to be a director?

SS: You have to really have a passion and a drive, and you can't be afraid to take chances. You can't just wait around for someone to hire you; you've got to create your own work. And that's the way it should be. There is a collaborative passion in the theatre that I don't think exists in any other business. All of us are in a swimming pool together, and we either drown together or we win an Olympic medal together. It is passion and drive that make a show work. And the drive toward an opening night: there is nothing like it, nothing like people coming together with a goal to move an audience. It's an amazing feeling. I am very fortunate to be in the theatre. I love the theatre so much!

5. All directors have individual ways of communicating with actors. Stroman's signature style is to write down individual cast notes on three-by-five cards and then pass them out to the actors—Patrick and Katrina in this case—after each rehearsal unit concludes.

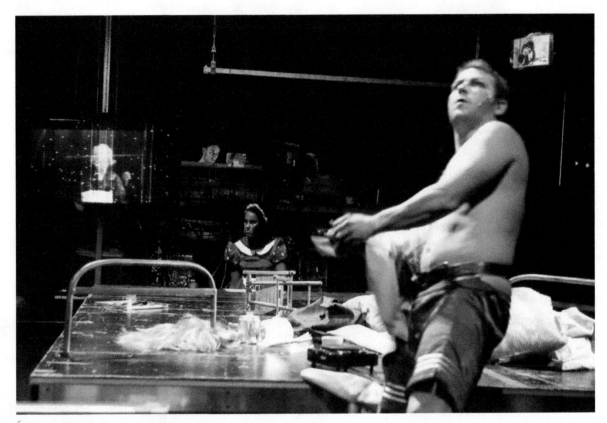

Director Elizabeth LeCompte's 2011 production of what was called "The Wooster Group's version of *Vieux Carré,*" adapted from the 1977 play by Tennessee Williams, retained much of Williams's original text, but wholly reconceived the play in a mixed-media contemporary environment. Premiering in Strasbourg, France in 2009, it has since played in New York, Los Angeles, Antwerp, Amsterdam, and, in 2012, at the World Stage Harbourfront Centre in Toronto.

Today's director understands realism and antirealism and feels free to mix them with impunity. At the beginning of a production, he or she faces a blank canvas but has at hand a generous palette. At the director's disposal are not only the underlying conventions of the time but also all those of the past, which can be revived for novel effects and stunning juxtapositions: our conglomerate theatre of today allows—indeed, encourages—Shakespeare in modern dress, Greek tragedy as a kabuki spectacle, theatre of the absurd as vaudevillian buffoonery, and romantic melodrama as campy satire. Thus, at the conception of a theatrical idea today—in the first moments of imagining a specific production—no question can be answered automatically, no style is obligatory, no interpretation is definitive. Philosopher-playwright Jean-Paul Sartre said about the whole of modern life that "man is

condemned to be free"; in the theatre the director's freedom in the face of almost limitless possibilities leads to a certain existential anxiety that is both chilling and thrilling in its challenge.

THE DIRECTING PROCESS: STEP BY STEP

Directing a play is a long process and does not begin when the director walks into the rehearsal room for the first time.

Indeed, the director may spend a year or more preparing and staging a production, and then more years restaging it in different theatres, in cases where the production begins in one theatre and then moves on to others—as *Avenue Q*, which began at the Eugene

O'Neill Theater Center in Connecticut, then transferred to the off-Broadway Vineyard Theatre, and then to the John Golden Theatre on Broadway, all three productions directed by Jason Moore during a three-year period.

This extended process of directing a play, then, has two quite different periods. The first, and ordinarily the longest, is the *preparation period*. The second, normally shorter, is the *implementation period*. We shall look at these in the rough order that they take place—"rough" because the ordering of events may be quite different from one director to another, and from one production (or theatre organization) to another.

Preparation Period

In the preparation period, a play is selected, its text may be translated or adapted, a producer is found, and the director begins to conceptualize the play's production so as to guide a production team dramaturgically (this is the story we want to tell), intellectually (this is *why* we want to tell it), and aesthetically (this is *how* we want it to look, sound, and feel), and assembles a team of designers technicians, and—of course—actors.

This preparation period does not normally take place in a theatre and often not even in a theatre facility. Rather it takes place in homes and offices, in e-mail exchanges and telephone conversations, at meetings in coffee shops and restaurants and theatre lobbies, and in the privacy of one's own reading. It takes place while reading scripts, seeing and participating in play productions, and discovering the world events—current or historical—that present important and potentially dramatic conflicts. Any of these activities may plant the seed of a possible new production of either a new or old play, and the desire to move on to the next step.

Finding a Producer   The first step most directors take at this point is to find a *producer* to finance the production, raise money to finance the production themselves and become its *producer-director,* or be invited by a producer to stage a play that could very well be this one. Indeed, most productions in American regional theatres today are initiated not by directors but by producers, who then hire directors to stage them.

The producer may be a single individual, such as the artistic director of a resident theatre, or a Broadway impresario, or the dean or chairperson of a university theatre department. Or it may be a number of individuals consolidated into a "producing entity"—such as a

corporation (such as Disney), a loose partnership of individuals (or "backers," as they are often informally called on Broadway), a committee (as in a university), or board of directors (as of a regional theatre). Whoever produces will certainly play a major role at the onset of the production, having a significant (and probably the final) say in its play selection, the assembling of its artistic team and cast, and, of course, the selection of the director.

The producer's role, however, is quite different than the director's. Typically, in a regional or university theatre, the producer's primary goal is to safeguard the long-term interests of the institution that hosts the production—whether it is an American regional company, a European national theatre, or a university drama department. Any of these established groups could face a decline in future attendance if the local audience and press reviewers deemed a single production too shocking or too boring. So producers generally maintain a close eye on the productions they oversee, making suggestions and giving notes to the director during the preparation period and later sitting in on rehearsals—particularly technical and dress rehearsals, when the production is taking final form. Producers cannot exactly "overrule" a director's decision, but they can certainly fire him or her, even at the last moment, and this happens with some regularity in the professional theatre world—quite famously before the (eventual) Broadway premiere of *Spider-Man: Turn Off the Dark.*

In addition to hiring (or firing) the director, and providing and distributing the financial resources, the producer's functions include creating and managing the budget, choosing and acquiring the theatre facility, and establishing the play's rehearsal and performance dates. They also generally handle the legal and business aspects of the production: negotiating its performance rights, and engaging and contracting the artistic staff (designers, composers, translators, technicians) and business staff (publicists, accountants, company managers). In addition, the producer is largely responsible for overseeing publicity, casting, ticketing, the house staff, and the creation of theatre programs. Although some of those latter functions may seem relatively distant from "theatrical art," each is absolutely crucial to theatrical success and thus plays a critical artistic role. The director's collaboration with the entity, whether one person or a team, is ongoing throughout the production process and is often critical.

Choosing the Play   The selection of a script may originate with the director or the producer. But certainly both producer and director must "buy into" the script if its production is to have a reasonable chance of succeeding. The play itself is the essential theatrical product. It is the basic element to which the audience responds—or thinks it responds—and it is universally perceived as the core of the theatrical experience.

Three basic considerations go into selecting a play: the director must have an eagerness to mount it (whether or not he or she first selected it); a confidence that it can be successfully cast, conceptualized, budgeted, and staged; and a belief that the production will engender genuine enthusiasm among the artistic team, the cast, and, eventually, its intended audience.

It is thus the director's job to seek the excitement latent in a script and to imagine its fullest theatrical potential. It is the audience, after all, that makes the theatre possible, and the director's ability to assess an audience's needs and wants is absolutely fundamental, both for pragmatic reasons (to ensure that an audience turns out to see the play) and for artistic reasons (to ensure that the play is satisfying, pertinent, and—one always hopes—thrilling to those who come to see it). It is also one of the primary determinants as to whether the director will be again invited to direct.

Simply because a director should consider audience interest when selecting a play, however, hardly means she or he should rely on the tried and true. Quite the contrary, the best directors provide their audiences with fresh, fascinating, vigorous, and exciting theatrical work. For some, these ingredients can be provided by musicals, thrillers, and domestic comedies; for others, by ancient classics, works of the European avant-garde, plays of social protest and reform, or new plays hot off the laptops of yet unknown authors. There is an audience for every sort of play, and it is the director's job to find that audience and attract it to their theatre. The audience demands to be challenged as well as confirmed—and, in the long run, directors who lead their audiences are far more likely to gain artistic recognition than are those who either follow the audience blindly or ignore it completely.

The director's capability to produce the play adequately with available resources is the final requisite for sound play selection, and here the director's collaboration with the producer is vital. Can the production rights to the play be acquired? Can a suitable cast be brought together? a production staff? a theatre? Is there enough money? Are the available actors experienced enough to master the play's style? Is the costume budget adequate for the size of the cast and the period of the play?

And do you, the director, understand this play well enough to bring out its ideas? A realistic consideration of one's own capabilities, together with an ability to assess the potential of one's expected collaborators, must be a significant factor in the critical decisions of play selection.

Adapting the Play   Often, particularly when the play is not covered by copyright,* a director may wish to adapt the script. The most common adaptation is "cutting" the text—deleting lines to compress the play's action and limit its duration. This is particularly true in the current era, when the average length of stage productions is closer to two hours than the two-and-a-half to three hours that was common in the past century. There are probably hundreds of *Hamlets* produced in America every year, but very few (if any) will include all of its 4,072 lines, which would take at least four hours to present in its entirety. The vast majority of American Shakespearean productions are therefore cut, these days, usually by five to fifteen percent of their original length. And not only cut: archaic words may be replaced with more commonly understood ones, scenes may be rearranged or eliminated altogether, and characters may be combined to reduce cast size. These revisions hold a potential danger—audience members familiar with the play may consider them distortions of what they had come to see—but general audiences rarely notice them and, when they do, may be more grateful than disappointed.

Along with changing the script, directors may change fundamental aspects of a play's dramaturgy—sometimes with shocking results. Indeed, leaner and more radical adaptations of classics are becoming almost common. Charles Marowitz may have led this movement, raising shock waves in London and Los Angeles in the 1970s and 1980s with his drastically revised version of Shakespeare's *The Taming of the Shrew*. Paring the title to simply *Shrew*, Marowitz deleted two-thirds of the text, added a few scenes of his own, and stripped Shakespeare's cast to merely five characters—Kate, the strong-willed "shrew" of the title, and four men, who not only taunted and domesticated her, as in Shakespeare's original, but brutally terrorized and finally sodomized her—driving her insane in the process.

---

*American copyright law currently covers an author's work until seventy years after his or her death.

In director Karen Henkel's radically revised and multi-lingual version of Shakespeare's *Macbeth* at the Munich Kammerspiele in 2011, Banquo and Macbeth intentionally bloody each other in order to appear as war heroes when they rejoin their company. Banquo (with the microphone, played by actor Benny Claessens) here sings of his woes while Macbeth (played by actress Jana Schulz) bashes him with his (or her!) staff. Such severe reconceptualizing of classical works can be controversial: many in the Munich audience attending the production's opening night performance booed loudly during the curtain call.

By retitling the play, Marowitz had warned the audience in advance that they would be seeing a reimagined version of Shakespeare's work, but more recent directors, particularly in Europe, don't always bother changing the titles. Karen Henkel's 2011 *Macbeth*, at the Munich Kammerspiele in Germany, was also stripped to five characters, who spoke only a tiny fraction of Shakespeare's actual text. In Henkel's modern-dress production, the witches sing "Rock-a-bye-Baby" (in English) to start the show, after which Macbeth (played by a woman) gives TV interviews that reference the killing of innocent Afghanis by a "kill team" of American soldiers. Actors in Elizabeth LaCompte's 2007 *Hamlet* with The Wooster Group in New York delivered a good deal of the Shakespearean text, but almost wholly in synch (and often in competition) with the 1964 filmed version, featuring Richard Burton,

projected onto the stage behind them. The projections were spiced up with intermittent interjections of cheap porn movies, Hawaiian hula dancing, and jerky kabuki movements. Nor are classic plays the only ones being overhauled today. The great 1935 American folk opera *Porgy and Bess*, retitled *The Gershwins' Porgy and Bess* (after its composer and lyricist, George and Ira Gershwin) was substantially revised by its adapter (Suzan Lori-Parks) and director (Diane Paulus) for its 2012 Broadway premiere. And in Germany, Tennessee Williams's 1947 *A Streetcar Named Desire* was, with the permission of the playwright's estate, radically adapted by both directors Frank Castorf (in Berlin, 2004) and Sebastian Nübling (Munich, 2011) with added and deleted scenes that led to astonishing results. These adapted productions are, and are intended to be, controversial, of course, and audience

Eastern European theatre—particularly in Romania—produced many brilliantly original high-concept directors during the cold war years because more straightforward plays displaying potentially liberal themes were discouraged by political authorities during the Soviet era. Since the fall of the iron curtain, many of these directors have brought their stylistic innovations to the world stage. Andrei Serban is one of the most distinguished. Here, the trial scene for his Parisian production of Shakespeare's *Merchant of Venice* at the Comédie-Française in 2001 combines words of the text on a blood-red back wall with an abstracted courtroom and its symbolically costumed personnel: the Christian defendant Antonio in white; the Jewish plaintiff Shylock in black; and the imposter judge Portia hatless and sporting a white tie beneath her black-and-pinstripe suit.

members often leave the theatre muttering something on the order of "Shakespeare (or Williams) must be rolling in his grave!" Nonethless, the "adaptation-option" has now become a clear possibility for stage directors around the world.

Conceptualizing the Production

More has been written in modern times about the director's role in conceptualizing a play than about any other directorial task; entire books are devoted to the creation of a central concept that focuses and unifies an entire production. There are two different sorts of directorial concept, however: the *core concept* and the *high concept*. All plays require the first; not all require the second.

The *core concept* is the director's determination of the most important of the many images, ideas, and emotions that should emerge from the play. Why should there be only one core concept when every play, when read, presents a multiplicity of important images, ideas, and emotions? Chekhov's *The Three*

Romanian director Gábor Tompa is represented here by this abstract and ritualized 2006 production of *Rhinoceros* by fellow Romanian playwright Eugène Ionesco. A hallmark of the theatre of the absurd, originally written and produced in Paris, *Rhinoceros* is now considered a global masterpiece: a savagely comic portrayal of the dehumanization of modern society, which turns humans into the equivalent of clumsy, brawling, thick-skinned animals—portrayed here by masked and trench-coated robotic creatures behind the one remaining human holdout, Ionesco's signature character of Beringer. The performance was produced by the Radu Stanca National Theatre and staged at the Sibiu International Theatre Festival in 2006.

Sisters, for example, can be seen as a play variously about love, ambition, sisterhood, despair, the oppression of women, rivalry between social classes, the social freedom of professional men, the oppression of rural Russian domesticity, the agony of unfulfilled hope, the corruption of provincial czarist bureaucracy, the seeds of a coming revolution. A director who tried to give equal weight to all those themes would create what most audiences and critics would consider a "mess"—a production that is unfocused and "all over the place." It can be staged as a comedy, a tragedy, or a romance. A production may incorporate most or even all of those themes and styles,

and indeed many more, but they must be prioritized, and one of them should be given the highest priority. That highest-priority image, idea, style or emotion becomes the *core organizing principle* that will give the production shape, meaning, importance, and momentum. It will help audience members clarify, at least to themselves, what the play is "about" and what it "means." It will ensure that the production *signifies something,* instead of, paraphrasing Shakespeare's Macbeth, being merely "full of sound and fury [but] signifying nothing."

How does a director decide on the core principle? There can be no universally "correct" answer to that question. Although research is important, the decision making is essentially a *creative* task. One way to approach it—to cut through the sound and fury of a complex play and settle on a single focal point before embarking into production—is to ask, "What should a poster for this production look like?" Should a poster of *Three Sisters* show the image of Masha's final embrace with her lover? the sisters abandoned by the soldiers at the final curtain? Natasha hiding in shame from the sisters gossiping about her in the next room? a birthday party of gaily laughing women and military officers, with the image of Lenin smirking at them from above? And should the poster's typeface be old-fashioned or modern? Should a few Cyrillic (Russian) letters be used to emphasize the play's Russian setting? Should the colors be primary or pastel, earth-toned or black-and-white, distressed, fragmentary, or faded? Should the design of the poster be clean or grimy, bold or subtle, abstracted or detailed? Should the mood be hopeful or despairing, the style elegant or grim? Answers to these "poster" questions point the director toward a possible core concept of the production.

Taglines—single statements that might serve as an informal subtitle for the play when produced—are also useful for creating a production's core concept. A tagline may be a social statement ("this is a play about tyranny") or a philosophical one ("a play about self-knowledge"). It may signal a specific interpretation ("a play about a man who cannot make up his mind") or invoke an invented dramatic genre ("a revenge melodrama"). A director may state the core concept in psychodramatic ("a primitive ritual of puberty"), historical ("a play about fratricide in the Middle Ages"), imagistic ("a play about swords, sables, and skulls"), or metatheatrical ("a play about playing") terms. Sometimes the tagline mentions a basic tone ("sad," "heroic," "royal") or a basic texture ("rich," "cerebral," "stark"). Diverse as those core-concept examples may seem, they all fall within the range of possibilities for conceptualizing a single play. Indeed, any one of them could be applied to Shakespeare's *Hamlet*—and every one of them has been, at some point, as have hundreds of others besides.

A *high concept* is another matter altogether. Contemporary directors can make a familiar play surprising—even astonishing—by introducing highly unexpected insights into character, story, or style. In its most simple form, a high concept may mean nothing more than moving a play out of the period in which it is set and placing it in another: for example,

resetting Molière's seventeenth-century *Tartuffe* from the Catholic-oriented France of the playwright's time and placing it in the Islamic-dominated, contemporary Middle East (as French director Arianne Mnouchkine did in 1995), or producing *Macbeth* as if taking place during Russia's Stalinist era (as British director Rupert Goold did in 2007). But today mere "relocation" hardly makes a play astonishing or even surprising. Twenty-first-century audiences have become quite used to high concepts and even expect them.

Like it or not (and there are many who do not), audiences and critics today are much more likely to admire (and remember) productions such as those of Robert Wilson and Peter Sellars (American), Peter Brook and Katie Mitchell (English), Ariane Mnouchkine and Dominique Serrand (French), Peter Stein and Frank Castorf (German) and Andrei Serban, Mihai Maniutiu, Silviu Purcarete, and Gábor Tompa (Romanian) that aim for unique and revelatory rethinkings of major works in the theatrical repertoire. (See also the section titled Four Global Luminaries in the chapter titled "Global Theatre Today.")

High-concept productions captivate audiences worldwide by transcending their plays' original conventions and presenting profound, moving, new, and uniquely illuminating theatricalizations that make telling references to current issues. High-concept theatre also avoids the "museum production" onus of traditional staging by taking actors out of, say, Elizabethan doublet and hose (traditional wear of the Shakespearean era) and putting them instead into something more contemporary, or making clearer references to the contemporary: if King Claudius (in *Hamlet*) looks like Muammar Gaddafi , the audience, without actually thinking about it, will quickly understand that this character is a brutal tyrant. A director known for brilliant high concepts will also discourage prospective attendees from declining to see his or her latest production of, for example, *King Lear* on the grounds that "I've already seen it," since they can be pretty sure they will have never seen anything like *this* production of it!

It is certainly no exaggeration, therefore, to say that *most* productions of classic plays in the twenty-first century, not just in experimental theatres but in the theatre's mainstream, seek high concepts. Directors (and directing students) are inevitably drawn to them, and audiences and critics, though sometimes skeptical, are almost always intrigued. Indeed, "So what's your concept for the show?" is likely to be the first question a colleague or a reporter asks a director engaging in a new production of a well-known play.

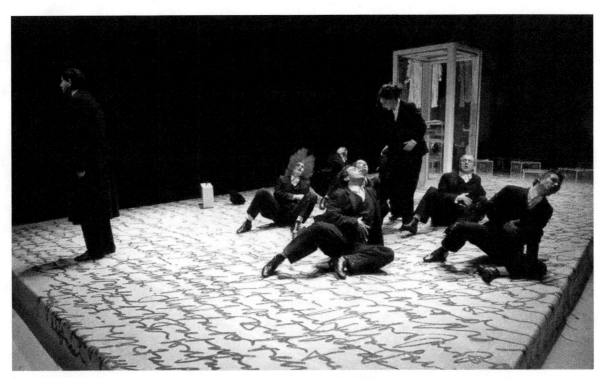

Directors often work very closely with dramaturgs, as when Romanian director Gábor Tompa collaborated with dramaturg Visky András in adapting Nobel Prize–winner Imre Kertész's introspective Hungarian novel about a Holocaust survivor, *Kaddish for an Unborn Child*, into a production that won critics' awards in Romania in 2008 and at France's Avignon Theatre Festival in 2009. Titled *Long Friday* (*Naître à jamais* in French), the play is a meditation on the survivor's refusal to have children since, as he says repeatedly, "Children were born at Auschwitz." Tompa's performers tackled the deeply provocative work with astounding athleticism, continually crashing to the floor and bouncing back again amid the singing of baleful dirges in Hebrew, Hungarian, Romanian, Greek, Italian, French, English, Spanish, and German. The design was by Carmencita Brojboiu.

Arriving at a high concept is no easy task. Once selected, the concept must "work" for the entire play. If *Othello* is set in World War II, what does the actor (or the property designer) do with Othello's "Put up your swords" line? How much can freshness add to a show without diminishing—or even obliterating—it? And how does the high concept actually improve the play—at least for its intended audience? What new ideas, readings of the text for the actors, and images for the designers does the high concept arouse? Heavy-duty research, and a comprehensive thinking-through of the entire script, are essential for the director trying to come up with an effective, workable, and genuinely inspiring high-concept production.

When approaching any play, the director should consider both core and high concepts. But because high concepts are prized for their unexpected insights into *familiar* plays, they probably should be avoided in the production of a *new* play. In a new play, the playwright

(presumably) is providing the fresh and unexpected insights, and the director of a new play probably should concentrate on the *core* concept.

The formation of both core and high concepts takes place at conscious and unconscious levels. In fact, it takes place whether the director wishes it to or not. It simply begins when the director first hears of a certain play, and it grows and develops as she or he reads the play, considers producing it, imagines its effects on an audience, and mentally experiments with possible modes of staging. Either sort of directorial concept is a product not only of the director's intelligence and vision but also of his or her personal experiences that relate to the matters portrayed by the play. Core and high concepts also call into play (and into the play) the director's personal likes and lusts, appreciations and philosophical leanings, and hopes for audience and critical reactions to the final product. A great directorial concept is personal; it is, finally, the director's studied and unique vision.

◉Spotlight

Dramaturg Jerry Patch

One of America's leading and longtime dramaturgs, Jerry Patch has played a role in the development of four Pulitzer Prize–winning plays (David Lindsay Abaire's *Rabbit Hole*, Donald Margulies's *Dinner with Friends*, Margaret Edson's *Wit*, and Lynn Nottage's *Ruined*), four other Pulitzer-nominated ones (Amy Freed's *Freedomland*, Richard Greenberg's *Three Days of Rain*, and Donald Margulies's *Sight Unseen* and *Collected Stories*), and about 150 other plays.

Most of this work took place in his three-plus decades as head dramaturg at South Coast Repertory in Southern California, but he also spent eight seasons as artistic director of the Sundance Theatre Program in Utah, which includes the noted Sundance Playwrights Laboratory, and he was coartistic director of San Diego's Old Globe Theatre for three years until, in 2008, he was invited to New York to assume the post of director of artistic development at the distinguished Manhattan Theatre Club (MTC), where your author interviewed him for this profile.

One of Patch's greatest successes was discovering Margaret Edson's *Wit* in the mid-1990s. It was one of the hundreds of plays submitted annually "over the transom" (unsolicited, unrepresented by an agent, and written by a beginning playwright unknown to the theatre's management) to South Coast Repertory.

"When we got it," Patch said, "its core was there, but elements in the first draft showed the playwright's inexperience. I knew there was an intelligence there, and the story that moved me was very human, and I was impressed that for all of Vivian Bering's [the lead character's] intelligence, she was most comforted by the nurse giving her a Popsicle. For a woman in her twenties to write this work was pretty amazing, so even though it wasn't seaworthy at that time, it was full of potential. So we took a couple of years—maybe three—working with Maggie to get the play to where it made sense for us to produce it. During that time we gave her regular dramaturgical feedback, we gave it a public reading, and finally we put it into rehearsal, during which we encouraged her to trim it from two acts and over two hours to a ninety-minute one-act—a very different structure. It was absolutely amazing, and she's an amazing woman."

Wit has enjoyed enduring success: it opened in New York in 1998, won the Pulitzer Prize in 1999, and made its Broadway premiere, starring Cynthia Nixon, in 2012. You can see an excerpt of the script in the chapter titled "The Playwright."

Patch acknowledges that today's New York theatre is at least as much about star actors as it is about new plays. He says it was difficult to get Lynn Nottage's *Ruined* produced in New York because it had "no stars, and, with eleven actors and understudies and a couple of musicians, it was not a cheap show to put on. And what's it about? A woman who gets raped in the Congo! So

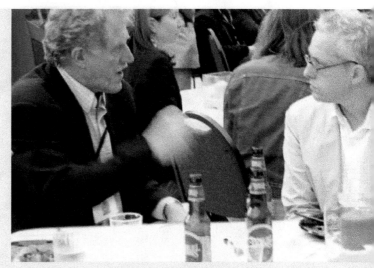

Dramaturgs don't always work in theatres! Here, over a couple of beers, dramaturg Jerry Patch and playwright Donald Margulies talk through a moment in Margulies' *Time Stands Still,* which the Manhattan Theatre Club, where Patch serves as Director of Artistic Development, brought to Broadway in 2010, where it enjoyed a year's run and won a Tony nomination.

at first we had to paper the hell out of the house [give away free tickets] to get audiences. But once people saw it, they became its advocates. The play became a grand event and we extended it several times; nearly everyone who saw it recommended it."

Patch had worked with Nottage before, at Sundance on her earlier *Crumbs from the Table of Joy*, and then at South Coast for the copremiere (in a coproduction with Baltimore's Centerstage) of her *Intimate Apparel*. The latter won "every critics' prize that year *except* the Pulitzer," Patch says wistfully.

Ruined first opened at Chicago's Goodman Theatre, where it remained in development until its New York debut at Manhattan Theatre Club. Before its MTC opening, Patch—along with his MTC colleague Mandy Greenfield—"mostly just went to the rehearsals and gave notes. We just asked questions, such as 'This is what I'm getting—is it what you want?' and 'Could this be shorter?' Lynn took it from there, and the play went all the way." In all, *Ruined* received thirteen best-play awards—including the Drama Desk, New York Critics, Outer Critics, and Obie awards, as well as the 2009 Pulitzer Prize.

Patch well remembers being told at the start of his career, "No kid ever dreamed of growing up to be a dramaturg." With the enormous contribution dramaturgs now make to the American theatre—and, indeed, to American culture—it is not surprising that students around the country are now contradicting that observation.

It is also specific, appropriate, evocative, visual, theatrical, concrete, and original, as well as a bit mysterious and a bit amusing. It leads the actors and the designers; and if it is truly inspired, it leads the director as well.

Many directors and producers today engage special theatre artists to assist the director in this conceptualizing period (and often in the play selection period as well). The usual title for this position is *dramaturg* (sometimes spelled "dramaturge"), although the terms "literary advisor" or "research assistant" are occasionally used.

A dramaturg is essentially a specialist in dramatic analysis who serves as a bridge between the director and the playwright. In some cases, if the play is a new one, the dramaturg may have already assisted the playwright in preparing the manuscript for production, whether the play is new or old. However, the dramaturg may help the director (and sometimes the actors) research the play; conceptualize the directorial approach; and better understand the play's structure, meanings, and historical context. The dramaturg's contributions are always advisory, but a well-trained and well-schooled dramaturg's advice often makes the difference between a bad production and a good one, and between a good one and a great one.

Implementation Period

As the production segues from preparation to implementation, the next task, if it has not often already been initiated (or even completed), is the assembling of a complete *artistic team* that will collaborate in the creation of the production. This will include, in addition to a dramaturg who may already be on board, the production's designers, stage managers, casting directors, actors, chief technicians, and various other personnel.

The director becomes the active head of this artistic team. He or she now bears the burden of sharing with the team the production's conception, giving their work a point of focus (a "direction," quite literally) and motivating the team to move toward it. From this time forward, the tasks of a play director are not unlike those of a corporate manager or chief executive: to set goals, establish priorities, facilitate communication, maintain the schedule, monitor progress, encourage the timid, rein in the errant, heighten the stakes, build team morale, and inspire excellence from everyone. No two directors will fulfill these functions in the same way or to the same degree, but, for most, a confident, natural, inspirational, and *collaborative* way of working with these teammates is at least as important as mastery of staging techniques. Artistic sensitivity, interpersonal skills, and eagerness

to accept responsibility—along with exercising needed authority—are always expected of professional play directors.

The steps of implementing the production's direction are many. Most are discussed in the following pages. Bear in mind, however, that in practice they are less clearly segmented than they appear here, as each of the separate elements (acting, lights, scenery, costumes, makeup) affects each of the others. And abstract concepts, once they are turned into an actual physical existence (such as a piece of scenery), often generate an unexpected impact on a production's other elements—for good or bad—and therefore on the production as a whole. So the sequence you are about to read is rarely as smoothly executed as it is described.

Selecting the Designers   The concept is the director's own creation, but its refinement and realization rest equally in the hands of designers, whose personal artistry and inclinations inevitably play an enormous role in the shape and impact of the final product. Hence the selection of these individuals is by no means a mechanical or arbitrary task; it is a central directorial concern of great artistic consequence.

Ordinarily directors make every effort to work with designers with whom they feel not only personal compatibility but also mutual respect and a synchrony of artistic and intellectual vision. Like all true collaborations, the most effective director-designer relationships result in a give-and-take of ideas, plans, feelings, and hypotheses—a sense of sharing and complementary support.

Collaborating with the Designers   Designing a production marks the first step toward transforming vision into actuality: at this stage, people turn ideas into concrete visual realizations. The director's work in designing a production is generally suggestive and corrective; how well she or he succeeds in this delicate task is highly dependent on the personalities and predilections of the individuals involved. In theory, the director's and designers' goals are identical: actable space, wearable costumes, and an evocative, memorable, and meaningful appearance of the whole. In practice, each of the principals has an independent perspective on what is actable, what is memorable, and what is evocative; moreover, each may have a different sense of the importance of sometimes contradictory values. A costume designer, for example, may place a higher value on the appearance of a garment than does the director, who may be more concerned with the actor's ability to move in it. A lighting designer may be greatly interested in the aesthetics of murkiness, whereas the director may be

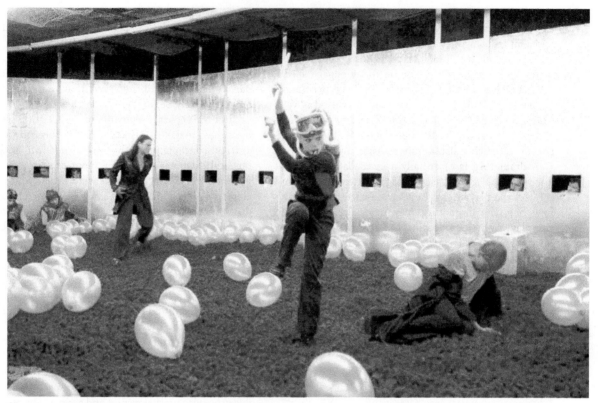

Staging sometimes begins with a reformulating of the nature of the playing space itself. Today's directors may completely redefine the relationship between audience and actor, either by placing the audience on the stage and the actors in the "audience" or by making other variations on the conventional theatrical arrangement. In Mihai Maniutiu's *Job Experiment*, for example, which the director adapted from the Old Testament book of Job, the play's actors— perhaps echoing Satan's Biblical question to God, "Have you not put a fence around him and his house?"—are surrounded by a closed-in polygonal wall (codesigned by Maniutiu and Christian Rusu) that is pierced by forty-four windows through which audience members, one to a window, peer in on the action. Here Job (*kneeling, right*—"he sits among the ashes," says the Bible) is in anguish as an angel of death kills his herd of cattle, represented by gold balloons. Maniutiu explained his goal was "not to bring old rites to life but to create a ritual fiction." The production was presented at the 2008 Romanian National Theatre Festival in Bucharest.

more concerned that an actor's face be clearly seen at a particular moment. These are the sorts of artistic perspectives that must be reconciled in the design process, which is essentially a collaboration whose decisions are less about finding the "right" or "wrong" solution and more a matter of subjective choice.

Production design normally takes place in a series of personal conferences between director and designers, sometimes on a one-on-one basis and sometimes in group meetings. (Increasingly, in America's regional professional theatres of the 2010s, many of these conferences take place electronically, via e-mail attachments and conference calls, because a given production's freelance director and designers may be working in different parts of the country—or world.) These are give-and-take affairs, for the most part, with the director doing most of the giving

at the beginning and the designers taking over shortly thereafter. Often the first step is a collective meeting— the first design conference—at which the director discusses his or her concept in detail and suggests some possibilities for its visual realization: colors, images, spaces, textures, and technological implementations.

In the ensuing conferences, which are often conducted one-on-one and sometimes on an ad hoc basis, designers normally present their own conceptions and eventually provide the director with a progressive series of concrete visualizations: sketches (roughs), drawings, renderings, models, ground plans, working drawings, fabrics, technical details, and devices. During these conferences the design evolves through a collaborative sharing in which the director's involvement may range from minimal to maximal, depending on

Trevor Nunn's 2004 production of *Hamlet* at the Old Vic in London employed the revolutionary casting of a very young man, twenty-three-year-old Ben Whishaw, in the title role. Forgoing the standard practice of using a famous older actor, Nunn's production—with a consequently younger-than-usual actress, Imogen Stubbs, as Hamlet's mother—made Hamlet's sulkiness and indecision far more affecting than is customary in this play.

how well the initial concept and the developing design seem to be cohering. Periodically—whenever the over-all design effort reaches a stage requiring coordinated planning—full design conferences are called to review and compare current plans for scenery, costume, light-ing, and properties; these conferences afford opportu-nities for the designers to collaborate with each other instead of simply with the director.

The director's function at this stage of design is to approve or reject, as well as to suggest. As the person who sits at the top of the artistic hierarchy, the direc-tor has the last word on design matters, but that does not mean she or he can simply command the show into being; theatre design, like any creative process, cannot be summoned forth like an obedient servant. More-over, wholesale rejection of a designer's work after the initial stages inevitably involves serious time loss and budgetary waste—not to mention the risk of provoking

some important staff resignations. For these reasons, the directorial effort must be committed from the out-set to sound collaborative principles. Once under way, the director-designer collaboration must take the form of shared responsibility in a developing enterprise, not confrontation between warring artists attempting to seize the reins of aesthetic control.

Casting the Actors   An old cliché states that "casting is 90 percent of directing"; while certainly a simplification, it contains more than a germ of truth. The people in a play—the actors—not only attract more audience attention than any other aspect of the play but also represent what the audience *cares* about and will remember the next day. They garner about 90 percent of all the interest an audience expends on a play, and if they squander that interest they can destroy the effectiveness of any theatrical presentation.

Photo Essay: Casting Director James Calleri

How can a professional director choose a cast from the more than 150,000 professional actors in the United States with any accuracy—much less seek out newcomers from the even larger number of student actors hoping to enter the professional world? The answer is simple: through the intercession of a casting director.

Casting directors became a vital part of the theatre and film worlds of New York and Los Angeles in the latter half of the twentieth century, and they now exist in theatre companies and, wherever professional theatres and film companies are active, in independent offices. The basic job of the casting director is to study scripts going into production, meet with producers and directors to assess what sorts of actors they're looking for, and, through interviews and preliminary tryouts, assemble a pool of outstanding performers to audition for the directors and producers. James Calleri, founding president of Calleri Casting in New York, has cast dozens of Broadway, off-Broadway, and regional theatre productions as well as hundreds of film and television roles. Your author asked him for his thoughts in 2009, soon after he had cast 33 *Variations* on Broadway with Jane Fonda and, off-Broadway, *The Seagull* with Diane Wiest and Alan Cumming. By this edition's time of writing, he has won eight Artio awards for outstanding achievement in casting from the Casting Association of America.

"My interest in casting started when I was in grad school," Calleri began. "I tended to be somewhat opinionated, and a little bossy with my teachers about who should be playing what roles (particularly when I didn't like somebody in something), and I remember speaking up about it. I thought somebody must know how to do this better, and so I packed up my car and moved to New York the day after I graduated. I didn't know anybody when I first got there, but I was lucky to get a job as an assistant at a talent agency, and that put me in the middle of everything. I developed a great relationship with the casting directors I met, and pretty soon I went to work for them, first sweeping floors and filing pictures and soon casting shows myself.

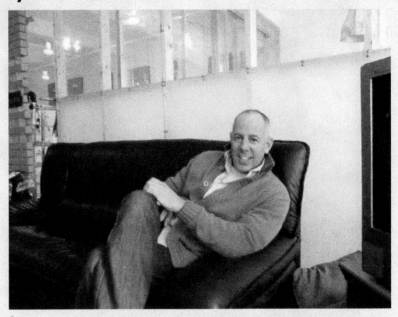

1. James Calleri, founding president of Calleri Casting in New York, in the informal interview room of his lower Manhattan office.

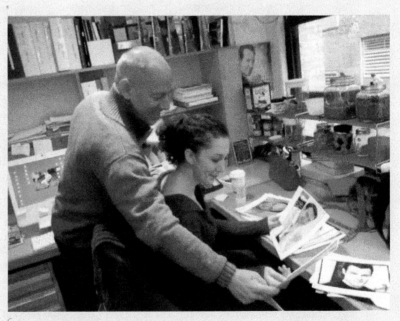

2. With assistant Katya Zarolinski, Calleri looks through headshot photographs of male actors he is considering for a new off-Broadway production.

"What do I look for in an actor? Of course, I want to see a person who's terrific in his or her craft, but I'm also hoping to see a fascinating personality, a mystique, a unique point of view about life. Equate this to dating: What is it about a person that keeps him or her in your mind? What drives you to ask that person for a second date? Well, an actor having that quality makes me confident that an audience will want to spend two to three hours watching him or her onstage or in multiple episodes of a TV series. For camera media, particularly TV, I'm looking primarily for personality. With theatre casting, it's much more about where you went to school, who you've worked with, what shows you've done, what theatres you've performed in, what type of roles you've played, what your voice is like and your body's like—all those things. And of course on Broadway, name recognition in the cast is pretty crucial. A play doesn't get to Broadway today unless the producers have a name they can hitch it to."

How can a beginning actor break into New York theatre? "You have to try to find work. Join a company, do a show that our agency would cover, perhaps in the fringe festival [an annual array of low-budget productions mounted around the city in late August], or a showcase, or a downtown theatre company that we frequent. That's where we find most people."

How has modern technology changed the business of casting? "We do a lot more looking at an actor's reels [short compilations of video clips of the actor's performance distributed on DVDs or via the Internet] these days, and we share video clips of our New York auditions with the producers and directors

3. Most of the submissions from actors and agents now come through the Internet. Here Calleri examines one of hundreds of digital headshots of actresses under consideration for the show's initial auditions.

in other cities. When I started at ABC, we would tape our auditions in New York and then ship the reels overnight to our colleagues at the studios in Los Angeles. Now we record them digitally and have them uploaded, edited, and sent out right to the L.A. set, where the producers can go into their trailers, watch the clips on their iPhones, and (we hope) say, 'Yes, that's exactly who I want!'"

How does Calleri like his job? "Casting? I love it. It's great, it's always different, it's always challenging, it never gets old."

The theatre as a medium has many individual standardized and predictable elements: flats are made according to formula, lighting instruments are factory calibrated to conform to precise specifications, color media are mathematically measured and numbered, and one theatre's jet black "velours" (plush draperies) are nearly identical to those of another. But the one unique ingredient of the theatre—as the audience sees it—is the actor. Actors are people, and as people they are exquisitely individual; moreover, the audience, being human itself, is particularly attuned to the actor's human and idiosyncratic uniqueness. We would never mistake the Hamlet of Mel Gibson for the Hamlets of Kenneth Branagh, Ethan Hawke, Kevin Kline, or Jude Law. The actor's personality, physical and vocal characteristics, technical abilities, and sheer talent and "presence" weigh mightily in the final realization of every individual performance and in every ensemble of performances. A miscast or untalented or untrained actor can mar the effectiveness of any production, even in a minor role; in a major role a poor performance simply ruins the play. Casting may not, in the end, account for 90 percent of the director's contribution, but there can be no doubt that bad casting renders all other efforts immaterial.

In professional theatre, initial casting decisions are often made by a *casting director,* who seeks and screens potential actors for the parts being cast, and often considers *submissions* (mainly photos and résumés) from actors who wish to be considered for one or more of the roles. The actual casting then takes place during a series of *auditions* in which the actor—either by his or her own application or on the recommendation of a casting director—can be seen and heard by the director, either in a reading of material from the play to be produced, or in a previously prepared dramatic monologue. The director's ability to detect an incipiently brilliant performance in either of these contrived audition formats is a critical factor in effective casting.

Depending on the specific demands of the play and the rehearsal situation, the director and casting director will, in this first audition, pay special attention to any or all of the following characteristics: the actor's training and experience, physical characteristics and vocal technique, suitability for the style of the play, perceived ability to impersonate a specific character in the play, personality traits that seem fitted to the material at hand, ability to understand the play and its milieu, personal liveliness and apparent stage "presence," past record of achievement, and apparent cooperativeness and "directability" in the context of an acting ensemble.

And the director might well be looking for a great many other things besides.

What is astonishing about the casting process is that the vast majority of these first audition decisions—which are the dreaded dismissal words "Thank you very much"—are often made in the first five or ten seconds of the actor's audition! That is because experienced directors and casting directors are quick to assess actors as being, at least in their opinions, wrong for the play, wrong for the part, or lacking in the desired level of proficiency. Others may be winnowed out on the subjective ground of apparent attitude—a dangerous ground because the director might mistake shyness for hostility or "audition jitters" for an exaggerated reserve.

Actors who survive the first audition then "read" again, sometimes several times, and at this stage the director is involved more and more in the audition process, often coaching the actors to determine how rapidly they can acquire the qualities needed. Such "callbacks" can go on for days and even weeks in the professional theatre, limited only by the union requirement that actors receive pay after a certain point. The frequency with which such payments are made amply attests to the care that attends final casting decisions in the professional theatre.

There is good casting and bad casting, of course, and there is also inspired casting. Many of the greatest performances in theatre history have been achieved by actors who at first glance appeared unsuited to their roles. When, for example, director Anthony Page cast the gangly Janet McTeer (the *New York Times* critic called her "a woman of towering height") as Nora (whose husband Torvald calls her his "little love-bird") in his Broadway production of Ibsen's *A Doll's House,* it seemed to many an odd choice, but Page's notion and McTeer's dazzling performance brilliantly underscored Page's notion that Torvald and, by inference, all men of his ilk who shortchange their wives' capabilities, are themselves severely diminished. And director Lee Breuer's casting of his Mabou Mines company's production of the same play with actors four feet tall or less in all the male roles and tall women for the female ones proved an equally brilliant stroke. Breuer's casting was complemented by the show's miniaturized "Alice-in-Wonderland" setting, and it expanded the personal and marital themes of the Page production to a more general social analysis of male-female relations in both Ibsen's and our own times. The ability to see beyond traditional casting options, and to imagine the unique and unexpected relationships actors can create with

Director Sebastian Nübling's 2010 staging of Tennessee Williams's *A Streetcar Named Desire* at the Munich Kammerspiele put the play in a modern setting yet maintained the author's realistic and powerfully focused struggle between the rough and tumble world of Stanley (Steven Scharf, standing), his wife Stella (Katja Buerkle, in blue) and his boldly tattooed, poker-playing friends, who are shown in complete contrast to the isolated and affected Blanche (Wiebke Puls) at lower right. The stage picture clearly reveals the social discords inherent in Nübling's directorial concept.

even "standard repertoire" roles, has always been the mark of the most daring and most successful directors.

Rehearsals

With the play selected and conceptualized, with the designers chosen and the designs under way, and with the actors auditioned and cast, the production begins to take physical, emotional, and *dramatic* shape. This is the period of rehearsal. During the coming weeks, the play will be read aloud, memorized, staged, and rehearsed—often in a room with makeshift "rehearsal furniture" and the walls of the setting indicated by taped marks on the floor. The actual sets, costumes, and props will be designed and built in shops available for those purposes. Sound, lighting, and special effect cues will be created and eventually worked into the rehearsals. The acting will be coached, detailed, and

drilled into the actors' muscle memories. By the end of the rehearsal period all the production's elements—acting, sets, lights, costumes, props, sound, scene shifts—will have been integrated into their final form in technical run-throughs, dress rehearsals, previews on some occasions, and the legendary "opening night."

The director's ability to maintain both leadership and creative inspiration through this period becomes more crucial every day, for from the time of that first company meeting, the director controls the focus and consciousness of the entire cast and staff. As head of an ambitious and emotionally consuming enterprise, the director will be the repository of the company's collective artistic hopes—and the focal point for the company's collective frustration, anxiety, and, on occasion, despair. The director is the company's shield against the intrusions of an outside world, as well as the spokesperson for the enterprise to which the company has

Fight scenes are not always duels or military battles. Here actors Roger Allam and Jodhi May have at each other with ordinary office chairs, as staged by Fight Director Malcolm Ranson in David Harrower's *Blackbird*, an intense drama about pedophilia and its horrific aftermath. The play, directed by the acclaimed German director Peter Stein, was performed at the Edinburgh Festival in 2006.

collectively dedicated itself. Directorial power or influence cannot be substantially altered by any attempt the director may make to cultivate or repudiate it—it simply comes with the job and with the need for every theatrical company to have a head, a focus, a direction. The manner in which the director uses that power, and the sensitivity with which she or he brings the production into being, determines the nature of each director's individual brand of artistry.

Staging   Positioning the actors on the set and having them move about in a theatrically effective manner is the most obvious of directorial functions. Directorial *composition*, as it is sometimes called, is the one thing directors are always expected to do and to do well, and it is the one they are most often *seen* doing; it is no wonder traditional textbooks on directing tend to be largely devoted to this function.

The medium of staging is the actor in space and time—with the *space* defined by the acting area and settings and the *time* defined by the duration of the theatrical event and the dynamics of its dramatic structure. The goals of staging are multiple and complementary: to create focus for the play's themes, to lend credibility to the play's characters, to generate interest in the play's actions, to impart an aesthetic wholeness to the play's appearance, to provoke suspenseful involvement in the play's events, and, in general, to stimulate a fulfilling theatricality for the entire production.

The basic architecture of staging is called *blocking*, which refers to the timing and placement of a character's entrances, exits, rises, crosses, embraces, and other major movements of all sorts. The "blocking pattern" that results from the interaction of characters in motion provides the framework of an overall staging; it is also the physical foundation of the actors' performance—and

One of the major problems in staging realistic plays is letting the audience see the expressions of important characters—and hence the faces of the actors playing them—while still maintaining the credibility of those characters, who are (supposedly) talking to each other and not to the audience. Director Guy Masterson solves this by having all actors focus on a key prop in this jury-room scene in Reginald Rose's *12 Angry Men*, produced at the Edinburgh Festival in 2003.

many actors have difficulty memorizing their lines until they know the blocking that will be associated with them.

The director may block a play either by preplanning the movements ("preblocking") on paper or by allowing the actors to improvise movement on a rehearsal set and then "fixing" the blocking sometime before the first performance. Often a combination of these methods is employed, with the director favoring one method or the other depending on the specific demands of the play, the rehearsal schedule, rapport with the acting company, or the director's own stage of preparation. Complex or stylized plays and settings and short rehearsal periods usually dictate a great deal of preblocking; simple domestic plays and experienced acting ensembles are often accorded more room for improvisation. Each method can produce highly commendable results in the right hands and at the right time; both can present serious problems if misapplied or ineptly handled.

For the most part, the blocking of a play is hidden in the play's action; it tends to be effective insofar as it is *not* noticed and insofar as it simply brings other values into play and focuses the audience's attention on significant aspects of the drama. By physically enhancing the dramatic action and lending variety to the play's visual presentation, a good blocking pattern can play a large role in creating theatrical life and excitement. But beyond this, there are moments when inspired blocking choices can create astonishing theatrical effects—effects that are not hidden at all but are so surprising and shocking that they compel intense consideration of specific dramatic moments and their implications. Such a coup de théâtre was achieved, for example, by director Peter Brook in his celebrated 1962 production of *King Lear*, when Paul Scofield, as Lear, suddenly rose and, with one violent sweep of his arm, overturned the huge oak dining table at which he had been seated, sending pewter mugs crashing to the floor as he raged at his daughter Goneril's treachery. This stunning action (though it might seem almost timid today) led to a reevaluation of the character of both Lear and Goneril and of the relationship between this tempestuous and sporadically vulgar father and his socially ambitious daughter. It also instantly established Brook as one of England's greatest living directors and, still talked about to this day, propelled his career to its extraordinary heights.

Some plays require specialized blocking for specialized movements such as dueling, dancing, or flying effects—as in *Peter Pan* or *Spider-Man*. Such scenes require particularly skilled direction and coaching, so the director may wish to engage a choreographer, fight director, or flying specialist to create the highly detailed moment-to-moment movements that scenes as these require. Such specialized dramatic situations are hardly rare. Almost every play written before the nineteenth century includes a dance, a duel, a battle, or some combination of all of them, and the ability to create or at least to oversee a captivating dance number or an exciting battle or flying scene is clearly requisite for any director aspiring to work beyond the strictly modern-realistic mode.

Directors are often thought of as commanding presences in a stage production, but Ariane Mnouchkine, the founding director of France's highly distinguished Théâtre du Soleil, has always believed in full collaboration, and the members of her company eat and in most ways live together, creating their works in a living artistic ensemble. In Soleil productions, the audience is invited to wander through the actors' makeup rooms before the show, and often—as in *Les Éphémères*—to enjoy beverages and cookies with the actors during intermissions. All Soleil company members are paid identical wages, from the assistant stage managers to Mnouchkine herself, shown here with company members before a *Les Éphémères* rehearsal.

Business is a theatre term that refers to the small-scale movements a character performs within the larger pattern of entrances and crosses and exits. Mixing a cocktail, answering a telephone, adjusting a tie, shaking hands, fiddling with a pencil, winking an eye, and drumming on a tabletop are all "bits of business" that can lend a character credibility, depth, and fascination. Much of the stage business in a performance is originated by the actor—usually spontaneously over the course of rehearsal—although it may be stimulated by a directorial suggestion or request. The director ultimately must select from among the rehearsal inventions and determine what business will become a part of the finished performance; when this determination is made, bits of business become part of the blocking plan.

Staging, then, in the largest sense, includes both hidden and bold blocking effects, specialized movements, and small idiosyncratic behaviors, all combined into a complex pattern that creates meaning, impact, and style. Skillful staging unites the design elements of a production with the acting, creating an omnidynamic spatial interaction between actors, costumes, scenery, and audience, infusing the stage with life. Getting a play "on its feet," as the theatrical jargon puts it, is usually the first step in allowing the actors to experience the full human vitality of the playwright's characters, both in the actions they take and the words they utter.

Actor-Coaching   The director is the actor's coach and both initiates and leads the various activities—discussions, improvisations, games, exercises, lectures, research, blocking, polishing—that will occupy the actors during each rehearsal. Like a football or hockey coach, the director seeks to stimulate proactive teamwork among the "players," as well as develop individual craft excellence and artistry in each one of them. And because the work of the theatre inevitably demands of the actor a good measure of emotional, psychological, and even irrational investment, the director has an opportunity (if not an obligation) to provide an atmosphere in which actors can feel free to liberate their powers of sensitivity and creativity. Good directors lead their casts; great directors inspire them.

Guiding the actors through the script may be important in the early stages of rehearsal, particularly if the language is complex, the historical period unfamiliar, or the play's characters unlike persons known to the actors themselves. Sometimes the director will invite the dramaturg, if one is on the artistic team, to provide appropriate readings or give a company lecture on the more elusive points of the text, helping integrate them into the production's conception. The director may ask voice coaches, dance and fight choreographers, and others to provide assistance where specialized performance techniques are desired.

The ways in which directors go about coaching actors are various and probably more dependent on

Stagecraft

"This Is How It's Done!"

Publicity photographs taken in rehearsal frequently show a director onstage with a few actors, demonstrating a bit of business and "showing them how it's done." This kind of publicity has probably fostered a certain misunderstanding of the director's role among the general public, for demonstration is only a part of directing, and a distinctly small part at that. Indeed, some directors scrupulously avoid it altogether.

Demonstration as a way of teaching an actor a role has a long history in the theatre and was a particularly common practice in those periods when directing was carried out chiefly by retired actors. Even today, young actors rehearsing for classical plays at the Comédie-Française (founded in 1680) are expected to learn their parts by mimicking the performance of their elders down to the last detail of inflection, tone, gesture, and timing. And many contemporary American directors occasionally give "line readings" to an actor or demonstrate the precise manner of gesturing, moving, sitting, or handling a prop if they perceive that a specific desired behavior might not come naturally.

But demonstration as an *exclusive* method of coaching an actor in a role is very much a thing of the past. Most contemporary directors make far greater use of discussion, suggestion, and improvisation. These methods seek to address the inner actor and to encourage the individual to distill his or her performance out of self-motivated passions and enthusiasms. Because they know that a purely imitative performance is all too likely to be a mechanical performance, today's directors tend to rely on methods more creative than "getting up there and showing how it's done."

personality than on planning. Some directors are largely passive; they either "block and run," in the jargon of commercial theatre, or function primarily as a sounding board for actors' decisions about intention, action, or business. Conversely, there are directors closer to the popular stereotype, mercurial fanatics whose approaches at times verge on the despotic: they cajole, bully, plead, storm, and rage at their actors; involve themselves in every detail of motive and characterization; and turn every rehearsal into a mixture of acting class, group therapy session, and religious experience. Both methods, as experience teaches, can produce theatrical wizardry, and both can fail utterly. Probably the determining factors either way are the strength of the director's ideas and the extent to which the cast is willing to accept his or her directorial authority.

Too little direction, of course, can be as stultifying to an actor as too much. The passive director runs the risk of defeating an actor's performance by failing to confirm it, that is, by withholding constructive response. Similarly, the extremely active director may, in a whirlwind of passion, overwhelm the actor's own creativity and squelch his or her efforts to build a sensitive performance, thereby condemning the production to oppressive dullness. For these and other reasons, most directors today strive to find a middle ground, somewhere between task mastery and suggestion, from which they can provide the actor with both a goal and a disciplined path toward it while maintaining an atmosphere of creative freedom.

Directors need not be actors themselves, but they must understand the paradoxes and ambiguities inherent in that art if they are to help the actor fashion a solid and powerful performance. The greatest acting braves the unknown and flirts continuously with danger (the danger of exposure, of failure, of transparency, of artifice). The director must give the actor a careful balance of freedom and guidance to foster the confidence that leads to that kind of acting. Directors who are insensitive to this requirement—no matter how colorful their stormings and coaxings or how rational their discussions of the playwright's vision—are almost certain to forfeit the performance rewards that arise from the great actor-director collaborations.

Pacing Despite all the director's responsibilities, pace is perhaps the only aspect of a theatrical production for which general audiences and theatre critics alike are certain to hold the director accountable. Frequently, newspaper reviews of productions devote whole paragraphs of praise or blame to the actors and designers and evaluate the director's contribution solely in terms of the play's pace: "well paced" and "well directed" are almost interchangeable plaudits in the theatre critic's lexicon; and when a critic pronounces a play "slow" or "dragging," everyone understands he or she is firing a barrage at the director.

To the novice director (or critic), however, pace appears to be simply a function of the rate at which lines are said; hence a great many beginning directors attempt to make their productions more lively simply

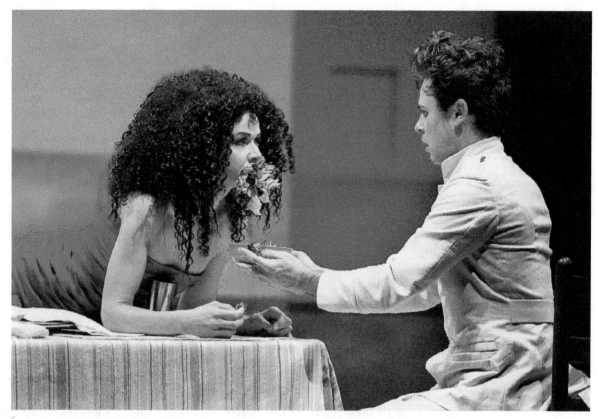

Directing comedy is an art in itself, and Dominique Serrand scored a brilliant success in a Shakespearean play that demands theatrical humor in its very title: *The Comedy of Errors*. Serrand directed this play at the Guthrie Theatre in 2002 with what one reviewer called "fantastical . . . madcap panache"—as clearly shown in the mouth-stuffing scene between Laura Esping as an irate Luciana and Judson Pearce Morgan as a bewildered Antipholus.

by instructing everyone to speak and move at a fast clip: "Give it more energy!" "Make it happen faster!" But dramatic pace is not determined solely by a stopwatch; rather, it is created on the basis of a complex and composite time structure that incorporates many variables: credibility, suspense, mood, style, and the natural rhythms of life, such as heartbeat, respiration, the duration of a spontaneous sob, and the suddenness of an unexpected laugh. How much time is properly consumed, for example, by a moment of panic? a pregnant pause? a flash of remembrance? an agonized glance? a quick retort? These are the true ingredients of pace, and they are not subject to the generalized "hurry-up" of the director who has not first discovered the pattern of rhythms inherent in the play.

What are those patterns of rhythms? In a farce, the audience needs almost no time to synthesize information; therefore, farce generally is propelled rapidly, with information coming as fast as the actors can get it out.

Political drama, on the other hand, demands of us a critical inquiry into our own societies, and demands time for the audience to linger over certain well-poised questions before moving on to speedier scenes as the play's arguments escalate toward climaxes. Deeply psychological dramas present a third pattern, often profiting by an even slower pace that fosters the audience's deeper understanding of the play's characters and their issues. Sympathy in these plays is more likely to be engendered when audience members have an opportunity to compare the characters' lives with their own, and are able to put themselves in the characters' situations, and ponder the subtle meanings emerging from the onstage actions.

But no pace is simply mechanical or unvaried. Just as a symphony is composed of several movements, so a well-paced theatrical production inevitably has its adagio, andante, and allegro tempos. Faster tempos tend to excite, bedazzle, and sharpen audience attention;

Tony-winning director Daniel Sullivan has established a firm and glowing reputation—in twenty-six Broadway productions and countless off-Broadway and regional ones —for extracting and conveying these dramas' most powerful emotional components. His 2011 production of David Lindsay-Abaire's *Good People*, set in a kitchen in a rundown South Boston apartment—the epitome of old-fashioned "kitchen sink realism" —consequently won the New York Drama Critics Award and a Tony nomination for Best Play of the Year, and Frances McDormand (*center*, flanked by Becky Ann Baker [*left*] and Estelle Parsons) received the Tony for Best Actress. John Lee Beatty designed the smartly detailed kitchen and David Zinn the working-class costumes.

slower ones give audience members a chance to consider and to augment the play's actions and ideas with their own reflections. Often directors speak about "setting up" an audience with a rapid pace and then delivering a "payoff" with a powerful, more deliberately paced dramatic catharsis. The sheer mechanics of theatrical pacing demand the greatest skill and concentration from both actor and director, and for both, the perfection of dramatic timing (and most notably comic timing) is a mark of great theatrical artistry.

Directors vary in their manner of pacing plays. Some wait until final rehearsals and then, martinet-like, stamp out rhythms on the stage floor with a stick or clap their hands in the back of the house. Some work out intricate timing patterns in the early rehearsals and explore them in great detail with the

actors as to motivation, inner monologue, and interpersonal effect. Directorial intervention of some sort is almost always present in the achievement of an excellent dramatic pace; it rarely occurs spontaneously. Actors trained in the realist manner often tend to work through material slowly and to savor certain moments all out of proportion to the information they convey; actors trained in a more technical manner just as often are "off to the races" with the dialogue, leaving the audience somewhat at sea about the meaning or importance of the matters at hand. And when a variety of actors, trained in different schools, come together in production for the first time, they can create such an arrhythmic pace that the play becomes unintelligible until the director steps in to guide and control the tempo.

Coordinating In the final rehearsals the director's responsibility becomes more and more one of coordination: of bringing together the concept and the designs, the acting and the staging, the pace and the performance. Now all the production elements that were developed separately must be judged, adjusted, polished, and perfected in their fuller context. Costumes must be seen under lights, staging must be seen against scenery, pacing must include the shifting of sets, acting must coalesce with sound amplification and the size of the performance hall, and the original concept must be reexamined in light of its emerging realization. Crucial questions must be answered: Is the theme coming across? Are the actions coming across? Can the actors be heard and understood? Do the costumes read? Is the play focused? Is the play interesting? Do we care about the characters? about the themes? about anything? Does the production seem to *work*?

Timing and wholeness are governing concepts in this final coordinating phase of production. In assessing the play's overall timing, the director must be prepared to judge the play's effectiveness against its duration and to modify or eliminate those parts of the production that overextend the play's potential for communicating information, feelings, or ideas. Last-minute cutting is always a painful process—much labor and creative spirit have gone into the parts that will be cut—but many a production has been vastly improved by judicious pruning at this time. And in the interest of providing wholeness—the quality that unifies a play and gives it the stamp of taste and aesthetic assurance—the best and bravest directors are willing in these final moments to eliminate elements that fail to cohere with the play's overall appearance and significance. Often these elements hold a special meaning for the director; they may even have figured into his or her earliest conception of the production. But now, in the cold light of disciplined analysis, they may rather look painfully like directorial indulgence or extraneous showing off. The best directors are those who can be most rigorous with themselves at this stage, for they are the ones who are capable not only of generating ideas but also of refining and focusing artistic form.

In the final rehearsals—the *technical rehearsals,* when scenery, lighting, and sound are added, and *dress rehearsals,* when the actors don costumes and makeup for the first time—the director arrives at a crossroads: though remaining fundamentally responsible for every final decision about the timing and balance of theatrical elements, she or he must now "give over" the core of the production to the actors and technicians who will execute it. In these rehearsals the director's presence becomes more a matter of finessing the show's details, delivered to the cast and staff in hundreds of last-minute notes, rather than general concepts or inspirational speeches. Yet it is in just these minute details that a production develops the refinement that distinguishes the outstanding from the mediocre.

What an extraordinary exchange of power has taken place between the first meeting of the cast and director and these final days! Whereas earlier the entire production was in the director's head and the cast waited in awe and expectation, now the actors hold the play in their heads and everyone confronts the unknowns of the play's reception. The actors have a new master now: the audience. It is in these days that even the most experienced actors confront their fundamental nakedness in performance: they must face the audience, and they must do it without benefit of directorial protection, with nothing to shield them save their costumes, characters, and lines. To the actor, the director is no longer a leader but a partner, no longer a parent but a friend. Actors may indeed experience a certain feeling of betrayal; the director, after all, has abandoned them to face the audience alone, just as in the medieval play Good Deeds accompanies Everyman only to the brink of the grave—she does not enter with him. Like death, acting is a trial that cannot be shared.

Presenting It is an axiom of the theatre that nobody is more useless on opening night than the director. If all has progressed without major catastrophe and the production has successfully been "given over" to those who will run it and perform in it, the director's task on opening night consists chiefly in seeing and evaluating the production and gauging the audience response. This night may, of course, prove to be nothing but a calm between storms. When there are preview performances, as there are in all professional theatres and some academic and community ones, the director has the opportunity (and responsibility) to evaluate the production in terms of its audience response, and institute changes during the previews where desirable—including cuts and changes in the text if it's a new play and the playwright is on hand and willing—right up to the opening performance. The director may invite the dramaturg, if one is on the team, to provide comments throughout this final period, and be an "in-house critic" to spot moments in the production that may not be coming through as strongly as they could be, and also to prepare the printed program for the production, including his or her own dramaturgical notes on the play, perhaps alluding to its historical context and thematic resonances that would guide the audience as to what they might want to look for in the performance they are about to see.

And although in professional theatre a director's contract normally terminates on opening night, most directors try to see performances periodically during the run, and may follow up their visits with notes to the actors—either to encourage them to maintain spontaneity or to discourage them from revising the original directorial plan. One perhaps apocryphal show-business story has it that the American director George Abbott once posted a rehearsal call late in a play's run in order to "take out the improvements."

Just as the actor might feel alone and somewhat betrayed in those empty moments prior to the opening performance, so might the director feel a twinge of isolation at the ovation that follows it. For it is in that curtain-call ovation that the audience takes over the director's critic-mentor function and the director is consigned to anonymity. The actors, heady with the applause, suddenly remember that they provide the essential ingredient of theatre, while the director, cheering the ensemble from the back of the house, suddenly realizes he or she is now just one of the crowd, one witness among many to the realization of his or her own intangible and now remote plans and ideas. In the professional theatre, it is at this moment the director's contract really expires—a fitting reminder of the "giving over" that occurs in the direction of all plays. Only directors who can derive genuine satisfaction from creating art out of the medium of others' performance will thrive and prosper in directorial pursuits; those who aspire to public acclaim and adulation will most likely face perpetual frustration as practitioners of this all-encompassing yet all-consuming craft.

THE TRAINING OF A DIRECTOR

Traditionally, directors have come to their craft from a great many areas, usually after achieving distinction in another theatrical discipline: for example, Elia Kazan was first an actor, Susan Stroman a choreographer, Harold Prince a producer, Peter Hunt a lighting designer, Franco Zeffirelli a scene designer, Robert Brustein a drama critic, Mike Nichols an improvisational comedian, and Robert Wilson an architectural student. Still,

in addition to a specialty, most of these directors have brought to their art a comprehensive knowledge of the theatre in its various aspects. Having distinction in one field is important chiefly insofar as it gives directors a certain confidence and authority—and it gives others confidence in their exercise of that authority. But it is *comprehensive* knowledge that enables directors to collaborate successfully with actors, designers, managers, playwrights, and technicians with facility and enthusiasm.

Directors entering the profession today, therefore, are more likely than not to have been trained in a dramatic graduate program or conservatory—and often they have supplemented this training with an apprenticeship at a repertory theatre. One of the most remarkable recent developments in the American theatre has been the emergence of a cadre of expertly trained directors: men and women with a broad understanding of the theatre and a disciplined approach to directorial creativity.

Well-trained directors will possess—in addition to the craft mastery of staging, actor-coaching, pacing, and production coordinating—a strong literary imagination and an ability to conceptualize intellectually and visually. They will be sensitive to interpersonal relationships, which will play an important role in the onstage and offstage collaborations under their control. They will have a thorough working knowledge of the history of the theatre, the various styles and masterworks of dramatic literature, the potential of various theatre technologies, and the design possibilities inherent in the use of theatrical space. They will have at their command resources in music, art, literature, and history; they will be able to research and closely analyze plays to investigate production possibilities without starting at absolute zero; and they will be able to base ideas and conceptions on sound social, psychological, and aesthetic understandings.

All of these advanced skills can be effectively taught in a first-rate drama program, and for that reason today's top-flight theatre directors, more than any other group of stage artists, are likely to have studied in one or another of the rigorous drama programs now in place across the country. The accomplished director is perhaps the one all-around "expert" of the theatre; this is not to deride his or her function as a creative and imaginative force but to emphasize the director's responsibility over a broad and highly complex enterprise. Nothing is truly irrelevant to the training of a director, for almost every field of knowledge can be brought to bear upon theatre production.

Photo Essay: The School for Wives

Molière's 1662 comedy, *The School for Wives*, directed by the author of this book, was produced by the Tony Award-winning Utah Shakespearean Festival in the city of Cedar City during the summer of 2008. The production ran from June 27 through August 30 of that year but was put together during a full year preceding its opening performance. These photos show some of the work involved in putting this production together.

1. *Conceiving.* The director and principal designers were engaged for this production during the summer and fall of 2007, and each began immediately to conceive the basic look, tone, and feel of the production. Since these artists are based far from Cedar City (New York City, Los Angeles, Tampa, and Ogden, Utah), almost all of the initial collaborations were accomplished by e-mail and attached digital images and sound samples. Here in October, Director Robert Cohen, in his Laguna Beach home, looks over a first "rough model" that Scenic Designer Jo Winiarski digitally photographed and then e-mailed to him from her New York studio.

2. *Planning.* In two midwinter meetings, one in Salt Lake City and this one in Cedar City, the director and the principal artistic and technical staffs share and coordinate their ideas for the show. Here, Scene Designer Winiarski shows her latest model, quite evolved from her earlier version, to the festival's producers and artistic staff.

3. (*Left*) *Detailing.* The show's costume designer, Janet Swenson, shows her rendering of the proposed costume for the character of Enrique, a dandy "recently arrived from New Spain," to the director for his comments and suggestions.

4. (*Top right*) *Casting.* The festival's casting director, Kathleen Conlin, discusses with the director the actors whom she is interested in casting in the play's nine roles.

5. (*Bottom right*) *Approvals.* Scott Phillips, the festival's executive director, meets with Cohen to evaluate and approve decisions made at the winter meetings, and also to discuss the proposed "Americanization" of a few words in the new translation, which is by British author Ranjit Bolt. The word changes for the Utah production will be developed by Cohen in consultation with Bolt.

6. *Director's and Designers' Presentations.* When cast and artistic staff finally assemble at the Cedar City theatre on May 5, 2008, the director and then the individual designers present their various concepts and plans for the production. Here Costume Designer Swenson shows her costume renderings to the assembled company.

7. *The First Reading.* The directing and design presentations are followed by a reading of the entire play by the actors, seated around a table and working from the scripts mailed to them several weeks previously. Other members of the production team have remained for this reading: they include the casting director, the vocal and dialect coach, the dramaturg, and members of the festival's artistic directorate. This reading is followed by a discussion of the play's details, and everyone around the table is encouraged to speak, comment, and ask questions. The first reading may be followed by a second, third, or even more readings in the ensuing days. In this case, the rehearsals moved directly into the staging of the action.

8. *Staging, or "Blocking."* After the reading phase, the play is given its initial staging. The director, in collaboration with the actors, "blocks" out the play's physical action—each character's entrances and exits, stands and sits, and other major moves. Actors pencil down this blocking in their scripts to be able to repeat it the next time through the scene. These rehearsals take place not on the theatre stage but in a nearby rehearsal hall. No scenery or costumes are yet available, so these rehearsals make do with substitutes: a table stands for a railing actors will lean against; a rectangular, stock step unit represents the curvilinear staircase they will descend. The locations of walls and doorways are marked on the rehearsal-room floor with strips of masking tape. If more than one play is rehearsed in the same hall, the different "sets" are indicated by different strip colors: in this case yellow represents the set pieces for *School for Wives*, green those for *Fiddler on the Roof.* Many actors wear "rehearsal costumes" to simulate the bulk of the costumes they will wear in the play. Here Betsy Mugavero wears a billowing rehearsal skirt to mimic the skirt she will wear as Agnès in the production, and Tim Casto has donned a rehearsal cape as her guardian (and would-be husband) Arnolphe. As he stages the play, Director Cohen refers regularly to planned moves he has already penciled into his script, on the music stand; he may change these plans in an instant if the actors make moves he likes better. Visible in the background are a costume rack for the rehearsal garments, a stack of shelves for rehearsal props, and a rehearsal schedule for the entire repertoire of the festival's plays currently in preparation.

9. (*Right*) *Scenic Construction.* In one of the festival's scene shops, the "deck"—scenic flooring—is being constructed under the oversight of Scenery Supervisor Benjamin Zimmer.

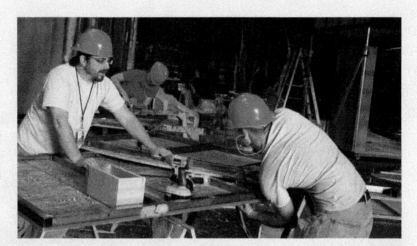

10. (*Below*) *Costume Transfer.* Costume Designer Swenson has transferred her costume designs—the dozen-plus individual renderings she has been sharing with the director and cast at various meetings—to the costume shop, where they now hang on the wall to guide the drapers, first hands, seamstresses, and embroiderers who will construct various garments. Here Swenson is giving special instructions to Costume Artisan Jennifer Biehl.

11. *Sewing.* Seamstress Eleanor Kingsley works on the fancy lace collar to be worn by Enrique, a Spanish dandy who arrives in the play's final scenes.

12. *Costume Fitting.* In the costume shop's dressing room, Betsy Mugavero is fitted for her first act Agnès costume by the production's draper, Louella Powell. First Hand Aria Thornton, seen in the mirror, takes notes from Powell on what, if anything, should be changed.

14. *Hanging.* Lighting Technician Bradley Carson, on a pneumatic lift that hoists him to the lighting battens twenty feet above the stage, hangs and focuses one of the more than three hundred lighting instruments that will be used in this production.

13. *Lighting Transfer.* The light plot (instrument chart), designed by Lighting Designer Stephen Boulmetis, lies on the stage floor as Assistant Lighting Designer Michael Pasquini studies it to determine exactly where each instrument should be hung.

15. *Millinery.* In the crafts shop, Assistant Costume Crafts Supervisor Jessica Crowden sews feathers onto the elaborate wide-brimmed hat that Enrique will wear in the last act.

16. *Cobbling.* Crafts Artisan Gregory Horton, also in the crafts shop, fashions leather shoes and other accessories that complete the costumes.

17. *Sound.* Sound Designer Palmer Jankens, in the sound design studio, records and assembles digital soundtracks of the harpsichord music (by seventeenth-century composer Jacques Duphly) that will be used in the production, along with other offstage sounds, including a horse's hoofbeats and whinnying, crashing dishes, breaking vases, and the footsteps of three persons racing up a flight of stairs.

18. *Voice Recording.* The director decided to add to the digital soundtrack Arnolphe's ad-lib grunts and yelps as he runs into a horse offstage, so Sound Designer Jankens has brought Tim Casto into the sound studio to record the actor's voicing of such nonverbal utterances, which Jankens will later combine with the horse whinny and crashing sounds.

19. (*Left*) *Acting Rehearsal.* In the rehearsal room, actors rehearse the second of the four farcical interludes that the director has interpolated between the acts of Molière's play. Here Agnès, at the demand of Arnolphe, is throwing a large "stone" down from her "balcony" at her lover Horace, played by Kevin Kiler, as the comic servants Alain and Georgette (Rick Ford and Lillian Castillo) egg her on from each side. These interludes are mimed by the actors, who use exaggerated commedia dell'arte–style movements but do not speak (because Molière wrote no lines for them).

20. (*Left*) *Fight Rehearsal.* This rehearsal of the third interlude, in which Alain and Georgette attempt to beat Horace as he ascends a ladder to rescue Agnès from her guardian's captivity, is overseen by Fight Director Christopher Villa. Trained—and desirably certified—fight directors are employed whenever stage actions involve potentially dangerous movements such as dueling, hitting, or falling, to make such actions theatrically vivid (realistic, convincing, dramatic, and/or hilarious, depending on the production's style) yet absolutely safe for the actors executing them in performance after performance.

21. *Painting.* In the paint shop, Scenic Charge Artist Michelle Fullerton, with Winiarski's rendering (finished sketch) in hand, paints the "portal" that, when erected vertically, will frame the scenic picture.

22. *Scenic Assembly.* Now in the Randall Theatre, where the play will be presented, the scenery is being erected and assembled on the actual stage.

23. *Scenic Detailing.* Scene Designer Winiarski demonstrates to Scenery Supervisor Zimmer precisely how she intends the window hinges to be fitted.

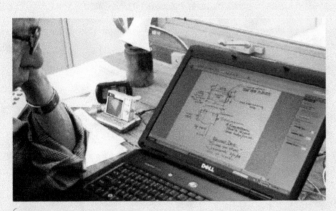

24. *Scenic Revision.* An early version of a stage prop—a portable desk that is to be carried and used by the "Notary"—is tested in rehearsal and found to be too bulky; it must be redesigned immediately. Since Scene Designer Winiarski is completing a project in New York that week, the redesign—as a simpler lap desk—is accomplished through a series of overnight e-mail exchanges. In Cedar City the next morning, Director Cohen approves—and sends to the prop shop—the new version.

25. *Props.* In the prop shop, the redesigned lap desk is sanded by Properties Construction Artisan Ryan McAlpine.

26. *Photo Call.* Neither scenery nor costumes are fully finished, nor have all the lighting instruments been installed, but selected pieces have been completed and temporary lighting has been set up so key scenes from the play may be photographed for the souvenir program and upcoming publicity releases. Publications Art Director Phil Hermansen frames a shot that will include Arnolphe and his two servants in front of the house where Agnès is lodged.

27. *Tech Rehearsal Setup.* The production is now ready to move into technical rehearsals, in which the acting and the scenery, props, sound, and lighting are brought together on the stage. Here, Scenery Supervisor Zimmer determines with Assistant Stage Manager Nicole Lalonde which upper windows in the scenery the actors will use when making certain appearances.

28. *Tech Walk.* Assistant Stage Manager Lalonde invites the actors to "walk the set." Having previously rehearsed only in a bare room with stray tables and strips of masking tape marking out the scenery elements, the actors now have to "feel the scenery" with their hands and feet as they navigate the various doors, windows, and railings that will actually be used.

29. *Cue Lights.* Production Stage Manager Angi Weiss-Brandt "calls" the show—that is, she times and calls the lighting, sound, and scene-shift cues to the appropriate operators over an intercom system. She herself blinks the thirty-plus cue lights in different backstage locations, letting individual actors know the precise moments when they should make their entrances or offstage cries and other sounds. Such remote cuing is frequently necessary because actors behind the scenery cannot see the onstage action. During technical rehearsals the stage manager's console is a table placed across the back rows of the audience, as shown here; by the time the show opens, the stage manager will be at a console in a glassed-in booth in the back of the house.

30. *Tech Tables.* Other work tables are set out in the audience so lighting, sound, and scenic designers can set and adjust cues as the actors "stop and go" through the play during two ten-hour technical rehearsals. In the foreground, Electrics Director Scott Palfreyman, at his table, talks to the stage manager through his intercom system. At the tech table in front of Palfreyman, Sound Designer Jankens readies his cues; other tech tables are to his left and right. Onstage, a crew member tapes the rough edges of a temporary wooden rail that represents a brass railing that has not yet been finished in the scene shop.

31. *Setting Light Cues.* At their tech table, Lighting Designer Boulmetis (*foreground*) and Assistant Lighting Designer Pasquini communicate by intercom with the stage manager, light-board operator, and follow-spot operators, while establishing and timing out the more than three hundred light cues that are to be executed in the production.

32. *Follow-spot.* Lighting Technician Cristine White operates one of the production's two follow-spots, lighting instruments that are hand-positioned by their operators to follow one or more actors as they move about the stage—or, in this production, up and down the theatre aisles.

33. *Gobos.* These oddly named devices are filters placed inside lighting instruments to create patterns that can be projected onto floors and walls to give added texture—to create the impression, for example, of moonlight shining through leafy trees. During technical rehearsal, these gobo-produced patterns will be added to the lighting of a nighttime interlude.

34. *ASM.* The stage manager will call the show from a booth behind the audience. Assistant Stage Manager Lalonde will stay backstage, where she can make visual cues to the actors, oversee the placement of the props, and in general trouble-shoot the production and respond to backstage emergencies.

35. *Dress Rehearsal.* After the lighting, sound, and scene-shift cues have been folded into the production, two dress rehearsals will complete the production's integration of its many elements. How do the costumes look in front of the set and under the lights? Do the garments overly restrain the actors' movements? Down in a dressing room, Lillian Castillo is being laced into Georgette's undergarment by a costume wardrobe assistant.

36. *Makeup.* Stage makeup is added during dress rehearsals. Here Betsy Mugavero, in the dressing room before the rehearsal begins, touches up her makeup after putting on her Agnès costume for the first act.

37. *Wig Preparation.* Tim Casto "makes horns" (puts his two forefingers flat against his forehead) to make it easier for Wigmaster Karen Craven to slip his Arnolphe wig over his scalp.

38. (*Above*) *Wig Setting.* The wig is securely placed.

39. (*Right*) *Facial Hair.* Assistant Wigmaster Devon Ash secures Casto's "billygoat" goatee and mustache to his face with spirit gum.

40. *Final Adjustments.* Before the first dress rehearsal begins, First Hand Thornton adjusts Casto's costume in his scene with Chrysalde, played by Dennis Elkins.

41. *Dress Check.* Rick Ford, in his Alain costume, checks the door handle before practicing, in full costume for the first time, his rapid (and highly comedic) entrances and exits prior to the run.

42. *Lights Up!* The audience area is a sea of computers—those of the stage manager and designers and their assistants—as the lights rise on the bare stage for the dress rehearsal's first scene.

43. *Quick Change.* Backstage, behind the door to Agnés's house, two dressers assist Tim Casto with the costume and wig change he must make in just five seconds.

44. *Publicity Interview.* The play will open tomorrow, and some of the actors—including Betsy Mugavero—have been asked to do interviews on regional television stations.

45–47. *Production Stills.* These three photographs from actual productions show the finished product—scenery, costumes, lighting, wigs, and actors all together. In the first, Rick Ford and Lillian Castillo are seen as the servants Alain and Georgette; and in the second, Tim Casto and Dennis Elkins are seen as Arnolphe, the central character, and Chrysalde, his best friend. In the final photo, Kevin Kiler, as Horace, expounds to Arnolphe as the servants watch from separate windows above the arch.

Chapter **7**

Theatre Traditions: East and West

THEATRE, WHICH CONSISTS OF LIVE actors who perform in real time before live audiences, is a unique art form because it exists "in the present." However, theatre is also deeply rooted in its past; many plays seen today are revivals, adaptations, or parodies of earlier ones. Even when wholly original, new plays are inevitably compared to earlier works. Likewise, contemporary actors—like contemporary baseball players—also are compared to their predecessors. Theatre is a living art but also a living tradition.

Some plays travel through time effortlessly, reappearing in new guises at dozens of points throughout history. *The Lot Drawers*, a fourth-century B.C. Greek comedy by Diphilos concerning an old man foolishly in love with a young girl, was revised a century later by the Roman Plautus as *Casina*—and a thousand years later Plautus's version was revised by the Italian playwright, Niccolò Machiavelli, as *Clizia*. Nor did it end there: scenes and gags from *Clizia* later appeared in the plays of Shakespeare and Molière, and continue to be seen in American comedies on stage, film, and television right up to the present day. ▶

Indeed, many of the world's greatest plays—in both East and West—are closely based on preceding ones. Dozens of eighteenth-century Japanese *kabuki* dramas are based on fourteenth-century Japanese *nō* scripts (often bearing the same titles), and most traditional Indian and Chinese plays are based on dramas from prior millennia. French neoclassic tragedies of the seventeenth century, as well as comedies of the twentieth century, were often based on Greek and Roman models more than two thousand years old. At least three of William Shakespeare's best-known plays—*King Lear, Hamlet,* and *The Taming of the Shrew*—were revisions of earlier English plays with nearly the same names by other authors. And Shakespeare's plays, in turn, have been a source for literally hundreds of modern dramas, including Tom Stoppard's *Rosencrantz and Guildenstern Are Dead,* Lee Blessing's *Fortinbras,* Paul Rudnick's *I Hate Hamlet,* Richard Nelson's *Two Shakespearean Actors,* Ann-Marie McDonald's *Goodnight Desdemona (Good Morning Juliet),* Amy Freed's *The Beard of Avon,* Stephen Sondheim's *West Side Story,* Neil Simon's *The Goodbye Girl* and *Laughter on the 23rd Floor,* and Punchdrunk's

2011 *Sleep No More,* all of which parody or creatively extend portions of Shakespeare's plays. Indeed, the theatre continually resurrects its past traditions, just as it always seeks to extend and surpass them.

Therefore it is helpful, when looking at the theatre of today, to look to the traditions of the theatre in the past, from the West (Europe and the Americas) and the East (Asia and the Indian subcontinent). What follows is a capsule history of eleven important theatre traditions, from both East and West, that together outline the major world developments prior to the start of the modern theatre in the nineteenth century.

THE ORIGINS OF THEATRE

How did drama begin?

No one knows for sure, but the theatre, along with human civilization itself, almost certainly began in Africa. The first known dramatic presentations occurred in northern Africa, alongside the Nile River in ancient Egypt, as much as five thousand years ago, possibly as early as 3300 B.C.

DNA studies have shown that the San Bushmen, seen here in a ritual trance-dance in their native Botswana, are direct descendants of the first evolved *Homo sapiens* from more than 100,000 years ago. The San remain hunter-gatherers; after a kill, the whole group chants and dances in a prehistoric desert ritual, summoning spiritual powers into each person's stomach to heal both physical and psychological illnesses.

But African theatre is far older than that. There are indications of ritual performances in the activities of literally hundreds of ancient African tribal groups, dating as far back as 6000 B.C. And although we know very little about such performances—which, unlike the arts of painting and sculpture, left behind no permanent records—it is very likely they resembled tribal performances widely performed in rural Africa today. From such present-day performances, we can see the two foundations of the theatre as it has been known and enjoyed throughout the course of human civilization: *ritual* and *storytelling*. Both have existed since ancient times, and both remain apparent—though in different forms—wherever theatre is performed today.

Ritual

A *ritual* is a collective ceremony, performed by members of a society, normally for religious or cultural reasons.

The most ancient rituals were primarily intended to summon gods and influence nature, as with rain dances and healing ceremonies. But tribal rituals also arose to observe important life events, such as the changing of the seasons, and to provide public witness to life passages such as birth, death, marriage, and coming of age. Contemporary Christian baptism and Jewish bar mitzvah (coming-of-age) rituals, along with funeral rites in nearly all cultures, are descendants of these ancient tribal ceremonies. Other rituals reenact defining moments of a culture's religious history—such as the birth, death, or resurrection of divine beings—thus allowing adherents to experience directly the passion of their culture's sacred heritage.

Over time, early tribal rituals began incorporating elements we would now consider essential to the theatrical event, such as staging, costuming, masks, makeup, music, dance, formalized speech, chanting, singing, and specific physical props, such as staffs, spears, and

Mudmen of the South Pacific, isolated from the rest of the world until the twentieth century, still cover their bodies in mud and wear homemade clay masks for their ancient hunting ritual, performed in their villages and also, as shown here, at a biannual September gathering of tribes in the town of Goroka.

Dogon performers of the *dana* ritual, dancing on six-foot stilts, represent larger-than-life forces in the most literal way: by being double human size.

skulls, that could contain totemic or spiritual properties. Though performed solely for the collective worship of the participants themselves, such theatricalized rituals also played a role in educating observers, including the children of the tribe and tribal visitors.

Not all rituals are based in religion. Secular rituals exist in Western society today that give a spiritual or "larger-than-life" dimension to more culturally significant events. Elements of secular rituals include the black robes of courtroom judges, the precisely choreographed changing of the guard at the Tomb of the Unknown Soldier, the daily recitation of the Pledge of Allegiance in American classrooms, and even the lowering of the ball in New York's Times Square on New Year's Eve.

Perhaps the wedding ceremony is the most common collective ritual in Western culture, with its costumes (tuxedo or T-shirt), elevated language (psalms or sonnets), symbolic gift exchanges (ring or rings), and traditional music (Brahms or Black Eyed Peas). And the slow march down the aisle retains the ancient symbolism of father figures giving their child away to their new partner, even though such symbolism has lost much (if not all) of its original meaning over the years.

Ritual is at the very origin of theatre. It is the act of performers re-creating, intensifying, and making meaningful the myths, beliefs, legends, and traditions common to their collective lives.

Storytelling

The art of storytelling emerged soon after the arrival of ritual activity; quickly, the two forms began intermingling. Since humans developed coherent speech, they have sought to recount their own (and others') daily adventures, including stories of the hunt and histories of the tribe. Indeed, such storytelling was essential to the development of speech itself. Why invent words like *glorious* and *brave* and *beautiful* if not to augment a story being told?

Storytelling is more personal than collective ritual performance because it generally relies on a single voice—and therefore a single point of view. While rituals may attract an audience, storytelling *requires* one: every tale must, by definition, have "hearer-spectators" who either don't know the story being told or are eager to hear it again. Storytelling thus generates elements of *character,* both in its use of impersonation—the creation of voices, gestures, and facial expressions that reflect the personalities of the individuals portrayed—and its desire to convey different emotions to the hearer-spectators. It also seeks to entertain, and thus provides a *structured narrative,* rather than a random series of

observations, which in turn helps encourage audience engagement through suspense, graphic details, and a calculated momentum of escalating events. These elements of structured action, in drama, combine to become the *plot.* Today, the ancient foundations of great storytelling live on, both in surviving tribal cultures and in modern storytelling performances.

If ritual makes an event larger than life, storytelling makes it personal and affecting. The ritual of marriage gives wedlock a halo of dignity, incorporating its participants into larger cultural and historical traditions. But marrying couples also tell the audience their own story through choosing the event's dress, language, music, setting, and staging. The resulting event thus combines collective formality with personal narrative, conveying their status both as members of a group and as unique individuals.

Shamanism, Trance, and Magic

The ancient form of theatre known as dance-drama began with the combination of ritual and storytelling. Dance-dramas appeared first on the African continent and afterward in tribal cultures around the world, and they continue to be performed in, among other places, Siberia, South America, Southeast Asia, Australia, and Native American enclaves. Storytelling provided these performances with audience-attracting narratives and links to events in daily human life, with a freshness of detail and ability to highlight each performer's special creativity. But ritual provided the intensity of the celebrants who could commit, body and soul, to the impersonation of divine spirits and reenactment of what they believed to be real, though otherworldly, events. Belief in the power of such spirits to animate objects has been called *animism*, a catchall term describing the basic religious impulse of tribal culture in prehistory. Humans who assume an animist role, mediating between spirit and earthly realities, are—in a similarly general way—called *shamans*.

Shamans have been identified in the tribal cultures of the Upper Paleolithic era since at least 13,000 B.C. and possibly even earlier. In the eyes of his community, the shaman (almost always male in the ancient world) can cure the sick, aid the hunter, make the rain come, and help the crops grow. Shamans may also appear as mediums, taking the forms of unearthly spirits, often animal or demonic. In most shamanic practices, the shaman performs his acts of travel between the human and spirit worlds, and his incarnation of spiritual presences, in a state of trance.

Since the shaman's trance leads him to otherworldly realms, his performance takes on a magical appearance. Ecstatic dancing and rapturous chanting are often

Storytelling, an art more ancient than theatre, is still practiced as a public performance form, nowhere more successfully than at the annual Jonesborough, Tennessee, storytelling festival.

primary features of shamanism, usually climaxing in violent shaking at astounding speeds. Acrobatic feats are common: in the *pegele* dance of Nigeria, shamans leap high in the air, spin around horizontally, and then come down far from where they left the ground. Sleight of hand may be involved in this "magic," as when the Formosan shaman "stabs" himself but really only pierces a blood-filled animal bladder hidden beneath his clothes. But genuine transformation, both physical and psychological, apparently takes place as well, permitting the execution of hitherto inhuman feats. The San Bushmen of Namibia and Botswana eat live snakes and scorpions during hunting rituals. The Indian *fakir* (Arabic for "poor man"; the word is not related to fakery) hangs suspended from a hook through his flesh. The Muslim dervish places glowing coals in his mouth, seemingly anesthetized from pain.

Costumes, body paint, headdresses, and—above all—masks disguise the shaman-performer, sometimes completely, transforming him (often to himself as well as to observers) into a spirit presence. Masks, common in almost all tribal cultures, initially adapted themselves from the ecstatic contortion of the shaman's face during trance and subsequently served to represent the particular spirit that the trance-liberated shaman inhabited. But the mask has outlived the rituals that spawned it and remains today a prominent symbol of drama around the world.

The Beginnings of Traditional Drama

When spoken dialogue comes into shamanistic rites, true traditional drama begins. The Sri Lankan *sanniyakuma,* a traditional, all-night curing ceremony of drumming and "devil dancing," portrays a suffering patient who seeks exorcism of the devil and includes this exchange:

YAKKA (*DEMON*)**:** What is going on here? What does this noise mean?

DRUMMER: Somebody has fallen ill.

YAKKA: What are you going to do about it?

DRUMMER: We will give him a medicine.

YAKKA: That will not be of any use! Give me twelve presents and I will cure him.

The dialogue creates suspense, conflict, danger, and action.

The antiwitchcraft *kponiugo* mask of the Poro secret society of the Senufo tribe in West Africa's Ivory Coast is believed to protect the community from sorcerers and soul-stealers. Groups of Poro-maskers seem to spit fire between the alligator teeth of their open jaws. Wild boar tusks and antelope horns represent ferocity and gentleness.

Traditional Drama in Sub-Saharan Africa

Theatrical performances almost certainly began in Sub-Saharan Africa, where we can see—even today— a vast variety of traditional drama in which ritual and storytelling continually interweave. More than eight hundred languages are spoken here, and each language represents a culture with roots in the past and social community in the present. Many of these cultures have long-standing traditions of dance-dramas. The Dogon performers of Mali are celebrated for their stilt walking and brightly colored masks. The Senufo of Ivory Coast and Burkina Faso have animal masks to frighten witches—with the tusks of wild boars, the teeth of alligators, and the horns of antelopes—and brightly colored masks for certain women characters (played by men). Such masks feature arched eyebrows, visible teeth, and scar marks on the cheeks, and the

characters' hand props often include horsetail whisks, perhaps the forerunners of today's pom-poms. In the Yacouba country of Ivory Coast, traditional performers may wear elaborate beaded headdresses and full-face makeup instead of masks, or, as in the panther dance-drama, cover their entire heads in painted cloth with panther ears. Acrobatics feature in Burundi performances; rain-dance rituals are common in Botswana.

Egyptian Drama

After theatrical performances began in Sub-Saharan Africa, they soon drifted northward, down the Nile River to what we now know as Egypt, and then spread to Mesopotamia, Canaan, and eventually throughout the Middle East. Although the first written records we have of this activity are in Egypt, dating at least as far back as 2500 B.C., performances may have occurred as much as eight hundred years before that.

The first known Egyptian drama, known as the *Abydos Passion Play,* was apparently staged each spring in a boat procession on the Nile, with performances taking place at several temples along the way. The play tells the story of the murder of the wheat-god Osiris by Set, the god of death, incorporating scenes of lamentation by the priestesses Isis and Neptys, the tearing asunder of Osiris's body (which is then thrown into the Nile), Osiris's resurrection in the person of the god Horus, and fierce combat between Horus and Set. Dialogue, dance, animal sacrifices, elaborate offerings of royal treasure, mimed violence, a coronation ceremony, and sacred fertility rites were all part of the action, complemented with bold stage effects. Beads of carnelian (a translucent red stone) represented the great Eye of Horus, which was bloodied when Set plucked it out in the combat between the two demigods. Two maces represented Set's testicles, which Horus tore off and engrafted onto his own body to become stronger. The lowering and raising of ceremonial pillars into the Nile represented the burial and rebirth of Osiris.

Modern anthropology has discovered this Egyptian springtime resurrection drama derives from even more ancient ritualized reenactments of the coming of spring that celebrated the rebirth of vegetation in the fields, such as the Babylonian play *Baal,* in which the god Baal dies, goes to the equivalent of Purgatory, and rises again on the same day. These plays, performed in the springtime, are ultimately joyous, not sad. The deaths of Osiris and Baal are not permanent, and after Osiris's body is torn apart and thrown into the river, he will be revived—as will the coming year's wheat crop after its seeds are scattered by the wind and submerged in the annual flooding of the Nile. The tragedy of death, therefore, yields life, and the tears of lamentation become nourishment for the seeds of life's renewal. However painful, such tragedy brings with it rejuvenation and hope.

THEATRE IN THE WEST

Drama did not continue to flourish in the Middle East, however. While many artistic forms persisted, much of the ancient theatre tradition there had disappeared by the third century B.C., and the religion of Islam, which originated early in the seventh century A.D., generally viewed depictions of humans—in both the visual and the performing arts—as irreligious. But the dramatic arts moved on: from their Egyptian and Middle Eastern origins, they spread rapidly both east and west. In India and Attica (now Greece), cultic rituals took place well before the first millennium B.C. And by the middle of that millennium, there arose a spectacular theatre in the city-state of Athens, which over the course of 150 years produced four of the greatest playwrights and the most important dramatic theorist in the theatre's long history. Greek drama established the formal foundations of Western theatre, shaping and defining the essential concepts—such as tragedy, comedy, characters, and plotlines—that remain essential to drama as we know it today.

Greek Drama

The drama of Athens in the fifth century B.C. still stands as one of the greatest—some would say *the* greatest—bodies of theatrical creation of all time. A magnificent and vigorous blend of myth, legend, philosophy, social commentary, poetry, dance, music, public participation, and visual splendor, Athenian drama created the forms of tragedy and comedy. Its characters have become cultural archetypes in successive eras, laying the foundation not only of future Western drama but also of continuing debates as to how—and to what purposes—life should be lived.

Aristotle and later scholars tell us Greek tragedy derived from *dithyrambs,* ancient orgiastic rites that consisted of wine-drinking, phallus-worshipping, and chanting ancient poems. Dithyrambs honored Dionysus, the demigod of fertility and wine who, according to myth, had arrived by way of the Middle East. Dionysus was the counterpart of Egypt's Osiris and, like the Egyptian wheat-god, was believed to have been dismembered in the winter and resurrected in the spring, proving a semi-divine analogue to the rebirth of vegetation on the Attic peninsula. When classic Greek dramas came to be staged on the Athenian acropolis by the latter part of the sixth century B.C., it was at the Great Theatre of Dionysus, during the annual springtime festival known as the City Dionysia (or Great Dionysia), that the demigod's apparent rebirth was celebrated. Dionysus has, ever since, been considered the founding deity of Western drama.

Although the transition from orgiastic celebrations to tragic drama is decidedly obscure, we do know that by the end of the fifth century B.C. three great tragedians—Aeschylus, Sophocles, and Euripides—had written and

Peter Hall's production of Euripides' *The Bacchae* played at England's National Theatre in 2002, and then to an audience of eleven thousand at the ancient theatre of Epidaurus in Greece. Hall and his designers employed bold and uniform colors—blood orange and sea green—to emphasize the masklike uniformity of members of the chorus as they collectively, not individually, wrestle with the play's giant spiritual themes.

produced close to three hundred plays. Thirty-three have come down to us, and most of them are on every theatre scholar's list of the world's greatest dramatic masterpieces. Furthermore, there was a brilliant author of comic dramas—Aristophanes—from whom eleven plays survive, one of which (*The Frogs*) is a biting and vastly informative satire about the three great tragedians who shared his times. Other authors of Greek comedy, including Menander, and literary theorists, including Aristotle (with his *Poetics*, a treatise on dramatic theory), plied their trades in the century that followed, making for one of the richest bodies of dramatic work ever created.

Greek tragedies explored the social, psychological, and religious meanings of the ancient gods and heroes of Greek history and myth, as well as current events; the comedies presented contemporary issues affecting all Athenians. Both types of drama were first staged in a simple wheat-threshing area on the ground (the *orchestra*), with a dressing hut (*skene*) behind it; the audience was seated on an adjacent hillside (the *theatron*). As Greek culture expanded, however, huge amphitheaters—the largest of which seated upward

of fifteen thousand people—were built in Athens and subsequently throughout the growing Greek empire. Many of those later theatres remain today, in various stages of ruin and renovation, in parts of Greece, Italy, and Turkey, and the terms *orchestra, scene,* and *theatre* remained to define the theatre of future eras.

All ancient Greek actors were male. They performed in masks, partly to indicate the age, gender, personality, and social standing of the characters they were playing and partly to amplify their voices. (The word *person* derives from the Latin *per sonum*, or "for sound," which initially referred to the amplification of the actor's voice and later became the root of the term *dramatis personae,* or "cast of characters.") Each tragic actor wore elevated shoes (*kothurnoi*), an elaborate headdress (*onkos*), and a long, usually colorful gown (*himation*) with a tunic (*chlamys*) over it to enhance the larger-than-life struggles between royal heroes, gods, and demigods. Plays were performed with only two (later three) principal actors, who, by changing masks, could play several parts each during the course of a play. The actors were supported by a Greek invention, a chorus of

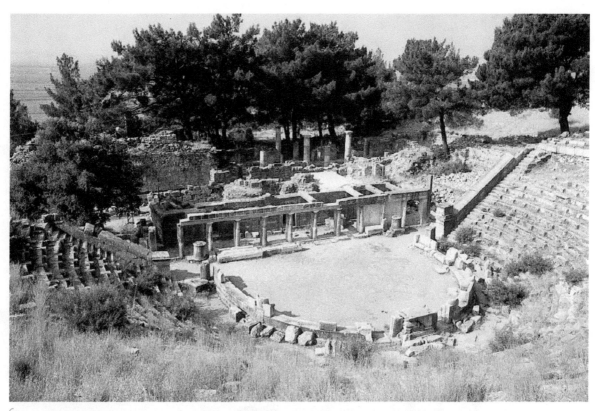

The Greek theatre of Priene, in modern-day Turkey, dates from about 300 B.C. Unlike most Greek theatres, Priene was never rebuilt by the Romans and thus remains one of the best examples of a hillside Greek *theatron*. The standing row of columns and connecting lintel once made up the front of the stone *skene*, or stagehouse.

twelve or fifteen singer-dancers (usually representing the local populace) who chanted their lines in unison or through a single chorus leader. When the skene became an elevated stage for the principal actors, the chorus members remained in the orchestra below, separated from the main interactions of the principals.

Greek tragedy was chanted or sung, not spoken; unfortunately, the music has not survived. And the chorus danced, as it did in the dithyrambic ceremonies, sometimes formally, sometimes with wild abandon. Greek tragedy, therefore, is the foundation not merely of Western drama but of Western musical theatre, including opera. Greek comedy, in contrast, is the foundation of burlesque, satire, and television sitcoms. The plays of Aristophanes, referred to as Old Comedy, are filled with broad physical humor, gross sexual gags and innuendos, and brilliant wordplay and repartee, often at the expense of contemporary politicians and celebrities. The later plays of Menander, known as New Comedy, gave rise to "stock characters" (such as the

bumbling suitor and the timid warrior) and comic plot devices (such as mistaken identity) that supply the elements of many contemporary television shows.

The City Dionysia was a weeklong festival of celebrations and dramatic competitions. On the first day, during introductory ceremonies, each playwright (selected in advance by civic authorities) introduced his cast and announced the theme of his work. The second day featured processions, sacrifices, and the presentation of ten dithyrambs; on the third day, five comedies were played. On the fourth, fifth, and sixth days, the three competing playwrights presented—each on a separate day—three related tragedies (a *trilogy*), followed by a comic variation or parody (a *satyr play*) on the same theme. The authors served as the directors of their works. On the seventh, and final, day, judging took place, and prizes for the best play and best leading actor were awarded. It appears that the entire population of freeborn males, and perhaps of freeborn females (we don't know this for certain), attended

In the dithyrambs that preceded ancient Greek tragedy, there was a chorus of fifty performers. Romanian director Silviu Purcarete, at the National Theatre of Craiova, employed a chorus of double that number—fifty men and fifty women—in his innovative production of *Les Danaïdes,* adapted from Aeschylus's war tetralogy, *The Suppliants.* Purcarete's highly stylized production, performed (in French) in Manhattan's Damrosch Park as part of the Lincoln Center Theatre Festival in 1997, had clear overtones of current problems in eastern Europe and the Balkans and a strong emphasis on political terrorism, sexual assault, and the ambiguity of gender and cultural identity.

these performances and rooted for their favorites; judging by later commentaries, outstanding dramatists and actors were as famous then as are today's best-known film directors and movie stars. Clearly the City Dionysia of fifth-century Athens was a monumental and glorious undertaking that led to some of the most thrilling dramas and theatrical spectacles in history.

Roman Drama

Greek civilization, battered by internal wars, had lost its leading edge by the end of the fifth century B.C., and the power balance in the Mediterranean shifted, in succeeding centuries, to the growing Roman Empire. Excelling in architecture and engineering more than in dramatic creativity, the Romans created some astonishing stage buildings, of which more than two hundred (most dating

from the first centuries A.D.) survive to the present day. Roman architects dispensed with the Greek hillside theatron and threshing-circle orchestra and designed a theatre that was an entirely integrated structure set on a level plain. They also cut the orchestra in half and created tunnel entrances (*vomitoria*) to it on both sides. The simple Greek skene became an elaborate three-story wall (the *frons scaenae*) decorated by dozens of statues.

Rarely as impressive as Roman architects, Roman dramatists almost always drew upon Greek sources for their work; indeed, most Roman plays are about Greek characters and Greek struggles. The Roman comic playwrights Plautus and Terence were quite popular in their time, however, and many of their works survive and are performed occasionally today, as are (albeit more rarely) the chamber tragedies of Seneca, a protégé (and victim) of Emperor Nero. All three of these Roman dramatists,

The most ancient theatre is often the most modern. This 1996 English production of Sophocles' *Oedipus Tyrannos*, with Greg Hicks shown here as Tiresias, premiered at the ancient Greek theatre of Epidaurus before reopening at the National Theatre in London. Packed houses greeted it with rousing acclaim in both locations.

in fact, were very popular and much admired by writers and audiences during the European Renaissance. Roman theatre, however, degenerated into sheer spectacle and decadence by the end of the empire, as many theatres were converted into arenas for gladiatorial combat, pitched sea battles, and gruesome public massacres. Together, Greek and Roman drama form a "classical theatre" tradition that has been referenced over and over in Western drama from the Renaissance right up to the present day.

Medieval Drama

The fall of Rome (around the middle of the first millennium A.D.) brought the classical era of theatre to an end. The early Christian religion banned theatrical representations altogether, partly in reaction to the excesses of late Roman theatre. When Western drama reappeared, as it did in Europe in the tenth century, it was an altogether different product, sponsored by the same Christian Church that had once forbidden it. The earliest known dramatization of that period was not a play in the ordinary sense but rather a brief moment in the church's Easter service, when officiating monks would reenact the story, adapted from the Bible, of the Three Marys visiting the tomb of Jesus. "Whom seek ye?" (*Quem queritis?*) an angel asks. "Jesus of Nazareth," reply the Marys, whereupon they are told, "He is not here, He has risen." They then break into a chorus of hallelujahs. Thus medieval European drama, like the drama of ancient Egypt and ancient Greece, began with the springtime celebration of a divine resurrection. This simple liturgical playlet, now known as the *Quem Queritis*, became the first of literally hundreds of church-sponsored dramatizations depicting and celebrating traditional Judeo-Christian stories, from the Creation of the Universe and Adam and Eve to Doomsday and the Harrowing of Hell.

Medieval drama remained in church liturgy for nearly two centuries, but by about 1250, Bible-based

As the sympathetic chorus peers out at the audience for help, Prometheus struggles against his imprisonment in New York's Classic Stage Company production of *Prometheus Bound*, a Greek tragedy of unknown authorship but long attributed to Aeschylus.

drama had moved outdoors, first to churchyards, then public streets throughout Europe. By this time the medieval "mystery plays," as they were then called, were performed in the common languages of French, English, Spanish, German, and Italian rather than Latin, and they included scenes that were more secular than purely religious, often with contemporary political overtones. The actors were no longer monks but ordinary citizens, and some of them—those who had mastered the leading parts—were well paid for their efforts. Though anonymous to us, the authors were highly prized by their communities, as they converted the formal prose of the Bible to comic interplay, jesting repartee, swash-buckling bluster, and intricate versification.

Entire festivals of such plays, numbering in the dozens, were presented in hundreds of European towns every spring, dominating city life where and when they were played and attracting rural audiences from all around. On the European continent, such drama festivals lasted for many days or even weeks, with huge casts

performing on a series of stages (known as *mansions*) set up next to each other in the town plaza or marketplace. Audiences could stroll from one play to the next as they were performed in sequence. In England, however, the plays were performed on wagon-mounted stages, one for each play, that were wheeled from one audience site to another during a daylong springtime festival known as Corpus Christi.

At first glance, these mystery plays may appear stylistically primitive, at least in contrast to the splendor of the classic Greek tragedies, but twenty-first-century productions have demonstrated their tremendous dramatic impact, even to today's religiously diverse audiences. The scale of medieval theatre production—with its mansions, rolling stages, and casts of hundreds—was simply astonishing. Like the great Gothic cathedrals—also created anonymously and at roughly the same time—the Bible-based medieval theatre was a monumental enterprise that affected the lives of the entire culture that created and experienced it.

Adam and Eve (Alessandro Mastrobuono and Erin Jellison) take their instructions from God (Tom Fitzpatrick) in Brian Kulick's 2003 *The Mysteries* in Los Angeles. The actors would probably have worn flesh-colored body stockings in medieval times, but contemporary theatre is able, on this occasion, to express their innocence before the Fall more literally.

The Oberammergau Passion Play, depicting the trial and crucifixion of Jesus, is certainly the most attended medieval play in the world today, as it has been produced in that southern Bavarian city every ten years (with a few exceptions) since 1634, where it is viewed by tens of thousands of mainly foreign visitors. Here Frederik Mayet, one of the 2,000 Oberammergau residents that take part in the production, plays Jesus speaking his last words to God in the 2010 production directed by Christian Stückl.

Renaissance Drama

Medieval drama was created in ignorance of its classical predecessors, but when, in the High Middle Ages, Roman and then Greek texts began to be translated and published, their influence—on all arts and culture, not merely the theatre—proved overwhelming. This period in which ancient culture was "reborn" and fused, sometimes uneasily, with the medieval and Gothic forms that had been dominant for centuries is called the Renaissance.

By most reckonings, the Renaissance began in Italy, where the plays of Plautus and Seneca were first translated in the 1470s. Amateur productions of these Italian translations soon became popular, giving rise to freer adaptations, which are now known as *commedia erudita*, or "learned comedies." By the 1520s, the Florentine diplomat and essayist Niccolò Machiavelli was famous throughout Italy for his learned comedies based on—and taking off from—Roman forebears, and by the middle of the sixteenth century, groups of itinerant professional actors began performing a semi-improvised variation of that comedy, known as *commedia dell'arte,*

throughout the Italian peninsula and even beyond. Soon both commedia dell'arte and scripted plays in modern European languages—based on classic or current themes rather than Biblical ones—became common throughout Europe.

It was in England that the Renaissance brought forth the greatest dramatic masterpieces of that (or perhaps any) era, in the works of William Shakespeare (1564–1616). Coming of age during the reign of Queen Elizabeth I, Shakespeare began his career in a vibrant and diverse theatrical culture, with palatial court theatres, freestanding outdoor "public theatres" that dominated the London skyline, and companies of professional actors who entertained court and public at home and on tour. The theatre of the Renaissance featured dozens of playwrights whose works remain popular today. While Christopher Marlowe, Ben Jonson, and John Webster are three of Shakespeare's most prominent contemporaries, and brilliant authors in their own right, none fully compared to Shakespeare himself. Alone among the world's greatest authors, Shakespeare was equally adept at producing exemplary masterpieces of both comedy and tragedy. Four centuries after they

An eighteenth-century illustration of Italian *commedia dell'arte.*

⚫Spotlight

Did Shakespeare Write Shakespeare?

Students occasionally wonder about the so-called authorship question, which challenges the commonly accepted belief that Shakespeare's plays were written by Shakespeare. Yet although several books and a 2011 film have argued against Shakespeare's authorship, and some distinguished thinkers (among them Mark Twain and Sigmund Freud) have shared their doubts as well, there is simply no question to be posed: the evidence that Shakespeare wrote Shakespeare's plays is absolutely overwhelming. No shred of evidence has appeared thus far to indicate that anyone else wrote them. Not a single prominent Elizabethan scholar has accepted the "anti-Stratfordian" (as proponents of other authors are called) argument, which one of America's most noted Shakespearean scholars, Harold Bloom, simply dismisses as "lunacy."

How can there be a question? Shakespeare's name appears as author on the title pages of 37 editions of plays published between 1598 and 1622, far more frequently than that of any other poet or dramatist of this period. Eleven of his plays are cited (and praised) in a book published when he was thirty-four. He is credited as the author of the First Folio in its title, *Mr. William Shakespeare's Comedies, Histories, and Tragedies,* published just seven years after his death. The Folio's editors were his acting colleagues, who describe Shakespeare as fellow actor, author, and friend, and their preface also includes four poems—one by dramatist Ben Jonson—each unequivocally referring to Shakespeare as the author of its plays. Surviving records show him performing in his plays at the courts of both Queen Elizabeth and King James, and he was buried, along with his wife, daughter, and son-in-law (and no one else), in the place of greatest honor in his hometown church. An inscribed funeral monument, mentioned in the Folio and showing him with pen in hand, looks down on Shakespeare's grave and was regularly visited in the coming years by persons wishing to see, as one wrote, the last resting place of "the wittiest poet in the world." Birth, marriage, death, heraldic, and other legal records, plus dozens of citations during and shortly after his life tell us more about dramatist William Shakespeare than we have collected for all but a few common-born citizens of his era.

So, what is left to argue? Anti-Stratfordians maintain that the evidence doesn't paint the picture we should expect of such a magnificent playwright: he apparently didn't go to college; his name was spelled in several different ways and sometimes hyphenated; his signatures indicate poor handwriting; his wife and daughters were probably illiterate; he didn't leave any books in his will; no ceremony marked his death; he never traveled to Italy, where many of his plays were set; and an early engraving of the Stratford monument looks different—lacking its pen—than the monument does now.

Little of this is provable, however, and none of it is remotely convincing even if true. Aeschylus, Euripides, Henrik Ibsen, and George Bernard Shaw didn't go to college, either. Shakespeare's knowledge of Italy is nothing an intelligent person couldn't have picked up in an afternoon's conversation—and it wasn't that geographically accurate (Shakespeare writes of one who could "lose the tide" sailing from Verona to Milan—where no water route exists). Many people have unreadable signatures, and in Shakespeare's day neither spelling nor hyphenation was standardized, nor was literacy a norm among country women. That we don't know of a memorial ceremony doesn't mean there wasn't one, and evidence clearly indicates the engraving of a penless monument was simply one of many errors in a hastily prepared book. And if Shakespeare maintained a library, he could simply have given it to his son-in-law (a doctor) before his death or left it to be passed on to his wife along with his house and furnishings, or perhaps he kept books in a private office at The Globe theatre in London, which burned to the ground three years before his death. And who actually knows that he didn't travel to Italy or even study at a university for that matter? We know next to nothing about Shakespeare between the ages of twenty-one and twenty-eight; he could have been anywhere and done anything.

But we do know he was a man of the theatre. And obviously a genius. What else need we know? Why must we insist that he have good handwriting? or literate relatives? Because *we* do? But we're not Shakespeare, and Shakespeare doesn't have to be like us.

And absolutely no evidence exists that anyone *else* wrote any of the plays—which explains why there are nearly a half dozen claimants to this phantom position of the "real" Shakespeare.

It is impossible to represent the entirety of either argument in a few paragraphs (one of the books, proposing the Earl of Oxford, runs more than 900 pages), but the entire anti-Stratfordian case, diverting as it may be, is painstakingly and effectively refuted in Irvin Leigh Matus's relentlessly straightforward *Shakespeare, in Fact* (1994) and James Shapiro's *Contested Will: Who Wrote Shakespeare?* (2010).

It is, of course, possible that all the evidence we now have—*all* of it—has somehow been fabricated. This would mean Shakespeare managed to fool—or buy off—almost everyone in his town, everyone in his church, everyone in his theatre company, everyone at two royal courts, everyone in the London theatre world, and most of the printers and booksellers in England, in addition to everyone these people talked to. We would be asked to believe that this gigantic lie (for which we have not a trace of evidence) *never* got out, not through three subsequent printings of the First Folio, not through the revival of his plays after his death and then later during the Restoration era. It would have been the most stupendous hoax in human history, incomparable to the insignificant hoax proffered to us by anti-Stratfordians today.

Like its predecessor, the modern Globe Theatre replica in London schedules performances by daylight, come rain or shine. As in Shakespeare's day, a sizable portion of the audience (the "groundlings," as they were called in Elizabethan times) observes from a standing-room pit in front of the stage; everyone else sits on hard wooden benches in the surrounding galleries. Shown here, the concluding dance of the Globe's 1998 *As You Like It* enchants the audience on all sides of the stage, which is "thrust" into their midst.

The Comedy of Errors may be Shakespeare's first play. In this work, based on a comedy/farce by the Roman playwright Plautus—but even funnier—Shakespeare clearly proved he could entertain an audience in the 1590s, and he can certainly do so today. This scene from the 2009 Chicago Shakespeare Theatre adaptation shows the stock characters, exaggerated physical characterizations, hilarious costumes and makeup, and super-rambunctious action that have always been factors of farcical performance. Pictured are Kymberly Mellen (*center*) as the (presumed) wronged wife, Kevin Gudahl as the quavering servant who faces her wrath, and Angela Ingersollas, the terrified servant peeking through the kitchen cupboard. David Bell adapted and directed.

The balcony scene from the 2006 Royal Shakespeare Company production of *Romeo and Juliet* took an athletic turn within and without Katrina Lindsay's unconventional design, up and down which the actors—Rupert Evans and Morven Christie—clambered with alacrity and grace. Nancy Meckler directed and Katrina Lindsay designed the spare scaffold that represented the balcony and much more.

Matthew Rhys (*left*) as Romeo and Tam Mutu as Tybalt duel in this 2004 Royal Shakespeare Company production of *Romeo and Juliet*, directed by Peter Gill.

Calderón's *Life Is a Dream* is one of the great classics of the seventeenth-century Spanish stage. Noted Cuban American playwright Nilo Cruz (*Anna and the Tropics*) adapted the play, and Kate Whoriskey directed its world premiere at South Coast Repertory in Costa Mesa, California. "I've always adored the poetic language of *Life Is a Dream* and its mythical landscape," said Cruz. "The play is full of questions, and I think Calderón's greatness as a playwright lies in the rich humanity of his characters, and the questions they pose." Daniel Breaker plays the banished prince, Segismundo; the designers were Walt Spangler (sets), Ilona Somogyi (costumes), and Scott Zielinski (lighting).

were written (from approximately 1580 to 1610), his plays are the most-produced dramas in literally thousands of theatres around the world and comprise the primary repertoires of more than a hundred theatre companies named after him.

Shakespeare was not only an author; he was also an actor and part owner of his own theatre company, the King's Men, and of The Globe theatre in London, which his company built and operated. A new Globe has now been built near the original site and, since its 1997 opening, has been used for the presentation of Shakespearean-era (and occasionally other) plays. With its "thrust stage" and standing-room "pit" open to the sky and surrounded by thatched-roof seating galleries on three levels, the modern Globe may not—because of fire regulations—seat the three thousand people accommodated by the original building, but its restoration

helps us better understand the vigor of Shakespearean-era staging and the potential of the drama to electrify a large and diverse audience with profound intelligence and passion, as well as comically expressive hijinks. Shakespeare's plays are well known to literary scholars for their poetic brilliance, relentless investigation of the human condition, and deeply penetrating character portrayals, but they are also filled with music, dancing, ribaldry, puns, satire, pageantry, and humor, which only performance truly brings to life. They are both great dramatic art and magnificent theatrical entertainment.

The Royal Theatre

If the Renaissance was the rebirth of classical civilization, the age that followed was a vast consolidation and refinement of what had come before, organized

Michel Vuillermoz plays Cyrano, the famously hook-nosed poet-warrior in Edmond Rostand's romantic 1897 masterpiece, *Cyrano de Bergerac*, here shown kneeling above his young friend Christian (Éric Ruf), who is dying in the arms of Roxanne (Françoise Gillard), a woman tragically fated to love them both. This 2006 Comédie-Française production was directed by Denis Podalydès in 2006; Ruf served also as the scenic designer.

intellectually by emerging empirical sciences and rational philosophies and politically by the increasing importance of European royalty. The seventeenth-century European theatre enjoyed powerful royal support, as it featured the dramas of Pedro Calderón de la Barca at the court of King Philip IV in Spain, the tragedies of Jean Racine and Pierre Corneille and the comedies of Molière under the patronage of King Louis XIV in France, and the Restoration comedies of William Wycherley and William Congreve under English king Charles II—who was crowned when the English royal family was restored to the throne after eleven years of Puritan rule.

Plays of this era were generally aimed more at the aristocracy than at the general populace and reflected the gentility of the seemingly refined taste of courtly patrons. Rational sensibility dominated the times: theories of drama, adapted from Aristotle and hence called "neoclassic," sought to regularize plays within "reasonable" frameworks of time and place, establish strictly measured structures for dramatic verse, unify styles around set genres, and eliminate onstage depictions of physical violence. Indoor theatres, lit by candles instead of sunlight, replaced the outdoor public theatres of earlier times, providing more intimate and comfortable surroundings for an increasingly well-dressed audience. Furthermore, protection from wind and weather permitted elaborately painted scenery and stage machinery. Several of these theatres are architectural gems that have remained in continuous use to the present day. Style, wit, grace, and class

distinction became not merely the framework of drama but its chief subject, and aristocratic items such as the fan and the snuffbox became signature props. This was also the Western world's first era of extensive theatrical commentary and thus the first from which we have detailed reports and evidence—both textual and visual—of the era's dramatic repertoires, acting styles, artists' lives, and manifestos that attempt to define the art of drama.

The Romantic Theatre

Every era in theatre is, to some extent, a rebellion against the previous one, and the romantic theatre of the eighteenth and nineteenth centuries was, in the main, a bold rejection of the rational decorum of the preceding royal era and its spirit of ordered, elegant, and enlightened debate. Romanticism, in contrast, was florid, exotic, grotesque, sprawling, and imbued with the free-flowing spirit of the individual rather than the social organization of class, court, or scientific or aesthetic academy. Compassion, rather than style and wit, was central to the romantic creed, and authors such as Johann Wolfgang von Goethe and Friedrich von Schiller, in Germany, and Victor Hugo, in France, intrigued audiences with their deep humanitarian concerns in plays that dealt with devils and monsters, robbers and priests, hunchbacks and heroes.

Romanticism gave rise to melodrama and grand opera, and supplied much of the anarchic passion and sprawling sentiment of modern realism as well. More-over, the romantic quest for the foreign and exotic represented Western drama's first serious reengage-ment with the theatre of the East. This, then, is a good point at which to return to drama's earlier years—to the Eastern strain of theatre that sprang from Egyptian and Canaanite beginnings and soon resurfaced on the Indian subcontinent and thereafter throughout Asia.

THEATRE IN THE EAST

It is misleading to refer to *an* "Asian theatre," for drama in Asia is as rich and diverse as theatre in the West, if not more so. Asia, after all—with nearly three-fifths of the world's population—comprises dozens of countries, hundreds of languages, and thousands of identified theatre forms. Nevertheless, although Asian dramatic forms differ markedly from each other, they generally adhere to many fundamental principles, mostly in strong contrast to Western traditions:

- Asian drama is never just "spoken"; rather, it is danced, chanted, mimed, and very often sung. Mere spoken drama, when it does occur in the East, is generally recognized as Western in origin or influence.

- Asian dramatic language is invariably rhythmic and melodic, and appreciated for its sound as much as (or more than) for its meaning. Alliteration, imagery, rhyme, and verbal juxtaposition are often as important in Asian dramatic dialogue as logic, persuasive rhetoric, and realism are in Western drama; the sonic value of words is as valued by an Asian audience as their semantic value is by a Western audience.

- Asian theatre is ordinarily more visual and sensual than literary or intellectual. Although some Asian dramatists are known for their literary gifts (and several are mentioned in the following discussion), few Asian plays have been widely circulated for general reading or academic study. Most Asians would consider the act of reading a play—separate from seeing it in performance—a rather odd pastime. Rather, Asian drama is inextricable from the modes of performance that bring it to life: dance, song, mime, gesture, acrobatics, puppetry, music, sound, costume, and makeup.

- Asian theatre has a strong emphasis on storytelling and myth, yet it is not tightly plotted, as Western drama is, and rarely leads to escalating incidents, stunning reversals, crescendoing climaxes, or elaborate plot closures. Asian theatre, whose metaphysical roots lie in those timeless meditations on human existence that are at the very heart of Hindu and Buddhist cultures, instead may seem, to Western tastes, leisurely and almost wandering in its structure. Certainly, Asian theatre's dramatic appeal is more continuous and rapturous than cathartic or arresting.

- Asian theatre is broadly stylized. As one might expect of a dramatic form imbued with music and dance, slice-of-life realism is practically unknown. Brilliantly colored costumes and makeup, long and obviously artificial beards, elegantly danced battle scenes, and live instrumental accompaniment are almost standard in traditional Asian theatre.

- Actors train in traditional Asian dramatic forms through an intense apprentice system beginning in early childhood and lasting into early middle age. Most Asian actors, indeed, are born or adopted into their trade.

- The Asian theatre is deeply traditional. Although there are modern and avant-garde theatre movements in most Asian countries—and some Western influence is evident in many of them—what is most remarkable about Eastern theatre is its near-universal consonance with folk history, ancient religions, and cultural myths.

Indian Sanskrit Drama

Asian drama probably began in India, where it sprang from the same Middle Eastern roots as its Western counterpart; some scholars even believe the Greek god, Dionysus, had an Indian heritage. India's oldest dramatic form is Sanskrit dance-theatre, which seems to have been created around the second century B.C. and remained popular for more than a thousand years thereafter. Sanskrit plays survive from about A.D. 100, and a comprehensive book of dramatic theory, the *Natyasastra,* or "treatise on theatre," ascribed to Bharata Muni, dates from somewhere between 200 B.C. and A.D. 200. The most comprehensive study of theatre surviving from the ancient world, the *Natyasastra* contains detailed analyses of Sanskrit dramatic texts, theatre buildings, acting, staging, music, gesture, dance, and even theatre-company organization. The treatise describes ten major genres of Sanskrit drama, including two primary ones: the *nataka,* which was based on well-known heroic stories of kings or sages, and the *prakarana,* based on the theme of love. The greatest Sanskrit poet, Kalidasa, wrote his masterpiece, *Sakuntala and the Ring of Recollection,* in the nataka style somewhere around the fifth century A.D. *The Little Clay Cart,* attributed to Sudraka, is the best known of two surviving examples of prakarana.

Sanskrit theatre, as far as we can tell (no ruins or drawings survive), was performed indoors, within roofed buildings. Rectangular in structure and fitted with a stage of about 48 by 24 feet, these buildings could seat somewhere between two hundred and five hundred spectators. Two doors, with an onstage orchestra between them, provided access to the dressing area behind the stage, and four columns held up the roof or an upper pavilion. Carved wooden elephants, tigers, and snakes adorned the pillars and perhaps the ceiling. Sanskrit drama was danced and acted with an onstage instrumental and percussive accompaniment, and its performers, all from priestly castes and trained from early childhood, were virtuosos of this demanding art.

Sanskrit drama died out around the tenth century, as the broad-based Hindu court culture fragmented in the wake of repeated Mongol invasions and the peoples of India fell back into preexisting regional cultures and languages. In succeeding centuries, an abundance of provincial theatre forms became popular throughout the subcontinent, a vast number of which remain to the present day. Despite their many differences, all Indian drama forms share many of the fundamental theatre aesthetics of their Sanskrit predecessors and the doctrines of the ancient *Natyasastra.*

Indian Kathakali

Today the most widely known dance-drama form is the *kathakali* ("story play"). Originating in rural villages in the province of Kerala in the seventeenth century, Kathakali is currently performed in many urban centers in India and abroad. Its stories come from the two great Indian epics, the *Ramayana* and the *Mahabharata,* and its traditional performance can be somewhat of an epic itself, beginning at ten in the evening and lasting well past dawn of the following day. Audience members are free to leave, take naps, and eat during these performances, however, and in modern times, kathakali performances are more commonly confined to three-hour evening time blocks, just as Western theatre.

In the Indian *kathakali* dance-drama, royal characters wear an elaborate *kiritam,* or crown, which frames the actor's eye movements—one of the most intensively studied skills of kathakali performers. Kalamandalam Gopi, a senior kathakali maestro, is shown here in the role of King Rugmangada in *Rugmangadacharitam,* performed in Trichur, Kerala (India), in 1993.

In kathakali, the text is sung—to a percussion accompaniment of gongs, drums, and cymbals—by two singers seated at the side. Actors dance and pantomime the dramatic action; by employing precise and elaborate hand gestures, footwork patterns, distinctive eye movements, and postural contortions, they reveal subtleties of meaning and characterization that are barely suggested by the text. Consequently, actors train rigorously for kathakali performance from early childhood, achieving mastery—if at all—only by about age forty. Highly stylized makeup and costuming also convey characterization and attitude: red- or black-bearded characters represent evil, white-bearded ones the divine. No scenery is used in kathakali, as plays are presented in arbitrary sites, with four simple poles defining the acting area.

Chinese Xiqu

China, Asia's largest nation, is Asia's oldest continuous culture, as well as the home of Asia's oldest continuous theatre tradition. Like all Asian drama, Chinese theatre is more sung than spoken, but since Chinese speech itself is semimusical—it is based on tonal changes as well as syllabic pronunciation—all traditional Chinese theatre is known by the Chinese term *xiqu* ("tuneful theatre"), which we translate as "Chinese opera."

Although forms of xiqu existed in China before the first century A.D., the first well-defined Chinese opera form, known as *zaju* ("various plays"), appeared in China during the Song dynasty in the tenth century, reaching its golden age in the thirteenth century under the Mongol emperor Kublai Khan. Zaju was a comedic music-dance-drama, with acrobatics and clowning; it was so popular that a single amusement park in thirteenth-century

Professional-level acrobatics are a fundamental part of all *kunqu*, and indeed of all Chinese opera. Here, in Hell, a devil leaps high over Du Liniang to terrorize her in the Suzhou Kun Opera production of *The Peony Pavilion* at the University of California–Irvine in 2006.

Keifeng (then China's northern capital) featured at least fifty indoor zaju theatres, the largest holding several thousand people.

By the end of the Ming dynasty, in 1644, zaju had been succeeded by a more stately, aristocratic, and poetic opera known as *kunqu*, originating from the town of Kun-shan. Soon thereafter, kunqu became the favored theatre entertainment of the Chinese court; it is still performed today. More popular theatre developed around the same time in the form of a boisterous "clapper opera," characterized by the furious rhythmic beating of drumsticks on a hardwood block. Subsequent years saw the rise of other regional theatre styles, influenced by the zaju, kunqu, and clapper-opera forms; as a result, China today sports as many as 360 variations of Chinese opera, most of them—such as Cantonese opera, Sichuan opera, and Hui opera—known by their regional origins.

The most famous Chinese opera in modern times is Beijing (Peking) opera, which is known in Chinese as *jingju*, or "theatre of the capital." Jingju was founded in 1790, when, in celebration of the emperor's eighti-eth birthday, a group of actors from the mountains of Anhui—led by one Cheng Changgeng—came to Beijing and amazed the court with their brilliant and innovative style of singing, music, and acrobatics. As local actors assimilated the Anhui style with their own, a new "capi-tal" style was developed, reaching its current form by about 1850, by which time it had become the dominant popular theatre throughout China.

Because the stories and plots of Chinese opera are normally ancient and well known, their actual stagings become, above all, celebrations of their performers' individual skills; in particular, actors must master the classic fourfold combination of singing (*chang*), speech (*nian*), acting and movement (*zuo*), and martial arts and acrobatics (*da*). Nearly all Chinese opera perform-ers are proficient in all four of these arts; the greatest performing artists—who are famous throughout the country—have mastered each of them to virtuoso stan-dards. Indeed, it might be said that the equivalent of a great Chinese actor in the West would be someone who could perform for the American Ballet Theatre, La Scala Opera, the Royal Shakespeare Company, the Ringling Brothers Circus, and the French Foreign Legion—all on the same evening!

Chinese opera offers a spectacular visual feast, with dazzling costumes, huge glittery headdresses, and bril-liantly colorful face painting. Actors of both sexes wear multilayered gowns in bold primary colors; many of them have "water-sleeves," which fall all the way to the floor. Chinese opera singing, much of it in an extreme falsetto (originally employed, according to traditional accounts, so actors could be heard over the din of people talking during the performance), is accompanied by the near-constant clanging of gongs and cymbals, clapper claps, drumbeats, and the furious strumming of various two-stringed fiddles. Movement skills include a rapid heel-to-toe walk, contortionist bendings and swayings, sudden jerks and freezes, and thrilling displays of full-stage acrobatics: back-springing performers bound across the stage in a literal blur, and in battle scenes combatants repel spear thrusts—sixteen at a time, all from different directions—with both hands and both feet. Chinese opera has never been dependent on scenery—an actor who enters holding a paddle behind him is assumed to be on a boat; an actor entering with a riding crop is assumed to be on horseback—but its storytelling conventions and its spectacular musical, visual, and acrobatic displays offer audiences one of the world's most thrilling and magnificent theatrical experiences.

Japanese Nō

The island nation of Japan has created two great theatre forms, *nō* and *kabuki*. Each is virtually a living museum of centuries-old theatre practice. Nō and kabuki are performed today in very much the same fashion as in previous centuries, yet each is also an immensely satisfying theatre experience for modern audiences attuned to the Japanese culture.

Nō is Japan's most revered and cerebral theatre. It is also the oldest continuously performed drama in the world. Perfected in the fourteenth and fifteenth centuries almost entirely by a single father-son team (Kan'ami and Zeami), who between them wrote and produced approximately 240 of the surviving plays, nō is a highly ceremonial drama, mysterious and tragic, that almost always portrays supernatural events and characters. All nō plays center on a single character, the *shite* ("doer"—pronounced "she-tay"), who is interrogated, prompted, and challenged by a secondary character, called the *waki*. Whereas waki

The Monkey King—a ferocious scamp—is the most enduring character in *xiqu;* he is always dressed in yellow, as shown here in this Shanghai Jingju Theatre production of *Pansi Cave.*

Nō actors usually come from long-standing nō families that operate nō schools. Here one of Japan's "living national treasures," the venerable Otoshige Sakai of the Kanze Nō-gakudo school, which was founded in the fourteenth century, helps mask his son, Otaharu, before a 2004 performance in Tokyo.

characters are always living male humans—usually ministers, commoners, or priests—shite characters may be gods, ghosts, women, animals, or warriors. The shite role, unlike the waki, is played in a mask. Nō actors, all of them male, train for only one of these role types and then perform them throughout their careers. Extensive training provides actors with the precise choreography and the musical notations required of their danced and chanted performances.

The actual nō stage is a precisely measured square of highly polished Japanese cypress flooring, about eighteen feet across, supported from below by large earthenware jars that resonate with the actors' foot-stompings. A bridgelike runway (*hashigakari*) provides stage access from stage right; it is used for the solemn entrances and exits particularly characteristic of nō. An ornate, curved roof covers the stage and is reminiscent of the time when the stage was housed in a separate building, which the audience observed from a distance. The nō roof is supported by four wooden pillars, each with its own name

and historic dramatic function. A wooden "mirror wall" at the rear of the stage bounces back the sounds of music and singing to the audience; on the wall, a painted pine tree, delicately gnarled and highly stylized, provides the only scenery. A four-man orchestra—whose instruments include a flute, small and large hand drums, and a stick drum—provides continuous musical accompaniment at the rear of the stage, and a chorus of six to ten singer-chanters is positioned on a platform addition at stage left. The absolute precision of the theatre design and the stately performance choreography and musicality give nō a ceremonial quality that is unique in world drama.

Nō has never been a theatre of mass entertainment, and first-time patrons today—including many Japanese—often find it bewildering. Plotting, even in comparison to other Asian forms, is almost nonexistent. The language is medieval, elliptical, and often forbiddingly obscure. The cast is small, the action relatively static, and the pace, by modern standards, nearly glacial: the basic nō walk, said to be derived from tramping

In kabuki's famous dance-drama *Kagami Jishi* (*The Lion Dance*), the lion (played by Nakamura Kankuro V) is teased by butterflies (played by his sons Nakamura Kantaro II and Nakamura Schichinosuki II).

through rice paddies, is an agonizingly deliberate slip-slide shuffle, with the feet barely leaving the ground. The actors are trained to keep their faces immobile and expressionless at all times, even when unmasked. Certainly nō is produced today more for enthusiasts than for the general public, but the number of such enthusiasts—at least in Japan—is currently growing, not falling. In fact, it is claimed that nō performances are currently at their most popular level in the history of the art. Like the studies of martial arts, flower arranging, and the tea ceremony, nō remains a Japanese national passion. Its sublime mystery and serenity—reflective of deep Buddhist and Shinto values—resonate profoundly in contemporary Japanese life and have proven increasingly influential to Japanese as well as Western dramatists of the current era.

Japanese Kabuki

Created two hundred years after nō, kabuki has always been a more spectacular and accessible form of theatrical entertainment. Whereas nō is refined, dignified,

and designed for small, studious audiences, kabuki is gaudy and exhilarating; from its earliest days, it was created to delight large crowds of merchants, traders, courtesans, and ordinary city dwellers. Whereas nō is sober and ascetic and staged on a relatively small, bare platform, kabuki is a theatrical extravaganza of dazzling colors, flamboyant dance and recitation, passionate emotion, and elaborate stage machinery and effects. Japanese audiences often respond by shouting their favorite actors' names or other words of encouragement at key moments in the play.

Kabuki was created in Kyoto around 1600 by the legendary shrine maiden Izumo Okuni, whose flamboyant and dramatic style of dancing became hugely popular in Kyoto's brothels and teahouses. The lavishness of Okuni's costumes and the fact that women performed both male and female parts led the Japanese to name it *kabuku*, meaning "askew" (today we might translate it as "punk"). This fast-developing and exotic entertainment was transformed by midcentury through a series of government edicts from an

This *bunraku* (puppet theatre) version of *Yoshitsune and the Thousand Cherry Trees* was performed at the National Bunraku Theatre in Osaka, Japan. As many as three puppeteers, dressed in black, operate each puppet in bunraku. The principal operator of each major-role puppet is usually unmasked, though he remains expressionless throughout the performance. Most other operators, such as the one barely seen here on the far right, are covered in black from the head down, making them all but invisible. In bunraku, the puppet is the star.

all-female to an all-male performing art. More complex dramatic storytelling—with themes based on traditional myths, historical incidents, local sex scandals and suicides, and already ancient nō drama—was adapted into the evolving format, which was then renamed *kabuki,* a term made up of three ideographs: *ka* ("song"), *bu* ("dance"), and *ki* ("skill"), the three major ingredients of kabuki.

By the eighteenth century, kabuki staging had incorporated curtains and scenery, playwrights' names were being printed in kabuki programs, and star actors had emerged, creating the two principal kabuki acting styles: *wagoto* (the elegant and naturalistic "soft style" of actor Sakata Tōjūrō I, from Kyoto) and *aragoto* (the thundering "rough style" of Ichikawa Danjūrō I, from Edo, now Tokyo). The traditions of both these actors remain central to kabuki to the present day, as all kabuki actors are members of just eleven famous families and all can trace their lineage—familial and professional— back to their kabuki-performing ancestors. The current star Ichikawa Danjūrō XII, for example, is the great-great-great-great-great-great-great-great-great-grandson of Ichikawa Danjūrō I, born in 1660; the celebrated Danjūrō style has been directly passed, father to son, down through the centuries.

There are many types of kabuki dramas, but the major works fall generally into two categories: history plays (*jidaimono,* or "period things") and domestic plays (*sewamono,* or "common things"). The history plays dramatize—usually in spectacular fashion— major political events of the remote past; often, however, the historical distance was little more than a protective cover for past playwrights and actors, who were in fact reflecting—under the guise of an apparently historical depiction—various controversial issues among the nobles and political officials of their own time. Domestic plays, in contrast, deal with the affairs of the townspeople, merchants, lovers, and courtesans of the playwright's own era, often focusing on the conflicts—intense throughout Japanese culture—between affairs of the heart and the call of duty. A great many domestic plays end in suicide

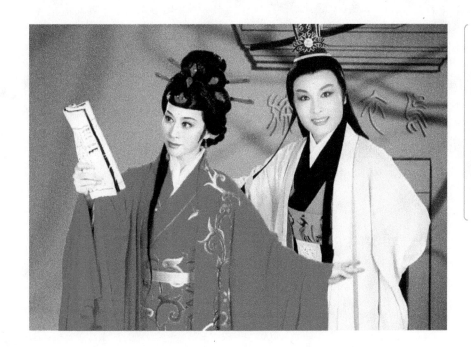

This fusion of Asian and Western theatrical styles was created by scholar/playwrights Sun Huizhu, Fei Chunfang, and Liu Lingzhi when they adapted Ibsen's *Hedda Gabler* into a *yueju*-style opera in which all roles are played by women. Retitled *Hedda, or Aspiration Sky High*, this blend of Ibsen and *xiqu* (Chinese opera) was produced by the Hangzhou Yueju Opera Company in Zhanjiang Gang in 2008; it also played in Germany, India, and Norway. Zhou Yujun (*left*) plays Hedda, looking over the manuscript of her would-be lover as her husband looks on.

(many, in fact, end in double suicides), with the lovers vowing to meet again in the world to come; such plays have been the subject of attempted bannings, since they have led to real suicides as a consequence.

Kabuki is mainly an actor's theatre; many of its plays are of unknown authorship and have been augmented over the centuries by actors' additions. One notable exception, however, is the kabuki author Chikamatsu Monzaemon (1653–1725). Considered the greatest Japanese dramatist of all time, Chikamatsu was also a famous playwright of the Japanese puppet-theatre *bunraku*.

THE THEATRICAL TRADITION TODAY: EAST AND WEST

These eleven great theatre traditions of the past—Greek, Roman, medieval, Renaissance, Royal, and romantic in the Western world, and Sanskrit, kathakali, xiqu, nō, and kabuki in the East—are all alive today, either in the form of regular and careful revivals or, happier yet in the case of the last four, by a continuous tradition of performance. All of these traditions have influenced the modern theatre, as we will see in the next chapter.

Chapter **8**

The Modern Theatre

THE THEATRE HAS EXPERIENCED MANY great periods, and one of its greatest is still going on. This is the period we call "modern," to which can be added the onrush of avant-garde movements we call (for the time being) "postmodern." Together, these make up the theatre of our times, a theatre that will likely be heralded for *all* times.

Modern drama can be said to date back to about 1875, and its roots lie deep in the social and political upheavals that developed in the eighteenth and nineteenth centuries, a time characterized by revolution. Political revolution in the United States (1776) and France (1789) irrevocably changed the political structure of the Western world, and the industrial-technological revolution overhauled the economic and social systems of most of the world. In the wake of these developments came an explosion of public communication and transportation; a tremendous expansion of literacy, democracy, and public and private wealth; and a universal demographic shift from countryside to city. These forces combined to create in Europe, the United States, and elsewhere mass urban populations hungering for social communion and stimulation: a fertile ground for the civilized theatre of our times. ▶

Simultaneously, an intellectual revolution—in philosophy, science, social understanding, and religion—was altering human consciousness. The intellectual certainty of Louis XIV, whose divine right to rule was unquestioned in the seventeenth and early eighteenth centuries, appeared ludicrous in an age governed by secular scientific investigation. The clear-sightedness of a playwright such as Molière seemed simplistic in an age of soul-searching and self-doubting philosophies. The intellectual revolution was an exceedingly complex phenomenon that occurred in many spheres of thought and was to gain momentum with each passing decade. It continues to this day.

The Copernican theory had already made clear that human beings do not stand at the geographic center of the universe but rather that our world, indeed our universe, is swept up in a swarm of interstellar movements. Later scientists would press further than that, until eventually the revelations of Albert Einstein, Werner Heisenberg, and others would remove our sense of stability and establish the human animal as little more than a transformation of kinetic energy, wobbling in a multigravitational atomic field marked by galaxies and black holes, neutrinos and quarks, matter and antimatter, all in a vast dance of inexplicable origin and doubtful destiny.

Nor was that "human animal" so vastly privileged over other species, it would seem. Darwin would argue that we *Homo sapiens* are directly linked to other mammals—descended not from Adam and Eve or pre-Hellenic demigods but from prehistoric apes. Our morals and religions, anthropologist Ruth Benedict would argue, were not handed down to all humanity from a single source but are instead a ranging complex of laws and traditions wholly relative to the climates and cultures we inhabit. The work of Sigmund Freud would posit the existence of the unconscious, a dark and lurking inner self filled with infantile urges, primordial fantasies, and suppressed fears and rages. Friedrich Nietzsche would argue that "there are no facts, only interpretations." The writings of Karl Marx would contend that social behavior has its basis in economic greed, class struggle, and political manipulation. "Everlasting uncertainty and agitation" is the nature of human interaction, according to Marx, and society comprises "two great hostile camps" continually engaged in civil war.

These and scores of other serious challenges to traditional thinking were accompanied everywhere by public debate and dispute. By the turn of the twentieth century, an investigative drive seized Western civilization: data were being collected on every conceivable topic, and scientific questioning and testing replaced intuition and dogma as the accepted avenues to truth. Experimentation, exploration, documentation, and challenge became the marching orders of the artist and intellectual alike.

The modern theatre has its roots in these political, social, and intellectual revolutions. Ever since its outset it has been a theatre of challenge, a theatre of experimentation. It has never been a theatre of rules or simple messages, nor has it been a theatre of demigods or of absolute heroes and villains. It has reflected, to a certain degree, the confusions of its times, but it has also struggled to clarify and to illuminate, to document and explore human destiny in a complex and uneasy universe.

REALISM

Thus far, the movement that has had the most pervasive and long-lived effect on modern theatre is, beyond question, realism. Realism has sought to create a drama without conventions or abstractions. *Likeness to life* is realism's goal; in pursuit of that goal it has renounced, among other things, idealized or prettified settings, versifications, contrived endings, and stylized costumes and performances.

Realism is a beguiling aesthetic philosophy. Indeed, the theatre has *always* taken "real life" as its fundamental subject, so realism seems at first glance to be the perfect style with which to approach the reality of existence. Instead of having actors represent characters, the realists would say, let us have the actors *be* those characters. Instead of having dialogue stand for conversation, let us have dialogue that *is* conversation. Instead of having scenery and costumes that convey a sense of time and place and atmosphere, let us have scenery that *is* genuinely inhabitable and costumes that *are* real clothes.

But, of course, realism has its limits: any dramatic piece must inevitably involve a certain shaping and stylization, no matter how lifelike its effect, and advocates of theatrical realism are well aware of this inevitability. The stylization and ideology of realism were tested, during the last years of the nineteenth century and the first years of the twentieth, in every aspect of theatre—acting, directing, design, and playwriting—and the results of those tests form a meaningful body of theatre and a style that remains enormously significant.

A Laboratory

In essence, the realistic theatre is conceived to be a laboratory in which the nature of relationships or the ills of society or the symptoms of a dysfunctional family are "objectively" set down for the final judgment of an audience of impartial observers. In its purest form, realistic theatre should strictly adhere to the "scientific method" of the laboratory; nothing must ring false. The setting is to resemble the prescribed locale of the play as closely as possible; indeed, it is not unusual for much of the scenery to be acquired from a real-life environment and transported to the theatre. Characters' costumes in the realistic theatre follow the dress of "real" people of similar societal status; dialogue recreates the cadences and expressions of daily life.

Early in the realist movement, the proscenium stage of the romantic era was modified to accommodate scenery constructed in *box sets:* three fully visible walls that featured real bookcases, windows, fireplaces, swinging doors, and so forth, built just as they are in a house interior. The audience was meant to feel as if they were eavesdropping, witnessing interactions within an actual private home. In the same vein, realistic acting was judged effective insofar as it was drawn from the behavior of life and insofar as the actors seemed to be genuinely speaking to each other instead of playing to the audience. A new aesthetic principle had spawned: the "theatre of the fourth wall removed" in which the life onstage was conceived to be the same as life in a real-world setting, except that, in the case of the stage, one wall—the proscenium opening—had been removed. Thus the theatre was like a laboratory microscope and the stage like a biologist's slide: a living environment presented for judicious inspection by neutral observers.

Realism presents its audience with an abundance of seemingly real-life "evidence" and permits each spectator to arrive at her or his own conclusions. There is some shaping of this evidence by author and performer alike, to be sure, but much of the excitement of the realistic theatre is occasioned by the genuine interpretive freedom it allows the audience and by the accessibility of its characters, whose behaviors are familiar enough to the average spectator that they may be easily assimilated and identified.

Moreover, in presenting its evidence from the surface of life, realism encourages us to delve into the mystery that lies beneath it. Realism's characters, like people in life, are defined by detail rather than by symbol or abstract idealization: like people we know, they are ultimately unpredictable—humanly complex rather than ideologically absolute. As such, while realism does not inherently advocate one political position—for the revelation of the messiness of life is too complex for a partisan position—its works inevitably have political

repercussions. The exposure of society's suppressed secrets can be potentially scandalous—but also, as history shows, extremely popular.

The success of realism is, in fact, well established; it remains one of the dominant modes of drama to this day. At its most profound, when crafted and performed by consummately skilled artists, realistic theatre can generate extremely powerful audience empathy by virtue of the insight and clarity it brings to real-world moments. In giving us characters, the realistic playwright gives us *companions*—fellow travelers on the voyage of human discovery with whom we can compare thoughts and feelings. In their uncertainties and trepidations, wistfulness, halting eloquence, and conversational syntax, we recognize ourselves; in that recognition we gain an understanding of our own struggles and a compassion for all human endeavors.

Pioneers of Realism

The realistic theatre had its beginnings in the four-year period that saw the premieres of three shocking plays by Norwegian playwright Henrik Ibsen: *A Doll's House* (1867), *Ghosts* (1881), and *An Enemy of the People* (1882). Already famous for historical and poetic dramas, including the magnificent *Peer Gynt* (1867), Ibsen (1828–1906), soon to be known as the "father of dramatic realism," turned his attention in these works to more contemporary and day-to-day themes: woman's role in society, hereditary disease, mercy killing, and political hypocrisy. Ordinary people populate Ibsen's realistic world, with issues that affect ordinary husband-wife, mother-son, and brother-brother relationships, as played out in the interiors of ordinary homes. Controversial beyond measure in their own time, these plays retain their edge of pertinence even today and still have the power to inform, move, and even shock. The reason for their lasting impact lies in Ibsen's choice of issues and his skill at showing both sides through brilliantly captured psychological detail.

The realistic theatre spread rapidly throughout Europe as the controversy surrounding Ibsen's plays stimulated other writers to follow suit. The result was a proliferation of "problem plays," as they were sometimes called, which focused genuine social concern through realistic dramatic portrayals. In Germany, Gerhart Hauptmann (1862–1946) explored the plight of the middle and proletarian classes in several works, most notably in his masterpiece *The Weavers* (1892). In England,

Lee Breuer's celebrated production of *Dollhouse* with the Mabou Mines company, which he co-heads in New York, was remarkable for casting all the male roles in this adaptation of Ibsen's play (usually translated as *A Doll's House*) with actors four feet tall or less, and with the play's women towering two feet above them. The setting (by Narelle Sisson) was also a "doll house," with miniature walls and furniture. Maude Mitchell plays Nora in this performance, seen at the 2007 Edinburgh Festival, with Mark Povinelli as her husband, Torvald.

Irish-born George Bernard Shaw (1856–1950) created a comedic realism through which he addressed issues such as slum landlordism (in *Widowers' Houses,* 1892), prostitution (in *Mrs. Warren's Profession,* 1902), and urban poverty (in *Major Barbara,* 1905). In France, André Antoine (1858–1943) created his Théâtre Libre in 1887 to encourage stagings of realistic dramas, including Ibsen's *Ghosts* and *The Wild Duck,* Hauptmann's *Weavers,* and the French plays of Eugène Brieux (1858–1932), including *Damaged Goods* (1902), about syphilis, and *Maternity* (1903), about birth control. By the turn of the century, realism was virtually the standard dramatic form in Europe.

If the realistic theatre came to prominence with the plays of Ibsen, it attained its stylistic apogee in the major works of Anton Chekhov (1860–1904). Chekhov was a physician by training and a writer of fiction by

vocation. Toward the end of his career, in association with realist director Konstantin Stanislavsky (1863–1938) and the Moscow Art Theatre, he also achieved success as a playwright through four plays that portray the last decades of the czarist era in Russia with astonishing force and subtlety: *The Seagull* (1896), *Uncle Vanya* (1899), *The Three Sisters* (1901), and *The Cherry Orchard* (1904). The intricate craftsmanship of these plays has never been surpassed; even the minor characters seem to breathe the same air we do.

Chekhov's technique was to create deeply complex relationships among his characters and to develop his plots and themes more or less between the lines. Every Chekhovian character is filled with secrets that the dialogue never fully reveals. As an example of Chekhov's realist style, examine the dialogue in the following scene from *The Three Sisters.* In this scene, Vershinin,

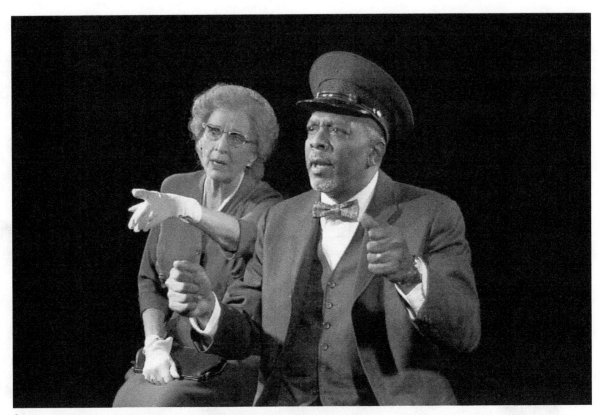

Realistic plays do not necessarily require realistic scenery. In Alfred Uhry's *Driving Miss Daisy*, the elderly southern Jewish woman of the title is driven around town by her African American chauffeur; over the years, they develop a profound—though mostly unstated—emotional relationship. It would be impossible to stage the moving car realistically, so this vital element must simply be mimed. But the costumes, dialogue, and acting are acutely realistic. Patricia Fraser and Ernest Perry Jr. are the actors in this 2000 Utah Shakespeare Festival production.

an army colonel, meets Masha and her sisters, Irina and Olga, whom Vershinin dimly remembers from past years in Moscow:

VERSHININ: I have the honor to introduce myself, my name is Vershinin. I am very, very glad to be in your house at last. How you have grown up! Aie-aie!

IRINA: Please sit down. We are delighted to see you.

VERSHININ: (*with animation*) How glad I am, how glad I am! But there are three of you sisters. I remember—three little girls. I don't remember your faces, but that your father, Colonel Prozorov, had three little girls I remember perfectly. How time passes! Hey-ho, how it passes! . . .

IRINA: From Moscow? You have come from Moscow?

VERSHININ: Yes. Your father was in command of a battery there, and I was an officer in the same brigade. (*To* MASHA) Your face, now, I seem to remember.

MASHA: I don't remember you.

VERSHININ: So you are Olga, the eldest—and you are Masha—and you are Irina, the youngest —

OLGA: You come from Moscow?

VERSHININ: Yes. I studied in Moscow. . . . used to visit you in Moscow.

Masha and Vershinin are destined to become lovers; their deepening, largely unspoken communion will provide one of the most haunting strains in the play. And how lifelike is the awkwardness of their first encounter! Vershinin's enthusiastic clichés ("How time passes!") and interjections ("Aie-aie!") are the stuff of everyday discourse; the news that he comes from Moscow is repeated so that it becomes amusing rather than informative, a revelation of character rather than of plot.

Masha's first exchange with Vershinin gives no direct indication of the future of their relationship;

Perhaps the seminal play of mid-century American realism is Clifford Odets's *Awake and Sing!* Initially produced by the Group Theatre in 1935, it led to a down-to-earth, gritty style of both playwriting and acting that dominated the American theatre for the next fifty years. The play, which details the hopes and dreams and emotional crises of a Jewish immigrant family living in a cramped Bronx apartment, established a pattern of American domestic dramas about urban, working-class life, and the actors who starred in the original production—Group Theatre members Luther and Stella Adler, Sanford Meisner, and Morris Carnovsky—later became legendary teachers of "the method" that was to inspire future generations of American performers. The production pictured was seen in 2010 at A Noise Within in Los Angeles: from left to right are Alan Blumenfeld as Uncle Morty, Len Lesser as Jacob, and Deborah Strang as Bessie Berger; Andrew Traister directed.

it is a crossed communication in which one character refuses to share in the other's memory. Is this a personal repudiation, or is it a teasing provocation? The acting, not simply the text, must establish their developing rapport. The love between Vershinin and Masha will demand that the actors who play them express deep feeling and subtle nuance, through the gestures, glances, tones of voice, shared understandings, and sympathetic rhythms that distinguish lovers everywhere. It is a theme that strongly affects the mood of the play but is rarely explicit in the dialogue.

Naturalism

Naturalism represents an extreme attempt to dramatize human reality without the appearance of dramaturgical shaping. The naturalists flourished primarily in France during the late nineteenth century. Émile Zola (1840–1902) was their chief theoretician. The naturalists based their aesthetics on nature, particularly humanity's place in the natural (Darwinian) environment. To the naturalist, human beings were merely biological phenomena whose behavior was determined

Incestuous desire hovers over Brooklyn dockworker Eddie Carbone's breakfast table in Arthur Miller's *A View from the Bridge* (1955), as Scarlett Johansson, playing Eddie's seventeen-year-old niece Catherine, plops impulsively onto her uncle's lap. Liev Schreiber is Eddie and Jessica Hecht plays his anxious wife Beatrice in this rapturously received 2010 Broadway revival. Though set in the early 1950s, Miller's intense family drama is structured as a Greek tragedy (complete with a one-man chorus) as it grapples with the sexual confusion, cultural tensions, and economic uncertainties of America's postwar period. The realistic settings and costumes were by John Lee Beatty and Jane Greenwood, respectively; the direction was by Gregory Mosher.

entirely by genetic and social circumstances. To portray a character as a hero, or even as a credible force for change in society, was anathema to the naturalists, who similarly despised dramatic conclusions or climaxes. Whereas realist plays at that time tended to deal with well-defined social issues—women's rights, inheritance laws, worker's pensions, and the like—naturalist plays offered nothing more than a "slice of life." The characters of the play were the play's entire subject; any topical issues that arose served merely to facilitate the interplay of personalities and highlight the characters' situations, frustrations, and hopes.

The naturalists sought to eliminate every vestige of dramatic convention: "All the great successes of the stage are triumphs over convention," declared Zola. Their efforts in this direction are exemplified by August Strindberg's (1849–1912) elimination of the time-passing intermission in *Miss Julie* (instead, a group of peasants, otherwise irrelevant to the plot, enter the kitchen setting between acts and dance to fill the time Miss Julie is spending in Jean's offstage bedroom) and by Arthur Schnitzler's (1862–1931) elimination of conventional scene beginnings, endings, and climaxes in the interlocking series of cyclical love affairs that constitute the action of *La Ronde*.

Inasmuch as sheer verisimilitude, presented as "artlessly" as humanly possible, is the naturalist's primary goal, the term *naturalism* is often applied to those realistic plays that seem most effectively lifelike. This is not a particularly felicitous use of the term, however, because it ignores the fundamental precept of naturalism—that the human being is a mere figure in the natural environment. Naturalism is not merely a matter of style; it is a philosophical concept concerning the nature of the human animal. Naturalist theatre represents a purposeful attempt to explore that concept, using life itself as its basic dramaturgy.

Eugene O'Neill (1888–1953), America's first great playwright, pioneered an earthy naturalistic style in his early plays, returning to that style in his autobiographical masterpiece, *Long Day's Journey into Night*—a play so true to life that O'Neill forbade its production or publication until many years after his death. In subsequent times, the dramas of Arthur Miller, Tennessee Williams, August Wilson, Wendy Wasserstein, Neil LaBute, and Theresa Rebeck are all strongly influenced by both realism and naturalism, which continue to have a commanding presence on the American stage.

ANTIREALISM

Realism and naturalism were not the only new movements of the late nineteenth century to make themselves strongly felt in the modern theatre, however.

A counterforce, equally powerful, was to emerge. First manifest in the movement known as symbolism, this counterforce evolved and expanded into what we will call antirealistic theatre.

The Symbolist Rebellion

The symbolist movement began in Paris during the 1880s as a joint venture of artists, playwrights, essayists, critics, sculptors, and poets. If realism was the art of depicting reality as ordinary men and women might see it, symbolism sought to explore—by means of images and metaphors—the *inner* realities that cannot be directly or literally perceived. "Symbolic" characters, therefore, would not represent real human beings but instead would symbolize philosophical ideals or warring internal forces in the human soul.

Symbolism had another goal as well: to crush what its adherents deemed to be a spiritually bankrupt realism and replace it with traditional aesthetic values—poetry, imagery, novelty, fantasy, extravagance, profundity, audacity, charm, and superhuman magnitude. United in their hatred for literal detail and for all they considered mundane or ordinary, the symbolists demanded abstraction, enlargement, and innovation; the symbolist spirit soared in poetic encapsulations, outsized dramatic presences, fantastical visual effects, shocking structural departures, and grandiloquent speech. Purity of vision, rather than accuracy of observation, was the symbolists' aim, and self-conscious creative innovation was to become their primary accomplishment.

The first symbolist theatre, founded in 1890 by Parisian poet Paul Fort (1872–1960), was intended as a direct attack on the naturalistic Théâtre Libre of André Antoine, founded three years earlier. Fort's theatre, the Théâtre d'Art, was proposed as "a theatre for Symbolist poets only, where every production would cause a battle." In some ways, the theatres of Antoine and Fort had much in common: both were amateur, gained considerable notoriety, and served as centers for "schools" of artistic ideology that attracted as much attention and controversy as any of their theatrical offerings.

But the two theatres were openly, deliberately, at war. While Antoine was presenting premieres of naturalistic and realistic dramas by August Strindberg, Émile Zola, and Henrik Ibsen, Fort presented the staged poems and poetic plays of both contemporary and earlier writers such as the French Arthur Rimbaud and Paul Verlaine, the Belgian Maurice Maeterlinck, and the American Edgar Allan Poe. Whereas Antoine would go to great lengths to create realistic scenery for his plays (for example, he displayed real sides of beef hung from meat hooks for his presentation of *The Butchers*), Fort would prevail upon leading impressionist painters—including Pierre Bonnard, Maurice Denis, and Odilon Redon—to dress his stylized stage. Silver angels, translucent veils, and sheets of crumpled wrapping paper were among the decors that backed the symbolist works at the Théâtre d'Art.

Fort's theatre created an immediate sensation in Paris. With the stunning success in 1890 of *The Intruder*, a mysterious and poetic fantasy by Maeterlinck, the antirealist movement was fully engaged and, as Fort recalled in his memoirs, "the cries and applause of the students, poets, and artists overwhelmed the huge disapproval of the bourgeoisie."

The movement spread quickly as authors and designers alike awakened to the possibilities of a theatre wholly freed from the constraints of verisimilitude. Realism, more and more critics concluded, would never raise the commonplace to the level of art; it would only drag art down into the muck of the mundane. As such, the symbolists reasoned, realism ran counter to all that the theatre had stood for in the past; it throttled the potential of artistic creativity. In fact, such naturalistic and realistic authors as Henrik Ibsen, August Strindberg, Gerhart Hauptmann, and George Bernard Shaw soon came under the symbolist influence and abandoned their social preoccupations and environmental exactitude to seek new languages and more universal themes. As an added element, at about this time Sigmund Freud's research was being published and discussed, and his theories concerning dream images and the worlds of the unconscious provided new source material for the stage.

By the turn of the century, the counterforce of theatrical stylization set in motion by the symbolists was established on all fronts; indeed, the half decade on either side of 1900 represents one of the richest periods of experimentation in the history of dramatic writing. Out of that period came Hauptmann's archetypal fairytale *The Sunken Bell* (Germany, 1896), Alfred Jarry's outrageously cartoonish and scatological *Ubu Roi* (France, 1898), Ibsen's haunting ode to individualism *When We Dead Awaken* (Norway, 1899), Strindberg's metaphoric and imagistic *The Dream Play* (Sweden, 1902), William Butler Yeats's evocative poetic fable *Cathleen ni Houlihan* (Ireland, 1903), Shaw's philosophical allegory *Don Juan in Hell* (England, 1903), and James Barrie's whimsical, buoyant fantasy *Peter Pan*

Robert Wilson (the director) and John Conklin (the costume designer) co-designed the scenery for this dreamlike American Repertory Theatre production of Ibsen's *When We Dead Awaken* in 1991.

(England, 1904). Almost every dramatic innovation that has followed since that time has been at least in part prefigured by one or more of these seminal works for the nonrealist theatre.

The realist-versus-symbolist confrontation affected every aspect of theatre production. Symbolist-inspired directors and designers, side by side with the playwrights, drastically altered the arts of staging and decor to accommodate the new dramaturgies that surged into the theatre. Realist directors such as Antoine and Stanislavsky suddenly found themselves challenged by scores of adversaries and renegades: a school of symbolist and poetic directors rose in France, and a former disciple of Stanislavsky, the "constructivist" Vsevolod Meyerhold (1874–1940), broke with the Russian master to create a nonrealist "biomechanical" style of acting and directing. At first, Meyerhold's techniques stood in sharp contrast to the more realistic styles established at Stanislavsky's Moscow Art Theatre, but by 1904 that theatre featured Stanislavsky himself producing the symbolist plays of Maeterlinck. With the advent of electrical stage lighting, opportunities for stylizing were vastly expanded: the new technology enabled the modern director to create vivid stage effects, starkly unrealistic in appearance, through the judicious use of spotlighting, shadowing, and shading. Technology, plus trends in modern art that were well established in Europe by 1900, led to scenery and costume designs that departed radically from realism. Exoticism, fantasy, sheer sensual delight, and aesthetic purity became the prime objectives of designers who joined the anti-realist rebellion.

In some respects, the symbolist aim succeeded perhaps beyond the dreams of its originators. Fort's Théâtre d'Art, although it lasted only two years, now has spiritual descendants in every city in the Western world where theatre is performed.

The Era of Isms

The symbolist movement itself was short-lived, at least under that name. *Symbolism,* after all, was coined primarily as a direct contradiction of *realism,* and movements named for their oppositional qualities—called for what they are *not*—can quickly lose their vitality, turning into mere critiques of art rather than as art itself.

Within months of the symbolist advances, therefore, symbolism *as a movement* was deserted by founders and followers alike. Where did they go? Off to found newer movements: futurism, dadaism, idealism, impressionism, expressionism, constructivism, surrealism, and perhaps a hundred other ism-labeled movements now lost to time.

The first third of the twentieth century, indeed, was an era of theatrical isms, rich with continued experimentation by movements self-consciously seeking to redefine theatrical art. Ism theatres sprang up like mushrooms, each with its own fully articulated credo and manifesto, each promising a better art—if not, indeed, a better world. It was a vibrant era for the theatre, for out of this welter of isms the aesthetics of dramatic art took on a new social and political significance in the cultural capitals of Europe and America. A successful play was not merely a play but rather the forum for a *cause,* and behind that cause was a body of zealous supporters and adherents who shared a deep aesthetic commitment.

Nothing quite like that ism spirit exists today, for we have lost the social involvement that can turn an aesthetic movement into a profound collective belief. In fact, one of the most prominent theatre movements in recent history, postmodernism, might be thought of as promoting "the death of isms" rather than a specific "ism" itself. Rather than create a singular event or communicate a unified point of view, postmodernism believes nothing is truly original. Instead, everything we see or hear onstage is just "quoted," much as a college essay quotes its sources. As such, while postmodernism intensifies key antirealist ideas—most notably a failure of communication, a break from recognizable reality, and an awareness of its status as theatre—it also abandons any attempt to ask the profound questions that characterized movements such as symbolism. A recent production of *Hamlet* by The Wooster Group

Willem Dafoe as the idiot and a friendly "Duck" tease the audience in Richard Foreman's postmodernist *Idiot Savant* presented by Foreman's Ontological-Hysteric Company performing at the New York Public Theatre in 2009.

exemplifies the postmodern style: the company performed Shakespeare's tragedy in front of a projection of a 1964 film version of the same play—and the film was, in turn, spliced together from recordings of three live performances of a Broadway production starring Richard Burton. Similarly, the postmodern director and playwright Richard Foreman's *Idiot Savant,* in 2009, begins with a disembodied voice reciting a list of comically diverse objects that will appear during the performance: two rowboats, a bloody towel, a spider, a golf ball, and a snake. Both of these productions arrange disparate elements without any connection—in fact, the lack of any connection is the point.

Isms have not completely vanished, however. They may have new names and be directed to new aims, but today's theatre movements retain the fundamental spirit of the artistic exploration of the isms. The experiments and discoveries of those early days of the twentieth century and the nonrealistic spirit of symbolism itself survive under a variety of formats such as ritual theatre, poetic theatre, holy theatre, theatre of cruelty, existentialist theatre, art theatre, avant-garde theatre, theatre of the absurd, theatre of alienation, dance theatre, and immersive theatre. These present-day groupings, unlike the early isms, are critic-defined rather than artist-defined; indeed, most theatre artists today reject any "grouping" nomenclature whatever. However difficult it may be to pin down their specific characteristics, though, the thriving and diverse artists that continue to move beyond realism can all trace their origins back to the drive in the late nineteenth century to rebel against convention, challenge traditional theatrical representation, and expand the potential of theatrical language. And that expansion has come in a variety of contemporary anti-realistic stylizations.

Stylized Theatre

Although disparate in its individual manifestations, all antirealistic theatre insists on transforming reality into a larger-than-life theatrical experience. We can thus refer to the entire spectrum of nonrealistic modern theatre as *stylized*. Theatre of all eras have had distinctive styles, but these in earlier times were largely *imposed* by then-current conventions while more recent dramatists have consciously *selected and created* styles to satisfy their aesthetic theories, their social principles, or simply their desire for novelty and innovation.

Antirealistic theatre attempts to create new theatrical forms, not merely to enhance the portrayal of human existence, but also to disclose the fundamental patterns underlying that existence: patterns of perception, association, and personal interaction. Such new forms come from anywhere and everywhere: from the past, from distant cultures, and from present and futuristic technologies. Present-day theatre artists have unprecedented reservoirs of sources to draw upon and are generally unconstrained by political, religious, or artistic traditions. Almost anything can now be put upon a stage, and in the twenty-first century it seems that almost everything is.

Antirealistic theatre does not altogether dispense with reality, however. Rather, it wields it in often unexpected ways and enhances it with symbol and metaphor, striving to elucidate by parable and allegory and to deconstruct and reconstruct by language, scenery, and lighting. Further, it makes explicit use of the theatre's very theatricality, reminding its audience members, both directly and indirectly, that they are watching a performance, not an episode in somebody's daily life. Stylization inevitably reaches for universality. It tends to treat problems of psychology as problems of philosophy, and problems in human relations as problems of the human condition. It reaches for patterns, not particulars; it explores abstractions and aims for sharp thematic focus and bold intellectual impact.

In the stylized theatre, characters usually represent more than individual persons or personality types. Like the medieval allegories, modern stylized plays often involve characters who represent forces of nature, moral positions, human instincts, and the like—entities such as death, fate, idealism, the life force, the earth mother, the tyrant father, or the prodigal son. The conflicts associated with these forces, unlike the conflicts of realism, are not responsive to changes in human behavior; more often than not, they represent permanent discords inherent in the human condition. The stylized theatre resonates with tension and frustration in the face of irreconcilable demands.

But that is not to say the antirealistic theatre is inevitably grim. On the contrary, it often uses whimsy and mordant wit as its dominant modes. Although the themes of the antirealistic theatre are anxious ones—for example, the alienation of humanity, the futility of communication, the loss of innocence, the intransigence of despair—it is not necessarily a theatre of pessimism or of nihilistic outrage. Indeed, the glory of the stylized theatre is that, at its best, its capacity to entertain refuses to be swamped by its themes. It transcends frustration, celebrating the victory of poetry over alienation, comedy over noncommunication, and artistry over despair. The antirealistic theatre aims at lifting its audience, not saddling them; even if it proffers no solutions to life's inevitable discords, it can provide us with a greater lucidity on the human adventure. To help us understand the diversity of stylized theatre that results from this philosophy, we will examine brief examples from plays written over the past hundred-plus years that establish the main lines of the antirealistic theatre.

Surrealism and the Avant-Garde: *Ubu Roi*   The opening of Alfred Jarry's *Ubu Roi* (*King Ubu*) at the Théâtre de l'Oeuvre in Paris on December 10, 1896, was perhaps the most violent dramatic premiere in theatre history: the audience shouted, whistled, hooted, cheered, threw things, and shook their fists at the stage. Duels were even fought after subsequent performances. The *avant-garde* was born.

The term avant-garde comes from the military, where it refers to the advance battalion, or the "shock troops" that initiate a major assault. In France the term initially described the wave of French playwrights and directors who openly and boldly assaulted realism in the first four decades of the twentieth century. Today the term is used worldwide to describe any adventurous, experimental, and nontraditional artistic effort.

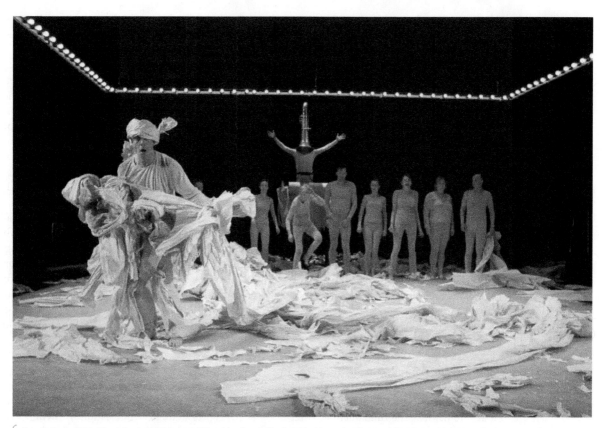

French director Alain Timar directed and designed this adaptation of *Ubu Roi* at the Hungarian Theatre of Cluj (Romania) in 2011. The twelve actors wear identical cream-colored long underwear and alternate in the roles of Ma and Pa Ubu while clothing themselves, and/or stuffing their costumes, with great sheaves of white paper torn from a giant "toilet roll" at the rear of the stage. "Merdre" indeed!

Alfred Jarry (1873–1907), a diminutive iconoclast ("eccentric to the point of mania and lucid to the point of hallucination," says critic Roger Shattuck), unleashed his radical shock troops from the moment the curtain rose. Jarry had called for an outrageously antirealis- tic stage—painted scenery depicting a bed with a bare tree at its foot; palm trees with a coiled boa constrictor around one of them; a gallows with a hanging skeleton; and falling snow. Characters entered through a painted fireplace. Costumes, in Jarry's words, were "divorced as far as possible from [realistic] color or chronology." And the title character stepped forward to begin the play with a word that quickly became immortal: *"Merdre!"* or "Shrit!"

This *mot d'Ubu* ("Ubu's word") more than anything else occasioned scandal, for although Ibsen had bro- ken barriers of propriety in subject matter, no play- wright had yet tested barriers of tasteful language in the Victorian age. Vulgar epithets, common enough in the works of Aristophanes and Shakespeare, had been

pruned from the theatre in the Royal era and abolished entirely in the lofty spirit of romanticism; far from try- ing to sneak them back in, Jarry simply threw them up, schoolboy-like, in the face of the astonished audience. The added "r" in *merdre* (or, in translation, the added "r" in "shrit"), far from "cleansing" the offending obscen- ity, only called more attention to it and to its deliberate intrusion onto the Parisian stage.

Ubu Roi was, in fact, quite literally a schoolboy play; Jarry wrote the first version at the age of fifteen as a lampoon of his high school physics teacher. Jarry was only twenty-three years old when the play astounded its Parisian audiences, and the juvenile aspects of the play's origins were evident throughout the finished product, which proved to be Jarry's sole masterwork: a savage and often ludicrous satire on the theme of power in which Father (later King) Ubu—a fat, foul-mouthed, venal, amoral, and pompous Polish assassin—proves one of the stage's greatest creations. The play sprawls; its thirty-three scenes are often just crude skits barely

Elmer Rice's *The Adding Machine* (1923) is one of America's most important expressionist plays, showing the dehumanization of employees trapped in a corporate accounting department. Anne Bogart directed this rambunctious version for the 1995 Classics in Context festival of the Actors Theatre of Louisville.

linked by plot, but the interplay of farce and violence is inspired, as in the famous dinner scene:

FATHER UBU, MOTHER UBU, CAPTAIN BORDURE and their followers enter the dining room.

CAPTAIN BORDURE: Hey, Mother Ubu! What delicacies have you for us today?

MOTHER UBU: Here's the menu: Polish soup, rat chops, veal, chicken, dachshund paté, turkey butt, charlotte russe . . .

FATHER UBU: Hey, that's enough!

MOTHER UBU: No, there's more! Iced cannonball, fruit salad, boiled artichokes, cauliflower à la shrit.

FATHER UBU: Hey, what do you think I am, the Emperor of Japan?

MOTHER UBU: (*to the others*) Don't listen to him; he's an imbecile!

FATHER UBU: Hah! I'll sharpen my teeth on your ankles!

MOTHER UBU: Eat this instead, Father Ubu. Good Polish soup!

FATHER UBU: (*sips a mouthful and spits it out*) Crap! That's terrible.

CAPTAIN BORDURE: Pretty awful, no?

MOTHER UBU: What's wrong with it, you pigs?

FATHER UBU (*striking his forehead*): I know what to do! Back in a minute! (*He leaves*).

MOTHER UBU: Gentlemen, it's veal time!

CAPTAIN BORDURE: It looks OK, but I'm all done!

MOTHER UBU: Turkey butt, then!

CAPTAIN BORDURE: Now that's terrific! Exquisite! Long live Mother Ubu. (*He leads the others in a cheer*)

EVERYONE: Long live Mother Ubu!!!

FATHER UBU (*returning furiously, waving a toilet brush in his hand*): You'll soon be crying, "Long live *Father* Ubu!" (*He throws the toilet brush onto the meat platter and stirs the food with it.*)

MOTHER UBU: You horrible man! What are you doing?

FATHER UBU: Go on! Taste it! (*Everyone takes a bite and falls down, poisoned.*

FATHER UBU: OK, Mother Ubu, gimme those rat chops, so I can hand 'em out.

MOTHER UBU: (*handing them over*) Here you go.

FATHER UBU: Captain Bordure, I need to talk to you. The rest of you, head for the door!

THE OTHERS: But we haven't finished our dinner!

FATHER UBU: You haven't? Why not? To the door! Not you, Bordure. (*No one moves.*) By my green candle, take your rat chops and get out of here! (*He starts throwing the rat chops an the rest of the food at them all.*)

EVERYONE: Oh! Ouch! Help! Save us! I've been hit! I'm dying!

FATHER UBU: Shrit! Shrit! Shrit! Out the door! (*to his wife*) See? I did it!

EVERYONE: Save yourselves! That horrible Father Ubu! He's a traitor! A rascal! A rogue!

FATHER UBU: At last! They're gone. I can breathe again. But what a terrible dinner! Let's go, Bordure.

They leave with *MOTHER UBU*

The deliberate use of toilet humor, juvenile satire, and a full-stage food fight make clear that *Ubu Roi* is a precursor of American comic films such as *The Hangover*. It is a little more difficult, however, to see the play as a precursor of a serious art and literary movement, but such is the case. *Surrealism*, a word that means "beyond realism" or "superrealism," was officially inaugurated by André Breton in 1924 but can be said to date from this play—which, its advocates claim, reaches a superior level of reality by tracing the unconscious processes of the mind rather than the literal depictions of observable life.

Expressionism: *The Hairy Ape* Of all the isms, expressionism is the one that has given rise to the most significant body of modern theatre, probably because of its broad definition and its seeming alliance with expressionism in the visual arts. The theatrical expressionism that was much in vogue in Germany during the first decades of the twentieth century (particularly in the 1920s) featured shocking and gutsy dialogue, boldly exaggerated scenery, piercing sounds, bright lights, an abundance of primary colors, a not very subtle use of symbols, and a structure of short, stark, jabbing scenes that built to a powerful (and usually deafening) climax.

In America, expressionist writers addressed the growing concern that the country's rapid industrial and financial successes were crushing human freedom—and human nature itself. During the 1920s, in the boldly expressionist dramas *Subway*, *The Adding Machine*, and *Street Scene*, Elmer Rice (1892–1967) angrily attacked what he considered the dehumanization of modern American life. And Eugene O'Neill, who had begun as a realistic playwright in the previous decades, wrote a play that became a landmark of expressionist theatre in 1921. O'Neill's *The Hairy Ape* is a one-act play featuring eight scenes. Its workingman-hero Yank meets and is rebuffed by the genteel daughter of a captain of industry. Enraged, Yank becomes violent and eventually crazed; he dies at play's end in the monkey cage of a zoo. Scene 3 illustrates the tenor of the writing:

The stokehold. In the rear, the dimly outlined bulks of the furnaces and boilers. High overhead one hanging electric bulb sheds just enough light through the murky air laden with coal dust to pile up masses of shadows everywhere. A line of men, stripped to the waist, is before the furnace doors. They bend over, looking neither to right nor left, handling their shovels as if they were part of their bodies, with a strange, awkward, swinging rhythm. They use the shovels to throw open the furnace doors. Then from these fiery round holes in the back a flood of terrific light and heat pours full upon the men who are outlined in silhouette in the crouching, inhuman attitudes of chained gorillas. The men shovel with a rhythmic motion, swinging as on a pivot from the coal which lies in

heaps on the floor behind to hurl it into the flaming mouths before them. There is a tumult of noise—the brazen clang of the furnace doors as they are flung open or slammed shut, the grating, teeth-gritting grind of steel against steel, of crunching coal. This clash of sounds stuns one's ears with its rending dissonance. But there is order in it, rhythm, a mechanical regulated recurrence, a tempo. And rising above all, making the air hum with the quiver of liberated energy, the roar of leaping flames in the furnaces, the monotonous throbbing beat of the engines. As the curtain rises, the furnace doors are shut. The men are taking a breathing spell. One or two are arranging the coal behind them, pulling it into more accessible heaps. The others can be dimly made out leaning on their shovels in relaxed attitudes of exhaustion.

PADDY: (*from somewhere in the line—plaintively*) Yerra, will this divil's own watch nivir end? Me back is broke. I'm destroyed entirely.

YANK: (*from the center of the line—with exuberant scorn*) Aw, yuh make me sick! Lie down and croak, why don't yuh? Always beefin', dat's you! Say, dis is a cinch! Dis was made for me! It's my meat, get me! (*A whistle is blown—a thin, shrill note from somewhere overhead in the darkness.* YANK *curses without resentment.*) Dere's de damn engineer crackin' de whip. He tinks we're loafin'.

PADDY: (*vindictively*) God stiffen him!

YANK: (*in an exultant tone of command*) Come on, youse guys! Git into de game! She's gettin' hungry! Pile some grub in her. Trow it into her belly! Come on now, all of youse! Open her up! (*At this last all the men, who have followed his movements of getting into position, throw open their furnace doors with a deafening clang. The fiery light floods over their shoulders as they bend round for the coal. Rivulets of sooty sweat have traced maps on their backs. The enlarged muscles form bunches of highlight and shadow.*)

YANK: (*chanting a count as he shovels without seeming effort*) One—two—tree—(*His voice rising exultantly in the joy of battle*) Dat's de stuff! Let her have it! All togedder now! Sling it into her! Let her ride! Shoot de piece now! Call de toin on her! Drive her into it! Feel her move. Watch her smoke! Speed, dat's her middle name! Give her coal, youse guys! Coal, dat's her booze! Drink it up, baby! Let's see yuh sprint! Dig in and gain a lap! Dere she go-o-es. (*This last in the chanting formula of the galley gods at the six-day bike race. He slams his furnace door shut. The others do likewise with as much unison as their wearied bodies will permit. The effect is of one fiery eye after another being blotted out with a series of accompanying bangs.*)

PADDY: (*groaning*) Me back is broke. I'm bate out—bate—(*There is a pause. Then the inexorable whistle sounds again from the dim regions above the electric light. There is a growl of cursing rage from all sides.*)

YANK: (*shaking his fist upward—contemptuously*) Take it easy dere, you! Who d'yuh tink's runnin' dis game, me or you? When I git ready, we move. Not before! When I git ready, get me!

VOICES: (*approvingly*) That's the stuff!
Yank tal him, py golly!
Yank ain't affeerd.
Goot poy, Yank!
Give him hell!
Tell 'im 'e's a bloody swine!
Bloody slave-driver!

YANK: (*contemptuously*) He ain't got no noive. He's yellow, get me? All de engineers is yellow. Dey got streaks a mile wide. Aw, to hell wit him! Let's move, youse guys. We had a rest. Come on, she needs it! Give her pep! It ain't for him. Him and his whistle, dey don't belong. But we belong, see! We gotter feed de baby! Come on! (*He turns and flings his furnace door open. They all follow his lead. At this instant the* SECOND *and* FOURTH ENGINEERS *enter from the darkness on the left with* MILDRED *between them. She starts, turns paler, her pose is crumbling, she shivers with fright in spite of the blazing heat, but forces herself to leave the* ENGINEERS *and take a few steps nearer the men. She is right behind* YANK. *All this happens quickly while the men have their backs turned.*)

YANK: Come on, youse guys! (*He is turning to get coal when the whistle sounds again in a peremptory, irritating note. This drives* YANK *into a sudden fury. While the other men have turned full around and stopped dumbfounded by the spectacle of* MILDRED *standing there in her white dress,* YANK *does not turn far enough to see her. Besides, his head is thrown back, he blinks upward through the murk trying to find the owner of the whistle, he brandishes his shovel murderously over his head in one hand, pounding on his chest, gorilla-like, with the other, shouting.*) Toin off dat whistle! Come down outa dere, yuh yellow, brass-buttoned, Belfast bum, yuh! Come down and I'll knock yer brains out! Yuh lousy, stinkin', yellow mut of a Catholic-moiderin' bastard! Come down and I'll moider yuh! Pullin' dat whistle on me, huh? I'll show yuh! I'll crash yer skull in! I'll drive yer teet' down yer troat! I'll slam yer nose trou de back to yer head! I'll cut yer guts out for a nickel, yuh lousy boob, yuh dirty, crummy, muck-eatin' son of a—(*Suddenly he becomes conscious of all the other men staring at something directly behind his back. He whirls defensively with a snarling, murderous growl, crouching to spring, his lips drawn back over his teeth, his small eyes gleaming ferociously. He sees* MILDRED, *like a white apparition in the full light from the open furnace doors. He glares into her eyes, turned to stone. As for her, during his speech she has listened, paralyzed with horror, terror, her whole personality crushed, beaten in, collapsed, by the terrific impact of this unknown, abysmal brutality, naked and shameless. As she looks at his gorilla face, as his eyes bore into hers, she utters a low, choking cry and shrinks away from him, putting both hands up before her eyes to shut out the sight of his face, to protect her own. This startles* YANK *to a reaction. His mouth falls open, his eyes grow bewildered.*)

MILDRED: (*about to faint—to the* ENGINEERS, *who now have her one by each arm—whimperingly*) Take me away! Oh, the filthy beast! (*She faints. They carry her quickly back, disappearing in the darkness at the left, rear. An iron door clangs shut. Rage and bewildered fury rush back on* YANK. *He feels himself insulted in some unknown fashion in the very heart of his pride. He roars.*) God damn yuh! (*And hurls his shovel after them at the door which has just closed. It hits the steel bulkhead with a clang and falls clattering on the steel floor. From overhead the whistle sounds again in a long, angry, insistent command.*)

O'Neill's forceful combination of expressionistic visual and auditory effects lends this play a crude, almost superhuman power. The use of silhouette in the staging and lighting, the "masses of shadows everywhere," the "tumult of noise," the "monotonous throbbing beat of the engines," the "fiery light," the "rivulets of sooty sweat," the massed chanting and the movements in unison, the "peremptory, irritating note" of the "inexorable whistle," the shouting of curses and sudden exclamations, the animal imagery, and the "horror, terror . . . of . . . unknown, abysmal brutality, naked and shameless" all typify the extreme stylization of early-twentieth-century expressionism. The scene also demonstrates how O'Neill and his followers in the American theatre turned away from realism and romanticism in their effort to arrive at a direct presentation of social ideology and cultural criticism.

Metatheatre: *Six Characters in Search of an Author*   First produced in 1921, *Six Characters in Search of an Author* expresses from its famous title onward a "metatheatrical" motif by which the theatre itself becomes part of the content of the play production, not merely the vehicle. Shakespeare may have announced that "All the world's a stage," but in this play Luigi Pirandello (1867–1936) explores how the stage is also a world—and how the stage and the world, illusion and reality, relate to and often blur with each other. In this still-stunning play, a family of dramatic "characters"—a father, his stepdaughter, a mother, and her children—appear as if by magic on the "stage" of a provincial theatre where a "new play" by Pirandello is being rehearsed. The "characters," claiming they have an unfinished play in them, beg the director to stage their lives so they may bring a satisfactory climax to their "drama." This fantasy treats the audience to continually shifting perceptions, for clearly a play-within-the-play is involved, but which is the real play and which the real life? There are actors playing actors, actors playing "characters," and actors playing "actors-playing-characters"; there are also scenes when the actors playing "characters" are making fun of the actors playing actors-playing-"characters." It is no wonder most audiences give up trying to untangle the planes of reality Pirandello creates in this play; they are simply too difficult to comprehend except as a dazzle of suggestive theatricality.

Pirandello contrasts the passionate story of the "characters"—whose "drama" concerns a broken family, adultery, and the suggestion of incest—with the artifice of the stage and its simulations. In the course of this exposition Pirandello's performers discuss the theatricality of life, the life of theatricality, and the eternal confusions between appearance and reality:

THE FATHER: What I'm inviting you to do is to quit this foolish playing at art—this acting and pretending—and seriously answer my question: WHO ARE YOU?

THE DIRECTOR: (*amazed but irritated, to his actors*) What extraordinary impudence! This so-called character wants to know who I am?

THE FATHER: (*with calm dignity*) Signore, a character may always ask a "man" who he is. For a character has a true life, defined by his characteristics—he is always, at the least, a "somebody." But a man—now, don't take this personally—A man is generalized beyond identity—he's a nobody!

THE DIRECTOR: Ah, but me, me—I am the Director! The Producer! You understand?

THE FATHER: Signore—Think of how you used to feel about yourself, long ago, all the illusions you used to have about the world, and about your place in it: those illusions were real for you then, they were *quite* real—But now, with hindsight, they prove to be nothing, they are nothing to you now but an embarrassment. Well, signore, that is what your present reality is today—just a set of illusions that you will discard tomorrow. Can't you feel it? I'm not speaking of the planks of this stage we stand on, I'm speaking of the very earth under our feet. It's sinking under you—by tomorrow, today's entire reality will have become just one more illusion. You see?

THE DIRECTOR: (*confused but amazed*) Well? So what? What does all that prove?

THE FATHER: Ah, nothing, signore. Only to show that if, beyond our illusions (*indicating the other characters*), we have no ultimate reality, so your reality as well—your reality that touches and feels and breathes today—will be unmasked tomorrow as nothing but yesterday's illusion!

These lines illustrate Pirandello's use of paradox, irony, and the theatre as metaphor to create a whimsical drama about human identity and human destiny. By contrasting the passion of his "characters" with the frivolity of his "actors," Pirandello establishes a provocative juxtaposition of human behavior and its theatricalization—and the whole fantastical style is nothing but an exploitation of the theatrical format itself.

Theatre of Cruelty: *Jet of Blood* Antonin Artaud (1896–1948) was one of drama's greatest revolutionaries, although his importance lies more in his ideas and

influence than in his actual theatrical achievements. A stage and film actor in Paris during the 1920s, he founded the Théâtre Alfred Jarry in 1926, producing, among other works, Strindberg's surrealist *A Dream Play* and, in 1935, an adaptation of Shelley's dramatic poem *The Cenci*. His essays, profoundly influential in the theatre today, were collected and published in 1938 in a book titled *The Theatre and Its Double*.

The theatre Artaud envisioned was a self-declared theatre of cruelty, for, in his words, "Without an element of cruelty at the root of every performance, the theatre is not possible." The "cruel" theatre would flourish, Artaud predicted, by

> providing the spectator with the true sources of his dreams, in which his taste for crime, his erotic obsessions, his savagery, his illusions, his utopian ideals, even his cannibalism, would surge forth.

In Artaud's vision, ordinary plays were to be abolished; there should be, in his words, "no more masterpieces." In place of written plays there should be

> cries, groans, apparitions, surprises, theatricalities of all kinds, magic beauty of costumes taken from certain ritual models; . . . light in waves, in sheets, in fusillades of fiery arrows. . . . Paroxysms will suddenly burst forth, will fire up like fires in different spots.

In a famous metaphor, Artaud compared the theatre to the great medieval plague, noting that both plague and theatre had the capacity to liberate human possibilities and illuminate the human potential:

> The theatre is like the plague . . . because like the plague it is the revelation, the bringing forth, the exteriorization of a depth of latent cruelty by means of which all the perverse possibilities of the mind, whether of an individual or a people, are localized. . . .
>
> One cannot imagine, save in an atmosphere of carnage, torture, and bloodshed, all the magnificent Fables which recount to the multitudes the first sexual division and the first carnage of essences that appeared in creation. The theatre, like the plague, is in the image of this carnage and this essential separation. It releases conflicts, disengages powers, liberates possibilities, and if these possibilities and these powers are dark, it is the fault not of the plague nor of the theatre, but of life.

Artaud's ideas were radical, and his essays were incendiary; his power to shock and inspire is undiminished today, and many contemporary theatre artists claim an Artaudian heritage. It is not at all clear from his writing, however, what final form his theatre of cruelty should actually take in performance, and it is readily apparent even to the casual reader that the theatre Artaud speaks of is much easier to realize on paper than on an actual stage. Artaud's own productions were in fact failures; he was formally "expelled" from the surrealist movement, and he spent most of his later life abroad in mental institutions. His one published play, *Jet of Blood* (1925), illustrates both the radically anti-realistic nature of his dramaturgy and the difficulties that would be encountered in its production. This is the opening of the play:

THE YOUNG MAN: I love you, and everything is beautiful.

THE YOUNG GIRL: (*with a strong tremolo in her voice*) You love me, and everything is beautiful.

THE YOUNG MAN: (*in a very deep voice*) I love you, and everything is beautiful.

THE YOUNG GIRL: (*in an even deeper voice than his*) You love me, and everything is beautiful.

THE YOUNG MAN: (*leaving her abruptly*) I love you. (*Pause*) Turn around and face me.

THE YOUNG GIRL: (*she turns to face him*) There!

THE YOUNG MAN: (*in a shrill and exalted voice*) I love you, I am big, I am shining, I am full, I am solid.

THE YOUNG GIRL: (*in the same shrill tone*) We love each other.

THE YOUNG MAN: We are intense. Ah, how well ordered this world is!

> *A pause. Something that sounds like an immense wheel turning and blowing out air is heard. A hurricane separates the two. At this moment two stars crash into each other, and we see a number of live pieces of human bodies falling down: hands, feet, scalps, masks, colonnades, porches, temples, and alembics, which, however, fall more and more slowly, as if they were falling in a vacuum. Three scorpions fall down, one after the other, and finally a frog and a beetle, which sets itself down with a maddening, vomit-inducing slowness . . .*
>
> *Enter a knight of the Middle Ages in an enormous suit of armor, followed by a nurse holding her breasts in both hands and puffing and wheezing because they are both very swollen.*

Artaud's apocalyptic vision has stimulated many subsequent theatre directors, including Jean-Louis Barrault and Roger Blin in France, Peter Brook in England, Jerzy Grotowski in Poland, and André Gregory in America; his influence can also be seen in the plays of Jean Genet and the productions of Robert Wilson. His notion of a theatre of cruelty, though not fully realized onstage in his lifetime, has been more closely approached by each of these artists and may still be achieved.

Philosophical Melodrama: *No Exit*   *No Exit* is one of the most compelling short plays ever written. In this one-act fantasy written in 1944, Jean-Paul Sartre (1905–1980), the well-known French existentialist philosopher, establishes a unique embodiment of Hell: a plain room without windows or mirrors. Into it come three people, lately deceased, all condemned to this netherworld because of their earthly sins. The three are brilliantly ill-matched in their sexual identities: Garcin, the sole man, leans toward homosexuality, as does Inez, one of the two women, while Estelle, the final occupant of this bizarre inferno, leans toward compulsive heterosexual desire—yet none of the characters are entirely clear about their or each other's leanings. Uncertainty reigns: Estelle pursues Garcin, Garcin pursues Inez, and Inez pursues the beautiful Estelle in a triangle of misdirected affections and failed connections that, one presumes, will continue maddeningly through eternity. The infinite bleakness of this play's fantastical situation and the numbing futility of each character's aspirations provoke Garcin to beg for torture, the traditional instrument of punishment in the underworld—but nothing quite so simple is forthcoming. Instead, he is forced to conclude: "Hell is other people." And the play ends with a line that is characteristic of the modern stylized theatre:

GARCIN: Well, well, let's get on with it.

Garcin's resignation suggests that although the play concludes, the situation continues, eternally, behind the drawn curtain.

No Exit is a classic dramatic statement of existentialism, of which Sartre was the twentieth century's leading exponent. Remove the fantastical elements—that this is Hell and the characters are ghosts—and we have Sartre's vision of human interaction: every individual forever seeks affirmation and self-realization in the eyes of everyone else, but fails to receive it. Each character in the play carries with him or her some baggage of guilt and expectation, each seeks from another some certification of final personal worth, and each is endlessly thwarted in their quests. We are all doomed to revolve around each other in frustratingly incomplete accord, suggests Sartre, or as he famously put it, we are all "condemned to be free."

One can accept or reject Sartre's view—which is perhaps more than usually pessimistic for having been written during the Nazi occupation of the playwright's beloved Paris—but no one can dispute the brilliance of his dramatic stylization: the fantastical Hell, an amusing "valet" who brings each character onto the stage, and the highly contrived assemblage of mismatched characters all serve to focus the intellectual argument precisely. Sartre's characters are philosophically representative rather than psychologically whole; there is no

In a poll of eight hundred playwrights, actors, directors, and theatre journalists taken by England's National Theatre in 1999, Samuel Beckett's *Waiting for Godot* was voted "the most significant play of the twentieth century." Yet its American premiere, at the Coconut Grove Playhouse in Miami, Florida, in 1956, was a complete disaster. On opening night, half the audience left at intermission, and the next morning when the box office opened, dozens of people were standing in line to return tickets they had bought for future performances! But times have certainly changed for this play about two elderly tramps who wait for a mysterious figure who never shows up. In 2009, major theatres in both New York and London presented *Godot* productions with superb casts, and each was completely sold out for its entire run. (Above) The American production with Nathan Lane (left) and Bill Irwin as the hapless tramps, Estragon and Vladimir, and between them John Goodman as the bullying pseudo-aristocrat, Pozzo. (Below) The London production with Patrick Stewart as Vladimir and Ian McKellan as Estragon.

intention on Sartre's part to portray individual people with interesting idiosyncrasies, and there is no feeling on our part that the characters have a personal life beyond what we see in the play. Biographical character analysis would be useless for an actor assigned to play one of these roles, and the author deliberately ignores the question of psychological motivation, even in this sexually charged atmosphere. What Sartre presents instead is a bleak, though compelling, philosophy of interpersonal relations.

Theatre of the Absurd: *Waiting for Godot*   The term *theatre of the absurd,* coined by English critic Martin Esslin in his 1962 book of that name, applies to a grouping of plays that share certain common structures and styles and are tied together by a common philosophical thread: the theory of the absurd as formulated by French essayist and playwright Albert Camus (1913–1960). Camus likened the human condition to that of the mythological Corinthian king Sisyphus, who because of his cruelty on Earth was condemned eternally in the afterlife to roll a stone up a hill, only to have it roll back down upon reaching the top. Camus saw the modern individual as similarly engaged in an eternally futile task: the absurdity of searching for some meaning or purpose or order in human life. To Camus, the inescapable irrationality of the universe is what makes this task absurd. On the one hand, human beings yearn for a "lost" unity and lasting truth; on the other hand, the world can only be seen as irrecoverably fragmented—chaotic, unsummable, permanently unorganized, and unorganizable.

The plays that constitute the theatre of the absurd are obsessed with the futility of all action and the pointlessness of all direction. These themes are developed theatrically through a deliberate and self-conscious flaunting of a sense of the ridiculous. Going beyond the use of symbols and the fantasy and poetry of other nonrealists, the absurdists have distinguished themselves by employing such devices as clocks that clang incessantly, characters that eat pap in ashcans, corpses that grow by the minute, and personal interactions that are belligerently noncredible.

The theatre of the absurd can be said to include mid-twentieth-century works by Jean Genet (French), Eugène Ionesco (Romanian), Friedrich Dürrenmatt (Swiss), Arthur Adamov (Russian), Slawomir Mrozek (Polish), Harold Pinter (English), Edward Albee (American), Fernando Arrabal (Spanish), and the Irish poet, playwright, and novelist Samuel Beckett. And although Paris is the center of this theatre—so much so that the works of Ionesco, Adamov, Arrabal, and Beckett are all written in French rather than in their native tongues—its influence is felt worldwide.

Samuel Beckett (1906–1989), the unquestioned leader of the absurdist writers, eschewed all realism, romanticism, and rationalism to create relentlessly unenlightening works that are indeed committed to a final obscurity. "Art has nothing to do with clarity, does not dabble in the clear, and does not make clear," argued Beckett in one of his earliest works, and his theatre was based on the thesis that man is and will remain ignorant regarding all matters of importance.

Born in Dublin, Beckett emigrated in 1928 to Paris, where he joined a literary circle centered on another Irish émigré, James Joyce. Beckett's life before World War II was an artistic vagabondage during which he wrote several poems, short stories, and a novel. After the war and his seclusion in the south of France during the Nazi occupation, he produced the masterworks for which he is justly famous: the novels *Molloy, Malone Dies,* and *The Unnamable,* and the plays *Waiting for Godot* and *Endgame.* By the time of his death in 1989, Beckett had received the Nobel Prize in Literature, and his works had become the subject of hundreds of critical books and essays. It was *Godot* that first brought Beckett to worldwide attention: the play's premiere in Paris in 1953 occasioned a great stir among French authors and critics, and its subsequent openings in London and New York had the same effect there.

Waiting for Godot is a parable without a message. On a small mound at the base of a tree, beside a country road, two elderly men in bowler hats—"Gogo" and "Didi"—wait for a "Mr. Godot," with whom they have presumably made an appointment. They believe that when Godot comes they will be "saved"; however, they are not at all certain Godot has agreed to meet with them or if this is the right place or the right day or whether they will even recognize him if he comes. During each of the two acts, which seem to be set in late afternoon on two successive days (although nobody can be sure of that), the men are visited by passersby—first by two men, a master (Pozzo) and his slave (Lucky), and subsequently by a young, unnamed boy who tells them that Mr. Godot "cannot come today but surely tomorrow." Gogo and Didi continue to wait as the curtain falls. Although there are substantial references in the play to Christian symbols and beliefs, it is not clear whether these imply positive or negative associations. The only development in the play is that all four adult characters seem to undergo a loss of adeptness while the setting blossoms in rebirth (the tree sprouts leaves between the acts).

What Beckett has drawn here is clearly a paradigm of the human condition: an ongoing life cycle of vegetation serving as the background to human decay, hope, and ignorance. Beckett's tone is whimsical: Gogo and Didi play enchanting word games with each other, they amuse each other with songs, accounts of dreams, exercises, and vaudevillian antics, and in general they make the best of a basically hopeless situation. Beckett's paradigm affords a field day for critical investigators: *Waiting for Godot* has generated a veritable library of brilliantly evocative discussions, and few plays from any era have been so variously analyzed, interpreted, and explored for symbolic meaning and content. Owing largely to the international critical acceptance of this play and its eventual public success, absurdist drama, as well as the whole of modern stylized theatre, was able to move out of the esoteric "art theatre" of the world capitals and onto the stages of popular theatres everywhere.

Theatre of Alienation: *The Good Person of Szechuan*

Contrasting vividly with the theatre of the absurd is the theatre of alienation (a term based on the German word *Verfremdung,* or "distancing"). Whereas the self-contained plays of absurdism highlight the essential futility of human endeavors, the sprawling, socially engaged "epic" theatre of alienation concentrates on humanity's potential for growth and society's capacity to effect change.

The guiding genius of the theatre of alienation was Bertolt Brecht (1898–1956), a theorist, dramatist, and director whose impact on modern theatre was overwhelming. Brecht brought to the theatre practices that openly defied many of the principles in use since the days of Aristotle, and by so doing he invigorated the post-war theatre with an abrasive humanism that reawakened the audience's sense of social responsibility and awareness of the theatre's capacity to mold public issues and events.

Brecht, who was born in Germany, emerged from World War I a dedicated Marxist and pacifist. Using poems, songs, and eventually the theatre to promote his ideals following the German defeat, Brecht vividly portrayed his country during the Weimar Republic as caught in the grips of four giant vises: the military, capitalism, industrialization, and imperialism. His *Rise and Fall of the City of Mahagonny,* for example, an "epic opera" of 1930, proved an immensely popular blending of satire and propaganda, music and expressionist theatricality, social idealism and lyric poetry. It was produced all over Germany and throughout most of Europe in the early 1930s as a depiction of a rapacious international capitalism evolving toward fascism.

Brecht was forced to flee his country upon Hitler's accession to the chancellorship in 1933. Thereafter he moved about Europe for a time and then, for much of the 1940s, settled in America. After World War II he returned in triumph to East Berlin, where the East German government established for him the Berliner Ensemble Theatre. There Brecht was allowed to consolidate his theories in a body of productions developed out of his earlier plays and the pieces he had written while in exile.

Brecht's theatre draws on a potpourri of theatrical conventions, some derived from the ancients, some from Eastern drama, and some from the German expressionist movement in which Brecht himself played a part in his early years. Masks, songs, verse, exotic settings, satire, and direct rhetorical address are all fundamental conventions Brecht adopted from other theatre forms. In addition, he developed many conventions of his own: lantern-slide projections with printed captions, speeches in which actors deliberately stepped out of character to comment on the action, and procedures aimed at demystifying theatrical techniques (for example, lowering the lights so the pipes and wires would be displayed). All of these innovations created what Brecht called a "distancing-effect" (*Verfremdunseffekt*)—the separation of the audience from involvement in the dramatic action.

The idea of the distancing-effect grew out of Brecht's distaste for sentimentality. Instead of encouraging audience empathy, he sought to create a performance style that was openly "didactic": the actors were asked to distance themselves from the characters they played—to "demonstrate" characters rather than to embody them in a realistic manner. In Brecht's view the ideal actor was one who could establish toward his or her character a *critical objectivity* that would make clear the character's social function and political commitment. In attempting to repudiate the "magic" of the theatre, Brecht demanded it be made to seem nothing more than a place for workers to present a meaningful "parable" of life, and he in no way wished to disguise the fact that the stage personnel—actors and stagehands—were merely workers doing their jobs. In every way possible, Brecht attempted to achieve audience distance, preventing his spectators from becoming swept up in an emotional bath of feelings: his goal was to keep the audience, like the actors, separated from the literal events the play depicted so they would be free to concentrate on the larger social and political issues the play generated and reflected. Brecht considered this theatre to be an "epic" one because it attempted, around the framework of a parable or an archetypal event, to create a whole new perspective on human history and to indicate the direction political dialogue should take to foster social betterment.

Brecht's theories were to have a staggering impact on the modern theatre. In his wholesale renunciation of Aristotelian catharsis, which depends on audience empathy with a noble character, and his denial of Stanislavsky's basic principles concerning the aims of acting, Brecht provided a new dramaturgy that

Many of Brecht's "demystifying" theatrical techniques—an onstage band, a visible handheld microphone, and broad banks of downlights that illuminate billowing stage smoke—are clearly evident in this image of the English National Theatre's 2009–2010 production of his 1939 play, *Mother Courage*, directed by Deborah Warner. Here Fiona Shaw, in the title role, is helmeted and singing on top of her sales wagon, where she conducts business with soldiers on all sides of the Hundred Years War.

encouraged playwrights, directors, and designers to tackle social issues directly rather than through the implications of contrived dramatic situations. Combining the technologies and aesthetics of other media—the lecture hall, the slide show, the public meeting, the cinema, the cabaret, the rehearsal—Brecht fashioned a vastly expanded arena for his *dialectics*: social arguments that sought to engender truth through the confrontation of conflicting interests. These ideas were played out, in Brecht's own works and in countless other works inspired by him, with bold theatricality, an open-handed dealing with the audience, proletarian vigor, and a stridently entertaining, intelligently satirical, and charmingly bawdy theatre. This theatre has proven even more popular today than it was in Brecht's time, because since then the world seems to have grown even more fragmented, more individualistic, and more suspicious of collective emotions and sentimentality.

No play better illustrates Brecht's dramatic theory and method than *The Good Person of Szechuan* (1943). This play, set in western China, concerns a kindhearted prostitute, Shen Te, who is astounded to receive a gift of money from three itinerant gods. Elated by her good fortune, Shen Te uses the money to start a tobacco business. She is, however, quickly beset by petty officials seeking to impose local regulations, by self-proclaimed creditors demanding payment, and by a host of hangers-on who simply prey upon her good nature. At the point of financial ruin, Shen Te leaves her tobacco shop to enlist the aid of her male cousin Shui Ta, who strides imperiously into the tobacco shop and rousts the predators, making it safe for Shen Te to return. But the predators come back, and Shen Te again has to call on the tyrannical Shui Ta to save her. A simple story—but Brecht's stroke of genius is to make Shui Ta and Shen Te the same character: Shui Ta is simply Shen Te in disguise! The aim of the play is not to show there are kindhearted people and successful people but that a person must choose to be one or the other. What kind of society is it, Brecht asks, that forces us to make this sort of choice? And, as audience members, what choices do we face every day about being good in our own societies—choices, perhaps, we may have not even realized are choices at all?

Brecht was no mere propagandist, and his epic theatre is not one of simple messages or easy conclusions. At the end of *The Good Person of Szechuan*, Shen Te asks the gods for help, but they simply float off into the air reciting inane platitudes as the curtain falls. The gods do not have the answer—so the audience must provide it. In the play's epilogue, a character comes forward and addresses us:

> Hey, honorable folks, don't be dismayed
> That we can't seem to end this play! You've stayed
> To see our shining, all-concluding moral,
> And what we've given you has been this bitter quarrel.
> We know, we know—we're angry too,
> To see the curtain down and everything askew.
> We'd love to see you stand and cheer—and say
> How wonderful you find our charming play!
> But we won't put our heads into the sand.
> We know your wish is ever our command,
> We know you ask for *more*: a firm conclusion
> To this alarming more-than-mass confusion.
> But what is it? Who knows? Not all your cash
> Could buy your way—or ours—from this mishmash.
> Do we need heroes? Dreams? New Gods? Or none?
> Well, tell us—else we're hopelessly undone!
> The only thing that we can think to say
> Is simply that it's *you* must end this play.
> Tell us how our own good woman of Szechuan
> Can come to a good ending—if she can!
> Honorable folks: you search, and we will trust
> That you will find the way. You must! You must! You *must*!

Brecht's parables epitomize the conflicts between social classes; they do not presume to solve these conflicts. Indeed, the problems Brecht addresses are to be solved not on the stage but in the world itself: the audience must find the appropriate balance between morality and greed, individualism and social responsibility. Brecht's plays reenact the basic intellectual dichotomy posed by Marx's dialectical materialism; thus they are, in a sense, Marxist plays, but they certainly are not Leninist, much less Stalinist. They radiate faith in the human potential. Yet although they are both socially engaged and theatrically eclectic—qualities not particularly noticeable in the theatre of the absurd—they still resound with the fundamental human uncertainty that pervades all of modern stylized theatre.

Comedy of Contemporary Manners: *Bedroom Farce* One less obvious form of stylized theatre is comedy, perhaps because of its enduring reputation as a "popular" genre, rather than an intellectually engaging one. Yet such a reputation is unfounded: Comedy has a distinguished tradition as one of the greatest staples of the theatre; since the days of Aristophanes in ancient Greece and Plautus in Rome, comedians have entertained the public with puns, antics, lighthearted social commentaries, and a host of other amusing reflections on the human struggle. It is an axiom of the theatre that "comedy is serious business," and the true comedian is understood to be as inspired an artist as any who labors under the lights. Comedy is rarely accorded its fair share of academic consideration, however, partly because it tends to be topical and therefore less than universal, and partly because the very thing that makes comedy popular—its accessibility—also makes it seem relatively simple. But simple does not mean simple-minded, and the relative scarcity of fine comic plays originating in any generation attests to the enormous talent it takes to write, direct, and act comedically.

In America, Neil Simon (born 1927) has, for decades, exhibited enormous talent and success as a writer of light comedy for the stage (and film), and in England, Alan Ayckbourn (born 1939) has demonstrated comparable mastery. Ayckbourn's *Bedroom Farce* was first produced in 1975 by the Library Theatre in Scarborough, England, with which Ayckbourn is associated; the play was subsequently produced by the National Theatre in London in 1977 and came to Broadway and various other American cities shortly thereafter.

Like all of Ayckbourn's works, *Bedroom Farce* is an ingenious comedy of current manners, novel in its dramatic structure and reasonably true to life in its concerns. The setting for *Bedroom Farce* is three bedrooms, all in view simultaneously. The characters consist of four couples who, for reasons cleverly worked out in the plot, find themselves rotating through one bedroom after another. Although the innuendos of this play are highly sexual, the action consists primarily of animated verbal exchanges and comic business and pratfalls; thus the play lives up to the farcical structure promised by its title.

The opening scene of *Bedroom Farce*—an exchange of dialogue between Ernest and Delia, the oldest couple in the play—typifies the witty and very British repartee mastered by Ayckbourn. The scene takes place in

Alan Ayckbourn has written 76 plays to date, winning him Tony, Olivier, and Molière awards (the top playwriting prizes in the United States, England, and France) and a truly global reputation for his intricate dramaturgy, multilevel plots, and great comic skill. His *Bedroom Farce,* directed by Peter Hall in London in 2010, involves four married couples and takes place in three of their bedrooms—all on the same night and mostly at the same time. Pictured are Daniel Betts as Malcolm and Finty Williams as Kate.

a bedroom described as a "large Victorian" room "in need of redecoration":

. . . DELIA sits in her bedroom at her dressing table mirror. She is going out. She is in her slip and finishing her make-up. An elaborate operation. ERNEST wanders in. Birdlike, bumbling, nearly sixty. He is in evening dress. He stares at DELIA. They are obviously going to be late but ERNEST has learnt that impatience gets him nowhere.

DELIA: It would appear that things between Susannah and Trevor are coming to a head.

ERNEST: Ah.

DELIA: He was always a difficult boy. I sometimes think if you hadn't ignored him quite as much—

ERNEST: I did?

DELIA: Of course you did. You hardly said a word to him all the time he was growing up.

ERNEST: I seem to remember chatting away to him for hours.

DELIA: Well. Chatting. I meant conversation. Conversation about important things. A father should converse with his son. About things that matter deeply.

ERNEST: Doesn't really leave them much to talk about then, does it?

DELIA: And that if I may say so is typical. No. Let's admit it. We weren't good parents. You did nothing and I tried to make up for it, and that's why he's like he is today. I mean if he'd had a stable childhood, he'd never have completely lost his sense of proportion and married Susannah. I mean, I sometimes feel on the rare occasions one does see them together that she's not really—awful thing to say but—not really resilient enough for Trevor. He wants somebody more phlegmatic. That Jan girl for instance would have been ideal. Do you remember her?

ERNEST: Jan? Jan? Jan?

DELIA: Nice little thing. Beautifully normal. She came to tea, do you remember? You got on very well with her.

ERNEST: Oh yes. She was jolly, wasn't she? She was very interested in my stamps. What happened to her?

DELIA: Oh, she married—someone else, I think. She still writes occasionally.

ERNEST: I must say I preferred her to Susannah. Never really hit it off with her, I'm afraid.

DELIA: Well, she's a very complex sort of girl, isn't she? Hasn't really made up her mind. About herself. I mean, I think a woman sooner or later has simply got to make up her mind about herself. I mean, even if she's someone like Carolyn—you know, Mrs. Brightman's Carolyn—who looks at herself and says, right, I'm a lump. I'm going to be a lump but then at least everyone can accept her as a lump. So much simpler.

ERNEST: I think he should have married this other one.

DELIA: Jan? I don't think she was that keen.

ERNEST: She was altogether much jollier.

DELIA: Well, we're saddled with Susannah as a daughter-in-law—at least temporarily. We'd better make the best of it—I think I've put these eyes on crooked—we'd better make the best of it.

ERNEST: It's their bed. They can lie on it.

DELIA: Yes. I think that's one of the problems.

ERNEST: Eh?

DELIA: B—E—D.

ERNEST: B—E—D? Bed?

DELIA: Enough said.

ERNEST: Good lord. How do you know?

DELIA: One reads between the lines, darling. I've had a little look around their house. You can tell a great deal from people's bedrooms.

ERNEST: Can you? Good heavens. (*He looks about.*)

DELIA: If you know what to look for.

There is nothing obscure or difficult in *Bedroom Farce*, which stands out in the contemporary theatre mainly for its capacity to entertain, titillate, and dazzle with cleverness. Indeed, Ayckbourn makes clear his purely comedic intentions in the selection of his title. What the author has created in *Bedroom Farce* is, however, something more ambitious than its title indicates. It is more than just another series of hijinks, physical incongruities, and dramatic clichés, instead becoming a wry combination of social satire, middle-class insights, and boisterous good fun. The modern stylization can be seen in the intricacy of the plot design, which is echoed if not exceeded in Ayckbourn's other plays (*Absurd Person Singular* takes place, successively, in the kitchens of three married couples; *The Norman Conquests* consists

of three interlocking plays involving the same cast of characters in three parts of the same house; *House and Garden* is in fact two plays, meant to be performed simultaneously in connected theatre buildings with the same cast) and reflects a skill at construction that borders on pure genius. This kind of craftsmanship alone would suffice to elevate any comedy far beyond the usual level of television skit or sitcom; in Ayckbourn's case, it enables his stage works to reach the heights of truly inspired hilarity.

Political Satire: *Serious Money*   Since the classical era, playwrights have used the theatre as a broad public platform to criticize the social world of their times—most often in a way that is both biting and entertaining. Criticism gives such works an edge, but a playful or whimsical tone renders even the harshest criticism palatable—and, in exceptionally dangerous times, may also protect a playwright from political retribution. We use the term *satire* to distinguish such works, which have been popular in the theatre of most cultures.

British playwright Caryl Churchill (born 1938) has been a unique exemplar of socially conscious dramatic satire since the 1970s, with trenchant and brilliantly innovative works on a wide variety of issues: sexual orientations and their attendant prejudices and hypocrisies (*Cloud 9*), gender discrimination throughout history (*Top Girls*), the post–cold war chaos in eastern Europe (*Mad Forest*), and the literal, apocalyptic end of the world (*Far Away*). In each of these works, Churchill has reinvestigated—and in some cases reinvented—the dramaturgical format itself. In *Cloud 9*, for example, she double-casts actors in both male and female—and youthful and elderly—roles, putting a wholly new slant on the complex perspectives gender and age cast on our notions of personal identity. And in all of her plays, Churchill reexamines the syntax of stage dialogue, often creating new conversational punctuation systems to identify just how characters—like people in real life—frequently overlap, interrupt, and abort their own and each other's speeches.

In *Serious Money* (1987), Churchill employs a racy rhyming verse—in an exceptional glib patter that lies somewhere between e. e. cummings and hip-hop—to explore the vagaries of arbitrage stock trading on the London market and of international finance:

ZACKERMAN [an international banker in London]:
There's some enterprising guys around and here's an example.

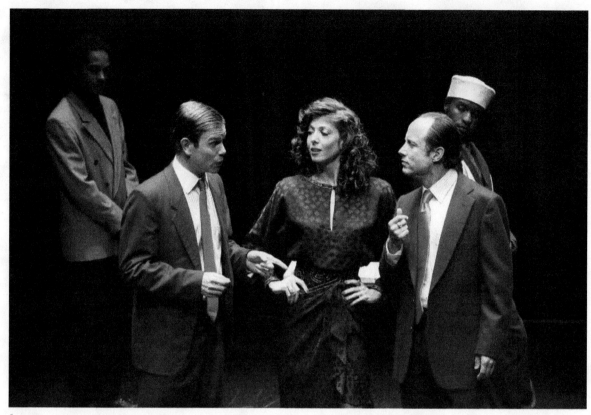

Caryl Churchill's *Serious Money*, a savage, satirical comedy about international finance—partly in verse and occasionally in song—had a well-received revival at New York's Atlantic Stage 2 in 2012. Here Jeanne LaSala Taylor plays Jacinta Condor, a sultry Peruvian drug trafficker, surrounded by David Barlow as an ultra-greedy financier (*left*) and Alex Draper as his British counterpart. Cheryl Faraone was the director.

You know how if you want to get a job in the
    states you have to give a urine sample?
        (This is to show you're not on drugs.)
There's a company now for a fifty dollar fee
They'll provide you with a guaranteed pure,
    donated by a churchgoer, bottle of pee.
        (They also plan to market it dehydrated
        in a packet and you just add water.)
And AIDS is making advertisers perplexed
Because it's no longer too good to have your
    product associated with sex.
But it's a great marketing opportunity.
Like the guys opening up blood banks where
    you pay to store your own blood in case of an
        accident and so be guaranteed immunity.
        (It's also a great time to buy into rubber.)
Anyone who can buy oranges for ten and sell at
    eleven in a souk or bazaar
Has the same human nature and can go equally
    far.

The so-called third world doesn't want our charity
    or aid.
All they need is the chance to sit down in front
    of some green screens and trade.

The witty rhymes, punctuated by parenthetical "ad libs," and the complicated frenzy of *Serious Money*'s plot and staging (much of the play takes place on a stock brokerage's trading floor, bursting with stock monitors, telephone banks, and continuous, shouted deal-making) create a mesmerizing enchantment. Yet Churchill's views of economic exploitation on an international level beam through loud and clear. Satire is a topical dramatic form that often does not outlive its topics, but when the content is compelling and the form brilliant—as it was with Aristophanes and is with Churchill—the play usually survives its merely political utility and makes its way into the lasting theatrical repertoire.

Chapter **9**

The Musical Theatre

MUSICAL THEATRE—A THEATRE THAT includes music and songs, and usually dance—is certainly "anti-realistic" in the most obvious sense. Its special nature, however, derives not from a rebellion against verisimilitude (and thus it does not fall into the category of "anti-realistic theatre," as described in the preceding chapter), but rather from its own unique performance aesthetic. Hence we treat musical theatre (or music theatre, as it is increasingly called) in a chapter of its own.

THE ROLE OF MUSIC IN THEATRE HISTORY

It could be argued that drama has always been at least partly musical. As we saw in the chapter titled "What Is a Play?" Aristotle considered music the fifth component of tragedy (by which he meant all serious drama). Classic Greek tragedy was sung and danced; it was accompanied by the *aulos* (flute) and other instruments, and Aeschylus, who directed his own plays, was particularly noted for his choreography in the choral entrance of *The Eumenides*. Most Renaissance and commedia dell'arte plays included songs and instrumental music, and twenty-five of Shakespeare's thirty-eight plays contain at least some singing (*The Tempest* alone has nine scripted songs). Moreover, Shakespeare's comedies, as well as those of his contemporaries, seem to have ended with full-stage company dances. ▶

Cole Porter's 1934 musical, *Anything Goes,* is a romantic shipboard comedy that has remained popular for 80 years, never more so than in this Broadway revival directed and choreographed by Kathleen Marshall which won the "Best Revival" Tony Award in 2011, and provided Sutton Foster (center front, as Reno Sweeney) a Tony for "Best Performance by a Leading Actress in a Musical."

In the seventeenth century, English dramatist Ben Jonson wrote musical *masques* (dance-dramas) for the court of King James I, and in France, Molière wrote *comédie ballets* for King Louis XIV. Each of the five acts of *The Bourgeois Gentleman,* for example, ends with a fully orchestrated and choreographed mini-opera. And, of course, all major Asian dramatic forms involve singing, dancing, and instrumental music—sometimes continuously throughout the performance.

Although spoken text predominates in modern Western drama, singing and dancing make frequent appearances there, too, certainly in the antirealistic theatre. Most of the plays in Bertolt Brecht's theatre of alienation involve songs (his *The Threepenny Opera, Happy End,* and *The Rise and Fall of the City of Mahagonny* are fully orchestrated musical works), and brief songs are included in the texts of Samuel Beckett's theatre of the absurd plays *Waiting for Godot* and *Happy Days.*

Still, musical theatre has become a distinct genre over the past 150 years of Western drama, not so much

as a reaction to (or against) prevailing theatre traditions but as a medium calculated—at first, anyway—to provoke audience merriment. Absorbing elements of light opera and ballet and, even more significantly, popular nineteenth-century entertainments such as the English music hall and American minstrel and variety shows, the modern musical theatre brings to the contemporary dramatic repertory a proven and widely enjoyed form of entertainment with global commercial appeal.

Nowhere is that commercial and entertainment success better known than in New York, which remains the international capital of the world's musical theatre—although London, Toronto, and Sydney are currently hot competitors. In New York, during the past two decades, as much as 80 percent of Broadway's box-office income has derived from musicals alone. Several of them (*Phantom of the Opera, The Lion King, Wicked*) seem all but permanently installed in the theatres where they play eight times a week. At the time of this writing, twenty-five full-scale musicals were performing on Broadway, and more were waiting in the wings. And the income from "road" (touring) versions of these shows attests to an even greater dominance of musicals in larger performing halls around the country. Furthermore, New York's less-capitalized off-Broadway theatres are also home to musicals, many of them smaller pieces with simpler stagings, reduced casts, and more minimal orchestras. *The Fantasticks*, with an eight-member cast and an "orchestra" of piano and harp, opened in 1960 and ran for forty-two years, closing in 2002—and then reopening in 2006!

Not-for-profit regional theatres are increasingly drawn to musicals, too, as are university, community, and dinner theatres and even Shakespeare festivals. Musical theatre is also now a staple of major theatres abroad, including government-subsidized houses such as the National Theatre of England, which in the past three decades has become a major producer of American musicals (*Guys and Dolls, Carousel, Oklahoma!, My Fair Lady, South Pacific, Anything Goes*, and *Caroline, or Change*). Indeed, up to a third of the main theatres in Berlin, Budapest, London, Tokyo, Sydney, and Stockholm (many of them government subsidized) are at any given time hosting engagements of such world-popular musicals as *Phantom of the Opera, Rent, Chicago, Jekyll and Hyde, The Lion King, Les Misérables*, and *The Sound of Music*. Such musical theatre engagements can form the commercial backbone of an entire theatre community's offerings.

But commercial appeal is hardly the sum of musical theatre's international importance. Musical theatre is a dramatic form of great variety, vitality, and—on many occasions—artistic significance. The Pulitzer Prize has been awarded to nine musical dramas to date (*Of Thee I Sing, South Pacific, Fiorello!, How to Succeed in Business without Really Trying, A Chorus Line, Sunday in the Park with George, Rent*, and the 2010 *Next to Normal*). Using techniques as old as Greek tragedy and as inspired as those of Mozart and Wagner, musical theatre authors and artists have created both aesthetic innovations and social impact through brilliantly integrated disciplines of melody, cadence, choreography, and rhyme.

THE DEVELOPMENT OF THE BROADWAY MUSICAL: AMERICA'S CONTRIBUTION

What we now know as the Broadway musical has roots deep in the nineteenth century, beginning with singing and dancing shows known as *extravaganzas*—such as *The Seven Sisters*, marketed as a "Grand Operatic,

Spectacular, Musical, Terpsichorean, Diabolical, Farcical Burletta" when it premiered in 1860 at the fabled Niblo's Garden in downtown New York City. Such lavish extravaganzas were soon joined by increasingly popular *vaudeville* entertainments (collections of musical and variety acts, originally performed in brothels and drinking parlors but becoming more respectable by that time) and *burlesques* (broadly comedic parodies of serious musical works, often involving cross-dressing). All of these led to a rapidly growing profession of musical performers adept at singing, dancing, acting, and comedy.

Burlesque and vaudeville lasted well into the twentieth century. Florenz Ziegfeld became one of America's great showmen with his annual Ziegfeld Follies—a musical review dedicated to "Glorifying the American Girl" that made stars of vaudevillian comics W. C. Fields, Eddie Cantor, Will Rogers, and Fanny Brice. But it was at Niblo's Garden that what is regarded as America's first true musical, *The Black Crook*, opened in 1866. This play was a rather ordinary melodrama, but when a French dance company, stranded in the city, was added to the show to give it some extra spice, *Crook* became a sexy spectacle, with dances, songs, and a bevy of scantily clad young women.

The popularity of staged musical entertainments featuring a wide diversity of performers grew by leaps during the nineteenth and early twentieth centuries. Challenging the old custom of white actors' "blacking up" (with burnt-cork makeup) for minstrel shows, a new black musical comedy arose, employing the emerging ragtime musical syncopations of earlier black vaudeville reviews. Bob Cole's 1898 *A Trip to Coontown* (*coon* was, at the time, the common term for a black actor who played stereotyped black characters) was one of the most successful: a full-length black musical comedy written and performed by African Americans (some in whiteface!), it played to large mixed-race audiences in New York. Though an unapologetic farce—with ethnic humor, girlie numbers, and semi-operatic inserts—Cole's play included at least one song of direct social protest: "No Coons Allowed!" tells of a young man unable to bring his date to the "swellest place in town" because of the club's racist policy.

By the end of the nineteenth century, New York also proved a hospitable site for sophisticated musical theatre works from abroad. The super-witty and still-popular satirical light operas of the English duo W. S. Gilbert and Arthur Sullivan (*HMS Pinafore, The Pirates of Penzance, The Mikado*), the *opéra bouffe* (satirical comic opera) of French composer Jacques Offenbach

(*La Périchole, La Belle Hélène, Orpheus in the Under-world*—which introduced the cancan), and the Viennese operetta of Franz Lehar (*The Merry Widow*) all demonstrated that musical theatre could tell a story in a delightfully appealing way. Audiences flocked to these musicals, and American writers and composers emerged to create homegrown products that could compete with these imports. Irish-born Victor Herbert, an émigré to the United States at twenty-seven, became America's first great composer for the stage. Herbert's major hits, *Babes in Toyland* (1903) and *Naughty Marietta* (1910), proved immensely successful, introducing songs such as "Ah, Sweet Mystery of Life" to America's popular music repertoire. More prominent still was Rhode Island–born vaudevillian George M. Cohan, whose *Little Johnny Jones* (1904), in which Cohan also starred, provided what became his—and some of his country's—signature songs: "I'm a Yankee Doodle Dandy" and "Give My Regards to Broadway." By the first decade of the new century, American musical theatre was becoming the world leader in a newly defined theatrical form: musical comedy.

Musical Comedy: Gershwin, Kern, *Darktown Follies*, and Rodgers and Hart

The first third of the twentieth century was the great age of *musical comedy*—a genre that emphasized comedy as well as singing but also portrayed youthful romance. It featured sexy (and lightly clad) girl choruses, liberal doses of patriotic jingoism, and, in response to the "dance craze" of the early 1900s, spectacular dancing—including the show-offy "tap"—to a jazzy or ragtime beat.

By the 1920s and 1930s, American musical comedy had dozens of starring composers, lyricists, and performers. Tourists from all over the country flocked to midtown Manhattan to see such musical works as the brothers George (music) and Ira (lyrics) Gershwin's cool and still-memorable *Lady Be Good, Oh, Kay!, Funny Face,* and *Girl Crazy*; Vincent Youmans's sweetly romantic *Hit the Deck* and *No, No, Nanette* (with "Tea for Two"); Jerome Kern's bouncy *Very Good Eddie* and *Sunny*; Cole Porter's wittily engaging *Anything Goes* and *DuBarry Was a Lady*; and a series of especially droll and delightful musical comedies by Richard Rodgers (music) and Lorenz Hart (lyrics), including *A Connecticut Yankee, On Your Toes,* and *Babes in Arms.* What all these works had in common were a laughably simple plot, a cast composed strictly of romantic and comedic characters, a wholly unchallenging

theme, lots of "pretty girls" in revealing costumes, and abundantly cheerful singing and dancing that had little or no connection to the plot. And although these works were often silly as dramas, there can be no mistaking the musical glories of the best of them, with music that remains enchanting to the present day. The Gershwin songs ("Embraceable You," "But Not for Me," and "Bidin' My Time") and those of Rodgers and Hart ("The Lady Is a Tramp," "Small Hotel," and "Bewitched, Bothered and Bewildered") and the shows they came from have been regularly revived; the songs themselves have become a staple of the repertories of literally hundreds of modern jazz singers and musicians.

Up in Harlem, meanwhile, Bert Williams and J. Leubrie Hill drew large mixed-race audiences for their *Darktown Follies of 1914* (introducing the hit number "After the Ball"). And in 1921 a black musical dominated a full Broadway season for the first time: composer Eubie Blake and lyricist Noble Sissle's wildly successful *Shuffle Along* ran more than five hundred performances and introduced such songs as "In Honeysuckle Time" and "I'm Just Wild about Harry." Popular high-stepping, side-slapping "black-bottom" dancing was a feature of many black musicals of the 1920s, as was the epoch-defining dance known as "the Charleston." Introduced in the 1923 black musical *How Come?* (composed by Maceo Pinkard), the Charleston started a national craze in the hit show *Runnin' Wild* (by James P. Johnson and Cecil Mack) later that year.

A Golden Age

By 1925 the American musical was beginning to dominate New York's cultural life—and the country's. That September, four great musicals opened on Broadway in four days: Youmans's *No, No, Nanette,* Rudolf Friml's *The Vagabond King,* Jerome Kern and Oscar Hammerstein II's *Sunny,* and Rodgers and Hart's *Dearest Enemy.* Each of these shows was wildly popular and went on to run for hundreds of performances, and well into the following year. What is widely considered a "golden age of musicals" had begun.

The golden age ushered in a new genre—musical *drama*—characterized by increasingly serious *books* (spoken texts) and sophisticated musical treatments. *Show Boat,* written by Jerome Kern (music) and Oscar Hammerstein II (book and lyrics) in 1927, was an early masterpiece of musical drama. It represents one of the great pieces of fully acted—and not just sung—vocal literature in the American theatre. Adapted from a gritty novel by Edna Ferber, *Show Boat* has a

The Gershwin's Porgy and Bess is the new title of this 2012 musical theatre revision (by playwright Suzan-Lori Parks and director Diane Paulus) of George and Ira Gershwin's 1935 American opera, set in Charleston, South Carolina, in the 1930s. Audra McDonald, in red, is Bess, with her friends on Charleston's fictitious "Catfish Row." The production won the Best Revival of a Musical Tony Award for the year, and McDonald received the Tony for Best Performance by an Actress in a Leading Role in a Musical.

complex plot that is carried by the music and dancing as well as by the work's spoken dialogue; the musical touches significantly on race relations in America. Indeed, the famous "Ol' Man River" referred pointedly to the then-current racial divisions as sung by a black actor in front of the show's (largely white) 1927 audience:

> Colored folks work on de Mississippi,
> Colored folks work while de white folks play,
> Pullin' dem boats from de dawn to sunset,
> Gittin' no rest till de Judgment Day—
> Don' look up
> An' don' look down—
> You don' dast make
> De white boss frown.
> Bend your knees
> An' bow your head,
> An' pull dat rope
> Until yo' dead.

Meanwhile, the Gershwin brothers' *Strike Up the Band* and *Of Thee I Sing* moved this fraternal team into the arena of political satire and proved so successful that the latter production received the 1932 Pulitzer Prize—the first musical to do so. The Gershwins followed with the full-out folk opera *Porgy and Bess* (1935), which remains a staple of international opera companies today and was revived on Broadway in 2012.

The second serious phase of the musical's golden age came into full flower with Rodgers and Hart's startling *Pal Joey* (1940), adapted from grimly ironic and sophisticated *New Yorker* stories by John O'Hara and featuring an amoral gigolo and his often unsavory companions in a musical pastiche of the contemporary urban nightclub scene. Tame by today's standards, *Joey* shocked prewar audiences with its blithely suggestive lyrics about sexual infidelity and shady business ethics and with a show-stopping song ("Zip!") belted out by an intellectual stripteaser—who sang out her thoughts while doing her act.

Many serious musicals followed, straining the word *comedy* wholly out of the musical's then-current nomenclature. Marc Blitzstein's *The Cradle Will Rock* (1938), which concerns the struggle to organize a union of steelworkers in "Steel-town" against the opposition of Mr. Mister, the town's leading capitalist, was canceled an hour before its New York opening by U.S. government officials who objected to the play's "left-wing propaganda" (the government provided funding for the sponsoring theatre). The play was performed later that night at another theatre, oratorio-style and without scenery or costumes, to tremendous enthusiasm—as memorialized in Tim Robbins's film *Cradle Will Rock.* *Lady in the Dark* (1941)—with a book by dramatist Moss Hart, lyrics by Ira Gershwin, and music by Kurt Weill (Brecht's colleague, who, like Brecht, had fled to America from Nazi Germany)—concerns itself with psychoanalysis and dream analysis and the perilous situation of a career woman (Liza Elliott) in a world dominated by old-fashioned ideas of marriage and women's roles; the musical numbers were all contained in Liza's three long dream sequences. *Oklahoma!* (1943), with music by Richard Rodgers and lyrics by Oscar Hammerstein II, deals with social and sexual tensions in the opening of the western states. Dispensing with the accepted convention of decorative dancing girls, *Oklahoma!* featured content-laden balletic choreography by Agnes de Mille to advance the plot and treated its historical subject—which included an onstage killing and the quick dispensing of frontier justice—with romantic passion and a new level of social intensity.

By the end of the Second World War, seriously themed Broadway musicals dominated the commercial American theatre. Rodgers and Hammerstein followed *Oklahoma!* with one success after another: *Carousel* (dealing with spousal abuse), *South Pacific* (racial prejudice), *The King and I* (gender prejudice and ethnocentricity), *Flower Drum Song* (East-West assimilation), and *The Sound of Music* (Nazism), all marked with social and intercultural conflict, richly romantic settings and songs, beautiful solo numbers and love duets, and thrilling choral, choreographic, and orchestral ensembles. Leonard Bernstein, one of America's leading orchestral conductors and composers, left a considerable mark on the musical's golden age with his *On the Town*, about World War II sailors on leave in Manhattan, and *West Side Story* (with lyrics by Stephen Sondheim), a powerfully emotional retelling of the *Romeo and Juliet* story with a contemporary Polish American (Tony) as his Romeo and a Puerto Rican American (Maria) as Juliet. And Jerry Bock and Sheldon Harnick conveyed a profoundly moving version of Jewish shtetl life in tsarist Russia with *Fiddler on the Roof.*

Not all musicals were deeply sober and serious, of course. More-lighthearted and satirical musicals of the 1940s and 1950s—first-rate works that still featured well-integrated plots, characters, themes, and musical styles—included Frank Loesser's *Guys and Dolls,* based on the idiosyncratic urban stories of Damon Runyon; Cole Porter's *Kiss Me Kate,* based on a backstage romance during a tour of Shakespeare's *The Taming of the Shrew;* and Irving Berlin's *Annie Get Your Gun,* based on the life of American folk heroine Annie Oakley. Richard Adler and Jerry Ross's *Pajama Game* (about union organizing in a pajama factory) and *Damn Yankees* (a Faustian tale about baseball) featured superlative jazz dancing choreographed by Bob Fosse. Alan Jay Lerner (book and lyrics) and Frederick Loewe (music) first successfully collaborated on the fantasy *Brigadoon,* about a mythical Scottish village, and then followed up with their brilliant musical revision of George Bernard Shaw's *Pygmalion,* renamed *My Fair Lady,* which wittily explores and exploits heroine Eliza Doolittle's proper and improper pronunciation of spoken English.

The best of these musicals during Broadway's golden age were commercially successful beyond anything in the theatre's previous history. Hit plays ran not for weeks or months, as before, but for years. They were, indeed, more than just "plays"; they were world-renowned cultural phenomena. For the first time, theatre tickets were sold as far as six months in advance, and business travelers returning from Manhattan were expected to provide a full report on "the new musicals in town." Touring companies brought the best of these shows to the rest of the country: first-class national tours, with the Broadway stars intact, and, subsequently, "bus and truck" tours, with less-familiar performers—nonetheless advertising "straight from Broadway!"—traveled around the nation. It is likely that most Americans during these years first experienced live theatre in the form of a road version of a Broadway musical, as did the author of this book. Songs from the best musicals—and even from some mediocre ones—routinely made the radio "hit parade" (forerunner of the "top forty" listings of today) and gained an instant national audience. Film versions of many musicals—*Oklahoma!, Carousel, My Fair Lady, Guys and Dolls, The Sound of Music*—were also widely popular. For a couple of decades, at least, it seemed as if everyone in America was whistling the latest creation from the tunesmiths of Broadway. And the stars of Broadway Golden Age musicals—Jimmy Durante, Eddie Cantor, Mary Martin, Ethel Merman, Julie Andrews, Carol Channing, Pearl Bailey, Bob Hope, and John Raitt—achieved national celebrity status;

Leonard Bernstein's and Stephen Sondheim's 1957 *West Side Story* was revived on Broadway in 2009 as directed by Arthur Laurents, who had written the book for the original production. For this production, Laurents revised some of the words and lyrics to be delivered in Spanish, heightening the famous tension between the gangs of Jets (Italian Americans, shown here) and Sharks (Puerto Rican Americans).

many becoming the pioneer performers on America's new entertainment medium, television. It is certain that the theatre had never played such a central role in American popular culture before; it is questionable if it ever will again.

THE CONTEMPORARY MUSICAL

No golden age lasts forever, and in retrospect no such age is unquestionably remembered as golden; the glittery epithet may in fact become little more than a quaint historical milepost. It is unquestionable, however, that the bulk of musicals produced in America today, not just by amateur groups but on Broadway as well, are revivals of the great musicals of mid-twentieth-century America. Today, however, a new and more contemporary musical theatre—at once less sentimental and more ironic, less rhapsodic and more choreographic—has come onto the scene.

The Emergence of Choreographer-Directors

The past half century has seen a tremendous escalation in the importance of choreography in American musicals. Agnes de Mille was instrumental in initiating this movement with her plot-advancing dance numbers in Rodgers and Hammerstein's *Oklahoma!* But later years saw the emergence of several choreographers who became more widely known than the directors they worked with—indeed, who *became* their productions' directors.

Jerome Robbins (1918–1998), trained in both ballet and acting, was the first of these. His "Small House of Uncle Thomas" ballet—a deliberately quaint, Siamese-themed version of *Uncle Tom's Cabin*—in *The King and I* and his vigorous teenage "street rumble" dances in *West Side Story* earned him national critical fame, leading to his combining directorial and choreographic chores

The iconic "musical about musicals" is Michael Bennett's *A Chorus Line* (1975), which portrays New York musical performers auditioning for a show—in part created from true stories told to Bennett by just such performers. This 2006 Broadway revival was directed by Bob Avian (the original production's choreographer); the costumes were designed by Theoni V. Aldredge, who also designed the originals.

in the seriocomic Broadway musicals *Gypsy*, about the lives of striptease artist Gypsy Rose Lee and her mother, and *Fiddler on the Roof*, about Jewish life in pre-revolutionary Russia. In 1989 Robbins put together a retrospective collection of his dances in *Jerome Robbins' Broadway*, winning the Tony Award for best musical.

Gower Champion (1921–1980) and Bob Fosse (1927–1987) were of Robbins's generation but utterly unlike him, or each other. Champion, a veteran dancer (with his wife, Marge) in many Broadway shows and Hollywood films, returned to the stage in 1960 to both stage and choreograph the energetic, crowd-pleasing *Bye Bye Birdie*. He followed this up with the romantic *Carnival* (1961) and the brashly presentational *Hello, Dolly!* (1964), in each case placing dance at the center of the dramatic entertainment. Champion's final show—he died tragically on its opening night—was *42nd Street*, a virtual valentine to the Broadway theatre and particularly to tap dancing; the show enjoyed a long run

after its 1980 opening and was brought back in a Tony Award–winning revival twenty years later. Fosse, also a golden-age choreographer (*The Pajama Game* and *Damn Yankees*, 1954 and 1955, respectively), went on to develop a highly idiosyncratic style—quick, jerky moves that suddenly segue to slow, sinuous come-ons; bumps and grinds from the striptease; white gloves and black bowler hats from minstrel and vaudeville; dance-as-sex and sex-as-dance—in, particularly, *Chicago* (1975) and *Dancin'* (1978), as well as in the film of *Cabaret* and his own filmed autobiography, *All That Jazz*. A post-humous retrospective of Fosse's dances, simply titled *Fosse*, opened on Broadway in 1999, running two years and winning the Tony Award for best musical.

Tommy Tune (born 1939) and Michael Bennett (1943–1987) are of a later generation. The lanky Tune, a brilliant tap dancer, even performs in some of the productions he also choreographs or directs; indeed, he is the only person to have won Tony Awards in four categories—director, choreographer, leading actor, and featured actor. Tune's *My One and Only* (1988), in which he also starred, *Grand Hotel* (1989), and *Will Rogers Follies* (1991) were celebrations of dance entertainment. Bennett's artistic goals were somewhat more conceptual: his masterwork (after choreographing and codirecting Stephen Sondheim's *Company* and *Follies*) was *A Chorus Line* (1975), a musical that, conceived, staged, and choreographed by Bennett, takes place in a dance audition and consists largely of dances interspersed with "interviews" of the auditioning dancers. It was initially developed off-Broadway using improvisations with performers, many of whom landed in the show itself. *A Chorus Line* was Broadway's longest-running show for many years.

At the top of the twenty-first century, Susan Stroman practically seized at least temporary control of the Broadway musical stage, winning every award in sight for her extraordinary direction and choreography of the hit Broadway production of Mel Brooks's *The Producers*, which won a record-shattering 12 Tony Awards, two for Stroman herself; she also received Tonys for her choreography of the wordless, all-dance *Contact*, which she also conceived, and for a remarkable revival of Rodgers and Hammerstein's *Oklahoma!*—all within a three-year period! What is remarkable about Stroman's choreography is its combination of humor, exuberance, inventiveness, and down-to-earth accessibility across an enormously wide-ranging stylistic palette. The clever deployment of "dancing props" is as close as Stroman comes to having a trademark: rustic mining implements in *Crazy for You*, hurtling trays of dishes in the restaurant scene of *Contact*, eye-popping rope tricks in *Oklahoma!*, tap dancing by old ladies hanging on to metal walkers in *The Producers*, and a "Putting on the Ritz" chorus dressed in top hats, tails, and rugged combat boots in the 2008 *Young Frankenstein*. Yet Stroman resists such easy characterization: her 2010 *The Scottsboro Boys*, treating the 1931 arrest of nine African American men and boys arrested for rapes they never committed, and staged by the director-choreographer with huge irony as a mock-minstrel show, displayed a profound sensitivity to cultural divisions in American culture of that time—and employed a setting mainly composed of simple silver chairs.

Stephen Sondheim

No one has had greater influence on the modern musical than the composer and lyricist Stephen Sondheim (born 1930), whose first important work, mentioned earlier, was the composition of lyrics for Leonard Bernstein's 1957 *West Side Story*. After one more assignment as a golden-age lyricist (for Jule Styne's *Gypsy*), Sondheim turned composer as well, winning high praise and success for both the lyrics and music to the songs in the highly novel *A Funny Thing Happened on the Way to the Forum*, drawn from the Roman comedies of Plautus.

In his work from 1970 onward, however, Sondheim departed from the standard formats of those early shows to develop a radically new style, marked by a disturbing plot, an ironic and sometimes even cynical tone, brutal skepticism about conventional morality, and highly sophisticated, adult, and intricately rhymed lyrics integrated within a score which brought surprising new rhythms to popular music. Sondheim's first works in this style include *Company* (1970), a devilishly clever and incisive look at sexual pairings and partings in the Manhattan of the time; *Follies* (1971), set at an onstage reunion of able but aging musical theatre performers, also set in Manhattan ("I'm Still Here" is the famous number from this show); and *A Little Night Music* (1973), adapted from an Ingmar Bergman film about summer sexual dalliances on a country estate in Sweden. These works were widely heralded for their brilliantly acerbic but always entertaining portrayal of the inevitable and eternal conflicts between social mores and romantic idealism (or, more bluntly, between laws and lust). Furthermore, particularly as all have been revived on Broadway twice since their premiere productions, they established Sondheim's supremacy in the American musical form for the entire generation that followed.

Sondheim continued to break new boundaries in three amazing creations. His *Pacific Overtures* (1976) employs kabuki-inspired music and stage techniques to trace the history of relations between Japan and the United States since Commodore Perry's "opening" of Japan in 1853. His *Sweeney Todd* (1979) integrates Brechtian distancing techniques and blends elements from Italian grand opera, the English music hall, and Victorian melodrama in a wildly morbid story of a barber's revenge. *Sweeney*'s score is so powerful and its actions and images so compelling that the work has been staged by several European opera companies. Conversely, his *Sunday in the Park with George* (1984) is an elegant musical play about the pointillist painter Georges Seurat; for this production, Sondheim invented a "pointillist" style of music to echo Seurat's painting style. These shows too have received Broadway revivals in the twenty-first century.

○Spotlight

Musical Lyrics through the Eras

This sampling of lyrics from different eras clearly indicates the changing styles of musical theatre popular in America.

W. S. Gilbert's lyrics tend toward lighthearted satire and revel in their own cleverness and literary showmanship. With multisyllable rhymes and a mocking attitude toward all pomposity, Gilbert amusingly skewers official British pretension, as in the Major General's self-explanatory "patter song" (so called because its singing requires rapid enunciation) from *The Pirates of Penzance* (1879):

STANLEY: I am the very model of a modern major general,
　I've information animal and vegetable and mineral,
　I know the kings of England and I quote the fights historical,
　From Marathon to Waterloo in order categorical.
　I'm very well acquainted too with matters mathematical,
　I understand equations both the simple and quadratical,
　About binomial theorems I am teeming with a lot of news,
　With many cheerful facts about the square of the
　　hypotenuse! . . .

Ira Gershwin's lyrics are openly romantic and tender; rather than call attention to the lyricist's own wit, Gershwin's clever wordplay reveals a charming emotional complexity in the characters' feelings as they sing his songs. The following excerpt from "'S Wonderful" was coauthored by Ira and his brother George (music) for the musical *Funny Face* (1927). Like most songs, it is divided into a verse, which sets up the situation, and a refrain, which is the musical (and emotional) heart of the song:

PETER: Life has just begun:
　Jack has found his Jill.
　Don't know what you've done,
　But I'm all a-thrill.
　How can words express
　Your divine appeal?
　You could never guess
　All the love I feel.
　From now on, lady, I insist,
　For me no other girls exist.

(Refrain)

　'S wonderful! 'S marvelous
　You should care for me!

　'S awful nice! 'S Paradise—
　'S what I love to see!
　You've made my life so glamorous
　You can't blame me for feeling amorous.
　Oh, 'S wonderful! 'S marvelous—
　That you should care for me! . . .

Perhaps no lyricist in the field has conveyed thwarted love and ironic longing as well as Lorenz Hart, the first partner of Richard Rodgers. In "Bewitched, Bothered and Bewildered" (*Pal Joey*, 1940), Vera, a society lady, drunkenly sings of her going-nowhere affair with a sexy but good-for-nothing nightclub owner:

VERA: After one whole quart of brandy,
　Like a daisy I awake.
　With no Bromo Seltzer handy.
　I don't even shake.
　Men are not a new sensation;
　I've done pretty well, I think.
　But this half-pint imitation's
　Put me on the blink.

(Refrain)

　I'm wild again,
　Beguiled again,
　A simpering, whimpering child again—
　Bewitched, bothered and bewildered am I.
　Couldn't sleep
　And wouldn't sleep
　Until I could sleep where I shouldn't sleep—
　Bewitched, bothered and bewildered am I.
　Lost my heart, but what of it?
　My mistake, I agree.
　He's a laugh, but I love it
　Because the laugh's on me . . .

By the time of Hart's death in 1943, Rodgers had begun a new partnership, with Oscar Hammerstein II, already the lyricist for Jerome Kern's *Show Boat* and many other musicals. Hammerstein wrote that he barely dared "place a timid encroaching foot on the territory" of the "masters" Gilbert and Hart, and sought to write instead what he himself termed "a more primitive type of lyric . . . expressing my own true convictions and feelings." His lyrics for the opening song in *Oklahoma!* (1943) clearly convey this:

CURLEY: There's a bright, golden haze on the meadow,
　There's a bright, golden haze on the meadow.

Sondheim's most controversial works are *Assassins* (1991) and *Passion* (1994). The first is a musical review of presidential assassinations (and assassination attempts), which cascades through two centuries, portraying the quirks and oddities of John Wilkes Booth, Lee Harvey Oswald, Lynette "Squeaky" Fromme, and John Hinckley Jr., among other unlikely musical theatre protagonists. *Passion*, a nineteenth-century gothic tragedy ("one long love song," Sondheim calls it) tells the strange story of Giorgio, a handsome Italian army officer who, though deeply in love with his beautiful mistress Clara, is relentlessly pursued by his superior's cousin Fosca, a homely, ailing, and pathetically obsessive woman. The play begins with Giorgio and Clara naked in bed, singing to each other: "I'm so happy, / I'm afraid I'll die / Here in your arms." But Giorgio soon

The corn is as high as an elephant's eye,
An' it looks like it's climbin' clear up to the sky.

(Refrain)

Oh, what a beautiful mornin'!
Oh, what a beautiful day!
I got a beautiful feelin'
Ev'rythin's goin' my way...

Hammerstein derived the verse of this song from a written stage description in Lynn Riggs's *Green Grow the Lilacs*, the source play for *Oklahoma!* Riggs had described the scene as "a radiant summer morning... cattle in the meadow, blades of the young corn... their images giving off a visible golden emanation that is partly true and partly a trick of imagination." Deciding it was a shame to waste Riggs's images on the reading audience only, Hammerstein made them the source of his famous opening lyric.

Stephen Sondheim, who enlarged the musical's palette more profoundly, perhaps, than any artist in the field, is most noted for a deeply ironic and antiromantic tone that, nonetheless, remains amusing and surprisingly good-spirited. Somehow he has managed to leaven his gloomy message with buoyant music, penetrating observation, and fiendishly clever rhymes and rhythm breaks. In "The Little Things You Do Together" (*Company,* 1970), Sondheim mocks the too-easy sentimentality of marital "relationships":

JOANNE: It's the little things you share together,
Swear together,
Wear together,
That make perfect relationships.
The concerts you enjoy together,
Neighbors you annoy together,
Children you destroy together,
That keep marriage intact.

(Refrain)

It's not so hard to be married
When two maneuver as one
It's not so hard to be married,
And, Jesus Christ, is it fun.

Jonathan Larson in *Rent* (1996) brought a new style to lyric writing altogether and, with it, a new audience for the Broadway musical. With rhythms borrowed from hip-hop and rock music (Larson wrote his own music) and with a script and staging that derived in part from cast improvisations, the musical scored an enormous success. "Contact" is one of the show's closing songs, sung to and in part by the character of Angel, a young drag queen dying of AIDS. Its language is coarse (it was deleted from the school edition until 2010), but its theatrical power is immense. Because it does not easily divide into verse and refrain stanzas, none are noted here:

ROGER, MARK, JOANNE, & BENNY: Hot-hot-hot-sweat-sweet
Wet-wet-wet-red-heat
Hot-hot-hot-sweat-sweet
Wet-wet-wet-red-heat
Please don't stop please
Please don't stop stop
Stop stop stop don't
Please please please please
Hot-hot-hot-sweat-sweet
Wet-wet-wet-red-heat
Sticky-licky-trickle-tickle
Steamy-creamy-stroking-soaking

COLLINS: Touch!

MAUREEN: Taste!

MIMI: Deep!

COLLINS: Dark!

MAUREEN: Kiss!

COLLINS: Beg!

MIMI: Slap!

MIMI, MAUREEN, & COLLINS: Fear!

COLLINS: Thick!

COLLINS, MIMI, & MAUREEN: Red, red
Red, red Red, red—please

MAUREEN: Harder!

ANGEL: Faster!

MAUREEN: Wetter!

MIMI: Bastard!

COLLINS: You whore

MAUREEN: You animal

MIMI & ANGEL: More

MAUREEN, COLLINS, & MIMI: Fluid no fluid no contact yes no contact

ALL: Fire fire burn—burn yes!
No latex rubber rubber
Fire latex rubber latex bummer lover bummer

yields to the intensity of Fosca's passionate fixation, much to Clara's (and the audience's) despair. There being little for the Broadway audience to "root for" in this romantic tangle, *Passion* closed less than eight months after its Broadway premiere. Its innovations, however, are exhilarating, and the musical won the 1994 Tony Awards for Musical, Best Book of a Musical, and Best Original Score, while subsequent productions, including the nationally televised 2005 Lincoln Center concert version and a 2010 Donmar Warehouse London revival, have won great praise and new awards.

Black Musicals

More than a dozen major "black musicals" (musicals largely by, about, and performed by African Americans)

For his 2005 Broadway revival of Stephen Sondheim's *Sweeney Todd,* director John Doyle had his reduced cast of only ten actors play the orchestral instruments as well as perform the characters' roles. The astonishing innovation proved a great sensation, and the show was nominated for six Tony Awards, with Doyle winning one for Best Direction of a Musical.

have excited Broadway audiences since the 1970s, attracting large "crossover" (i.e., black and white) audiences and indeed helping to pave the way for cultural integration at every level of the country's social structure. In the last decade of the twentieth century these included Charlie Smalls's *The Wiz* (an African American version of *The Wizard of Oz*), *Bubbling Brown Sugar* and *Eubie* (both based on the music of ragtime composer/pianist Eubie Blake, who in 1921 wrote Broadway's first black musical, *Shuffle Along*); *Ain't Misbehavin'* and *Sophisticated Ladies* (featuring, respectively, the music of Fats Waller and Duke Ellington); *Dreamgirls* (celebrating a Supremes-like singing group and their struggles to succeed in an environment of racism and civil strife); *Jelly's Last Jam* (about jazz pioneer Jelly Roll Morton, written and directed by George C. Wolfe); and *Bring in 'Da Noise, Bring in 'Da Funk* (a capsule history of racial injustice in America, conceived and directed by George C. Wolfe and choreographed by Savion Glover, who also performed).

More recent black Broadway musicals like *Memphis, Fela!,* and *The Scottsboro Boys* celebrate—and often criticize—the interaction between black music and white culture. *Memphis* (2009) deals with the transition from African American rhythm & blues to white American rock & roll in Tennessee during the 1950s. *Fela!* (2009) showcases the legendary, and politically radical, Nigerian singer/musician Fela Anikulapo Kuti and the mesmerizing Afrobeat music he pioneered in his Lagos nightclub in the 1970s. *The Scottsboro Boys* (2010) tells the true story of young black southern men—some of them just boys—who were falsely accused and convicted of raping two white women on a train in 1931; the events are recalled in the format of a minstrel show, with a white "Interlocuter" and an otherwise all-black cast (some comically assuming white roles). And more recently yet, the great 1935 Gershwin opera *Porgy and Bess,* set among the black inhabitants of Charleston's Catfish Row of the 1930s, having been revised by black playwright Suzan-Lori Parks and director Diane Paulus

Sahr Ngaujah plays the title role of Nigerian Afrobeat performer Fela Anikulapo Kuti in the 2009 Broadway musical *Fela!*, which treats Fela's political, social, and marital views as well as his musical genius. The director, choreographer, and coauthor of the book was Bill T. Jones.

(with music adapted by Diedre Murray) into a more conventional music theatre format, opened on Broadway in 2012 with the new title, *The Gershwins' Porgy and Bess.*

Foreign Invasions: British, French, and Disney

American-born musicals dominated Broadway's musical theatre scene for the first six decades of the twentieth century. Then, beginning in 1970, European composers, lyricists, and directors came to the musical theatre forefront. Leading the "foreign invasion" of America's music theatre capital was English composer Andrew Lloyd Webber, first with his Bible-themed *Joseph and the Technicolor Dreamcoat* in 1982, followed by *Cats* (also 1982, based on poet T. S. Eliot's *Old Possum's Book of Practical Cats*) and the now nearly legendary *Phantom of the Opera* (1988), the latter two becoming the longest-running musicals in Broadway history. Lloyd Webber's works—also including the successful *Jesus*

Christ Superstar, Evita, Starlight Express, and *Sunset Boulevard*—are known for their lush musical scores more than for their books or lyrics. Most are "sung-through" (with no spoken dialogue), so they are easily accessible to global audiences who need little in the way of translation. The staging of these musicals has also tended to extravagance: *Starlight Express* featured a cast speeding on roller skates around an elevated track encircling the audience. In *Phantom*, a chandelier seems to fall right in the midst of the audience, and the masked Phantom and his beloved cruise in a gondola on a fiery subterranean "lake" in the basement of the Paris Opera House. Lloyd Webber's most recent music theatre creation, which opened in London in 2011, is *The Wizard of Oz*, a lushly staged adaptation and augmentation of the celebrated 1939 film.

Following closely in Lloyd Webber's trans-Atlantic steps were French composer Claude-Michel Schönberg and lyricist Alain Boublil. Their *Les Misérables* (1987, revived 2006) and *Miss Saigon* (1991) both became

Mary Poppins is only one of the spate of Disney musicals that have transformed Broadway in recent years (others are *The Lion King, Beauty and the Beast, Tarzan,* and *Aida*). The show's designs by Bob Crowley (see the chapter titled "Designers and Technicians" for some of Crowley's working process on this show) and its choreography by the innovative Matthew Bourne made the stage production, which is darker than the Disney movie on which it is based, a success in its 2005 London premiere (pictured here with Laura Michelle Kelly as Mary) and even more popular on Broadway in 2006.

megahits in America and around the world, rivaling Lloyd Webber's productions with both their luxuriant scores and their spectacular staging, capped by the helicopter descending onto the roof of the American Embassy to rescue fleeing diplomats in *Miss Saigon.* Not only were composers and lyricists of these shows European, but the productions were in the main staged by top-tier British directors: Nicholas Hytner (*Miss Saigon*) and Trevor Nunn (*Cats, Les Misérables, Sunset Boulevard,* and *Starlight Express*).

No one has more mastered the global theatrical musical, however, than the very American corporation known as Disney, which since the 1990s has all but saturated theatres worldwide with its productions of *The Lion King, Beauty and the Beast, Aida, Mary Poppins, The Little Mermaid,* and *Tarzan*—indeed, *Tarzan,* though a relative flop in the United States, was subsequently overhauled in Europe where it became a great success in both the Netherlands and Germany. Disney musicals, mostly adaptations of very successful Disney films, profit commercially from Disney's bottomless financial resources and worldwide name recognition. The celebrated "Mouse" also has been credited with great theatrical art, however, particularly in the designs of Bob Crowley for *Mary Poppins* and the amazingly innovative designs and staging of *The Lion King* by longtime avant-garde director-designer Julie Taymor. (See the chapter titled "Global Theatre Today" for more on Taymor's work.) This show (with music by Elton John), opened on Broadway in 1997 and, in April 2012, surpassed *The Phantom of the Opera* to become the

highest-grossing Broadway play of all time. *The Lion King* has grossed $4.8 *billion* worldwide in box-office income and currently plays in London, Hamburg, Madrid, and Tokyo, with plans to expand to Sao Paulo in 2013. Clearly the musical theatre, in the twenty-first century, has become a global phenomenon.

Musicals of the Twenty-first Century

Our new century's musicals have had their share of great commercial success, as noted above, and offered comedy as broadly entertaining as in any previous age—Mel Brooks's *The Producers,* Marc Shaiman's *Hairspray,* David Yazbek's *Dirty Rotten Scoundrels,* David Bryan's *Memphis,* and Trey Parker, Matt Stone, and Robert Lopez's *The Book of Mormon* are all prime examples.

But the musicals of this century are increasingly tackling serious subjects. Gang violence (*The Beautiful Game,* 2000), unemployment and its sexual consequences (*The Full Monty,* 2000), infidelity and betrayal (*The Wild Party,* 2000), environmental degradation (*Urinetown,* 2001), immigration and assimilation (*Flower Drum Song,* revised version by David Henry Hwang, 2002), the exploitation of scandal and sexual anomalies in American popular culture (*Jerry Springer, the Opera,* 2003), oppression in race relations (*Caroline, or Change,* 2004), sexual ignorance and its ramifications (*Spring Awakening,* 2006), the challenges of barrio life in New York City's Washington Heights (*In the Heights,* 2007), government corruption in Nigeria (*Fela!,* 2009), and blatant judicial malfeasance (*The Scottsboro Boys,* 2010) have been explored in today's musical dramas with sharp, even brutal, insight and penetration.

Some of these plays have been not only serious but downright grim. John Lachiusa and George C. Wolfe's *The Wild Party* (the second of two Broadway musicals in the 2000–2001 season with that title, each derived from the same 1928 poem) cynically depicts the raucous goings-on at a late-night drinking party, providing a menu of sexual infidelities and emotional betrayals. "People like us, we take lovers like pills/Just hoping to cure what we know we can't fix," says one character at the party. "You're out in the clubs/Paradin' your meat/Spending all your advance/On snatch off the street/You seen more ass/Than a toilet seat," says another. And the party ends with the conclusion:

You can make a fortune doing next to nothing:
You can sit there on your ass and screw your friends:
But you better know how to kick—kick—kick your way
Outta the burning room
When it ends.

The musical *Spring Awakening*, based on Frank Wedekind's 1891 play, astonished audiences and critics in its 2006 Broadway opening, winning eight Tony Awards and having reviewers arguing over whether it was the best musical of the year or the best in a generation. The production, directed by Michael Mayer, retains the basic story, characters, and oppressive social-sexual morality of the nineteenth-century German original while coupling them with modern (and postmodern) elements: a brazenly contemporary rock score by Steven Slater and Duncan Sheik, electrifying modern choreography by Bill T. Jones, a "theatre-within-a-theatre" setting by Christine Jones complete with onstage band and an onstage audience, and nonstop lighting magic by Ken Adams that pulses with the music and cavorts with the performers. The performers, whose average age at the time of opening was under nineteen, created an impressive ensemble. "I can't think of a better bonding experience than to be able to sit onstage and to watch your fellow performers perform on stage every night," said Jonathan Groff, who played Melchior.

The Hell of *The Wild Party*, conveying the message of the medieval *Everyman* with a contemporary American bite, is echoed by Ben Elton's lyrics for the ironically named *The Beautiful Game* (with music by Andrew Lloyd Webber) as it addresses English-Irish terrorism with this prisoner's lament:

> You're in the death zone. Satan sits on his throne.
> Even the strongest are frightened.
> This is the dark zone. We see in monochrome.
> Nothing is good or enlightened.
> Happiness is ended. All hope is suspended.
> We are the damned, we are all despised.

Other recent musicals combine cultural unease with social protest and personal anguish. The 2005 *Billy Elliott*, written by Lee Hall and with music by Elton John, tells the story of an English coal miner's son who wants to become a ballet dancer during the raucous turmoil of labor unrest and violent class antagonism in the north of England during 1984. Termed a "protest musical," it became an enormous success on London's West End and won thirteen Tony Awards when it opened on Broadway in 2008. Richard Thomas's *Jerry Springer* presented—only to London and Chicago audiences thus far—the chamber of horrors existing on America's outermost sexual fringes, with rambunctious (and scatological) song titles and lyrics such as "Chicks with Dicks," "Sex with My Sister," and "I got shit pouring outta my ass" in the first act alone. And the second act takes place in Hell. It was "the most explosive theatrical event in years" said the *London Observer*. Tony Kushner's *Caroline, or Change* is awash in bleak depression from beginning to end. Its characters' hopes are continually dashed, and the title

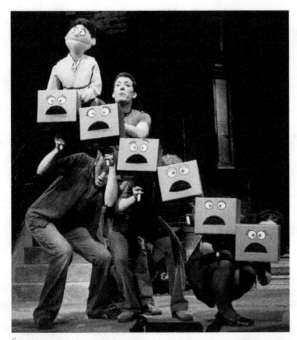

Avenue Q, an ironic and risqué musical of current life—animated by both humans and puppets—walked away with five Tony Awards in 2004.

Alice Ripley won the Tony for Best Actress in a Musical for her leading role as a mother with bipolar disorder in the 2009 *Next to Normal*. Here Ripley is seated next to Robert Spencer, who plays her stage husband, while Aaron Tveit, as the living image of their grown son—a son who had actually died in infancy—hovers over them both, as a nightmare that simply will not go away. Directed by Michael Greif; the scenic design is by Mark Wendland.

character—a black maid working for a white Jewish family in the American South—never smiles during the entire play (nor, in the performance this writer attended, even during the curtain call ovation). Caroline's defining solo, at her ironing board, is practically a funeral dirge:

> I'm gonna slam that iron
> down on my heart
> gonna slam that iron
> down on my throat
> gonna slam that iron
> down on my sex
> gonna slam it slam it slam it down
> 'til I drown the fire out
> 'til there ain't no air left anywhere!

Dare we applaud? Of course, we do—but we sure don't feel like it.

Spring Awakening, based on Frank Wedekind's 1891 German drama about teenagers kept sexually ignorant by their parents and teachers with disastrous results, received outstanding reviews for its pop-rock score by Duncan Sheik (music) and scalding lyrics by Stephen Slater, as from the song "Totally Fucked":

> There's a moment you know you're fucked
> Not an inch more room to self destruct
> No more moves, oh yeah, the dead end zone
> Man you just can't call your soul your own

But the thing that makes you really jump
Is that the weirdest shit is still to come
You can ask yourself, "Hey what have I done?"
You're just a fly the little guys, they kill for fun.

And *Next to Normal* (music by Tom Kitt, book and lyrics by Brian Yorkey) is a powerfully realistic musical about a housewife with bipolar disorder bordering on schizophrenia, and the dreadful impact her illness has on her husband and teenage daughter, Natalie, who sings:

> So it's times like these I wonder how I take it
> And if other families live the way we do?
> If they love each other or if they just fake it
> And if other daughters feel like I feel too?
> 'Cause some days I think I'm dying
> But I'm really only trying
> To get through
> For just another day . . .

This musical, ten years in development on its road to receiving three 2009 Tony Awards, the 2010 Pulitzer Prize, and a sixteen-city national tour, was greatly prized for its alternately delicate and soaring portrayal of a deeply troubled but ultimately admirable family battling with tragic psychic ailments and the hope and anguish that come with them.

Seriousness, of course, need not be conveyed through profanity or mental breakdowns, but the intensity of passion that radiates through most of these works leads to an unpitying vigor that makes the current musical theatre angrier and more genuinely shocking than the musicals of previous eras. And the rock-inspired music increasingly employed by the

Spotlight

The Book of Mormon

Many musicals have been truly groundbreaking in the current century, and many extremely popular, but no musical has achieved *both* of these encomiums to the extent as did *The Book of Mormon* in 2011. This show is "blasphemous, scurrilous and more foul-mouthed than David Mamet on a blue streak. But . . . its heart is as pure as that of a Rodgers and Hammerstein show," said critic Ben Brantley in the *New York Times*. Though a "raucously funny . . . nonstop fusillade of obscenities," the play "is earnestly about the power of faith," said Steven Suskin in the trade magazine *Variety*. "Some of the sweetest poison ever poured," said Peter Marks in the *Washington Post*.

Indeed, all the reviews were rapturous, and the Tony Award voters overwhelmed, by this outlandish comedy by *South Park* creators Trey Parker and Matt Stone, who teamed with Robert Lopez of *Avenue Q*—a similarly wildly successful and irreverent musical that employs puppets to depict highly adult and scandalous situations—to create their first Broadway production. The script, as mentioned, treats white, male, Mormon missionaries transported to black Uganda, Africa, and while the social, sexual, economic, religious, and cultural differences between these peoples are as extreme as could possibly be imagined, human linkage somehow seeps into every miscommunication, irritation, disappointment, and conflict that arises among them until the audience erupts, time and again, into joyous laughter and applause. Every group is riotously satirized—not just Mormons and Africans but Jews, gentiles, gays, straights, thugs, wimps, believers, atheists, intellectuals, and ignoramuses—and everyone somehow comes out a hero.

Two Morman missionaries, played by Andrew Rannells and Josh Gad, meet the Ugandan sorcerer Mafala Hatimbi, played by Michael Potts, in *The Book of Mormon*, 2011.

composers of these shows—which were preceded in this regard by the epoch-making *Hair* (1968)—has created a contemporary musical context (even for the nineteenth-century setting of *Spring Awakening*), and it has brought to Broadway a younger audience as well as the technology of the contemporary rock concert era, with its heart-pumping sound amplification and lighting dazzle. The music theatre of the twenty-first century in all likelihood will continue to intrigue and entertain and perhaps will spread its influence deeper into the general populace of an increasingly interracial and intercultural American community.

Chapter **10**

Global Theatre Today

THE THEATRE OF TODAY EXISTS onstage, not in the pages of this or any other book. The theatre of today is being performed right now, in the multimillion-dollar theatres of the world's great cities as well as on simpler stages at schools, community theatres and nightclubs, and in city parks, streets, and even streetcars around the world.

The theatre of today is all around us, waiting to be discovered, seen, heard, felt, and experienced. The best way to tap into its fundamental impulse is to go out and see it.

WHAT'S HAPPENING?

It's not easy to say what's happening in the theatre today. We cannot evaluate the current theatre with the same objectivity that we bring to the theatre of the past—even the recent past. Theatre is a business as well as an art, and the increasingly feverish pitch of promotion, publicity, and puffery that surround each current theatrical endeavor make a cool perspective difficult. Whereas poets and painters are often ignored until years following their deaths, the opposite is more often true of theatre artists: they may be lionized in their own time and forgotten a few years later. A permanent place in the repertory of world theatre is the achievement of very few; among the playwrights once deemed equal to Shakespeare are such dimly remembered figures as John Fletcher, Joseph Addison, and Maxwell Anderson. ▶

The 2009 Broadway revival of *Hair*—by James Rado and Gerome Ragni (book and lyrics) and Galt McDermot (music)—brought back to New York the iconic musical that boldly introduced nudity, profanity, rock music, and interracial casting to mainstream American theatre in the mid-1960s. Originally a product of the hippie era's sexual revolution and virulent antiwar protest, this 2009 Broadway revival—pictured above with Will Swensen (*center*) as Berger and Alison Case (*kneeling at his right*) as his sometime girlfriend Crissy—went on to receive the Tony Award for Best Revival and then to have a London triumph as well, with critics and audiences alike acknowledging that while *Hair* may have been a creation of its rambunctious era, neither its social impact nor its entertainment value had lessened over the ensuing decades.

Which of our present-day writers and actors and other theatre artists will achieve more than ephemeral glory? Which, if any, will leave a mark on future generations? No one can answer either question with any certainty.

From a practical point of view—looking at stage practice rather than theory—theatre is a fairly conservative institution. Theatre companies around the world present plays from the past as well as from their own time and also conserve many of the theatre's traditional ways of working. Nearly all the plays mentioned in the previous chapters will be performed somewhere in the world this season, and the vigorous debates among today's actors and directors often repeat dialogues from the days of Aristophanes, Shakespeare, and Stanislavsky. Nevertheless, in the twenty-first century, a new era seems to be emerging. The previous century

was a violent one: two world wars, assassinations of political and cultural leaders (Mohandas Gandhi, Martin Luther King Jr., John and Robert Kennedy, Anwar Sadat, Yitzhak Rabin, John Lennon), the Holocaust, the threat of nuclear annihilation, the proliferation of alluring but dangerous drugs and sex-linked diseases, and the threatened destruction of Earth's vital resources. The arts responded to these social changes with an artistic freedom often frightening in its extremity—nowhere more so than in the theatre, where by the 1970s Dionysian ecstasy had returned to the stage with a force almost equal to that of the ancient dithyramb. As play-licensing laws fell in England and legal censorship became locally unenforceable in America, profanity, nudity, at least simulated copulation, violence, and libelous accusation—all unknown on the legitimate stage since ancient times—became almost commonplace. Plays popular in America in the last third of the twentieth century featured accusations of a sitting president of murder (*MacBird*) and a recent pope of genocide (*The Deputy*), a farm boy copulating with his pig (*Futz*), teenage boys stoning a baby to death in its crib (*Saved*), and actors undressing and marching naked out into the street (*Paradise Now*). Some of this Dionysian frenzy reached right into the theatre's mainstream when the rock Broadway musical *Hair* (1968) ended its first act with its actors—who had already sung rapturously about sodomy, fellatio, and cunnilingus—brazenly stripping off their clothes and facing the audience in a posture of mocking defiance.

Nor were theatre audiences themselves immune from such changes in theatrical convention. In the experimental theatre of the 1970s and 1980s, spectators almost routinely found themselves sat upon, fondled, assaulted, hurled about, handed lit joints of marijuana, and, in at least one case (in Finland), urinated upon. These and other extreme behaviors had become part of the license claimed by a theatre purportedly trying to make itself heard above the societal din of war, riots, and corruption. Or, as many asked, were its adherents merely "acting out" to get attention? In any event, it was an era of dramaturgical violence and abandon that brought the age of "modernism" to a crisis, if not to a conclusion: the once-rebellious conventions of realism and antirealism seemed tame compared to this newfound drive to create shocking, immersive theatre events.

Well before the century's end, however, this mood of violent protest was largely spent, and the theatre turned its focus from assaulting the audience to raising its social awareness. Profanity and nudity no longer seemed novel and, having lost their power to shock, became conventional tools for addressing serious issues. The American theatre, in particular, responded to the era's pervasive (and largely knee-jerk) prejudices and privileges associated with gender, race, class, and sexual orientation that were then were coming under increasing fire as various movements—civil rights, feminism, gay pride—were gaining a more prominent cultural voice.

On the international scene, the end of the twentieth century saw an explosion of new social and political alignments and an overwhelmingly broadened spectrum of new technologies. With the cold war ended, the newly globalized economy challenged local cultures with enhanced but often troubling prospects, and astonishing advances in telecommunications—social networks, weblogs, satellite telecasting, text-messaging, and smart phones—revolutionized (and continue to revolutionize) the way the world's populations could connect. Huge technological advances in sound and lighting design, spurred by globally touring rock concerts, created ear-splitting and eye-popping effects with the flick of a console button. A mere year into the new millennium, whatever political stability seemed to have been achieved at the century's end was staggered by a terrorist attack on New York and Washington that was said to have "changed everything" and that soon led, if indirectly, to military invasions, suicide bombings, regime changes, civil wars, insurrections, threats of nuclear proliferation, a "global war on terror," and worldwide economic crises.

This brings us to the present moment: on the one hand, a time of increased communication, broadening civil rights, and stunning technological innovation, but on the other, of political instability and insecurity. The theatre—a tool of live communication—has responded quickly to these new freedoms and opportunities. Once again, as in the days of the ancient Greeks and Shakespearean England, the stage has surfaced as an arena in which new thoughts, fashions, feelings, morals, theologies, and aesthetics can be enacted, and new methods explored, in order to bring lucidity and structure to the confusions that beset us all.

Although generalizations about an era still upon us must be tentative, some major themes have clearly emerged in today's theatre, and we look at several of them in the ensuing pages.

An Open Theatre

It is safe to say that, particularly in the United States, theatre audiences and practitioners alike have opted for an "open" theatre—open, that is, for an infinitely wider range of interests, cultures, and individuals than existed during any other period in theatre history. This openness—the word comes from Joseph Chaikin's short-lived but extremely influential Open Theatre of the 1960s and 1970s—makes us painfully conscious of the theatre's challenge, after two world wars, to fully reflect the humanity inside us and the society around us. For although Shakespeare (for instance) was certainly able to create magnificent female and minority characters (Beatrice and Cleopatra, Othello and Shylock) and his acting company was apparently skilled at bringing them vividly to life, the notion of an all-white (and all-male) theatre company following Hamlet's famous demand to hold "a mirror

Robin Williams plays the title role—a snarling tiger in an Iraqi cage—in the 2011 Broadway premiere of Rajiv Joseph's Pulitzer Prize finalist, *Bengal Tiger at the Baghdad Zoo,* set in the chaos that immediately followed the fall of Saddam Hussein. Molsés Kaufman directed.

up to nature" has proven generally unsustainable. How can an exclusively male or an exclusively white—or even an exclusively single-ethnicity company—wholly "mirror" the hopes and concerns of all human nature: women as well as men, gays and straights, Asians and blacks and Native Americans as well as whites?

Postwar authors and directors, therefore, have increasingly sought to open the theatre to all comers. Emphasizing a disconnect between actor and character is helpful in creating this openness, as many playwrights or directors tend now to create "roles" more than characters, inviting the audience to see an actor not *as* a character but rather as an actor *playing* a character. So today a woman may play a king, a grown-up a five-year old child, a white actor a black and a black one a white, and Robin Williams can star on Broadway as a Bengal tiger—all without compromising the integrity of the theatrical experience. Casting considerations now radically bend gender distinctions, cross racial lines, and span age ranges and living species.

Chaikin's Open Theatre pioneered these developments for more than a decade, combining social improvisation with Brechtian techniques, developing plays in which performers glided into and out of their characters (they also played pieces of the scenery and individual props, and often simply "played" themselves), and using story and character merely as vehicles for direct interactions with audiences. Their plays, which included Megan Terry's *Viet Rock,* Susan Yankowitz's *Terminal,* and the company-authored *Mutation Show,*

were continually evolving workshop performances that addressed immediate audience concerns. The Open Theatre toured Europe, as well as American campuses and prisons, making alliances with the New Lafayette Theatre in Harlem, El Teatro Campesino in San Juan Bautista (California), and the Women's Collective Theatre in San Francisco. Although it ended its existence in 1973, the Open's influence lasts to this day, and its name may well stand to represent the larger "opening" of our contemporary stage to the great diversity of our contemporary cultures, and to our diverse personal identifications and orientations.

A Diverse Theatre

From top to bottom, in gender, race, and ethnicity, in playwrights, performers, producers, and directors, the American theatre is now broadly heterogeneous. Indeed, the United States, known as a "melting pot" of races, cultures, and religions from around the globe, is clearly the leader in creating such diversity in its theatre—as America has the most broadly diverse population of any country in the world.

Women were practically unrepresented in the theatre until the seventeenth century (except in the commedia dell'arte and some medieval English pageant productions), and even afterward they were relegated mainly to acting, copying scripts, and building costumes. Now women comprise a major force at every level of the American theatrical arts. Since the 1980s, seven women

Tom Stoppard's *The Invention of Love* portrays various events in the life of the English classical scholar and poet A. E. Housman from age eighteen to seventy-seven, not only by jumping backward and forward in time but also by imagining through intriguing same-time conversations between the young Housman (played by Robert Sean Leonard, *right*) and Housman as a just-deceased old man (played by Richard Easton), here shown—along with their reflections—sitting on a fallen antique monument (another postmodern touch) on the River Styx in Hades (the land of the dead). Both Leonard and Easton won Tony Awards for their Housman portrayals in the 2001 Broadway season. Sets and costumes are by Bob Crowley; lighting is by Brian MacDevitt.

playwrights (Paula Vogel, Beth Henley, Marsha Norman, Wendy Wasserstein, Margaret Edson, Suzan-Lori Parks, Lynn Nottage) have received Pulitzer Prizes and four (Anna Deveare Smith, Naomi Wallace, Mary Zimmerman, Sarah Ruhl) have been honored with MacArthur "genius" awards. Women directors, once a rarity, now represent at least one-third of the nation's total field and a comparable percentage are now artistic directors as well. Meanwhile, feminist theatre ensembles—groups of women presenting plays by, about, and for women—have been founded throughout the United States. While diverse in their approaches, such theatre companies share a broad goal of presenting plays about women's experiences, focusing on topics such as gender-role stereotyping, abortion, pregnancy, motherhood, rape, mother-daughter relationships, lesbianism, domestic violence, women's history, violence against women, and female incarceration.

Racial diversification of American theatre shows a similar development. Until the mid-1950s, the American dramatic repertoire was almost entirely written by, for, and about whites. Talented black writers were

Denzel Washington plays Troy Maxson, a retired Negro League baseball star, and Viola Davis plays Rose, his wife, in one of the happier moments during August Wilson's most famous play, *Fences*. Kenny Leon directed this 2010 Broadway revival.

to American society but also to the American stage. In 1967, actors Robert Hooks and Douglas Turner Ward created the Negro Ensemble Company, bringing forth dramatist Lonne Elder III's eloquent *Ceremonies in Dark Old Men* in 1969 and continuing to flourish to the present day, and in 1982 Charles Fuller's *A Soldier's Play*, about the murder of a black soldier in the American South, received the Pulitzer Prize.

The early 1980s brought to the fore the extraordinary August Wilson, whose ten-play dramatic cycle (see the chapter titled "The Modern Theatre: Realism") is an unparalleled achievement, treating aspects of American black life in each of the ten decades of the twentieth century. Wilson's plays received dozens of awards—including two Pulitzer Prizes—and have been regularly revived on Broadway and in regional theatres since his untimely death in 2005. And in the current century, two African American women dramatists have received Pulitzer awards: Suzan-Lori Parks for *Topdog/Underdog* in 2002 and Lynn Nottage for *Ruined* in 2009, while in the 2011–2012 Broadway season, three black women playwrights—Parks (with her adaptation of *Porgy and Bess*), Katori Hall (*The Mountaintop*), and Lydia R. Diamond (*Stick Fly*)—also had their works presented on the "Great White Way." As black playwrights, directors, and actors increasingly populate mainstream Broadway and regional American theatre, the movement to create dedicated black ensembles has faded, though certainly not disappeared.

Latino theatre, often distinguished by its language as well as its ethnic roots, has also blossomed in today's open environment. Spanish-speaking theatre is hardly a new innovation in North America—indeed, the first play staged on this continent was *Los Moros y Los Cristianos* (*The Moors and the Christians*) at the San Juan Pueblo near Santa Fe in the sixteenth century. But the 1965 founding of El Teatro Campesino by Mexican American Luis Valdez became the impetus to a truly national movement to create homegrown Latino theatre in the United States. Created in conjunction with the United Farm Workers union in rural California, Valdez's Teatro and its powerful creative and political thrusts electrified California audiences and won national acclaim, particularly for its groundbreaking *Zoot Suit* (1978), written by Valdez about riots in the Los Angeles barrio that pitted Mexican American migrants against the Los Angeles police and politicians in the early 1940s. In this work, Valdez employed Brechtian techniques to raise social, political, and economic questions, while retaining the music, whimsy, and verve of full-blooded theatrical entertainment.

hardly ever able to secure productions, and even the best black actors were often reduced to playing the roles of servants and "exotics." But in the decades following World War II, black-themed, black-authored, and black-acted drama began to surge forward in American culture. Lorraine Hansberry's 1959 *A Raisin in the Sun*, a realistic study of black family life, became the first black-authored play to appear on Broadway, and its director, Lloyd Richards, became the first black director in the American theatrical mainstream. Soon, the black theatre had become a truly revolutionary force with the startling work of African American Amiri Baraka, whose *Dutchman* and *The Toilet* appeared off-Broadway in 1964 and confronted American racism with astonishing ferocity. Baraka (then known as LeRoi Jones) refused to shrink from his subject's violent ramifications, and his gut-wrenching urban plays—set, respectively, in a subway car and a high school restroom—provided a startling wake-up call not only

Lorainne Hansberry's modern classic, *A Raisin in the Sun,* was beautifully revised by the Ebony Theatre Company in Los Angeles in 2012. Staged by Felicia Rashad, the production featured (*left to right*) Deidrie Henry, Kevin T. Carroll, Kim Staunton, Kenya Alexander, and Brandon David Brown as the first black American family to move into an all-white neighborhood in 1959 Chicago.

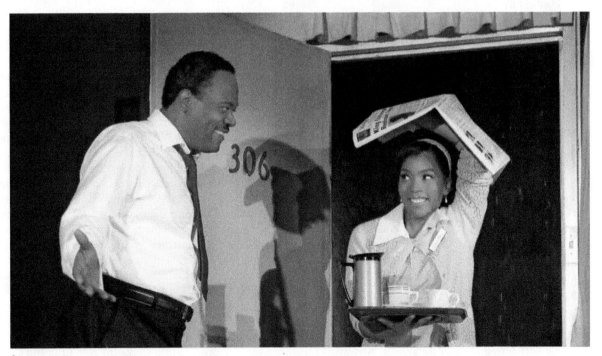

Samuel L. Jackson plays Dr. Martin Luther King Jr. and Angela Bassett plays a motel maid bringing him coffee in African American playwright Katori Hall's *The Mountaintop*, which takes place during the evening preceding the Nobel Prize-winner's 1986 assassination at the Lorraine Motel in Memphis, Tennessee. The 2011 Broadway premiere was directed by Kenny Leon.

El Paso–born Octavio Solis moved into the top tier of American playwrights with his brilliant, Pulitzer-finalist *Lydia* in 2009. This production, directed by Juliette Carrillo and performed in a mixture of English and Spanish at the Mark Taper Forum in Los Angeles, starred Onahuoa Roderiguez (*left*) as Ceci, a young girl whose brain was shattered in a car accident days before her quinceañera (traditional fifteenth birthday celebration). We mainly see Ceci, however, in her dreams of her past life as a vivacious young woman. Stephanie Beatriz plays the mysterious Lydia, a young Mexican "illegal" (unlawful immigrant) who uses magical powers to comfort Cici and translate her unexpressed thoughts to her bewildered parents and brothers.

The play went on to Broadway (making a star out of Edward James Olmos) and was eventually adapted into a feature film. "In a Mexican way," wrote Valdez in 1966, "we have discovered what Brecht is all about. If you want unbourgeois theatre, find unbourgeois people to do it." El Teatro Campesino continues to perform, at least intermittently, at its permanent home in San Juan Bautista, California.

Today, the works of dozens of Latina and Latino dramatists can be seen around the country. Cuban-born Nilo Cruz received the 2003 Pulitzer Prize for his enchanting *Anna in the Tropics*, portraying Cuban émigré workers in a Florida cigar factory. His rapturous adaptation of Calderón's classic *Life Is a Dream* successfully premiered in California in 2007. Octavio Solis,

born of Mexican immigrant parents in El Paso, Texas, was nominated for a 2009 Pulitzer for his intense *Lydia*. This realistic yet often mystical drama of a family not unlike Solis's own had earned extravagant praise in its initial productions in Denver and Los Angeles. Puerto Rican–born José Rivera is another nationally heralded Latino playwright. His *Marisol* (1992), a fantasy about a woman and her guardian angel in the tradition of magic realism, has been produced throughout the country, as has his *References to Salvador Dali Make Me Hot* (2003). And Chicana author Josefina López is known for, among other works, her *Real Women Have Curves* (1990), which after its stage success became an award-winning entry at the Sundance Film Festival.

Since Latino theatre is closely linked to its Spanish-speaking roots (*Lydia, Zoot Suit,* and Valdez's *I Don't Have to Show You No Stinkin' Badges* all employ a mixture of spoken Spanish and English), permanent and semipermanent bilingual Latino theatre companies flourish throughout the country, particularly in areas with significant Spanish-speaking populations. California's Culture Clash, cofounded in San Francisco in 1984 by Richard Montoya, Ric Salinas, and Herbert Siguenza, has become the most noted Chicano/Latino performance company in the United States, producing a wide-ranging repertoire in major theatres around the country (Lincoln Center, Kennedy Center, Seattle Repertory, Mark Taper Forum) comprising plays that range from *Water and Power,* an exposé of the hidden influence of business on local Los Angeles politics, a riotous adaptation of Aristophanes' comedy *The Birds,* and *American Night: The Ballad of Juan José,* about a young Mexican man's fantastical dream as he falls asleep while preparing for his American citizenship exam. Premiering at the Oregon Shakespeare Festival in 2010, this play occasioned the company, for the first time in its history, to add performances to meet the extraordinary demand for tickets. The Culture Clash founders—who are also the company's leading actors and directors—describe their methods as making a "performance collage" of "history, geography, 'urban excavation,' 'forensic poetry,' and storytelling—together in a contemporary, movable theater narrative through a Chicano point of view." And in New York, Repertorio Español, founded in 1968 by René Buch, regularly produces classical Spanish drama (including plays by Garcia Lorca, Calderón de la Barca, and Lope de Vega), along with contemporary Latino works (by Nilo Cruz and Carmen Rivera, among others) in both English and Spanish, seeking to fulfill artistic director Buch's dream to create a theatre that "instills cultural pride among Hispanics

Gloria Garayua is Gracie in Octavio Solis's Christmas play, *La Posada Mágica* (*The Magic Journey*), which echoes the traditional Latin American procession honoring Joseph and Mary's search for lodging in which to bear the Christ child. This 2008 production, directed by playwright Solis himself, was presented for the fifteenth consecutive year at South Coast Repertory in Costa Mesa, California.

from all Latin American countries, challenges misconceptions and ignorance about Spanish language, culture and traditions, and hopefully, creates and inspires the next generation of theatergoers and theatre artists."

Asian American theatre has claimed its share of the American theatrical scene as well; its quantum leap forward was David Henry Hwang's *M. Butterfly,* which received both a Tony Award and a Pulitzer Prize during its 1988 Broadway premiere. Hwang's play boldly reinterprets the story of Giacomo Puccini's opera *Madama Butterfly,* with careful attention to its political and sexual prejudices, while incorporating both Western and Beijing opera (xiqu) techniques into a contemporary, highly postmodern play that explodes "Orientalist" stereotypes about Asians as viewed by Westerners. Hwang's career continues to flourish (see the chapter titled "The Playwright") with his *Golden Child,* about

the conflict between Chinese traditions (foot-binding in particular) and contemporary values, which was nominated for a best-play Tony Award, and his semiautobiographical 2008 *Yellow Face,* which covers his own career as an Asian American playwright, including his winning the Tony and then losing his battle to keep a white actor from playing the lead role of an Asian character in the Broadway *Miss Saigon.*

Hwang is only the most prominent of the many Asian Americans now solidly ensconced in the American repertoire, however. Philip Kan Gotanda, Lonnie Carter, Diana Son, and Elizabeth Wong are among the others writing about relations between American and, respectively, Japanese, Filipino, Korean, and Chinese cultures.

Finally, Native American theatre is rapidly entering the American national theatre repertoire. The California-based Native Voices theatre

Photo Essay: Theatre in the Borderlands

1.

1. In a public assembly room in the city center, the audience gathers, sitting on folding chairs that surround the acting area. A handful of lights illuminate the hand-painted setting.

2. In the performance, "Little Brother" (Bryant Ranier Enriquez, *standing*) thinks he sees a ghost in his bedroom, as "Big Brother" (Rafael E. Martinez) rolls over in mock dismay.

Not all—or even most—Latino theatre activity in the United States is found in America's largest cities. The Borderlands Theatre was founded in Tucson, Arizona, in 1986, to provide theatrical entertainment for the local Mexican American population and create interchange among members of the Latino and Anglo communities in the Arizona-Sonora "borderlands"—the area that at times links and at other times divides Mexico and the United States.

Borderlands has no permanent theatre and owns minimal equipment, but it recruits plays, performers, and directors from both countries with the aid of National Endowment of the Arts funding along with a body of loyal community supporters. The pictured production, presented in English and Spanish versions on alternate nights, is Mexican playwright Javier Malpica's *Papá está en la Atlántida* (*Our Dad Is in Atlantis*), directed by Eva Tessler. It was a great success for the company in 2009, telling the heartbreaking story of two preteen Mexican brothers—played by adult actors Rafael E. Martinez and Bryant Ranier Enriquez—who, after their mother's death, try to walk through the Sonoran desert to find their father, who has illegally crossed the border to Atlanta (which the younger brother thinks is the magical kingdom of Atlantis).

Similar bilingual theatre companies can be found in most cities along America's southern frontier—Teatro Promoteo in Miami, Latino Teatro in Los Angeles, the Latino Theatre Alliance in Austin, Texas—as well as in northern cities including Teatro Pregones in New York City, the Gala Hispanic Theatre in Washington, and the all-female Teatro Luna in Chicago.

2.

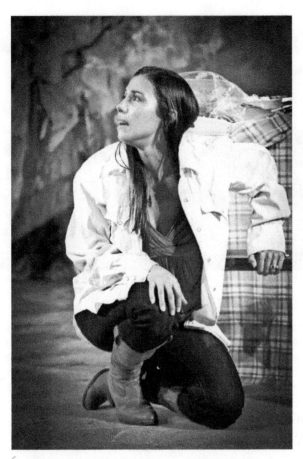

Choctaw-American actress Shyla Marlin plays Carlisle in Caroyln Dunn's *The Frybread Queen* in the 2011 premiere production in Los Angeles by Native Voices. The playwright and cast members were all of Native American heritage.

company performs Native American plays regularly at its Autry Theatre home base in Griffith Park, Los Angeles, and tours plays and play readings to the La Jolla Playhouse in San Diego; the company's 2011 world premiere of Cherokee Carolyn Dunn's The *Frybread Queen*—with an all-Native American cast— was one of the highlights of the Southern California theatre season (see photo). The Thunder Theatre, operated by the Haskell Indian Nations University in Lawrence, Kansas, is also devoted to producing Native American plays and training Native American theatre artists; its Web site lists more than one hundred Native American dramatists working around the country. Native American theatre, which is certainly the oldest form of performance on the North American continent, has once more come to public attention in the current century.

An International Theatre

Few countries, if any, have anywhere near the diversity of America's theatre. The Comédie Française, France's historic theatre founded in 1680, accepted its first black actor, Bakary Sangaré, only in 2002; he is still the only nonwhite person in the sixty-member company. Most European theatre companies (Ariane Mnouchkine's Théâtre de Soleil is an exception) have few or no black or Asian members; virtually all classical Asian companies have no European or North or South American members. But today's theatre is increasingly international, wherever you go.

Of course during much of its history theatre has crossed regional and national borders. In ancient Greece, nearly all of the diverse and often warring city-states on the Hellenic peninsula participated in the Great Dionysia in Athens, which, held in the spring, also attracted traders and visitors from throughout the Mediterranean world. In 326 B.C., Alexander the Great's armies brought Greek theatre all the way to the Ganges River in India, influencing the theatre that was to develop throughout all of Asia. In the sixteenth century, Shakespeare's London audiences included a broad mix of foreigners from throughout Europe; some of his plays toured Denmark and Germany during his lifetime. And Shakespeare's plays were set in many foreign lands—Italy, France, Egypt, Bohemia, Greece, Austria, Denmark, Scotland, and a fantasy island in the Mediterranean (or perhaps the Atlantic)—so his audiences must have had an interest in faraway places.

In the nineteenth century, with the advent of steamships, actors and even entire theatre companies began touring the world. American audiences became accustomed to seeing celebrated foreign actors performing in the great classic roles, sometimes even in their own native languages, and American actors toured abroad. The 1923–1924 American tours of Konstantin Stanislavsky's Moscow Art Theatre, which eventually played—in Russian—380 performances in Manhattan, Brooklyn, Newark, New Haven, Hartford, Chicago, Boston, Cleveland, Detroit, Pittsburgh, and Washington, provided an opportunity for American audiences to discover modern Russian theatre and revolutionized this country's acting style for decades to come. And the vastly increased speed and lowered cost of global travel in recent decades have allowed many of the world's greatest theatre companies to perform not only in the major centers of New York (at the Brooklyn Academy of Music and the summer Lincoln Center Theatre Festival) and Los Angeles (at the UCLA Center for the Art

The three-week Avignon Theatre Festival in the south of France, founded by Jean Vilar in 1947, uses the 2,000-seat "Honor Court" in the city's fourteenth-century Papal Palace, pictured here, as its major venue for productions it imports from around the world. But the Festival also hosts twenty or thirty additional productions that perform in more than a dozen other theatres in Avignon at the same time and oversees a "Festival du Off" that presents more than a thousand self-invited productions that spring up in the streets, parks, courtyards, and cafes of the city. As a truly international festival, it regularly appoints associate artistic directors from other countries to aid in its selections; these have included the German director Peter Ostermeier, the Lebanese playwright Wajdi Mouawad and, for 2012, the English director Simon McBurney.

of Performance) but also in smaller cities such as Ann Arbor, Michigan; and Davidson, North Carolina.

And for Americans able and willing to travel abroad, literally dozens of major international theatre festivals provide vast samplings of some of the greatest theatrical achievements of our time in a host of cities: Amsterdam, Edinburgh, Singapore, Berlin, Avignon, Paris (France), Spoleto (Italy), Tampere (Finland), Gdansk (Poland), Ibiza (Spain), Toga (Japan), Adelaide (Australia), Pècs (Hungary), and Curitiba (Brazil), and—in the most globally ambitious country of them all, Romania—in the cities of Sibiu, Cluj, Craiova, and Bucharest. In some cases these festival productions are provided with English translations (by earphones or supertitles), but most often the productions brought to international festivals are well-known classic plays that audiences can appreciate without proficiency in the production's language.

Nothing could prove more valuable for the world today than such cultural exchanges, for drama's capacity to serve as a vehicle for international communication goes beyond mere rhetoric and allows theatre artists and audiences from around the world to share—person to person—in the universals of human experience: hopes, fears, feelings, and compassion for the living.

A Macaronic Theatre

There is no single language sacrosanct in the theatre of today, as plays are increasingly written in multiple tongues. Critic Marvin Carlson uses the term *macaronic*—originally referring to the *maccarone*

(macaroni) of Latin and Old Italian as they were interwoven in the speech of medieval Italy—to describe plays that employ such a mingling mix of languages.

The European theatre has long been macaronic: even Shakespeare's plays include many lines (and a large part of two entire scenes) in French, Italian, Latin, or Welsh. Postmodern plays take this multilingualism much further. Canadian playwright David Fennario's *Balconville*, about the relationship of French-speaking and English-speaking Canadians, is presented in both languages of officially bilingual Canada. The French comedy *Les Aviateurs* is performed entirely in English—the language of aviation—although it is a thoroughly French play that (so far) has been performed only in France. *Endstation Amerika*, Frank Castorf's adaptation of Tennessee Williams's *A Streetcar Named Desire* for Berlin's Volksbühne ("People's Theatre"), was performed in a roughly equal mixture of German, French, and English. British dramatist David Edgar's *Pentecost* (the word refers to the Biblical "tongues of fire" of multiple languages) portrays a mix of frightened Kurdish, Romani, Azeri, Mozambican, Hindi, Afghan, and Bosnian refugees, all speaking their own languages along with their individual versions of English. The American macaronic theatre has recently generated Octavio Solis's Spanish-English *Lydia*, Lonnie Carter's English-Tagalog (Filipino) *The Romance of Magno Rubio*, David Henry Hwang's Chinese-English *Chinglish*, and Tony Kushner's French-Arabic-Pashto-Dari-English-Esperanto *Homebody/Kabul*.

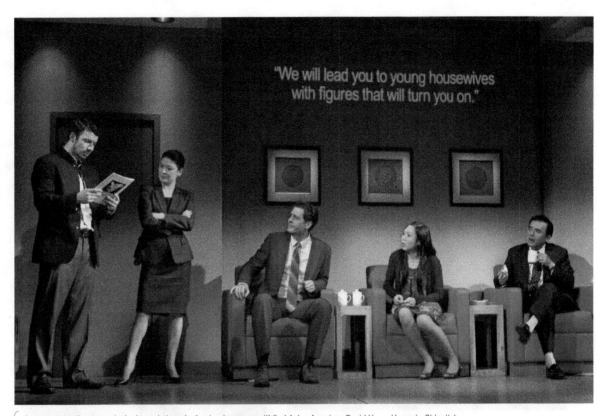

"We will lead you to young housewives with figures that will turn you on."

Anyone struggling to read a bad translation of a foreign language will find Asian American David Henry Hwang's *Chinglish* a very funny play. About an American businessman who seeks to expand his entreprenurial enterprise in China, the play is written in both Chinese and (fractured) English, helped (and often hindered, as above) by projected supertitles. Premiering at Chicago's Goodman Theatre, the play afterward enjoyed a three-month 2011–2012 Broadway run. Direction was by Leigh Silverman and scenic design by David Korins.

It is both realistic and poignant for the characters in all those plays to speak in different languages, for in each case linguistic variety conveys differing aspects of cultural identity—as well as the difficulties inherent in intercultural communication—while still propelling the dramaturgical basics of plot, character, and the creation of audience empathy. Many of us face these linguistic challenges in our increasingly multicultural lives, and a macaronic theatre mirrors our evolving nature. It is hard to overestimate the importance of this movement, which can powerfully depict conflicts between cultural survival and assimilation, and give voice to the multiple perspectives of societies rent with factionalism and longing for harmony.

A Theatre of Difference

Gender, race, ethnicity, geography, and language are not the only sources of the new voices entering the theatre's mainstream in the current era. Sexual preference has emerged as a defining issue for many theatre groups, festivals, and publications that seek to examine the political, cultural, and aesthetic implications of gay- and lesbian-themed drama. Sexual preference remained buried deeply in the closet during most of the theatre's history. As recently as 1958 the representation of homosexuality was illegal in England and widely (though not legally) suppressed in America. The love that "dared not speak its name" came to the stage only through authors' implications and audiences' inferences. Gay playwrights, such as Oscar Wilde, Tennessee Williams, Gertrude Stein, Edward Albee, William Inge, and Gore Vidal, were forced to speak—at certain critical moments in their work—only by innuendo and through oblique code words.

Dramatic changes occurred in the late 1960s, when gay and lesbian life and gay and lesbian issues began to be treated as serious dramatic subjects, most notably by Mart Crowley in his groundbreaking

Martin Sherman's 1979 *Bent* received a Tony nomination for its harrowing tale of the treatment of German homosexuals during the rise of Adolf Hitler, and it paved the way for the serious—even tragic—theatrical treatment of homophobia. In this 2006 English revival at the Trafalgar Studios in London, Max (Alan Cumming, *right*) and Rudy (Kevin Trainor) are gay men imprisoned by the Nazis. Max pretends to be Jewish under the misapprehension that he will be treated less harshly. Costumes are by Mark Bouman.

Jefferson Mays, as German transvestite Charlotte von Mahlsdorf and his treasured antique record player in Doug Wright's multiple-award-winning *I Am My Own Wife*. Charlotte is one of thirty-three roles Mays plays in the show, which crosses gender, linguistic, and time barriers.

American comedy *The Boys in the Band* (1968). Since then, sexual-preference issues have become principal or secondary topics in hundreds of plays, including mainstream Broadway musicals (*La Cage aux Folles, Falsettos, Kiss of the Spider Woman, The Wild Party, Avenue Q*), popular comedies (*Love! Valour! Compassion!, Jeffrey, The Little Dog Laughed*), and serious dramas (*Bent, M. Butterfly, Gross Indecency, The Laramie Project, Take Me Out, I Am My Own Wife*). Gay actors have come out of the closet (most of them theatrically) to advocate gay rights worldwide, as did the British classical star Ian McKellen in his one-man performance "A Knight Out" at the Gay Games in New York in 1994. Gay plays have entered the global mainstream as well, as exemplified by the Shameless Theatre company, which opened a theatre

in London's Victoria district in 2008 wholly dedicated to plays on gay themes, and the annual Gay Theatre Festival in Dublin, Ireland, which has presented gay-themed plays from Poland, Germany, Zimbabwe, France, Spain, Australia, South Africa, Venezuela, Canada, America, England, and Ireland since its creation in 2004.

In the wake of a new and terrible illness, a growing genre of AIDS plays, most notably Larry Kramer's 1985 *The Normal Heart*, addressed the tragic human consequences of this disease, whose initial victims in the United States and Europe were predominantly gay. Although AIDS has now become an arguably manageable disease, the issue has remained a hot one on the American stage: in 1992, Tony Kushner's *Angels in America*, treating AIDS as central to what Kushner

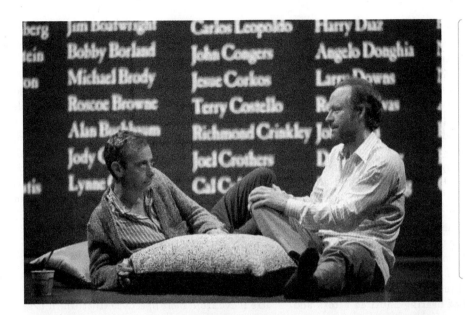

Larry Kramer's 1985 off-Broadway production of *The Normal Heart* was very instrumental in making the American public, and then the government, far more responsive to the AIDS crisis than it had been. The play's 2011 revival, on Broadway this time, won three Tony Awards. Shown are Joe Mantello (*left*), as Ned Weeks, an AIDS activist, and John Benjamin Hickey as Felix, Ned's love interest. Looming behind them are the names of the dead and dying. George C. Wolfe and Joel Grey codirected the production; Kramer, whose activism on this issue has never slowed, was out front after most performances, handing out blistering letters to exiting audience members so as "to get the word out, again."

Deaf West is a Los Angeles theatre for the hearing-impaired, and its production of the musical *Big River*, in which characters alternately speak, sing, and sign their roles, began on the company's tiny home stage. From there it moved to the much larger Mark Taper Forum and then to Broadway, winning critical acclaim not merely for overcoming its "handicapped" label but for creating an altogether new theatre aesthetic of hearing and "seeing" musical drama at the same time. Tyrone Giordano (*left*) plays Huckleberry Finn, with Michael McElroy as Jim, at the American Airlines Theater in 2003.

termed his "gay fantasia on national themes," proved the country's most celebrated stage production of the decade, while in 2011, Kramer's *Normal Heart* won the Tony Award for Best Revival.

Differently-abled people are also represented by new plays as well as by theatre companies that were created specifically for these voices and for expanding differently-abled audiences. In New York, Theatre Breaking Through Barriers (until 2008 known as Theatre by the Blind) employs blind and/or otherwise disabled actors for all of its productions. The National Theatre of the Deaf in Connecticut and Deaf West in Los Angeles are two of several groups that create theatre by and for the hearing-impaired, employing American Sign Language (ASL) as their primary verbal dramatic medium. With Mark Medoff's prize-winning *Children of a Lesser God,* the challenges of the hearing-impaired reached a broad popular audience, and a number of hearing-impaired actors and actresses found national recognition.

Nontraditional Casting

In America, particularly, color-blind or deliberately cross-color casting—once thought of as daring—has become almost routine, especially in the classics. As audiences more easily accept the notion that they are watching "performances of characters" rather than "characters" themselves, the theatre has increasingly cast African Americans in roles once thought to be reserved for whites, and, occasionally, vice versa, as when the white actor Patrick Stewart played the black Othello opposite a black actress playing the white Desdemona.

The New York Shakespeare Festival has been a leader in nontraditional casting, choosing Angela Bassett for Lady Macbeth, Morgan Freeman for Petruchio, and Denzel Washington for Richard III. This is not limited to New York: in Los Angeles, the black actress Fran Bennett played King Lear and in Oregon, a state with less than 6 percent African Americans and Asian Americans combined, the Oregon Shakespeare Festival recruits and engages an acting company in which a full one-third of the members are non-Caucasian. Black, Asian, and Hispanic actors are often cast in American productions today as Elizabethan royalty, French aristocrats, Greek gods, or Judeo-Christian Bible figures, thus dispensing fully with stereotypes of received images.

Cross-gender casting is also commonplace in the current era in most countries, as in the case of Bennett's *King Lear* in Los Angeles and Mark Rylance's *Cleopatra and Olivia* at London's Globe Theatre. By now, female Hamlets, Prosperos, Richard IIs and Richard IIIs are everywhere apparent—as are male Rosalinds and Lady Bracknells. And in *Bridge and Tunnel* on Broadway in 2006, the black, Baltimore-born actress Sarah Jones played fourteen different roles—male and female, black and white, Pakistani, Lithuanian, Mexican, Russian, Jamaican, Jordanian, Chinese, and African American—all with uncanny accuracy, charm, and respectful admiration of the shared problems and challenges of immigration and assimilation, the "bridges and tunnels," that affect a great majority of our current national corpus.

A Spectacular Theatre

Aristotle considered spectacle the least of his six components of theatre, but the past decades have seen theatre move from mere spectacle (that which is seen) to the totally spectacular (that which astounds). In part, this shift reflects the development of new technologies, affecting both visual and sound design; and in part, it reflects the emergence of a new aesthetic.

Some of the new theatre technology (see the chapter titled "Designers and Technicians") comes from cinema, with its dazzling computer graphics, animations, and digitized motion-capture, and from the contemporary circus. The effects to be seen in films like *Star Wars* and *Lord of the Rings,* and in Cirque du Soleil productions like *O* and *Kà,* have encouraged stage directors and designers to discover computerized technologies that in a matter of nanoseconds can create and remove lakes and replace them with tall buildings or vast cauldrons of hellfire, can move lights and change their colors second by second, and can produce seemingly magical illusions and even upend whole stages, plunging the actors into the unknown below. And the pop/rock concert stage has created sound systems capable of reaching ear-blasting volume while still maintaining clarity of tone and mellowness of timbre, reaching every seat in the house simultaneously and in the process overthrowing, as it were, the very speed of physical sound.

Such spectacular effects reach their apex in the high-budget (and high-priced) Broadway musicals, with their high-wire flying actors (*Spider-Man*), falling chandeliers (*Phantom of the Opera*), and ascending helicopters (*Miss Saigon*), and in Canada's Cirque du Soleil extravaganzas with their gyrating stages and loudspeakers fitted behind every seat in the audience. But audiences have come to expect these effects in

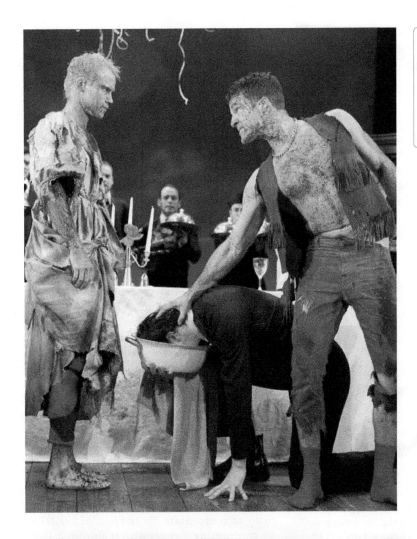

Copying the format of Shakespeare's own theatre, England's Propeller is an all-male acting company directed by Edward Hall. Thus in Hall's 2006 production of Shakespeare's *The Taming of the Shrew*, Dugald Bruce Lockhart (*right*) plays Petruchio (the tamer) and Simon Scardifield plays Katherine (the "shrew"). This is no mere novelty, however, as it allows the play to seriously engage with the real-life implications of marital cruelty and abuse.

In the Globe Theatre of Shakespeare's time, men played all the roles. As the Artistic Director of the "new" Globe Theatre in London from 1995 to 2005, Mark Rylance continued the tradition from time to time—in this case by playing Lady Olivia in *Twelfth Night,* for which he received England's Olivier Award, the equivalent of America's Tony.

In Karin Henkel's radically adapted 2011 production of Shakespeare's *Macbeth* at the Munich (Germany) Kammerspiele (Chamber Theatre), the bloody Macbeth is played by the female actor Jana Schulz (*left*), with Katja Bükle playing his Lady—as well as one of the witches. The production emphasizes Lady Macbeth's famous "unsex me here" line, making gender as well as political points as it goes, and the production's languages are also mixed, including German, Flemish, Swiss-German, and English. Despite the startling text and plot changes, the production was still titled "Macbeth von William Shakespeare," making clear that German (and Eastern European) theatergoers no longer expect productions of classic plays to always stick to their original texts.

theorist Antonin Artaud argued fiercely in the 1930s that theatre should have "no more masterpieces," and that words in dramas should be valued more for their vibrations than for their meanings and have only the importance they have in dreams. Artaud's proposed theatre was one of overwhelming sounds and visual images that would dominate the stage. His arguments, not fully tested in his own time, have proven greatly influential in ours, starting with the unscripted *happenings* of the 1960s and the more lasting *performance art* that followed in the 1980s and continues to this day.

Performance Art

Performance art is another kind of spectacle: it is primarily visual and conceptual, and all but anti-dramatic with its lack of concern for plot, character development, or dramaturgical structure. Successful performance art is, instead, arresting, shocking, and provocative, often with a political thrust. The movement became prominent in a famous presentation by noted performance artist Karen Finley in the late 1980s in which she smeared her naked body with chocolate to represent the exploitation and sexual abasement of women; this performance stimulated the National Endowment for the Arts (NEA) to revoke the funding they had awarded her in 1990. For her subsequent *Shut Up and Love Me*, Ms. Finley again smeared herself with chocolate, this time inviting audience members to lick it—at twenty dollars a lick—to compensate for the loss of her NEA grant. By confronting viewers with their own lust, and disgust, Finley creates a vividly memorable unease.

Many other performance artists are active today, among the best known being Laurie Anderson, a master of many voices, musical instruments and original ideas since the 1970s; and Serbian-born Marina Abramović, whose 2010 performance entitled "The Artist is Present" at New York's Museum of Modern Art consisted of her sitting, in complete silence, all day every day, for a month and a half—716 hours and 30 minutes in all—while museum-goers took a seat across from her one at a time to have a silent conversation" with the woman many call "the mother of performance art."

Verbatim Theatre

Theatre has always dealt with current politics. Indeed, the potentially short lead time between

such shows—pricey as they are—to the extent that audiences for Broadway musicals willingly accept that the "characters" whose lives and fortunes they're presumably following have visible microphones pasted on their foreheads (or, in the case of the naked actors in Stephen Sondheim's *Passion,* wires running down their backs), in return for the amplified and digitally processed sound they enjoy in return.

There is also an aesthetic behind the theatre's current turn from spectacle to spectacular. The French

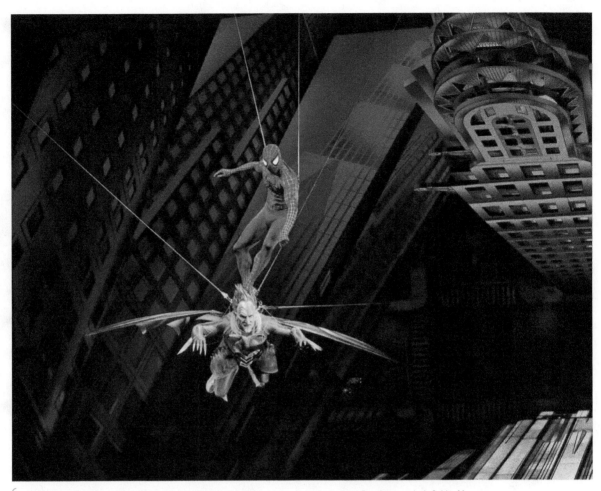

Spider-Man and the Green Goblin grapple with each other high above the audience in the 2011 Broadway musical, *Spider-Man, Turn off the Dark*. The aerial choreography was by Daniel Ezralow.

initial conception and finished product is one of the advantages live theatre has over film. But the twenty-first century has seen a virtual explosion of up-to-the-minute dramas performed on major stages, particularly in England. Many of these may be called "verbatim theatre," as they have been developed from transcripts of real-life speeches and interviews. Here are a few examples:

- *My Name Is Rachel Corrie* was compiled from the diaries and e-mail messages of American peace activist Corrie, who died in Gaza in 2003 while trying to stop an Israeli bulldozer from demolishing a Palestinian home. Despite its success at London's Royal Court Theatre in 2005,

its scheduled New York opening was "postponed" (in effect canceled) the following year in deference to reactions from persons opposed to the play's theme.

- *Stuff Happens*, by celebrated British playwright David Hare, deals with the creation of the British-American coalition during the buildup to the Iraq War; the play's title comes from U.S. Defense Secretary Donald Rumsfeld's response, during a press conference, to the looting of Baghdad.

- *Sin, a Cardinal Deposed* was created by playwright Michael Murphy from a thousand pages of court deposition by Boston's Cardinal Bernard Law,

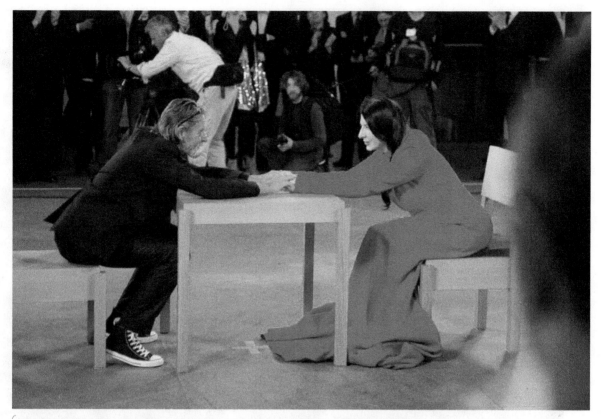

In this 2010 performance art piece, "The Artist Is Present" by Marina Abramović, the distinguished Serbian artist sat silently, all day every day during its run, across from individuals who came to view the work. Performance art is clearly not theatre—rather it is something close to "theatre without drama"—but it has had a broad influence on theatre artists around the world.

plus letters and public documents from priests, doctors, and sexual-abuse victims. The verbatim script was performed by six actors of the Bailiwick Theatre in Chicago in 2004 to great—and often tearful—acclaim.

- *Black Watch* was compiled by Gregory Burke from intensely gripping verbatim interviews he conducted with soldiers from Scotland's 72nd ("Black Watch") regiment after their return from the war in Iraq. Premiered by the National Theatre of Scotland in 2006, it won four Olivier Awards and has since toured the world, with a four-city American tour in 2011.

A Dangerous Theatre

A theatre that is drawn directly from today's news, that is open and diverse, experimental and macaronic, is

likely to be shocking as well. And so the late modern and postmodern theatre has increasingly been seen as a dangerous one.

The nudity and sensory assault of contemporary theatre stagings no longer cause much consternation. Audiences in the twenty-first century generally take these in stride; indeed, the 2009 revival of *Hair* proved a mainstream Broadway hit, with most of the audience considering its famous full-cast frontal nudity tableau ending the first act more quaint than electrifying. Danger in today's theatre is more apt to come from violence and vehemence than the breaking of social codes. Physical torture, in particular, has become an increasingly popular theme in modern world drama, as in Christopher Durang's *Why Torture Is Wrong, and the People Who Love Them*. In this 2009 play, Durang frames the brutality of his subject into a genre that might be termed lunatic farce and virtually turns members of

Paul James Corrigan, Paul Rattray, and Emun Elliott play members of Scotland's Black Watch in the verbatim drama by that name that dealt with the horrors of the Iraq war. Created by the National Theatre of Scotland in 2006, it has been performed around the world, enjoying a sold-out, four-city American tour in 2011.

the audience into pretzels as they find themselves laughing hysterically—despite themselves—at the cruelest scenes imaginable. Other recent plays on torture, such as Martin McDonagh's *Lieutenant of Inishmore* and *The Pillowman* (both nominated for Tony Awards); David Wiener's *Extraordinary Chambers* about the tortures and killings of Cambodia's Khmer Rouge regime, premiering at Los Angeles's Geffen Playhouse in 2011; and the New Haven Long Wharf's reading of Philippe Sands's book *Torture Team* in the same year, are also dark, ironic works

in which the agonies of the victims are emotionally distanced from the audience, in Brechtian fashion. As a result, each play's political message is evoked indirectly rather than through empathy alone. Other, more direct plays about actual human savagery—during World Wars, the Holocaust, at Abu Ghraib prison in Iraq, and on the battlefield—have also proliferated worldwide. Violent and unwanted sex in Africa is the central subject of Lynn Nottage's *Ruined*, the 2009 Pulitzer Prize winner (the title refers to the mutilation of a young woman's genitalia

No playwright in recent years has caused more controversy than England's Sarah Kane, whose postmodern, largely expressionistic works are filled with gruesome violence and carnality. Her first play, *Blasted*, presents shocking images of rape, racism, and cannibalism that caused a theatre scandal at its 1995 London premiere—which led to hundreds of productions of this and her four other plays throughout the theatre world. Kane was certainly England's most talked-about new playwright when, tragically, she took her own life in 1999, just weeks after her twenty-eighth birthday. In this production, directed by Thomas Ostermeier and seen at the Avignon Theatre Festival in 2005, Katharina Schüttler plays Cate, kneeling over her rapist Ian (played by Ulrich Mühe), who by this time has himself been raped, blinded, and battered to near-death by a soldier in the play's wartime environment. Scenery is by Jan Pappelbaum; costumes are by Almut Eppinger.

With Daniel Radcliffe in the leading role, *Equus* proved a solid success at both London's National Theatre and its 2008–2009 Broadway engagement. Based on a true story, Shaffer's play treats an engaging but disturbed teenage boy, Alan Strang, whose passion for horses has displaced his more conventional sexual development. *Equus* (Latin for "horse") achieves its astonishing climax when, totally naked in a horse-filled stable, Alan fails to consummate an impromptu sexual encounter with a naked girl and, in a fit of maniacal despair, blinds the onlooking "horses" with a hoof pick. The play's twenty-first-century revival made clear that nudity on stage, though perhaps no longer shocking, retains its tremendous power to create an intense theatrical impact.

threats and the eventual cancellation of a planned 1998 New York opening of Terrence McNally's *Corpus Christi*, in which a Jesus-like character was to have sexual relations with his disciples. (The play finally opened in New York ten years later, causing no disturbance at all.) And Neil LaBute's violent, baby-murdering *The Distance from Here* was met with outrage by some subscribers and loud screams from at least one audience (as well as plaudits from many critics) at its Manhattan Theatre Club premiere. Theatre today continually treads on toes—and sometimes the toes kick back.

A Theatre of Community

Although most of the theatre discussed and pictured in this book was created by trained professional artists, we must never forget that theatre's origins are located in performances created not by theatre professionals but by social communities—religious and ethnic—whose works were intended not for the entertainment of spectators but for the benefit, and often the rapture, of their own participants. The African dance-drama, the Egyptian resurrection plays, the Greek dithyrambs, and the medieval *Quem Queritis* trope were basically celebrations of their societies' cultures, and their performers were the primary celebrants. Such theatres—whose works are created not only *for* a community but *by* it—continue today. They eventually may attract audiences, attain box office income, and pay professional salaries, but they are primarily expressions, celebrations, and sometimes critiques of the cultures of their creators.

In America, such groups have existed in tribal Native American cultures since before the landing of Columbus. In twentieth-century America, several "workers' theatres" in the 1930s created theatre pieces by and for the American laborer. The most famous, Clifford Odets's *Waiting for Lefty*, was produced in 1935 by the Group Theatre, which became one of the country's first prominent theatre ensembles dedicated to social causes. Other such theatre ensembles followed, many devoted not merely to creating theatre works by and for members of their community, but also to touring their productions to localities previously unserved by the theatre at all, including Luis Valdez's El Teatro Campesino (the "farmworkers' theatre," mentioned earlier) and the Free Southern Theatre founded in New Orleans by African American playwright John O'Neal in 1965.

One of the most gripping contemporary plays about urban British violence is Mark Ravenhill's shockingly titled *Shopping and Fucking*. Andrew Clover is the besieged actor in the original London production, at the Royal Court Theatre, in 1996.

when she is raped with a bayonet), and rapes, killings, dismemberments, and cannibalism are the subjects of the late Sarah Kane's *Blasted*, which, though premiering in 1995, became a worldwide success with its 2001 London revival following Kane's suicide.

Even the language of theatre has become violent, perhaps starting in America with David Mamet's 1983 *Glengarry Glen Ross*—with lines like "*Fuck* marshalling the leads. What the fuck talk is that?" The trend caught on quickly, and now even the titles of Mark Ravenhill's 1996 *Shopping and Fucking* and Stephen Adly Guirgis's 2011 *The Motherf**ker With the Hat* have forced family newspapers to puzzle out how to list such works in their pages. A play's theme or plot can be dangerous as well; accusations of religious defamation led to bomb

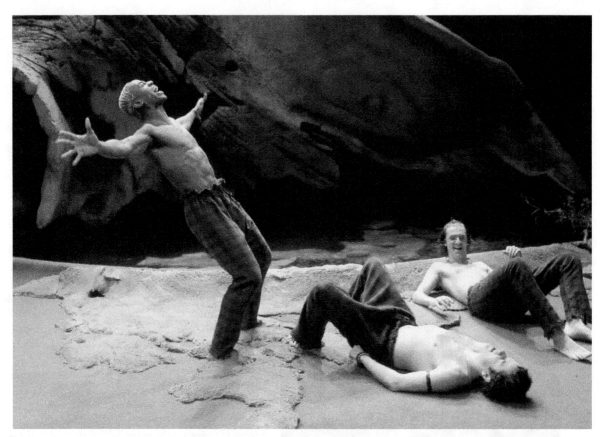

The director of Howard Brenton's *Romans in Britain* was hauled into Old Bailey—the venerable British court—when the play first opened at England's National Theatre in 1980. He was accused of creating an act of "gross indecency" when actors simulated the rape of a naked Celt male by a naked Roman soldier during the Roman occupation two thousand years previously. The director (Michael Bogdanov) won his case, but Brenton's powerful play, which draws parallels with modern-day English rule in Northern Ireland, still sparks furious controversy. This Sheffield, England, revival in 2006, with its luxuriously verdant setting by Ralph Koltai, may suggest an even deeper parallel that the author did not consider: the rape of the natural planet by civilization. Samuel West directed.

Unique in this movement, however, is the Cornerstone Theater, founded in 1986 by Harvard graduates Bill Rauch and Alison Carey and now headed by Michael John Garcés. The Cornerstone's goal has been to engage with local cultural groups in creating new theatrical works (often based on classic dramas) adapted to each group's interests, fears, and aspirations. These works are then performed—by the merged Cornerstone and community groups—within the community, usually on a free or pay-what-you-can basis. The response is usually electric: not only are these plays heralded as absorbing and entertaining, but they initiate new cultural discourse and even social change in almost every community where they have been engaged. Examples

of Cornerstone's work are as varied as American culture itself, as, for example:

- *Tartoof:* Molière's *Tartuffe,* adapted to portray a disintegrating farm family with a cast and crew of fifty-five Kansans; performed in Norcatur, Kansas (population 215).

- *Romeo & Juliet:* performed by a racially integrated cast in Port Gibson, Mississippi (population 2,371).

- *The House on Walker River:* an adaptation of Aeschylus's trilogy *The Oresteia,* staged on an Indian reservation in Schurz, Nevada (population 325).

- *Steelbound:* adapted from the tragedy *Prometheus Bound,* featuring steelworkers at a defunct Bethlehem Steel plant in Pennsylvania and staged in a vacant factory.

- *The Toy Truck:* adapted from a Sanskrit epic and performed in English, Spanish, Mandarin, and Korean with residents of the nation's largest low-income housing complex for seniors.

- *Touch the Water:* written by Julie Hébert, directed by Juliette Carrillo, and created in collaboration with, according to the Cornerstone, "local river residents, engineers, biologists, environmentalists, activists, advocates and patrons who walk, fish, bike and ride horses on the Los Angeles River." Staged in 2009 next to the river—which is mostly a vast ribbon of concrete through the city's downtown, with barely a trickle of water—the play seeks to explore the ways laws "shape and disrupt communities."

Theatre, Cornerstone's founder Rauch believed, is "a rehearsal for changing the world." In asserting this goal, Rauch reached back to the most ancient role of theatre as the broadest possible community forum—not merely an entertainment for an elite "theatergoing" class but a participatory ceremony involving truth, fiction, struggle, and art, welded together into performance and witnessing. His successors are clearly continuing in this tradition.

Movement Art and Dance-Theatre

With emphases in postmodern performance shifting from verbal semantics to the sheer sensory impact of images and sound, contemporary "theatre" listings now often include stage events consisting almost entirely of expressive movement, dance, music, and lighting—events in which rhythm, color, sound, and athleticism reign over plot, character, and language. Many of these groups enjoy enormous popularity and have been fully embraced by the commercial as well as the experimental theatre communities.

At least in the popular mind, *movement art* might be said to date from the early 1990s when Luke Cresswell, a percussionist and composer, and Steve McNichols, an actor and writer, created *Stomp,* a storyless and purely percussive performance piece in 1991; it proved a great success in both London and New York and has run ever since in those cities and many others around the world. *Stomp* employs an assortment of garbage can lids, pipes, brooms, and other everyday objects for its drumming; its rhythms are furious, its choreography is explosive, and its intensity is relentless—and often comic.

Blue Man Group, which followed, is a similarly plotless, percussive performance that also employs riotous clowning, interaction with the audience, and amazing food fights; it is performed by three head-shaved actors

Blue Man Group, now running lavish and apparently permanent productions in six cities in the United States and Europe, began as an unknown three-man percussion ensemble performing in the streets and eventually in a tiny off-Broadway theatre. Extraordinary drumming, lighting, physical dexterity, and the now-famous iridescent blue makeup have characterized Group performers since the beginning.

Martha Clarke's *The Garden of Earthly Delights,* based on a painting (from about 1503) by Hieronymus Bosch, was a seminal creation in American dance-theatre in 1984. Shown here is Clarke's re-creation of the work in 2008 in the same theatre (the off-Broadway Minneta Lane) where it sparked even greater public enthusiasm than at its premiere.

Susan Stroman directed and choreographed *Contact,* one of the first musical hits of the twenty-first century. Debra Yates is the dazzling dancer in the yellow dress who attracts the life-changing attention of Boyd Gaines (*spotlighted behind her*), who plays a burnt-out advertising exec.

covered from the neck up in super-glossy blue goop. The avant-garde group was created in New York City by former school pals Chris Wink, Matt Goldman, and Phil Stanton, who opened their first show, *Tubes,* at the tiny off-Broadway Astor Place Theatre in 1991. They (and their professional heirs) are now a near-permanent fixture in New York, Boston, Chicago, Berlin, Orlando, and Las Vegas, and may also be seen on tour in more than fifty American cities each year and on board the Norwegian Cruise Line.

Dance theatre, the mixture of speech and dramatic choreography, was popularized by Pina Bausch in Germany and has reached prominence in America through the work of Martha Clarke, a veteran of the Pilobolus dance troupe. Clarke first received wide acclaim for her dance-theatre pieces in the late 1980s, particularly *The Garden of Earthly Delights,* based on the famous painting by Hieronymus Bosch; she refashioned and revived this production to wide acclaim in 2008–2009. Her major works in the current century include *Vienna: Lusthaus,* which evoked the artistic and sexual ferment of Vienna at the time of painter-designer Gustav Klimt, and *Kaos,* a dance-theatre piece based on stories by Italian playwright Luigi Pirandello, which includes a spoken Italian text (with projected English translations) conveying tales of tragic madness, sexual passion, and despair among the inhabitants of a dusty Sicilian village.

Despite the tragic story, dance and minstrelsy play major roles in director/choreographer Susan Stroman's production of *The Scottsboro Boys*, which dramatically explores the 1931 conviction and jailing of nine black teenage boys on charges of a "gang rape" on the Southern Railroad that quite obviously never took place.

The dance-theatre of the present has also been enhanced by innovative choreographers who work in pure dance. A prize example of this is Susan Stroman, who has choreographed for the New York City Ballet as well as choreographing and directing Broadway's *The Producers* and *The Scottsboro Boys*. The versatile Stroman scored an immense success with her all-but-wordless *Contact* in 2000, which surprisingly won the Tony Award for best play while Stroman took the Tony for best director. Billed as a "dance play," *Contact* consists of three separate pieces connected only by the theme of romantic linkups: "Swinging," in which Fragonard's famous eighteenth-century French painting of a girl on a swing comes to life as a three-way sex romp; "Did You Move?", a housewife's seriocomic fantasy in a chaotic, outer-borough, 1950s New York restaurant; and the title piece, "Contact," in which an alcoholic and burnt-out advertising executive tries to commit suicide after failing to make contact, in a high-voltage dance club, with a sexy lady dazzlingly dressed in brilliant yellow. (For more on Susan Stroman, see the photo essay in the chapter titled "The Director.")

Solo Performance

Although Anton Chekhov wrote a short play for a single actor (*On the Harmfulness of Tobacco,* in which the character is a lecturer addressing his audience), only in recent times have authors seriously entertained the possibilities of full-length plays employing a single actor. Sometimes these are little more than star vehicles or extended monologues, often based on historical characters, as, for example, Hal Holbrook's long-running portrayal of America's great writer in *Mark Twain Tonight,* James Whitmore's rendition of America's feisty thirty-third president in *Give 'Em Hell, Harry!,* and Julie Harris's recurrent tours as Emily Dickinson in *The Belle of Amherst.* More fully dramatized works followed in the 1990s, however, when Jay Presson Allen wrote two intriguing and generally successful Broadway plays for solo actors, most notably *Tru,* about novelist and society darling Truman Capote in his last, despairing days. Other noteworthy solo performance plays include Lily Tomlin's portrayal of all seventeen characters in Jane Wagner's wonderfully amusing and affecting

The Argentine movement art company De La Guarda was founded in 1993 by a group of theatre students who, unable to find acting jobs upon graduation, created their own, highly original form of expression in interactive aerial ballet. Company performers mostly fly over and into their standing, swaying audience—which is simultaneously assaulted by rain, smoke, and wind and blasted by pummeling music and sound. The company's most recent production, *Fuertzabruta* (*Brute Force*)—seen here in its run at the Edinburgh International Festival in Scotland—has elements of circus, rave, rock concert, striptease, and fraternity party and has been performed around the world.

Search for Signs of Intelligent Life in the Universe, Patrick Stewart's one-man presentation of Charles Dickens's *A Christmas Carol,* in which the celebrated Shakespearean actor (and *Star Trek* star) played all the roles, and Ed Harris's great performance in Neil LaBute's *Wrecks,* a modern and solo version of *Oedipus Rex* that premiered in Ireland in 2005.

More socially engaged solo performances, however, have redefined the genre. Jeff Weiss's epic narratives of (presumably) his life on the Lower East Side, *. . . And That's How the Rent Gets Paid,* probably began the trend at the Performing Garage in New York's SoHo during the 1970s and 1980s. In the next decade, Eric Bogosian's series of intense and penetrating performances, savage and comic by turns, with their indelible cast of American low-life characters—pimps and whores, addicts and agents, executives and rock stars, panhandlers and jocks (*Drinking in America; Sex, Drugs, and Rock & Roll; Wake Up and Smell the Coffee*)—created a giant social panorama of life on the social fringes. Anna Deveare Smith's *Fires in the Mirror, Twilight: Los Angeles 1992,* and most recently (2011) *Lay Me Down Easy* are all solo narratives, in multiple voices, that respectively portray the days of rage in Crown Heights, Brooklyn, following the violent deaths of an African American and a Hassidic Jew; the Los Angeles riots following the acquittal of white police officers charged with the beating of the black motorist, Rodney King; and the current crisis in health care. Many solo performances are autobiographical; Colombian-born John Leguizamo's performances of

Danny Hoch is one of today's most exciting solo performers. He is seen here in a collage of three of the nine characters—black and white, male and female, English- and Spanish-speaking—that he plays, without change of makeup, in his *Taking Over.* The play premiered at Berkeley Repertory Theatre in 2008, then was performed in the Bronx, in Queens, and at the Public Theatre in Manhattan. The play concerns the gentrification—too rapid in Hoch's opinion—of his Williamsburg neighborhood in Brooklyn.

Freak and *Sexaholix,* both set in Leguizamo's childhood borough of Queens (New York), are hugely comic and often deeply poignant autobiographical journeys of his childhood and adolescence; his 2011 Broadway hit, *Ghetto Klown,* describes his later battles trying to combine a stage and film career with fame, family, and friendships. And Danny Hoch, who came to public attention with his *Jails, Hospitals & Hip Hop* in the late 1990s, is the most recent solo performer on the national scene. Hoch's 2008 *Taking Over,* a series of eight monologues on the theme of urban gentrification (elite classes "taking over" ethnic urban neighborhoods), thrilled audiences in its Berkeley Repertory Theatre (California) premiere and subsequent engagements at New York's Public Theatre and the Mark Taper Forum in Los Angeles. Specializing in luminous portrayals of loudmouthed social outcasts—of both sexes and all

races and persuasions—who habituate New York's working-class boroughs, and fluent in both English and a handful of Latin American dialects, Hoch gives a brief history of every technique and innovation discussed in this chapter: a glorious theatrical mashup of the postmodern, nonlinear, multicultural, macaronic, foul-mouthed, and politically engaged styles of performance that characterize our times.

Puppet Performance

The theatre does not always limit itself to human performers, and puppet theatre in one form or another has flourished since ancient Egyptian times. In the eastern forms of Indonesian *wayang kulit* and Japanese *bunraku,* puppetry has been a major format for more than a thousand years; in the West, it has provided children's entertainment since the *commedia dell arte,* with Punch and

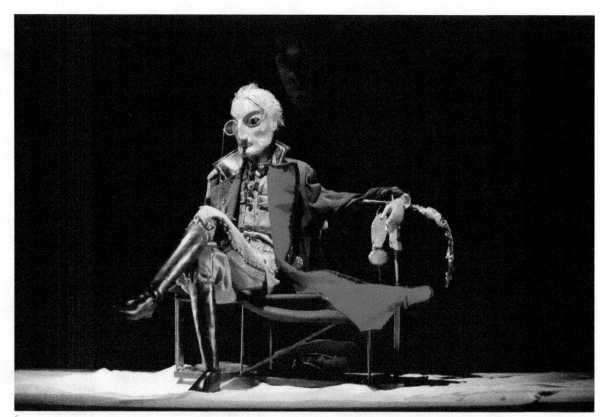

The brilliant puppetry (*shown above and at right*) of theatre artist Rezo Gabriadze, from the Tblisi National Theatre Studio in formerly Soviet Georgia, is abundantly evident in his production of *The Battle of Stalingrad*, which was presented in New York by the Lincoln Center Theatre Festival in 2010. A fantasy about the intermingling of undying love and a hideous war, of the interactions of men, women, horses, and even ants, it creates a dream-like atmosphere that could never be realized solely by human actors.

A puppet leads the live actor in this 2009 Paris production of *Oedipus Rex,* where the blind seer Teiresias (Stéphane Dausse) is led onto the stage by his puppet guide. Philippe Adrien directed.

Judy shows in England and "Guignol" performances in France still performed regularly. Today's global theatre, however, has seen a considerable increase in puppetry for adult audiences in the West and East alike, particularly in the avant-garde, where Peter Schumann's Bread and Puppet Theatre has become prominent in America since the 1960s, and *Shockheaded Peter,* a British adaptation of the nineteenth-century German classic *Strewelpeter* (in which bad little boys have their fingers chopped off—a scene difficult to stage effectively with live actors) toured the world in 1998. In more recent times, puppets have appeared in adult mainstream as well as experimental theatre, in the works of Julie Taymor (see the section titled Four Global Luminaries), the Broadway musical *Avenue Q* (see the chapter titled "The Musical Theatre"), and in many countries around the world.

Theatre Beyond Theatre and Site-Specific Performance

Who says theatre must take place in a theatre?

Many plays today are staged in environments quite beyond the formal theatrical facilities with curtains and theatre seats. For more than a decade, the New York Classical Theatre has staged Shakespearean and other dramas in Manhattan's Central Park, with the audience gathering at a designated point and following the actors as they move about the trees, park benches, and rock outcroppings. The company has recently expanded their performance venues to include Battery Park, the World Financial Center, and, in a 2011 production of *Henry V,* on a ferryboat across the Hudson River to Governor's Island.

The notion of an "itinerant theatre" has clearly caught on. The 2011 Romanian production of *The Cioran Temptation,* written and directed by Gavriil Pinte, was staged in a streetcar traveling from the city of Sibiu, Romania, to Rasinari, where the actual Emil Cioran (a twentieth-century Romanian philosopher) was born: as the play progressed, the character of Cioran escorted the audience to and from his hometown, sharing his reactions to his town, his country, and his life. This style of performance is called *site-specific,* as the actual site of the performance is where actions described in the play are actually considered to take place.

And one of the biggest hits in the New York 2011–2012 season was the "theatre beyond theatre" *Sleep No More,* an extraordinarily imaginative new work inspired by *Macbeth.* Staged by England's

Punchdrunk company in three interconnected, long-abandoned Manhattan warehouses, the audience was invited to wander wherever they wished among some 100 rooms in the six floors of the building, each room elaborately decorated in a 1920s, film noir style. Audience members, who were given full-face masks and instructed to wear them throughout, were also encouraged to follow whatever actor interested them, and to actually interact with the "scenery" they found in the various rooms: to sit in the chairs, lie on the beds, type on the typewriters, and open the cabinets and study their contents. As the core play (*Macbeth*) is a tragedy with ghosts and witches, *Sleep No More* is both brooding and blood-soaked, with ominous music, occult images, and violent, seminaked sex. The power of the production, however, is that you are not just observing it, you are in it. This sense of co-participation between actor and audience has led to a new genre in today's dramatic repertoire: immersive theatre.

Founding Artistic Director Stephen Burdman calls his New York Classical Theatre, founded in 1999, a creator of "panoramic theatre," as its works are staged outdoors in public venues. Here Teresa Pond has staged the Duke of Gloucester courting Lady Anne in a 2010 production of *Richard III* in New York's Central Park.

Gavriil Pinte's *The Cioran Temptation,* seen at the 2011 Sibiu International Theatre Festival, is literally staged in and around a streetcar that travels, during the performance, to and from the same Romanian cities that its title character, the Romanian philosopher Emil Cioran, visited often as a young man.

Sleep No More, presented in New York in 2011 by England's Punchdrunk company, is a radical reconstruction of Shakespeare's *Macbeth*. The production requires audience members to don identical masks, then invites them to follow—and occasionally interact with—individual actors as they move from floor to floor and room to room in a bizarrely decorated five-story "hotel." The fascinating action—impossible to follow in its entirety—climaxes in a scene where the spectators are herded together to see Macbeth and Lady Macbeth wash the murderous blood from their bodies in a basement bathtub.

FOUR GLOBAL LUMINARIES

Once every decade or two, a playwright or director develops a reputation that is not merely local or national but global. This is necessarily rare; for it to happen, a playwright's work must be translated into multiple languages and a director's stage productions must be transported to multiple countries so these works achieve international prestige. But the globalization of today's communication systems, the increase in transcontinental tourism and the proliferation of international theatre festivals have vastly increased the global reach of theatre arts everywhere. Theatrical luminaries, such as Peter Brook (English), Ariane Mnouchkine (French), Matthais Langhoff (German), Tadashi Suzuki (Japanese), and Robert Wilson (American), each famed for their creation of new styles, new techniques, and new theories of performance, have therefore enjoyed broad international acclaim throughout the past five decades and, now, in their 70s and 80s, continue to create and tour productions around the world. Their work has been featured in this section in previous editions of this book.

This tenth edition features four younger theatre artists—playwright Yasmina Reza (French), and directors Silviu Purcarete (Romanian), Katie Mitchell (English), and Julie Taymor (American)—each of whom has reached international acclaim in this first decade of the twenty-first century and become a luminary in the era we now live in. And as a testament to our current global culture, each balances a unique voice reflective of his or her home country while simultaneously communicating in a universal artistic language.

Yasmina Reza

While foreign language translations and productions of plays by living American playwrights, including Tony Kushner, Neil LaBute, Edward Albee, Theresa Rebeck, and even your author, are relatively common in theatre capitals throughout Europe and Asia, the reverse is rarely the case, as very few foreign-language plays by living dramatists are translated and staged professionally in America's major theatres. There are some exceptions, of course: *Death and the Maiden* by the Argentinean-Chilean playwright Arial Dorfman (translated from Spanish), and both *Boeing-Boeing* and *Don't Dress for Dinner* by Swiss-French Marc Camoletti (translated from French) have played on Broadway in recent years. But no dramatist has broken the mold like the French-born Yasmina Reza, who has had three of her plays performed on Broadway, two winning its "Best Play" Tony Awards—as well as two "Best Play" Olivier Awards in London's West End. These awards were for her 2006 *God of Carnage* and her 1994 *Art*; the

Great actors as well as great plays attract audiences, and an all-star cast of Marcia Gay Harden, Hope Davis, Jeff Daniels, and James Gandolfini was assembled—all are onstage almost the entire evening—for the Broadway production of *God of Carnage* by French playwright Yasmina Reza, which won the 2009 Tony for best play. Seeming at first a realistic drama—two couples politely trying to come to terms about a playground fight between their eleven-year-old sons—the play quickly becomes a riotous farce about social and gender differences in the contemporary urban upper-middle class. The distinguished actors excelled in every role. Harden received the Tony for her performance, and Gandolfini was nominated for one. The brilliantly paced direction was by Matthew Warchus, who also won the Tony; Mark Thompson designed the highly stylized contemporary apartment.

latter has already been translated into no fewer than thirty-five languages and produced in hundreds of cities around the world. Reza is clearly, as Amanda Giguere writes in her book on her, "a global phenomenon."

Born in Paris in 1959 of a Hungarian mother and a Russian-Iranian-Jewish father, one can almost say Reza has been an international figure since birth. Trained initially as an actress, her first theatrical coup was as a translator, converting Steven Berkoff's English *Metamorphosis* (based on Franz Kafka's German novel) into French; it earned her the 1988 Molière award for translation. *Art,* her most famous play to date, premiered not in France but in Berlin, where it then quickly moved to London and New York, then Tokyo, Bombay, Buenos Aires, Johannesburg, and the world. Her 2000

Life X 3 premiered simultaneously in Vienna, Paris, and Athens before heading to New York's Great White Way, and *God of Carnage* premiered (in German) in Zurich. But playwriting only represents a part of Reza's accomplishments: she is also a successful novelist and screenwriter, and, in 2007, she spent a year traveling around the world with former French President Nicolas Sarkozy and wrote a book on him. (Her work revealed her dramatist's eye: "I think he is a tragic personality, a man bent on self-destruction," she reported).

But drama, so far, is her forte. *Art* is an easy-to-produce one-act masterpiece, with only three characters and a single set which, with only slight modifications (the positions of two paintings), represents the living rooms of all three men. These are middle-aged men and

This 2011 production of Yasmina Reza's *Art* was directed by Matthew Gardiner at the Signature Theatre in a Washington, D.C., suburb. The very clever scenic design is by James Kronzer.

longtime school friends. The situation is simple: Serge, a dermatologist, has just bought an all-white painting for two hundred thousand francs (about $30,000 in U.S. currency at the time). Marc, an aeronautical engineer, is bewildered by what he finds an idiotic purchase ("You paid two hundred thousand francs for this shit?"), and grows furious thinking about it. Yvan, who is soon to be married but has no stable profession, wants only to keep this three-way friendship from breaking apart because of this quarrel. And that's the entire "plot" of the play.

What is thrilling about *Art* is not the plot itself, but the intricacy with which these male friendships are put to task, and the wit and delicacy with which Reza analyzes human interactions. The tactical interplay of ordinary laughter, for example, comes under her close scrutiny, as in this extended (and slightly edited) example:

YVAN: We had a laugh.

MARC: You had a laugh?

YVAN: We had a laugh. Both of us. We had a laugh . . . a good laugh, both of us.

MARC: You told him it was shit and you had a good laugh.

YVAN: No, I didn't tell him it was shit; we laughed spontaneously.

MARC: You arrived, you looked at the painting and you laughed. And then he laughed. . . . A genuine laugh, was it?

YVAN: Perfectly genuine. . . . It was Serge who laughed first.

MARC: It was Serge who laughed first?

YVAN: Yes.

MARC: He laughed first and you joined in.

YVAN: Yes.

MARC: But what made him laugh?

YVAN: He laughed because he sensed I was about to laugh. . . . He laughed to put me at my ease.

MARC: It doesn't count if he laughed first. If he laughed first, it was to defuse your laughter. It means it wasn't a genuine laugh.

YVAN: It was a genuine laugh.

MARC: It may have been a genuine laugh, but it wasn't for the right reason. . . . He wasn't laughing because his painting is ridiculous; you and he weren't laughing for the same reasons—you were laughing at the painting and he was laughing to ingratiate himself, to put himself on your wavelength, to show you that on top of being an aesthete who can spend more on a painting than you can earn in a year, he's still your same old subversive mate who likes a good laugh.

YVAN: Mm hum . . .

Seventeen lines about two people laughing—and yet Reza has made a different point with each one, carrying along the audience with a brilliantly provocative analysis of laughter as a deliberate act people often perform specifically to engage support or to humiliate adversaries.

Art, however, is basically a comedy, and a commercial comedy at that. The highlight of most productions—certainly those on Broadway and in London's West End—is a three page, one-sentence speech rattled off by Yvan as he bursts into the room to announce that both his and his fiancée's stepmothers want their names on the wedding invitation. No production of this play that your author has seen (on Broadway, in the West End, and in American regional theatres) has failed to draw a spontaneous and sustained ovation when the rant concludes.

In her work, Reza also mixes the realistic gloss of commercial comedy with a solidly Brechtian sense of distancing: between scenes in this play, the characters often appear alone and talk directly to us, providing us information ("I'm Yvan," says Yvan) and asking us questions ("What possible difference can it make to me if Serge lets himself be taken in by modern art?" Marc asks). In the next-to-final scene, Marc takes a felt-tip pen to the painting and draws a skier skiing down a hill on it—while in the scene that follows Serge washes off the defacement. "Why does my relationship with Marc have to be so complicated?" Serge then asks us—and we begin to ask ourselves about our own relationships well before the play concludes. That *Art* has excited critics and thrilled huge audiences in dozens of countries is a testament to its ability to tap into not merely the debates of art patrons and dealers, but universal aspects of ordinary human friendships, conflicts, and communications.

God of Carnage is Reza's other mega-hit, and the first to become a major film (the 2011 *Carnage*). Close to the format of *Art,* it has an elegant, urban, in-home setting where two couples, meeting for the first time, try to decide what to do about a playground fight occurring earlier that day between the couples' eleven year-old sons, injuring one seriously. What begins over coffee and cordial conversation ends with fury, threats, drunken slurs, marital discords, and vomiting on the coffee table. "You could describe my plays as being a theater of nerves," Reza has said, referring to this play. And yet her results are hilarious. Once again Reza, like Shakespeare, Molière, and Chekhov, has turned deep-set aggression in social behavior into the farce of everyday human life.

The great success of Reza's *Art* and *God of Carnage* should not obscure her other fine plays that are regularly performed today in Europe and America, including *Conversations After a Burial,* which won her the Molière Award, France's equivalent of the Tony, and *Life X Three,* in which one couple unexpectedly arrives a day early to another's dinner party—in three different versions—that had a short Broadway run in 2000. And the film *Carnage,* with Jodie Foster and Kate Winslet, and directed by Roman Polanski, has brought her rare genius to new audiences around the world. Readers of this edition should look forward to her newest play, *How You Talk the Game,* which premiered in 2012 at Berlin's Deutsches Theatre and concerns "a writer who comes to present his latest work in a small town."

Silviu Purcarete

Born in 1950, Silviu Purcarete is the eldest of the four featured luminaries, and the one with the broadest international profile. A Romanian, Purcarete was severely limited in his foreign travel under the Soviet control of his country during the Cold War, and again by the autocratic regime of Nicolae Ceausescu that followed, but after his country's revolution in 1989 he began touring his productions to international festivals in France, Scotland, Japan, Australia, Canada, England, Poland, and Bulgaria. By the mid-1990s he had moved to France, where he still lives, and in 1996, after an eleven-country tour, he brought his production of *Les Danaïdes,* an adaptation of Aeschylus's *The Suppliant Maidens,* to the Lincoln Center Festival in New York where he and his 100-member cast were met with both great acclaim and fierce controversy.

Purcarete is known for creating mammoth visual spectacles. His *Les Danaïdes* (pictured earlier in this book) used fifty flaming torches to illuminate the action, which actually heated up the outdoor audience in the cool New York summer night. The production featured mass rape (fifty men raping fifty women) and

(*Top photo*) One of a band of fire-eaters ignites and blows clouds of flame in the "Walpurgisnacht" (Feast of Witches) scene in Silviu Purcarete's monumental production of Goethe's *Faust*. But the fire-spewer is only one of the 110 performers in this production, which is presented on two gigantic stages (the audience is shuffled from one to the other and back again) in an abandoned factory outside the city limits of Sibiu, Romania, where the production was created in 2007 and is still playing at the time of this writing—and attracting audiences from throughout the world because of its spectacular reviews for its 2009 appearance at Scotland's famed Edinburgh Festival. Purcarete's "Walpurgisnacht" also includes a giant rhinoceros with two dandified eighteenth-century aristocrats riding on its back; a 90-actor chorus playing a grotesque army of hogs, whores, witches, and clowns; a rock band that plays at full volume above the audience and actors; white-gowned "virgins" hanging from the ceiling on grappling hooks. (*Bottom photo*) A blood-soaked Gretchen, who carries a hog's head on a platter atop her head, is leered at by Mephistopheles, played by a woman (the actress Ofelia Popil). This is no Feast of Witches; it is sheer Hell.

mass murder—all overseen by the six observant Greek gods, who were dressed in mock eighteenth-century finery (a signature Purcarete design). What did this all mean? "I don't think my productions make statements," said Purcarete in an interview with this book's author. "I don't think theatre has any manifest power to really change human beings. For thousands of years everybody has hoped to change human beings, but there is no sign of that ever happening. So live theatre shouldn't try to do that. Theatre is important, not to change things, but rather to celebrate the imperfection of God's creation."

Purcarete's masterpiece of the twenty-first century is unquestionably his 2007 adaptation and production of Goethe's *Faust,* which at time of this writing is being performed for its fifth consecutive year in Sibiu, Romania. Taking up two vast stages in an abandoned factory outside the city (the audience being transported, during the performance, from one stage to the other and back again), this *Faust* is filled with live rock music, riotous dancing, fire-eating and fire-spewing, and serial stripping, gyrating, and copulating, all in the presence of a dozen grotesque hogs, a giant rhinoceros, and a giant scaffold with bodies hanging and twirling high above the heads of the audience. Reviewer Euan Ferguson in *The Guardian,* seeing its appearance at the Edinburgh Festival, called this *Faust* "the most blisteringly stunning theatrical experience of this (or, appropriately enough, any other) life." The production, Ferguson continued, "seared and stuck like hot tar on bare skin, and . . . left me saddened only in one perverse way: I may never see a grander, more theatrical event in my life."

Other recent Purcarete productions include a 2005 *Waiting for Godot* in which only the roots of Beckett's famous tree were visible—way above the heads of the characters—while a three-piece combo in rabbit suits played at the rear of the stage, all utterly in conflict with the playwright's strict instructions; the production later toured to England and Croatia. And in 2011, Purcarete staged an epic, outdoor presentation of Ovid's *Metamorphoses* in which twenty-eight male and female characters in white underwear splashed around a giant, man-made lake, occasionally playing musical instruments; at the play's conclusion its giant white backdrop burned to the ground.

Purcarete's work is certainly controversial—his *Danaïdes* was largely panned by New York critics for a lack of emotional complexity and thematic development, but the *New York Post* critic added that "Purcarete . . . is a name we will *not* be able to forget." The

dazzling power of his theatricality is simply unquestionable and his worldwide reputation continues to expand, with his 2011 *Tempest* being performed at Shakespeare festivals in Romania, Hungary, and Poland and his *Waiting for Godot* appearing at the 2012 Latin American Theatre Festival in Bogota, Colombia, and his new *Gulliver's Travels* having its world premiere at the famous Edinburgh Festival in Scotland, also in 2012.

Julie Taymor

The general public may know Julie Taymor as the director who was dismissed, under a cloud of controversy, from the Broadway production of *Spider-Man: Turn Off the Dark* during the show's previews, but the theatre world knows her as one of the most imaginative, inventive, and successful stage directors of our time. Her 1997 stage production of *The Lion King,* which she both directed and designed, earned her Tony Awards in each of these categories; fifteen years later, the show continues to play to packed Broadway houses, and has already become the biggest box office hit in American theatre history. And, as it turned out, a year after its opening *Spider-Man* had joined—and even surpassed—*Lion King* in the list of Broadway's three top-selling shows.

But Taymor is far more than the creator of commercial blockbusters. Indeed, she began her career deeply involved in the avant-garde. After graduating high school, she went to Paris to study with mime artist Jacques Lecoq. After college (Oberlin), where she worked with avant-garde theorist/director Herbert Blau, her interest turned to puppetry as she apprenticed at the Bread and Puppet Theatre in New York and studied Javanese shadow puppetry at the American Society for Eastern Arts in Seattle. A fellowship then allowed her to travel to Eastern Europe and Asia, where, settling in Indonesia for four years, she created her own international performing troupe, Teatr Loh, reporting, "I have never seen theatre as potent, powerful, and overwhelmingly theatrical as I have in Indonesia."

Finally returning to America in the late 1970s, Taymor began designing and directing at regional theatres on the east coast and eventually in New York, where she designed *The Haggadah, a Passover Cantata* at the off-Broadway Public Theatre, for which she won the 1980 Henry Hewes Award for her scenic, costume, and puppet designs. Fifteen years and dozens of productions later, Taymor made her Broadway premiere

Patrick Page as the Green Goblin in the center of his villains, Carnage, Electro, Kraven the Hunter, Lizard, Swarm, and Swiss Miss in *Spiderman: Turn off the Dark*. In addition to being the original conceiver and director of the production, Julie Taymor is cocredited for the script and solely credited with the elaborate mask designs.

with *Juan Darien* and received Tony nominations for Best Direction of a Musical and Best Scenic Design. In her production of the play, which she had adapted from a Uraguayan short story, the South African jaguar cub that serves as the play's title character was played both by both a puppet and a boy, while other characters were represented by shadow and hand puppets. The critical excitement and Tony nominations that greeted this experimental but still mainstream theatre project quickly caught the eye of Disney Corporation executives, who had a new project in their sights. This was *The Lion King*, and the avant-garde Taymor soon became the director, costume designer, and codesigner of masks and puppets of what was to become arguably the most spectacular, and certainly the most expensive, production in Broadway's history up to that time.

The opening moments of *The Lion King* displayed a theatre magic previously unknown in live theatre.

Twenty-six-foot-tall giraffes loped soulfully across the vast African plain and a thirteen-foot-long elephant, more than eleven feet high, made an astonishing entrance down the auditorium aisle. By play's end, the audience had seen fifty-three performers and two-hundred-thirty-two puppets representing twenty-five different species of animals, birds, fish, and even insects. Spectators gawked at gazelles leaping in staggered unison, birds courting wildly in midair, warthogs wobbling across the stage, wildebeests stampeding, flowered vines descending from the trees, and an enormous, latticed sun rising to reveal the radiant African dawn. But none of this was created realistically. With masterful, Asian-based techniques, Taymor revealed the blatant theatricality of the puppetry. Her puppets' heads were located above the faces of the actors who wore them, so the audience was always aware of the actors who manipulated (and often spoke for) each animal. All the strings,

Julie Taymor's *The Lion King* forges a profound alliance between experimental theatre, African ritual, Asian dance and puppetry, and American mass-market entertainment (namely, the Disney Corporation and Broadway). Here, South African vocalist Tsidii Le Loka plays the role of Rafiki, the singer-narrator, amid leaping gazelles and a menagerie of other animals.

wheels, and sticks of puppetry mechanics were in full sight.

The Lion King proved to be a global show that attracted a global audience. Designing the play's characters (costumes, masks, and puppets) and cleverly staging their movements, Taymor ingeniously mixed Javanese rod puppetry and Balinese headdresses with African masks and stilts. The music (by the English Elton John and South African Lebo M) and lyrics (by Lebo M, the English Tim Rice, and American Taymor herself) combined Western and African rhythms and languages. The orchestra was not buried in a below-stage pit but rather extended into audience boxes on both sides of the stage, each box holding costumed African drummers and chanters. In this work, Taymor seemed to put the entire world—and the world's living species—on a single Broadway stage. And the world responded: at the time this edition is going to press, *The Lion King* is not only on Broadway and midway through a fourteen-city tour of the United States,

but also playing in major theatre capitals in Europe (London, Hamburg, Madrid) and Asia (Tokyo), with plans to open in Sao Paulo. By April 2012—when *The Lion King* became the highest-grossing Broadway show of all time—it had earned $4.8 billion in box office receipts worldwide.

Taymor did not rest on her laurels after *Lion King*, however, but went right into new experimental works in several media. Her films included the 1999 *Titus* (after *Titus Andronicus*), a remarkable if controversial version of one of Shakespeare's earliest, least-liked, and certainly most savage plays; her 2002 *Frida*, about the life of Mexican artist Frida Kahlo, which received six Academy Awards; and her 2009 *The Tempest*, based on Shakespeare's play, which featured the celebrated British actress Helen Mirren as Prospera and African actor Djimon Hounsou as Caliban. In the world of opera, she staged a lavish production of Mozart's *Magic Flute* at New York's Metropolitan Opera, which was sent by satellite to movie theatres throughout the United States and Europe, and the world premiere of *Grendel* in Los Angeles, receiving high plaudits for both works. Her theatre designs have been showcased separately from their productions in a major exhibition of her work, "Julie Taymor: Playing with Fire," seen at the National Museum of Women in the Arts in Washington and at the Field Museum in Chicago. By the end of the first decade of this century, the avant-garde adventurist had established herself as one of the world's best-known stars across the broadest possible spectrum of performing arts.

But it was *Spider-Man* that made front-page (as opposed to arts-page) headlines in 2011. The $75 million Broadway musical that Taymor coconceived, coauthored, and directed for four years ran into serious problems during both its preparation and preview performances. The sudden death of its initial producer, cost overruns while developing the play's extensive and complex flying sequences, actor injuries in rehearsals and then in preview performances, and finally some negative reviews—particularly of the plot—in early blogs from preview viewers, led to cancelled performances and deferred opening dates until major press reviewers decided it was time for them to weigh in before opening night, despite customary protocols prohibiting this. The critics' mixed reactions led the producers to shuffle their team, a process that concluded with Taymor's departure and replacement.

Nonetheless, Ms. Taymor has nothing to worry about. *Spider-Man* (for which she is now credited as "original director") opened after a record 186 previews to somewhat better "re-reviews" from the New York critics, and during the 2011 Christmas week it earned the highest ticket income in Broadway history. In a 2012 settlement with the producers, she received full royalties for her work throughout its run (though litigation continues), and the American theatre community has continued its admiration of her work. After her departure from the team, veteran Broadway actor Patrick Page—*Spider-Man's* Green Goblin—wrote, "For me, any day Julie is not in the rehearsal room is a day that I'm going to miss her. No one in the world has her creative vision, her energy and her unique take on things."

Katie Mitchell

The youngest of the theatre artists in this section, Katie Mitchell, was born in England in 1964 and quickly earned a reputation as an exciting, if highly controversial, stage director—primarily of the classics. Although Mitchell has not yet created a blockbuster success (and may never do so), she has gained extraordinary plaudits from discerning audiences and press critics in several countries, receiving an Order of the British Empire (OBE) citation in England in 2009 and a "New Theatrical Realities" prize in Russia in 2011.

Educated at Oxford University and by touring throughout continental Europe, Mitchell was influenced greatly by the great German dance-theatre innovator Pina Bausch, whom she has described as "my great heroine," and by world-renowned avant-garde directors in Eastern Europe, including Lev Dodin and Anatoli Vassiliev in Russia and Tadeusz Kantor in Poland. She began her professional career in London, first as a stage manager and then assistant director; by 1990 she had created her own company (Classics on a Shoestring) which she ran for six years. Soon she was directing regularly at London's esteemed Royal Court Theatre, then for a decade at the Royal Shakespeare Company (RSC) in Stratford, and most recently at the Royal National Theatre (NT) in London—England's premier and, indeed, "royal" theatrical venues. But there is nothing royal about Mitchell's work, which is gritty, intense, socially provocative, and searingly intellectual.

Mitchell's first major award was a "best director" prize for her adaptation and staging in 1995 of Euripides' *The Phoenician Women* at the RSC's "Other Place," an experimental stage then across the street from the company's major theatre. And "experimental" this production certainly was: audience members wandered into a cold, dark, black-box theatre and were guided by ushers to tiers of hard, backless benches on three sides that had replaced the theatre seats normally positioned there. Instead of programs, the ushers handed sprigs of thyme to the audience—at which time the "ushers" turned out to be the play's actors. There was no scenery on the stage, apart from some three candle-lit Cycladic statues on the back wall, and the lighting cables and instruments hung in full sight above and around the action. Soon the actor-ushers turned into chorus-principals, alternately speaking in synchronized choruses, singing and dancing to polyphonic Balkan music (the play drew deliberate parallels to the war then going on in Bosnia-Herzegovina), and playing the principal roles of Euripides' play, or as much of the play that Mitchell chose to present. Critics were largely ecstatic about the production, describing it as "eloquent and enthralling," "magnificent and devastating," and "chillingly, compellingly contemporary." But reactions from the general audience and a few conventional critics were often a lot less enthusiastic—particularly about

Sandy McDade (center) is Susan, the title character of Thomas Heywood's 1603 domestic tragedy, *A Woman Killed with Kindness,* as directed by Katie Mitchell at the Royal National Theatre in 2011. Mitchell updates the play to the early twentieth century, as if it were an example of early realism and modern feminist ideology, but she also employs contemporary and postmodern ploys such as speeding up and slowing down the action as suits her theatrical purposes. It was, as customary with Mitchell's work, controversial: "A brilliant example of Mitchell's genius" said *Timeout;* "cold and curiously unrewarding," said *The Telegraph.*

With its bright colors and cardboard scenery, Katie Mitchell's production of *The Cat in the Hat* at the National Theatre in 2009 proved a delight for the children who were her major intended audience. Mitchell brought groups of children to her rehearsals, including her own four-year-old daughter Edie, explaining, "If they look away and get distracted for more than 15 seconds, what we are doing needs to be sharpened." Angus Wright is The Cat in this charming photograph of the production.

Paul McCleary plays the grossly nightmarish dictator Ubu in Katie Mitchell's 2012 staging of *Trial of Ubu*, an updated version by Simon Stephens of Alfred Jarry's 1896 pre-absurdist classic. The production begins with a puppet version of Jarry's play and then moves to an international trial that references the one of Slobodan Milosevic then taking place at The Hague in The Netherlands.

the inconsistency of the actors' roles, Mitchell's revision of the classic text, and above all the uncomfortable seating, made worse by the deliberate lack of an intermission for the two-hour-plus production, leading one reviewer to say, "the emotional agony experienced by the characters in the tragedy was matched by the physical suffering of the audience." The combination of rave and panning reviews led one reviewer to call her "a director who polarizes audiences like no other," a reputation that still lingers.

Yet great theatre is not for the dainty. Mitchell's NT productions have included cutting-edge renditions of powerful ancient Greek classics (*The Oresteia, Women of Troy, Iphegenia at Aulis,* in addition to *Phoenecian Women*), all channeling examples of twentieth-century warfare. Her 2004 *Iphegenia* production, for example, told the classic story of Agamemnon's sacrifice of his daughter—with Agamemnon wearing a Nazi SS uniform as a chorus of five fashionable 1930s society ladies, in shiny black dresses, handbags, and high-heeled shoes trade barbs and pleasantries as the hapless Iphegenia is stripped of her bridal gear and murdered at the demand of this Greek Führer.

"Mitchell delivers a mind-bending intensity" said the reviewer for the *Guardian.*

But Mitchell, while clearly in the avant-garde, also has strong roots in traditional Stanislavsky realism, which she studied in Russia. Directing *Iphegenia at Aulis,* for example, she asked the actors to recall a situation in their lives when they were deeply afraid, and then to reenact it in front of the entire company. "In this way," Mitchell reports, "you encourage the actors to think about using very precise physical information from real-life situations to communicate the moments in the action of the play." Now, mostly as an Associate at the NT, she has clearly varied her repertoire with acclaimed—and sometimes castigated—productions of Chekhov (*Ivanov, The Seagull, Three Sisters*), along with rarely performed plays from the past (Thomas Heywood's 1603 *A Woman Killed with Kindness,* Ferdinand Bruckner's 1923 *Pains of Youth,* Alfred Jarry's 1896 *Ubu Roi*), and multimedia adaptations of novels by Dostoevsky and Virginia Woolf. She has also, surprisingly, tried her hand staging children's plays, an adaptation of Dr. Seuss's *The Cat in the Hat* and an original version of *Beauty and the Beast*—both created at the suggestion of her then-four-year-old daughter, Edie. When not directing at the NT, where she is now an Associate, Mitchell has been staging plays for Stockholm's Dramaten Theatre, Berlin's Schaubühne, and Cologne's Schauspielhaus, along with operas at London's Royal Opera and both the English and Welsh National Operas. And she has written an outstanding textbook on directing, *The Director's Craft.* With the expectation of decades ahead of her, Katie Mitchell promises to lead the English—and global—theatre in new and exciting directions for a long time to come.

THEATRE TODAY: WHERE CAN YOU FIND IT?

Theatre happens all over the world: in villages, campuses, prisons, resorts, and parks; at local and international festivals; on ocean liners and at suburban dinner theatres; on temporary stages in rural churchyards and within historic ruins; and, increasingly, at site-specific venues such as a Manhattan apartment, a worker's meeting hall, a parking lot, or, as we saw earlier in this chapter, on a moving streetcar or ferry boat.

But mostly, current theatre is found in cities, and cities in almost every country on the globe.

FINDING THEATRE IN THE UNITED STATES

The American theatre is one of the world's most active, and while it takes place in every state in the union, its unquestioned capital is the small island of Manhattan, in America's largest city.

Theatre in New York

New York is the site of more performances, more openings, more revivals, more tours, and more dramatic criticism than any half dozen other American cities put together. The city's hundred-plus playhouses are a prime tourist attraction and a major factor in the local economy.

Moreover, in the minds of most theatre artists—actors, directors, playwrights, and designers—New York is the town where the standards are the highest, the challenges the greatest, and the rewards the most magnificent. "Will it play in Peoria?" may be the big question in the minds of film and television producers, but "Will it play in New York?" remains a cardinal concern in the rarefied world of American professional theatre.

The professional New York theatre, however, comes in three different and quite distinct categories: Broadway, off-Broadway, and off-off-Broadway.

Broadway   Mapmakers know Broadway as the longest street in Manhattan, slicing diagonally down the entire length of the island borough. Nearly everybody else knows Broadway as the historic and commercial apex of the American theatre, however. It is the "Great White Way" (referring to its bright lights), where tourists from around the world head, sometimes on their first day of arrival, to catch a "Broadway show." And rightly they do so: the forty-four theatres that make up today's official Broadway Theatre District, all within a dozen blocks north of Times Square, house a concentration of theatrical excitement unique in the world. The great growth of twentieth-century American drama took place right here: the Broadway district is where Eugene O'Neill, Arthur Miller, Tennessee Williams, William Inge, and Edward Albee premiered their masterpieces; where George M. Cohan, Ethel Merman and Liza Minelli sang and danced their hearts out; and where Marlon Brando, Barbra Streisand, Sean Penn, Meryl Streep, Robert Redford, and thousands of others acted their

Bright lights, big city! Though often thought of as Times Square, this is actually Duffy Square in New York; five blocks north and between these two squares lie almost all the theatres in the Broadway district. Behind the giant red staircase, which has become a well-populated overlook for the intense Broadway action, is the TKTS booth, where theatergoers can get same-day, half-price tickets to many of the current shows playing both on and off-Broadway. Looming above the booth are the giant posters of the shows playing in December 2011 when the photo was taken.

way into America's hearts and, subsequently, into Hollywood's films. Broadway flourishes now as never before, and in 2011 recorded its highest ticket income (more than a billion dollars) and highest attendance (more than 12.5 million) in history. And the Broadway "Road"—the collection of Broadway productions that tour to major cities throughout North America—extends the "Broadway experience" to audiences almost as numerous as those attending the same shows in "the Big Apple."

Yet Broadway is hardly the sum of American theatre. Broadway's lure is its dazzling visual and social excitement, its heady mix of bright lights and famed celebrities, its trend-setting fashions, big-buck entertainments, and ceremonial Tony Awards. The Broadway stakes are higher than anywhere else in theatre ("If you can make it there, you'll make it anywhere"), and its energy is electric. Most excitingly, its glamour is readily accessible: the TKTS Booth (Broadway at 47th Street) and several Web sites sell half-price tickets for many shows, making the Broadway experience affordable for almost everyone. But the Great White Way is no longer the place where new plays routinely originate, as it was in 1947 when Tennessee Williams's *A Streetcar Named Desire* and Arthur Miller's *All My Sons* debuted there. Today, Broadway is primarily the staging ground for extravagantly produced musicals, both new (*Billy Elliot, The Book of Mormon, Spider-Man*) and revived (*Anything Goes, Follies, Godspell*). Second, Broadway is the showcase for the best (or at least the most commercially promising) new plays from America's off-Broadway (David Auburn's *Proof*, John Patrick Shanley's *Doubt*, Neil LaBute's *Fat Pig*); for new plays from abroad (from France, Yasmina Reza's *Art* and *God of Carnage*; from Ireland, Conor McPherson's *The Weir* and *The Seafarer*; from England, Jez Butterworth's *Jerusalem* and Tom Stoppard's *The Coast of Utopia*); and for new works that premiered earlier at America's top-ranking non-profit theatres—including the Pulitzer Prize winners *August: Osage County*, which had premiered at Chicago's Steppenwolf; *Wit*, initially produced by South Coast Repertory in California; and *Clybourne Park*, which had its premiere a few blocks away at Playwrights Horizons.

Finally, Broadway is the site of many major revivals from the international dramatic repertory, including recent star-heavy productions of ancient and modern classics such as *Waiting for Godot* with Nathan Lane and John Goodman, *The Merchant of Venice* with Al Pacino, *The Seagull* with Kristin Scott Thomas, *Hamlet* with Jude Law, and *A Life in the Theatre* with Patrick Stewart.

Rarely does a new play premiere directly on Broadway today. The costs are usually far too high to risk on an untested product, for despite high ticket prices, which in 2012 ascended to as much as $155 for straight plays and $277 for best-selling musicals (not to mention "premium" tickets at close to double these prices or more for patrons seeking front-and-center seats at the last minute), the majority of Broadway productions fail to recoup their expenses. Increasingly, therefore, Broadway producers look for new plays whose worth has been "proven" in less-expensive off-Broadway, or in the subsidized European (chiefly English) theatre, or on a not-for-profit American regional stage. Only a star-studded revival or a new

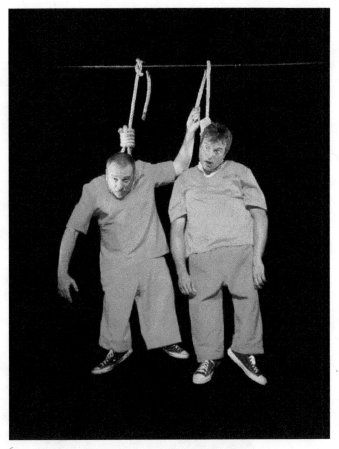

One of the highlights of the 2009 "off-off" Fringe Festival in New York was *666*, a one-hour piece created and performed in pantomime by Madrid's self-styled "slapstick theater company" Yllana. The wordless play, raucously hysterical, treats four death-row inmates, the crimes they committed, and their attitudes about the death penalty they each face. The actors, said a *New York Times* reviewer, "pester the audience, laugh themselves silly killing one another and dedicate considerable creative resources to plumbing the comic possibilities of urine." This is exactly what one might expect from a performance at the American (or Spanish) theatre's "fringe."

musical with Tony Award potential is otherwise likely to be "bankable" and offer sufficient opportunity for commercial success. Nonetheless, Broadway remains the primary showcase for the most fully realized theatrical entertainment—and often inspiration—that America has to offer.

Off-Broadway and Off-Off-Broadway   Not all of New York theatre is performed in the forty-four theatres that, as defined by their contracts with Actors' Equity Association and other unions, constitute "official" Broadway. At least two hundred New York theatres are not in the "Broadway" category, many of them fully professional and most of the others semi-professional (that is, they engage professional actors

Regional theatre produces much of America's greatest drama. Tracy Letts's *August: Osage County,* a large-scale (thirteen actors, three-plus hours) realistic comedy about a wildly dysfunctional Oklahoma family, was created by Chicago's Steppenwolf Theatre Company, long famed for its ensemble acting. Following its Chicago premiere, the show went on to Broadway, where it was awarded the 2008 Pulitzer Prize for Drama, along with the Tony, New York Critics Circle, and Drama Desk Awards. Steppenwolf artistic director Anna D. Shapiro ingeniously staged the quarrelings and couplings—of the many characters shown here in the now-famous dinner scene in the second act—so audience members felt they knew each one of the characters personally and probably also felt they knew someone in their own lives exactly like them. Deanna Dunagan (*center, with pearl necklace*) plays the central role of Violet, the drug-addicted family matriarch, for which she received the Tony Award for best actress. Steppenwolf-based designers included Todd Rosenthal (scenery), Ana Kuzmanic (costumes), and Ann G. Wrightson (lighting).

and other artists who, by mutual agreement, are not paid minimum union salaries). The symbolic centrality of Broadway, however, is so strong that these theatres are named not for what they are but for what they are not: some are "off-Broadway" theatres, and others are "off-off-Broadway."

Off-Broadway is a term that came into theatrical parlance during the 1950s and now includes forty to sixty theatres found throughout New York neighborhoods—with concentrations on West 42nd Street, Greenwich Village, the SoHo area, Chelsea, Union Square, and Manhattan's Upper East and Upper West Sides. Several

of the best off-Broadway houses, ironically, are in the Broadway geographic area itself (American Place Theatre, Manhattan Theatre Club, Playwrights Horizons) but operate in somewhat smaller theatres and therefore under off-Broadway contracts. Some of the best theatre in America—including eventual Tony and Pulitzer Prize winners—has come out of these companies in recent years.

Off-off-Broadway, a term dating from the 1960s, denotes semi-professional or even amateur theatres located in the metropolitan area, often in church basements, YMCAs, coffeehouses, and converted studios or garages. The actors' union oversees off-off productions under its "Showcase Code," which allows union actors to perform for next to nothing (essentially bus fare to and from the theatre), allowing them to enjoy the public exposure and press reviews that could lead to the off-Broadway and eventually Broadway roles to which they aspire.

Other off-off Broadway habitués, however, find the anticommercialism, artistic excitement, experimental spirit, and cultural camaraderie of the off-off more appealing than the monetary benefits of its alternatives. The annual Obie Awards, given by the *Village Voice*, recognize outstanding work in both off- and off-off Broadway theatres and often are more accurate indicators of national theatre trends than are the more glamorous Tonys.

The non-Broadway New York theatre generates passionate and vigorous theatrical creativity. Leaner

Many American regional theatres fill their houses with family audiences in December with productions of a Christmas play—nearly always an adaptation of Charles Dickens' novel *A Christmas Carol*. This production, with South Coast Repertory veteran Hal Landon front and center as Scrooge, is from the final scene of South Coast's twenty-ninth annual production of the play, adapted by Jerry Patch, in 2008.

and less costly than their Broadway competitors, off and off-off productions attract audiences of their own, many of whom would never think of going to Times Square to see a play. And with their lower ticket prices (particularly in the off-off), and subscription seasons (particularly in the off), many companies have lured successive generations of audiences to new and exciting works before they reach the Broadway masses.

Regional American Theatre: Not for Profit

Very little professional theatre was produced on a regular basis outside of New York City until 1950, when the Arena Stage was founded in Washington, D.C. In the next fifteen years other "regional" theatres opened, including Houston's Alley Theatre, San Francisco's Actors' Workshop, and Minneapolis's Guthrie Theatre. In the following decade theatres opened almost weekly around the country, until now there are nearly *five hundred* such professional theatres, operating in almost every state.

These theatres, though professional to varying degrees, are nearly all not-for-profit (or nonprofit)—meaning they are in business not to make money but to create art. Not-for-profit theatres receive box-office revenue, of course, but they supplement that income with government and foundation grants and from private donations that, if the theatre has been legally registered as a nonprofit corporation, provide tax deductions to the donors. Some of these theatres, such as the Public Theatre, the Manhattan Theatre Club, and Playwrights Horizons, operate as part of New York's off-Broadway. The vast majority, however, are scattered throughout the country and produce more than two thousand productions each year, providing Americans in hundreds of cities and towns an opportunity to see professional theatre, often at its very best. An annual Tony Award for regional theatre cites the most distinguished of these groups, and thirty-six such theatres have been so honored, some in large cities such as Washington, Chicago, Los Angeles, Denver, Minneapolis, Seattle, Boston/Cambridge, and some in smaller ones, including Williamstown (Massachusetts), Waterford (Connecticut), and Costa Mesa (California).

Nonprofit theatres vary enormously in character. Some concentrate on world classics, some on new American plays, some on specific ethnic repertories, some on the European avant-garde, many on theatrical experiments. Some operate in ninety-nine-seat spaces with extremely modest five-figure budgets; others on multiple stages with funds to match: the Music Center in Los Angeles, for example, ran its three-theatre 2010 season on a $44.5 million budget.

What was simply a "movement" during the 1960s and 1970s has now become, quite simply, America's national theatre, for the regional theatre is where the vast majority of America's best-known plays have first been shaped and exposed since the 1970s. More and more, the American national press is attuned to major theatre happenings in the nonprofit sector. More and more, the Broadway audiences, while admiring the latest "hit," are aware they are seeing that hit's second, third, or fourth production. National theatre prizes such as the Pulitzer, once awarded only for Broadway productions, are now increasingly claimed by off-Broadway theatres (David Lindsay-Abaire's *Rabbit Hole,* Lynn Nottage's *Ruined,* Bruce Norris's *Clybourne Park*) and by regional companies (Steppenwolf's *August: Osage County* and Hartford Stage's *Water by the Spoonful*). World-renowned actors such as Al Pacino, John Mahoney, Dianne Wiest, Mary Louise Parker, Maggie Gyllenhaal, Matthew Broderick, and Brian Dennehy, once seen live only on Broadway stages and on tour, now also appear in many of the country's nonprofits. For the first time in America's history, the vast majority of Americans can see first-class professional theatre created in or near their hometowns, and professional theatre artists can live in any major city in the country—not only in New York.

Shakespeare Festivals

In Broadway's mid-twentieth-century heyday there was also *summer stock,* a network of theatres, mainly located in resort areas throughout the mountains of the Northeast, that provided summer entertainment for tourists and assorted local folks. This "straw-hat circuit," as it was called, produced recent and not-so-recent Broadway shows, mainly comedies, with a mix of professional theatre artists from New York and young theatrical hopefuls from around the country; it was America's vacation theatre and professional training ground.

Summer stock is mostly gone today, but in its place has arisen another phenomenon that, like summer

Most American Shakespeare festivals make a point of being, indeed, festive—none more so than the Utah Shakespeare Festival, which each year performs *The Greenshow* before each evening performance. Staged beside the Festival's replica of a Shakespearean-era theatre and performed by interns selected from applicants around the country, the show is free to all comers—those attending the play and those just showing up to see a family-friendly show that mixes Elizabethan singing and dancing with comic skits reflecting early English entertainment. This bouncy 2008 USF *Greenshow* was directed by Kirsten Sham.

stock, is unique to the United States. This is the vast array of Shakespeare festivals, begun during the Great Depression and now flourishing in almost every state. The Oregon Shakespeare Festival, in rural Ashland, is the much-heralded grandparent of this movement. Founded by local drama teacher Angus Bowmer, whose three-night amateur production of *The Merchant of Venice* in 1935 was preceded by an afternoon boxing match "to draw the crowds," the Oregon festival, which immediately discovered that Shakespeare outdrew the pugilists, now produces no less than eleven plays each year, attracting 350,000 spectators during a ten-month season in a town of less than 20,000 people! There are now more than two hundred North American Shakespeare festivals, many of them largely or partially professional, with two of them (Oregon's and Utah's) winning regional Tony Awards. Characteristic of each is a core of two to four Shakespearean productions, normally performed outdoors, together with more contemporary plays often performed on adjacent indoor stages—an arrangement not unlike that of Shakespeare's King's Men, which by the end of the playwright's career performed plays of many authors at both the outdoor Globe and the indoor Blackfriars. In addition to providing exciting classical and modern theatre to audiences around North America, these Shakespeare festivals provide a bridge for aspiring performers and designers segueing from college training to professional employment.

Summer and Dinner Theatres

There remain some notable professional summer theatres without the word *Shakespeare* in their names. The Williamstown Theatre Festival in Massachusetts is the most notable, as it employs many of New York's better-known actors, designers, and directors, eager to leave the stifling city in July and August to spend a month or two in this beautiful Berkshire village, where they play Chekhov, Brecht, Ibsen, Williams, and newer plays in elegantly mounted productions. The Berkshire Theatre Festival in Stockbridge, Massachusetts, is also a highly accomplished professional summer theatre, located in a culturally rich area just two hours north of New York, where, in the afternoons, visitors can also drop in at Tanglewood to see the Boston Symphony Orchestra rehearsing in shirtsleeves.

Dinner theatres were introduced to suburban America in the 1970s, offering a "night-on-the-town" package of dinner and a play in the same facility. Their novelty has worn thin, however, and only a few of them remain, generally offering light comedies, mystery melodramas, and pared-down productions of golden-age Broadway musicals.

Amateur Theatre: Academic and Community

There is an active amateur theatre in the United States, some of it operating in conjunction with educational programs. More than a thousand U.S. colleges and universities have drama (or theatre) departments offering degrees in these fields, and another thousand collegiate institutions put on plays, or give classes in drama, without having a full curriculum of studies. Several thousand high schools, summer camps, and private schools also teach drama and mount plays. Much of this dramatic activity is directed toward

general education. The staging of plays has been pursued at least since the Renaissance as a way to explore dramatic literature, human behavior, and cultural history—as well as to teach skills such as public speaking, self-presentation, and foreign languages. Practical instruction in drama has the virtue of making the world's greatest literature physical and emotional; it gets drama not only into the mind but into the muscles—and into the heart and loins as well. Some of the world's great theatre has emerged from just such academic activity. Four or five "University Wits" dominated Elizabethan playwriting before Shakespeare arrived on the scene, and Shakespeare's company competed with publicly presented school plays that had become popular in London during his career (such plays "are now the fashion," says a character in *Hamlet*). Several plays that changed theatre history—such as Alfred Jarry's *Ubu Roi* and Tom Stoppard's

Snow falls on a barren landscape in this 2011 University of California–Irvine production of Samuel Beckett's *Waiting for Godot*, set in wintertime. The portrayed actors (*from left*, Ben Jacoby as Vladimir and Chris Klopatek as Estragon) and the designers (Robin Darling, scenery; Gwyn Conoway Bennison, costumes; Karen Lawrence; lighting, Patricia Cardona, sound) were all graduate drama students.

Rosencrantz and Guildenstern Are Dead—were first conceived as extracurricular college projects.

The founding of the Yale Drama Department (now the Yale School of Drama) in 1923 signaled an expanded commitment on the part of American higher education to assume not merely the role of theatre educator and producer but also that of theatre trainer. Today, the majority of American professional theatre artists receive their training in American college and university departments devoted, in whole or in part, to that purpose. As a result, academic and professional theatres have grown closer together, and many artists are working as both theatre professionals and theatre professors. For this reason, performances at many university theatres may reach sophisticated levels of excellence and, on occasion, equal or surpass professional productions of the same dramatic material.

Community theatres are amateur groups that put on plays for their own enjoyment and for the entertainment or edification of their community. There are occasions when these theatres, too, reach levels of excellence. Some community theatres are gifted with substantial funding, handsome facilities, and large subscription audiences, and some (such as the Laguna Playhouse in California) become professional. One should always remember that many of the greatest companies in the theatre's history, including Konstantin Stanislavsky's Moscow Art Theatre and André Antoine's Parisian Théâtre Libre, began, essentially, as amateur community theatres. One should also remember that the word *amateur* means "lover" and that the artist who creates theatre out of love rather than commercial expedience may in fact be headed for the highest, not the lowest, levels of art. Community theatre has, then, a noble calling: it is the theatre a community makes out of and for itself, and it can tell us a lot about who we are and what we want.

The Global Theatre

While this book is published in America, and is in some measure aimed at American readers, the reduced cost of travel has now made the world of global theatre increasingly available to a global audience. Few spectator experiences are as challenging and fascinating as seeing plays from a culture—and a country—other than your own. Theatre from other countries—and continents—presents a variety of styles, techniques, and ideas that will make your eyes pop and your mind explode. The global theatre transcends local ideologies;

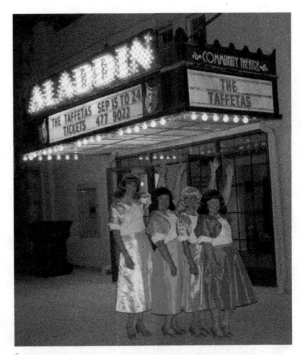

The Aladdin Theatre is a community theatre in the town of Parowan, Utah, population 2,790. Built in the 1920s and proclaimed a "Community Theatre" on its marquee, the theatre is maintained by the city corporation and its board of community residents; shown here are the stars of the theatre's 2011 fall production of *The Taffetas* ready to greet their audience.

it can make antagonists into partners and turn strangers into friends. As theatre once served to unite the ten tribes of ancient Attica, so it may serve in the coming era to unite a world too often fractured by prejudice and divided by ignorance. Nothing could be more vital in today's world than sharing popular "entertainment"—and being reminded of the original meaning of *entertain*: "to bring together."

A trip to an international drama festival, in the United States or abroad, is a superb way to sample the theatres of several countries within a short period of time. But nothing can quite match a theatre tour abroad, where an adventurous theatergoer can see the theatrical creativity of another culture in its own setting and with its own, intended audience. Seeing kabuki in Tokyo, with the audience shouting *kakegoe* (cries of approval) at climactic moments, or attending an Igbo *mmonwu* (masquerade) under the African sun, with the audience sitting and standing around the performers, cheering them on and swaying to the beat of their drums, is an experience that cannot be equaled.

theatrical cultures are never more than a brief train ride away, is a venture upon which more and more Americans embark.

Literally millions of Americans each year find their way to England for this very reason. Indeed, Americans often account for up to one-third of the theatre audiences in London, where productions, in addition to revered classics and extravagant musicals, may in any given year feature new and provocative works by such celebrated current English dramatists as Tom Stoppard, Mark Ravenhill, Alan Ayckbourn, Charlotte Jones, Martin McDonagh, Howard Brenton, David Hare, and Caryl Churchill. Highlighting London's mainstream theatre scene are the government-subsidized National Theatre (NT), which houses three stages in a modern complex on the south bank of the Thames; the nearby Globe Theater, a replica of Shakespeare's original outdoor playhouse that highlights Shakespearean-era drama during the summer months; and the West End theatre district on and around Shaftesbury Avenue and Covent Garden, which is comparable to New York's Broadway in its mix of musicals, new dramas, and classical revivals, sometimes playing long commercial runs after their initial premieres at the National. There is also a London "Fringe" of smaller theatres, roughly comparable to off-Broadway, which is often where the most exciting action is, particularly at the always-adventurous Almeida, Cheek by Jowl, Complicite, Donmar Warehouse, and Royal Court theatres. And in Shakespeare's hometown of Stratford-upon-Avon, little more than an hour's train ride away, you can see productions by the Royal Shakespeare Company, which produces their namesake's work (and much more) in three theatres in that town, as well as seasonally in London and on tours throughout the United Kingdom. Theatre ticket prices in England are less than in the United States, and an official half-price TKTS Booth, comparable to the one in New York, may be found in London's Leicester Square.

World travelers can explore other English-speaking dramatic centers as well. Ireland has provided a vast repertoire to the stage since the seventeenth century. Indeed, most of the great "English" dramatists of the eighteenth and nineteenth centuries—George Farquhar, Oliver Goldsmith, Richard Sheridan, Oscar Wilde, and George Bernard Shaw—were actually Irish by birth. In the twentieth century, a genuinely Irish drama became immensely popular in the hands of William Butler Yeats, Sean O'Casey, and Brendan Behan. But possibly no period of Irish drama is as rich

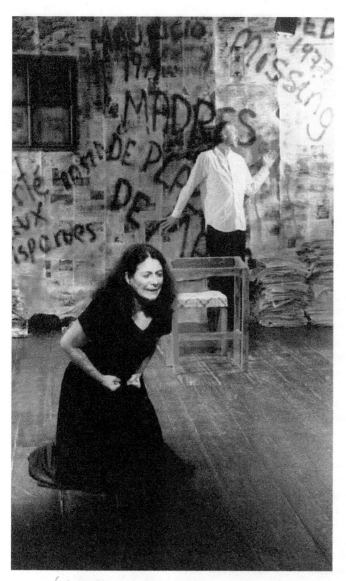

Current Latin American theatre is usually experimental and often intensely political. Here, in the Teatro Ubu (San José, Costa Rica) premiere of Argentinian-Quebecois Luis Thenon's *Los Conquistadores*, Maria Bonilla (director-actor at Costa Rica's National Theatre) kneels in anguish at the plight of her son, whom she discovers listed among citizens who mysteriously "disappeared" but were generally known to have been tortured and killed by official goon squads.

Admittedly, few Americans are able or willing to devote the time and resources to travel to Asia or Africa solely for theatergoing, and those who do will find the theatrical attractions on those continents far apart, and hard to get to, one from the other. A theatre trip to Europe, however, where dozens of distinct and dazzling

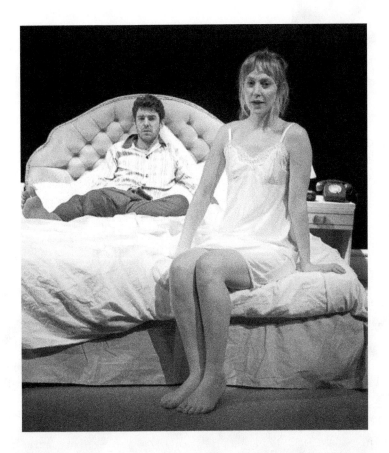

Caryl Churchill has been one of England's most prominent avant-garde playwrights for more than three decades; her *Three More Sleepless Nights* (1980), which presents the convoluted conversations of two different couples, one young and the other not, was revived with great success in 2009 by England's National Theatre. Paul Ready plays Pete and Hattie Morahan is Dawn in the production directed by Gareth Machin.

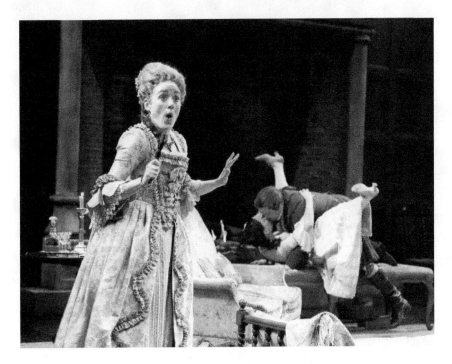

One can always count on the London theatre to present, in addition to new plays and avant-garde productions of older ones, "conventional" but still intensely stimulating productions of classic plays, both comedies and tragedies. Here the English National Theatre presents Oliver Goldsmith's eighteenth-century classic *She Stoops to Conquer* with Sophie Thompson as the hilariously scandalized Miss Oldcastle; this production, which was probably not very different from its premiere in Goldsmith's time, was so popular it was telecast live (by National Theatre Live) after its 2012 London opening.

"Panto" is a traditional English Christmastime entertainment for both adults and children. (The word is short for "pantomime" but bears little relation to the American art of that name.) Here the distinguished classical actor Ian McKellen (*right*) plays Widow Twankey (cross-gender casting is essential to panto), and Roger Allam plays Abbanazar in a 2004–2005 version staged at London's Old Vic. "Panto has everything theatrical—song, dance, verse, slapstick, soliloquy, audience participation, spectacle, cross-dressing and a good plot, strong on morality and romance—what more could you want from a family outing?" says McKellen. The outrageous panto costuming is by Mark Bouman.

Tourist literature portrays the island of Ireland as a peaceful and beautiful land, but unfortunately it has suffered fiercely contentious rule for most of its political history. Martin McDonagh, English-born but of Irish parents, writes about the island's notorious "troubles," as they are famously called there, and his 2002 *The Lieutenant of Inishmore,* a dark (and many say tasteless) comedy of violence, torture, and killings (of both humans and animals), both shocked and fascinated London audiences. Paul Lloyd (*hanging upside down*) and Peter McDonald are shown here in one of the play's grimmer scenes.

The Druid Theatre of Dublin has specialized in staging the classic works of Irish dramatist John Millington Synge, whom Garry Hynes, the Druid's artistic director, jocularly calls the company's "house playwright." *Playboy of the Western World*, which caused riots at its 1907 premiere, is Synge's masterpiece: a profoundly realistic portrayal of the language, customs, morality, and sense of humor of rural Ireland—specifically the Aran Islands, where Synge spent many summers and generally set his plays. Hynes first staged the play in 1975. This scene is from her 2008 reprise of that production as seen in Los Angeles. Scenery was by Francis O'Connor, and costumes were by Kathy Strachan.

as the current one, which includes major established playwrights such as Brian Friel (*Philadelphia, Here I Come; Translations; Dancing at Lughnasa*) and newer ones such as Sebastian Barry (*The Steward of Christendom, Whistling Psyche*), Conor McPherson (*The Weir, The Seafarer*), and English-Irish Martin McDonagh (*The Beauty Queen of Leenane, The Cripple of Inishmaan, The Pillowman, A Behanding in Spokane*). Most of these plays make their way to the United States, but seeing them in their natural surroundings, as at the Abbey or Gate Theatres of Dublin and the Druid Theatre of Galway, is a special treat.

In Canada, theatre flourishes in every province. The city of Toronto alone boasts two hundred professional theatre companies and is, after London and New York, the largest professional theatre metropolis in the English-speaking world. But Canada is a bilingual country, and its major playwrights cover a broad international spectrum; its dramatists today include the veterans Michel Tremblay (a French Canadian writing in French) and Daniel David Moses (a Delaware Indian identifying himself as an "Aboriginal Playwright Poet" and writing in English), and relative newcomers including Wajdi Mouawad (born in Lebanon, educated in Quebec, and writing in French). Canada is also known for its globally prominent playwright/director Robert Lepage, its two major theatre festivals (one for Shakespeare in Stratford, the other for George Bernard Shaw in Niagara-on-the-Lake), a strong network of repertory companies and avant-garde groups throughout the country, and its spectacular and world-famous Cirque du Soleil performance troupe. With a virtual

The Stratford Shakespeare Festival is Canada's best-known theatre company, and one of the greatest companies in the Americas. Founded in 1953 and opening its first season in a tent in this small Ontario town named after Shakespeare's birthplace, it has since grown into a five-theatre operation producing fourteen productions a year. This spectacular 2011 production of the Andrew Lloyd Webber musical, *Jesus Christ Superstar*, proved enormously successful in Canada, and transferred to Broadway in 2012.

flood of new playwrights, directors, and theatre critics working in multiple languages, Canadian theatre, in addition to its growing popularity at home, is developing a very wide recognition abroad.

Australia also has a fine theatrical tradition and a lively contemporary scene. Veteran playwrights David Williamson (his *At Any Cost,* a dark comedy on end-of-life contemporary medicine opened at Sydney's Ensemble Theatre in 2011) and Louis Nowra (*The Emperor of Sydney* in 2007) have long flooded that country's stages with provocative plays. They are now supplemented by a host of younger writers who flourish in both standard repertory and offbeat, alternative theatres in Melbourne, Sydney, and Brisbane—as well as at Australia's biennial Adelaide Arts Festival.

And South Africa has given the world one of its most prominent living playwrights, Athol Fugard, whose *Sizwe Banzi Is Dead, The Island, Master Harold . . . and the Boys, A Lesson from Aloes, Valley Song, My Children! My Africa!,* and *Playland,* mostly premiered at the Market Theatre of Johannesburg. Both Fugard and the Market Theatre have won their reputations not only for the outstanding quality of their work but also for their courageous and effective confrontation of that country's now-concluded policy of apartheid. In the post-apartheid era, Fugard has written new plays, often autobiographical, dealing with his continuing struggles to reconcile contemporary Africa with both its roots and its future; these include the notable *Valley Song* (1996) and its sequel, *Coming Home* (2009). Now living in California, his *The Train Driver* opened in Los Angeles in 2010 and went on to play in London, earning rave reviews in both venues, and will be enjoying a New York premiere in 2012.

South African playwright Athol Fugard cowrote *The Island* with actors John Kani and Winston Ntshona, who played the two roles—of convicts at hard labor in South Africa's brutal Robben Island prison—in the play's 1973 Cape Town premiere and in London and Broadway showings the following year, which attracted international attention to the play and, in New York, earned Tony Awards for the two actors. Here Kani and Ntshona repeat their roles in a 2003 revival at the Brooklyn Academy of Music.

For travelers willing to manage a foreign language, France and Germany—the countries that spawned the theatre of the absurd and the theatre of alienation, respectively—are immensely rewarding theatre destinations. Each country provides an outstanding mix of traditional and original theatre. French and German theatre, like that of most European countries, enjoys strong government support, which keeps ticket prices at a fraction of what they are in the United States and England.

France has five fully supported national theatres. Four of them are in Paris—including the historic Comédie-Française, founded in 1680 out of the remains of Molière's company shortly after his death; the historic Odéon, now a "Theatre of Europe," presenting home-based plays as well as productions from around the continent; and the Théâtre du Chaillot, which focuses on new plays and dance pieces and whose

Web site includes outstanding video clips of current productions.

In Germany, where major dramatic activity is spread more broadly throughout the country (there is no recognized German cultural "capital" remotely comparable to London or Paris), federal and city governments support more than 150 theatres, and about sixty theatre festivals, in just about every large city on the map. The modern German theatre, often called "post-Brechtian" because the brash, experimental style of most productions takes off from the influence of Bertolt Brecht, is considered revolutionary in its breaking of theatrical stage conventions. German directors Peter Stein, Matthais Langhoff, Claus Peymann, and Frank Castorf have pioneered in theatrical innovations that have influenced theatres around the world. In addition to the Berliner Ensemble, currently headed by Peymann, Berlin boasts Castorf's super-radical Volksbühne and each May mounts an annual *Theatertreffen* (Theatre Meeting), bringing what a jury of critics selects as the ten best German-language theatre productions (out of the four hundred they evaluate) from Germany, Austria, and Switzerland. Theatertreffen productions are chosen almost entirely for their innovative direction and design, and for their contribution to the future of theatre in the German-speaking world. Attending such events puts the audience in contact with the most adventurous theatre in western Europe.

Other western European countries—particularly Spain, Italy, Sweden, Denmark, Finland, Switzerland, Belgium, and the Netherlands—also have extremely active theatre communities and their own legendary actors and directors. And they too are wonderful places to engage in the theatre of the present and see a glimpse of the theatre of the future. The most exciting theatre in Europe today, however, according to many observers (including your author), is in Eastern Europe.

Because the theatres of eastern European countries faced strict government censorship during the post-war Soviet era (from 1945 until the early 1990s), their playwrights were relatively muffled in comparison to their western European counterparts, and it was directors who took the lead in creating both the "new theatre" that all audiences crave and the "dangerous theatre" discussed earlier in this chapter that expresses subversive political ideas in artistically flamboyant styles. They did this by mounting radical reconstructions of classical plays—for what Communist party official would dare complain about a director who wanted to stage a two-thousand-year-old Greek tragedy, even one that treated the overthrow of a despotic government? Thus, Eastern European theatre (including the theatre of what was then East Germany and some of the German directors discussed above who began there) became a "director's theatre." The art of directing—and the acting and design that emanated from it—created a theatre of ancient plays produced "in code," with their hidden, often subversive meanings clear to intelligent audiences but opaque to Soviet censors. Indeed, the Eastern European theatre played a major role in the sweeping away of Communist rule in the Soviet bloc, particularly in Czechoslovakia, where in 1989 the "Velvet Revolution" led by Václav Havel, a prominent dissident Czech playwright, brought about the overthrow of the Communist government and the election of Havel as president of Czechoslovakia.

Within Eastern Europe, the country of Romania deserves special recognition, because, with a population smaller than that of Texas, it has produced an extraordinary collection of world-famous directors. Andre Serban, Mihai Maniutiu, Gábor Tompa, and Silviu Purcarete have international reputations for innovative brilliance and creativity. "In the field of directing, it is not Romania but America that needs to catch up," said Senior Editor Randy Gener in a 2007 cover story on Romanian theatre for *American Theatre,* the country's most distinguished publication in that field.

Each of those Romanian directors seeks not only to produce plays but to reinvent the theatre itself: the way it works, the way it thinks, the way it projects ideas and images to its audiences. Each has worked frequently in Europe, Asia, and the United States. Serban directs regularly at the American Repertory Theatre in Cambridge, Massachusetts, and teaches at Columbia University in New York. Purcarete's internationally renowned work has been considered earlier in this chapter, while Tompa and Maniutiu (respectively) head the Hungarian-language and Romanian-language national theatres of Cluj, where both of those languages are spoken; each also now teaches and directs at the University of California campuses at (respectively) San Diego and Irvine. All four continue to direct in their home country, however, where they face increasing competition from a new generation of Romanian disciples who are actively building on their discoveries.

Romanian theatre is intellectually bold, stylistically innovative, physically demanding of its performers, and emotionally demanding of its audiences. There is no doubt that Gener's estimate of Romania's importance to the theatre's future is accurate; the entire Spring 2009 issue of Yale University's *Theater* journal was also devoted to Romanian theatre today, and the international festivals Romania now hosts annually in Bucharest, Cluj, Craiova, and Sibiu are attended by theatre practitioners, students, and fans from all over the world.

And for those readers—the vast majority, of course—who aren't making foreign theatre tours this year, the Internet provides a wonderful way to catch a glimpse of and a feeling for the works described in these pages. A quick Web search—beginning with the theatre companies or the directors named here—quickly leads to photos and in many cases videos of their latest work, plus archival photos of many of the productions mentioned.

CONCLUSIONS ABOUT THEATRE TODAY?

Can we draw any conclusions about theatre today? No, we cannot, because what is current is never concluded. The current theatre is in process; it is *current* in both senses, a river that is continually running, continually replenished with fresh rainwater and snowmelt. What is hot today may be cold tomorrow. But the theatre of today is *our* theatre and it is *your* theatre: there to apprehend, to enjoy, to appreciate, and to respond to. It is not just a series of plays, or a spectrum of performances, but a communication between individuals and peoples that raises levels of human discourse and artistic appreciation. It responds to individual impulses of creativity and collective demands for human contact and understanding. It synthesizes the impulses of artists and audiences, and it fosters a focused interaction that incorporates our human experience, aspirations, and values. Like a river, theatre began long before the advent of recorded history and "keeps on rolling."

And it is always new. As Heraclitus said twenty-five hundred years ago, "We cannot step twice in the same river; for when I step in the river for a second time, neither I nor the river are the same."

Chapter

11

The Critic

IT IS 10:30 P.M. THE lights fade a final time, the curtain falls, the audience applauds, and the play is over. The actors go back to their dressing rooms, take off their makeup, and depart. The audience disperses into the night. But the theatrical experience is not over; in many ways, it is just beginning.

A play does not begin and end its life on a stage. A play begins in the mind of its creator, and its final repository is the minds and memories of its audiences. The stage is simply a focal point where communication in the form of theatrical performance takes place.

After the performance is over, the play's impact remains. It is something to think about, talk about, fantasize about, and live with for hours, days, and years to come. Some plays we remember all our lives: plays whose characters are as indelible in our memories as the people in our personal lives, whose settings are as deeply experienced as our childhood locales, and whose themes resonate with many of our most crucial decisions. Should we take up arms against a sea of troubles? Can we depend on the kindness of strangers? What's in a name? Shall we be as defiant as Prometheus? as determined as Oedipus? as passionate as Romeo? as accepting as Winnie? as noble as Hecuba? What is Hecuba to us, or we to Hecuba? We talk about these matters with our fellow theatregoers—our ▶

friends who accompanied us, and perhaps other audience members, former strangers with whom we have shared this experience—once the curtain has fallen.

We also talk about the production—about the acting, the costumes, the scenery, the sound effects. Were we convinced? impressed? moved? transported? changed? Did the production hold our attention throughout? Did our involvement with the action increase during the play, or did we feel a letdown after the intermission? Did we accept the actors as the characters they were playing, or were we uncomfortably aware they were simply "acting" their parts rather than embodying their roles?

We do not need to be in a theatre to engage deeply with a play. The printed text can also prompt important questions. That play the teacher or director asked you to read yesterday: Did it "get to" you? Could you follow the story? Were you interested in the characters? Did it move you emotionally or stimulate you intellectually? Did it make you want to take action politically? Why? Why not? Could you visualize its actions, its settings, its impact on a theatre audience? Could you imagine casting it with actors you have seen on stage or screen? Were there aspects of the play you thought could be changed for the better?

When you address any of those sorts of questions about a performance or a play text, you are engaging in *dramatic analysis*. Some people do this for a living. A person who does so publicly, explaining to readers or listeners his or her reactions to a play or a play performance, is a creator of *dramatic criticism* and is called a *drama critic* or a *play reviewer*.

Dramatic analysis is the informed, articulate, and communicative response of the critic or reviewer to what he or she has seen in the theatre. It can appear as production reviews in newspapers, blogs, periodicals, or on television; as feature newspaper or magazine articles about individual theatre artists or companies; as essays in scholarly books about dramatic literature, history, or theory; and simply as class discussions or social gatherings in a home or restaurant after the show. Sharing your post-performance responses to a theatre experience can provide, in fact, some of the most illuminating discussions life can offer.

CRITICAL PERSPECTIVES

What makes a play particularly successful? What gives a theatrical production significance and impact, and what makes it unforgettable? What should we be looking for when we read a play or see a dramatic production?

We have, of course, complete freedom in making up our minds, for the price of theatrical admission carries with it the privilege of thinking what we wish and responding as we will. But five perspectives can be particularly useful in helping us focus our response to any individual theatrical event: the play's social significance, human or personal significance, artistic quality, theatrical expression, and capacity to entertain.

Social Significance

Theatre, as we have seen throughout this book, is always tied to its culture. Many theatres have been directly created or sustained by governments and ruling elites: the Greek theatre of the fifth century B.C. was a creation of the state; the medieval theatre was generated by the church, the township, and the municipal craft guilds; and the Royal theatre was a direct extension of monarchical power. Even in modern times, government often serves as sponsor or silent benefactor of the theatre. But the intellectual ties between a theatre and its culture extend well beyond merely political concerns: thematically, the theatre has at one time or another served as an arena for the discussion of every social issue imaginable. In modern times, the theatre has approached such issues as alcoholism, gay rights, overseas labor, venereal disease, prostitution, public education, racial prejudice, health care reform, capital punishment, overseas labor, thought control, prison reform, political assassination, civil equality, political corruption, and war crimes. The best of these productions have presented the issues in all of their complexity and have proffered solutions not as dogma but as food for thought—for great theatre has never sought to purvey pure propaganda.

The playwright is not necessarily brighter than the audience or even better informed. The playwright and his or her collaborators, however, may be able to focus public debate, stimulate dialogue, and turn public attention and compassion toward social injustices, inconsistencies, and irregularities. The theatre artist traditionally is something of a nonconformist; the artist's point of view is generally to the left or right of the social mainstream, and her or his perspective is of necessity somewhat unusual. Therefore, the theatre is in a strong position to force and focus public confrontation with social issues, and at its best it succeeds in putting members of the audience in touch with their own thoughts and feelings about those issues.

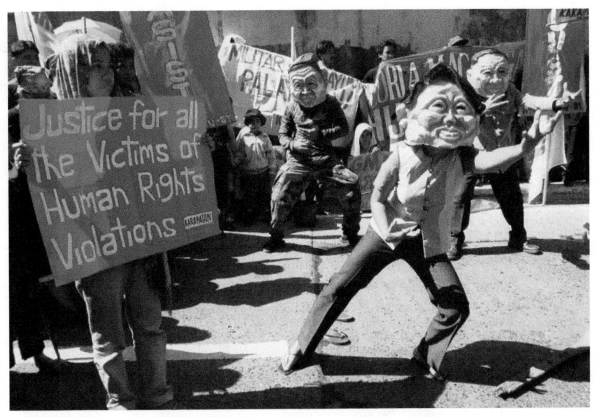

Some theatre is openly and primarily political. This outdoor event is part of a protest march in downtown Manila, where a Filipino theatre troupe—one member masked as now-former President Gloria Arroyo—condemn what they believe was the government's rigging the country's 2007 election and other abuses of human rights. Such street theatre protests can be effective; Arroyo, at this time of writing (2012), is on trial for just these accusations.

Human Significance

The theatre is a highly personal art, in part because it stems from the unique perspectives of its artists. The greatest plays transcend the social and political to confront the hopes, concerns, and conflicts faced by all humankind: personal identity, courage, compassion, fantasy versus practicality, kindness versus self-interest, love versus exploitation, and the inescapable problems of growing up and growing old, of wasting away and dying. These are some of the basic themes of the finest plays and of our own stray thoughts as well; the best plays simply link up with our deepest musings and help us put our oftentimes random or suppressed ideas into some sort of order or philosophy. The theatre is a medium in which we invariably see reflections of ourselves, and in the theatre's best achievements those reflections lead to certain discoveries and evaluations concerning our own individual personalities and perplexities.

Artistic Quality

The theatre is an art of such distinctive form that even with the briefest exposure we can begin to develop certain notions as to what that form should be. We quickly come to know—or think we know—honesty onstage, for without being experts we feel we can recognize false notes in acting, in playwriting, and even in design.

Beyond that, we can ask a number of questions of ourselves. Does the play excite our emotions? Does it stimulate the intellect? Does it surprise us? Does it thrill us? Does it seem complete and all of a piece? Are the characters credible? Are the actors convincing? enchanting? electrifying? Does the play seem alive or dead? Does it seem in any way original? Is it logically sound? Is the action purposeful, or is it gratuitous? Are we transported, or are we simply waiting for the final curtain? In the last analysis, does the play fit our idea of

☉Spotlight

Performance Studies

"All the world's a stage, and all the men and women merely players," said Shakespeare, and one of the growing areas in theatre education is the area of *Performance Studies*—or how we "perform" in everyday life.

Rather than examine staged theatre, Performance Studies encompasses all human action as its object of study. As a result, everything we do—make war, play sports, take museum tours, engage in political activism—is seen as a kind of performance. Even everyday events, such as buying groceries, become part of an exhibition. We perform with dialogue ("I'll be paying with credit") and follow blocking (when the customer ahead is finished, we move up one place in the line), and we depend on proper costumes and properties to complete our actions. By becoming aware of our constant dependence on the theatre, we are encouraged to study performance as a way of understanding the entire world.

Performance Studies is open-ended, and draws influences from many different disciplines. But its two most prominent forefathers are anthropology and linguistics. From anthropology, it draws an interest in ritual and ancient practices from all parts of the world. From linguistics, it focuses on the construction of meaning through language. Other important influences are avant-garde art, sociology, and cognitive psychology. What unifies this diverse set of inspirations is the rejection of solely text-based knowledge. Instead, Performance Studies embraces the medium of our bodies in time and space. Rather than pore over the written word, performance studies looks at the moving actor.

As it has risen in popularity, more universities and colleges have begun offering classes and degrees in Performance Studies, and several academic journals specialize in its practice. By giving us a theatrical vocabulary to describe our lives, this exciting discipline places us all onstage, and encourages us to think critically about the entrances, exits, and scenes that we make every day.

The motto of Konstantin Stanislavsky, who directed the original production of Chekhov's *The Three Sisters* in 1901, was "Live the life of your character onstage," and the depth of the human values expressed in that play have never been surpassed. Here you can glimpse in a single moment the deep feelings of these sisters, beautifully performed in 2011 at the Classic Stage Company, by (left to right) Jessica Hecht as Olga, Maggie Gyllenhaal as Masha, and Juliet Rylance as Irina. The very skilled director was Austin Pendleton, the period costumes by Marco Piemontese.

An audience does not bring absolute standards into the theatre—and certainly any standards it brings are not shared absolutely. The theatrical response is a composite of many individual reactions. But each of us has an aesthetic sensibility and an aesthetic response. We appreciate colors, sights, sounds, words, actions, behaviors, and people that please us. We appreciate constructions that seem to us balanced, harmonic, expressive, and assured. We appreciate designs, ideas, and performances that exceed our expectations, that reveal patterns and viewpoints we didn't know existed. We take great pleasure in sensing underlying structure: a symphony of ideas, a sturdy architecture of integrated style and action.

Relationship to the Theatre Itself

As we've already discussed, plays are not simply things that happen *in* the theatre; they *are* theatre—which is to say that each play or play production redefines the theatre itself and makes us reconsider, at least to a certain extent, the value and possibilities of the theatre itself. In some cases the playwright makes this reconsideration mandatory by dealing with theatrical matters in the play itself. Some plays are set in theatres where plays are going on (Luigi Pirandello's

what a play should be—or, even better, does it force us, by its sheer luster and power, to rewrite our standards of theatre?

Aesthetic judgments of this sort are necessarily comparative, and they are subjective as well. What seems original to one member of the audience may be clichéd to another; what seems an obvious gimmick to a veteran theatergoer can seem brilliantly innovative to a less jaded patron. None of this should intimidate us.

Few plays are as probing, fascinating, and thought-provoking as Shakespeare's *Hamlet*, and the play is produced with regularity throughout the theatre-going world. But how do directors and designers make it fresh and exciting to see again and again? How do they make it a work of contemporary art? This 2009 production by the Kolyada Theatre of Yekaterinberg, Russia, portrayed the Danish prince at the beginning of the play as a fragile and spoiled child who bites his nails but later assumes the role of an avenger and eventually a national hero. The production, directed by Nikolai Kolyada, who considers himself a "great provocateur," surprised and generally thrilled French audiences in its 2011 showing at the Odéon Theatre in Paris with its imaginative imagery and novel ideas. Kolyada also designed the scenery; the costumes were by Elena Getsevich, lighting by Denis Novoselov, and the grinning child-Hamlet was played by Oleg Yagodine.

Six Characters in Search of an Author, Michael Frayn's *Noises Off,* Mel Brooks's *The Producers*); other plays are about actors (Jean-Paul Sartre's *Kean*) or about dramatic characters (Tom Stoppard's *Rosencrantz and Guildenstern Are Dead*); still other plays contain plays within themselves (Anton Chekhov's *The Seagull,* William Shakespeare's *Hamlet*) or the rehearsals of such plays (Shakespeare's *A Midsummer Night's Dream,* Molière's *The Versailles Rehearsal,* Jean Anouilh's *The Rehearsal*).

We use the term *metatheatre,* or *metadrama,* to describe those plays that specifically refer back to themselves in this manner, but in fact all plays and play productions can be analyzed and evaluated on the way they use the theatrical format to best advantage and the way they make us rethink the nature of

theatrical production, for all plays stand within the spectrum of a history of theatre and a history of theatrical convention (see the chapter titled "What Is a Play?"). All plays and productions can be studied, often with illuminating results, from the perspective of how they adopt or reject prevailing theatrical conventions, how they fit into or deviate from prevailing dramatic genres, how they echo various elements of past plays or productions—and what theatrical effects, good and bad, such historical resonances may have.

Entertainment Value

Finally, we look upon all theatre as entertainment. Great theatre is never less than pleasing. Even tragedy delights. People go to see *Hamlet* not for the purpose of

Since 1982, Gerard Alessandrini's *Forbidden Broadway* has been spoofing Broadway shows. A classic piece of metatheatre, it makes clear that theatre is able to poke fun at itself—which it has done for many, many years, in plays by Aristophanes (*The Frogs*), Molière (*The Versailles Rehearsals*), Shakespeare (*A Midsummer Night's Dream*), and Chekhov (*The Seagull*), among numerous others. In 2009 *Forbidden Broadway* closed in New York and reopened in London—with Anna-Jane Casey shown here in a parody of the hit musical *Wicked*—and, after an American tour, it reopened at New York's 47th Street Theatre in the summer of 2012, covering new musicals including *The Book of Mormon, Anything Goes*, and *Sister Act*—"a godsend," raved the *New York Times*.

self-flagellation or to wallow in despair but, rather, to revel in the tragic form and to experience the liberating catharsis of the play's murderous finale. Hamlet himself knows the thrill of staged tragedy:

HAMLET: What players are they?

ROSENCRANTZ: Even those you were wont to take such delight in, the tragedians . . .

What is this entertainment value that all plays possess? Most obviously, the word *entertainment* suggests "amusement," and so we think immediately of the hilarity of comedy and farce; indeed, most of the literature regarding theatrical entertainment concentrates on the pratfalls and gags that have been part of the comic theatre throughout its history. But entertainment goes far beyond humor. Another definition for *entertainment* is "that which holds the attention" (from the French *entre* [between] and *tenir* [to hold], thus "to hold together" or "to bring together"). This definition casts more light on our question. It means entertainment includes the enchantment of romance; the dazzle of brilliant debate, witty epigram, and biting repartee; the exotic appeal of the foreign and the grotesque; the beauty and grandeur of spectacle; and the nuance and crescendo of a musical or rhythmic line. It accommodates suspense and adventure, the magic of sex appeal, and the splendor of sheer talent.

Finally, of course, it includes any form of drama that profoundly stirs our feelings and heightens our awareness of the human condition. It is no wonder that Hamlet delights in the performance of tragedians—and that we delight in *Hamlet*—for the mixture of ideas, language, poetry, feelings, and actions that constitute great tragedy confers one of life's sublime entertainment experiences.

Indeed, the theatre is a storehouse of pleasures, not only for the emotional, intellectual, spiritual, and aesthetic stimulation it provides, but also for its intrinsic social excitement. Theatre is a favored public meeting place for people who care about each other. "Two on the aisle" implies more than a choice seating location; it implies companionship in the theatrical experience, for the theatre is a place to commune in an especially satisfying way with strangers. When in the course of a dramatic performance we are gripped by a staging of romantic passion or stunned by a brilliantly articulated argument or moved by a touching denouement, the thrill is enhanced a hundredfold by the certainty that we are not alone in these feelings, that possibly every member of the audience has been stirred to the same response. Theatre, in its essence, serves to rescue humankind from an intellectual and emotional aloneness, and therein lies its most profound "entertainment" value.

David Ives's *Venus in Fur* is both a two-character play and a two-character play within that play, in which an actress (played by Nina Arianda) is auditioning for a director (Hugh Dancy). In the course of the action, the actor and director go back and forth between performing the "play's" roles and "being themselves," with the "performed" and the "real" behaviors becoming, by the play's conclusion, almost impossible to separate. This highly metatheatrical 2011 Broadway production was directed by Walter Bobbie.

CRITICAL FOCUS

Those five perspectives on the theatre experience—on its social, personal, artistic, theatrical, and entertainment values—are all implicit in the responses of any audience, regardless of its training or theatrical sophistication. Those are the five angles from which we view and judge plays—and judge them we do, for our involvement with a play naturally generates a series of comparisons: the play exists in relation to other plays, our personal experiences, and other things we might have done that evening. Judging plays and performances, which has been done formally since ancient Greek times and continues today through the well-publicized Tony and Obie awards, Pulitzer Prizes, and Critics Circle citations, is one of the fundamental aspects of theatrical participation—and it is participation open to professional and amateur alike.

Professional Criticism

Professional criticism takes the basic form of production reviews and scholarly books and articles written, for the most part, by people who specialize in this activity, often for an entire career.

Newspaper reviews of play productions remain common throughout the theatre world; indeed, the box-office success of most theatres depends on favorable press coverage. In the commercial Broadway theatre, favorable newspaper reviews—particularly from the extremely influential *New York Times*—are almost essential to guarantee a successful run, and sternly unfavorable reviews may mean a closing within a week or two. Although newspaper theatre coverage has diminished somewhat (indeed, newspapers themselves have been diminishing in the twenty-first century), any decline in press reviews has been more than made up for by an explosion of theatre Web sites and blog reviews. If you type "Henry V review 2012" into an online search engine, you will come up with hundreds of reviews—from both newspapers and theatre blogs—for productions of *Henry V* around the world in that year. If you add the name of a city or theatre where such a production was staged, you will find the full complement of critical response the work has so far engendered.

In New York (and most theatre capitals around the world), newspaper reviews generally appear the morning after the opening performance, which usually takes place in late afternoon rather than evening to meet the paper's press deadline. Customarily, after that performance, actors and producers and their fans gather at Sardi's restaurant in Broadway's Theatre District, where they pretend to eat dinner while awaiting the first TV reviews, generally appearing on the eleven o'clock news program, and advance copies of the following morning's *Times,* published just blocks away. As they wait for the print copy, some are checking their phones to see if the review has been posted on the newspaper's Web site. The televised and printed reviews are examples of "instant criticism," and the reporters or journalists who tackle such assignments must be very fluid at articulating their impressions immediately. Outside New York, critics may take from two days to a week to review a production, allowing themselves the luxury of considered opinions and more polished essays.

Still, the journalist's or blogger's review must be limited to a brief, unstudied reaction rather than a detailed or exhaustive study. It provides a firsthand, audience-oriented response to the production, often vigorously and wittily expressed, and may serve as a useful consumer guide for the local theater-going public. Writing skill rather than dramatic expertise is often the newspaper critic's principal job qualification, and at many smaller papers, staff reporters with little dramatic background are assigned to the theatre desk. But many fine newspaper critics throughout the years—New York's Ben Brantley and Los Angeles's Charles McNulty, for example—have proven extremely subtle and skillful at transcending the limitations of their particular profession and have written highly intelligent dramatic criticism that remains pertinent long after its consumer-oriented function has run its course.

More scholarly critics, writing without the deadlines or strict space restrictions of journalists, are able to analyze plays and productions within detailed, comprehensive, and rigorously researched critical contexts. They are therefore able to understand and evaluate, in a more complex way, the achievements of playwrights and theatre artists within any or all of the five perspectives we have discussed. Scholarly critics (and by *scholarly* we mean only "relating to the act of studying") seek to uncover hidden aspects of a play's structure, analyze its deep relationships to social or philosophical issues, probe its various meanings and dramatic possibilities, define its place in cultural history, amplify its resonance with earlier works of art, shape its future theatrical presentations, and theorize about larger issues of art and human understanding. Such criticism is itself a literary art, and the great examples of dramatic criticism have included brilliantly styled essays that have outlasted the theatrical works that were their presumed subjects: Aristotle, Goethe, Shaw, and Nietzsche are among the drama critics who, simply through their analyses of drama, have helped shape our vision of life itself.

The scholarly critic, ordinarily distinguished by her or his broad intellectual background and exhaustive research, writes with a comprehensive knowledge of the specific subject—a knowledge that includes the work of all important previous scholars who have studied the same materials. The professional scholar is not content to repeat the opinions or discoveries of others but seeks to make fresh insights from the body of literature (play texts and productions, production records, previous scholarship) that constitutes the field of study.

Scholarly critics tend to work within accepted frameworks of engagement—or "methodologies"—which develop and change rapidly in contemporary academic life. Traditional methodologies include historical and biographical approaches, thematic and rhetorical analyses, studies of character and plot, examinations of staging and theatrical styles, and detailed explications of meaning. More contemporary methodologies include systems and theories developed since the 1970s, particularly structuralist, semiotic, and psychological approaches; these bypass traditional questions of history, biography, and character, focusing instead on the internal relationships of various dramatic ingredients. Such methodologies, which draw heavily from the fields of philosophy, linguistics, anthropology, and critical theory, are intellectually demanding and difficult to master; they provide, however, stunning insights to those properly initiated.

Amateur Criticism

Anyone who watches a play can be a critic. For students, writing dramatic criticism for a school paper is a wonderful way to affect—and become a part of—the theatre. Writing a play review, in fact, is a common

Of course a great deal of theatre is created mainly, if not solely, to provide sheer audience entertainment. Although it deals with appalling subject matter, Mel Brooks's farcically satirical *The Producers* was designed purely for pleasure—as if to allow its audience to shake off, once and for all, the horrors of the Nazi regime with its parody play-within-the-play called "Springtime for Hitler." Matthew Broderick is shown here surrounded by a bevy of beautiful chorus girls.

class assignment, and a relatively easy way to get published and read within your local community. Similarly, writing a review on a blog is an easy way to share your thoughts and impressions with a large audience; more and more, impassioned theater writers in the "blogosphere" have become respected and prominent critical voices. Choosing one or more (but not all!) of the five perspectives cited earlier in this chapter can provide a good starting point for writing an analysis of a production. Some simple but effective methodologies for writing both class essays and production reviews for local or school newspapers are provided in the Online Learning Center for *Theatre* at www.mhhe.com/cohen10e and in *Enjoy the Play!* which accompanies this text.

WE ARE THE CRITICS

Whether we are professional writers, students, or just plain theatergoers, we are all critics of the theatre. As audience members, we are a party to the theatrical experience, not passive receptacles for its contrived effects. The theatre is a forum of communication, and communication demands mutual and active participation.

To be an *observant* critic, we need only go to the theatre with an open mind and sharply tuned senses. Unfettered thinking should be a part of every theatrical experience, and provocative discussion should be its aftermath.

To be an *informed* critic, we need sufficient background to provide a context for opinion and evaluation. A play may be moving, but is it as moving as *The Three Sisters*? as passionate as *Prometheus Bound*? as romantic as *Romeo and Juliet*? as funny as *The Bourgeois Gentleman*? as intriguing as *Happy Days*? An actor's voice may be thrillingly resonant, but how does it compare with the voice of Patrick Stewart? If our opinions are to have weight and distinction, they may do so only against a background of knowledge and experience. If we are going to place a performance on a scale ranging from one to ten, our friends (or readers) must know what is our "one" and what is our "ten."

To be a *sensitive* critic, we must be receptive to life and to artistic experience. The most sensitive criticism comes from a compassionate approach to life, to humankind, and to artistic expression; this approach elicits and provokes a personalized response to dramatic works. Sensitive criticism admits to the critic's needs: it begins from the view that life is difficult and problematic and that relationships are demanding. Sensitive critics are questing, not smug; humane, not self-absorbed; eternally eager for personal discovery and the opportunity to share it. They recognize that we are all groping in the dark, hoping to encounter helping hands along the way in the adventure of life—that this indeed is the hope of theatre artists too.

To be a *demanding* critic is to hold the theatre to the highest standards of which it is capable, for, paradoxically, in the theatre's capacity to entertain, to supply immediate gratification, lies the seed of its own destruction. As we have seen so often in the preceding pages, the theatre wants to be liked. It has tried from its very beginning to assimilate what is likable in the other arts. Almost scavenger-like, it has appropriated for itself in every era the most popular music and dance forms, the most trendy arguments, vocabularies, philosophies, technologies, and fashions in dress. In the process, alas, it often panders to tastelessness and propagates the meanest and most shallow values of its time. And here the drama critic in each of us can play a crucial role. The very need of the theatre to please its patrons tends to beget crass insecurity: to resort to simple sensationalism in exchange for immediate approval. Cogent, fair-minded, penetrating criticism keeps the theatre mindful of its own artistic ideals and its essential responsibility to communicate. It prevents the theatre from either selling out completely to the current whim or bolting the other way into hopeless self-absorption.

To be an *articulate* critic is to express our thoughts with precision, clarity, and grace. An utterance of "I loved it" or "I hated it"—or, perhaps most deadly of all, "I don't get it"— is not criticism but rather a crude expression of a general opinion—or an admission of not having an opinion at all. Articulation means the careful building of ideas through a presentation of evidence, logical argument, the use of helpful analogy and example, and a style of expression neither pedantically turgid nor idiosyncratically anarchic. Good criticism should be a pleasure to write, a pleasure to read; it should make us want to go deeper into the mysteries of the theatre and not suffocate us with the prejudices or egotistical displays of the critic.

In sum, the presence of a critical focus in the audience—observant, informed, sensitive, demanding, and articulate—keeps the theatre honest. It inspires the theatre to reach its highest goals. It ascribes importance to the theatrical act. It telegraphs the expectations of the audience to producer, playwright, director, and actor alike, saying, "We are out here, we are watching, we are listening, we are hoping, we care: we want your best—and then we want you to be better yet." The theatre needs such demands from its audience. The theatre and its audience need to be worthy co-participants in a collective experience that enlarges life as well as art.

If we are to be critics of the theatre, then, we must be knowledgeable, fair, and open-minded; receptive to stimulation and excitement; open to wisdom and love. We must also admit that we have human needs.

In exchange, the theatre must enable us to see ourselves in the characters of the drama and in the performers of the theatre. We must see our situations in the situations of plays and our hopes and possibilities in the behavior staged before us. We must be drawn to understand the theatre from the *inside* and to participate in thought and emotion in a play's performance.

Thus do we become critics, audience, and participants in one. The theatre is then no longer simply a remote subject encountered in a book, in a class, or in the entertainment columns of the world press; the theatre is part of us.

It is *our* theatre.

Glossary

Within the definitions, terms that are defined in this glossary appear in *italic*.

absurd The notion that the world is meaningless, derived from an essay, "The Myth of Sisyphus," by Albert Camus, which suggests that human beings have an unquenchable desire to understand but that the world is eternally unknowable. The resulting conflict puts individuals in an "absurd" position, like Sisyphus, who, according to Greek myth, was condemned for eternity to push a rock up a mountain, only to have it always roll back down before it reached the top. The philosophical term gave the name to a principal postwar dramatic *genre: theatre of the absurd*.

act (*verb*) To perform in a play. (*noun*) A division within a play. Acts in modern plays are separated by an *intermission*. Full-length modern plays are customarily divided into two acts, sometimes three. Roman, Elizabethan, and neoclassic plays were usually printed in five acts, but the actual stage productions were not necessarily divided by intermissions, only stage clearings.

ad-lib A line improvised by an actor during a performance, usually because the actor has forgotten his or her line or because something unscripted has occurred onstage. Sometimes an author directs actors to ad-lib, as in crowd scenes during which individual words cannot be distinguished by the audience.

aesthetic distance The theoretical separation between the created artifice of a play and the "real life" the play appears to represent.

agon "Action," in Greek; the root word for "agony." Agon refers to the major struggles and interactions of Greek *tragedy*.

amphitheatre In Rome, a large elliptical outdoor theatre, originally used for gladiatorial contests. Today the term is often used to designate a large outdoor theatre of any type.

anagnorisis "Recognition," in Greek. Aristotle claimed that every fine *tragedy* has a recognition scene in which the *protagonist* discovers either some fact unknown to her or him or some moral flaw in her or his character. Scholars disagree as to which of these precise meanings Aristotle had in mind. See also *hamartia*.

angle wing A flat wing to which is hinged a second flat wing at an angle—usually between 90 and 115 degrees. Used extensively in seventeenth-century scenery, where it was painted to represent, among other things, diagonal walls on either side of the stage or exterior corners of buildings. See *flat; wings*.

antagonist In Greek *tragedy*, the "opposer of the action"; the opponent of the *protagonist*.

Apollonian That which is beautiful, wise, and serene, in the theories of Friedrich Nietzsche, who believed *drama* sprang from the junction of Apollonian and *Dionysian* impulses in Greek culture.

apron The part of the stage located in front of the *proscenium;* the forward-most portion of the stage. The apron was used extensively in the English *Restoration* period, from whence the term comes. Today, it is usually called the *forestage*.

aragoto The flamboyant and exaggerated masculine style of acting employed in certain *kabuki* roles.

arena stage A stage surrounded by the audience; also known as "theatre-in-the-round." Based on a Latin term meaning "sand," the *arena* originally referred to the dirt circle in the midst of an *amphitheatre*.

aside A short line in a play delivered directly to the audience; by dramatic convention; the other characters onstage are presumed not to hear it. Popular in the works of William Shakespeare and dramatists of the *Restoration* period, the aside has made a comeback and is used to good effect, in conjunction with the longer *direct address*, by contemporary American playwrights such as Margaret Edson and Neil LaBute.

audition The process whereby an actor seeks a role by presenting to a director or casting director a prepared reading or by reading from the text of the play being presented.

avant-garde Artists who abandon conventional models and create works that are in the forefront of new movements and styles.

backstage The offstage area hidden from the audience that is used for *scenery* storage, for actors preparing to make entrances, and for stage technicians running the show. "Backstage plays," such as *The Torchbearers* and *Noises Off,* "turn the set around" and exploit the furious activity that takes place backstage during a play production.

biomechanics An experimental acting system, characterized by expressive physicalization and bold gesticulation, developed by the Russian director Vsevolod Meyerhold in the 1920s.

black musical See *black theatre*.

black theatre In America, theatre that is generally by, with, and about African Americans.

black-box theatre A rectangular room with no fixed seating or stage area; this theatre design allows for a variety of configurations in staging plays.

blocking The specific staging of a play's movements, ordinarily by the director. Often this is worked out ("blocked out") on paper by the director beforehand.

book In a *musical,* the *dialogue* text, apart from the music and song lyrics.

border A piece of flat *scenery,* often black velour but sometimes a *flat,* which is placed horizontally above the set, usually to *mask* the lighting instruments. Borders are often used with side *wings,* in a scenery system known as "wing and border."

box set A stage set consisting of hard scenic pieces representing the walls and sometimes the ceiling of a room, with one wall left out for the audience to peer into. This set design was developed in the nineteenth century and remains in use today primarily in *realistic* plays.

Broadway The major commercial theatre district in New York, roughly bordered by Broadway, Eighth Avenue, 42nd Street, and 52nd Street.

bunraku A Japanese puppet-theatre, founded in the sixteenth century and still performed today.

burlesque Literally, a *parody* or mockery, from an Italian amusement form. Today the term implies broad, coarse humor in *farce,* particularly in parodies and *vaudeville*-type presentations.

business The minute physical behavior of the actor—fiddling with a tie, sipping a drink, drumming the fingers, lighting a cigarette, and so forth.

Sometimes this is controlled to a high degree by the actor or the director for precise dramatic effect; at other times the business is *improvised* to convey *verisimilitude*.

call An oral command, normally whispered over an intercom by the stage manager to the appropriate operator, to execute a specific lighting, sound, or scene-shift cue as, for example, "Sound cue number 121—go!" See also *cue sheet; tech run-through*.

call book or calling book See *prompt book*.

callback After the initial *audition*, the director or casting director will "call back" for additional—sometimes many—readings by the actors who seem most promising. Rules of the actors' unions require that actors be paid for callbacks exceeding a certain minimum number.

caricature A character portrayed very broadly and in a stereotypical fashion, ordinarily objectionable in *realistic* dramas. See also *character*.

catharsis In Aristotle's *Poetics*, the "purging" or "cleansing" of the terror and pity that the audience feels during the *climax* of a *tragedy*.

character A "person" in a play, as performed by an actor. Hamlet, Oedipus, Juliet, and Willy Loman are characters. Characters may or may not be based on real people.

chiton The full-length gown worn by Greek tragic actors.

choral ode See *ode*.

chorus (1) In classic Greek plays, an ensemble of characters representing the general public of the play, such as the women of Argos or the elders of Thebes. Originally, the chorus numbered fifty; Aeschylus is said to have reduced it to twelve and Sophocles to have increased it to fifteen. More recent playwrights, including Shakespeare and Jean Anouilh, have occasionally employed a single actor (or a small group of actors) as "Chorus," to provide narration between *scenes*. (2) In *musicals*, an ensemble of characters who sing or dance together (in contrast to soloists, who mostly sing or dance independently).

chou In *xiqu*, clown characters and the actors who play them.

classic drama Technically, plays from classical Greece or Rome. Now used frequently (if incorrectly) to refer to Elizabethan, Jacobean, and French *neoclassical* masterpieces. See also *modern classic*.

climax The point of highest tension, when the conflicts of the play are at their fullest expression.

comedy Popularly, a funny play; classically, a play that ends happily; metaphorically, a play with some humor that celebrates the eternal ironies of human existence ("divine comedy").

comic relief In a *tragedy*, a short comic scene that releases some of the built-up tension of the play—giving the audience momentary "relief" before the tension mounts higher. The porter scene in Shakespeare's *Macbeth* is an often-cited example; after the murder of Duncan, a porter jocularly addresses the audience as to the effect of drinking on sexual behavior. In the best tragedies, comic relief also provides an ironic counterpoint to the tragic action.

commedia dell'arte A form of largely improvised, masked street theatre that began in northern Italy in the late sixteenth century and still can be seen today. The principal characters—Arlecchino, Pantalone, Colombina, Dottore, and Scapino among them—appear over and over in thousands of commedia stories.

company A group of theatre artists gathered together to create a play production or a series of such productions. See also *troupe*.

convention A theatrical custom that the audience accepts without thinking, such as "when the curtain comes down, the play is over." Each period and culture develops its own dramatic conventions, which playwrights may either accept or violate.

cue The last word of one speech that then becomes the "signal" for the following speech. Actors are frequently admonished to speak "on cue" or to "pick up their cues," both of which mean to begin speaking precisely at the moment the other actor finishes.

cue sheet A numbered list of lighting, sound, or scene-shift changes coordinated with precise moments marked in the stage manager's *prompt book*.

curtain call The last staged element, in which the actors, after the play ends and the audience has begun to applaud, come forward to graciously accept the applause by bowing.

cycle plays In medieval England, a series of *mystery plays* that, performed in sequence, relate the story of the Judeo-Christian Bible, from the Creation of the Universe to the Crucifixion to Doomsday. The York Cycle includes forty-eight such plays.

cyclorama In a *proscenium theatre*, a large piece of curved *scenery* that wraps around the rear of the stage and is illuminated to resemble the sky or to serve as an abstract neutral background. It is usually made of fabric stretched between curved pipes but is sometimes a permanent structure made of concrete and plaster.

dada A provocative and playful European art movement that followed World War I and is characterized by seemingly random, unstructured, and "anti-aesthetic" creativity. It was briefly but deeply influential in poetry, painting, and theatre.

dan In *xiqu*, the female roles and the actors who play them.

denouement The final *scene* or scenes in a play devoted to tying up the loose ends after the *climax* (although the word originally meant "the untying").

deus ex machina In Greek *tragedy*, the resolution of the *plot* by the device of a god ("deus") flying onstage by means of a crane ("machina") and solving all the characters' problems. Today, this term encompasses any contrived play ending, such as the sudden arrival of a long-lost husband or father. This theatrical element was considered clumsy by Aristotle and nearly all succeeding critics; it is occasionally used ironically in the modern theatre, as by Bertolt Brecht in *The Threepenny Opera*.

dialogue The speeches—delivered to one another—of the *characters* in a play. Contrast with *monologue*.

diction One of the six important components of *drama*, according to Aristotle, who meant by the term the intelligence and appropriateness of the play's speeches. Today, the term refers primarily to the actor's need for articulate speech and clear pronunciation.

didactic drama Drama dedicated to teaching lessons or provoking intellectual debate beyond the confines of the play; a dramatic form espoused by Bertolt Brecht. See also *distancing effect*.

dim out To fade the lights gradually to blackness.

dimmer The electrical device that regulates the amount of light emitted from lighting instruments.

Dionysia The weeklong Athenian springtime festival in honor of *Dionysus*; after 534 B.C., it was the major play-producing festival of the ancient Greek year. Also called "Great Dionysia" and "City Dionysia."

Dionysian Characterized by passionate revelry, uninhibited pleasure-seeking; the opposite of *Apollonian*, according to Friedrich Nietzsche, who considered *drama* a merger of these two primary impulses in Greek culture.

Dionysus The Greek god of *drama* as well as the god of drinking and fertility. Dionysus was known as Bacchus in Rome.

direct address A character's speech delivered directly to the audience, common in Greek *Old Comedy* (see *parabasis*), in Shakespeare's work (see *soliloquy*), in *epic theatre*, and in some otherwise *realistic* modern plays (such as Tennessee Williams's *The Glass Menagerie*).

discovery A *character* who appears onstage without making an entrance, as when a curtain opens. Ferdinand and Miranda are "discovered" playing chess in Shakespeare's *The Tempest* when Prospero pulls away the curtain that was hiding them from view.

distancing effect A technique, developed by German playwright Bertolt Brecht, by which the actor deliberately presents rather than represents his or her character and "illustrates" the character without trying to embody the role fully, as *naturalistic* acting technique demands. This effect may be accomplished by "stepping out of character"—as to sing a song or to address the audience directly—and by developing a highly objective and *didactic* mode of expression. The actor is distanced from the role in order to make the audience more directly aware of current political issues. This technique is highly influential, particularly in Europe.

dithyramb A Greek religious rite in which a *chorus* of fifty men, dressed in goatskins, chanted and danced; the precursor, according to Aristotle, of Greek *tragedy*.

divertissement A French term, now accepted in English, for a frothy entertainment, intended to "divert" the audience from more serious matters.

documentary drama Drama that presents historical facts in a non-fictionalized, or slightly fictionalized, manner.

doggerel Coarse, unsophisticated poetry, usually with short lines and overly obvious rhymes, often used comically by Shakespeare to indicate simplistic verse written or performed by characters in his plays, such as Orlando's amateurish love poems to Rosalind in *As You Like It* or the play of "Pyramus and Thisbe" presented by inexperienced performers in the last act of *A Midsummer Night's Dream*.

domestic tragedy A *tragedy* about ordinary people at home.

double (*verb*) To play more than one role. An actor who plays two or more roles is said to "double" in the second and following roles. Ordinarily the actor will seek, through a costume change, to disguise the fact of the doubling; occasionally, however, a production with a *theatricalist* staging may make it clear that the actor doubles in many roles. (*noun*) To Antonin Artaud, the life that drama reflects, as discussed in his book *The Theatre and Its Double*. See also *theatre of cruelty*.

downstage The part of the stage closest to the audience. The term dates back to the eighteenth century, when the stage was *raked* so that the front part was literally lower than the back (or *upstage*) portion.

drama The art of the theatre; plays, playmaking, and the whole body of literature of and for the stage.

dramatic Plays, scenes, and events that are high in conflict and believability and that would command attention if staged in the theatre.

dramatic criticism A general term that refers to writings on drama, ranging from journalistic play reviews to scholarly analyses of dramatic *genres*, periods, *styles*, and theories.

dramatic irony The device of letting the audience know something the characters don't, as in Shakespeare's *Macbeth*, when King Duncan remarks on his inability to judge a person's character—while warmly greeting the man (Macbeth) who we already know plans to assassinate him.

dramaturg (also spelled "dramaturge") A specialist in play construction and the body of dramatic literature, dramaturgs are frequently engaged by professional and academic theatres to assist in choosing and analyzing plays, to develop production concepts, to research topics pertinent to historic period or play production *style*, and to write program essays. The dramaturg has been a mainstay of the German theatre since the eighteenth century and is becoming increasingly popular in the English-speaking world.

dramaturgy The art of play construction; sometimes used to refer to play structure itself.

drapery Fabric—often black—mainly used as neutral *scenery* to *mask* (hide) actors when they leave the lit (active) area of the stage. Also refers to a front curtain (a "main drape"), which is often red.

dress rehearsal A *rehearsal* in full costume; usually also with full *scenery*, *properties*, lighting, sound, and technical effects. Such rehearsals are ordinarily the last ones prior to the first performance before an audience.

drop A flat piece of *scenery* hung from the *fly gallery*, which can "drop" into place by a flying system.

emotion memory A technique in which an actor stimulates emotion by remembering the feelings he or she experienced during a previous, real-life event. Employed since ancient times, it was developed and named by Konstantin Stanislavsky (who, however, subsequently disowned it) and was promoted in America by Lee Strasberg. Also called "affective memory."

empathy Audience members' identification with dramatic characters and their consequent shared feelings with the plights and fortunes of those characters. Empathy is one of the principal effects of good drama.

ensemble Literally, the group of actors (and sometimes directors and designers) who put a play together; metaphorically, the rapport and shared sense of purpose that bind such a group into a unified artistic entity.

environmental theatre Plays produced not on a conventional stage but in an area where the actors and the audience are intermixed in the same "environment" and there is no precise line distinguishing stage space from audience space.

epic theatre As popularized by Bertolt Brecht, a *style* of theatre in which the play presents a series of semi-isolated episodes intermixed with songs and other forms of *direct address*, all leading to a general moral conclusion or set of integrated moral questions. Brecht's *Mother Courage* is a celebrated example. See also *distancing effect*.

epilogue In Greek *tragedy*, a short concluding *scene* of certain plays, generally involving a substantial shift of tone or a *deus ex machina*. Today, the epilogue is a concluding scene set substantially beyond the time frame of the rest of the play, in which characters, now somewhat older, reflect on the preceding events.

episode In Greek *tragedy*, a *scene* between characters and between choral *odes*. The word literally means "between odes."

existential drama A play based on the notions of existentialism, particularly as developed by playwright/philosopher Jean-Paul Sartre. Existentialism, basically, preaches Sartre's principal tenet in *No Exit* that "you are your acts, and nothing else" and that people must be held fully accountable for their own behavior.

exodos In Greek *tragedy*, the departure *ode* of the *chorus* at the end of the play.

exposition In play construction, the conveyance, through *dialogue*, of story events that occurred before the play begins.

expressionism An artistic *style* that greatly exaggerates perceived reality in order to express inner truths directly. Popular mainly in Germany between the world wars, expressionism in the theatre is notable for its gutsy dialogue, piercing sounds, bright lighting and coloring, bold scenery, and shocking, vivid imagery.

farce Highly comic, lighthearted, gleefully contrived drama, usually involving *stock situations* (such as mistaken identity or discovered lovers' trysts), punctuated with broad physical stunts and pratfalls.

flat A wooden frame covered by fabric or by a hard surface and then painted, often to resemble a wall or portion of a wall. The flat is a traditional staple of stage *scenery*, particularly in the realistic theatre, because it is exceptionally lightweight, can be combined with other flats in various ways, and can be repainted and reused many times over several years.

fly (verb) To raise a piece of *scenery* (or an actor) out of sight by a system of ropes or wires. This theatre practice dates back at least to ancient Greek times. See also *deus ex machina*.

fly gallery The operating area for flying scenery, where fly ropes are tied off (on a pinrail) or where ropes in a counterweight system are clamped in a fixed position.

follow-spot A swivel-mounted spotlight that can be pointed in any direction by an operator.

footlights In a *proscenium theatre*, a row of lights across the front of the stage, used to light the actors' faces from below and to add light and color to the setting. Footlights were used universally in previous centuries but are employed only on special occasions today.

forestage See *apron.*

found object In scene or costume design (and art in general), an item that is found (rather than created) and is incorporated into the finished design.

full house Audience seating filled to capacity. See also *house.*

gel Short for "gelatin," a sheet of colored plastic placed over a light source to color the beam emitted from a lighting instrument. Also used as a verb: to insert gels into the instruments.

genre A French noun meaning "kind"; a term used in dramatic theory to signify a distinctive class or category of play—*tragedy, comedy, farce,* and so on.

geza The *stage right,* semienclosed musicians' box in *kabuki* theatre. This term also refers to the music that is played in this box.

gidayu The traditional style of chanting in *kabuki* and *bunraku* theatre.

gobo A perforated sheet of metal that, when placed in front of the lens of a sharply focused lighting instrument, projects designs on the floor or wall the light falls on.

greenroom A room near the stage where actors may sit comfortably before and after the show or during scenes in which they do not appear. This room is traditionally painted green; the custom arose in England, where the color was thought to be soothing.

ground plan A schematic drawing of the stage setting, as seen from above, indicating the location of stage-scenery pieces and furniture on (and sometimes above) the floor. A vital working document for directors in *rehearsal,* as well as for technicians in the installation of *scenery.*

hamartia In Aristotle's *Poetics,* the "tragic flaw" of the *protagonist.* Scholars differ as to whether Aristotle was referring primarily to a character's ignorance of certain facts or to a character's moral defect.

hanamichi In the *kabuki* theatre, a long narrow runway leading from the stage to a door at the back of the auditorium that is used for raised and highly theatrical entrances and exits through the audience. For some plays, a second hanamichi may be added.

Hellenistic theatre Ancient Greek theatre during the fourth and third centuries B.C. The surviving stone theatres of Athens and Epidaurus date from the Hellenistic period, which began well after the great fifth-century tragedies and comedies were written. The Hellenistic period did produce an important form of comedy (*New Comedy*), however, and Alexandrian scholars during this period collected, edited, and preserved the masterpieces of the golden age.

high comedy A comedy of verbal wit and visual elegance, primarily peopled with upper-class characters. The *Restoration* comedies of William Congreve (1670–1729) and the Victorian comedies of Oscar Wilde (1854–1900) are often cited as examples.

hikimaku The traditional striped curtain of the *kabuki* theatre.

himation The gownlike basic costume of the Greek tragic actor.

house The audience portion of the theatre building.

hubris In Greek, "an excess of pride"; the most common *character* defect (one interpretation of the Greek *hamartia*) of the *protagonist* in Greek *tragedy.* "Pride goeth before a fall" is a Biblical expression of this foundation of tragedy.

improvisation *Dialogue* or stage *business* invented by the actor, often during the performance itself. Some plays are wholly improvised, even to the extent that the audience may suggest situations that the actors must then create. More often, improvisation is used to "fill in the gaps" between more traditionally memorized and rehearsed scenes.

inciting action In play construction, the single action that initiates the major conflict of the play.

ingenue The young, pretty, and innocent girl role in certain plays; also used to denote an actress capable of playing such roles.

interlude A *scene* or staged event in a play not specifically tied to the *plot;* in medieval England, a short moral play, usually comic, that could be presented at a court banquet amid other activities.

intermission A pause in the action, marked by a fall of the curtain or a fade-out of the stage lights, during which the audience may leave their seats for a short time, usually ten or fifteen minutes. Intermissions divide the play into separate *acts.* In England, known as "the interval."

jing In *xiqu,* the "painted-face" roles, often of gods, nobles, or villains.

jingju "Capital theatre" in Chinese; the Beijing (Peking) opera is the most famous form of *xiqu.*

kabuki One of the national theatre styles of Japan. Dating from the seventeenth century, kabuki features magnificent flowing costumes; highly stylized *scenery,* acting, and makeup; and elaborately styled choreography.

kakegoe Traditional shouts that *kabuki* enthusiasts in the audience cry out to their favorite actors during the play.

kathakali Literally, "story play"; a traditional dance-drama of India.

kōken Black-garbed and veiled actors' assistants who perform various functions onstage and off in *kabuki* theatre.

kunqu (sometimes *kunju*) The oldest form of Chinese *xiqu* still performed, dating from the sixteenth century.

kyōgen A comic, often farcical, counterpoint to Japanese *nō* drama, to which it is, surprisingly, historically related.

lazzo A physical joke, refined into traditional *business* and regularly inserted into performances of *commedia dell'arte.* "Eating the fly" is a famous lazzo.

LED The recently developed light-emitting diode is a light source that, because of its extremely long life, is beginning to replace incandescent sources in a variety of stage lighting instruments.

Lenaea The winter dramatic festival of ancient Athens. Because there were fewer foreigners in town in the winter, comedies that might embarrass the Athenians were often performed at this festival rather than at the springtime *Dionysia.*

light plot The layout—on paper—showing the positions where stage lights are to be hung and how they are wired (connected) into the numbered electrical circuits of the theatre facility.

liturgical drama *Dramatic* material that was written into the official Catholic Church liturgy and staged as part of regular church services in the medieval period, mainly in the tenth through twelfth centuries. See also *mystery play.*

low comedy Comic actions based on broad physical humor, scatology, crude punning, and the argumentative behavior of ignorant and lower-class *characters.* Despite the pejorative connotation of its name, low comedy can be inspired, as in the "mechanicals" scenes in Shakespeare's *A Midsummer Night's Dream.* Good plays, such as this one, can mix low comedy with *high comedy* in a highly sophisticated pattern.

mask (*noun*) A covering of the face, used conventionally by actors in many periods, including Greek, Roman, and *commedia dell'arte.* The mask was also used in other sorts of plays for certain occasions, such as the masked balls in Shakespeare's *Romeo and Juliet* and *Much Ado about Nothing.* The mask is a symbol of the theatre, particularly the two classic masks of Comedy and Tragedy. (*verb*) To hide backstage storage or activity by placing in front of it neutrally colored *flats* or drapery (which then become "masking pieces").

masque A minor dramatic form combining dance, music, a short allegorical *text,* and elegant *scenery* and costuming; often presented at court, as in the royal masques written by Ben Jonson, with scenery designed by Inigo Jones, during the Stuart era (early seventeenth century).

melodrama Originally a term for *musical* theatre, by the nineteenth century this became the designation of a suspenseful, plot-oriented *drama* featuring all-good heroes, all-bad villains, simplistic *dialogue,* soaring moral conclusions, and bravura acting.

metaphor A literary term designating a figure of speech that implies a comparison or identity of one thing with something else. It permits concise communication of a complex idea by use of associative imagery, as with Shakespeare's "morn in russet mantle clad."

metatheatre Literally, "beyond theatre"; plays or theatrical acts that are self-consciously theatrical, that refer back to the art of the theatre and call attention to their own theatrical nature. Developed by many authors, including Shakespeare (in plays-within-plays in *Hamlet* and *A Midsummer Night's Dream*) and particularly the twentieth-century Italian playwright Luigi Pirandello (*Six Characters in Search of an Author, Tonight We Improvise*), thus leading to the term "Pirandellian" (meaning "metatheatrical"). See also *theatricalist* and *play-within-the-play*.

mie A "moment" in *kabuki* theatre in which the actor (usually in an *aragoto* role) suddenly "freezes" in a tense and symbolic pose.

mime A stylized art of acting without words. Probably derived from the *commedia dell'arte*, mime was revived in France during the mid-twentieth century and is now popular again in the theatre and in street performances in Europe and the United States. Mime performers traditionally employ whiteface makeup to stylize and exaggerate their features and expressions.

modern A difficult term to pin down because it literally refers to work of "the present"—which, however, is always changing. The term popularly means "up-to-date," but arts scholars employ it mainly in reference to works created between approximately 1890 and 1945, which were called modern in their own time (e.g., "Modern art") and now—in contrast to *postmodern* works—can be roughly categorized into identified various artistic *styles* (e.g., realism, naturalism, expressionism, absurdism, epic theatre) of those years.

modern classic A term used to designate a play of the *modern* era that has nonetheless passed the test of time and seems as if it will last into the century or centuries beyond, such as the major works of Anton Chekhov, George Bernard Shaw, and Samuel Beckett. Contrast with *classic drama*.

monologue A long unbroken speech in a play, often delivered directly to the audience (in which case it is more accurately called a *soliloquy*).

morality play An allegorical medieval play in which the characters represent abstractions (Good Deeds, Death, and so on) and the overall impact of the play is moral instruction. The most famous in English is the anonymous *Everyman* (fifteenth century).

motivation That which can be construed to have determined a person's (or a *character's*) behavior. Since Konstantin Stanislavsky, actors have been encouraged to study the possible motivations of their characters' actions. See also *objective*.

music theatre A dramatic *genre* that employs, normally in addition to spoken dialogue (but see *sung-through*), a musical score with a dozen or more songs and dances. Also called "musical theatre."

musical (*noun*) A single work of *music theatre*—such as *Oklahoma!* or *The Producers*.

musical comedy A *musical* intended mainly as light comic entertainment, emphasizing comedy and youthful romance as well as singing.

mystery play The most common term referring to medieval plays developed from liturgical drama that treated Biblical stories and themes. (They were also known as "pageant plays" in England, as "passion plays" when dealing with the Crucifixion of Jesus, and as "Corpus Christi plays" when performed in conjunction with that particular festival.) Unlike *liturgical dramas*, which were in Latin, mystery plays were written in the vernacular (English, French, German, Italian, Spanish, and Russian versions exist) and were staged outside the church.

naturalism A version of *realism* advancing the notion that the natural and social environment, more than individual willpower, controls human behavior. Its proponents, active in the late nineteenth and early twentieth centuries, sought to dispense with all theatrical convention in the search for *verisimilitude*—or, as the naturalists would say, a *slice of life*.

neoclassicism Literally, "new classicism." A renewed interest in the literary and artistic theories of ancient Greece and Rome and an attempt to reformulate them for the current day. A dominant force in seventeenth-century France, neoclassicism promoted restrained passion, balance, artistic consistency, and formalism in all art forms; it reached its dramatic pinnacle in the tragedies of Jean Racine.

New Comedy Greek comic dramas—almost all of which are now lost—of the late fourth to the second centuries B.C. Considerably more realistic than the *Old Comedy* of Aristophanes, New Comedy employed *stock characters* and domestic scenes; it strongly influenced Roman author Plautus and, through him, Renaissance comedy.

nō The classical dance-drama of Japan. Performed on a bare wooden stage of fixed construction and dimensions and accompanied by traditional music, nō is the aristocratic forebear of the more popular *kabuki* and has remained generally unchanged since its fourteenth-century beginnings.

objective The basic "goal" of a *character*. Also called "intention," "goal," or "victory." Since Konstantin Stanislavsky, the actor has been urged to discover his or her character's objectives and, by way of "living the life of the character," to pursue that character's objective during the course of the play.

ode In Greek *tragedy*, a song chanted or sung by the *chorus* and often accompanied by dance. Also called "choral ode."

off-Broadway The New York professional theatre located outside the *Broadway* district; principally in Greenwich Village and around the Upper East and West Sides. Developed in the 1950s, when it was considered *avant-garde*, the off-Broadway theatre is now more of a scaled-down version of the Broadway theatre, featuring *musicals* and commercial *revivals* as much as (or more than) original works.

off-off-Broadway A term designating certain theatre activity in New York City, usually nonprofessional (although with professional artists involved) and usually experimental and *avant-garde*. Off-off-Broadway developed in the 1970s as a supplement to the commercialism of both Broadway and, increasingly, off-Broadway.

Old Comedy Ancient Greek comedy of the fifth century B.C., mainly known to us through the bawdy, satirical, and even slapstick comedies of Aristophanes.

onnagata "Women-type" roles in *kabuki*, which, like all the roles, are played by men.

"Open the house!" A direction to admit the audience. See also *house*.

orchestra (1) In the ancient Greek or Roman theatre, the circular (in Rome, semicircular) ground-level acting area in front of the stagehouse, or *skene*. It was used primarily by the *chorus*. (2) In modern U.S. theatre buildings, the ground-level section of the audience, which usually slopes upward at the rear. Distinct from the mezzanine and balconies and ordinarily containing the more expensive seats. In England, known as "the stalls."

parabasis The "coming-forward" of a *character* in Greek *Old Comedy* who then gives a *direct address* to the audience in the middle of the play. In Aristophanes' plays, the parabasis is often given in the author's name and may have been spoken by Aristophanes himself. The parabasis was often unrelated to the *plot* and dealt with the author's immediate political or social concerns.

parados (1) The *ode* sung by the *chorus* entering the orchestra in a Greek *tragedy*. (2) The space between the stage-house (*skene*) and audience seating area (*theatron*) through which the chorus entered the orchestra.

parody Dramatic material that makes fun of a dramatic *genre* or mode or of specific literary works; a form of theatre that is often highly entertaining but rarely has lasting value.

passion play A medieval play about Jesus and his trial and crucifixion, still performed in many towns and villages around the world during Easter week.

pathos "Passion," in Greek; also "suffering." The word refers to the depths of feeling evoked by *tragedy*; it is at the root of our words "sympathy" and "empathy," which also describe the effect of drama on audience emotions. See also *empathy*.

peripeteia The change of course in the *protagonist's* fortunes that, according to Aristotle, is part of the *climax* of a *tragedy*.

platform A tablelike construction of any height, built to be stood upon, that creates raised flooring for a designated portion of the stage.

play-within-the-play A play "presented" by characters who are already in a play, like "The Murder of Gonzago," which is presented by the "Players" in *Hamlet*. Many plays are in part about actors and plays and contain such plays-within-plays; these include Anton Chekhov's *The Seagull*, Jean Anouilh's *The Rehearsal*, and Shakespeare's *A Midsummer Night's Dream* and *The Taming of the Shrew*.

plot The events of the play, expressed as a series of linked dramatic actions; in common terms, the story of the play. Plot is the most important component of a play, according to Aristotle.

postmodern A wide-ranging term describing certain post–World War II artistic works characterized by nonlinearity, self-referentiality if not self-parody, and multiple/simultaneous sensory impressions.

practical A *property* that works onstage the way it does in life. For example, a "practical" stove, in a stage setting, is one on which the characters can actually cook. A "nonpractical" stove, by contrast, is something that only looks like a stove (and may in fact be a stove without insides).

preview A performance prior to a production's formal opening, primarily intended to allow the director and cast to make final changes in response to audience reactions. There may be one preview or many; the musical *Spider-Man* had 183 of them before its opening night.

problem play A realistic play that deals, often narrowly, with a specific social problem. George Bernard Shaw's *Mrs. Warren's Profession*, for example, is virtually a dramatic tract on prostitution. The term was most popular around the beginning of the twentieth century.

producer (1) In America, the person responsible for assembling the ingredients of a play production: financing, staff, theatre, publicity, and management. Not ordinarily involved in the day-to-day artistic direction of the production, the American producer nonetheless controls the artistic process through her or his authority over personnel selection and budgeting. (2) Until recently in the English theatre, the theatre artist whom Americans refer to as the director.

prologue In Greek *tragedy*, a speech or brief *scene* preceding the entrance of the *chorus* and the main action of the play, usually spoken by a god or gods. Subsequently, the term has referred to a speech or brief scene that introduces the play, as by an actor in certain Elizabethan plays (often called the chorus) and in the *Restoration*. The prologue is rarely used in the modern theatre.

prompt book The annotated script maintained by the production stage manager during rehearsal identifying the cues—chiefly lighting, sound, and scene changes—to be implemented during the production. When performances begin, this book is often renamed the *call book* or the *calling book*.

properties Or "props"; the furniture and handheld objects (hand props) used in play productions. These are often real items (chairs, telephones, books, etc.) that can be purchased, rented, borrowed, or brought up from theatre storage; they may also, particularly in period or stylized plays, be designed and built in a property shop.

proscenium The arch separating the audience area from the main stage area. The term derives from the Roman playhouse, in which the proscenium (literally, *pro skene*, or "in front of the stage") was the facing wall of the stage. Modern *thrust* and *arena stages* have no proscenium.

proscenium theatre A rectangular-roomed theatre with a *proscenium arch* separating the audience on one end from the stage at the other. The proscenium theatre was first popular in the late seventeenth century and reached its apogee in the late nineteenth and early twentieth centuries. Still the basic theatre architecture of America's Broadway and of major European theatre companies.

protagonist In Greek *tragedy*, the "carrier of the action"; in any drama, the principal *character*, often opposed by an *antagonist*.

raked stage A sloped stage, angled so that the rear (*upstage*) area is higher than the forward (*downstage*) area. A raked stage was standard theatre architecture in the seventeenth century and is often used today in scene design but rarely in a theatre's permanent architecture.

realism The general principle that the stage should portray, in a reasonable facsimile, ordinary people in ordinary circumstances and that actors should

behave, as much as possible, as real people do in life. Although the roots of realism go back to Euripides, it developed as a deliberate contrast to the florid *romanticism* that swept the European theatre in the mid-nineteenth century. See also *naturalism*, which is an extreme version of realism.

recognition See *anagnorisis*.

rehearsal The gathering of actors and director to put a play into production; the period in which the director stages the play and the actors develop and repeat their *dialogue* and actions; etymologically, a "reharrowing," or repeated digging into. In French, the comparable term is *répétition*.

repertory The plays a theatre company produces. A company's current repertory consists of those plays available for production at any time.

Restoration In England, the period following the restoration of the monarchy in 1660. In the theatre, the period is particularly noted for witty and salacious comedies, through to William Congreve's brilliant *The Way of the World* in 1700.

revival The remounting of a play production after its initial closing.

rising action In play construction, the escalating conflict; events and actions that follow the *inciting action*.

ritual A traditional cultural practice, usually religious, involving precise movements, music, spoken text, or gestures, that serves to communicate with deities. Ritual is often incorporated into plays, either as *conventions* of the theatre or as specific dramatized actions.

romanticism A nineteenth-century European movement away from *neoclassic* formalism and restraint and toward out-sized passions, exotic and grotesque stories, florid writing, and all-encompassing worldviews. Supplanted late in the century by *realism*, romanticism survives today primarily in grand opera and nineteenth-century-based *musicals*.

rotating repertory The scheduling of a series of plays in nightly rotation. This is customary in most European theatres and in many American Shakespeare festivals; it is otherwise rare in America. See also *repertory*.

samisen The three-stringed banjolike instrument used in *kabuki* and *bunraku*.

satire A play or other literary work that ridicules social follies, beliefs, religions, or human vices, almost always in a lighthearted vein. Satire is not usually a lasting theatre form, as summed up by dramatist George S. Kaufman's classic definition: "Satire is what closes on Saturday night."

satyr A mythological Greek creature, half man and half goat, who attended *Dionysus* and represented male sexuality and drunken revelry; goatskin-clad followers of Dionysus who served as the *chorus* of the *satyr play*.

satyr play The fourth play in a Greek *tetralogy*. Satyr plays were short bawdy *farces* that parodied the events of the *trilogies* that preceded them.

scansion The study of verse for patterns of accented and unaccented syllables; also known as "metrics."

scene (1) The period of stage time representing a single location during a continuous period of time, now usually marked by a stage clearing and a noticeable change in the lighting; the subdivision of an *act*. (2) The locale where the events of the play are presumed to take place, as represented by *scenery* (as in "the scene is the Parson's living room"). (3) Of scenery, as "scene design."

scenery Physical constructions that provide the specific acting environment for a play and that often indicate, by representation, the locale where a *scene* is set; the physical *setting* for a scene or play.

scenography *Scene* design, particularly as it fits into the moving pattern of a play or series of plays. Scenography is four-dimensional, comprising the three physical dimensions plus time.

scrim A theatrical fabric woven so finely that when lit from the front it appears opaque and when lit from behind it becomes transparent. A scrim is often used for surprise effects or to create a mysterious mood.

script The written version of a play.

semiotics The study of signs, as they may be perceived in literary works, including plays. Semiotics is a contemporary tool of *dramaturgical* analysis that offers the possibility of identifying all the ingredients of *drama* (staging as well as language) and determining the conjunctions between them.

set piece A single piece of *scenery* that represents a fixed object, such as a tree or a bathtub.

setting Or "set"; the fictional location where the play's action is presumed to take place, e.g., "a forest."

sheng In *xiqu*, the male roles and the actors who play them.

shite The principal *character* (the "doer") in *nō*.

skene The Greek stagehouse (and root word of *scene*). The skene evolved from a small changing room behind the *orchestra* to a larger structure with a raised stage and a back wall during the Greek period.

slapstick Literally, a prop bat made up of two hinged sticks that slap sharply together when the bat is used to hit someone; a staple gag of the *commedia dell'arte*. More generally, slapstick is any sort of very broad physical stage humor.

slice of life Pure *naturalism*: stage action that realistically represents an ordinary and arbitrary "slice" of the daily activity of the people portrayed.

soliloquy A *monologue* delivered by a single actor with no one else onstage, sometimes played as the *character* "thinking aloud" and sometimes as a seeming *dialogue* with the (silent) audience.

sound effects A term referring to single sounds, normally played from offstage and often prerecorded, that represent specific (and usually realistic) sounds, such as a telephone ringing, a car braking, or a cannon firing. Today, such effects are mostly incorporated into a play's overall sound design.

stage business See *business.*

stage directions Scene descriptions, *blocking* instructions, and general directorial comments written, usually by the playwright, in the *script.*

stage left Left, from the actor's point of view.

stage machinery A variety of mechanical devices, including hoists, cranes, rolling carts, and turntables, used to move or change actors or *scenery*. Many, though now electric, date from ancient Greek times.

stage right Right, from the actor's point of view.

stasimon A choral *ode* between scenes (*episodes*) in a Greek *tragedy.*

stock character A *character* recognizable mainly for his or her conformity to a standard ("stock") dramatic stereotype: the wily servant, the braggart soldier, the innocent virgin, and so on. Most date from at least Roman times.

stock situation One of a number of basic *plot* situations—the lover hiding in the closet, twins mistaken for each other, and so on—that, like *stock characters,* have been used in the theatre since Plautus and before.

storyboard A series of rough preliminary drawings that, when looked at in sequence, visually illustrate an imagined order of stage moments—the sequencing of the *scenery* and the flow of the action—in a play being prepared for production.

style The specific manner in which a play is shaped, as determined by its *genre,* its historical period, the sort of impact the director wishes to convey to the audience, and the skill of the artists involved. The term generally refers to these aspects inasmuch as they differ from *naturalism,* although it could be said that naturalism is a style.

stylize To deliberately shape a play (or a setting, a costume, etc.) in a specifically non-naturalistic manner.

subplot A secondary *plot,* usually related to the main plot by play's end. The Gloucester plot in *King Lear* and the Laertes plot in *Hamlet* are examples.

subtext According to Konstantin Stanislavsky, the deeper and usually unexpressed "real" meanings of a *character's* spoken lines. Of particular importance in the acting of realistic plays, such as those of Anton Chekhov, where the action is often as much between the lines as in them.

summer stock Theatre companies, located mostly in vacation areas of the American Northeast, that produce a season of plays (often one per week) during the summer months. Particularly popular in the three decades following World War II, when they mainly offered light, Broadway-styled comedies and provided pleasant entertainment for vacationers, salaries for unemployed New York actors, and break-in opportunities for student apprentices. The surviving companies, such as the Williamstown Theatre Festival in Massachusetts, have since become much more artistically ambitious.

sung-through (*noun*) A *musical* that has no spoken *dialogue.*

surrealism An art movement of the early twentieth century, in which the artist sought to go beyond *realism* into superrealism.

symbolism The first major antirealistic movement in the arts and in the theatre. Symbolism, which emphasizes the symbolic nature of theatrical presentation and the abstract possibilities of drama, flourished as a significant movement from the late nineteenth century to the early twentieth century, when it broke into various submovements: *expressionism, surrealism,* theatricalism, and many others.

tableau A "frozen moment" onstage, with the actors immobile, usually employed at the end of a *scene,* as the curtain falls or the lights dim.

technical rehearsal A stop-and-start *rehearsal,* in which a play's technical elements—mainly scene shifts, lighting, and sound cues—are precisely timed and integrated with the acting. See also *cue sheet.*

tech run-through A nonstop *rehearsal* of the play with all technical elements called by the stage manager and executed. See also *call; cue sheet.*

tetralogy Four plays performed together in sequence. In ancient Greek theatre, this was the basic pattern for the tragic playwrights, who presented a *trilogy* of tragedies, followed by a *satyr play.*

text A play *script.* This term is sometimes used to indicate the spoken words of the play only, as apart from the stage directions and other material in the script.

theatre—and drama These words are often used interchangeably, yet they also have distinct meanings. "Theatre" is the broader term and can denote all of the elements of theatrical production (plays, scenery, staging, acting). "Drama" mainly focuses on plays performed in a theatrical environment. This difference in meaning reflects the words' separate etymologies: theatre is that which "is seen," and drama is that which "is done." So "theatre" can mean a building, but "drama" cannot. And "dramatic" suggests actions, in both plays and life, that are compelling; but "theatrical," when referring to real-life behavior, implies overly showy or sensationalistic.

theatre—and theater *Theatre* is the French and British spelling; *theater* the German. Both spellings are common in the United States.

theatre of alienation See *distancing effect; epic theatre.*

theatre of cruelty A notion of theatre developed by the French theorist Antonin Artaud (1896–1948). Artaud's goal was to employ language more for its sound than for its meaning and to create a shocking stream of sensations rather than a coherent *plot* and cast of *characters.* Although Artaud's practical achievement was slight, his theories have proven extraordinarily influential.

theatre of the absurd A theatrical style, named by Martin Esslin in his 1961 book of that title, that has been applied to the post–World War II plays of Samuel Beckett, Eugène Ionesco, Jean Genet, and others, mostly Europeans. Esslin employed the term, derived from an essay by Albert Camus (see *absurd*), to describe plays with unrealistic and illogical plots, repetitious and disconnected language, and unclear themes, reflecting a world in which humans "absurdly" seek meaning but never find it.

theatre-in-the-round See *arena stage.*

theatricalist A contemporary style that boldly exploits the theatre itself and calls attention to the theatrical contexts of the play being performed. This term is often used to describe plays about the theatre that employ a *play-within-the-play.* See also *metatheatre.*

theatricality A quality of particularly vivid and attention-grabbing showmanship, either on stage or in daily life.

theatron The original Greek theatre; from the Greek for "seeing place."

thespian Actor; after Thespis, the first Greek actor.

thrust stage A stage that projects into the seating area and is surrounded by the audience on three sides.

tragedy From the Greek for "goat song," originally meaning a serious play. Tragedy was later refined by Greek playwrights (Thespis, sixth century B.C., being the first) and subsequently the philosopher Aristotle (384–322 B.C.) into the most celebrated of dramatic *genres:* a play that treats, at the most uncompromising level, human suffering. The reason for the name is unclear; a goat may have been the prize, or the *chorus* may have worn goatskins.

tragic flaw See *hamartia*.

tragicomedy A play that begins as a *tragedy* but includes comic elements and ends happily. Tragicomedy was a popular *genre* in the eighteenth century but is rarely employed, at least under that name, in the modern theatre.

traveler A curtain that, instead of flying out (see *fly*), moves horizontally and is usually opened by dividing from the center outward.

trilogy Three plays performed in sequence; the basic pattern of ancient Greek tragedies, of which one—Aeschylus's *The Oresteia* (*Agamemnon, The Libation Bearers,* and *The Eumenides*)—is still extant.

trope A written text, usually in dialogue form, incorporated into the Christian worship service. In the tenth century A.D. tropes became the first *liturgical dramas*.

troupe A group of actors who perform together, often on tour. See also *company*.

unit set A set that, by the moving on or off of a few simple pieces and perhaps with a change of lights, can represent all the scenes from a play. The unit set is a fluid and economical staging device, particularly useful for Shakespeare productions.

unities The unity of place, unity of time, unity of action, and unity of tone were the four "unities" that *neoclassic* critics of the seventeenth century claimed to derive from Aristotle; plays said to "observe the unities" were required to take place in one locale, to have a duration of no more than one day (in an extreme interpretation, in no more time than the duration of the play itself), and to concern themselves with no more than a single action. Aristotle made no such demands on playwrights, however, and very few authors have ever succeeded in satisfying these restrictive conventions.

upstage (*noun*) In a *proscenium theatre,* the part of the stage farthest from the audience; the rear of the stage, so called because it was in fact raised ("up") in the days of the *raked stage*. (*verb*) To stand upstage of another actor. Upstaging is often considered rude, inasmuch as it forces the *downstage* actor to face upstage (and away from the audience) in order to look at the actor to whom she or he is supposed to be speaking. Figuratively, the term may be used to describe any sort of acting behavior that calls unwarranted attention to the "upstaging" actor and away from the "upstaged" one.

vaudeville A stage variety show, with singing, dancing, comedy skits, and animal acts; highly popular in America from the late 1880s to the 1930s, when it lost out to movies, radio, and subsequently television.

verisimilitude Lifelikeness; the appearance of actual reality (as in a stage *setting*).

wagoto In *kabuki,* "soft-style" acting performed by certain male romantic characters.

waki The secondary *character* in *nō*.

well-made play *Pièce bien faite* in French; in the nineteenth century, a superbly plotted play, particularly by such gifted French playwrights as Eugène Scribe (1791–1861) and Victorien Sardou (1831–1908); today, generally used pejoratively, as to describe a play that has a workable *plot* but shallow characterization and trivial ideas.

West End The commercial theatre district of London, England.

wings In a *proscenium theatre,* vertical pieces of *scenery* to the left and right of the stage, usually parallel with the *footlights*.

working drawings Designer's drawings that show how a prop or a piece of *scenery* looks, and indicate how it should be constructed. See also *properties*.

xiqu Chinese for "tuneful theatre"; the general term for all varieties of traditional Chinese theatre, often called "Chinese opera."

zadacha Russian for "task" (though commonly translated as "objective"); according to Konstantin Stanislavsky, a character's (fictional) tasks (or goals), which the actor must pursue during the play.

Selected Bibliography

Historical Surveys of Theatre and Drama

Banham, Martin, ed. *The Cambridge Guide to Theatre*. 9th ed. Cambridge: Cambridge University Press, 1995.

Boardman, Gerald, and Thomas S. Hischak. *The Oxford Companion to American Theatre*. New York: Oxford University Press, 2004.

Brockett, Oscar G., and Franklin J. Hildy. *History of the Theatre*. Boston: Allyn & Bacon, 2003.

Deeney, John F., and Maggie B. Gale, eds. *The Routledge Drama Anthology and Sourcebook: From Modernism to Contemporary Performance*. New York/Routledge, 2010.

Gerould, Daniel. *Theatre/Theory/Theatre: The Major Critical Texts from Aristotle and Zeami to Soyinka and Havel*. New York: Applause Books, 2003.

Hill, Errol. *The Theatre of Black Americans*. New York: Applause Books, 1987.

Kanellos, Nicolás, ed. *A History of Hispanic Theatre in the United States: Origins to 1940*. Austin: University of Texas Press, 1990.

Kennedy, Dennis. *The Oxford Encyclopedia of Theatre and Performance*. Oxford: Oxford University Press, 2003.

Lee, Esther Kim. *A History of Asian American Theatre*. Cambridge: Cambridge University Press, 2006.

Nagler, Alois M. *A Source Book in Theatrical History*. New York: Dover, 1959.

Pavis, Patrice. *Dictionary of the Theatre: Terms, Concepts, and Analysis*. Toronto: University of Toronto Press, 1999.

Sanders, Leslie C. *The Development of Black Theater in America*. Baton Rouge: Louisiana State University Press, 1988.

General Studies of Theatre and Drama

Armstrong, Anne Elizabeth, and Kathleen Juhl, eds. *Radical Acts: Theatre and Feminist Pedagogies of Change*. San Francisco: Aunt Jute Books, 2007.

Bentley, Eric. *The Life of the Drama*. New York: Applause Books, 1991.

Chinoy, Helen, and Linda Jenkins, eds. *Women in American Theatre*. 3d ed. New York: Theatre Communications Group, 2006.

Esslin, Martin. *An Anatomy of Drama*. New York: Hill & Wang, 1977.

Granville-Barker, Harley. *On Dramatic Method*. New York: Hill & Wang, 1956.

Hayman, Ronald. *How to Read a Play*. 2nd ed. New York: Grove Press, 1999.

Mamet, David. *Three Uses of the Knife: On the Nature and Purpose of Drama*. New York: Columbia University Press, 1998.

Proehl, Geoffrey S., with D. D. Kugler, Mark Lamos, and Michael Lupu. *Toward a Dramaturgical Sensibility*. Madison, NJ: Fairleigh-Dickinson Press, 2008.

Schechner, Richard. *Environmental Theatre*. 2nd ed. New York: Applause Books, 1994.

———. *Performance Studies*. 2nd ed. New York: Routledge, 2006.

Styan, J. L. *Drama, Stage, and Audience*. New York: Cambridge University Press, 1975.

———. *The Elements of Drama*. New York: Cambridge University Press, 1960.

Worthen, W. B. *Drama: Between Poetry and Performance*. Hoboken: Wiley, 2010.

Specialized Studies

The Ancients

Arnott, Peter D. *Public and Performance in the Greek Theatre*. New York: Taylor and Francis, 1991.

Ashby, Clifford. *Classical Greek Theatre: New Views of an Old Subject*. Iowa City: University of Iowa Press, 1998.

Beacham, Richard C. *The Roman Theatre and Its Audience*. Cambridge, MA: Harvard University Press, 1996.

Duncan, Anne. *Performance and Identity in the Classical World*. Cambridge: Cambridge University Press, 2011.

Hall, Edith. *The Theatrical Cast of Athens*. New York: Oxford University Press, 2006.

Hart, Mary Louise. *The Art of Ancient Greek Theater*. Los Angeles: Getty Publications, 2010.

Kirby, E. T. *Ur-Drama: The Origins of Theatre*. New York: New York University Press, 1975.

Ley, Graham. *A Short Introduction to the Ancient Greek Theatre*. Chicago: University of Chicago Press, 2006.

Pickard-Cambridge, Sir Arthur. *The Dramatic Festivals of Athens*. 2nd ed., revised by John Gould and D. M. Lewis. Oxford: Oxford University Press, 1989.

Rehm, Rush. *The Play of Space: Spatial Transformation in Greek Tragedy*. Princeton, NJ: Princeton University Press, 2002.

———. *Radical Theatre: Greek Tragedy and the Modern World*. London: Duckworth, 2003.

Roselli, David Kawalko. *Theater of the People: Spectators as Society in Ancient Athens*. Austin: University of Texas Press, 2011.

Stewart, Roberta. *Plautus and Roman Slavery*. Hoboken: Wiley, 2012.

Storey, Ian C., and Arlene Allan. *A Guide to Ancient Greek Drama*. London: Blackwell, 2005.

Taplin, Oliver. *Greek Tragedy in Action*. 2nd ed. London: Routledge, 2002.

———. *The Stagecraft of Aeschylus*. 2nd ed. Oxford: Clarendon Press, 1990.

Ugonna, Nnabuenyi. *Mmonwu: A Dramatic Tradition of the Igbo*. Lagos, Nigeria: Lagos University Press, 1983.

Webb, Ruth. *Demons and Dancers: Performance in Late Antiquity*. Cambridge, MA: Harvard University Press, 2009.

Wiles, David. *Greek Theatre Performance*. Cambridge: Cambridge University Press, 2000.

Zimmerman, Bernhard. *Greek Tragedy: An Introduction.* Translated by Thomas Marier. Baltimore: Johns Hopkins University Press, 1991.

The Middle Ages

Butterworth, Philip. *Theatre of Fire: Special Effects in Early English and Scottish Theatre.* London: Society for Theatre Research, 1998.

Chambers, E. K. *The Medieval Stage.* 2 vols. Oxford: Clarendon Press, 1903.

Clopper, Lawrence M. *Drama, Play and Game: English Festive Culture in the Medieval and Early Modern Period.* Chicago: University of Chicago Press, 2001.

Enders, Jody. *The Medieval Theater of Cruelty: Rhetoric, Memory, Violence.* Ithaca: Cornell University Press, 2002.

———. *Murder by Accident: Medieval Theater, Modern Media, Critical Intentions.* Chicago: University of Chicago Press, 2009.

Gusick, Barbara I., and Edelgard E. DuBruck. *New Approaches to European Theatre of the Middle Ages.* New York: Peter Lang, 2004.

Johnston, Alexandra F., and Margaret Rogerson. *Records of Early English Drama: York.* Toronto: University of Toronto Press, 1979.

Kupfer, Marcia, ed. *The Passion Story: From Visual Representation to Social Drama.* University Park, PA: Pennsylvania State University Press, 2008.

Muir, Lynette R. *The Biblical Drama of Medieval Europe.* Cambridge: Cambridge University Press, 1995.

Ogden, Dunbar H. *The Staging of Drama in the Medieval Church.* Newark: University of Delaware Press, 2002.

Symes, Carol. *A Common Stage: Theater and Public Life in Medieval Arras.* Ithaca: Cornell University Press, 2007.

Tydeman, W. *The Theatre in the Middle Ages.* New York: Cambridge University Press, 1979.

Wickham, Glynne. *The Medieval Theatre.* London: St. Martin's Press, 1974.

The Renaissance

Bate, Jonathan. *Soul of the Age: A Biography of the Mind of William Shakespeare.* New York: Random House, 2009.

Bevington, David. *This Wide and Universal Theater: Shakespeare in Performance, Then and Now.* Chicago: University of Chicago Press, 2007.

Bloom, Harold. *Shakespeare: The Invention of the Human.* New York: Riverhead Books, 1998.

Chambers, E. K. *The Elizabethan Stage.* 4 vols. London: Oxford University Press, 1923.

David, Richard. *Shakespeare in the Theatre.* New York: Cambridge University Press, 1981.

Donaldson, Ian. *Ben Jonson: A Life.* Oxford: Oxford University Press, 2012.

Forcione, Alban K. *Majesty and Humanity: Kings and Their Doubles in the Political Drama of the Spanish Golden Age.* New Haven: Yale University Press, 2009.

Garber, Marjorie. *Shakespeare after All.* New York: Random House, 2005.

Greenblatt, Stephen. *Shakespearean Negotiations: The Circulation of Social Energy in Renaissance England.* Berkeley: University of California Press, 1989.

Henke, Robert. *Performance and Literature in the Commedia dell'Arte.* Cambridge: Cambridge University Press, 2010.

Hildy, Franklin J., ed. *New Issues in the Reconstruction of Shakespeare's Theatre.* New York: Peter Lang, 1990.

Howard, Jean. *Theater of a City: The Places of London Comedy, 1598–1642.* Philadelphia: University of Pennsylvania Press, 2006.

Kahn, Coppélia. *Man's Estate: Masculine Identity in Shakespeare.* Berkeley: University of California Press, 1981.

Kiernan, Pauline. *Staging Shakespeare in the New Globe.* New York: St. Martin's Press, 1999.

Mann, David. *The Elizabethan Player.* New York: Routledge, 1991.

Stern, Tiffany. *Documents of Performance in Early Modern England.* Cambridge: Cambridge University Press, 2009.

Worthen, W. B. *Shakespeare and the Force of Modern Performance.* Cambridge: Cambridge University Press, 2003.

Asian Theatre

Akihiko, Senda. *The Voyage of Contemporary Japanese Theatre.* Honolulu: University of Hawai'i Press, 1997.

Brandon, James R., ed. *Nō and Kyōgen in the Contemporary World.* Honolulu: University of Hawai'i Press, 1997.

Emmert, Richard. "Expanding Nō's Horizons." In *Nō and Kyōgen in the Contemporary World,* edited by James R. Brandon. Honolulu: University of Hawai'i Press, 1997.

Ernst, Earle. *The Kabuki Theatre.* New York: Grove Press, 1956.

Fenollosa, Ernest, and Ezra Pound. *The Noh Theatre of Japan: With Complete Texts of 15 Classic Plays.* New York: Dover, 2011.

Goldman, Andrea. *Opera and the City: The Politics of Culture in Beijing, 1770–1900.* Palo Alto: Stanford University Press, 2012.

Gunji, Masakatsu. *Kabuki.* Tokyo: Kodansha International, 1988.

Huang, Alexander C. Y. *Chinese Shakespeares: Two Centuries of Cultural Exchange.* New York: Columbia University Press, 2009.

Immoos, Thomas. *Japanese Theatre.* Translated by Hugh Young, photographs by Fred Mayer. London: Studio Vista, 1977.

Keene, Donald. *Nō and Bunraku.* New York: Columbia University Press, 1970.

Kominiz, Laurence R. *The Stars Who Created Kabuki.* Tokyo: Kodansha International, 1997.

Leiter, Samuel L. *Frozen Moments: Writings on Kabuki 1966–2001.* Ithaca, NY: Cornell University Press, 2002.

———. *New Kabuki Encyclopedia.* Westport, CT: Greenwood Press, 1997.

Ma, Qiang. *The Pictorial Album of Costumes in Chinese Traditional Opera.* Shanxi, China: Shanxi Education Press, 1992.

Mackerras, Colin. *The Performing Arts in Contemporary China.* 2nd ed., London: Routledge, 2005.

Maruoka, Daiji, and Tatsuo Yoshikoshi. *Noh.* Translated by Don Kenny. Osaka: Hoikusha Publishing, 1992.

Miettinen, Jukka O. *Classical Dance and Theatre in South-East Asia.* Oxford: Oxford University Press, 1992.

Nakamura, Matazo. *Kabuki, Backstage, Onstage: An Actor's Life.* Translated by Mark Oshima. Tokyo: Kodansha International, 1990.

Ortolani, Benito. *The Japanese Theatre: From Shamanistic Ritual to Contemporary Pluralism.* Leiden: E. J. Brill, 1990.

Richmond, Farley P., Darius L. Swann, and Phillip B. Zarilli, eds. *Indian Theatre: Traditions of Performance.* Honolulu: University of Hawai'i Press, 1990.

Scott, A. C. *The Classical Theatre of China.* London: Simson Shand, 1957.

———. *The Theatre in Asia.* London: Weidenfeld and Nicholson, 1972.

Seizer, Susan. *Stigmas of the Tamil Stage: An Ethnography of Special Drama Artists in South India.* Durham: Duke University Press, 2005.

Shindo, Shigero. *Kunisada (The Kabuki Actor Portraits).* Tokyo: Graphic-sha Publishing, 1993.

Toita, Yasuji, and Chiaki Yoshida. *Kabuki.* Translated by Don Kenny. Osaka: Hoikusha Publishing, 1992.

Van Erven, Eugène. *The Playful Revolution: Theatre and Liberation in Asia.* Bloomington: Indiana University Press, 1992.

Wang-ngai, Siu, with Peter Lovrick. *Chinese Opera*. Vancouver: University of British Columbia Press, 1997.

Wichmann, Elizabeth. *Listening to Theatre: The Aural Dimension of Beijing Opera*. Honolulu: University of Hawai'i Press, 1991.

Royal Theatre

Bradby, David, and Andrew Calder. *The Cambridge Companion to Moliere*. Cambridge: Cambridge University Press, 2006.

Holland, Peter. *The Ornament of Action: Text and Performance in Restoration Comedy*. New York: Cambridge University Press, 1979.

Nicoll, Allardyce. *History of English Drama, 1660–1900*. 6 vols. London: Cambridge University Press, 1955–1959.

Nussbaum, Felicity. *Rival Queens: Actresses, Performance, and the Eighteenth-Century British Theater*. Philadelphia: University of Pennsylvania Press, 2010.

Scott, Virginia. *Women on Stage in Early Modern France: 1540–1750*. Cambridge: Cambridge University Press, 2010.

Modern and Postmodern Theatre

Artaud, Antonin. *The Theatre and Its Double*. Translated by Mary C. Richards. New York: Grove Press, 1958.

Bentley, Eric. *The Playwright as Thinker*. 4th ed. Minneapolis: University of Minnesota Press, 2010.

Bigsby, C. W. E. *A Critical Introduction to Twentieth-Century American Drama*. 3 vols. Cambridge: Cambridge University Press, 1985.

Bradby, David. *Modern French Drama 1940–1980*. Cambridge: Cambridge University Press, 1984.

Brecht, Bertolt. *Brecht on Theatre*. Translated by John Willett. New York: Hill & Wang, 1965.

Brook, Peter. *The Empty Space*. New York: Atheneum, 1968.

Brotchie, Alastair. *Alfred Jarry: A Pataphysical Life*. Cambridge, MA: The MIT Press, 2011.

Craig, Edward Gordon. *On the Art of the Theatre*. 2nd ed. Boston: Small, Maynard, 1924.

de Jongh, Nicholas. *Not in Front of the Audience: Homosexuality on Stage*. London: Routledge, 1992.

Esslin, Martin. *The Theatre of the Absurd*. Rev. ed. New York: Vintage, 2004.

Grotowski, Jerzy. *Towards a Poor Theatre*. Eugenio Barba, ed. Rev. ed. New York: Routledge, 2002.

Hercher, Jutta and Peter Urban, eds. *Chekhov on Theatre*. London: Nick Hern Books, 2012.

Innes, Christopher. *Modern German Drama: A Study in Form*. New York: Cambridge University Press, 1979.

Marranca, Bonnie, and Gautam Dasgupta, eds. *Interculturalism and Performance*. New York: PAJ Publications, 1991.

Murphy, Brenda. *American Realism and American Drama, 1880–1940*. Cambridge: Cambridge University Press, 2008.

Puchner, Martin. *Stage Fright: Modernism, Anti-Theatricality, and Drama*. Baltimore: The Johns Hopkins University Press, 2011.

Roose-Evans, James. *Experimental Theatre: From Stanislavski to Peter Brook*. 4th ed. New York: Routledge, 1996.

Salamon, Julie. *Wendy and the Lost Boys: The Uncommon Life of Wendy Wasserstein*. New York: Penguin Press, 2011.

Savran, David. *Breaking the Rules: The Wooster Group*. New York: Theatre Communications Group, 1993.

Shaw, George Bernard. *The Quintessence of Ibsenism*. London: Constable, 1913.

Vanden Heuvel, Michael. *Performing Drama/Dramatizing Performance*. Ann Arbor: University of Michigan Press, 1991.

Wekwerth, Manfred. *Daring to Play: A Brecht Companion*. New York: Routledge, 2011.

Williams, Mance. *Black Theatre in the 1960s and 1970s*. Westport, CT: Greenwood Press, 1985.

Music Theatre

Bloom, Ken. *American Song*. 2nd ed. New York: Schirmer, 1996.

Bordman, Gerald. *American Musical Theatre*. 2nd ed. New York: Oxford, 1992.

Bradley, Ian, ed. *The Complete Annotated Gilbert and Sullivan*. New York: Oxford University Press, 1996.

Everett, William A., and Paul R. Laird. *The Cambridge Companion to the Musical*. Cambridge: Cambridge University Press, 2002.

Ganzl, Kurt. *The Encyclopedia of Musical Theatre*. Oxford: Blackwell, 1994.

Hammerstein, Oscar. *Lyrics*. New York: Simon and Schuster, 1949.

Hischack, Thomas S. *Boy Loses Girl: Broadway's Librettists*. Lanham, MD: Scarecrow Press, 2002.

Hollis, Alpert. *125 Years of Musical Theatre*. New York: Arcade Publications, 1991.

Jones, John Bush. *Our Musicals, Ourselves: A Social History of the American Musical Theatre*. Waltham, MA: Brandeis University Press, 2003.

Knapp, Raymond. *The American Musical and the Formation of Personal Identity*. Princeton, NJ: Princeton University Press, 2005.

———. *The American Musical and the Performance of Personal Identity*. Princeton, NJ: Princeton University Press, 2006.

Most, Andrea. *Making Americans: Jews and the Broadway Musical*. Cambridge, MA: Harvard University Press, 2004.

Naden, Corinne. *The Golden Age of the American Musical Theatre: 1943–1965*. New York: Scarecrow Press, 2011.

Peterson, Bernard L. *A Century of Musicals in Black and White*. Westport, CT: Greenwood Press, 1993.

Wolf, Stacy. *A Problem Like Maria: Gender and Sexuality in the American Musical*. Ann Arbor: University of Michigan Press, 2002.

Global Theatre Today

Erven, Eugene van. *Community Theatre: Global Perspectives*. New York: Routledge, 2001.

Giguere, Amanda. *The Plays of Yasmina Reza on the English and American Stage*. Jefferson, NC: McFarland, 2010.

Harvie, Jen, and Andy Lavender, eds. *Making Contemporary Theatre: International Rehearsal Processes*. Manchester (UK): Manchester University Press, 2010.

Kuftinec, Sonja. *Staging America: Cornerstone and Community-Based Theater*. Carbondale: Southern Illinois University Press, 2003.

Majumdar, Ramendu, and Mofidul Hoque, eds. *The World of Theatre: 2008 Edition*. Dhaka, Bangladesh: Bangladesh Centre of ITI, 2008.

Pearson, Mike. *Site-Specific Performance*. New York: Palgrave Macmillan, 2010.

Roman, David. *Performance in America: Contemporary U.S. Culture and the Performing Arts*. Durham: Duke University Press, 2005.

Acting and Directing

Acker, Barbara, and Marion Hampton, eds. *The Vocal Vision*. New York: Applause, 1997.

Benedetti, Jean. *Stanislavski: An Introduction, Revised and Updated*. 2nd ed. New York: Routledge, 2004.

Berry, Cecily. *Voice and the Actor*. London: Harrap, 1973.

Bogart, Ann. *And Then, You Act: Making Art in an Unpredictable World*. New York: Routledge, 2007.

Boleslavski, Richard. *Acting: The First Six Lessons*. New York: Theatre Arts Books, 1933.

Carnicke, Sharon Marie. *Stanislavsky in Focus*. Amsterdam: Harwood Press, 1998.

Chaikin, Joseph. *The Presence of the Actor.* 2nd ed. New York: Theatre Communications Group, 1993.

Cohen, Robert. *Acting One/Acting Two.* New York: McGraw-Hill, 2007.

———. *Acting Power: The 21st Century Edition.* London: Routledge, 2013.

———. *Acting Professionally* (with James Calleri). London: Palgrave Macmillan, 2009.

Cohen, Robert, and John Harrop. *Creative Play Direction.* 2nd ed. Englewood Cliffs, NJ: Prentice-Hall, 1984.

Cole, Toby, and Helen K. Chinoy, eds. *Actors on Acting.* Rev. ed. New York: Crown, 1995.

———. *Directors on Directing.* Rev. ed. Indianapolis: Bobbs-Merrill, 1963.

Diderot, Denis. "The Paradox of Acting." In William Archer, *Masks or Faces?* New York: Hill & Wang, 1957.

Donnellan, Declan. *The Actor and the Target.* 2nd ed. London: Nick Hern Books, 2005.

Giannachi, Gabriella and Nick Kaye. *Performing Presence: Between the Live and the Simulated.* Manchester: Manchester University Press, 2011.

Gordon, Robert. *The Purpose of Playing: Modern Acting Theories in Perspective.* Ann Arbor: University of Michigan Press, 2006.

Hagen, Uta. *Respect for Acting.* 2nd ed. Hoboken: Wiley, 2008.

Hethmon, Robert. *Strasberg at the Actors Studio.* New York: Viking, 1965.

Lewis, Robert. *Advice to the Players.* New York: Theatre Communications Group, 1980.

Linklater, Kristin. *Freeing the Natural Voice: Imagery and Art in the Practice of Voice and Language.* Rev. ed. New York: Drama Publishers, 2006.

Mitchell, Katie. *A Director's Craft: A Handbook for the Theatre.* New York: Routledge, 2008.

Roach, Joseph R. *The Player's Passion: Studies in the Science of Acting.* Newark: University of Delaware Press, 1985.

Shevtsova, Maria and Christopher Innes. *Directors/Directing: Conversations on Theatre.* Cambridge: Cambridge University Press, 2009.

Spolin, Viola. *Improvisation for the Theatre.* 3rd ed. Evanston, IL: Northwestern University Press, 1999.

Stanislavsky, Konstantin. *An Actor Prepares.* Translated by Elizabeth Reynolds Hapgood. New York: Theatre Arts Books, 1936.

———. *An Actor's Work.* Translated by Jean Benedetti. London: Routledge, 2008.

Design

Aronson, Arnold. *American Set Design.* New York: Theatre Communications Group, 1985.

Bicat, Tina. *Costume and Design for Devised and Physical Theatre.* Marlborough (UK): Crowood Press, 2012.

Collins, Jane, and Andrew Nisbet. *Theatre and Performance Design: A Reader in Scenography.* New York: Routledge, 2010.

Corson, Richard. *Stage Make-up.* 8th ed. Englewood Cliffs, NJ: Prentice-Hall, 1989.

Crabtree, Susan, and Peter Beudart. *Scenic Art for the Theatre.* 3rd ed. Waltham: Focal Press, 2011.

Essig, Linda. *Lighting and the Design Idea.* Belmont, CA: Thomson/Wadsworth, 2005.

Goodwin, John, ed. *British Theatre Design: The Modern Age.* London: Weidenfeld & Nicholson, 1989.

Izenour, George C. *Roofed Theaters of Classical Antiquity.* New Haven, CT: Yale University Press, 1996.

———. *Theatre Design.* 2nd ed. New Haven, CT: Yale University Press, 1996.

Jones, Robert Edmund. *The Dramatic Imagination.* New York: Meredith, 1941.

Mielziner, Jo. *Designing for the Theatre.* New York: Atheneum, 1965.

Motley. *Designing and Making Stage Costumes.* Rev. ed. New York: Routledge, 1992.

Oddey, Alison, and Christine White, eds. *The Potentials of Spaces: The Theory and Practice of Scenography and Performance.* Bristol, UK, and Portland, OR: Intellect Books, 2006.

Payne, Darwin Reid. *Computer Scenographics.* Carbondale: Southern Illinois University Press, 1994.

———. *Scenographic Imagination.* Carbondale: Southern Illinois University Press, 1993.

Pecktal, Lynn. *Costume Design.* New York: Back Stage Books, 1993.

Reid, Francis. *Designing for the Theatre.* New York: Routledge, 1996.

———. *The Stage Lighting Handbook.* 5th ed. New York: Routledge, 1996.

Smith, Ronn. *American Set Design 2.* New York: Theatre Communications Group, 1991.

Sofer, Andrew. *The Stage Life of Props.* Ann Arbor: University of Michigan Press, 2003.

Svoboda, Joseph. *The Secret of Theatrical Space.* New York: Applause Theatre Books, 1993.

Walne, Graham, ed. *Effects for the Theatre.* New York: Drama Book Publishers, 1995.

Credits

TEXT CREDITS

Chapter 2 p. 37 Excerpt from *Waiting for Godot*, English translation copyright © 1954 by the Estate of Samuel Beckett. Used by permission of Grove/Atlantic, Inc., and Faber & Faber, Ltd.

Chapter 3 pp. 46, 48 Excerpts from Jean Benedetti, *An Actor's Work: A Student Diary*. Copyright © 2008 Jean Benedetti. Reprinted by permission of Routledge/Taylor & Francis.

Chapter 4 p. 70 Excerpt from *Glengarry Glen Ross*, copyright © 1982, 1983 by David Mamet. Used by permission of Grove/Atlantic, Inc. p. 71 Excerpt from *Silence* by Harold Pinter, copyright © 1969 by H. Pinter Ltd. Used by permission of Grove/Atlantic, Inc., and Faber & Faber Ltd. p. 71 Excerpt from *Dirty Linen*, copyright © 1976 by Tom Stoppard. Used by permission of Grove/Atlantic, Inc., and Faber & Faber, Ltd. p. 73 Excerpt from *Wit* by Margaret Edson. Copyright © 2000. Published by Faber & Faber Ltd. All rights reserved. p. 75 By Tennessee Williams, from *Cat on a Hot Tin Roof*, copyright ©1954 by The University of the South. Reprinted by permission of New Directions Publishing Corp. and Georges Borchardt Literary Agency. p. 75 Excerpts from *Joe Turner's Come and Gone* by August Wilson. Copyright © 1988 by August Wilson. Used by permission of Dutton Signet, a division of Penguin Group (USA) Inc. p. 79 *Angels in America Part Two: Perestroika*: "the world's oldest living Bolshevik" from *Angels in America* by Tony Kushner. Copyright © 1993 Tony Kushner. Published by Theatre Communications Group. Used by permission of Theatre Communications Group. p. 80 *Homebody/Kabul* by Tony Kushner. Copyright © 2005 Tony Kushner. Published by Theatre Communications Group. Used by permission of Theatre Communications Group. p. 87 Excerpts from Frank Rich's review of *Spike Heels*, *New York Times*, June 5, 1992. Copyright © 1992 New York Times Company, Inc. Used with permission.

Chapter 5 p. 116 From "The Fantasticks" by Tom Jones and Harvey Schmidt. Copyright © 2000. Reprinted by permission of Hal Leonard Corporation. p. 121 Excerpt from *Waiting for Godot*, English translation copyright © 1954 by the Estate of Samuel Beckett. Used by permission of Grove/Atlantic, Inc., and Faber & Faber, Ltd. p. 121 By Tennessee Williams, from *A Streetcar Named Desire*, copyright © 1947 by The University of the South. Reprinted by permission of New Directions Publishing Corp and Georges Borchardt Literary Agency. p. 139 Excerpt by Tennessee Williams, from *The Glass Menagerie*, copyright 1944 by The University of the South. Reprinted by permission of New Directions Publishing Corp.

Chapter 6 p. 156 Excerpt from *The Music Man* by Meredith Willson. Copyright © 1962. Reprinted with permission from Hal Leonard Corporation. All rights reserved.

Chapter 7 p. 199 From E. T. Kirby, *Ur-Drama: The Origins of Theatre*. Copyright © 1975 New York University Press. Used with permission.

Chapter 8 p. 238 Excerpts from "No More Masterpieces" in *The Theatre and Its Double* by Antonin Artaud, copyright © 1958 by Grove Press, Inc. Used by permission of Grove/Atlantic, Inc. p. 241 Excerpt from *Waiting for Godot*, English translation copyright © 1954 by the Estate of Samuel Beckett. Used by permission of Grove/Atlantic, Inc., and Faber & Faber Ltd. pp. 245–246 Excerpts from Alan Ayckbourn's *Bedroom Farce, Act One*. Copyright © 1975 Alan Ayckbourn. Reprinted by permission of Grove/Atlantic, Inc., and Random House, Ltd. pp. 246–247 Excerpts from *Serious Money* by Caryl Churchill. Copyright © 1987 Caryl Churchill. Reprinted by permission of Bloomsbury Publishers.

Chapter 9 p. 253 Lyrics to "Ol' Man River" from *Show Boat*, 1927, Jerome Kern & Oscar Hammerstein. Copyright 1927 by PolyGram International Publishing, Inc. Copyright renewed. Reprinted by permission of Hal Leonard Corporation. p. 258 George and Ira Gershwin, "'S Wonderful" from *Funny Face*. Copyright 1927 (renewed) WB Music Corporation. All rights reserved. Used by permission of Alfred Publishing Company. p. 258 "Bewitched, Bothered and Bewildered" from *Pal Joey*. Words by Lorenz Hart Music by Richard Rodgers. Copyright 1941 (renewed). Chappell & Co., Inc. Rights for extended renewal term in U.S. controlled by the Estate of Lorenz Hart (administered by WB Music Corp.) and the Family Trust U/W/ Richard Rodgers and the Family Trust U/W Dorothy E. Rodgers (administered by Williamson Music, a division of The Rodgers & Hammerstein Organization, an Imagem Company). All rights reserved. Used by permission. p. 258 Excerpt from "Passion" by Stephen Sondheim. Copyright © 1994. Reprinted with the permission of Hal Leonard Corporation. All rights reserved. International copyright secured. p. 259 Richard Rodgers and Oscar Hammerstein II, "Oh, What a Beautiful Mornin'" from *Oklahoma!* Copyright 1943 by Williamson Music. Copyright renewed. International copyright secured. All rights reserved. Used by permission of Williamson Music, a division of The Rodgers & Hammerstein Organization, an Imagem Company. p. 259 "Little Things You Do Together" written by Stephen Sondheim. Used by permission of Herald Square Music, Inc. on behalf of Range Road Music, Inc., Jerry Leiber Music, Silver Seahorse Music, LLC and Rilting Music, Inc. p. 259 Excerpt from *Green Grow the Lilacs* by Lynn Riggs. Copyright 1931 Lynn Riggs. Used with permission from The Barbara Hogenson Agency. p. 259 Jonathan Larson, "Contact" from *Rent*. Copyright © 1996 by Finster & Lucy Music Ltd., Co. All rights controlled by and administered by Emi April Music, Inc. All rights reserved. International copyright secured. Reprinted with permission. p. 262 Michael John LaChiusa and George C. Wolfe, excerpt from "When It Ends" from *The Wild Party*. Copyright © 2000 by Fiddleback Music Publishing Company, Inc. All rights reserved. Used by permission of Alfred Publishing Co., Inc. p. 263 Ben Elton excerpt from "Dead Zone" from *The Boys in the Photograph*. Copyright © 2000. Reprinted with the permission of Hal Leonard Corporation. All rights reserved. International copyright secured. p. 263 Review: *Jerry Springer—The Opera*, by Susannah Clapp, *The Observer*, 4 May 2003. Copyright © Guardian News & Media, Ltd., 2003. p. 264 Tony Kushner, excerpt from "Lot's Wife" from *Caroline, or Change*. Copyright © 2004 by Tony Kushner. Published by Theatre Communications Group. Used by permission. p. 264 Duncan Sheik and Steven Sater, excerpt from "Totally F*cked" from *Spring Awakening*. Copyright © 2000. Reprinted with the permission of Hal Leonard Corporation and Warner Chappell Music. All rights reserved. International copyright secured. p. 264 Lyrics "Just Another Day" from *Next to Normal* (music by Tom Kitt, book and lyrics by Brian Yorkey). Copyright © 2009. Reprinted by permission Alfred Publishing Co., Inc. p. 265 Excerpt from Steven Suskin's review of *The Book of Mormon*, *Variety* 2011. Copyright © 2011. Used with permission.

Chapter 10 pp. 284 Excerpts from "No More Masterpieces" in *The Theatre and Its Double* by Antonin Artaud, copyright © 1958 by Grove Press, Inc. Used by permission of Grove/Atlantic, Inc. p. 304 Excerpt from *Waiting for Godot*, English translation copyright © 1954 by the Estate of Samuel Beckett. Used by permission of Grove/Atlantic, Inc., and Faber & Faber, Ltd.

PHOTO CREDITS

Index